CW00521249

THE ULTIMATE EU TEST BOOK
Administrator (AD) Edition 2011

Also from John Harper Publishing

The Ultimate EU Test Book now exists in separate ADMINISTRATOR and ASSISTANT editions.

The companion edition to this book is *The Ultimate EU Test Book – Assistant (AST) Edition 2011*, ISBN 978-0-9564508-2-1

To keep up to date with developments on EPSO exams and any updates on *The Ultimate EU Test Book*, visit ***www.eu-testbook.com***, from which you can also link to the *Ultimate EU Test Book* Facebook page to gather information from and make contact with others taking the exams.

For the latest details of other John Harper Publishing titles on the government and politics of the European Union, including our guides to the institutions of the European Union, visit ***www.johnharperpublishing.co.uk***

THE ULTIMATE EU TEST BOOK

ADMINISTRATOR (AD) EDITION 2011

András Baneth

Published by John Harper Publishing
27 Palace Gates Road
London N22 7BW, United Kingdom.

www.johnharperpublishing.co.uk

The Ultimate EU Test Book
First edition, November 2005
Second edition, May 2007
Third edition, March 2008
Fourth edition, April 2009
Fifth edition, March 2010
1st Assistant edition, November 2010
1st Administrator edition, February 2011

ISBN 978-0-9564508-3-8

Typeset in 9 & 10/11pt Palatino

Printed and Bound in Malta at the Gutenberg Press.

TABLE OF CONTENTS

PART I: GETTING AN EU JOB

PART II: PRE-SELECTION – PSYCHOMETRIC TESTS

PART III: THE ASSESSMENT CENTRE

INTRODUCTION

Purpose of the Book

The purpose of *The Ultimate EU Test Book* is to help candidates prepare and practise for the European Personnel Selection Office (EPSO)[1] recruitment competitions, often called by their French name, the *concours*.

The 2005-2009 editions of this book comprised extensive tests of EU knowledge, with some verbal and numerical reasoning questions, reflecting the character of the (first-phase) pre-selection tests of the time. The 2010 edition was the first to cover the radically new EPSO system introduced that year. As this reform is now in place it seemed appropriate to create specialised editions for Assistant and Administrator exams.

This new Administrator edition has been based on the foundations of the 2010 edition, updated and revised to reflect the experience gained from the first full cycle of EPSO exams in 2010. It therefore covers not only the full range of tests of reasoning ability used at pre-selection (including methodologies and a total of 400 verbal, numerical and abstract reasoning questions with detailed answers) but also the suite of new tests introduced in the second, assessment phase. All the abstract reasoning questions, and most of those in the verbal and numerical tests, are different from those that appeared in the 2010 edition as we have sought to fine-tune the questions more exactly to specific AD competition levels.

The aim is to give you, the candidate, a thorough understanding of what the tests involve and how to tackle them. While the main purpose is to help you pass the tests, without doubt an understanding of the qualities and behaviours the examiners are seeking to identify in candidates will also stand you in good stead to be "operational from Day One" when starting to work in an EU institution or body.

The Three Parts

The *Ultimate EU Test Book Administrator Edition* is divided into three parts.

Part I starts with a short overview of the "EU affairs" jobs arena, including the various types of permanent and temporary contracts available when working for the EU institutions and other bodies. It then moves on to a detailed step-by-step guide with timeline describing each stage of the new EU recruitment process. Including dozens of useful tips and hints, it signposts you to all the areas covered in greater detail later in the book.

Part II deals with the pre-selection phase of the testing system, which is the stage where the majority of candidates tend to fail. Pre-selection involves computer-based testing of verbal, numerical and abstract reasoning skills and non-eliminatory situational judgement tests. Many candidates find verbal, numerical and abstract reasoning tests difficult and intimidating and the aim is to help you gain the technical skills and confidence to achieve the best you are capable of. With this in mind, individual chapters are devoted to detailed methodologies for succeeding in each of these test types, followed by comprehensive test question exercises and a detailed key.

Candidates who do not reach the required level in these three tests will not be offered the chance to proceed further in the competition. It is therefore vital to study carefully the methodology to learn the principles and shortcuts involved and then make sure to practise to increase your speed, accuracy and ratio of correct answers.

Part II also covers situational judgement tests: these are included in the pre-selection on a non-eliminatory basis, but those candidates who succeed at pre-selection will have their results in the situational judgement test taken into account in the subsequent assessment phase, so this is an important new aspect of the exam system that you can read about in detail.

Part III deals with the second stage of the testing system, called the Assessment Centre (AC).

Until 2010, EPSO used ACs only for head of unit and more senior posts, but since the reform, ACs are used for all levels, including entry-levels of Administrator, Linguist and Specialist profiles who have passed the pre-selection phase (or in the case of most Specialist profiles, the preselection phase is integrated into the AC itself). Consequently, based on a detailed competency framework that has been established for each profile, you will find a full set of sample questions to help you prepare for the probing questions that the assessors will most likely challenge you with.

In this part you can find an in-depth description of each exercise that you can expect to encounter, including the case study, group exercise and oral presentation, with numerous useful tips and with sample exercises to test yourself against. Moreover, the situational judgement tests you will have taken in the pre-selection exams are taken as a basis for the so-called "structured interview", on which you can also find a detailed chapter with tips and samples. Finally, Part III includes sample Assessment Centre reports, based on current best practice, which will help you get an idea of how assessors will approach their task and what they will be looking for.

Important Notice

Despite my and the contributing authors' best efforts to be thorough and up-to-date to the fullest possible extent, some information may become outdated over the course of 2011. The book describes a major reform launched in 2010 that is still being fine-tuned – therefore adjustments may occur after going to press. Make sure therefore that you keep up-to-date with the EPSO website and other EU news sources, including www.eu-testbook.com and The Ultimate EU Test Book Facebook page. This book being a preparation and testing tool, it is also highly recommended to read widely on EU affairs as part of your study process – as well as taking every opportunity to practise and rehearse.

The task that lies ahead of anyone seeking to pass an EPSO recruitment competition is undoubtedly very challenging. Each competition brings many good candidates contesting for a finite number of places. I hope that *The Ultimate EU Test Book* will be an ever-useful guide to help you on the road ahead.

András Baneth

Brussels, February 2011

1 *www.epso.eu or www.eu-careers.eu*

ABOUT THE AUTHORS

András Baneth wishes to express his appreciation to all those who made this book happen by contributing ideas and checking its content. Special thanks are due to Christine J. Ruzicka for her invaluable proof-reading and comments.

András BANETH is currently an independent author, lecturer and speaker on EU policies, institutions, online communication and recruitment. His bestselling *Ultimate EU Test Book* has helped thousands of candidates prepare for EPSO competitions. A former policy officer at the European Commission, András had previously worked at the Hungarian Parliament, at the European Court of Justice in Luxembourg and then as briefing coordinator for Commission President Barroso and later as a member of the cabinet of Commissioner Kovács. Fluent in English, French and Spanish, he holds an M.A. in law and political sciences and the degree of Master of European Public Administration from the College of Europe, Bruges, Belgium. He is the author of several articles and a frequent guest lecturer at academic seminars in Europe and beyond. If you wish to contact András to request a speech or presentation at your conference or event, please get in touch with him at andras@baneth.eu

Gábor MIKES: With an M.A. in English Language and Literature and former Kellner Scholar at Trinity College in Hartford, Connecticut (USA), Gábor has worked at an NGO specialising in EU affairs communication and at Ericsson, the Swedish telecom giant. With a keen passion for psychometric tests, Gábor has held dozens of training courses for hundreds of people around Europe on verbal, abstract and numerical reasoning, many of whom are now working for various EU institutions. Being an expert on successful methodologies, including both the theory and practice of passing pre-selection tests, he has been the managing director of Europe's leading training company on EPSO exam preparation.

Benjamin WILLIAMS is an HPC Registered Occupational Psychologist and a Chartered Associate Fellow of the British Psychological Society (BPS). Ben has led the design and implementation of Assessment Centres for over 300 public and private sector clients across Europe and the Middle East. Ben began his career reading Experimental Psychology at Oxford University followed by a Masters in Organisational and Occupational Psychology. After his studies, Ben joined SHL, the UK's largest Occupational Psychology firm, then began working for PSL as a Senior Consultant before launching his freelance career in 2006. Ben is an active member of the Division of Occupational Psychology within the BPS and has lectured at the Universities of Greenwich and Surrey on a range of assessment-related topics.

Thomas A. WILLIAMS, with over 20 years' experience teaching Writing, Translation and Business English, is currently involved in teacher education at the University of Szeged, Hungary. He has an MA from the University of Reading (UK) and is now working towards a PhD in English Applied Linguistics. He has published articles on a range of topics as well as a test prep book.

PART I

GETTING AN EU JOB

1. Working "with" or "for" the EU

Dealing with EU Affairs

Before a presentation on EU affairs, I sometimes ask participants why they would like to work in this field and in particular, why they would like to become civil servants of an EU institution.

There are multiple motivations, ranging from the salary benefits to the desire to work in a multicultural environment, but in almost all cases there is a certain (much appreciated) idealism that people would like to work for a united Europe. Despite being an abstract concept, this is in fact a very strong driving force for many professionals who leave their home countries behind and move to Brussels, Luxembourg or other locations where EU institutions are present and where "European" policies are formulated.

Salary issues apart, I have tried to assemble in what follows some of the factors why the field of EU affairs seems attractive to many. It is also important for European Personnel Selection Office (EPSO) competition participants to examine their own motivation: not only isthis a question in the online application form and in the structured interview at the Assessment Centre; it also helps everyone understand which type of position or job profile would suit their needs best.

Seeing how the EU Works in Practice: An important motivational factor for many who have started or are planning careers in both the public and private sectors is to see at first hand the day-to-day operation of the institutions and learn how EU policies are shaped. A national expert dealing with rural development funds for an Italian region, an official in charge of transposing the Services Directive in Latvia, a Portuguese lobbyist covering European research policy on behalf of a pharmaceutical company or a Japanese diplomat following European trade policy issues will all understand the power relations and everyday operation of the system only when having closely observed it and actively taken part in the decision-making procedures and policy formulation. With some hands-on experience, this can add both personal and professional benefits that can be taken advantage of in your later career.

Multicultural Environment: Brussels and Luxembourg are known for their international atmosphere with well over one hundred thousand "expats" living there on a long-term (or permanent) basis. This has a strong influence on the EU affairs working environment where even small firms and NGOs may have, say, just three employees who have four different citizenships and speak five languages. Apart from the opportunity to learn new languages or improve existing ones by interacting in those on a daily basis, this multicultural context has its rather positive influence on work morale and creates a truly intercultural environment.

This also has some very practical consequences. When applying for an EU affairs job or sitting an EPSO Assessment Centre, all candidates must be aware of the cultural and linguistic sensitivities of their fellow candidates and those of the interviewers; stereotypes or national prejudices are taboo. (I once heard about a candidate who, when asked which language he would consider learning if accepted for the job, said that "I don't really like German because it sounds too harsh" – unluckily for him, one of the jury members was Austrian. A hint: he could have formulated it in a positive way by saying

"In fact I like Italian because of its musical sound", without stating a negative opinion or hurting anyone's sensitivity.)

Paradigm Shift: Many people agree that one of the great benefits of working in EU affairs is that their scope of thinking is not limited to their home country or region. It is a broadening experience to learn the different perspectives of people from other countries. EU-wide issues inevitably demand a broad pan-European approach, enlarging the lens through which events are viewed. Moreover, most jobs in this field require travelling in Europe to meet decision- and policy-makers in Member States, which further contributes to how people look at events.

International Networks: Like other international organisations, EU institutions attract a large number of foreign diplomats, businessmen and political activists who interact with each other and their official counterparts on a daily basis. Enlarging your personal and professional network is another motivational item for many; a mutually beneficial relationship with organisations that have offices in a number of European countries and beyond may prove useful for both parties. For instance, someone dealing with fisheries regulations can easily develop contacts with national experts covering this topic, along with other interest representatives such as Greenpeace or the European Association of Fish Producers' Organisations – contacts which can be highly useful in future endeavours.

With the above motivational factors in mind, let's now take a brief overview of EU affairs jobs grouped into two major categories: those that offer work *"with"* the EU and those where employees work *"for"* the EU.

Working "with" the EU

European Union affairs cover a number of different policies, issues and interests; this is well reflected in the Brussels public affairs arena. Thousands of professionals deal with EU public affairs on a daily basis without being employed by one of the EU institutions. For some, undertaking any of the job profiles below is only a stepping stone into the EU institutions themselves. For others public affairs positions and organisations may be better suited to their personality even in the long run, and they may have no intention of joining EU insititutions.

Here are a few examples of working "with" the EU:

Diplomatic Jobs

Diplomatic jobs refer to job profiles that require a certain diplomatic status or involve a (local or national) government official being sent to Brussels or elsewhere for a multi-year period. The recruitment channel is almost exclusively through the national administration, though there are some exceptions as detailed below.

Permanent Representations: All 27 EU Member States and some other countries have a so-called "permanent representation" (or in case of most non-EU countries, so-called "missions") in Brussels dealing exclusively with EU affairs. (These are different from bilateral embassies which represent a country in Belgium rather than to the European Union as an entity.) Each "PermRep" employs a large number of diplomats (from 40 to well over 200) who are both diplomats and experts in fields ranging from money laundering through pesticide regulations to fiscal matters. During their stay in Brussels their status is that of a diplomat; many are in fact civil servants from various ministries.

While administratively speaking these are officials recruited in their home country, they have been seconded to Brussels for a certain number of years to represent their Member State in the working groups and political bodies of the Council of Ministers. (In the case of non-EU countries this obviously does not happen but those diplomats serve as the contact points for technical and political negotiations which affect their country's interests). Those having an expertise in a certain field and with the ambition of becoming a seconded diplomat can enquire at the Permanent Representation of the country of their citizenship or ask the national ministries or government offices' EU department whether they are in need of EU experts.

Regional Representations: Several EU regions and capitals (such as Lower Saxony's or the city of Budapest's Brussels representation office) have their outposts in Brussels to follow EU policy developments, send information home, organise events aiming to increase the visibility of the city or region they represent and network with others to create partnerships for project consortia. These offices sometimes employ civil servants who were sent from home to Brussels for a longer period of time, while others tend to work with any professional who can offer them the right expertise in their field, regardles of their nationality. Those familiar with a certain region's political priorities, language and culture can successfully apply for positions and thus deal with EU affairs from a special regional perspective.

Seconded National Experts: Such experts, also referred to as ENDs (derived from the French abbreviation of "*Expert National Détaché*") work in EU institutions on a temporary basis, mainly the European Commission, while being formally employed by their home government administration. Accordingly, seconded experts may work in any Agency or Directorate General of the European Commission doing similar work to that of EU officials, for example in DG Environment to cover the Slovenian perspective on a certain special protection zone regulation, or in the European Medicines Agency as an expert in the veterinary medicines sector.

EU institutions and Agencies generally publish calls for ENDs and have these also published by the Permanent Representations from which they expect applications, so it is worth checking your PermRep's website or contacting the relevant personnel to notify you in case of vacancies. In most cases ministries or governmental offices in the Member States are also aware of vacancies; it is therefore worth asking around in the Prime Minister's office, Ministry of Foreign Affairs or other national bodies dealing with horizontal coordination of EU affairs as well.

International Organisations: Apart from the EU institutions, Brussels and various other European capitals host a number of international organisations that have formal and permanent contacts with EU bodies. These include NATO, the Council of Europe, the European Free Trade Association (EFTA), the World Trade Organisation (WTO), the United Nations (UN) and its various specialised bodies such as the Food and Agriculture Organisation (FAO) or the International Atomic Energy Agency (IAEA) and others.

These international organisations, while their primary agenda is obviously different from that of the EU, have official links and employ several people to liaise with European institutions. Their recruitment system and job profiles exceed the limits of this book, but those with an interest in EU affairs may be tempted to discover these related fields well. The status of those employed by the above institutions is in most cases comparable to a diplomatic status with various degrees of immunity, specialized tax regime and other benefits.

Political Jobs

The label "political" refers to a rather different job profile than those of diplomats, though in the EU arena this distinction is not as sharp as it may be in a national context. Political jobs have more to do with high-level policy-making than technical rules or project dossiers. Some people are attracted to these positions given their visibility and the high-level issues tackled while others dislike them for the occasional involvement of party politics and allegedly limited focus on execution.

Assistant to a Member of the European Parliament (MEP): One of the most common ways to start a career in the EU arena is to become a personal assistant to an MEP. Given that currently there are 736 Members in the European Parliament and each MEP has at least one or rather two or even three assistants, there are more than 1500 assistants with this job profile. Though since June 2009 parliamentary assistants are formally employed by the European Parliament and therefore do not fully fit the "working with" category, they do represent a special group inasmuch as the decision about selection rests entirely with the MEP. This way, while the Staff Regulations have been amended to cover the assistants' status, they do not need to pass a recruitment competition to be eligible for appointment; on the other hand, their contracts are always only for a temporary period.

This job in fact offers a truly exciting first-hand experience of how European politics are made, though it must not be forgotten that working for a single person requires a very good "chemistry" between the assistant and the MEP, not to mention the need for perseverance and stamina to be always available in case something comes up (and it always does).

Assistants are in no way limited to working only for their fellow compatriots – so as long as they possess the required linguistic skills and subject matter expertise, they have the opportunity to be offered a position by an MEP of any nationality. Thus a Czech university graduate speaking fluent French may be hired by a Belgian MEP or a Bulgarian junior professor may get to work for a British MEP given his English skills and familiarity with Balkans issues which the MEP happens to be involved with.

Given the European Parliament's profile as a political institution and the fact that it is politically active MEPs who are seeking assistants, the way to approach this job is often via political parties; some MEPs require political affiliation or party membership while others seek expertise in a certain policy they are responsible for.

Political Groups in the European Parliament: The European Parliament has seven political groups (and some non-attached members), each of which has its own secretariat and staff. These political groups, such as the Group of the European People's Party or the European Conservatives and Reformists, have specialists who, depending on their policy field expertise and their linguistic-cultural background, variously deal with relations with the media and affiliated political parties and political organisations in the Member States or follow legislative dossiers in the European Parliament's committees and assist the MEPs belonging to the given political group. Most of the groups organise their own recruitment competitions (announced on their websites from time to time) and offer similar benefits to those EU officials enjoy but, unlike in the case of EPSO exams, political affiliation understandably plays an important role in the selection process.

Advocacy Groups: Similarly to Washington D.C., Brussels has a large number of advocacy groups aiming to make their voice and agenda heard. While one may argue whether they truly fit into this category of "political" jobs, Greenpeace, Oxfam and various human rights, religious, pro-democracy and other organisations have indeed strong political views they wish to voice. Job seekers sharing these ideas can certainly find the opportunity to work with EU affairs on a continent-wide basis while representing a cause they sympathize with.

As an example, the campaign by Humane Society International and others to ban the seal trade from Canada required intensive contacts with the European Commission's DG Trade and DG Environment, along with senior diplomats dealing with animal welfare and trade issues in the Council of Ministers, and liaising with MEPs in the relevant Parliamentary committees and making contacts with other advocacy groups and officials to achieve their goal.

Academic Jobs

There are dozens of think-tanks and research institutes covering and analysing EU affairs, many in Brussels and several located around European centres of EU studies.

Think-tanks: The best-known think tanks in Brussels include the Bertelsmann Stiftung, Bruegel, the Centre for European Studies (CEPS), the European Policy Centre (EPC), Madariaga - College of Europe Foundation and the Stiftung Wissenschaft und Politik (SWP) to name just a few. Research institutes in Florence, Warsaw or London are also widely known. These think-tanks carry out research projects in a large number of policy fields in order to provide forward thinking and critical review to EU decision-makers.

By analysing existing policies and offering strategic proposals for legislation, think-tanks and research institutes play a crucial role in European policy making. Those individuals having a more academic interest with skills to carry out interviews, organise conferences and speak in various forums will have good chances to fill vacancies offered by these organisations.

Interest Representation Jobs

Interest representation, or as generally referred to, lobbying companies employ thousands of people interested in EU affairs approached from a sectoral perspective. Private sector contracts are obviously subject to the conditions offered by each individual company.

Consulting Companies: Large international public affairs (PA) consultancies such as Fleishman-Hillard or Hill & Knowlton are all present in the Brussels arena along with their smaller counterparts, active in all sectors including e.g. renewable energy or the aerospace industry. Their tasks mainly include monitoring legislative changes on the EU public affairs scene, offering strategic forecasts, organising consultations with policy makers, carrying out advocacy campaigns, raising awareness of their perspective and presenting briefings to senior officials in the framework of representing their clients.

The contacts with EU officials are rather close, regulated on both sides by strict codes of conduct and ethical rules to respect the principle of impartiality and transparency. Consulting companies offer a great way to learn about EU affairs in a practical way and understand how a policy change can affect a certain sector.

Law Firms: International law firms dealing with EU affairs tend to have competition law or regulatory affairs as their chief focus given their clients' needs and the European Commission's extremely powerful role in formulating and enforcing EU rules in these fields. Lawyers dealing with state aids, mergers and acquisitions, cartels and related issues can always find vacancies, though they must bear in mind that the workload in these firms tends to be very challenging.

In some cases law firms carry out other tasks related to EU affairs such as legislative monitoring or interest representation towards EU officials and MEPs. This is generally in relation to issues that have more legal implications than public affairs concerns so a law firm is considered to be better placed to tackle them than a lobbying firm.

Industry and Trade Associations: Along with the above companies dealing with issues and clients on a horizontal basis, there are hundreds of industry associations such as the European Chemical Industry Council (ECIC), the American Chamber of Commerce Office to the European Union (AmCham-EU) or the European Federation of Pharmaceutical Industries and Associations (EFPIA) and many others.

These associations, while dealing with a single sector, may touch upon several related issues: for instance, the EFPIA deals with intellectual property legislation, research issues, internal market (free movement of goods) issues, smuggling and counterfeiting challenges, public health efforts and even trade policy issues towards third countries in relation to medicine exports. Trade and industry associations usually have close contacts with those EU institutions that are relevant to their agenda, and they employ professionals with a background in natural, political or legal science.

Working "for" the EU

Working in an EU institution may be possible under different contracts, which generally depends on the recruitment method used: to become a *permanent official*, one must without exception pass EU competitions organised by the European Personnel Selection Office, while e.g. EU trainees may be accepted based solely on their online applications. As regards the place of work, the vast majority of the approximately 40,000 EU employees are located in Brussels and Luxembourg, while Commission and Parliament representation offices and EU Agencies located in the Member States also host a certain number of people. Some 5000 temporary agents and EU officials are posted to European External Action Service representations around the world.

Within this category of working "for" the EU, I think it is worth separating out the "formal" part of employment (*the type of contracts available*) and the "content" part of the work, i.e. *the specific job profiles*. First, let's see a short description of the various positions and contracts EU institutions can offer.

Contract Types

Trainee (also commonly called by its French name "*stagiaire*"): An EU traineeship is a very common and popular way to gain first-hand experience of the institutions in Brussels or Luxembourg. Traineeships last five months with two intakes a year, the first batch between 1 March and 31 July while the second batch starts on 1 October and lasts until 28 February the following year; candidates must have at least a Bachelor's degree to apply.

Trainees are offered a modest monthly allowance to cover their living and subsistence expenses, though some traineeships in the European Parliament and elsewhere may be non-remunerated. The largest number of trainees, about 600 per intake, are welcomed by the European Commission in Brussels and Luxembourg, while all other institutions and advisory bodies, including the European Parliament, the Court of Justice of the EU, the Court of Auditors, the Committee of the Regions, the European Economic and Social Committee, the European Investment Bank, European Central Bank, the European Ombudsman and the European Data Protection Supervisor, offer a limited number of traineeships each year.

Having done a traineeship in an EU institution or body can be a very positive element in a CV when seeking a position after successfully passing an EU recruitment competition. Trainees are always allocated to posts throughout the organisation and depending on their background, are assigned tasks such as preparing background briefings, researching certain legislation, carrying out financial analysis or note-taking in meetings, all of which offers a real insight to how institutions operate. (Please see the websites recommended at the end of this chapter for further information.)

Temporary Agent, Contract Agent: As their names suggest, both of these contracts offer *fixed-term* employment for clerical, administrative or policy-making tasks, depending on the job profile and the candidate's background. EU Agencies, located all over the EU, almost exclusively only offer temporary agent contracts that are concluded for three years, renewable for another two; permanent officials are seldom posted or recruited to an Agency though such cases do occur.

On the other hand, EU institutions do employ a large number of temporary and contract agents both for reasons of replacing staff on maternity leave or to fill temporary vacancies in positions that have been newly created and where no permanent official or successful recruitment competition candidate can be found at short notice. Temporary and contract agent recruitments are based on candidates' CVs and a selection interview; however, from time to time EPSO organises so-called CAST ("Contract Agents for Specific Tasks") exams related to an upcoming enlargement or an expected rise in demand for certain short-term tasks. These exams follow the same pattern as general EPSO exams, though in some cases candidates may only be required to pass the pre-selection phase such as verbal and numerical reasoning tests.

Temporary or contract agents of non-EU citizenship may also be employed by Commission or European Parliament representations in EU Member States or in EU delegations around the world to become, for instance, assistant to the Head of EU Representation in Tokyo or carry out political reporting in the Commission's Prague representation office. At the time of writing, it seems that the European External Action Service will also offer such contracts to Member State diplomats who are temporarily seconded to the EEAS. Vacancies are usually announced on EPSO's website or on the EU Agencies' individual websites; it is also worth registering in the EU CV database (link listed in the recommended websites section). You can also make use of a number of websites that offer one-stop-shop information on current vacancies so those in search of jobs do not need to browse through dozens of links.

Permanent Posts (AD, AST): To become a permanent or established EU official of any grade, candidates must pass the recruitment selection competition organised by EPSO. In most cases these are open competitions where anyone with the required citizenship and meeting the formal criteria can apply; however, EU institutions occasionally organise internal competitions where established officials of a lower grade may have fast-track advancement in the hierarchy or temporary agents may become permanent officials. The detailed selection procedure is discussed in the next chapter: here I will only describe the positions and job profiles a permanent official may have. EU officials are always grouped into two major categories called "Assistants" (AST) and "Administrators" (AD).

AST profiles require a high school diploma for AST1 level and a certain number of years of work experience for AST3 level , while AD profiles require at least a Bachelor's level degree. In both cases applicants must have an EU citizenship, though in case of competitions linked to enlargement (e.g. Croatia), the citizenship requirement is extended to the would-be Member State. In both the AST and AD profiles there are multiple levels; thus we can talk about AST1 or AST3, all the way until AST11 while the AD category may go from AD5 (entry level Administrator) until AD16, the latter being the most senior level in the hierarchy of EU officials (Commissioners and MEPs have their own statute, therefore they are not ranked according this system).

Assistant job profiles include, for instance, performing organisational and human resource-related tasks for a Head of Unit in the European Parliament's Committee on Foreign Affairs or coordinating translation files at the Council of Ministers' Estonian lawyer-linguist unit. Administrators may be policy officers in charge of the banking supervision legislation in DG Internal Market or head of unit (minimum AD9 level) at the Committee of the Regions dealing with cross-border cooperation projects and supervising a team of 15 people.

Senior managers having at least 15 years of work experience and significant managerial skills are recruited from outside the institutions or selected from among staff having reached the required level of seniority (minimum AD12) and placed in positions such as Director of Air Transport in the Commission's DG Transport.

For further information on the benefits, allocations, health insurance and pension schemes for EU officials, please refer to the EU civil service website at the end of this text.

Qualifications and Job Profiles

Whatever a candidate's qualifications or type of contract may be, EU institutions offer a wide range of exciting job profiles. Though it may not be possible to get the desired position as the very first place of employment, being already on the "inside" offers the opportunity of internal mobility (transfers) between the institutions after an initial period of time while employees can keep their acquired administrative level, salary and other benefits.

Setting out with the desire to work "somewhere" in an institution is not necessarily the right approach: the goal is to match the right profiles and skills with relevant professional careers to avoid frustration, increase productivity and make it a win-win endeavour for both the employer and employee. That being said, many candidates with e.g. a linguistic background have decided to sit a competition for Public Administrators and consequently got to work in non-linguistic areas; similarly, someone with a veterinary diploma may be invited to work on the Common Agricultural Policy at the European Commission as long as they have passed the required open competition. This is just to underline that the original qualification is less limiting in the choice of career than many might assume.

At the end of this chapter is my intuitive (and certainly non-official) collection of some "typical" positions in various EU institutions and bodies for those wishing to work in one of them. The aim is to give you a flavour of the type of jobs available and help you decide which job type or institution to target on the basis of your degree, work experience and personal profile. This will hopefully be useful not only to identify the type of positions that exist "in" the EU but also to provide a practical compass for those who have successfully passed a recruitment competition and wish to know where to ideally start their EU career.

Recommended links:

EU jobs and EPSO exams:
http://www.eutraining.eu/eujobs

EU civil service jobs website:
http://ec.europa.eu/civil_service/job/index_en.htm

Uploading a CV into the EU institutions' database (to be eligible for a temporary contract):
http://ec.europa.eu/civil_service/job/cvonline/index_en.htm

Middle management posts special bulletin board:
http://ec.europa.eu/dgs/personnel_administration/working_middle_mgt_en.htm

Senior management posts special bulletin board:
http://ec.europa.eu/dgs/personnel_administration/working_senior_mgt_en.htm

European Commission traineeships:
http://ec.europa.eu/stages/index_en.htm

European Parliament traineeships:
http://www.europarl.europa.eu/parliament/public/staticDisplay.do?id=147

European Central Bank traineeships:
http://www.ecb.int/ecb/jobs/apply/html/index.en.html

European Investment Bank internships:
http://www.eib.org/about/jobs/internship/index.htm

European Court of Auditors traineeships:
http://eca.europa.eu/portal/page/portal/aboutus/workingatthecourtofauditors/Traineeship

European Economic and Social Committee traineeships:
http://www.eesc.europa.eu/organisation/tgj/trainees/index_en.asp

Committee of Regions traineeships:
http://www.cor.europa.eu/pages/DetailTemplate.aspx?view=search&id=traineeships

European Ombudsman traineeships:
http://www.ombudsman.europa.eu/recruit/en/default.htm

Court of Justice of the EU traineeships:
http://curia.europa.eu/jcms/jcms/Jo2_7008/

Name of institution (examples only, non-exhaustive list)	Political Science, Social Science Profiles	Lawyers, Legal and Paralegal Profiles	Economist, Auditor, Financial Profiles	Natural and Physical Science, Medical, Veterinary Profiles	Linguistic, Interpretation Profiles	Clerical, Administrative Profiles
European Commission						
DG Environment	Policy officer in charge of revising the EU emission trading system (ETS)	Desk officer responsible for infringement procedures in the field of water pollution standards	Auditor of environmental communication programmes provided via national tendering authorities	Policy officer in charge of mixture toxicity and international aspects of chemical policy		Assistant to the Director responsible for civil protection
DG Research	Administrator responsible for the development of biotechnology research policies	Lawyer in charge of the legal and financial aspects of research contracts	Economist in charge of the financial and budgetary aspects of the 7th Framework Programme	Engineer programme officer in charge of contacts with industrial and academic stakeholders		Assistant in charge of organising conferences and management of publications
DG Legal Service	Coordinator of inter-institutional relations and horizontal coordination with other DGs	Member of the legal service in charge of agricultural and fisheries legislation/policy	Internal auditor in charge of evaluating risk management and governance issues		Italian reviser and linguistic proof-reader of draft legislative acts	Secretary of the legal service in charge of institutional affairs
DG Translation	Policy officer in charge of translation studies and multilingualism		Financial assistant coordinating the invoice processing of external translators		Dutch translator and reviser	Assistant to the Head of Unit in charge of human resource management and coordination
EU Agencies						
European Chemicals Agency	Administrator in charge of risk assessment of products and policy development	Legal officer in charge of public tenders and legal affairs of the Agency	Finance expert to supervise operational budget and respect of the financial regulations	Chemist in charge of scientific support and supervision of market authorisations	Communication officer in charge of web publishing and information dissemination	Secretary in charge of correspondence with stakeholders
European Food Safety Authority	Policy officer in charge of monitoring international food safety trends and strategy	Lawyer in charge of appeals and legal representation of the Authority	Economist responsible for scientific analysis of authorisation decisions' effect on the internal market	Agricultural engineer in charge of scientific risk evaluation		Personal assistant to the director for administration and personnel

Name of institution (examples only, non-exhaustive list)	Political Science, Social Science Profiles	Lawyers, Legal and Paralegal Profiles	Economist, Auditor, Financial Profiles	Natural and Physical Science, Medical, Veterinary Profiles	Linguistic, Interpretation Profiles	Clerical, Administrative Profiles
European Parliament						
Directorate for Structural and Cohesion Policies	Policy officer providing support for the Committee on Regional Development	Legal officer in charge of legal aspects of initiatives under the transport policy	Economist in charge of analysis and forecast of policy changes in the field of tourism			Assistant in the Committee on Fisheries providing clerical support
DG Translation	Coordinator in charge of planning and translation demand management	Swedish lawyer-linguist in charge of translation and revision of parliamentary acts	Financial supervisor in charge of information and technology contracts		Interpreter in charge of simultaneous interpretation into Estonian	Secretary to the Head of Unit in charge of the terminology service unit
DG Communication	Policy officer in charge of public opinion monitoring and improvement	Legal officer in charge of online copyright issues	Economist in charge of budgetary control of human resources		Administrator in charge of publishing multi-lingual print brochures	Assistant coordinator of audiovisual projects
Other Institutions and Bodies						
Council of Ministers	Policy officer in charge of relations with the EU office of the United Nations	Lawyer in charge of financial services legislation	Economist in charge of assisting the Eurogroup meetings	Coordinator in charge of industrial policy initiatives	Danish linguist in charge of proof-reading of proposals for linguistic consistency	Event coordinator in charge of training and personnel development
Committee of the Regions, European Economic and Social Committee	Policy coordinator of the "employee" group's secretariat in charge of contacts with Member organisations	Legal supervisor in charge of decision-making procedures and respect of procedural obligations	Administrator in charge of internal audit of both CoR and EESC services		German translator for both CoR and EESC services dealing with employment, regional policy and social affairs documents	Secretary at the Culture and Education unit of the EESC in charge of preparing and organising meetings
Court of Justice of the EU	Administrator in charge of institutional protocol and visitor groups	Law clerk in charge of drafting judgments and legal assistance to judges	Economist in charge of research, documentation and assistance to judges		Linguist in charge of coordinating and developing translation tools for lawyer-linguists	Assistant providing logistical support to the Registry

2. The European Union's Personnel Selection and Recruitment Process

Introduction

There are thousands of applicants, including trainees and those already working for the EU with a fixed term contract, who attempt to pass the open competitions knowing that this is the only way to become a permanent official of the European Union institutions and bodies. EPSO, being aware of the high interest from candidates and also from its "clients", the EU institutions and bodies, realised the need for strategic and transparent planning. It has consequently made radical changes to the competitions by introducing annual (therefore regular) cycles.

Given that this reform was launched as of last year (2010), significant changes have been introduced compared to the previous system that had been in place for decades with only minor adjustments over the years. In this chapter, I provide a detailed overview of the system, the candidates, the eligibility criteria, the exam steps and other relevant information with numerous practical tips and hints that I hope may improve your chances of success.

The Recruitment Procedure since 2010

Applications in General

Owing to the exclusive nature of open competitions, EPSO cannot consider any ad hoc applications or CVs that are submitted outside the framework of an official competition. On the other hand, vacancies for non-permanent posts or a limited number of senior positions (director level and above) that do not require the below selection procedure are regularly posted on the EPSO website with links to the given Agency or body where applications should be submitted directly. You can find more information about non-permanent jobs below and in the chapter concerning EU jobs.

Planning and Transparency

Further reinforced by the European Ombudsman and the European Court of Auditors' analysis, in 2008 EPSO adopted a Development Programme[1] that outlined a number of improvements and changes to the selection procedure. One of the key elements was to make recruitment as transparent as possible by giving more information to candidates about the stages and methodology of recruitment, along with detailed and timely feedback about the applicants' very own performance in the tests.

It is in this framework that strategic human resource planning was introduced in all institutions, meaning that each Directorate General or high-level administrative unit must signal a forecast of its staffing needs for the upcoming three or so years. This is to help EPSO to plan competitions and it should also help to decrease frustrations that occur when a successful laureate receives no job offer for months or even years. Planning is further reinforced by analysing employee fluctuations, political developments (e.g. the creation of the European External Action Service) or other factors affecting staff turnover or intake.

Increasing transparency is an ongoing effort that includes detailed information about the flagging system (see below), disclosing the names of Selection Board members, the aim to communicate test results and Assessment Centre reports to candidates and help candidates plan their preparation efforts by knowing a relatively precise timeline of exam schedules. This trend is certainly highly appreciated by all applicants.

Skills vs. Knowledge

The most significant element in the recruitment system is a shift from primarily knowledge-based testing to a greater emphasis on competencies (meaning that multiple choice tests and essays focused on memorising facts such as the infamous "How many women Commissioners are there in the Barroso Commission?" type of question are completely a thing of the past).

EPSO has instead created a competency framework against which candidates are evaluated. This way EU-specific and domain-specific knowledge is only of secondary importance and these aspects are only tested to evaluate a candidate's final suitability for the job, provided they possess all the required skills.

While this may look like a novel approach to recruitment, it has in fact been demonstrated by numerous studies that job performance predictability is best provided by a unique mix of skill and knowledge testing, jointly called "competency testing" (see especially Part 3, chapter 1). While not contradicting the above, EPSO nonetheless wishes to recruit candidates who are "operational from day one", therefore the case study and the oral presentation (or in the case of Assistants, e-tray exercise or the practical linguistic tests for linguists), which are the items most closely related to the specific knowledge required for the job, will gain in their relative importance, being the main elements of testing on-the-job suitability.

Core Competencies

According to EPSO[2], the following are considered as core competencies (which are required for all profiles independent of the competition):

- **Analysis and Problem Solving** – Identifies the critical facts in complex issues and develops creative and practical solutions
- **Communicating** – Communicates clearly and precisely both orally and in writing
- **Delivering Quality and Results** – Takes personal responsibility and initiative for delivering work to a high standard of quality within set procedures
- **Learning and Development** – Develops and improves personal skills and knowledge of the organisation and its environment
- **Prioritising and Organising** – Prioritises the most important tasks, works flexibly and organises own workload efficiently
- **Resilience** – Remains effective under a heavy workload, handles organisational frustrations positively and adapts to a changing work environment
- **Working with Others** – Works co-operatively with others in teams and across organisational boundaries and respects differences between people
- **Leadership** – Manages, develops and motivates people to achieve results (only for Administrator grades)

One or two further competencies may be identified for specific job profiles or competitions, depending on the analysis of the given position. The above general competencies are always tested by two different exercises to ensure their validity and reliability as organisational psychologists and human resource experts have created a specific method to ensure the above quality criteria. For more details on what each competency means, how it is measured and how to best improve your performance on them, please refer to the relevant chapters on the Assessment phase in Part III.

Duration

Given candidates' frustration with the extremely long recruitment process under the previous system (where it could easily take two years or more from the exam announcement until actual recruitment), EPSO decided to radically cut down the recruitment cycle by streamlining and professionalizing it. This in practice means that instead of ad hoc competitions, exams are announced each year on a regular, cyclical basis, complemented by exams for Specialists based on resource needs. The annual cycles start with the announcement of Administrator exams in March, followed by the publication of exams for Linguists in July, and closing with the call for application of Assistants in November. It is nevertheless essential to check the EPSO website for the latest information on the schedule as changes in policy or priorities may always happen.

The duration of each cycle is planned not to exceed 9 months from announcement until the publication of the reserve list, which still means however that the actual recruitment may take a bit longer. In any case, it is possible to plan ahead your preparation as it is clear what type of competition is to be announced and when. On a related note, it is advisable to focus your efforts on only preparing for the given upcoming exam phase (pre-selection or Assessment Centre) and not the entire procedure as such from the very beginning.

Soon-to-be Graduates Welcome

A significant improvement in the new system is that the so-called "cut-off date", meaning the date by which a candidate must meet all eligibility criteria, especially that of possessing a diploma or qualification, has been moved to the publication date of the reserve list (i.e. the list of successful candidates) instead of the application deadline.

Take a practical example. EPSO announces the Administrator exams in March 2011. The change means that if you are a graduating student and you expect to receive your diploma in June 2011 but the exam, where a university diploma is a pre-requisite, has its application deadline in April, you could still apply as long as the diploma is obtained by the time the reserve list is established, in around the following January. The rationale behind this change is to offer soon-to-be graduates the opportunity to apply in their last year of studies, thus broadening the scope of the candidate pool, which I think is a great step forward.

Candidates with Special Needs

European Union institutions have always been keen to respect the principles of equal access and non-discrimination given this policy's pivotal place in the EU Member States' legislation and obviously inside the institutions themselves. Therefore in the EU recruitment procedure candidates with special needs, such as seriously limited eyesight, physical disability or other issues that require adaptation in the test centres, should notify EPSO well in advance to make sure that both their access to the testing and the scoring of their exams are adapted to their condition. In its Development Programme, EPSO has also referred to the possibility of introducing supervised one-on-one tests or other measures to encourage such candidates to apply.

Chances of Succeeding

The total number of applications per year is very high – it reached 57,000 for the 2010 Administrator exams. This should, however, not discourage anyone from applying as this figure is far better once put into perspective. Consider that about 10% of these applicants never actually show up at the test centre (they change their minds, were not really serious about sitting the exam, could not make it due to personal reasons etc.) and thus your chances are already higher.

Further, the pre-selection phase is very challenging for those who see verbal, numerical and abstract reasoning questions for the first time at the exam centre. Those having done their "homework" to prepare well are therefore immediately at an advantage. This is the stage at which most will drop out.

EPSO estimates[3] that for the Assessment Centre stage of the exams 1200 Administrators, 600 Linguists and 300 Specialists are to be tested in a year; in addition 900 Assistant candidates will be assessed. This means that the odds are against passing the pre-selection phase and proceeding further (varying largely among the profiles of course, which is discussed further below). It also means that it is not enough to just pass – you have to aim for the highest possible score to do better than others who also reach the pass mark. This is primarily true for the pre-selection phase as those candidates who win through to the Assessment Centre are measured more against the pre-established competencies and less against each other.

Competition and Sifting-in

In the new system, the concept of "sifting-in" is introduced: this means that after looking at the overall results and the number of candidates, the Selection Board determines the threshold score above which all candidates are *considered* for the next phase. This does not mean that all those having scored above this limit will be admitted to the Assessment Centre; however the Selection Board will examine their formal qualifications, eligibility and CVs, and only invite a certain pre-determined number of them for the upcoming stage of recruitment.

This also means that you must consider carefully which exam profile to apply for. For example, if you have a diploma in sociology, you can certainly sit a Public Administration AD5 exam and a Specialist exam if that fits your profile. Similarly, if you are an economist who considers that, based on the earmarked figures disclosed in the Notice of Competition (published on EPSO's website and in the Official Journal), you have more chances in the Economist profile than in the Public Administration segment, you are free to choose either one as long as your diploma and other formal criteria make you eligible for both.

Let's consider an imaginary but practical example. Depending on your profile, you may look at the Notice of Competition and discover that EPSO plans to create a reserve list of 500 Public Administration profiles and 280 lawyer profiles in the framework of an Administrator (AD5) competition. If you have a legal background, you are thus eligible to compete in either of the two categories.

While at first glance it might seem logical to apply for the one where more people are taken and thus your chances seem higher, practice shows that far more candidates apply in the "generalist" Public Administration profile – which changes the equation. If we assume that 9,000 people apply in the Public Administration profile and 3000 people apply for the lawyer one, your chances are 500:9000 compared to 280:3000 for the lawyers, therefore the latter is the smarter choice. The only problem in this logic is the lack of actual statistics: nobody knows exactly how many applicants *will* apply until the deadline is up; therefore this is a unique mix of logical reasoning and chance.

Another aspect to consider is the long-term repercussions of your choice: not only will your exam profile determine the required professional knowledge but it will also affect your recruitment prospects once placed on the reserve list. It is for obvious reasons that EPSO creates sub-profiles and specialist profiles in the recruitment: if an expert on environmental infringement cases is sought, those on a lawyers' reserve list have far better chances of being offered a job than those on a Public Administration list (though this is not a formal rule of course and depends on other external factors as well).

Deciding on which exam profile to sit is therefore a tough decision for many, given its repercussions on the chances to succeed. Nevertheless, as long as you are aware of these aspects, you can evaluate the position better for yourself – this will, in fact, be your first numerical reasoning practice exercise!

Feedback and Complaints

When discussing feedback and complaints, it must be borne in mind that given the significant number of candidates, both are handled in an automated way in the first place until human intervention is required.

Feedback (on test results) is only available in an automated format for the pre-selection phase while those who take part in an Assessment Centre are to be offered more comprehensive feedback in the form of a written report (see a sample detailed positive and negative sample report in Part III, Chapter 6). EPSO also requests feedback online from time to time, so as to improve its procedures.

For complaints, only well founded and serious ones can be taken into account by the Selection Board, for the above reasons. This also means that individual cases are always examined by the Selection Board and EPSO as a body. Moreover, complaints can only concern the lack of respect for the exam rules or other administrative procedures but they cannot relate to the "revision" of the scores or exam results. As an example, if you missed the mark by one point, you cannot argue in favour of leniency or flexibility unless there was an error in one of the exam questions and it must be "neutralised" (more on this below). Another scenario when your complaint may be substantiated is when an exam rule was not respected, e.g. your relevant diploma was not accepted by the Selection Board even though the issuing university is accredited and recognized by your Member State.

As mentioned above, the first place to lodge a complaint with is the Selection Board, but both the Ombudsman and the Civil Service Tribunal may deal with the case. While the Ombudsman can only deal with "maladministration" (this term refers to a situation when an EU institution or body fails to respect the exam rules or procedures – as opposed to individual exam results or evaluations of the selection board), the EU Civil Service Tribunal does examine individual cases on their merits but acts only as a second level judicial review body after the Selection Board has refused your formal complaint. It must nevertheless be borne in mind that these are long and cumbersome procedures that are only worth the effort if you are truly and reasonably convinced that you have been discriminated against or that your application's treatment can be challenged on legal grounds.

On a positive note regarding the feedback that you are given, the best thing is that it opens the way to identifying areas where you may need to improve. Should you not succeed, try to honestly analyse and work on the issues that the assessors pointed out as weaknesses. This will not only help in a subsequent application but, given the nature of such reports, it can help in your own personal development as well, independent of EU competitions.

Another important aspect is that regardless of any failed efforts to pass the exams you can apply for new ones without any limitations. If you do not pass an exam, EPSO does not retain your scores or keep a file on your results, therefore you can start with a "clean slate" if you decide to re-attempt passing the exams.

The Selection Boards

Selection Boards have traditionally been composed of EU officials who volunteer to take part in such tasks. Their background, motivation and interests vary greatly which ensures an objective and fair treatment based on strict guidelines that each of them must follow. Selection Boards, including most assessors, are still going to be chosen from among volunteering active and even retired personnel, though some expertise may be provided by external contractors. EPSO has been trying to professionalize the Selection Boards by extending the scope of their members' assignment for several months or even years instead of using them on an ad hoc basis, thus ensuring the accumulation of more insight and knowledge on their part.

Members of the Selection Boards generally perform the entire administration of an exam on behalf of EPSO but in an independent manner (hence EPSO always denies any responsibility for specific competitions and refers you to the given Selection Board), such as preparing the tests, admitting candidates on the basis of their files or marking the exercises. You, of course, may never approach a Selection Board member for any additional information other than that formally communicated to you even though the board members' names are always made public on EPSO's website for reasons of transparency. Some candidates think that a quick online search to find the professional background of board members could help identify their favourite topics (e.g. if a member works in DG Competition of the European Commission, it may have some bearing on the questions they ask), though this is rarely the case especially since the Assessment Centres have a very different approach in testing candidates.

Venues and Costs

The exams usually take place in Brussels and Luxembourg or, in the event that an open competition is related to the EU's recent or upcoming enlargement or when several Member States' citizens are eligible (e.g. in the case of an EU-10 or EU-27 competition), the capital city of the affected Member States or to-be Member State all host an exam centre. As almost all exams under the EPSO system are administered on computers, exams are generally held over a certain period of time at the designated centres.

Candidates are required to pick and book a date and venue online that suits them most within this period, though you must be very careful in your first choice as revisions or changes are almost never allowed after the booking period is over (the very few exceptions may include issues such as childbirth or medical events).

After you validate your application (i.e. submit it formally), booking will be made available shortly thereafter. The minute the booking is opened, be sure to sign up as soon as possible given that places tend to fill up fast and to avoid any last minute internet blackout or server crash that may prevent you from securing your place in time. On the other hand, be aware that the sooner you validate (submit) your exam application, the sooner your available exam date range will be. If you feel you need more time to prepare, validate your application towards the end of the application period (but certainly not on the last day) so that your exam dates can be towards the end of the exam period. The risk in this approach is that many other candidates think the same way and places may be limited on the date of your preference.

For the assessment phase, you will be given a specific date some time in advance with limited or no option to amend it unless compelling events prevent you from attending and you can duly justify the reason.

As a rule, no contribution is made towards any travelling or subsistence expenses associated with the pre-selection phase of the exam. As these exams take place in the exam centres located in the capital of each Member State and in case of larger countries, also in other large cities, travelling from your home to these centres is always on your own budget.

Assessment Centres are located centrally in Brussels. Candidates who need to travel there are reimbursed for their travel costs and also given some daily subsistence allowance for hotel and food. The specific rules are always communicated in advance either as early as in the Notice of Competition or later to those who actually make it through to the assessment phase. The underlying principle is that nobody should suffer any disadvantage in attending the competitions due to budgetary issues. The same rule of equal opportunities applies for those flying in or travelling to a specific job interview unless a telephone or videoconference is a feasible alternative.

Motivation

Before applying, it is useful to reflect on what factors motivate you in wanting to work for an EU institution. Usually it is a mixture of various considerations – such as the desire to work on international affairs, the opportunity to travel, getting an attractive salary and benefits, having an interesting and varied job, speaking and learning foreign languages, job security etc. Realising which factors are the most important for you can help better identify which profile to apply for and it should also help in the structured interview when assessors try to find out more about your personality. "Being part of something larger than yourself" is a vital aspect that you may also emphasize in your application's motivation section.

The Candidates

It is very hard, if not impossible, to outline a "typical" candidate profile given the large number and diverse backgrounds of applicants. However, I have formed the impression that most of the serious applicants have five things in common. They:

- Are interested in EU affairs, committed to European integration and wish to work for a "good cause"
- Have a solid knowledge of at least two foreign languages
- Are flexible and willing to work abroad in a multi-cultural environment
- Have strong motivation to study for and pass the exams to get into the EU institutions
- Understand and accept that EU institutions are different from the private sector inasmuch as they are a hybrid of a diplomatic corps, an international organisation and a government administration that is based on a hierarchic model

The above qualities will also be looked at by assessors if only on an indirect or informal level. Should you feel that any of the above features does not relate to you, you may wish to reconsider your application or divert your attention to the other sorts of EU-related jobs described in the previous chapter. In any case, EU institutions deal with such a wide variety of issues that you can certainly find the job that best suits your interests and personality if your motivation is right.

Age

There is no limitation on an applicant's age as long as it is not overly close to the retirement age (minimum age is determined by the requirement of a diploma or work experience, therefore minimum age is never formally spelled out). Obviously the EU is keen on ensuring a level playing field in terms of candidates' backgrounds, ensuring equal opportunities for all based on merit, regardless of whether they belong to any particular religious, sexual, ethnic or other minority, social segment or age group.

Whatever your age, you will be required to pass a medical check that will serve as a benchmark for your social security and health insurance file before taking up an EU job. This also serves to ensure that you are physically capable of doing the job you are to be required to perform.

Quotas

It is frequently asked whether EU institutions apply a quota system for allocating posts to a certain number of officials from each Member State. In fact the Staff Regulations provides that officials are to be "recruited on the broadest possible geographical basis from among nationals of Member States of the Communities"[4], which explains the special treatment of so-called EU-10 and EU-2 candidates (nationals of EU Member States that joined in 2004 and 2007, namely Central and Eastern European countries, Malta and Cyprus; later Romania and Bulgaria) and explains why some niche competitions aimed at a limited number of nationalities (including to-be Member States such as Croatia or exams aimed only at Polish and Czech candidates) are announced from time to time.

Apart from the above, this provision in practice means an ongoing effort to maintain a proportional allocation of posts that more-or-less reflects the ratio of each Member State's population and size in the EU, both for ASTs and ADs, including those for senior management. Yet, despite the above principle, there are no hard-coded quotas for Irish or Cypriot citizens given the merit-based competition system. Natural imbalances therefore always exist and they could only be challenged by the introduction of specific staff allocations, which would then likely infringe upon the principle of non-discrimination based on nationality. This is certainly not an easy issue to handle politically as it touches on the very essence of the principles guiding European integration.

Language Rules

One of the most common misunderstandings regarding EU competitions is the language regime: what is the exact meaning of the so-called first and second language? In fact the first language refers to your mother tongue, as long as it is an official EU language. The reason why this needs to be specified is because a Latvian candidate may have Russian as their mother tongue but that cannot be considered as their first language since it is not an official EU language.

In some cases, especially for enlargement-related or linguist exams, the candidate's citizenship or the given exam's specific language profile automatically determines the *required first language* (e.g. exams for Croatian candidates will require the first language to be Croatian, or compulsory French as first language for translator exams in the French language), whereas in other instances you are free to choose your first language as long as the above rules on citizenship and the official EU language requirements are respected (for instance if you have Luxembourgish citizenship, your first language may just as well be French or German; Luxembourgish is not an official EU language). It is important to note that "mother tongue" can also mean that you have a perfect command of a language that you "learned", and if you are confident that your speaking and writing is close to perfect in that language, you can indicate it as your first language (e.g. your citizenship is Slovak but you speak Greek perfectly, and you wish to apply for an exam where one of the first language choices is Greek [and probably there is no option of Slovak as a first language], feel free to do so).

The *second language* is in fact *your first foreign language* and in most cases it must be English, French or German. However, for linguist exams (and sometimes for certain Assistant exams) the second language is usually the one for which candidates are sought. For example, if EPSO announces a linguist exam for Bulgarian translators, the first language is required to be Bulgarian, the second language may be any other EU official language, and there may be a third language (in fact, second foreign language) requirement as well. Note that I did not mention any Bulgarian citizenship requirement here as the goal is the perfect command of a language regardless of which EU citizenship you may have. This is a fundamental rule in the system: the citizenship requirement is almost always different from the language requirements.

An important development is that from 2011 onwards, EPSO plans to require all pre-selection tests (abstract reasoning, verbal reasoning and numerical reasoning) to be done in your first language. This shows that the aim of the pre-selection is not to test your linguistic knowledge but to assess your psychometric reasoning skills, which can be done best in your "EU mother tongue". Situational judgement tests and other tests (e.g. domain specific tests for Specialists, Assessment Centre exams and others) will still be in English, French or German.

A special situation is when your first language is English, French or German - either because your first language in reality is one of these, or for instance in the case of the 2010 Assistant (AST1) exams, the number of first language choices was limited to only a few options. Note that there was no limitation on citizenship, so that anyone having any of the EU27 citizenships could apply, but they had to choose one of the available first languages. This way an Estonian candidate could apply for the AST1 exam in Dutch as long as she spoke that language well enough. In such cases, the rule provided that the second language had to be different from the first one, therefore those with English as their first language were limited to choosing French or German as their second language. This situation will likely be the same in *all* exams from 2011, therefore if your main language is any of these three, make sure to improve your skills in either of the other two!

Once recruited, AD level officials will also need to demonstrate their ability to work in a second foreign language (their "third language") before their first promotion, though many candidates already show this ability at the exam if such an option is available. In any case, always be very mindful which language(s) you select when signing up for the exam, as you would certainly not like to decode French abbreviations in your test if you had intended to take the exam in English!

Another crucial piece of advice to bear in mind is that once you know which language you will take the exam in (i.e. the choice for "second language"; in case of linguists/interpreters, your first language will also be tested), read all preparation materials only in that/those language(s). Needless to say, French, German and all other names of EU institutions, abbreviations, programmes and concepts may differ significantly from each other, and you certainly do not wish to mix up the European Council with the Council of the EU because of a language issue.

Formal Criteria

As a candidate applying for EU exams, you must meet certain formal (objective) criteria. These, as a general rule, say you must:

- Be a citizen of a Member State of the European Union (though exceptions occur as in the case of enlargement-related competitions)
- Be entitled to full rights as such a citizen (e.g. no legal limitations as a result of criminal acts or other issues)
- Have fulfilled any obligations imposed by the laws on military service (only relevant for those Member States where such service is compulsory, and even there you may prove that you were exempted from the service)
- Have a thorough knowledge of one of the official languages of the European Union and a satisfactory knowledge of a second (this is the minimum requirement but further linguistic prerequisites may be set out in the given Notice of Competition as also mentioned above)

- Have the sufficient minimum education[5] and/or work experience[6] as set out in the Notice of Competition

These formal criteria are required for all profiles, regardless of the specific provisions of an exam announcement; meeting these does not lead to passing any stage but their lack certainly leads to non-eligibility or if discovered later, disqualification from the exam.

The Four Profiles

The EPSO system comprises four main segments generally referred to as profiles. These can be summarised in the following table:

	Administrators (AD)	Linguists (AD)	Assistants (AST)	Specialists (AD or AST)
Minimum Qualification	Diploma (min. BA level or 3 years of studies, EPSO may require it to be related to the chosen sub-profile, e.g. Audit)	Diploma (min. BA level or 3 years of studies)	High school degree or post-secondary degree (a minimum of 3 years study-related work might also be required)	Same as for ASTs and ADs
Work Experience	None (AD5); 6 years (AD7); 12 years (AD9) (exception: see Specialists' column)	None (AD5); 6 years (AD7); 12 years (AD9)	None or 3 years, depending on the qualification (AST1-3)	Same as for ASTs and ADs (with possible exceptions, e.g. AD7 lawyer-linguists may have only 3 years of work experience instead of 6)
Type of Qualification (in many cases, though not always, qualifications are eliminatory, so make sure to read EPSO's Notice of Competition carefully)	Arts, Law, Economics, Political Science, Statistics etc.	Language Studies, Interpreting	Clerical Studies, Arts, Finances, IT, Technical skills etc.	Lawyers, Linguists, Engineers, Scientists, Doctors, Veterinaries

Please note that the above table is for information purposes only and the actual requirements may differ; please always consult EPSO's official communications for up-to-date information. Examples of actual job tasks for each profile can be found in the previous chapter.

Choosing a profile is determined by both objective and subjective reasons: depending on your qualifications and work experience (which are "objective" facts you cannot change overnight), you may be limited to only one "choice"; it may nevertheless happen that you are formally eligible for multiple profiles and it remains your individual choice which one to sit for (e.g. a lawyer with three years' experience and fluent knowledge of three languages might be eligible for all the above profiles, including Specialists [lawyer-linguists]).

Multiple Applications

A general approach taken by many candidates is to apply for all competitions they are eligible for, this way increasing their chances. This is in fact a highly recommended strategy though you should be very careful not to apply for two exams in parallel that are mutually exclusive.

Such rules are usually indicated in the Notice of Competition and are limited to the sub-profiles of a given exam: an Administrator (AD5) competition in the annual cycle may have 4-5 domains such as Public Administration, Law, Economics, Audit, Finance and Statistics where candidates are required to pick only one of these options. Apart from the risk of being disqualified from both, it is also technically impossible to choose two domains at the same time given the features of the online application form. If in doubt whether you may run parallel applications for different competitions (for example an AD exam and a Specialist exam), better to ask EPSO than lose out on both counts.

The Exam Procedure Step-by-Step

Having overviewed the above general principles and hints, below are the elements and possible pitfalls of the new EPSO system.

The system comprises the following elements for the four main profiles:

Month(s)	Administrators	Assistants	Linguists	Specialists
0	Notice of competition + self-assessment	Notice of competition + self-assessment	Notice of competition + self-assessment	Notice of competition + self-assessment
1	Online registration	Online registration	Online registration	Online registration
2-4	Pre-selection: verbal/numerical/abstract reasoning tests + situational judgement tests	Pre-selection: verbal + numerical + abstract reasoning tests + secretarial tests (for AST1) + situational judgement tests (for AST3)	Pre-selection: verbal + numerical + abstract reasoning tests + cognitive ability tests	CV sift
5-7	Admission + Assessment Centre: case study + group exercise + oral presentation + structured interview	Admission + professional skills test + structured interview	Admission + Assessment Centre: practical linguistic tests + structured interview	Admission + detailed case study +structured interview + group exercise (+verbal + numerical + abstract reasoning tests)
8-9	Reserve lists/recruitment	Reserve lists/recruitment	Reserve lists/recruitment	Reserve lists/recruitment

As seen in the above table, the exam system comprises essentially four main phases:

1. Notice of Competition, Self-Assessment, Registration
2. Pre-selection Phase
3. Assessment Centre
4. Reserve List, Recruitment

Below I have tried to provide an introduction to each of the stages and tests, along with some practical advice. Later chapters in this book provide sample tests with detailed answer keys on these components.

Phase 1: Notice of Competition, Self-Assessment, Registration

The Notice of Competition

As mentioned earlier, the Notice of Competition (NoC) is a special administrative notice addressed to all EU citizens and it is therefore published in the Official Journal of the EU both in print and online. It is important to underline that the NoC is the only official source of information, therefore if you see any contradicting or different interpretation in the press or on a website, make sure to check the original authentic source which is always referenced on EPSO's website.

The NoC is a rather extensive document that sets out all the formal eligibility criteria, language requirements, deadlines and other practical arrangements linked to the exam. Even more importantly, the NoC contains a wealth of information that you can use to your benefit by reading it attentively, such as the size of the reserve list (so you can estimate your chances and thus decide which sub-profile or domain to apply for after analysing the earmarked number of applicants to be accepted for the assessment phase and how many people are to be placed on the reserve list).

The job description, also detailed in the NoC, is particularly interesting as it is not only an indication of what sort of tasks you would need to carry out once inside but you can deduce lots of hints about the topics to cover when preparing for the domain-specific parts of the assessment phase.

Below is a sample extract of a Public Administration/Human Resources competition's NoC[7]. The comments I have added indicate what type of documents and information sources you should research and focus on when preparing. I suggest using the same method for your specific NoC once the exam you wish to apply for has been published.

Field 1: EPA/HR The general role of administrators in the field of European Public Administration is to support the decision-makers in fulfilling the mission of their institution or body.
The main duties involved, which may vary from one institution to another, include:
— Design, implementation, follow-up and control of programmes and action plans
[Meaning: You will need to be familiar with the EU institutional structure, the main principles of stakeholder consultation, transparency rules, major EU policies currently on the political agenda, legislative procedures including impact assessment and decision-making procedures, and be familiar with shared and exclusive EU competencies]
— Management of resources including staff, finances and equipment
[Meaning: Know the EU Staff Regulations' main provisions on staff rights and obligations, its principles and key formal rules related to the above issues; research some general, non-EU human resources concepts regarding employee satisfaction, training needs, equal opportunities and promotion; revise the EU financial regulations on handling administrative budgets and allocations]
— Assisting decision-makers by means of written or oral contributions
[Meaning: Understand the main organs, bodies and structure of the European Commission, the Council and the European Parliament, be familiar with the key elements of its internal operations; know how to draft notes and highlight policy priorities and link them to organisational objectives]
— Drafting policy analysis briefings
[Meaning: You will most likely need to read about EU competencies in concluding agreements, major initiatives such as the EU2020, economic governance, trade, environment, foreign policy and others, and the main institutions involved in formulating, implementing and controlling these policies]
— External communication as well as internal reporting and communication
[Meaning: What are the EU's efforts to improve its communication, which are the flagship proposals of information and communication policy, be familiar with initiatives, communications and policy papers in this field; internal reporting to the hierarchy, how to present EU policies and achievements to citizens]
— Interservice and interinstitutional coordination and consultation, as well as relations with external stakeholders.
[Meaning: Know what the rules are on the European Transparency Initiative, how stakeholder consultations are done, Green papers, White papers, European Citizens' Initiative, have a basic understanding of intra- and inter-institutional decision-making procedures in all major EU institutions]

It is therefore crucial to understand and analyse every detail provided in the NoC to make sure you can gain valuable insights. This also helps you avoid seemingly evident pitfalls that might lead to disqualification (such as a requirement to submit a certain certificate or sign a submitted document) – you would be surprised to know how many people get rejected on formal grounds by accidentally overlooking a date, a provision or a prerequisite.

Self-Assessment

Self-assessment as a tool is widely used in international organisations and multinational private companies (such as the Canadian civil service, universities, pharmaceutical companies etc.) and EPSO also decided to introduce it from 2010 onwards. Its goal is to make candidates realise what EU jobs are really about and dispel misconceptions or misperceptions at the earliest stage. This is hoped to result in a reduction in non-eligible applications and candidate frustration and so to decreasing overhead expenses related to the organisation of exams caused by registered applicants not showing up or refusing job offers because they had a very different idea of what working for the EU means.

Self-assessment is non-eliminatory, meaning that you cannot pass or fail based on your answers. Expect questions about your willingness to relocate to Brussels, Luxembourg or elsewhere if you are successful in the competition; your interest in working in a multicultural environment; your capacity to handle complex tasks, and various other issues related to values. This latter group of questions may include a check on whether your personal values (such as integrity, hard-work, ethics and others) and personality (flexible, self-driven, confident, autonomous etc.) match those honoured by the EU institutions (working for a public administration, serving the public interest, involvement in policy making, travelling, reward etc.).

This exercise serves both to raise awareness about the rights and obligations that come with an EU job and also to sift out those who may not be so serious about sitting the exam after all. When filling out the self-assessment, there is no real trick to it – simply be honest, think carefully about the issues and bear in mind the above comments on candidate profiles.

Registration

Registration is done exclusively online on the EPSO (EU Career) website at the start of the procedure, which also means that you will not need to hand in *any* proof, paper or document at this stage – you only need to make an honest declaration. The first step is to create an EPSO account, which is an online personal profile where your correspondence with EPSO will take place. If you change your postal or e-mail address during the procedure or any other contact information becomes obsolete, make sure to update your online account immediately.

If, after registration, the confirmation e-mail does not arrive in your inbox within a few hours, check your spam or bulk mail folder as it may have been misfiled by your e-mail application; should you still not receive anything, ask EPSO for technical assistance. Make sure, however, that you do not register twice as it may lead to confusion or even to potential disqualification if other signs show you had second thoughts when doing so.

As in all other steps of the exam, make sure to re-read all input you provide as a wrong click with your mouse can lead to sitting the exam in a different language than intended or an error in choosing your citizenship from a drop-down menu may even result in you being refused for the pre-selection. Lastly, never leave anything for the final moment as many candidates may rush to complete their account in the last few days of application and it may cause service interruptions or outages and prevent you from securing your place – which is every candidate's worst nightmare!

Phase 2: Pre-Selection

Having taken the above steps and provided that you meet all formal eligibility criteria, you should receive an official invitation to the pre-selection phase, communicated to you in your online EPSO profile. Once this eagerly awaited message arrives, you should start planning seriously your preparation as the booking period will open shortly and the exam is imminent. Once the booking starts, you can choose a venue and a time from the available exam centres and time slots. If you live overseas, that is, outside Europe, you can choose an exam centre outside the Member States; most recently EPSO has extended the reach of exam centres to other continents via international test centres in China, the USA and elsewhere, which is a welcome development.

When choosing an exam centre, make sure you are fully aware of the logistical issues: print the map of its location, find out which public transport goes there on the exam day, make sure that no strike or service interruption is foreseen for that day, and have a fall-back plan in case you are running late, such as the phone number of a reliable taxi company.

My general advice for test-takers is to start practicing as early as you can; preferably straight after deciding to sit for an EPSO exam. Even though you will not need any EU knowledge in the pre-selection phase, competition is still fierce and you must achieve the highest possible score. For those who have not dealt with maths since high school (as is the case for most of us), some refreshing courses or online research can always help for the psychometric tests. Various websites provide online preparation tests and courses, and a number of companies offer training in Brussels and elsewhere in Europe.

As also detailed in the relevant chapters, I strongly advise creating a concrete study plan where you allocate sufficient time for the upcoming weeks and months for practice, revision, simulation and preparation. Simply saying "I'll find the time whenever I have nothing else to do" will not lead to tangible results as watching the next episode of *Desperate Housewives* always seems more fun than dealing with rhombuses in abstract reasoning quizzes.

Scoring

In the new EPSO system, some of the multiple choice tests may have as many as six answer options, thus reducing your guessing chances from 25% (in the case of four options) to a bit more than 16% in cases where you are unsure of the answer and need to randomly pick one from six. In any event, as opposed to the system commonly used in French competitions and exams, there is only one correct answer for any given test except for Situational Judgement Tests (see below).

A small but very important piece of advice is to read the question extremely carefully to avoid overlooking words such as "not" in a question that reads "Which of the following is not an EU policy?" I have been told more than a dozen times that a certain question in the previous editions of this book was wrong when it turned out that the readers had misread the question. This of course relates to verbal and numerical reasoning tests as much as other multiple choice questions.

Another important aspect to note is that EPSO is going to evaluate your scores separately for each exercise, which means that you must reach at least 50% (or whatever pass mark is required by the NoC) in each of the tests. It will still of course be your overall score that is going to decide whether or not you make it to the next round but verbal, numerical and abstract reasoning are no longer considered as "single" tests, therefore the threshold must be reached in each of them and not just in aggregate. A piece of good news is that the number of questions and available time limits are different in each test type.

Computer Screens

As all tests in the pre-selection phase are administered on computers located in accredited exam centres, you should be prepared for the difficulties this entails. Reading a text is always slower on a computer screen than on paper, speed being also influenced by the font size and screen resolution. Highlighting, underlining or adding comments on screen is technically not available, therefore you need to take notes on the scrap paper the exam centres provide. Even though an on-screen calculator is usually available, handling it is less easy than using a physical one, especially if you could not practice such operations beforehand.

Computer-based exams do have a few advantages however. The display of the available time (which is not meant to put pressure on you but rather to help time management); the automatic registration of answered and unanswered questions (which should help you keep track of the questions); the flexibility of choosing a convenient exam day (as opposed to having a single exam day); and the faster (and more reliable) correction of your answers given the electronic evaluation, are among the advantages of computer based exams.

Verbal and Numerical Reasoning Tests

The verbal and numerical reasoning tests, along with abstract reasoning, are commonly known as psychometric tests. These are one of the most popular methods to evaluate cognitive skills and the intelligence of prospective employees. They are widely used by multinational companies and civil service recruiters around the world given their flexible application, cost-effectiveness and proven relevance to gauge candidates' skills. The relevant chapters of this book provide a full methodology and hundreds of practice exercises: what follows here is more of a description of how these tests are administered along with some general advice on how to tackle them.

Verbal reasoning tests are essentially reading comprehension tests where you are required to answer a question based on an 8-15 line-long text. A fundamental rule is to only consider information contained in the text and ignore all prior knowledge you may have of a given topic unless it is a law of nature or common knowledge (e.g. that the Earth revolves around the Sun or that the EU has 27 Member States).

Numerical reasoning, on the other hand, is a calculation exercise based on statistical charts and graphs based on which you are required to find a certain percentage, figure, or decide on relative values (e.g. "Based on the table, which country had the highest relative birth rate in 2008?"). Questions can be tricky as in many cases no calculation is required given that you can simplify the riddle by applying calculation methods and short-cuts. A comprehensive toolkit is offered in the relevant chapter of this book regarding the above.

EPSO has been using verbal and numerical reasoning tests for several years in its competitions and they have proven to be one of the most challenging parts of the exam procedure. The likely reason is that while EU knowledge could be memorised by dedicating sufficient time to this end, succeeding in verbal and numerical reasoning requires a completely different approach. Extensive practice is only part of the solution as applying a few fundamental principles and understanding the methodology are essential to succeed.Lots of practicing and learning the methodology is therefore crucial to succeed.

As mentioned above in the languages section, from 2011 all verbal and numerical reasoning tests are most likely going to be in your first language (along with abstract reasoning, but there the choice of language has no relevance). Linguists can expect to have three different verbal reasoning tests: one in their main language (which depends on which linguistic profile they had applied for, e.g. Bulgarian translator or German interpreter); while the other two depend on the source languages available for that given exam (English,

French and German have privileged status and almost always appear among the languages).

Work as hard as you can to improve your overall vocabulary in the exam's language by reading quality newspapers, boost your spelling skills for complex words, your understanding of measurement units (billions vs. millions, how many litres is one m^3 etc.) and revise basic mathematical operations. You can also find dozens of further hints and resources in this book.

Abstract Reasoning Tests

A new element in the reformed competition system is the abstract reasoning, which is another test type that various international employers commonly use; it is a common feature of popular IQ tests as well. Abstract reasoning is different from the other two tests as it requires no linguistic skills: there is only one main question for all tasks, such as "Which figure is the next in the series?"

Using these questions for personnel selection is practical for EPSO given that there is no need to translate the exercise into any language and also because abstract reasoning tests have been scientifically proven to be culture-neutral while effectively testing candidates' so-called "fluid intelligence". This latter term refers to the capability to solve new problems and understand the relationship between various concepts, independent of any acquired knowledge.

The main skill you need to efficiently resolve abstract reasoning tests is "imagination", that is, the ability to mentally rotate, flip or turn certain figures according to a certain logic or rule. This rule is one of the main challenges of this question type as you should be able to "dissect" a figure and identify its component elements. Those capable of performing such tasks are likely to be able to cope with unknown or new situations in the workplace: this skill therefore does have more practical value for predicting actual job performance than may seem at first glance. You can find a large number of abstract reasoning tests in the relevant chapter of this book, along with an in-depth methodology that is highly practical and applicable.

Situational Judgement Tests

Situational Judgement Tests (or SJTs for short), although a new element in EPSO preselection exams and which are to be used for most profiles, have been employed for decades by different organisations, such as the Canadian Civil Service, and companies that have wished to measure potential candidates in real-life work scenarios. The objective of SJTs is to create realistic work-related scenarios in which you must determine the proper course of action given the parameters and situation. In other words, the test basically asks what you would do in a particular circumstance.

An important element of SJTs is that there are no qualitatively right or wrong answers when testing your judgement. Rather, judgement is about your ability to assess a given situation and make clearly defined decisions on how to proceed from there, based on your own unique set of experiences in life, understanding of the EU institutions' culture and ethical rules, while applying a certain common sense to workplace situations.

For example, given a sample question about witnessing malpractice in your unit committed by a colleague, your reaction or response may be to confront that person first while another person may feel it is most appropriate to let your head of unit know about what has happened. This is therefore closely linked to the competencies that EPSO is seeking to find in future EU officials.

Since there are no right or wrong answers, the decision whether one answer is better than another would have to be in the hands of the test administrators; however, the benchmark for deciding the value of each answer is the competency list that EPSO has established (see above) and against which it evaluates candidates. SJTs therefore have the potential to measure various issues such as your organisation or team working skills, or your ability to prioritise.

It is important to point out that while real world situations can certainly be summarised into brief sentences or paragraphs, rarely do we come across situations in life that resemble these questions precisely. As in the above example, you may be confronted with a colleague who may be stealing and who may also be a friend, or someone with whom you are in direct competition for a promotion. This would certainly change your judgement and response.

For further background details on SJTs, how they are created, including a full sample that covers all competencies EPSO has determined, please refer to the relevant chapter in this book.

Notification of Results

After the pre-selection phase, or in the case of Specialist profiles, after the successful sifting-in of your CV, candidates are notified both of their positive or negative results. The scores and the answers you had given are communicated to you in all cases though for practical reasons EPSO cannot disclose the multiple choice questions themselves, only the answers you had marked.

Should you not make it to the structured interview in the assessment phase, your situational judgement tests are "lost" in the sense that your competency profile is not established. Otherwise a special algorithm interprets your SJT answers, which is then forwarded to the assessors for follow-up in the assessment phase.

Since the number of applicants in the pre-selection phase runs into the tens of thousands, EPSO decided some time ago to require the submission of supporting documents only for those who have passed the pre-selection or were "short-listed" Specialists based on their CV. This means that even those who have already cleared the first hurdle may not take their eligibility for the assessment phase for granted: EPSO will first of all require you to send in a completed and signed application form along with annexes listing your educational qualifications and if necessary, documents attesting your professional experience or other required information.

As soon as the above documents are validated and accepted, you receive an official notification in your EPSO profile that you have been admitted to the assessment phase. Shortly afterwards you will be required to confirm your presence at a given venue and date to undergo the assessment exams.

Phase 3: Assessment

An Assessment Centre, as the second round of exams for Administrators and Linguists (and in most cases, the first round for Specialists), consists of a standardized evaluation of behaviour based on multiple inputs[8]. This in practice means that several trained observers called "assessors" evaluate your performance throughout half a day or a full day of exercises that have been developed specifically for this purpose. EPSO is using multiple types of exercises based on their competency framework: the idea is that each competency (listed above such as "Delivering quality and results") will be tested by two types of exercises to make sure that the observations are valid.

The reason why different competencies are tested by using various exercises for various profiles is that EPSO has linked certain competencies to each profile and therefore only wishes to test you on those that are relevant for your field. Accordingly, Assistants will not be required to give an oral presentation as their job roles will not include giving presentations; similarly, a case study is used for Administrators and Specialists as it is a highly complex drafting/analytical exercise that other profiles do not need to be tested on.

Based on the above, EPSO uses the following catalogue of exercises in the Assessment phase of the recruitment competition:

Professional Skills Tests

Linguists' Skills Tests (Translators, Interpreters, possibly Lawyer-Linguists)

For the Linguist profiles, the pre-selection tests already include two extra verbal reasoning tests that concern their two "source" languages. The main verbal reasoning test is in their "target" language (which is the language of the chosen exam profile, e.g. for Spanish interpreters it is Spanish). More information on the languages is given in the section above on this topic.

As for the professional skills tests, they have not yet been organised at the time of writing but they are likely to be somewhat similar to a classic language exam, comprising either multiple choice tests on grammar, syntax, punctuation and synonyms or, as a more likely scenario, including the translation of two 500 to 1500-word-long texts from each of the source languages into the target language (for translators) and a "live" interpretation with the above language combinations (for interpreters). A listening comprehension test (answering multiple choice tests based on an audio recording) is also possible.

Translators and interpreters are also going to have various exercises in the assessment phase such as the structured interview, group exercise, oral presentation and the above-mentioned professional skills test. These exercises will not necessarily cover EU affairs, though they will certainly cover a wide range of topics such as economics, history or politics, given that these issues feature prominently in the day-to-day work of an EU translator or interpreter.

For lawyer-linguists the translation of a legal (though not necessarily EU) text is going to be maintained in the Assessment Centre phase, along with verbal, numerical and abstract reasoning tests and other competency tests (structured interview, group exercise). Traditionally, lawyer-linguists have not been allowed to use a dictionary for their translations, which made this testing more challenging than that of translators. Interestingly and importantly, lawyer linguists will have an extra test in the Assessment Centre which covers their general knowledge of and linguistic skills related to national (!) law. The reason for this test is not so much the knowledge of national paragraphs and regulations but the requirement to be familiar with the judicial and legal terminology that is a pre-requisite to performing a lawyer linguist's job well.

Specialists' Tests

It is important to note that for Specialists, the pre-selection exams described above may be moved into the Assessment Centre stage, depending on the number of applicants. As a general rule, EPSO says that if the number of specialist (e.g. nuclear scientist, cohesion policy expert, competition lawyer etc.) applicants exceeds 20 times the number of places available on the reserve list, it would organise a pre-selection round for specialists as well, otherwise these exam items would be included in the assessment phase. Moreover, specialists need to go through an online pre-screening questionnaire that tries to identify their work experience in the given field, whether they have had publications in academic journals, done research in the field and many other declarations that can help the Selection Board evaluate specialist candidates' suitability and eligibility for the post. (Even though these are declared on "word of honour", they may be checked by requesting supporting documents any time in the selection process or at recruitment.) Should a large number of such candidates remain even after the pre-screening, a pre-selection round may be organised to filter candidates further. For all other profiles (Administrators, Linguists and contract agent posts), a pre-selection phase is the default rule without any in-depth online screening other than basic formal eligibility criteria.

In the previous system, specialist knowledge was always tested in the second (written) phase of the exams in the form of multiple choice tests and an essay; in the current system this type of domain specific knowledge is tested in the assessment phase mainly in the form of a practical exercise or in the framework of the case study. This latter is closely related to the exam profile and the sub-profile or domain that you had chosen at the time of application.

EPSO sometimes decides to include multiple choice specialist (though almost certainly not EU knowledge) questions even in the pre-selection or later in the assessment phase of all profiles, especially for Assistants and Specialists (e.g. "office skills" tests for AST1 candidates). If applied, these questions cover practical issues such as financial or project management, public administration and human resources issues, depending on the profile sought. What seems more probable is that even if some aspect of the specialist knowledge is tested by multiple choice questions, these will take a less theoretical and more job-oriented approach than the tests used beforehand, though as a general rule, such knowledge is tested in the case study exercise.

In any case, specialist knowledge is going to be tested for all profiles as no capable candidate who otherwise lacks the proper knowledge of the chosen field can be recruited, given EPSO's wish that all new officials should be operational from "day one". Moreover, even specialists need a solid understanding of EU institutions, procedures and stakeholders, which can add valuable points to your performance in the assessment phase of the exam.

For instance, if you are familiar with the overall context of the EU's environmental policy, know which institutions and agencies are involved, which are the formal rules to enact policy in this field, which European associations and NGOs are taking an active part in influencing decision-makers and what the strategic thinking is on this policy's future, you are immediately in a position to make more out of the group exercise, the case study or the oral presentation than many other candidates who lack such knowledge would be able to do.

Here are a few further examples of EU and specialist questions to give you an idea of the wide range of issues that may be touched upon by the specialist tests and other exercises such as the case study (see below):

- What is an impact assessment and which are its governing rules?
- How can an EU tender procedure be launched and what are the exclusion criteria?
- What are the main competencies and tasks of the European Parliament?
- Which are the main EU institutions and what does each deal with?
- What is the ordinary legislative procedure? What other procedures exist?
- What does the European Investment Bank do?
- If you were asked to highlight 5 improvements introduced by the Treaty of Lisbon, which ones would you pick?
- What is the EU2020 plan?
- What is the so-called climate change and energy package?
- What is meant by the concept of "economic governance" and how is it being addressed?
- What should EU institutions do to improve access to EU documents for EU citizens?
- What are the sources of EU law?
- What instruments can EU institutions use against the non-respect of EU law?
- What is an Excessive Deficit Procedure and why is it used?

– Which institutions and bodies are involved in concluding an external trade agreement?
– What is performance audit and how is it used in the EU institutions?
– Which procedures ensure budgetary control in the EU?
– What is the European Arrest Warrant and how does it work?
– What are the rights and obligations of an EU official, based on the Staff Regulations?

Case Study

The case study exercise is meant to test your professional skills along with other behavioural items such as organisation and prioritisation skills. You will be given a comprehensive dossier including various policy communications, statistical data, legal and/or technical background information, based on which you will be required to answer some open-ended but profile-specific questions.

This type of exam item is very similar to an essay but in this case you are required to use the background file in a structured manner in order to produce a position paper, an analysis or a line of argument in favour of or against an initiative. This task is in fact the one where your professional skills related to the chosen profile (Economics, Law, Building Manager, Engineer etc) are tested as much as your competencies to structure your thoughts in a logical and compelling manner, argue in a convincing way and express yourself in writing to a high standard.

It is understandable that EPSO will want to see your ability to draft reports, understand complex files and provide similar input that your to-be superior may request from you one day. This book provides a large number of sample questions for a diverse range of profiles and a full exercise with scoring grid and sample answer file to help you understand how your performance is evaluated, and further tips on drafting effectively.

Oral Presentation

Your exam profile's tasks may require you to make an oral presentation. This is a special opportunity to speak in front of a small audience of assessors or possibly fellow candidates to present your case and answer challenging (and sometimes purposely probing) questions. Similarly to other Assessment Centre exercises, this one also relates to the competency catalogue items against which EPSO wishes to measure you.

The oral presentation is therefore a unique mixture – examining your professional knowledge and understanding of the European Union along with your ability to talk about a specialist topic in a clear manner and awareness of your vocabulary and body language while withstanding pressure from various "stakeholders". This is an exciting exercise in the Assessment Centre, but it certainly requires thorough preparation with friends or a professional coach, especially for those who have no experience in public speaking or giving presentations. Recording yourself while making a speech is a good first step to improve, followed by a careful analysis of your body language, choice of words, reactions to questioning and managing pressure.

In the relevant chapter we have included an in-depth collection of tips and hints on how to make the most out of your oral presentation.

Group Exercise

Unlike the case study, the group exercise is not specifically related to your chosen profile and its focus is purely on testing your competencies. Skills relevant to working in a team, interacting, arguing intelligently with and listening to others, cooperating and coming to an agreement are being assessed in this exercise. This emphasis on skills, however, does not mean that your EU knowledge and understanding of the various cross-cutting policies, terminology and institutional-political system would not be crucial to achieving a high score: the underlying scenario is likely to be related to EU affairs or a key policy such as the fight against climate change, enhancing the internal market, creating equal opportunities or the EU's global role.

While you perform other exercises individually, this one will test your ability to work with potentially stubborn, silent or extrovert candidates in an efficient manner: a true simulation of your future unit with a diverse personal and cultural background. You can find in the relevant chapter a full group exercise scenario with scoring guide and preparation tips to help you perform your best.

A common misunderstanding concerning the structured interview is to look at it as a job interview, which it is *not*. While a job interview focuses on your suitability for a very specific role such as "Case handler in DG Competition State Aid unit", the structured interview aims to gauge your skills and take on certain competency-related situations such as your skill to communicate with clarity or manage tight deadlines, reinforced by examples from your earlier work or other experience. This is the reason why the situational judgement tests form the basis of this interview by establishing a preliminary competency report on you, further fine-tuned in this exercise. Not only will your body language, oral expression and choice of words be evaluated, but the example situations and answers will also be listened to with great attention.

As candidates in *all* EPSO profiles will be required to undergo a structured interview, this chapter is one of the most comprehensive ones in this book, covering all eight competencies against which EPSO wishes to evaluate you. For each of these competencies we have included sample questions and follow-up probes, a thorough description, possible issues to think of and a scoring guide with sample answers. This should prove to be a valuable asset in your preparation as it should allow you to come up with examples that will likely be useful in the exam (e.g. it is certainly far better to consider a question such as "Tell me about a time when you experienced a difficulty in a working relationship with someone" beforehand rather than freeze at the exam if no good example comes to mind under pressure).

Assessment of Heads of Unit

The assessment for Head of Unit and Director posts has traditionally been carried out via an Assessment Centre, which is nevertheless likely to undergo changes based on the reformed selection of non-managerial candidates. In any case, potential Heads of Unit should prepare along the same lines as Administrators, even though the competency model against which they are evaluated will be somewhat different, having a strong focus on management-related issues.

This means that questions testing the candidate's people/time/team/financial/operational/conflict management skills will feature prominently in the structured interview and will possibly impact other exam items such as the group exercise and the case study as well. Moreover, candidates for these exams are advised to be familiar with the EU Financial Regulations and general principles of handling budgets and funds (see relevant links below).

Further to the samples described above and in the relevant chapters, here are a few example questions focusing on management issues:

- List a few examples of management challenges from your work experience.
- What approach would you adopt with your subordinates who are older than you?
- How can you motivate your staff within the framework of the Staff Regulations?
- How would you handle a situation in which you found out that a subordinate had applied for the same post as the one you were selected for and was acting rather jealously?
- How would you handle underperformance in your unit?

- Describe a project where you efficiently used your delegation skills.
- What methods would you use for internal communication in your unit or directorate?
- What is your negotiating experience? Please also provide examples.
- How would you react if a member in your unit had a serious medical problem and would need to be absent from work for several weeks?
- How do you prioritize tasks on a busy workday?
- If a member of your unit came to work dressed inappropriately, how would you react?

Assessment Report

After both the Assessment Centre and other forms of assessment, a report will be drawn up by the assessors to evaluate you against the pre-established competencies. This also means that first and foremost you will not be judged against other candidates but rather against the *objective* behavioural criteria EPSO seeks in candidates. The ranking of suitable candidates will come afterwards and will be largely influenced by your performance in professional knowledge metrics.

Based on a streamlined and structured methodology, assessors draw up a report that summarises your performance, along with your strengths and weaknesses. For the sake of understanding and to draw conclusions, you can find two such sample reports in this book (Part III chapter 6) relating to an imaginary candidate who performed well and one for a candidate who was not deemed to be suitable for the given profile.

Upon request or even automatically, EPSO plans to reveal this report to all candidates regardless of whether or not they were successful in the assessment phase. This report can add a lot to your self-development as it provides a comprehensive analysis of your personality traits as observed during the assessment. It can also be very helpful in deciding which of your skills or competencies may need to be developed.

Phase 4: Reserve List, Recruitment

For those candidates who successfully passed both stages and survived other potential pitfalls in the exam procedure, a notification including the words "we are happy to inform you" arrives in their virtual EPSO account's mailbox. This also means that your name will be published in the reserve lists that appear in the EU's Official Journal and on EPSO's website and your competency passport, based on the above assessment, will be added to your profile once you take up employment. Those who did not succeed this time should not despair as they can re-apply for any later exam with the advantage of being familiar with the working methods of the system.

Validity of the Reserve List

Once a reserve list is published, it is always clearly indicated when it expires, meaning until which date can you be recruited from it. However, EPSO has regularly extended the validity period of a reserve list to make sure that all available candidates are recruited from it. In the new system, the idea is to have the Administrator (AD) competitions' reserve list valid until the next annual cycle results in a new list; for linguists it is the same approach but instead of the next annual cycle, it will be the next competition in the same language that replaces the previous list; for Specialists, the lists are valid as long as they still contain recruitable (available) laureates.

Flagging

Once on the reserve list, candidates (or as they are called at this stage, "laureates") are "flagged" by the institutions. This means that your profile listed in the "E-laureates" database can be assigned different statuses (marked in colours) as follows:

- **Green**: Any institution may recruit the candidate; they are not reserved for any specific EU institution or body
- **Yellow**: A specific institution or EU body has a keen interest in the candidate or the candidate passed an exam which was specific for a given institution (e.g. a lawyer-linguist exam to recruit officials for the European Parliament); as a general rule, this reservation is valid for three months, after which the candidate regains a "green" flag
- **Orange**: It is similar to the yellow flag but an interview has already been scheduled with the laureate or an extension of the above 3-month rule has been requested
- **Blue**: It is again similar to the yellow flag but it also shows that the laureate is already employed by an EU institution (e.g. an Assistant who is working for DG SANCO has passed an AD5 exam)
- **Red**: The laureate has already been recruited or their recruitment is happening right now
- **Grey**: The laureate is temporarily not available (e.g. the person is interested in taking up a job but currently cannot due to family or work reasons)
- **No Flag**: The candidate is no longer available for an EU job despite having passed the competition and being on the reserve list

Job Interview

Once on the reserve list, you can try to lobby for yourself by indicating your exam's reference number and presenting your CV to targeted heads of unit; this, however, is seldom effective. EPSO much rather recommends that you wait to be contacted by interested institutions or if you wish to get in touch with them yourself, they provide a candidate contact service list on their website[9].

Any time between a few weeks and several months, you may receive a phone call or e-mail asking whether you would be interested in an interview for a position at x or y EU institution. Always make sure your contact data is up-to-date and that you regularly check your EPSO profile as well in order not to miss such important events.

Once offered the chance to attend a job interview, it is highly recommended to participate even if the job itself may not be the most appealing. You can always decide to decline and wait for a better or different offer, but it is better to have such options than decline flatly in the first place. You can also gain useful interview experience and find out more about the position; you might even realize that the job is in fact meant for you.

The job interview itself is different from other parts of the recruitment competition as it is focused on your suitability for the specific position and it does not include any general EU questions. If you apply for a consumer health expert position, you can expect a number of technical questions on this specific topic but nothing on e.g. the Treaty of Lisbon or the EU's immigration policy (unless the job in question is in the Commission's DG Home).

Your interviewers will most likely speak in English, French or German, unless you are applying for a translator or interpreter post where the rule is rather your second language (if different from the above three). Be aware, however, that questions may be put to you in any other language specified in your CV. Should you feel that you need to further clarify matters, take care not to patronise the interviewer and that your body language is also entirely respectful. It is very much recommended to review the hints and tips described in detail in the structured interview and oral presentation chapters of this book as they contain dozens of practical bits of advice for this stage as well.

Medical Check

A medical check is required for all new recruits; it may take place even before you know the result of your job interview. Should you not be chosen, the medical check results are valid for a few months so you will not need to re-take it if you attend another interview and you are accepted for another post. In any case, avoid the temptation of having that delicious-looking ham-and-eggs for breakfast or you risk further check-ups due to an excessive cholesterol level.

Travelling

You will most likely need to travel to Brussels or Luxembourg for the interview unless a video- or phone-conference call can be arranged at the EU representation or delegation office of your country of residence. Should you need to travel, all costs will be reimbursed and you will be given a modest daily subsistence allowance as well (based on strict formal conditions), but be prepared to receive the reimbursement only several weeks later.

Recruitment

If your interview was successful, you will be offered a job first by phone or e-mail, then formally by letter. Should this not arrive in time, make sure you ask your future EU institution's HR department or the unit in which you will work to send it to you. Generally you can agree on the starting date of employment with your future boss, so you can look for accommodation (if in Belgium, try www.immoweb.be) and arrange paperwork in due course.

Moving costs are paid for unless you have lived in the country where you were recruited to for more than a certain period of time (e.g. if you had done an EU traineeship at the Commission in Brussels right before you got recruited, this may prevent you from having your moving costs paid or being granted a so-called "expatriation allowance", though the rule is generally six months of residence and for traineeships, the duration is five months). The detailed rules can be found in the EU officials' Staff Regulations, listed in the section below on further resources.

Preparation Methods

Preparing for EPSO tests is far from being an easy exercise and experience has shown that most test takers have had feelings of apprehension as they prepared. The way of preparing for the tests is really an individual choice. You may find that simply looking at the tests' objectives and preparing on your own makes you feel confident; conversely, you may want to read text books, take web-based training courses, or actually go through instructor-led preparatory classes offered by a training centre such as Trainday (*www.trainday.eu*), the European Training Institute (*www.e-t-i.be*) or others. Another great way of preparing is forming a study group where you can evaluate each other's written and oral expression skills based on the guidelines of this book.

Whatever method you choose, know that timing and motivation are the linchpins. As you prepare for your test, make sure to start soon enough and take it very seriously all the way. Knowing when to begin your preparation process is critical to having enough time without feeling rushed. The change in EPSO's communication, where the timelines of subsequent exam phases are transparently published, will make the planning much easier than it has been in the past, and it is strongly advised to start preparation at least two months before the exam day.

The first thing that you must remember is that tests are not written with the intention of catching you out. In fact they are only meant to probe your skills and competencies in various "reasoning" exercises and assess whether you have a concise understanding of the chosen field while ensuring that you possess the right competencies at the same time.

What to Study

Regarding your EU knowledge, make sure to have a good understanding of the "Treaties", meaning the Treaty on European Union and the Treaty on the Functioning of the European Union. This is something that can add greatly to your performance and potentially impress the assessors (as long as you get all the other items right).

A solid knowledge of how EU institutions and decision-making procedures work and what the key priorities of the European Commission and Parliament are; an idea about some milestones in EU history; and familiarity with the latest European Council Presidency Conclusions, key judgements of the European Courts, basic Eurostat data, and strategic policy papers such as the EU2020 programme – these are all useful for learning the specific character and vocabulary of the EU. Lastly, reading EU news on a daily or weekly basis can help you understand how a seemingly abstract or complex piece of legislation works in real life.

Preparation Resources

For the pre-selection phase, I recommend reading through this book's concise methodology chapters and practicing the exercises multiple times. You can find further resources online as indicated above and in the collection of links below, while. EU specialist bookshops such as *www.eubookshop.com*, *www.libeurop.eu* and *www.eurobookshop.be* also offer a wide range of books. For the assessment phase, several YouTube videos can help you see real life examples and tips for each exercise, and this book should also help in identifying the key concepts to be aware of.

Browsing the Commission Directorates Generals' websites for "hot" issues and checking the relevant Commissioner's website and speeches on your topic will help you understand where to focus your attention; having a look at the various European Parliament committees' meeting reports can also serve as time-saving and efficient tools.

Linguists can find excellent resources on the Commission DG Translation's website regarding terminology; finding and comparing the terminology of various EU documents in different linguistic versions is also a powerful preparation method.

Having reviewed the above rules and general advice, let's get started with the preparation!

Endnotes

1 *http://europa.eu/epso/doc/epso_development_plan.pdf*

2 *http://europa.eu/epso/discover/selection_proced/selection/index_en.htm#chapter2*

3 *http://ted.europa.eu/Exec?DataFlow=N_one_doc_access.dfl&Template=TED/N_one_result_detail_curr.htm&docnumber=58794-2009&docId=58794-2009&StatLang=EN*

4 The wording "Communities" is likely to be changed soon to "Union" according to the changes introduced by the Treaty of Lisbon.

5 For the official list of diploma types accepted by EPSO, please refer to *http://europa.eu/epso/doc/diplomasfortheweb.pdf*

6 Regarding work experience, generally a copy of references from the current and previous employers is sufficient to demonstrate that the required level and length of professional experience have been attained

7 Extract from: *http://eur-lex.europa.eu/LexUriServ/LexUriServ.do?uri=OJ:C:2010:064A:0001:0008:EN:PDF*

8 *http://www.assessmentcenters.org/pdf/00guidelines.pdf*

9 *http://europa.eu/epso/success/recru/contacts/index_en.htm*

Further General Resources (see other specific resources in the relevant chapters)

Europa: *http://europa.eu*

EU Legislation Summaries: *http://europa.eu/legislation_summaries/index_en.htm*

EU CV Registration for Temporary Jobs:

https://ec.europa.eu/dgs/personnel_administration/open_applications/CV_Cand/index.cfm?fuseaction=account&langue=EN

European Parliament Fact Sheets:

http://www.europarl.europa.eu/parliament/expert/displayFtu.do?language=EN&id=73&ftuId=theme.html

European Court of Justice: *http://www.curia.europa.eu*

Council of the European Union: *http://www.consilium.europa.eu*

Presidency Conclusions: *http://europa.eu/european-council/index_en.htm*

European Court of Auditors: *http://www.eca.europa.eu*

European Environment Agency glossary: *http://glossary.eea.europa.eu/EEAGlossary*

Eur-lex: *http://eur-lex.europa.eu*

Treaties: *http:/eur-lex.europa.eu/en/treaties*

European Personnel Selection Office: *http://europa.eu/epso/*

EU Official Directory: *http://europa.eu/whoiswho/*

Staff Regulations: *http://ec.europa.eu/civil_service/docs/toc100_en.pdf*

Citizens' Europe: *http://ec.europa.eu/citizenship/*

Multilingual Terminology: *http://iate.europa.eu/iatediff/*

EU Financial Regulation: *http://europa.eu/legislation_summaries/budget/l34015_en.htm*

DG Translation Aids: *http://ec.europa.eu/translation/index_en.htm*

EU ABC: *http://en.euabc.com/*

Wikipedia: *http://www.wikipedia.org*

Euractiv: *http://www.euractiv.com*

EU Observer: *http://www.euobserver.com*

EU Politix: *http://www.eupolitix.com*

To find this list with updated information, visit ***www.eu-testbook.com***

PART II

PRE-SELECTION – PSYCHOMETRIC TESTS

PART II covers the PSYCHOMETRIC tests you will face in the EPSO recruitment pre-selection phase.

We can group these tests into two main types: classic psychometric tests (verbal reasoning, numerical reasoning and abstract reasoning) and situational judgement tests. While the first group of tests gauges candidates' skills in an indirect manner, situational judgement tests relate closely to real-life work situations while measuring competencies against a pre-established framework that EPSO has determined for each job profile.

Although situational judgement tests are described as "non-eliminatory" at pre-assessment, and may therefore seem less important at this stage, how well you do in them will be taken into account and "validated" in hands-on exercises when it comes to the assessment phase, so they also need to be taken seriously from the beginning.

We start Part II with a general overview of what verbal, numerical and abstract reasoning tests involve and how to approach them. These are tests that often strike alarm in candidates and a sound understanding of how they should be tackled is essential. For each of these test types methodological guidance is given, followed by plenty of practice questions designed to resemble AD level tests. In each case, answers are provided to help you understand where you may have gone wrong and so to improve your performance.

1. Verbal, Numerical and Abstract Reasoning Tests in EPSO Administrator Exams

Introduction

EPSO has, since its inception, used verbal reasoning and numerical reasoning tests in the so-called pre-selection or admission phase of open competitions (while for some Specialist profiles these are required in the assessment phase). Although it is often said that taking such tests does not require specific knowledge and they are therefore "easy" to pass, they have been dreaded by many candidates – and for good reasons.

From 2010 onwards, a new component, the so-called abstract reasoning test also became part of the pre-selection stage of the competitions. While this is a new test type that has only recently become part of EPSO exams, it has triggered the same kinds of mixed feelings in test-takers as the other two test types.

When it comes to abstract, verbal and numerical reasoning tests (commonly referred to as "psychometric tests"), it is important to answer the following questions:

- *What exactly are these tests like?*
- *What do they measure?*
- *What is the concept behind their design?*
- *What is the rationale for their use?*
- *What are the factors determining success?*
- *How are these tests scored?*
- *And finally: how to prepare and practice for them?*

An Overview of the Three Test Types

Each test type will be described in detail in the relevant upcoming chapters, but it is important to first get a sense of what these tests are like in general terms.

Format

All three test types, verbal, numerical and abstract reasoning, are in multiple-choice format. Based on EPSO's recent practice, verbal reasoning tests include four answer options, while abstract and numerical reasoning test feature five answer options; this is nevertheless not carved in stone and may be subject to change. In any case, there is always only one correct answer.

Verbal Reasoning

Verbal reasoning tests are designed to measure a candidate's ability to comprehend complex texts on various topics. These may vary from the description of an EU policy through current news, culture, history, or even natural sciences – in other words, the topic can be almost anything.

The length of the text is usually not more than 200 words (e.g. a similar length to the above "Introduction" section), and it is usually followed by one of the following two questions:

"Which of the following statements is correct?" (the expected format in AD competitions)
"Which of the following statements is incorrect?" (an alternative but less likely format)

The four (or more) answer options will then measure whether you:

- *...understood key concepts?*
- *...have the necessary vocabulary to comprehend a wide range of topics?* (Believe it or not, this may be an issue in your native language as well.)
- *...are able to deduce arguments from the text?*
- *...can accurately interpret key indicators (such as chronology, causality, quantities) in the text?*

For more information and practice tests, turn to the chapters on "Verbal Reasoning".

Numerical Reasoning

Numerical reasoning tests are designed to measure a candidate's ability to interpret data and numbers, with a special emphasis on the relationship between various data sets and on performing quick calculations based on intuitive insight. This means in practice that the focus is not on complex mathematics but on identifying how one can arrive at the figure in question in the most efficient way.

The data on which the test question is based is usually a table with several rows and columns. The rows usually indicate various groups (countries, age groups, regions, industries, and so on), while the columns often contain various metrics (GDP, average income, amount transported, percentages, and so on). Alternatively, the data can also be presented in the form of a chart or several charts (pie chart, bar chart, etc.), or any combination of the above-mentioned items.

The test question usually seeks either a figure ("200", "0.3", "45%", "1/5", etc.) or one of the groups in the data set ("France", "People aged between 15-64", "Europe", "Agriculture", etc.) as the answer.

By arriving at the answer in a timely manner, you can demonstrate your ability to:

- *identify relevant data*
- *understand the relationship between various metrics*
- *determine the level of accuracy needed to answer the question*
- *perform quick mental calculations, and*
- *make fast but relatively accurate estimates*

For more information and practice tests, turn to the chapters on "Numerical Reasoning".

Abstract Reasoning

Abstract reasoning tests always involve geometric shapes. Although there are test types where the shapes are three-dimensional, EPSO decided against using such tests and therefore candidates will only be given questions with two-dimensional objects.

The drawings in the questions can be geometrical ones, such as circles, rectangles, triangles, lines, and combinations of these, but they can also be the simplified representations of real-life objects, for example bodies, faces, vehicles, animals, and so on. Another important aspect is to avoid any gender, nationality or other bias regarding candidates' abilities to solve them; EPSO also made sure that those with visual challenges are not being discriminated against either.

The tests are designed so that there is some kind of relationship among the items in the set of illustrations included with the question. In general, such relationships in abstract reasoning tests can take several forms: one item can be the odd-one-out, the items in the set can form a meaningful series, and they can even be the visual representation of mathematical concepts like addition or subtraction. EPSO, however, decided to limit its test database to test items where the figures form a series and the test-taker is expected to select which of the five answer options would come next in the series.

Abstract reasoning tests measure your ability to:

- *interpret abstract concepts that do not carry actual real-life meaning*
- *draw conclusions in new and unfamiliar scenarios*
- *discover relationships between seemingly "unrelated" concepts, and*
- *use your so-called "fluid intelligence" and apply it to any intellectual problem*

For more information and practice tests, turn to the chapters on "Abstract Reasoning".

Why these Tests are Used

When someone first looks at verbal or numerical reasoning test questions, and especially in the case of abstract reasoning, a thought that often comes to mind is "*How is this related to my potential performance as an Administrator in the European Commission?*" It is a fair question and one which deserves a good answer.

According to one approach, these tests are generic indicators of intelligence. Their results are standardized and are simply good predictors of performance in any work situation where intelligence, creativity and independent thinking is required. While this is certainly true, it is also easy to identify much more concrete work scenarios where the "skills" measured by these tests can actually be put to good use.

As mentioned above, verbal reasoning tests measure a general ability to interpret texts, regardless of the topic. One can easily imagine the wide array of topics, formats and styles an Administrator at the European Commission or the Committee of the Regions will be expected to read about and make sense of in the course of their career. One day you might be reading about some new internal procedures to follow, the next day you might be asked by your superior to skim through a report on the effects of the increasing price of fertilizers on the Latvian farmers' standard of living. Regardless of the topic, one thing is certain: you will need to be able to make sense of the text in a timely manner, draw the right conclusions, avoid common misunderstandings and eventually summarize your findings. Sounds familiar? Hopefully it does as this is exactly what you will be expected to do in the verbal reasoning test as well.

You might also be given a statistical report one day at work. It may contain a mind-numbingly large number of tables and charts, and although you are looking for one single figure or piece of data, it's just not in there. There may be a wealth of other (irrelevant) data, but not the bit you are looking for though you are expected to come up with an answer based on that report and nothing else. What you will need to do is sort through all the data, disregard everything you do not need and find a way to "extract" the useful information. Again, this is exactly what you will do when taking the numerical reasoning tests.

When it comes to abstract reasoning, the above analogy will of course not work. Not even in an institution with as widespread responsibilities as the EU will you face a situation where you need to select a shape with four circles and one rectangle (as opposed to two rectangles) in order to get through the day. You do, however, stand a good chance of going to your office one Monday morning and facing a situation or being given a task that will be completely unfamiliar; it might be about something you have never even heard about. Situations like this are the ones where the above-mentioned "fluid intelligence", the ability to manage the "unfamiliar" and apply logic, patterns and common sense becomes useful and that is exactly what abstract reasoning tests measure, as proven by various psychological experiments.

The Factors Determining Success

Just as is the case with any other test, success and good performance in EPSO's pre-selection exam is determined by several factors. We will now briefly discuss the four most important ones:

- *Motivation*
- *Habits and hobbies*
- *Educational background*
- *Preparation and practice*

Motivation

EPSO's pre-selection exam is certainly an event that one must prepare for and set aside significant amounts of time for this purpose: expect to experience a lot of stress both in the process of preparing and in the exam itself. In short, it takes time and effort, and it is easy to be distracted or discouraged on the way. This is exactly why having a clear and strong motivation is so important.

I always found that one essential component of motivating myself is to know why am I expected to carry out a given task and how I can benefit from the effort that must be dedicated to it. Even if performing well at these tests is just a means to an end, it is still much easier to put in the required effort if we have a clear sense of why we are expected to do it and understand its objective benefits such as the potential of getting an EU job or performing much better in job tasks requiring psychometric skills.

The above section on how these test types can be related to actual work situations may be thought of as one component of the motivation needed to succeed – knowing why you are expected to do this at the exam, and not something else.

Motivation is also about setting clear and attainable goals. There is an acronym that nicely sums up this challenge: being SMART.

A SMART strategy is one that includes goals that are:

Specific – "I will practice X hours a day for X days a week in order to get the job I have always wanted. Each week I will do X number of tests and revise X previous tests. I will also start reading about EU affairs to familiarise myself with the institutions."

Measureable – "I will improve this or that much every week, and will be able to get X per cent at these tests by the time of the exam. I will do a benchmark test against which I can measure my progress."

Achievable – "I have never been particularly good with numbers so I will not try to score 100% at numerical reasoning, but I will make sure to score as much as possible above the 50% threshold and to make it up in the other test types."

Relevant – "I will do all of the above because my goal is to work in the Directorate General for Development of the European Commission. I would also like to get this job so I will have the financial means to pursue my long-time dream of visiting a friend in Australia. Even if I find these tests challenging or tedious at times, I understand that they are required for the exam and in any case I can improve my skills too."

Time-bound – "I will set aside this amount of time for the next X months to achieve this or that goal. I will have a clear timetable for the next two months where I indicate the days and hours I plan to spend on practicing. I will be able to stick to my schedule because I see the end of the tunnel."

Educational Background

Educational background is another important factor in success. In addition to the obvious fact that the quality of education one received can make a huge difference, there are various fields of study that provide a more relevant background for performing well at these tests than others. Mathematics or other disciplines that make use of logic and deduction may help in solving the test questions better under time pressure.

Obviously, your educational background is not something you can change at the time you decide to participate in an EPSO Administrator competition. If you have a more relevant background, so much the better – though if you do not, there is certainly no reason for despair either: there are numerous important factors in success, all of which you can improve significantly (see relevant tips below and in each consequent chapter).

Habits and Hobbies

Before turning to the "controllable" factors mentioned above, we must also mention that there are certain hobbies and activities that, if you are a fan of them, may provide some temporary advantage. When it comes to verbal, numerical and abstract reasoning, people who have done crossword puzzles, Sudoku and other mind games might be at some advantage.

Preparation and Practice

The factor, however, that is the single most important one is what this book is all about: ***the quality and quantity of preparation and practice you complete in the run-up to the exam.***

In the following chapters, we will introduce in detail:

- *the three test types and how they are designed*
- *the typical problems and challenges they pose*
- *the methods and tricks that can greatly improve your performance*
- *the best ways to approach and interpret the test questions, and*
- *the optimal way to prepare and practice for these tests*

With a clear grasp of the methods that can be used to efficiently take these tests and with the right amount of focused practice, powered by the correct motivation, even those candidates who feel that such tests are not their strong suit can improve significantly and pass this stage of the exam.

How these Tests are Scored

When you are preparing for the exam, you might often wonder exactly how well you are expected to perform in order to succeed. To answer this question, let us overview the marking system for these tests. The score candidates receive will have to satisfy two conditions:

Pass Mark – this is a simple "objective" barrier, for example 50% of the overall score in the test that must be reached in each test separately, to be considered for the shortlist. For some exams EPSO will set a pass mark for two or more tests combined (e.g. they will consider your numerical and abstract reasoning test scores as one and establish a 50% pass mark for the global score of these two tests) – this is an easier situation because you can compensate for poorer performance in one test by excelling in the other one(s).

The Best X – this is a "relative" barrier, meaning that in addition to scoring higher than the objective pass mark, you must also be among a given number of best-performing candidates in all tests collectively.

Mixed Version – EPSO may also use the "pass mark" approach to create a larger pool of potential candidates and then "sift in" a certain number whose qualifications match various objective, pre-determined criteria, though the "best X" may also be factored in the decision.

In Practice

- *Although you can count on compensating your weakness in one test type by performing stronger in another and thus still reaching a relatively high overall score, this option is limited by the requirement to reach the pass mark in each test separately*
- *A "good" score in the context of one group of candidates (e.g. those who sit AD exams for the audit sub-profile) might be an insufficient score in another group (e.g. those who have chosen the financial management sub-profile) – so examples of "successful scores" from the past are not really relevant*

The figure below shows what is known as a "bell curve". Although it is just an illustration and it is not based on statistics, it quite accurately shows the typical distribution of scores candidates get at such tests. As we can see, there are few candidates with very low scores and very high scores. Most of the candidates will get scores in a very narrow range, for example between 60% and 70%, or 70% and 80%.

If "successful" candidates are selected by the best X number of participants in the exam, you must certainly score higher than others. ***Looking at the bell curve, it is easy to see that only a few percentage points of improvement can mean that you have beaten a large number of additional candidates!***

Why is this important? The way we must approach this information is that the goals you set when you start preparing and practicing for these tests do not have to be unrealistic or unattainable. Also, you can take comfort in the fact that every small improvement will make a huge difference at the exam and will improve your chances exponentially – all thanks to the bell curve.

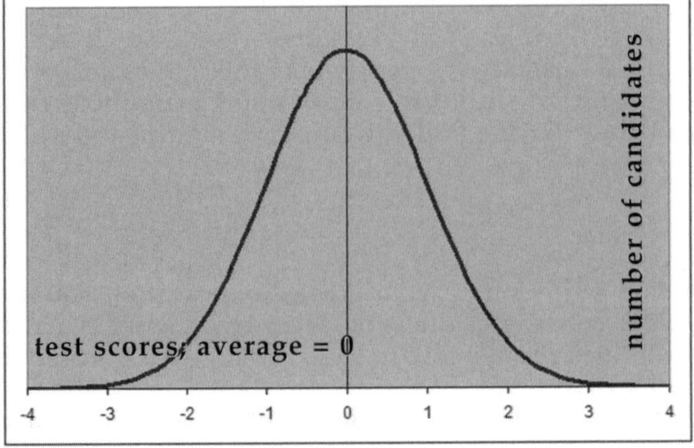

In the following chapters, we will see what the best methods and tricks to achieve success are, accompanied by a large number of quality practice tests.

After all, the best way of learning things is by doing them.

2. Succeeding in Verbal Reasoning Tests

In the world of standardized testing, the term "verbal reasoning" is commonly used to designate various test types relating to the interpretation and comprehension of texts. Although EPSO uses currently only one of these verbal reasoning test types, some of the models below measure skills that underlie the verbal reasoning tests EPSO uses to test candidates. It is therefore worth taking a quick look at each of them:

- **Spelling tests** are designed to test a person's ability to spell words correctly and also to differentiate between words with similar spellings yet completely or partially different meanings (for example, "their" and "there" or the correct spelling of "conscientious")
- **Word meaning tests** measure a person's vocabulary and their ability to select the best definition for words that have complex meanings (for example, to correctly identify the meaning of "preposterous" or "spill-over effect")
- **Word relationship tests** are designed to test a person's ability to determine the relationship between two concepts based on the analogy of another pair of concepts (for example, "what apple is to pear, a horse is to a ...")
- **Comprehension tests** measure a person's ability to comprehend complex texts and determine whether statements about a text are correct, incorrect, or impossible to tell (this is the "classical" type used by EPSO)
- **Verbal deduction tests** are the most advanced form of verbal reasoning exercises – they measure the reader's ability to make correct and logical conclusions based on the information provided (for example, a text describing Dubai's financial troubles followed by various questions such as "Who is the main investor in the country?", "Why did construction stall last year?" etc; this is a somewhat different approach from the "Which of the following statements is false?" question)

EPSO's verbal reasoning tests are closest in design to the comprehension test type. It is, however, easy to see how good performance in a comprehension test is based on the candidate's ability to identify correct spelling, the meaning of complex expressions and the relationship between various concepts. In this respect, this type of test is at the top in a hierarchy where success in comprehension depends on skills stemming from good performance on each of the lower levels.

We must also mention another particular feature of the way EPSO has implemented verbal reasoning tests. It is important to note that verbal reasoning tests are, by design, not language tests. They were not conceived to measure a candidate's command of or vocabulary in a second language (that is, the candidate's first foreign language). This is true even though up until 2010, likely due to various technical and organizational challenges, EPSO only offered verbal reasoning tests in three of the EU official languages: English, French and German. This will in future no longer be the case – starting with certain competitions in 2010, candidates are now expected to be able to take the verbal reasoning test (along with abstract and numerical reasoning tests) in their main (native) language, as long as it is one of the 23 official EU languages.

In the following, we will overview several issues to look out for in a text, as well as a number of methods and tricks that, once mastered, can greatly improve your performance. These include:

- *How verbal reasoning tests are designed*
- *The role of familiar and unfamiliar topics*
- *Sources of information*
- *Assumptions*
- *Correct versus incorrect statements*
- *Near-equivalent versus identical concepts*
- *Omission of information*
- *General versus particular*
- *Determiners and quantities*
- *Frequency*
- *Verbs: time and mode*
- *Causality versus chronology*

We must mention here that a few of the methods and tips discussed in this chapter are discussed in the context of English-language test questions – this does not mean, however, that they cannot be applied in taking tests in other languages as well. In addition, the overwhelming majority of test-taking strategies discussed here are language-independent and are extremely useful in taking these tests in any language.

We will also discuss the best way to deal with each test question, the suggested order of reading the various components of the test (the text, the question and the answer options) and the recommended methods to practice for the test.

The sample test below is representative of the type of test questions EPSO currently uses (though you might be given altogether six instead of four options) as well as the expected level of difficulty at an Administrator competition. It consists of:

- *A passage of text of between 100 and 200 words*
- *A standard question asking which of the supplied statements is correct*
- *Four statements as answer options, one being the correct answer, that is, the only correct statement*

We will now consider the factors and methods listed above one by one. Before we do that, however, I believe that it is essential to gain some insight into how verbal reasoning tests are designed by their authors – if you understand the concepts and strategies behind the creation of verbal reasoning tests, taking those tests will become incomparably easier.

How are verbal reasoning tests designed?

When psychologists whose specialty is the creation of psychometric tests design verbal reasoning items, they essentially follow two design steps:

1. Selecting an appropriate piece of text.
2. Authoring appropriate answer options.

Let us see what considerations go into each of these two steps.

1. Selecting an appropriate piece of text

A Sample Test

Rebuilt after an earthquake in 1963 wiped out most of the city, Skopje, the capital of the ex-Yugoslav republic of Macedonia, was for years characterised by ugly concrete blocks and strange empty spaces. But earlier this year Nikola Gruevski's conservative government produced a video that revealed the full ambition of "Skopje 2014", its plan for a radical reinvention of the city centre. Supporters of the plans said that, after decades of stagnation, Skopje would at last get the regeneration it deserves, its heroes commemorated in marble and bronze. Sceptical critics, used to a city where nothing much happens, sarcastically asked which triumph the proposed triumphal arch would be celebrating. Yet it is happening. New buildings are sprouting up along the banks of the Vardar river and a fresh statue is unveiled every few weeks (*The Economist*, Aug 26th 2010).

Which of the following statements is correct?

A Promoted by a conservative government, the "Skopje 2014" project has a nationalistic tone to it.

B Critics of Skopje's city regeneration plans have had their predictions of inaction come true.

C The Vardar river runs through Skopje, the capital of the former Yugoslav republic of Macedonia.

When selecting excerpts for a verbal reasoning text, several factors are considered, such as:

Does the text include a good variety of verbs, nouns, adjectives, and so on?

Is the difficulty of vocabulary appropriate for the purposes of the test (e.g. for assessing Assistant candidates for an EU job?)

Is the text free of jargon?

Are abbreviations explained at least once in the text?

Is the text free of topics that might be objectionable from a political, moral or ethical point of view?

The difficulty of the text and its vocabulary is a complex issue, suffice it to say that such things are considered as the length of the sentences (in number of words) or the length and complexity of the words themselves.

2. Authoring appropriate answer options

The creation of the answer options is the most difficult and most important task in the design of verbal reasoning tests. Let us overview what kind of answer options exist – being aware of the types of answer options that you might face will be highly useful in the EPSO pre-selection as well.

Patently true statements: Such statements are clearly and demonstrably correct based on the information in the text. No outside knowledge is required to prove their correctness; it is possible to determine that on the basis of the excerpt and by drawing well-founded conclusions. Obviously, each verbal reasoning test item features only one such statement, and that statement will be the correct answer. It is worth noting that the difficulty of the test item can be greatly influenced by how this statement is formulated:

- Does the correct answer use similar expressions to those found in the text? The more similar the wording, the easier it is to spot that it is the correct statement.
- Is the correct answer simply a reworded version of a statement in the passage, or is it a conclusion that can be drawn by utilizing several pieces of information from various parts of the excerpt?

Patently false statements: Such statements are clearly and demonstrably incorrect based on the information in the text passage. It is important to point out that these statements are not simply unfounded (that is, no evidence exists as to whether they are correct or incorrect) but can be clearly disproved by utilizing information in the text. The difficulty of spotting such statements is, again, dependent on several factors:

- Is part of the statement correct? If so, it may be more difficult to realize that it is an incorrect statement, because only part of the information contained in it makes it so.
- Is the topic of the text expected to be familiar to test-takers? If so, it is much easier to decide a statement is incorrect, because you know it to be false and it will immediately "stand out".

You may now think that the above two statement types are all there is to verbal reasoning tests, but we will see very soon that there is one more statement type which makes the whole thing much more complicated. Nevertheless, we can already see that the difficulty of test items that utilize only these two statement types can also vary greatly in difficulty based on the factors listed above.

"Insufficient information" statements: This is the statement which usually causes the greatest confusion and represents the most dangerous trap when taking a verbal reasoning test. "Insufficient information" statements can belong to one of two categories:

- Statements that are *incorrect* if assessed using outside knowledge: such statements are easier to handle, because they will "feel" incorrect – you might know the statement to be incorrect based on your knowledge of facts, but it is impossible to classify the statement as incorrect based solely in information in the test passage. Fortunately, you are not expected to do that – just remember that **any statement which cannot be clearly proven by information in the excerpt is "incorrect"** in the context of a verbal reasoning test
- Statements that are *correct* if assessed using outside knowledge: such statements are the hardest to spot because they will "feel" correct upon first reading. The reason they are dangerous is exactly because you instinctively want to agree with the statement you know to be true. The important thing to remember here is that the **only correct statement in a verbal reasoning test is one that is fully supported and proven by information in the text passage**.

We can now easily realize that verbal reasoning tests can be designed using any mixture of the above statement types.

Here are a few:

- 1 patently true statement, 3 patently false statements: this is probably the easiest type, as patently true and false statements are easier to spot
- 1 patently true statement, 2 patently false statements, 1 "insufficient information" statement: this test would be a bit harder, because in addition to the correct answer, one additional answer option might at first "feel" correct – remember the tips above and you will be able to easily avoid this trap
- 1 patently true statement, 3 "insufficient information" statements: this is the "crown jewel" of verbal reasoning tests – the most difficult type. This is because due to the

nature of the statement types used, you might feel that *all four statements* are correct upon first reading, but, again, you can discard those with insufficient information by remembering the principles described above

Based on experience and consulting with occupational psychologists, I expect that the overwhelming majority of verbal reasoning test questions that you will encounter at an EPSO Administrator competition will feature at least one "insufficient information" statement and it is quite likely that you will face at least a few questions where three of the four answer options will be of this type. You should, however, be aware of the existence of the other combinations listed above as well – better safe than sorry, as the saying goes.

Let us now consider a concrete example and return to the sample test item on page 51 above. Let us analyze the answer options based on the criteria we established.

A. Promoted by a conservative government, the "Skopje 2014" project has a nationalistic tone to it.

This is a typical "insufficient information" statement that is made even more difficult because it might "feel" correct. For many people, "conservative" might seem synonymous with "nationalistic", and the theme of the sculptures mentioned in the text (commemorating heroes) also could create the impression that the project has a nationalistic tone. Considering this statement correct, however, violates two important principles:

- we make unfounded assumptions about the nature of the project that are not supported by the text
- we also consider a subjective opinion to be patently true – a real correct statement will never be subjective unless the text passage itself is also subjective (which in this case it is not)

B. Critics of Skopje's city regeneration plans have had their predictions of inaction come true.

This is a *patently false* statement. Although the text does state that critics are used to inaction in the city, we also know that "[the project] is happening" and that new buildings are being erected in the city.

C. The Vardar river runs through Skopje, the capital of the former Yugoslav republic of Macedonia.

This is a *patently true* statement:

- the text passage states that Skopje is the capital of Macedonia
- the text passage states that the project involves new building and statues in the centre of Skopje
- the text passage states that these new buildings are erected along the banks of the Vardar river
- we can draw the well-supported conclusion that the Vardar river runs through Skopje

Consequently, this will be the correct answer.

D. Skopje's concrete blocks represent the legacy of rebuilding after the destruction of World War II.

This is a *patently false* statement. The text passage clearly establishes that the current state of the city is due to reconstruction after a devastating earthquake that occurred in 1963.

Now that we have analyzed the above four statements, we can see that our sample test item contains one patently true statement (the correct answer), one "insufficient information" statement, and two patently false statements. From a design perspective, the above test item is of medium difficulty, and I expect that the EPSO verbal reasoning test for Administrators will include items of comparable or greater difficulty.

Let us now turn our attention to the factors listed a few pages earlier – familiarity with such techniques as verb time and mode or generalizations will help you quickly determine which category each statement in a test belongs to, allowing you to find the correct answer in record time.

The Role of Familiar and Unfamiliar Topics

The topics of the texts in the verbal reasoning test can be varied. They may be closely EU-related (descriptions of policies, EU news) or they may be completely unrelated, dealing with history, art, nature, science and technology, music, and so on. Based on their interests or hobbies, most candidates have one or several preferred topics; however, the topic of the text should be completely irrelevant from the point of view of performing well in the test. While it is troubling to be faced with a topic that is completely alien to you, a familiar topic has its own dangers, because you must only use the information in the text, not your own knowledge.

Let us consider the pros and cons of familiar and unfamiliar topics.

As we can see, there is no significant argument either for or against wishing for familiar topics. Each has its distinct pitfalls and advantages.

As an example, if a candidate is very up to date in EU issues and reads a text on a topic she knows a lot about, for instance the Services Directive, it may seem a comfortable situation but may also backfire. Having a deep knowledge of a topic may make it hard to separate the information in the text from the information we already have about the subject – and, as we will see, it is one of the main mistakes test takers commit. In the above example, the candidate may be familiar with the regulations on cross-border healthcare services and "project" this into the text even if it does not mention this particular aspect at all.

On the other hand, many candidates panic when faced with a text about a subject they have never been interested in. There may even be several words and expressions that they have never even heard of. Yet it often happens that it is exactly the distance from the topic and "objectivity" that allows us to consider only the information in the text and select the correct answer quickly and correctly.

Familiar Topic (e.g. EU-related)		**Unfamiliar Topic (e.g. molecular biology)**	
Pros	***Cons***	***Pros***	***Cons***
Mainstream vocabulary	*Bias*	*No bias*	*May be colloquial*
Familiarity	*Technical vocabulary*	*May be everyday topic*	*May include exotic vocabulary*
No colloquialisms	*Assumptions*	*No assumptions*	*Not familiar*

Sources of Information

When we discussed the familiarity of the subject, we touched upon the fact that it is crucial to always keep in mind what information we use when assessing whether statements in the answer options are correct.

Let us consider the following sentence from an imaginary verbal reasoning text passage: *"small businesses employ almost half of all US workers."*

If the reader of this passage happens to have an encyclopaedic knowledge about the United States and knows the exact figure for how many workers there are in the country, he might unconsciously use that information when assessing whether a certain statement is correct. Let's see a theoretical answer option where this could cause a problem:

"Almost 100 million US workers are employed by small businesses." If the reader happens to know that there are approximately 200 million workers in the US and uses that assumption when taking the test, he might end up selecting the above answer option as correct – and lose a point, because the above answer cannot be correct if the text does not contain information about the actual number of people employed by small businesses.

It is thus crucial to remember that statements in the answer options must be assessed based solely on the information in both the main text and the answer itself.

Assumptions

In the previous example, we saw a situation where an assumption (regardless of whether correct or incorrect) was made about a statement based on "outside" knowledge. Let us consider another example.

"Consuming small amounts of healthy nuts improves the speed at which certain cognitive tasks can be performed."

A possible answer option:

"Consuming small amounts of peanuts improves, for example, performance in verbal and numerical reasoning tasks."

One might be tempted to select the above answer option as correct. If we do so, we make two assumptions:

1. Peanuts are a type of healthy nuts.
2. Verbal and numerical reasoning belongs to those types of cognitive tasks whose performance is boosted by consuming healthy nuts.

Whether the above answer option is indeed the correct one depends entirely on what other information regarding healthy nuts and the types of cognitive tasks is included in the text on which the answer options are based. For example, if there is no mention of peanuts in the text, considering them as healthy nuts will be a false assumption which will cause us to lose a valuable point in the test. Also, it is merely our interpretation (assumption) that verbal and numerical reasoning tests belong under "cognitive tasks" unless the text itself gives that information.

Correct versus Incorrect Statement

Although it is expected that the verbal reasoning test in Assistant competitions will only include items where the question is always *"Which of the following statements is correct?"*, I believe it is important to mention another possibility – when the question is *"Which of the following statements is incorrect?"*

The same principles that we discussed apply in this situation as well, but we will need to look for the patently false statement – that will be the "correct" answer. It is also important to point out that if the question is seeking the incorrect statement, we can still encounter "insufficient information" statements – in this case, however, such statements will often be designed to "feel" incorrect - thereby leading you to think that they indeed are. Just remember: if you are expected to pick the incorrect answer option, look for a statement that can be clearly and unambiguously disproved based on the information in the text passage.

As a final point, I would like to mention something that may seem so trivial that some readers will wonder whether it was even worth mentioning. Yet it is crucial to always carefully read the question (the one immediately after the text) and keep in mind whether you are supposed to look for the correct or incorrect statement. As simple as this may sound, hundreds of candidates have lost points in verbal reasoning tests by not taking the extra two seconds to read the question, especially under the stress and time pressure of the exam. This inattention happens more often than you would think and leads to the unnecessary loss of valuable points.

Near Equivalent versus Identical Statements

Consider the following example:

"Not many inventions last for more than 100 years without major modifications. One of these is the barometer."

A possible answer option:

"Since it was invented, the barometer has not been modified in any way."

The statement in the answer option is very similar to the information in the excerpt. It uses many of the same words and expressions, and it essentially conveys the same meaning. We could say that the two statements are nearly equivalent. Yet in the context of a verbal reasoning test, we cannot infer that "without major modifications" is equivalent to "not been modified in any way".

It is always dangerous to look for similar words and expressions in the answer option. Similarity can hide small but important differences in meaning and can prevent the reader from reading on and seriously considering other answer options among which the correct one can be found.

Another piece of advice is to always look for prefixes or adjectives that change the meaning or the scope of a statement, such as "some", "hardly", "almost", "not always", "any", "completely", "at all", "partially", "to some extent", "mostly", "generally", "exclusively", "sometimes", "largely", "arguably", "seemingly" and others (see more examples below).

If the situation changes and you end up being able to take the verbal reasoning test in your main language, it is still worth taking some time to think about words and expressions in your own language that slightly modify the meaning of the sentence in which they are included. This is especially true because we use our native language much less consciously than a second language and slight shifts in meaning are often overlooked in everyday speech.

Omission of Information

Here is an excerpt from another text:

"Verdi's operas continue to be extremely popular. This year, over 50 opera houses have staged Verdi's various works with great success all over the world."

A possible answer option:

"Verdi's operas are still being played in a number of opera houses."

Note that the above answer option has a completely different approach than the excerpt from the text. Having read the text, readers might be inclined to look for answer options that emphasize how extremely popular Verdi's operas still are. Our example answer option does not do that, it simply states that Verdi's operas are still being played in certain places.

At first reading, the statement in the answer option seems to be in conflict with the excerpt by not conveying the extreme popularity of these operas. Yet it is a perfectly valid and correct statement.

We must, then, remember that the fact that a statement fails to convey all the information that was included in the text about something does not mean that it is an incorrect statement. In short and all other factors being equal, omission of information is not necessarily disagreement or contradiction.

General versus Particular

Another typical mistake many candidates make has to do with the difference between general categories and particular instances. This mistake can take one of two forms:

- *Generalisation*
- *Over-specification*

Let us consider an example.

"Deserts are the driest habitats on Earth. Average precipitation in deserts is 5% of the amount we are used to in Western Europe. Some deserts in Central America do not experience rain for several years in a row."

A possible answer option:

"Deserts do not experience rain for several years in a row."

The above statement is an example of a generalisation where a statement made about certain instances of a category (in this case, Central American deserts) is assumed to be correct about the entire category (that is, deserts).

Let us consider another example.

"Some deserts do not support any plant life whatsoever; others, such as those that get limited rainfall every year, support some plant life."

A possible answer option:

"Some deserts support some plant life, depending on the season."

The above answer option is correct in stating that some deserts support some plant life, but it is overly specific in stating that the supported plant life depends on the season – this is unfounded information not included in the text which makes the statement incorrect.

Determiners and Quantities

We now come to more language-specific problems. While most of the points raised so far are valid in all languages the test is administered in, there are always language-specific issues to consider. If the test is administered in English these tips will be directly useful to your preparation.

If you take your test in another language, the following few sections can serve as a guideline along which you can consider the peculiarities of your own language and come up with a list of things to look out for. A good way of doing this is to read newspaper articles with higher than usual attention – professional journalists are always careful about how they formulate their statements and use many of the linguistic devices demonstrated here to make their statements more accurate.

Determiners and words expressing certain or uncertain quantities can be hard to notice; many candidates tend not to attribute much meaning to them in everyday situations even though they may greatly alter the meaning of a statement in the context of a verbal reasoning test.

Be mindful of the exact meaning of some of the most common determiners:

- "the" usually signifies one concrete object or person, or one concrete group: "the girl", "the Member States", "the books [on the table]", and so on.
- "a/an" and nouns without any determiner usually refer to one unspecified object or person, or an unspecified group of objects or persons, "a girl", "a Member State", "Countries around the world", and so on.

When the answer option lacks the determiner found in the text or features a different one, we must always be suspicious and consider whether this distinction changes the meaning of the statement.

A similar pattern can be observed when it comes to quantities: "some", "many", "several", "a number of" refer to an unspecified number of objects of persons. "All", "the entire", "every", and "each" signifies that the statement is about every single member of a group, or an object in its entirety, without exception.

It is important to bear in mind that these determiners of quantity are not interchangeable and if the text mentions "many countries", an answer option that extends that claim to "all countries" will not be correct.

Frequency

A very similar situation can be created by the use of adverbs signifying the frequency at which an action takes place. Always pay special attention to the use of the adverbs "sometimes", "often", "usually", "frequently", "never", "hardly ever", "occasionally", "always" and so on.

Although the only two concrete indicators are "never" and "always", and it is very hard to define the difference between "sometimes" and "occasionally", we must be mindful of the fact that they do carry meaning and can significantly change the meaning of a statement.

The same also can be said about adjectives and adverbs expressing chronology:

- "before", "previously", "earlier", "prior to that" are hints that one event took place sooner than another one
- "meanwhile", "concurrently", "simultaneously", "meanwhile" and others indicate that two events occured at the same time
- "after", "subsequently", "followed by", "later", and similar words help us establish that one event followed another event in time

Think of the following statements: "He copied the document and left the office; subsequently he talked to the press." and "After he talked to the press, he copied the document and left the office." – the implied actions are very different in the two scenarios. Another example is "Birds have colourful feathers" versus "Birds occasionally have colourful feathers": the scope and extent are very different.

Verbs: Time and Mode

Closely related to the previous point, the tense of verbs also plays a crucial role in re-creating a series of events. Take an example:

"Prior to her sister Anne's marriage to King Henry VIII of England, Mary Boleyn was the most renowned member of her family due to her adulterous affair with the King."

A possible answer option:

"Mary is the most famous member of the Boleyn family."

The above option is incorrect because according to the text, she had been the most famous member of the family only until her sister became the wife of the King. This fact is indicated by the use of the expression "prior to" and also the past tense.

Verb mode also plays an important part in determining whether a statement is correct:

- Probability – "would happen" does not necessarily mean that something "will happen"; "would have happened" certainly means that the event did not in fact happen at all
- "Could happen" indicates that a certain event is only one of several possible outcomes

- "Should do something" indicates that a certain course of action is recommended or likely, but not necessarily unavoidable or mandatory
- "About to happen" shows that an event was going to take place but may or may not have actually happened
- "Was about to" (e.g. "he was about to go home when") refers to an intention or plan that was likely to take place when a certain event interrupted it or took place

Causality versus Chronology

As a last point, we must mention two phenomena that are frequently confused. Let us look at an example.

"Café Vian has been frequently visited by Hollywood celebrities since 2003 [...] In 2008, it finally received the highest rating in one of the world's most respected restaurant review guides."

A possible answer option:

"Hollywood celebrities frequently dine at Café Vian, which led to the restaurant receiving the highest rating in a respected restaurant review guide."

The statement in the above answer option incorrectly makes the assumption that there is a cause-and-effect relationship between the patronage of Hollywood celebrities and the rating the restaurant received in the review guide a few years after celebrities started going there. The relationship between the celebrity visits and the high rating is, in this case, merely chronological (one event happened before the other one), but there is no evidence that the earlier event led to the second event mentioned in the text.

It is often very easy to mistake a merely chronological relationship for a cause-and-effect one, but one thing that will help decide is the verbal clues mentioned above. Since test-makers tend not to include ambiguous information in tests, we can always count on indicators of a cause-and-effect relationship ("led to", "consequently", "resulted in") or a mere chronological relationship to appear in the text.

Methods for Approaching the Test Questions

Let us return to our sample text:

Rebuilt after an earthquake in 1963 wiped out most of the city, Skopje, the capital of the ex-Yugoslav republic of Macedonia, was for years characterised by ugly concrete blocks and strange empty spaces. But earlier this year Nikola Gruevski's conservative government produced a video that revealed the full ambition of "Skopje 2014", its plan for a radical reinvention of the city centre. Supporters of the plans said that, after decades of stagnation, Skopje would at last get the regeneration it deserves, its heroes commemorated in marble and bronze. Sceptical critics, used to a city where nothing much happens, sarcastically asked which triumph the proposed triumphal arch would be celebrating. Yet it is happening. New buildings are sprouting up along the banks of the Vardar river and a fresh statue is unveiled every few weeks (The Economist, Aug 26th 2010).

Which of the following statements is correct?

A Promoted by a conservative government, the "Skopje 2014" project has a nationalistic tone to it.

B Critics of Skopje's city regeneration plans have had their predictions of inaction come true.

C The Vardar river runs through Skopje, the capital of the former Yugoslav republic of Macedonia.

D Skopje's concrete blocks represent the legacy of rebuilding after the destruction of World War II.

When somebody first looks at a verbal reasoning test like the one above, the natural instinct is to start reading the text, then read the question, and finally read the four or more answer options. If we wish to consider all the factors we discussed in this chapter and make mental "notes" of them by underlining the key expressions in the text using the above method, it would look like this:

Rebuilt after an earthquake in 1963 wiped out most of the city, Skopje, the capital of the ex-Yugoslav republic of Macedonia, was for years characterised by ugly concrete blocks and strange empty spaces. But earlier this year Nikola Gruevski's conservative government produced a video that revealed the full ambition of "Skopje 2014", its plan for a radical reinvention of the city centre. Supporters of the plans said that, after decades of stagnation, Skopje would at last get the regeneration it deserves, its heroes commemorated in marble and bronze. Sceptical critics, used to a city where nothing much happens, sarcastically asked which triumph the proposed triumphal arch would be celebrating. Yet it is happening. New buildings are sprouting up along the banks of the Vardar river and a fresh statue is unveiled every few weeks.

Which of the following statements is correct?

A Promoted by a conservative government, the "Skopje 2014" project has a nationalistic tone to it.

B Critics of Skopje's city regeneration plans have had their predictions of inaction come true.

C The Vardar river runs through Skopje, the capital of the former Yugoslav republic of Macedonia.

D Skopje's concrete blocks represent the legacy of rebuilding after the destruction of World War II.

The underlined expressions are "suspect phrases" because of the various factors we discussed.

But what if most of the factors that we concentrated on when reading the text for the first time later turn out to be completely irrelevant because the answer options do not relate to those bits of the text? In order to avoid wasting time on irrelevant information, it is a good idea to *read the question and the answer options first*, looking for keywords and key concepts, and *then read the text*, already focusing on and searching for those bits that we know we need to answer the question.

Our mental notes using this recommended method would therefore look like this:

Rebuilt after an earthquake in 1963 wiped out most of the city, Skopje, the capital of the ex-Yugoslav republic of Macedonia, was for years characterised by ugly concrete blocks and strange empty spaces. But earlier this year Nikola Gruevski's conservative government produced a video that revealed the full ambition of "Skopje 2014", its plan for a radical reinvention of the city centre. Supporters of the plans said that, after decades of stagnation, Skopje would at last get the regeneration it deserves, its heroes commemorated in marble and bronze. Sceptical critics, used to a city where nothing much happens, sarcastically asked which triumph the proposed triumphal arch would be celebrating. Yet it is happening. New buildings are sprouting up along the banks of the Vardar river and a fresh statue is unveiled every few weeks".

Using this method, answer option D can be discarded the moment we read "rebuilt after an earthquake in 1963", answer option B rejected the moment we read "Yet it is happening", and answer option A immediately after having read the entire text passage if we realize that the excerpt makes no characterizations about the tone of the project. Even if we are not entirely confident in the conclusion that the Vardar river must run through Skopje, we are quite simply left with that answer option as the only correct answer possible.

Let us summarize the above method in a few points:

1. Read the question first – are we looking for the correct or incorrect statement?

2. Read the answer options and make a mental note of the important keywords and themes included in those statements.
3. Read the text by focusing on the themes and keywords we made a mental note of when reading the answer options.
4. If you encounter a statement in the text that is clearly in agreement with an answer option (or in clear disagreement, if we are looking for the incorrect statement), and you are sure about your assessment, you can even stop reading and move on, thereby saving precious time.
5. If you are not sure about your assessment, you can continue reading and then eliminate the answer options one by one. This is where your knowledge of the possible statement types (patently false, insufficient information, etc.) will prove extremely useful – if you apply this knowledge right, and factor in the methods we discussed in this chapter, no amount of "witchcraft" on the part of the test item's author will confuse you.

Practice Methods

As a last point, it might be useful to make a few suggestions as to what the best methods are for preparing for the verbal reasoning test.

- Start practicing by taking your time, reading all kinds of high level English texts, making mental notes of the "suspect phrases" we covered in this chapter
- Continue by doing the same, this time with actual test questions, for example the ones in this book (for the sake of practicing, you may wish to underline or outline these concepts and also write down in your own words why a certain answer option is wrong)
- Once you have established the necessary routine in identifying the key phrases and concepts, you can start timing yourself – start by simply measuring how much time it takes for you to answer one test question
- Check how much time you will have at the exam, and how many questions you will need to answer
- Start decreasing the amount of time you let yourself use for answering one question – ideally, by the time of the exam, you should be able to answer more questions in the given time than required in the exam (this is necessary because you cannot re-create the stress of the exam, which can decrease performance, not to mention to slower pace when reading texts on a computer screen for the pre-selection exams)
- Try to re-create as much of the atmosphere and infrastructure of the exam as you can – do not interrupt the test, go to a quiet place, use an alarm clock, and so on
- If you have access to such a service, practice tests online, e.g. the *www.eutraining.eu* site – since the EPSO exam will also be computer-based, and it is a good idea to get used to the "interface" before going to the exam. Most such websites also offer the opportunity to revise the practice tests you took and look at detailed statistics, comparing your performance to others and measuring your improvement in a test type over time – experience shows that such statistics can have an extremely positive psychological effect as well as help to reveal the weaknesses and strengths of your skills in various tests.
- Try to read as much as possible on screen and measure the time it takes to read texts of comparable length (e.g. one page copied into Word) so you can measure and improve your performance.

In the following chapter you will find 150 verbal reasoning questions that you can use to start practicing straight away. The answers may be found following question 150.

For advice and tips on tackling verbal reasoning questions – see the previous chapter.

For the answers to this test – see at end of questions.

3. Verbal Reasoning Test

150 QUESTIONS – ANSWERS follow questions

In each question below, which statement is correct or can be best derived from the question text?
Please note that each question should be considered independently and no further information or knowledge should be considered when answering.

1. **British courts are being flooded with hundreds of trivial cases as a result of Europe's extradition laws, according to a damning report. The high volume of requests is placing an "unjustified burden" on police and prisons, the campaign group Fair Trials International (FTI) will warn.**

   The report comes amid growing criticism that judges are sending people abroad with "no questions asked" at the behest of foreign countries, often over allegations of petty crimes or offences committed many years ago, and with little regard to potentially-serious human rights abuses...

   FTI calls on ministers to introduce a new "proportionality test" that would slash the number of cases Britain has to process. The test would be applied by judges who would decide whether the offence in the requesting state was serious enough to merit extradition, taking into account factors such as the length of time that had passed, the length of prison sentence awaiting the individual, and the impact on their family life. *(The Telegraph, http://www.telegraph.co.uk/)*

A. The new "proportionality test" will result in fewer extradition requests being made to the British courts.

B. The majority of extradition requests to Britain come from countries in which human rights abuses are common.

C. The "proportionality test" would allow judges to consider a crime's gravity before granting extradition requests.

D. The report responds to a situation in which there are no guidelines governing extradition requests.

2. Russian and German scientists may have found a better way to treat infections than using antibiotics: cold plasma. Plasma - an ionized gas sometimes called the fourth state of matter - typically exists at thousands of degrees Celsius, and hot plasmas are regularly used to sterilize surgical equipment. Cold plasmas are closer to room temperatures. Only recently have researchers been able to make plasmas at a steady 35 to 40 degrees Celsius, cold enough to touch safely, and because the torch can be directed at a specific, small area of infection, surrounding tissue is left unharmed.

A research team in Moscow used a cold plasma torch in the lab to combat two common bacteria, Pseudomonas aeruginosa and Staphylococcus aureus, which show up frequently in wound infections but are resistant to antibiotics because they have a protective layer called a biofilm. After five minutes, the plasma torch killed 99 percent of bacteria grown in a Petri dish, and after ten minutes, it killed 90 percent of bacteria present in the wounds of a rat. (*Discovery News, http://news.discovery.com*)

A. One reason that hot plasmas have not proven effective in killing bacteria in wounds is because they cannot be directed at a small enough area and so burn tissue surrounding the wounds.

B. In laboratory tests, cold plasma was successful in killing most of the bacteria because it could penetrate the biofilm of the bacteria Pseudomonas aeruginosa and Staphylococcus aureus.

C. In laboratory tests, Pseudomonas aeruginosa and Staphylococcus aureus managed to survive cold plasma for several minutes thanks to their biofilm layers.

D. The two bacteria in this study, Pseudomonas aeruginosa and Staphylococcus aureus, seem to be more resistant to the effects of cold plasma when living in rat wounds than in a Petri dish.

3. Compact, ultra-blue galaxies spied for the first time in the deep universe are the most distant—and therefore the earliest—galaxies anyone has ever seen, astronomers announced today. These galaxies started forming just 500 million years after the big bang, which is thought to have occurred around 13.7 billion years ago. That pushes back the known start of galaxy formation by about 1.5 billion years.

The Hubble images, combined with data from the Spitzer Space Telescope, show that the newfound galaxies are relatively small, and they appear very blue, a colour linked to lighter elements such as hydrogen and helium. Hydrogen fusion inside active stars creates heavier elements such as iron and nickel, which get spread across the universe when massive stars explode. These elements cause modern galaxies to glow in a rainbow of colours, so the extreme blueness of the newfound galaxies suggests that they formed before very many massive stars had lived and died. (*National Geographic, http://news.nationalgeographic.com*)

A. As seen through the Hubble telescope, more recently formed galaxies glow in a wider range of colours than ancient galaxies due to the former's greater proportion of heavy elements.

B. The future discovery of additional, previously unknown galaxies will push back even further the date that scientists currently use to estimate the beginning of galaxy formation.

C. The appearance of a blue glow in a galaxy means that it is a relatively old galaxy with few active stars and a small proportion of light elements such as hydrogen and helium.

D. The galaxies that appear through the two telescopes to have the widest range of colors also have the greatest numbers of massive stars and the greatest number of heavy elements.

4. Developing the competitiveness of the European economy in line with the Lisbon agenda requires a renewed

commitment of the public and private sectors to the objective of investing 3% of GDP in research, with a particular emphasis on technological innovation including environmental technology, on developing human capital through higher investment in education and research, along the lines recommended by the Council on 22 September 2003. *(Presidency Conclusions, Brussels European Council, 2003)*

A. The current level of investment in research and technological innovation is currently less than three percent of GDP

B. The Council of Ministers with the portfolio for environmental issues held a meeting on 22 September 2003

C. Development of human capital means a greater investment into financial markets and education

D. The Lisbon agenda was aiming at boosting the European economy in order to make it the most competitive market in the world

5. **Unprecedented advances in the life sciences and the potential for the misuse of the scientific enterprise for bioterrorism or bio-warfare have created a pressing need for an international consensus on the steps that must be taken to reduce this grave threat to humanity. Counter-bioterrorism measures must include providing ethical guidance – especially for scientists, physicians, scientific institutions, and others engaged in research and development in the life sciences throughout the world. (*Science Magazine*)**

A. Ethical guidance is likely to stop scientists from getting involved in bio-warfare issues

B. There is an international consensus that bio-warfare is linked to terrorism

C. The latest progress in the life sciences has fostered the need for measures against the misuse of achievements

D. Scientists and physicians are more likely to be involved in bioterrorism than those not dealing with the life sciences

6. **So far this year, more than 90% of illegal migrants to Europe have entered through Greece, according to Frontex, the E.U.'s border-patrol agency. Until recently, Italy, France and Spain were the most popular entry points for illegal immigration into the continent. But increased coast-guard patrols in the past couple of years have blocked routes by sea, forcing migrants to find a new way in.**

Alarmed by the sudden influx of illegal migrants pouring into Greece, the E.U. sent Frontex forces to Orestiada in November to help Greek police patrol an especially troublesome eight-mile (13 km) section of the 128-mile (200 km) land border between Greece and Turkey. Some 31,400 people crossed just that portion of the border in the first nine months of 2010 — more than the numberof illegal crossings through all of the Canary Islands in 2006, a peak year for immigration to Spain. (*Time, http://www.time.com/*)

A. Before the recent increase in coast-guard patrols, more illegal immigrants had entered Greece by sea than over land from Turkey.

B. In the first nine months of 2010, 90% of illegal immigrants to Europe entered Greece through an eight-mile stretch near Orestiada.

C. Prior to 2010, the most heavily used entry point for illegal immigrants entering Europe was through the Canary Islands and into Spain.

D. In 2010 there were fewer illegal immigrants entering Europe through the Canary Islands and into Spain than there had been in 2006.

7. **Migration is well established as a mechanism by which animals cope with seasonal variations in food supply. It has also been suggested as a possible way of reducing the burden of parasitism in a range of hosts, either by weeding out**

infected individuals or by allowing them to escape from environments in which parasites have accumulated. Evidence has been provided that one of the more spectacular examples of migration – that of the monarch butterfly in North America – may have evolved at least in part as such a mechanism. *(Science Magazine)*

A. Parasitism may only be reduced by weeding out infected hosts

B. The monarch butterfly migrates every winter to North America

C. Evidence has shown that the real reason why the monarch butterfly migrates is to cope with seasonal variations in the food supply

D. Animals migrate in order to overcome difficulties caused by changing seasons

8. **After a period of uncertainty, some positive signs are emerging in Europe. An improvement in the international economic environment, low levels of inflation, stabilised oil prices and better conditions in the financial markets are key factors behind a pick-up in economic activity, which is expected to strengthen in the course of 2004. Since the situation remains fragile, a message of confidence in the European Union's economic potential is needed. Maintaining sound macroeconomic policies, accelerating structural reforms and promoting investment in infrastructure and human capital are key policies. (*Presidency Conclusions, Brussels European Council*, 2003)**

A. Reinforcing measures are needed to stabilise the positive tendencies

B. Oil prices have been fluctuating strongly in recent years

C. The uncertainty that has prevailed for several years does not seem to be abating

D. The key goals are to improve the financial markets, encourage the free flow of capital and keep inflation down

9. **A new study suggests that most people inhale substantially more organic contaminants, including cancer-causing benzene, than is indicated by standard environmental risk assessments based on outdoor measurements. "Ambient measurements at central sites aren't good predictors of [personal] exposure," says John Adgate of the University of Minnesota in Minneapolis. "Actual exposures are higher." To monitor urban air quality, environmental agencies typically measure pollutant concentrations in samples collected at centralized outdoor locations and extrapolate individuals' average exposures from those measurements. That's a reasonable approach for studying ozone and other pollutants that form out-of-doors or that come almost exclusively from identifiable industrial sources. (*Science News*)**

A. The extrapolation method of assessment is only reliable in the case of ozone

B. Urban air quality is usually measured at outdoor locations and conclusions are not as reliable as it had been presumed before

C. A recent study has shown that people inhale a lot more benzene than ten years ago

D. Environmental agencies have the exclusive right to measure pollutant concentrations in centralized areas

10. **Multifaceted and astonishingly productive, Domènech wore many hats. Besides being an architect and professor (Gaudí was his student at Barcelona's School of Architecture), he was also a prominent politician and Catalan nationalist and a pre-eminent scholar of heraldry.**

For architects, Barcelona at the turn of the 20th century was the right place at the right time. Nineteenth-century

industrialization brought tremendous wealth, and between the Universal Exposition of 1888 (for which Domènech created two of the most noteworthy buildings) and the construction of the Eixample — the vast grid of streets laid out in 1859 to decongest the old city — there was a heady mix of civic pride and social ascension in the air. The rising middle class was eager to make its mark on the rapidly growing city, and the new modernista style seemed perfectly suited to this task, rife as it was with neo-Gothic motifs that linked the newly minted mercantile titans to Barcelona's rich medieval history.
(*The New York Times, http://travel.nytimes.com*)

A. The construction of the Eixample in 1859 marked the beginning of a period of civic pride in Barcelona that lasted into the 20th century.

B. Although best known today for his architecture, Domènech was a professor of medieval history who specialized in the study of heraldry.

C. The architectural richness of Barcelona at the turn of the 20th century was made possible, in part, by wealth generated by industrialization.

D. Modernist architecture was the only way through which the rising middle class was able to connect with Barcelona's rich medieval history.

11. Shortly after finding arsenic-loving lifeforms, NASA astronomers have uncovered amino acids—the fundamental foundation for life—in a place where they shouldn't be. The acids—precursors of proteins—have been unexpectedly found inside fragments of previously superheated meteorites that landed in northern Sudan in 2008, a new study says.

Amino acids have already been found in a variety of carbon-rich meteorites formed under relatively cool conditions. But this is the first time the substances have been found in meteorites that had been naturally heated to 2,000 degrees Fahrenheit (1,100 degrees Celsius). That extreme a temperature should have destroyed any hint of organic material inside, said study leader Daniel Glavin, an astrobiologist at NASA's Goddard Space Flight Center in Maryland.

The discovery provides additional support for the theory that life's ingredients were delivered to the Earth by asteroids. (*National Geographic Daily News, http://news.nationalgeographic.com*)

A. The finding of amino acids was surprising because organic matter was not expected to survive the hot temperatures of the superheated meteorites.

B. The discovery of organic matter in the superheated meteorites was surprising because amino acids had never been found in any meteorites.

C. Scientists uncovered the amino acids in the superheated meteorites accidentally, in the course of conducting structural studies on the meteorites.

D. Some factor or condition unrelated to temperature allowed the amino acids to survive temperatures at which no organic matter can exist.

12. In the context of integrating migration issues in our Union's relations with third countries, the European Council reaffirms that the EU dialogue and actions with third countries in the field of migration should be part of an overall integrated, comprehensive and balanced approach, which should be differentiated, taking account of the existing situation in the different regions and in each individual partner country. In this respect, the European Council recognises the importance of developing an evaluation mechanism to monitor relations with third countries which do not cooperate with the EU in combating illegal immigration.
(*Presidency Conclusions, Thessaloniki European Council*, 2003)

A. Migration issues have been part of the EU's policy towards third countries

B. The EU has extensive relations with a number of third countries in various continents

C. The EU affirms its intention to reconsider relations with third countries that do not take steps against illegal immigration

D. The European Council considers it necessary to combat illegal immigration and establish a comprehensive approach in its foreign policy

13. The European Council calls in particular on the Council, along with the European Parliament where appropriate, to adopt as rapidly as possible during 2000 pending legislation on the legal framework for electronic commerce, on copyright and related rights, on e-money, on the distance selling of financial services, on jurisdiction and the enforcement of judgments, and the dual-use export-control regime. *(Presidency Conclusions, Lisbon European Council, 2000)*

A. The European Council expressed its wish to have legislation passed on several issues on, among other things, distance selling of financial services

B. The ever more widespread use of e-money makes ir necessary for the Council to urgently regulate it

C. The European Council voiced its concern over the lack of legislation in areas like international cooperation in criminal matters

D. The Council must always consult the European Parliament when passing legislation on copyright and related rights

14. The famous lifelike poses of many victims at Pompeii—seated with face in hands, crawling, kneeling on a mother's lap—are helping to lead scientists toward a new interpretation of how these ancient Romans died in the A.D. 79 eruptions of Italy's Mount Vesuvius. Until now it's been widely assumed that most of the victims were asphyxiated by volcanic ash and gas. But a recent study says most died instantly of extreme heat, with many casualties shocked into a sort of instant rigor mortis.

Volcanologist Giuseppe Mastrolorenzo and colleagues began by analyzing layers of buried volcanic ash and rock, then fed the data into a computer simulation of the Mount Vesuvius eruption. They concluded that the volcano, some six miles (ten kilometers) from Pompeii, produced six different pyroclastic surges—fast-moving, ground-hugging waves of hot, toxic gases and ash. Most of the hundreds of fatalities occurred during the fourth surge—the first to reach Pompeii—even though that surge was relatively slow and ash-poor. (*National Geographic Daily News, http://news.nationalgeographic.com*)

A. Mastrolorenzo and his colleagues are the first to conclude that the eruption resulted in multiple surges.

B. The new finding, if correct, would mean that most of the residents of Pompeii did not suffer a prolonged death.

C. The position of the victims at Pompeii is clear evidence that there had to be a cause of death other than asphyxiation.

D. Compared with the fourth, all other pyroclastic surges hit Pompeii more quickly and carried more ash.

15. The removal of technical barriers to trade is a precondition for the completion of the internal market. Since the adoption of the new approach to technical harmonisation and standardisation in 1985, the harmonisation of European industrial standards in the sixteen areas covered by European technical legislation has become an essential instrument for the achievement of this objective. This approach was subsequently complemented by a

coherent policy on certification and tests, setting out clear, consistent and transparent principles which apply to the product certification procedures to be used at Community level.
(ScadPlus)

A. There are more than twenty areas where technical legislation has to be implemented in order to remove technical barriers to trade

B. The completion of the internal market entails the harmonisation of industrial standards and a policy on certification and tests

C. Product certification procedures require the adoption of a new approach to technical harmonisation

D. The completion of the internal market was achieved in 1985 when technical standards were harmonised

16. About 5 percent of the world's carbon dioxide emissions arise from the cement kilns that make the key ingredient of civilization's hard surface areas, roughly double the amount from the jet fuel burned in all global air travel. Technically known as "Portland cement," named after the craggy peninsula where building stone was originally quarried in industrial-age England, cement is the binding agent, or glue, that makes concrete stick together and fastens one brick to another.

The problem lies in cement's chemistry, which is a sort of double-whammy of CO2 production. To turn Portland cement's key ingredient, calcium carbonate—found in limestone or chalk—into a finished product called alite, the minerals must be broken down in kilns heated to more than 2,550°F (1,400°C). The heating process uses tremendous amounts of energy, which is typically generated using coal, the most carbon-intensive fossil fuel. Then, the ensuing chemical process releases a second wallop of CO2 as a byproduct of turning calcium carbonate into calcium oxide.
(*National Geographic Daily News, http://news.nationalgeographic.com*)

A. All heating processes that are currently being used to produce alite result in significant CO2 emissions.

B. The only way to produce cement involves intense heat and a chemical process that both result in CO2 emissions.

C. Finding alternative heating sources to use in producing alite would reduce the world's CO2 emissions by five percent.

D. Two processes commonly used to produce cement, both of which emit CO2, cause 5% of the world's CO2 output.

17. In 1985, the Dooge Committee Report, drawn up in preparation for the Intergovernmental Conference which was to lead to the Single European Act (SEA), contained a number of proposals concerning foreign policy. The provisions introduced by the SEA established an institutional basis for the European Political Cooperation, the group of European correspondents and a secretariat working under the direct authority of the Council presidency.
(ScadPlus)

A. The Single European Act was signed in 1986 and entered into force in 1987

B. The Dooge Committee proposed to place the European Political Cooperation's secretariat under the Council presidency

C. The Intergovernmental Conference calls for the creation of the Dooge Committee to give proposals for the reform of foreign policy

D. It was the Single European Act that actually created a specialised group of European correspondents

18. The latest round of international talks on climate change broke up today (6 November). Little progress was made on defining emission-reduction targets for rich countries or on agreeing finance for

developing countries, the UN said at the end of five days of talks in Barcelona. The talks were the last formal round of negotiations before a climate conference in Copenhagen next month at which the UN hopes a pact to succeed the Kyoto Protocol will be agreed. "Without these two pieces of the puzzle in place, we will not have a deal in Copenhagen," said Yvo de Boer, executive secretary of the United Nations Framework Convention on Climate Change. The European Commission's chief negotiator, Artur Runge Metzger, added that developing countries needed to do more to curb the growth of their emissions. Referring to a pledge by Indonesia to cut emissions growth by 26% and up to 40% with outside help, Runge Metzger, said "we need to see more of that". (*European Voice*)

A. A deal in Copenhagen hinges on defining emission-reduction numbers for developed countries and agreeing on finance for developing countries.

B. The Commission's chief negotiator said that Indonesia's pledge of cutting emissions growth by 26% (or up to 40% with outside help) is not ambitious enough.

C. No progress was made in Barcelona, which was the last formal round of negotiations before the Copenhagen Climate Conference.

D. Indonesia would be able to double its emission-reduction pledge with outside help.

19. The proposed new European laws under the controversial Alternative Investment Fund Managers directive have been widely criticised for being unworkable and hugely damaging to the hedge fund and private equity industry – 80% of which is based in the UK. Although Sweden gave some concessions in the three most controversial areas – leverage, depositories and limits on marketing funds – it shocked hedge funds yesterday when it added bonus caps previously aimed at banks and applied them at the last minute to the hedge fund directive. The additions on pay are taken from the capital requirement limits proposals for the banking sector and include deferring as much as 60% of annual pay for up to three years. Insiders of the process say political pressure from the French, and increasing opposition to bonus payouts generally, meant that Britain was alone among member states in trying to stop the late inclusions. (*The Daily Telegraph*)

A. A new European directive aims at decreasing the annual pay of hedge fund directors by 60%.

B. The UK and France were the only Member States that opposed the new measures aimed at limiting the annual pay for hedge fund directors.

C. Sweden could not be persuaded to be flexible on the most controversial ideas.

D. Hedge fund directors may have to wait up to 3 years to receive a large portion of their annual pay.

20. Every day, Glen McNeil spends six or seven hours buzzing about the streets of London on his motorbike with a map clipped to the handlebars. McNeil, 28, is engaged in the years-long memory training required to earn his green badge and become a licensed London taxi driver. If McNeill fulfils his dream, his brain may be the bigger for it, at least in one part. The hippocampus, a seahorse-shaped structure that is part of the brain's limbic system, is critical to many functions of memory and learning, including processing spatial relationships in the environment. An MRI study published in 2000 by scientists at University College, London, showed that in London taxi drivers the rear portion of the hippocampus was enlarged compared with those of control subjects, confounding the long-held notion that the adult human brain cannot grow. But the bonus in brain tissue may not have come free of charge. On average, the

front portion of the hippocampus was smaller than normal in the taxi drivers, suggesting that the effort to build an increasingly detailed mental map of the city had recruited neighbouring regions to the cause. (*National Geographic*)

A. The adult human brain cannot grow.

B. The brain's limbic system is only responsible for processing spatial relationships in the environment.

C. McNeill dreams about making his brain bigger.

D. The growth of one part of the brain may come at the price of a decrease in the size of other parts of it.

21. In previous years, the International Energy Agency had predicted that crude oil production would continue to rise for at least another couple of decades. Now, because of rising oil prices, declines in investment by the oil industry, and new commitments by some nations to cutting greenhouse gas emissions, the new forecast says oil production is likely to be lower than the IEA had expected.

The projected flat crude oil production doesn't translate into an immediate shortage of fuels for the world's cars and trucks. IEA actually projects that the total production of what it calls "petroleum fuels" is most likely to continue steadily rising, reaching about 99 million barrels per day by 2035. This growth in liquid fuels would come entirely from unconventional sources, including "natural gas liquids," which are created as a by-product of tapping natural gas reservoirs. (*National Geographic Daily News, http://news.nationalgeographic.com*)

A. The steady increase in "petroleum fuels" that the IEA projects through 2035 would come entirely from "natural gas liquids."

B. The IEA projects that the production of "petroleum fuels" will remain flat or fall through 2035.

C. Market forces and new conservation commitments are both factored into the revised projection of crude oil production.

D. Natural gas reservoirs are the largest of the unconventional sources of "petroleum fuels" that factor into the IEA's predictions.

22. The mountains of discarded computers, cell phones and other electronic devices dumped off in the developing world are slated to triple in size over the next decade. The plastic encasings and metallic insides that make electronics work turn into non-biodegradable e-waste once they're tossed out and often exported to China, India and developing nations. As a result, an e-waste industry has developed as people mine the discarded devices for their valuable metallic innards, including gold, silver and copper.

But toxic elements, such as brominated flame retardants and lead in circuit boards, batteries and other components, along with caustic acids and burning methods used to dismantle the old electronics, pose serious environmental and health risks for the communities that subsist on the e-waste industry. (*Discovery News, http://news.discovery.com*)

A. The number of discarded cell phones and computers is projected to triple over the next decade.

B. The only valuable parts of discarded electronics are those made of copper, silver, and gold.

C. The hazards of e-waste arise from both the devices' materials and the methods used to dismantle them.

D. China and India are the two developing countries with the most advanced e-waste industries.

23. Belgian chocolates and pralines (chocolate with creamy or nutty fillings) need no introduction, but Brussels and Liege

waffles are appreciated just as much. The country's bakeries offer a great variety of different kinds of bread and a number of regional specialities. They include couque (sugary, spicy bread from Brussels and hard spiced bread with honey from Dinant), craquelin (sugar-filled brioche or enriched bread), noeud (butter biscuit with brown sugar), cramique (milk bread with raisins), pistolet (small round loaf), and mastel (rusk bread with aniseed).
(*Michelin Guide*)

A. Liege is mostly famous for its waffles, whereas Brussels is more known for chocolate and pralines

B. Craquelin and pistolet are both Belgian specialities that are like a small cake or loaf

C. The noeud is mainly sold in the Liege area and occasionally in other regions as well

D. Craquelin is a rusk bread with aniseed and a sugar topping

24. The protection of intellectual property is, of course, governed by many international conventions. The World Intellectual Property Organisation (WIPO) and, more recently, the World Trade Organisation (WTO) are responsible for implementing numerous international conventions and treaties. The first convention, the Paris Convention for the Protection of Industrial Property, dates back to 1883, and since then several conventions and treaties have been signed which cover various aspects of the protection of intellectual property, such as the protection of literary and artistic works (Berne Convention) and the protection of performers, producers of phonograms and broadcasting organisations (the Rome Convention).
(*ScadPlus*)

A. Artistic works and broadcasting organisations are protected by the Berne Convention

B. The first convention to protect industrial property was the Paris Convention

C. The World Intellectual Property Organisation and the World Trade Organisation have their headquarters in Paris and Rome

D. Performers are generally protected by the Paris Convention and, in some special cases, the Rome Convention

25. The transport industry occupies an important position in the Community, accounting for 7% of its GNP, 7% of its total employment, 40% of Member States' investment and 30% of Community energy consumption. Demand, particularly in intra-Community traffic, has grown more or less constantly for the last 20 years, by 2.3% a year for goods and 3.1% for passengers.
(*DG Transport*)

A. The transport industry accounts for a higher percentage of the Community's GNP than it does of the Community's total employment

B. The transport industry accounts for one-third of the Community's energy consumption and more than half of Member States' investment

C. Demand for transport services has grown more dynamically for passengers than goods in the last twenty years

D. Each Member State spends about 7% of its gross national product on transport services

26 For most of history even a first degree at a university was the privilege of a rich few, and many academic staff did not hold doctorates. But as higher education expanded after the Second World War, so did the expectation that lecturers would hold advanced degrees. American universities geared up first: by 1970 America was producing just under a third of the world's university students and half of its science and technology PhDs (at that time it had only 6% of the global population). Since then America's annual output of PhDs has doubled, to 64,000.

Other countries are catching up. Between 1998 and 2006 the number of doctorates handed out in all OECD countries grew by 40%, compared with

22% for America. PhD production sped up most dramatically in Mexico, Portugal, Italy and Slovakia. Even Japan, where the number of young people is shrinking, churned out about 46% more PhDs. Part of that growth reflects the expansion of university education outside America. Richard Freeman, a labour economist at Harvard University, says that by 2006 America was enrolling just 12% of the world's students (*The Economist*, Dec. 16th 2010).

A. The share held by US universities in producing the world's science and technology PhDs has grown twofold in about 40 years.

B. At 12 per cent, US universities were taking in the smallest portion of the world's students in 2006 compared to other OECD countries.

C. A proliferation in PhD production, particularly outside the US, also appears to be accompanied by a drop in standards worldwide.

D. In the eight years after 1998, the increase in the number of doctorates conferred by US universities stood below the average increase for OECD countries.

27. The notion that money can't buy happiness is popular, especially among Europeans who believe that growth-oriented free-market economies have got it wrong. They have drawn comfort from the work of Richard Easterlin, professor of economics at the University of Southern California, who trawled through the data in the 1970s and observed only a loose correlation between money and happiness. Although income and well-being were closely correlated within countries, there seemed to be little relationship between the two when measured over time or between countries. This became known as the "Easterlin paradox". Mr. Easterlin suggested that well-being depended not on absolute, but on relative, income: people feel miserable not because they are poor, but because they are at the bottom of the particular pile in which they find themselves.

But more recent work – especially by Betsey Stevenson and Justin Wolfers of the University of Pennsylvania – suggests that while the evidence for a correlation between income and happiness over time remains weak, that for a correlation between countries is strong. According to Mr. Wolfers, the correlation was unclear in the past because of a paucity of data. There is, he says, "a tendency to confuse absence of evidence for a proposition as evidence of its absence" (*The Economist*, Dec. 16th 2010).

A. More recent research has found that with globalization people are increasingly comparing their income to that of other people in countries different from their own.

B. Mr Easterlin found no strong link between money and happiness when measured between countries except among certain European countries with strong safety nets.

C. Mr Wolfers concludes that sufficient data are currently available to suggest a relationship between income and well-being when measured between countries.

D. When he considered a possible correlation between money and happiness, Mr Easterlin defined poverty in absolute rather than in relative terms.

28. Most people require about 8 hours sleep a night, but some lucky oddballs function well on 4 hours or even less. A new study in fruit flies provides evidence that genetics plays a strong role in determining who can get by with little rest. A single mutation in a gene that's also found in people can reduce the insects' sleep needs by about two-thirds. Although researchers have been studying sleep for decades, they've made little progress in teasing out the genetic components that control this phenomenon. A sleeping fly simply sits motionless, usually for many hours a day. *(Science News)*

A. Everybody needs at least four hours' sleep every day

B. A sleeping fly, as a recent study has found, does not move for more than 8 hours

C. Those who require four hours' sleep a night are likely to have a mutation in the same gene that also reduces the sleep needs of insects

D. Scientists have been researching insects' sleep needs for decades

29. Printer cartridges and air freight may be new, but lethal missives are not. The Bandbox Plot of November 4th 1712, foiled by Jonathan Swift (author of "Gulliver's Travels"), was an attempt to kill Robert Harley, Earl of Oxford and Lord Treasurer. A hatbox left at his door was configured to fire cocked pistols when the lid was lifted.

On January 19th 1764 a Danish diarist, Bolle Willum Luxdorph, described perhaps the first successful parcel bomb. A Colonel Poulsen received a box by post. "When he opens it, therein is to be found gunpowder and a firelock which sets fire unto it, so he became very injured."

Politicians have long been targets of such attacks. One was aimed at US Senator Thomas Hardwick and exploded (unsuccessfully) on April 29th 1919. It was the first of nearly 30 devices sent by anarchist groups to politicians, judges and businessmen, all intended to explode on May Day. A campaign in June of the same year involved eight larger bombs that killed several people, including one of the anarchists (*The Economist*, Nov. 4th 2010).

A. Bomb plots hatched by anarchists against government and business leaders resulted in casualties in the first half of 1919.

B. In 1764 Bolle Willum Luxdorph wrote boastfully in his diary about an explosive device he sent to cause great injury to a certain Colonel Poulsen.

C. Sending explosives through the post has represented a cause of great concern for the authorities since as long ago as the 17th century.

D. An assassination attempt on a top government official was uncovered by author Jonathan Swift after a careful investigation.

30. There is water on the Moon, scientists stated unequivocally on Friday. The confirmation of scientists' suspicions is welcome news to explorers who might set up home on the lunar surface and to scientists who hope that the water, in the form of ice accumulated over billions of years, holds a record of the solar system's history. The satellite, known as LCROSS, crashed into a crater near the Moon's south pole a month ago. The 9,000-kilometres-per-hour impact carved out a hole 20 to 30 meters wide and kicked up at least 90 litres of water. The LCROSS mission, intended to look for water, was made up of two pieces — an empty rocket stage to slam into the floor of Cabeus, a crater 96 kilometres wide and 3 kilometres deep, and a small spacecraft to measure what was kicked up. (*New York Times*)

A. Scientists now suspect that there might be water on the moon

B. When the LCROSS mission hit the south pole of the moon, the impact carved out a crater 96 kilometres wide and 3 kilometres deep on the lunar surface

C. The LCROSS mission confirms that there is at least 90 litres of water on the Moon

D. The water on the Moon has accumulated over billions of years in a liquid form

31. The idea that language influences thought is a profound, exciting and possibly disturbing one. It has often been used to exoticise other languages: in the 1930s, Benjamin Lee Whorf wrote that Hopi had no words for time (like days and months), and therefore perceived time far differently than European-language speakers do. The belief that language shapes thought also has political implications: in Nineteen Eighty-Four, George Orwell imagined a dystopia in which government banned subversive words, making the associated thoughts unthinkable. Even in this decade, a group of French activists have proposed making French the sole language of European law, because of its purported

great "rigour" and "precision". Using such a precise language, we are expected to believe, will lead to better law.

In the dominant school of post-war linguistics, such "Whorfian" thinking has traditionally had a bad reputation. (This is not least because Whorf's knowledge of Hopi proved to be hopelessly incomplete.) However, such thinking is still extremely common in the wider world. Most common is the "no word for X" trope, the idea that if a language does not have a single word for a symbolic English word, that people's thinking must differ significantly. No less a figure than Ronald Reagan once said that Russian has no word for "freedom", when of course it does: svoboda. Such myth-believing in high places can be worse than embarrassing (*The Economist*, Dec. 13th 2010).

A. Whorf felt that languages shape our thinking in the same ways that going to medical school or learning to fly a plane build expertise and transform our abilities.

B. Ronald Reagan was a firm believer in Whorf's ideas about the relationship between the language people speak and the way they think.

C. Even if Russian actually lacked a word for "freedom", most linguistic experts today would not conclude from this that Russian speakers think differently about that concept.

D. French activists see their country's laws as strong evidence of the efficacy of the French language in writing the most precise legislation possible.

32. The ecosystems surrounding us are the lifeblood of the planet, providing us with everything from the water we drink to the food we eat and the fibre we use for clothing, paper or lumber. Historically, agricultural production was stepped up by increasing land use and employing the best technologies available. Densely populated parts of the world, such as in China, India, Egypt and some regions of Europe, reached the limits of arable land expansion many years ago. Intensification of production has therefore become a key strategy — obtaining more from the same amount of land. Until recently, food output kept up with global population growth: in 1997 agriculture provided (on average) 24% more food per person than in 1961, despite the population growing by 89%. (*European Group on Ethics in Science and New Technologies to the European Commission*)

A. Agricultural production increased by only 24% between 1961 and 1997, while population grew by 89%

B. Global population almost doubled between 1961 and 1997

C. In China, increasing land use is still the best option for boosting production

D. In the past, agricultural production was increased solely by expanding land use

33. Jayaben Desai, who has died aged 77 after a long illness, defied stereotyping all her life. "A person like me, I am never scared of anybody," she told managers at the Grunwick film processing plant in the north-west London borough of Brent, shortly before she led a walk-out on the baking hot day of Monday August 23rd 1976. The events that followed contributed immeasurably to increasing the level of respect shown to newly arrived immigrant workers, many of them women – especially by their colleagues in the existing workforce.

Desperate for work, the newly arrived accepted long hours and low wages, though the need to do so, Mrs Desai said, "nagged away like a sore on their necks". When she decided she had had enough, this small woman employee told her tall and heavily-built manager, Malcom Alden, "What you are running is not a factory, it is a zoo. But in a zoo there are many types of animals. Some are monkeys who dance on your fingertips. Others are lions who can bite your head off. We are those lions, Mr Manager." As a result of her

passion and magical turn of phrase, 100 of her fellow workers joined her on strike (*The Guardian*, Dec. 28th 2010).

A. As an Indian immigrant, Mrs Desai was battling not only against unfair working conditions, but also against racism in the workplace.

B. Mrs Desai's choice of words played an important role in organising fellow workers at the Grunwick film processing plant in London.

C. Initially, Mrs Desai and her co-workers at the Grunwick film processing plant did not enjoy the support of any trade union.

D. Though Mrs Desai and fellow strikers eventually lost, their cause transformed the way workers viewed their immigrant colleagues.

34. The Empire State Building is a 102-story landmark Art Deco skyscraper in New York City at the intersection of Fifth Avenue and West 34th Street. Construction on the building started on March 17, 1930. The project involved 3,400 workers, mostly immigrants from Europe, along with hundreds of Mohawk iron workers, many from the Kahnawake reserve near Montreal. According to official accounts, five workers died during the construction. Governor Smith's grandchildren cut the ribbon on May 1, 1931. The construction was part of an intense competition in New York for the title of "world's tallest building". Two other projects fighting for the title, 40 Wall Street and the Chrysler Building, were still under construction when work began on the Empire State Building. Each held the title for less than a year, as the Empire State Building surpassed them upon its completion, just 410 days after construction commenced. The building was officially opened when United States President Herbert Hoover turned on the building's lights with the push of a button from Washington, D.C. (*Wikipedia*)

A. The Chrysler Building was finished more than a year earlier than the Empire State Building

B. The 3,400 workers took only about four days on average to finish one story

C. 40 Wall Street was finished before construction began on the Empire State Building

D. All 3,400 workers were from Europe

35. I visited the Liszt Museum when I was in Budapest last year. Although Liszt never really lived in the city, he rented three modest rooms that now form the museum. Used to receiving students, they are a monument to his simplicity – more a monk's cell than a prince's palace. I wasn't permitted to try any of the pianos (two Chickerings and a Bösendorfer), but if I had been, what might I have played? Possibly the first two bars of Wagner's Tristan und Isolde, not just because the Cornish knight's name was the last word Liszt spoke, but because Wagner was as much a musical son of the Hungarian Liszt as a legal one, through marriage to Liszt's daughter Cosima.

But if Liszt was the fountainhead of so much musical life in the later 19th and early 20th centuries, where did he himself come from? There are two main sources for his earlier musical style: his teacher Carl Czerny's generation of post-classical, pre-Romantic, fast-fingered pianist-composers; and the demonic virtuosity and mysterious personality of Paganini. Liszt married the dexterity of the first to the flamboyance of the second and created a new style. Indeed, Liszt's instinct for what sounds effective on the piano has never been equalled (*The Guardian*, Dec. 27th 2010).

A. Although Liszt never remained in Budapest for more than a few months at a time, he gave private lessons in three simple rooms he was renting there.

B. The effects of Paganini as well as of Carl Czerny could be felt on Liszt's early music just as Liszt had an impact on Wagner's style.

C. On his deathbed, the thoughts of the great composer-pianist Liszt turned to Tristan und

Isolde, Wagner's classic opera about a Cornish knight.

D. Liszt was a Hungarian Romantic composer and piano virtuoso, whose sense of what works well on the instrument remains unparalleled.

36. Below its icy crust Jupiter's moon Europa is believed to host a global ocean up to 160 kilometres deep, with no land to speak of at the surface. And the extraterrestrial ocean is currently being fed more than a hundred times more oxygen than previous models had suggested, according to provocative new research. That amount of oxygen would be enough to support more than just microscopic life-forms: At least three million tons of fishlike creatures could theoretically live and breathe on Europa, said study author Richard Greenberg of the University of Arizona in Tucson. "There's nothing saying there is life there now," said Greenberg, who presented his work last month at a meeting of the American Astronomical Society's Division for Planetary Sciences. "But we do know there are the physical conditions to support it." In fact, based on what we know about the Jovian moon, parts of Europa's seafloor should greatly resemble the environments around Earth's deep-ocean hydrothermal vents, said deep-sea molecular ecologist Timothy Shank. (*National Geographic*)

A. Europa supports at least three million tons of fishlike creatures in its global ocean

B. Microscopic life forms have been known to exist on Europa

C. There is no evidence that life exists on Jupiter's moon Europa

D. Jupiter has several moons

37. In Norway archeologists have found what is being described as a kind of "mini-Pompeii." The well-preserved site is by the seashore at Hamresanden in southern Norway. The "sealed" Stone Age settlement is thought to have been covered by a sandstorm, possibly in the course of a few hours. Under about a metre of sand, excavations uncovered an almost perfectly preserved example of a community from what is known as the Funnel Beaker Culture, so called because of the distinctive clay beakers used by the first Stone Age farmers, with a funnel-shaped rim. This was the major culture in north-central Europe from around 4000 BC to 2700 BC. Archeologists estimate that the Hamresanden site was buried by sand around 3500 BC – that is, about 5,500 years ago. At the time, Norway's climate was much more arid and geological formations have shown that sandstorms were not uncommon.

The location of the find may also provide the researchers with information about the ways in which the southern Norwegian shoreline has changed over time. When the settlement was inhabited, the ground was nine metres lower than it is today. As a result, archeologists believe they may find the remains of even older dwelling sites nearby, under water (*Der Spiegel*, Dec. 29th 2010).

A. The Hamresanden settlement belonged to a culture that had existed for approximately half a millennium by the time that community was completely enveloped in a sandstorm.

B The find is significant, in part, because it may clarify how the local topography has changed and provides the first evidence of the presence of Funnel Beaker Culture in what is today, Norway.

C. The archeological site at Hamresanden revealed that the Norwegian climate was far more arid in the past.

D . Due to the fact that the site was completely covered, artifacts being discovered there tend to be larger and more complete – if not entirely intact – than those from other sites.

38. Bustling modern-day Phnom Penh in Cambodia is a city rich with the legacies of kings and conquerors, both foreign

and Khmer. Legend has it that Phnom Penh was founded when a woman called Penh discovered five images of Buddha inside a log washed up on the bank of the Mekong River. In 1373, Wat Phnom was built to house them. The town that grew around it became known as Phnom Penh. With phnom in Khmer meaning hill, the name literally means Hill of Penh. Oudong, 40 kilometres north, usurped Phnom Penh as the capital between 1618 and the mid-19th century, but it was Phnom Penh that was the seat of government when the French arrived in 1863. Their influence is obvious in many of the grand colonial buildings that dot the city, especially in the French Quarter around the Old Market. Colonial rule brought stability. During this prosperous time, in 1892, King Norodom constructed the stunning Wat Preah Keo (Silver Pagoda), paved with 5,000 blocks of silver. (*Travel Channel*)

A. A woman called Penh found a log near the Mekong River with images of Buddha carved into it

B. The last time Phnom Penh was the seat of government was in 1618

C. Oudong today is still the seat of government in Cambodia

D. Phnom Penh is south of the city that was the capital of Cambodia for more than 200 years after 1618

39. **In the face of prejudice and rumour, it may be surprising to learn that there are places where the Roma feel at home. In Spain, the Roma and the payos ("whites") have demonstrated their capacity to live in peaceful coexistence, most notably in the southern region of Andalusia. The number of Roma, or Gitanos, as they refer to themselves there, is estimated to be between 500,000 and 800,000, and most of them live in Andalusia. Just as in France, there are also Central European Roma, but they number only about 40,000 and live mainly outside of Madrid. The Andalusian Gitanos have been in Spain for hundreds of years, through good times and bad, never far from the recurring threats of persecution, poverty and forced settlement. But today, Andalusia can serve as an example of successful Roma integration, and for one main reason.**

Professor Gunther Dietz, author of a report entitled "The State and the Roma in Spain", reveals that the traditional values of the Gitanos, such as the importance of family and clan, the notion of honour, and the authority accorded to family elders, are all compatible with the traditional rural culture of Spain. The integration of the Roma in Andalusian villages was therefore much easier than in the larger cities to the north (*Presseurop*, Sept. 6th 2010).

A. Like the value system of the Central European Roma, that of the Andalusian Gitanos is well-suited to that found in the Spanish countryside.

B. Having lived in Andalusia for centuries, most of Spain's half a million or more Gitanos have managed to live in peace with their non-Gitano neighbours.

C. Values held dear by the Gitanos include the central role of family and clan, the concept of honour, and great reverence for the recently deceased.

D. Due to the less compatible values of the local culture, Gitanos will never assimilate into the larger Spanish cities north of Andalusia.

40. **The rich cultural diversity of New Mexico has created a culinary melting pot. Finding something to eat is easy, but choosing from all of the options may take awhile. There are a variety of ethnic restaurants in Albuquerque, and for every one of these, there are at least three restaurants offering New Mexican cuisine. In the Old Town, offering the finest New Mexico beef, wild game and poultry, the High Noon Restaurant and Saloon serves gourmet meals in a casual atmosphere. No trip to this area of town would be complete without a stop at one of the restaurants on the plaza. Casa**

de Fiesta Mexican Grill offers fine New Mexican dining with a full view of the plaza. Old Town's bars and pubs reflect the quiet atmosphere of this historical district and rowdier nightlife needs to be sought in another part of town. (*Travel Channel*)

A. Many different cuisines have mixed in New Mexico.

B. New Mexico's culinary specialty is food cooked in a so-called melting pot.

C. The High Noon Restaurant and Saloon offers gourmet food and visitors can also play exciting games.

D. Albuquerque does not have a bustling night life.

41. Princess Hijab is Paris's most elusive street artist. Striking at night with dripping black paint she slaps black Muslim veils on the half-naked air-brushed women – and men – of the metro's fashion adverts. She calls it "hijabisation". Her guerrilla art has been exhibited from New York to Vienna, sparking debates about feminism and fundamentalism – yet her identity remains a mystery.

In secular republican France, there can hardly be a more potent visual gag than scrawling graffitied veils on fashion ads. Six years after a law banned headscarves and all conspicuous religious symbols from state schools, Nicolas Sarkozy's government has banned the veils from public spaces amid a fierce row over women's rights, Islamophobia and civil liberties. The "burqa ban", approved last month, means that from next year it will be illegal for a woman to wear full-face Muslim veils in public, not just in government offices or on public transport, but in the streets, supermarkets and private businesses. The government says it is a way of protecting women's rights and stopping them being forced by men to cover their faces (*Presseurop*, Nov. 12th 2010).

A. Princess Hijab's street art represents a protest against the use of Islamic religious clothing.

B. Critics of the burqa ban attribute such legislation to a mix of Islamophobia, feminism and resurgent nationalist sentiment.

C. France's moves to ban religious symbols in public stem from a tradition of secularism, set down in law over a century ago.

D. Princess Hijab applies black paint to ads in Paris under cover of night, drawing international attention both to her art and the issues it raises.

42. You smell the oil in the creeks and farmland of Ogoniland and the Niger delta long before you see it. Nigerian crude is a sweet oil which barely needs refining but in the sweltering tropical heat, it stinks of garage forecourts and rotting vegetation. We tried to find the source of one spill in a creek near the fishing village of Otuegwe. The further we swam into the warm shallow waters the more we became covered in a sheen of grease. The light brown and yellow liquid was coming from a buried, rusty pipeline. That was Ogoniland nearly 10 years ago. These days the 400 sq mile, densely-populated delta which provided Shell and the Nigerian government with some \$100bn (£64bn) of oil between its discovery in 1958 and the company being expelled by the community in 1994, is still badly polluted (*The Guardian*, Aug. 22, 2010).

A. Shell has offered to return to Ogoniland to repair the oil spills there, but the local community will not hear of it.

B. Oil had polluted Ogoniland and the Niger river delta ten years ago, but by now the area has been cleaned up.

C. Oil in Ogoniland had earned Shell and the Nigerian state a great deal of money, but the environmental impact is still being felt there.

D. Nigerian crude is full of impurities and must therefore undergo a relatively complex and expensive refining process.

43. In Germany, the introduction of Swedish-style parental leave, allowing a mother or a father to take 12 months off while still receiving 67% of his or her salary or a maximum of 1,800 euros per month, failed to make an impact on the country's fertility rate — 1.36 children per woman — which is still one of the lowest in Europe.

From a historical perspective, the reduction of fertility rates in many countries, not least in Europe, is positive news. However, when the fertility rate slumps below 2.1 children per woman, which is necessary for the ongoing renewal of a society, we should look at the underlying causes.

It is hard to argue with the hypothesis which attributes German women's limited desire to become mothers to a lack of sexual equality. Family policy in what used to be West Germany was highly conservative. The law identified fathers as providers, and for women, giving birth amounted to a de facto obligation to exit the labour market. Now the level of state support for children is increasing, but working mothers still have to contend with a hostile social context and a lack of infrastructure. The term "Rabenmutter" (bad mother) is still used to stigmatise women who put their children in the care of others so that they can continue working (*Presseurop*, Dec. 15th 2010).

A. Family policy that provides affordable child care and enables women to return to the labour market easily tends to boost the fertility rate.

B. Germany's family policy has also provided men with the option of taking a year's partially paid leave from work to take care of a child at home.

C. Often faced with a choice between family and work in many of the more conservative cultures, women appear to choose their jobs.

D. A 2.1 fertility rate assumes that more boys are born than girls and that women must thus give birth to 2.1 children on average to replace the population.

44. Symbolic gestures come in all shapes and sizes, but few as imposing as that of the USS George Washington, a ship more than three football-pitches long, and capable of carrying 85 aircraft and more than 6,200 people. But even symbols of such massive heft can be interpreted in various ways. The George Washington has just been in the South China Sea, off the coast of Danang, once home to one of the American army's biggest bases in Vietnam. Fifteen years after the opening of diplomatic relations, and 35 years since the end of the Vietnam war, the carrier's visit, and the joint naval exercises that followed, were striking tokens of reconciliation. But observers in China saw a different sort of gesture: not so much a handshake with a former enemy; more a brandished fist towards a potential one, their own country (*The Economist*, Aug. 12, 2010).

A. The US's warming military relations with a former enemy are a matter of great concern for China.

B. Diplomatic relations between China and Vietnam were only established fifteen years ago.

C. The US currently maintains one of its largest army bases in Vietnam at Danang.

D. The US sent an impressively large aircraft carrier to Vietnam in a show of defensive strength.

45. A team of researchers at Edinburgh Napier University's Biofuel Research Center led by the center's director, biology professor Martin Tangney, have spent the last two years experimenting with two byproducts of the whisky-making process. They took the byproducts, a liquid from copper stills called "pot ale" and spent grains, wonderfully named "draff," and turned it into a butanol "superfuel." The butanol could then be blended with regular gasoline or diesel, similar to the way small amounts of ethanol are blended now, meaning engines wouldn't need any

alterations.

The potential market for transforming this organic waste into fuel is actually sizable. According to the university, the $6.25 billion whisky industry produces more than 400 million gallons of pot ale and 187,000 tons of draff every year. So far, the scientists have filed a patent on the biofuel and plan to start a company that will develop it commercially. (*Discovery News, http://news.discovery.com*)

A. Butanol, much like ethanol, would work in regular gasoline and diesel engines without any modifications to the engines.

B. The butanol superfuel created from pot ale and draff, as well as the means used to produce it, are environmentally benign.

C. Similar amounts of butanol can be produced from both draff and pot ale, making them equally valuable.

D. Pot ale from iron as well as copper stills could equally be used to produce the butanol superfuel.

46. Whales and other marine mammals, fish, and even some invertebrates depend on sound, which travels much farther in water than light does. They use it to find food and mates, to avoid predators, and to communicate. But they face a growing problem: man-made noise is drowning them out.

Two years ago, the problem made it to the US Supreme Court. The Court's decision protected the right of naval vessels to test submarine-hunting sonar systems, whose intense sound pulses have been linked to several mass whale strandings. But the Navy is not the lone villain. Oil company ships towing arrays of air guns fire round-the-clock fusillades loud enough to locate oil buried under the seafloor – and also to be heard hundreds of miles away.

And most of the rising tide of noise – a hundredfold increase since 1960, in many areas – is created simply by the dramatic growth in shipping traffic. The problem is getting steadily worse for another reason. As we're making more noise, we're also making the ocean better at transmitting it. Seawater is absorbing less sound as carbon dioxide from fossil-fuel burning seeps into the ocean and acidifies it (*National Geographic*, Jan. 2011).

A. Certain marine invertebrates, such as sea urchins, starfish and squid, rely on sound to locate both food and mates, steer clear of predators, and communicate.

B. Sound is transmitted far greater distances in water than light is, more so now due to a process of ocean water acidification from increased carbon dioxide.

C. The US Supreme Court has considered the threat of naval operations to whale populations and has protected the interests of marine animals.

D. Sea life is disrupted by noise from the Navy testing sonar equipment, oil companies searching for oil with air guns, and commercial ships using increasingly powerful engines.

47. China has become the world's second biggest economy according to data released on Monday August 16th. Japan's economy fell behind China's at market exchange rates in the second quarter (it has been number three in purchasing power parity – PPP – terms for some time). These numbers are not strictly comparable: Japan's data have been seasonally adjusted while those for China have not. Quibbles aside, Japan will surely be eclipsed soon, if it has not been already. Data compiled by Angus Maddison, an economist who died earlier this year, suggest that China and India were the biggest economies in the world for almost all of the past 2000 years. Why they fell so far behind may be more of a mystery than why they are currently flourishing (*The Economist*, Aug. 16, 2010).

A. By all of the various standard economic measures, America's economy is larger than that of both China and Japan.

B. As China's economy grows and overtakes Japan's, tensions between the two neighbours have been growing.

C. China's flourishing economy seems to be in line with its economic performance over most of the last two millennia.

D. When measured according to PPP, China has been the third largest economy for a relatively long time.

48. By sequencing the full genome of a girl's fossil finger bone found in a Siberian cave, researchers concluded that there must have been a closely related sister group of Neanderthals living in central Asia about 40,000 years ago. The data also show that, like Neanderthals, the mysterious group interbred with modern humans, in this case leaving behind a genetic fingerprint in modern-day Melanesians of Papua New Guinea and Bougainville Island, nearly 10,000 kilometers (6,213 miles) from where the fossil was found.

As recently as a year ago, evidence suggested that modern humans spread throughout the world in a single migration out of Africa that wiped out any genetic traces of other early hominids. But the new study suggests that the lineage of modern humans is much more intertwined. The presence of the ancient group's genes in modern-day humans suggests that the new group, christened "Denisovans" after the Denisova Cave in southern Siberia where the finger bone was found, was once widespread throughout Asia. (*Discovery News, http://news.discovery.com*)

A. The discovery suggests that the Denisovans were the only early hominids to have interbred with modern-day humans.

B. Melanesians of Papua New Guinea and Bougainville Island are the only modern humans with genetic traces of early hominids.

C. The new discovery challenges even recent assumptions about the diversity, complexity and distribution of humans.

D. The distance between Siberia and Melanesia is the sole reason for believing that Denisovans were once widespread through Asia.

49. Huge dust storms, like the ones that blanketed Sydney twice last week, hit Queensland yesterday and turned the air red across much of eastern Australia, and are spreading lethal epidemics around the world. However, they can also absorb climate change emissions, say researchers studying the little understood but growing phenomenon. The Sydney storm, which left millions of people choking on some of the worst air pollution in 70 years, was a consequence of the 10-year drought that has turned parts of Australia's interior into a giant dust bowl, providing perfect conditions for high winds to whip loose soil into the air and carry it thousands of miles across the continent.
It followed major dust storms this year in northern China, Iraq and Iran, Pakistan, Saudi Arabia, Afghanistan, east Africa, Arizona and other arid areas. Most of the storms are also linked to droughts, but are believed to have been exacerbated by deforestation, overgrazing of pastures and climate change (*The Guardian*, Sept. 27, 2009).

A. Climate change is responsible for the droughts that are the exclusive cause of dust storms.

B. The primary causes of dust storms is the fact that too many trees are being cut down.

C. Dust storms in Australia and elsewhere are carrying not only loose soil, but also deadly diseases.

D. Parts of Australia have been suffering from a drought for much of the past 70 years.

50. Cahokia Mounds in the US state of Illinois represented the apogee, and perhaps the origin, of what anthropologists call Mississippian culture – a collection of agricultural communities that reached across the American Midwest and Southeast starting before A.D. 1000 and peaking around the 13th century.

Yet the idea that American Indians could have built something resembling a city was so foreign to European settlers that when they encountered the mounds of Cahokia, they commonly thought they must have been the work of a foreign civilisation: Phoenicians or Vikings or perhaps a lost tribe of Israel. Even now, the idea of an Indian city runs so contrary to American notions of Indian life that we collectively ignore Cahokia's very existence.

Our disregard has deep roots. The first person to write a detailed account of Cahokia's mounds was Henry Brackenridge, a lawyer and amateur historian, in 1811. "I was struck with a degree of astonishment, not unlike that which is experienced in contemplating the Egyptian pyramids," he wrote. But newspaper accounts of his discovery were widely ignored. He complained of this in a letter to his friend, former President Thomas Jefferson, and with friends in such high places, word of Cahokia did eventually get around. Unfortunately, it was not word most Americans were very interested in hearing. The US was trying to get Indians out of the way, not appreciate their history (*National Geographic*, Jan. 2011).

A. Brackenridge was the first person of European descent to discover Cahokia Mounds in 1811, upon which he compared them admiringly to the pyramids of Egypt.

B. When Cahokia Mounds are not being disregarded outright, myths of their having once been built by Phoenicians, Vikings or a lost tribe of Israel persist even today.

C. Mississippian culture stretched across the American Midwest and Southeast, spanning over something like three centuries, until its rapid downfall.

D. Once Brackenridge wrote to Thomas Jefferson, news of the Cahokia mounds started to spread although it often fell on deaf ears.

51. Donor conception involves having a baby or babies after undergoing fertility treatment using someone else's eggs, or sperm, or both, or another woman's embryo. In 2008 a total of 1,600 children were born in the UK as a result of donated sperm (977), eggs (541) or embryos (82). That represented 11% of the total of 15,237 births that year due to either in vitro fertilisation (IVF) or donor insemination (DI) – the highest number ever. In 2008 Britain's Human Fertilisation and Embryology Authority (HFEA) registered just 396 sperm donors – far fewer than experts say is needed to help women conceive. Although it was the highest since 1996, fewer men donate sperm than previously, mainly because donors lost their right to anonymity in 2005. Children born as a result of a donation are allowed to find out who their biological father is when turning 18 (*The Guardian*, Aug. 22, 2010).

A. In 2008 more children were born in Britain because of donated sperm than because of donated embryos.

B. In 2008 more babies were born in the UK due to in vitro fertilisation (IVF) than to donor insemination (DI).

C. Experts generally agree that about 400 sperm donors are sufficient in the UK to assist women in conceiving.

D. Changes in anonymity rules in 2005 have had little effect on the number of men who donate sperm.

52. Hidden beneath arabesque decorations, art experts have found what they believe is the earliest signature placed on a painting by the Renaissance master Raphael (1483-1520), who at the time was a 16-year-old boy. Featuring the words "RAPHAEL SANT" – Santi was Raphael's real surname – the signature has been detected in an obscure painting that has been kept in private collections for the past three centuries.

The 51.2 x 37.7 cm (20.1 x 14.8 inch) oil painting, called "The Mystical Marriage of St. Catherine" or "The Betrothal of St. Catherine to the Infant Jesus," dates 1499, when Raffaello

Sanzio, known as Raphael, was an unusually tall and handsome teenager.

Born in Urbino, 70 miles east of Florence, where the arts flourished under the patronage of the dukes of Montefeltro, Raphael learned the artistic rudiments by his father, the painter Giovanni Santi. At 17, he was already being described by his contemporaries as a "master" of his craft. (*Discovery News, http://news.discovery.com*)

A. At the time that Raphael produced the newly discovered painting, he was already hailed as a "master."

B. The oil painting called "The Mystical Marriage of St. Catherine" is Raphael's earliest work.

C. At around 1500, Raphael was described by others as a tall and handsome teenager already a master of his craft.

D. The painting is known by two titles because it has been in private hands for the past three centuries.

53. You are what you remember. It's difficult to imagine being you without some access to your remembered life story. But the new science of memory tells us that remembering is just that: a story. Memories are not stashed away, fully formed, in the vaults of the brain; they are constructed, when needed, according to the demands of the present. And they are soberingly fragile as a result. You can have vivid memories of things that never happened, and yet you can come away with the sketchiest recollections of events that actually did.

Memories of childhood are particularly suspect. When I recall my first day at school, I know I'm not remembering the event itself, but more my last act of remembering it. The brain stores autobiographical information in many different systems, and the sensory qualities of early experiences are likely stored accurately. It's the mental home movie into which they're assembled that may not bear much resemblance to reality (*The Guardian*, Aug. 22, 2010).

A. Our minds probably create a precise store of what our senses have picked up in our earliest days.

B. Normally, we can neatly and accurately call to mind most experiences from our past.

C. With special training, we can have far greater control over our memories than we normally do.

D. Even for someone with an active imagination, it is impossible to remember events that never happened.

54. A sedentary lifestyle, bad eating habits and alcohol consumption all kick in by the age of 19, but researchers found that 16 was the 'tipping point' for this type of behaviour. And they recommend that children under 13 should be targeted for health campaigns before it is too late to change.

The findings were presented in a doctoral thesis submitted by Marta Arrue to the University of the Basque Country in Spain. She said: "The least healthy habits turn out to be eating ones, followed by ingestion of alcohol, sedentarism, risks involving sexual relations, the consumption of tobacco and drugs and, finally, low quality or insufficient sleep.

"Special attention has to be paid to adolescents of 16 years. This is the point of no return, as it were, the age in which either healthy activities are opted for or risk behaviour patterns arise. "The data point to the fact that young persons show more risk behaviour than expected, more even than they themselves perceive, believing that they are healthier than they really are.

"It is notable that risk behaviour presents itself in early adolescence and that all the habits, except sleep, worsen with the passing of the years."

Ms Arrue studied 2,018 young people from the Basque region who were asked to fill in various questionnaires. With the gathered data, she collated and analysed habits of life according to sex

and age, adolescents from 13 to 17 and young persons from 18 to 26 (*The Telegraph*, Dec. 31st 2010).

A. In a survey of over 2,000 people between the ages of 13 and 26, Ms Arrue found that eating habits tend to be the least healthy.

B. A survey conducted by a PhD student of Basque descent concluded that the age of 16 was pivotal in terms of lifelong health behaviour patterns.

C. Recent research has found that young people display less unsafe behaviour than had been anticipated, particularly in terms of narcotics.

D. Ms Arrue's doctoral thesis dealt with young people's health habits based on data from various questionnaires as well as follow-up interviews.

55. After responsibility for security is handed over to Afghan police and soldiers in 2014, German police trainers will continue to teach local recruits. "That seems to me to be in tune with the sustainability of our current engagement," German Interior Minister Thomas de Maiziere told the DPA news agency. "But whether three, five, twenty or another number of police trainers will stay in Afghanistan, I can't yet say."

In July, Afghan President Harmid Karzai told international diplomats at a conference that 2014 was the date when Afghans "will be responsible for all military and law enforcement operations throughout our country." It is a non-binding date, but has been seized upon by Western politicians facing electorates at home who are increasingly opposed to sending soldiers to fight an increasingly powerful Taliban insurgency for a national government plagued by high levels of corruption (*Deutsche Welle World*, Aug. 22, 2010).

A. Afghan President Harmid Karzai has announced that he will expel all foreign troops from his country in 2014.

B. It has become expedient for Western politicians to refer to the statement made by the Afghan president.

C. Soldiers and law enforcement trainers from Germany will all pull out of Afghanistan in 2014.

D. Voters in Western countries increasingly back the fight against the Taliban because of their human rights abuses.

56. Most scholars have assumed that all prehistoric artists were male, but new evidence suggests women and even young girls produced at least some cave drawings, according to a study in the latest Oxford Journal of Archaeology. The study focused on finger flutings made on the walls and ceiling of Rouffignac Cave in the Dordogne, France.

Prior research had determined that relative finger length, also known as digit ratio, can be a marker for gender differences affected by hormones. Digit ratio theory holds that men tend to have ring fingers that are slightly longer than their index fingers. In women, these fingers are about the same length, or the index digit is slightly longer.

The researchers concluded that five of the artists were female and two were male. Based on the overall size of the flutings, they also believe patterns on the roof of one chamber in the cave were made by the fingers of children – both male and female – aged between two and five years old. (*Discovery News, http://news.discovery.com*)

A. Finger flutings were studied because digit ratio theory provides a widely accepted method of determining gender.

B. Finger flutings are the only prehistoric artwork ever discovered that is suspected of being produced by children.

C Digit ratio theory was first proposed as a method of distinguishing art created by women from that produced by men.

D. According to digit ratio theory, it is possible for a woman's index finger to be longer than her ring finger.

57. After the earthquake which hit Haiti in January this year, a number of European

officials called on the EU to create a European emergency force to react as a single body in international crisis situations. The EU came under fire for its lack of cohesion with critics lamenting the missed opportunity for the bloc to show its solidarity and project its image as a major player on the world stage. Eight months on from Haiti, the EU has yet to create a single emergency reaction force or aid fund and as such is running the risk of being labelled weak and inefficient again. Over the weekend, French President Nicolas Sarkozy called for the establishment of an EU disasters rapid reaction force in a letter to EU Commission President Jose Manuel Barroso (*Deutsche Welle World*, Aug. 16, 2010).

A. The Union has been criticised for not cooperating effectively in dealing with the crisis in Haiti.

B. The EU has established an office in Brussels to coordinate the Union's emergency relief efforts.

C. The EU set up an emergency force to assist in disaster relief after the Haitian earthquake in January.

D. Mr Sarkozy praised Mr Barroso for his efforts in setting up an EU disasters rapid reaction force.

58. People on the street in Ukraine say the rich are not paying their fair share of taxes. A new sign hung from a protest camp tent in the Ukrainian capital of Kyiv on Nov. 25 delivered this blunt message: "Veto or Revolution." Indeed, tens, perhaps hundreds, of thousands attended tax code protest rallies across Ukraine as pressure mounted on President Viktor Yanukovych to choose. The demonstrators on Nov. 25 made three demands: Veto the tax code, dismiss Prime Minister Mykola Azarov and his government, and call parliamentary elections in 2011, as required by the 1996 constitution now in force.

As this edition of the Kyiv Post went to press, about 10,000 protesters were rallying on Kyiv's Independence Square. Mass protests also took place in Donetsk, Cherkassy, Lviv, Ternopil and Sumy.

The non-partisan tax code protest campaign is setting a precedent, according to political analysts. As one foreign observer quipped, "We know this must be a genuine protest, because it's gone almost unnoticed in the western press and the CIA hasn't given it a colour" (*Spectrezine*, Nov. 29th 2010).

A. Ordinary Ukrainian citizens have been demonstrating their opposition to a system of taxation that spares the wealthy and is inconsistently enforced.

B. Known to give colour names to movements it supports in countries of the post-Soviet space, the CIA appears not to have taken a position on recent events in Ukraine.

C. Political analysts see Ukraine's protests, involving tens of thousands or more, as being independent of any political parties.

D. At least tens of thousands of protesters in Ukraine are demanding that their president veto a tax law and sack the prime minister after less than a year in office.

59. Every year, the Stockholm International Peace Research Institute (SIPRI) issues a report surveying international military expenditure. And if anyone thought that, this time, the financial crisis would have dampened the world's enthusiasm for bringing death and destruction upon their neighbours, they'll be disappointed. Military expenditure went up substantially. A SIPRI report released on Wednesday estimates expenditure in 2009 amounted globally to 1.5 trillion dollars, 5.9 percent more than in the previous year. In fact the crisis may have been one of the reasons for the increase. Dr Sam Perlo-Freeman, Head of the Military Expenditure Project at SIPRI, says that many countries increased public spending generally in 2009 as a way of boosting demand to combat the recession: "Although military spending hasn't been a big part of economic stimulus packages, public spending hasn't

been cut yet," he said (*Deutsche Welle World*, June 2, 2010).

A. Despite the tough economy, many governments may have increased defence spending partly in an effort to increase demand.

B. A survey on global military expenditure has found that many countries are causing more death and destruction than before.

C. The Stockholm International Peace Research Institute (SIPRI) publishes a biannual report on defence outlay.

D. Each surveyed country spent more money on weapons and equipment in 2009 than they did the year before.

60. The remains of a mighty Persian army said to have drowned in the sands of the western Egyptian desert 2,500 years ago might have been finally located, solving one of archaeology's biggest outstanding mysteries, according to Italian researchers. Bronze weapons, a silver bracelet, an earring and hundreds of human bones found in the vast desolate wilderness of the Sahara desert have raised hopes of finally finding the lost army of Persian King Cambyses II. The 50,000 warriors were said to be buried by a cataclysmic sandstorm in 525 B.C.

According to Herodotus (484-425 B.C.), Cambyses, the son of Cyrus the Great, sent 50,000 soldiers from Thebes to attack the Oasis of Siwa and destroy the oracle at the Temple of Amun after the priests there refused to legitimize his claim to Egypt. After walking for seven days in the desert, the army got to an "oasis," which historians believe was El-Kharga. After they left, they were never seen again. (*Discovery News, http://news.discovery.com*)

A. Sometime around 525 B.C., Cambyses wished to be the undisputed ruler of Egypt.

B. Since he had first-hand knowledge of the event, Herodotus is a trustworthy source.

C. The last site at which Cambyses' army was known to have visited was El-Kharga.

D. Whatever their identity, the remains belong to humans who died in a sandstorm.

61. No news is good news, it seems, if it comes from the Democratic Republic of the Congo (DRC). The kind of Western headlines that make mention of the vast central African country focus on corruption, mineral conflicts, war, mass-scale rape and slavery of women, and most recently the ambush and brutal murder of three United Nations peacekeepers. There is a lot to report on, but as the DRC's low ranking in the press freedom index compiled by Reporters Without Borders underscores, it is not a place where journalists have the freedom to say and write what they want. In 2009, the African country stood at 146th place in the table of 175 nations. Ambroise Pierre, head of the Africa desk of the Paris-based Reporters Without Borders, told Deutsche Welle that journalists working in the DRC are frequently silenced by intimidation and brutality, and sometimes even by murder (*Deutsche Welle World*, Aug. 21, 2010).

A. There is a great deal of news to report in the DRC and reporters there risk their lives covering it.

B. The DRC's low ranking in the press freedom index has shown a slight improvement recently.

C. Reporters Without Borders, which compiles a press freedom index, has its headquarters in Africa.

D. Three UN peacekeepers were recently killed in the DRC in a fire fight with Congolese rebels.

62. A Polish court on Thursday sentenced a Swedish neo-Nazi leader who admitted to masterminding the theft of the Auschwitz death camp entrance sign, to 32 months behind bars in his homeland. Anders Högström, 34, who had risked up to 10 years behind bars if convicted in Poland of plotting the theft, struck a plea deal announced late November before his case reached court.

Anders Högström was arrested in Sweden on a Polish warrant in February on suspicion of ordering the theft of the infamous "Arbeit macht frei" sign from the site of the World War II Nazi camp in the southern Polish city of Oswiecim. Polish police recovered the five-metre metal sign – which means "Work Will Set You Free" in German – two days after it went missing late last year. It had been chopped into three pieces. Five Polish men were arrested and charged with the actual theft of the sign, three of whom have already been sentenced to two-and-a-half years in prison. The two others are still to face trial. In 1994, Mr Högström founded the National Socialist Front, a Swedish neo-Nazi movement he subsequently ran for five years before quitting (*The Local*, Dec. 30th 2010).

A. Swedish neo-Nazi leader Anders Högström has confessed to organising and funding the theft of the "Arbeit macht frei" sign from the Auschwitz concentration camp.

B. When the "Arbeit macht frei" sign was stolen from the entrance to the former extermination camp at Oswiecim in Poland, it was cut up into its three constituent words.

C. Anders Högström faces 32 months' imprisonment for his role in stealing the Auschwitz entrance sign – a sentence only two months longer than three of his accomplices.

D. Until this recent case, Anders Högström had generally managed to keep out of the limelight since he left Sweden's neo-Nazi National Socialist Front in 1999.

63. Dutch teenager Laura Dekker has started her solo sailing trip around the world at the age of 14, with the intention of becoming the youngest person to sail solo around the world. There are conflicting reports on where she started her journey from on Saturday. Some reports say she sailed from Gibraltar, others say she set off from the south coast of Portugal. Ms Dekker ran into problems with Portuguese authorities, as it is against the law in Portugal for a minor to sail alone. Back home in the Netherlands, Ms Dekker had won a court case at the end of July that allowed her to make the trip alone. Dutch child welfare authorities had tried to prevent the voyage, insisting that it would stunt Ms Dekker's social and emotional development. The teenager wants to break the record currently held by Australia's Jessica Watson (*Deutsche Welle World*, Aug. 21, 2010).

A. Ms Dekker had some trouble with Portuguese authorities because she has no sailing licence.

B. Ms Dekker set out on her sailing trip from the Netherlands after winning a court case there.

C. In the end, Dutch child welfare officials voluntarily agreed to let Ms Dekker embark on her voyage.

D. Ms Watson is currently the youngest person to have sailed around the world on her own.

64. The same kind of peer-to-peer file sharing that made Napster famous – and infamous – is being used in a new research project in Europe that aims to pipe TV programs over the Internet. As part of the P2P-Next project, engineers from several European universities, research institutes, broadcast networks and manufacturers have agreed to pool their expertise to develop a file-sharing system, based on free open-source software. The system could someday allow users connected to the Internet to deliver videos from anywhere to anywhere – and to any number of people throughout the world.

The goal is to develop not only an entirely open P2P platform for delivering video on demand and live webcast streaming services but one that is also legal, secure and reliable. The project reflects a growing European interest in Internet-based television, including pioneering work by the state-owned Norwegian Broadcasting Corporation, which has launched a hugely successful TV series delivered via P2P. (*Discovery News*,

***http://news.discovery.com*)**

A. The Norwegian Broadcasting Corporation continues to offer the most advanced Internet-based television services currently available in Europe.

B. Currently, there are no P2P platforms available in Europe that can deliver video on demand and live webcast streaming services.

C. Existing P2P platforms capable of delivering video on demand and live webcast streaming are all illegal, unsecure or unreliable.

D. In developing the new system, engineers working on the P2P-Next project are looking to or adapting existing file-sharing systems.

65. In its purchasing managers' index of 4,500 Eurozone companies, the London-based economic research group Markit Economics revealed a dip from 56.7 to 56.1 points on Monday, the third in four months. Although the figures indicate a new downward turn, Markit said the reading was "consistent with a robust rate of expansion," adding that combined manufacturing and service sector output had been rising for 13 consecutive months. ING Bank economist Martin van Vliet said that although economic recovery was slowing down, it still retained "significant forward momentum." There is concern, however, that growth is restricted to the bloc's powerhouses, Germany and France. Markit head Chris Williamson said there was "little evidence" to suggest that "buoyant business conditions" in core economies were influencing weaker ones where austerity measures have been introduced to bring down budget deficits (*Deutsche Welle World*, Aug. 23, 2010).

A. According to Mr Williamson, positive developments in major European economies were also being felt in frailer ones.

B. Economic research group Markit's index shows an increase in Eurozone economies in line with 13 months of expansion.

C. Austerity measures taken to reduce budget deficits in certain Eurozone countries have significantly weakened those economies.

D. Mr van Vliet believes that the Eurozone economies are recovering less quickly than before but recovering nonetheless.

66. Parents in Britain will be able to see what proportion of a school's pupils achieve strong academic qualifications, or General Certificates of Secondary Education (GCSEs), in languages, sciences, history and geography from next month. Until now, school performance tables have measured the proportion who gain a middling grade C and above in English, maths and three or more other unspecified subjects. But ministers are worried that schools try to boost their score by putting a high proportion of pupils in for so-called "soft" subjects – a practice the government thinks fails to give pupils a rounded education.

From the beginning of 2011, schools will be measured according to how many pupils achieve good grades in five specified core subjects: English, maths, at least one science, a foreign language and a humanities subject. Ministers have described this set as the English baccalaureate – or "English bac". "If you get five GCSEs in those areas, I think you should be entitled to special recognition," education secretary Michael Gove said in September. He wants pupils who achieve the "English bac" to get a separate certificate. (*The Guardian*, Dec. 30th 2010).

A. Top government officials believe that schools do not encourage students to do GCSEs in easier or soft subjects.

B. As of January 2011, school performance will be assessed by pupils' achievement in five core subjects.

C. The "English bac" is named for similar secondary school baccalaureate systems operated in a number of European and Asian countries.

D. Conservative education secretary Michael Gove views a science, a foreign language and a humanities subject as part of a rounded education.

67. A flagship European Earth observation satellite has been struck by a second computer glitch and cannot send its scientific data down to the ground. The Goce spacecraft is on a mission to make the most precise maps yet of how gravity varies across the globe. In February, a processor fault forced operators to switch the satellite over to its back-up computer system. This too has now developed a problem and engineers are toiling to make the spacecraft fully functional again. The European Space Agency (ESA) remains confident the situation can be recovered, however. "There's no doubt about it: we're in a difficult situation, but we are not without ideas," Goce mission manager Dr Rune Floberghagen told BBC News (*BBC News*, Aug. 21, 2010).

A. A European Earth observation satellite has suffered a malfunction due to the effect of gravity.

B. The European Space Agency (ESA) is confident that a problem with its Goce spacecraft can be resolved.

C. A satellite is no longer functioning since it experienced a processor error in its back-up computer.

D. A satellite is no longer able to transmit data to Earth since it was struck by space debris.

68. According to a new study, the likelihood of having a healthy, full-term infant is five times higher in women who have just one embryo transferred than in women who opt for putting in two at once. That's mostly because doubling the embryo number vastly increases the chance of having twins, which carry far more complications than singletons do. Even though transferring two embryos increased the overall chance of having a baby, the study found that the difference just about disappeared when women followed a failed round of single-embryo IVF (in-vitro-fertilization) with another attempt also using one embryo.

As a growing number of people turn to assisted reproductive technologies, the new findings suggest that – putting financial complications aside – the safest strategy for many moms and babies is to try IVF with just one embryo at a time. (*Discovery News, http://news.discovery.com*)

A. In any given round of IVF, according to the study, the odds of having an infant were much greater when two embryos rather than one were transferred.

B. The findings suggest that financial considerations are less important to most parents than health considerations in determining the number of embryos to transfer.

C. A recent study suggests that it might be safer to try IVF with one embryo at a time.

D. Before this study, the prevailing medical wisdom was that the odds of bearing a healthy, full-term infant increased with the transfer of two embryos.

69. A Russian man suspected of selling arms to insurgent groups around the world is to be extradited to the United States, a court in Thailand has ruled. Viktor Bout, 43, is pleading not guilty on US charges of conspiracy to sell arms to Colombian rebels. Mr Bout – dubbed the Merchant of Death – was detained in a joint Thai-US sting operation in March 2008. Russia has condemned the decision and said it would work to secure his return. Russian Foreign Minister Sergei Lavrov described the ruling as "unlawful" and said his government believed it was made "under very strong external pressure". The ministry has summoned Thailand's ambassador to express its "extreme disappointment and bewilderment" at the verdict, the Agence France-Presse news agency reported. The US said it was "extremely pleased" at the news (*BBC News*, Aug. 20, 2010).

A. A Thai court has found Mr Bout guilty of conspiracy to sell weapons to Colombian insurgents.

B. Russia feels that Mr Bout must be brought to

justice but that this should not be done in the US.

C. America and Thailand have worked together to capture a suspected Russian arms merchant.

D. Russia accepted a court decision on Mr Bout and will cooperate on the matter in future.

70. If they stay at home in this kind of economic environment with unemployment at 11 per cent, many young Portuguese have concluded, they will not succeed in life. The economy is stagnant – the nation has been called the Sick Man of Europe – the older generation have a stranglehold on good jobs, and the future looks bleak.

Now, public spending is being slashed back in a way not seen for a generation, with a socialist government desperately trying to stop Portugal falling as the next domino in the euro crisis. José Sócrates, the prime minister, insisted last week that a bailout would not happen, much as Ireland's leaders did in the days before their own financial rescue. He may just cut spending enough to stave off an Irish-style humiliation, but most analysts doubt it. With markets sensing weakness and threatening to force up the price of its borrowing, in the next few weeks Portugal may have no choice but to take a bailout of around €50 billion from the EU and IMF, possibly twice as much.

The prospects for young people were bad even before their current economic woes. Their parents enjoy job security which makes them almost unsackable no matter how little work they do, especially in the bloated public sector. The young, who entered the workforce when perks and safe jobs had come to an end, must struggle through on short-term contracts and bad pay. So many of the best-educated and brightest depart – and Portugal loses the energetic, skilled people it desperately needs (*The Telegraph*, Nov. 27th 2010).

A. Portugal may be forced to accept a rescue package from the EU and the IMF that is at least as large as the €85 billion agreed earlier for Ireland.

B. With unemployment at 11 per cent and a dearth of attractive jobs, many young Portuguese are heading abroad to places like London and Brazil.

C. The socialist government of José Sócrates may ward off an EU/IMF bailout with major spending cuts such as a pay freeze for public sector workers.

D. Portugal may need more money to stay afloat, but with commercial lenders threatening to make borrowing too expensive, the country might have to turn elsewhere.

71. Official data released by European Union statistics agency Eurostat on Friday, Aug 13th, show that growth in the eurozone is chugging along at its fastest clip since 2006. And at the front of the European train is a German engine charging out of recession. Europe's largest economy accounted for about two-thirds of the eurozone GDP in the second quarter and is growing twice as fast as the rest of the bloc. Germany's economy, boosted by surging orders for its world-class machines, automobiles and other manufacturing products, expanded 2.2% in the second quarter over the previous quarter, pulling along behind it the rest of the eurozone, which posted growth of 1% in the same period. The German economy is now growing at its fastest rate since unification in 1990 (*Time*, Aug. 13, 2010).

A. The German economy has not grown as rapidly as it did in the second quarter of this year since 1990

B. Germany's expansion of 2.2% in the second quarter is principally due to an increased demand for its outstanding services.

C. Germany's economy grew faster than other eurozone countries in the second quarter, each of which also experienced some positive growth.

D. Leading the rest of the nations of the eurozone, Germany boasts a GDP that makes up around a third of that of the entire bloc.

72. During pregnancy and the post-partum period, women often feel their brains turning to mush. It's such a common phenomenon that women often call it "Mommy Brain." But studies in mice, rats, and other mammals have shown growth and other physical changes in the brains of new mothers.

To see if similar changes might happen in people, Pilyoung Kim, a developmental psychologist, and colleagues scanned the brains of 19 mothers a few weeks after giving birth and again three to four months later. Their results, published in the journal Behavioral Neuroscience, showed a small but significant amount of growth in a number of brain regions, including the hypothalamus, prefrontal cortex and amygdale. These are the areas that motivate a mother to take care of her baby, feel rewarded when the baby smiles at her, and fill her with positive emotions from simple interactions with her infant. These brain areas are also involved in planning and foresight, which might help a mother anticipate her infant's needs and be prepared to meet them. (*Discovery News, http://news.discovery.com*)

A. The study shows that women become more intelligent immediately after giving birth and that the results last for up to four months.

B. The study discovered growth in areas of women's brains responsible for influencing nurturing behaviors in caring for their infants.

C It is known that men also experience brain changes as a result of participating in the birth of or of interacting with their newborn children.

D. The study shows that what women sometimes call "Mommy Brain" is not based in changes to their actual brain structure or function.

73. During the 20th century, Switzerland appeared to combine deregulated low-tax economics with robust rule-of-law democracy. It was the first refuge for those fleeing communism after 1917 or Nazism after 1933 — just as it had offered safe haven to Voltaire, James Joyce and Lenin. Openness made Geneva a world capital, with the League of Nations, the International Red Cross, and then key U.N. agencies all settling there. The Alpine nation was an island of freedom during World War II. Churchill went to Zurich to appeal for European unity after 1945. Diplomats signed peace treaties in Switzerland in the 1950s and 1960s. The country sold itself as neutral, free of Cold War alignments and the snares of the European Union. Reagan and Gorbachev met there to begin ending the Cold War. Switzerland was where the world came to find solutions. Today, however, Switzerland's cities are grubby, its trains run late, its highways are always under repair, and its politicians often seem provincial (*Newsweek*, Feb. 5, 2010).

A. As it did in the 20th century, Switzerland continues to demonstrate to the world a strong model on which other countries might build.

B. Like those fleeing Nazism after 1917, Voltaire, James Joyce and Lenin all sought refuge in Switzerland in the 20th century.

C. Reagan and Gorbachev were attracted to Switzerland as a neutral place where they could begin to resolve the problems of the Cold War.

D. In the 1900s, Switzerland's economy was characterised by high taxes, but the revenue was used to ensure a good life for all Swiss citizens.

74. The Italian anarchists who have claimed responsibility for the letter bombs that exploded in the Swiss and Chilean embassies in Rome on Thursday want to make it clear that they consider themselves part of something bigger. "We've decided to make our voice heard once again, with words and with deeds," read a note written in Italian found in the remains of a crude bomb that exploded in the Chilean embassy. "We will destroy the system of domination."

The note was signed by the Informal

Federation of Anarchy, a loose union of Italian anarchist groups that authorities say is the largest such organisation in the country. It said the bombs were the work of the organisation's "Lambros Founas Cell," named after a Greek anarchist killed in a shootout with police in March, and expressed solidarity with other anarchist groups in Argentina, Chile, Mexico, Spain and Greece.

But while there's little doubt the group shares an ideological affinity with violent activists in other parts of the world, it's less certain that their capabilities rise to the level normally associated with international terrorism. The bombs, made from video cassette boxes stuffed with gunpowder and metal shards, were triggered by a nine-volt battery. Officials say they were mailed from within the country, using the Italian postal system, adding that the anarchists have few supporters in Italian society (*Time*, Dec. 24th 2010).

A. Constituting part of the Informal Federation of Anarchy, the Lambros Founas Cell was named for an anarchist who died in a shootout with the Italian police.

B. The Informal Federation of Anarchy always works in co-operation with other anarchist organisations in Argentina, Chile, Mexico, Spain and Greece.

C. The parcel bombs that blew up in the Swiss and Chilean embassies in Rome were crude compared to those typically used by international terrorists.

D. While officials downplay the significance of the recent bombings, they are concerned that the country will see an upswing in anarchist violence.

75. Fires left at least four people dead and hundreds homeless in two regions of central Russia, government officials said on Friday. At least 18 people were injured and 957 people were moved to temporary homes, according to authorities. The blaze started after severe windstorms, coupled with hot weather, disrupted electricity transmission lines, causing short circuits that led to the fires, the Russian Emergency Situations Ministry said. More than 2,500 fire-fighters and rescuers are battling the blazes. The ministry said it is increasing its efforts to localize and put out the fires. Russian Prime Minister Vladimir Putin signed a decree on Friday allocating 1 billion roubles (almost $33 million) in financial aid to the two regions. The funds will be used to replace houses lost in the fires and compensate for the loss of property. Families of those who died will receive a lump sum of 1 million roubles (almost $33,000), according to the decree (*CNN*, Sept. 3, 2010).

A. Deadly wildfires that have struck two regions in Russia have also affected a third.

B. Russian Prime Minister Vladimir Putin has approved funds to assist victims of the disaster.

C. More than 2,500 fire-fighters and rescuers have aided victims and extinguished all the fires.

D. The blazes started in nearby forests, which are especially susceptible to fires in hot weather.

76. Even before the "death ships" pulled into port at Messina, many Europeans had heard rumors about a "Great Pestilence" that was carving a deadly path across the trade routes of the Near and Far East. However, they were scarcely equipped for the horrible reality of the Black Death. "In men and women alike," the Italian poet Giovanni Boccaccio wrote, "at the beginning of the malady, certain swellings, either on the groin or under the armpits…waxed to the bigness of a common apple, others to the size of an egg, some larger and some smaller." Blood seeped out of these strange swellings, which were followed by a host of other unpleasant symptoms–fever, chills, vomiting, diarrhea, terrible aches and pains–and then, in short order, death. The Black Death was terrifyingly, indiscriminately contagious: "the mere touching of the

clothes," wrote Boccaccio, "appeared to itself communicate the malady to the toucher." (*History.com, "Black Death," http://www.history.com*)

A. The epidemic that became known in Europe as the Black Death originated in Italy.

B. At the time no treatments were available to combat the symptoms of the plague.

C. The Black Death appeared to afflict people without almost any discernible cause or pattern.

D. The swellings associated with the sickness were never smaller than an egg.

77. First there was the discovery of dozens of bottles of 200-year-old champagne, but now salvage divers have recovered what they believe to be the world's oldest beer, taking advertisers' notion of 'drinkability' to another level. Though the effort to lift the reserve of champagne had just ended, researchers uncovered a small collection of bottled beer on Wednesday from the same shipwreck south of the autonomous Aland Islands in the Baltic Sea. "At the moment, we believe that these are by far the world's oldest bottles of beer," Rainer Juslin, permanent secretary of the island's ministry of education, science and culture, told CNN on Friday via telephone from Mariehamn, the capital of the Aland Islands. "It seems that we have not only salvaged the oldest champagne in the world, but also the oldest still drinkable beer. The culture in the beer is still living." (*CNN*, Sept. 3, 2010).

A. Researchers first discovered bottles of champagne and then bottles of drinkable beer on a shipwreck in the Baltic Sea.

B . Champagne and beer were found on a ship that had sunk after leaving the port of Mariehamn in the Aland Islands 200 years ago.

C. Dozens of bottles of champagne had been lifted from one ship when a small collection of beer was found on another.

D. Having been bottled 200 years ago, the beer that was found under the sea would make one very ill if one were to drink it.

78. After years of unsuccessfully banging on the EU's door, Recep Tayyip Erdogan, Turkey's prime minister and leader of its governing AKP party, known for its economically liberal though moderately Islamic politics, decisively shifted Ankara's gaze toward the Ottoman empire's old stomping grounds east and south. He won plaudits among many in the Arab and Muslim world for his tough stance on Israel following an Israeli raid on ships heading to Gaza with relief supplies. Bucking a longstanding Israeli-Turkish alliance, he branded the raid an act of "inhumane state terrorism." Later, joining forces with Brazilian President Lula da Silva, Mr Erdogan met with Iran's embattled President Mahmoud Ahmadinejad and unveiled what's called the Tehran Declaration on May 17th. It offered a fuel swap as part of an alternative solution to US-backed sanctions on Iran as the world tried to rein in Tehran's nuclear program — the move was received as a mark of a burgeoning new world order.

On the down side, the Tehran Declaration was snubbed by the US and its allies, undermining Mr Erdogan's attempt at diplomacy power-brokering. In February, Mr Erdogan found himself in the midst of a political crisis, and had 31 former or current military officers arrested on charges of plotting to foment a coup. The struggle accentuated the divide between Mr Erdogan's more religious democratic party and secular-nationalists tied to the country's military, which has been a longstanding force in Turkish politics (*Time*, Nov. 10th 2010).

A. Mr Erdogan worked with the Brazilian president to hammer out an agreement with Iran, a move which America did not embrace.

B. Mr Erdogan 's arrest of 31 military officers served as a stark reminder of the not-so-distant past, when the army has overthrown the government.

C. Mr Erdogan won praise from Arabs and Muslims for his censure of Israel although Turkey's relations with the Jewish State remain strong.

D. Mr Erdogan is the head of Turkey's ruling AKP, a moderately Islamic, democratic party he established nearly a decade ago.

79. This week, Catalonia took a huge step forward in ending the cruel "sport" of bullfighting. Its parliament voted in favour of amending the animal protection legislation to abolish bullfighting in the region. The vote, passed with 68 in favour of the ban and 55 against, is a historic victory for animal welfare. It is also a vindication for the thousands of Catalonians who called on their parliament to include bulls in their animal protection law. Back in December 2009, the organization PROU presented a "popular legislative initiative" to the Catalonian Parliament with more than 180,000 signatures supporting the end to bullfighting. This action initiated the nearly yearlong process that led up to this week's vote. Many pro-bullfighting activists have argued that the "sport" is an important part of the Spanish culture and should not be banned. But cultural heritage is no excuse for inflicting pain on a frightened and confused animal (*CNN*, July 30, 2010).

A. The vote is very important for anti-bullfighting activists because Catalonia is the bullfighting hub of Spain.

B. The push to have the Catalonian animal protection law cover bullfighting had clear popular support.

C. The anti-bullfighting vote was initiated by a parliamentarian who favours greater animal protection.

D. The vote to outlaw bullfighting in the Catalonian parliament won by a handy two-thirds majority.

80. From around A.D. 800 to the 11th century, a vast number of Scandinavians left their homelands to seek their fortunes elsewhere. These seafaring warriors – known collectively as Vikings or Norsemen ("Northmen") – began by raiding coastal sites, especially undefended monasteries, in the British Isles. Over the next three centuries, they would leave their mark as pirates, raiders, traders and settlers on much of Britain and the European continent, as well as parts of modern-day Russia, Iceland, Greenland and Newfoundland.

Contrary to some popular conceptions of the Vikings, they were not a "race" linked by ties of common ancestry or patriotism, and could not be defined by any particular sense of "Viking-ness." Most of the Vikings whose activities are best known come from the areas now know as Denmark, Norway and Sweden, though there are mentions in historical records of Finnish, Estonian and Saami Vikings as well. Their common ground – and what made them different from the European peoples they confronted – was that they came from a foreign land, they were not "civilized" in the local understanding of the word and – most importantly – they were not Christian. (*History.com, "Vikings," http://www.history.com*)

A. It has been a widely-held belief among some people that the Vikings were a rather homogenous group.

B. For 300 years or more, all Vikings forcibly uprooted and displaced local inhabitants in order to settle new lands.

C. Vikings came exclusively from the areas now known as Denmark, Norway, and Sweden.

D. Religious beliefs were one area in which all Vikings, no matter where they originated, were the same.

81. West Nile Virus has killed 14 people in northern Greece and sickened 142, the Hellenic Centre for Disease Control and Prevention reported on Thursday. As of Wednesday, the health agency said, 32 people remained hospitalised, eight of

them in intensive care. West Nile Virus is usually transmitted by infected mosquitoes or blood transfusions. Severe symptoms can include high fever, headache, neck stiffness, stupor, disorientation, coma, tremors, convulsions, muscle weakness, vision loss, numbness and paralysis. About 80 per cent of people infected with the virus show no symptoms, health officials say. Authorities in central Macedonia, in northern Greece where most cases have been reported, said they would step up spraying programs in an attempt to ward off mosquitoes. Authorities also said they are taking steps to prevent transmission by blood transfusions. Blood donations in regions at high risk for West Nile Virus have been cancelled and people leaving the area are encouraged not to donate blood for up to 28 days (*CNN*, Sept. 2, 2010.)

A. In a severe case of West Nile Virus, a victim may even lose movement in his arms or legs.

B. Stagnant waters in central Macedonia may account for the high number of mosquitoes there.

C. The West Nile Virus can generally only be contracted through an infected mosquito.

D. Only one-fifth of those infected by the West Nile Virus escape all the symptoms.

82. The eastern half of the Roman Empire proved less vulnerable to external attack, thanks in part to its geographic location. With Constantinople located on a strait, it was extremely difficult to breach the capital's defenses; in addition, the eastern empire had a much shorter common frontier with Europe. It also benefited greatly from a stronger administrative center and internal political stability, as well as great wealth compared with other states of the early medieval period. The eastern emperors were able to exert more control over the empire's economic resources and more effectively muster sufficient manpower to combat invasion. As a result of these advantages, the Eastern Roman Empire–variously known as the Byzantine Empire or Byzantium–was able to survive for centuries after the fall of Rome. (*History.com, "Byzantine Empire," http://www.history.com*)

A. The emperors in the Western Roman Empire could not summon soldiers to repel invasions because they did not control the empire's economic resources.

B. Due to its geographic location, the Byzantine capital, Constantinople, saw fewer attempted attacks than did the capitals of the Western Roman states.

C. Although the Byzantine Empire lasted for centuries after the dissolution of the Roman Empire, the fall of Rome assured Byzantium's eventual fall.

D. Byzantium's geographic, economic and political situation afforded the Eastern Roman Empire a higher degree of protection.

83. Proud of its title as a cultural capital, Paris boasts some of the world's most iconic monuments. Littered with ancient obelisks, Gothic churches, classical bridges and modern masterpieces, the city has for centuries cultivated an extraordinary array of artists, writers, philosophers and architects.

The end result makes for a city of unparalleled beauty, which revels in its cultural heritage. But with more than 400 parks, 134 museums, 143 theatres and 242 floodlit churches, statues, fountains and national buildings, it's virtually impossible to see all the cultural highlights Paris has to offer. So, for a quick fix of Europe's most fashionable, exclusive and elegant city, follow our 24-hour culture vulture guide. It's a whirlwind tour packed with the "must-dos" on the cultural trail – giving you a true taste of Paris' cultural life, past and present (*CNN*, Aug. 11, 2010).

A. The culture vulture guide offers an all-in exhaustive tour of all the significant cultural sights of Paris.

B. Paris boasts more churches than museums and many more parks than either of them.

C. Paris is a cultural hub at least partly because of the high number of theatres and museums.

D. Paris was once home to a range of creative talents, but now only their spirits live on.

84. Last month, a small Islamic terrorist group named al Qaeda in the Islamic Maghreb (AQIM) made headlines when it executed Michel Germaneau, a French aid worker. He was not the first hostage to be executed by AQIM, but his death provoked France to declare war on al Qaeda. While Western nations like France are just starting to escalate their engagement against terrorist organizations in Africa, the Tuareg people of Niger – where Germaneau was kidnapped – have long been victims of the underdevelopment that nourishes fundamentalism. Often pretending to fight for communities like the Tuareg, groups like AQIM operate in the ungoverned regions of a continent that is struggling to establish centralized states and the rule of law. From the Sahel to the Horn of Africa, they thrive off of the symptoms of state collapse: drugs, weapons and grinding poverty (*Deutsche Welle World*, Aug. 23, 2010).

A. AQIM wish to create their own state to fill the void left in the ungoverned regions of Africa.

B. Where there are many poor people, organisations like AQIM tend to flourish.

C. Victimized people like the Tuareg have staunch allies in organisations like AQIM.

D. AQIM drew international attention when they killed their first hostage, Michel Germaneau.

85. As the 18th century drew to a close, France's costly involvement in the American Revolution and extravagant spending by King Louis XVI (1754-1793) and his predecessor had left the country on the brink of bankruptcy. Not only were the royal coffers depleted, but two decades of poor cereal harvests, drought, cattle disease and skyrocketing bread prices had kindled unrest among peasants and the urban poor. Many expressed their desperation and resentment toward a regime that imposed heavy taxes yet failed to provide relief by rioting, looting and striking.

In the fall of 1786, Louis XVI's controller general, Charles Alexandre de Calonne (1734-1802), proposed a financial reform package that included a universal land tax from which the privileged classes would no longer be exempt. To garner support for these measures and forestall a growing aristocratic revolt, the king summoned the Estates-General ("les états généraux")–an assembly representing France's clergy, nobility and middle class–for the first time since 1614. (*History.com, "French Revolution," http://www.history.com*)

A. The French king immediately preceding King Louis XVI had left the country in sound financial condition.

B. The aristocracy had probably not been asked to pay land taxes for an indeterminate period before the fall of 1786.

C The Estates-General wielded considerable influence over France's aristocracy at the time they were summoned.

D. Acts of civil unrest in France during the latter part of the 18th century were not limited to peasants and the urban poor.

86. After months of haggling over its involvement in the unprecedented European Union bailout to save Greece from defaulting, Germany finds itself at the centre of another financial tangle with the debt-ridden Mediterranean nation – this time involving defence contracts Greece could ill afford and the shadowy deals behind them. At the same time that German Chancellor Angela Merkel's cabinet was approving 22.4 billion euros ($29.7 billion) in aid to Greece, prosecutors in Germany began investigating whether defence contractors had paid millions of euros in bribes to Greek officials in connection with the sale of two German submarines in a

deal worth more than a billion euros (*Deutsche Welle World*, Aug. 12, 2010).

A. Germany's government is accused of corruption in connection with money given to Greece to help pay its debt.

B. Germany gave away two submarines worth over a billion euros to improve Greece's defensive posture.

C. Military contractors are suspected of having paid government officials in Greece to sweeten a procurement deal.

D. After the German government voted to give financial aid to Greece, investigators launched a corruption probe.

87. Nearly all nuclear power reactors in service around the world are fuelled with uranium; water is needed not only to cool the reactor, but also to slow the neutrons so fission will be effective. But dating back to the beginnings of nuclear power research, there have been efforts to deploy effective "fast" reactors, using a combination of plutonium and uranium. The neutrons were not cooled with water in these reactors; they remained "fast." The original idea was to create a chain reaction that would produce more fuel than the reactor consumed — a so-called "breeder" reactor. But the aim of the latest efforts in Integral Fast Reactor (IFR) technology is not to breed new fuel, but to fission the fuel as completely as possible — while producing a great deal of energy (*National Geographic*, Sept. 1, 2010).

A. The majority of nuclear power reactors today use a combination of plutonium and uranium.

B. The current purpose of the Integral Fast Reactor (IFR) technology is to create new fuel for later use.

C. Research has been conducted to develop nuclear power reactors that run on cold fusion.

D. The majority of nuclear power reactors today use water to slow down neutrons.

88. Amid the celebrations of the 20th anniversary of German reunification in October 2010, many former citizens of East Germany were likely asking themselves exactly what they had gained in the two decades since the two countries became one. Today, the states of eastern Germany still lag behind former West Germany in just about any social or economic indicator you can name, and many former East Germans still wonder if the reunification process could have gone differently.

At the time, after the fall of the Berlin Wall on Nov. 9, 1989, many East Germans wanted to reform their country rather than simply abolish it. But reunification was pushed through at a record pace by then-West German Chancellor Helmut Kohl, and the two countries officially became one on Oct. 3, 1990. Although a pro-unification grouping of parties received the most votes in East Germany's first, and only, free parliamentary election in March 1990, there was a perception among some East Germans that they had been steamrollered by powerful West Germany. (*Spiegel Online International*, English edition, 12/27/10)

A. A majority of East Germans favoured reform of their country over its abolition.

B. East and West Germany officially became a single political entity on Nov. 9, 1989.

C. Before Nov. 9, 1989, East Germany had never held a free parliamentary election.

D. Many East Germans view reunification as an economic, social and political failure.

89. Last year, a group of young Moroccans campaigning to change the law banning eating in public during the Muslim Ramadan fast made plans for a picnic via social networking site Facebook. They organised to meet in Mohammedia near Casablanca for the public feast. It was a risky move because under Moroccan law, eating in public during daylight hours in the holy month is considered a crime. Sure

enough, the authorities in Morocco monitored the Facebook group and cracked down before the demonstration could take off. "We were met by hundreds of police at the station in Mohammedia. They were like an army waiting for terrorists," Zineb Elghzaoui, one of the co-founders of the group called Alternative Movement for Individual Freedoms (MALI), remembered. "We were abused, forced back on the train and then we were arrested and interrogated for hours. It's only because the incident attracted international attention that the police finally closed our cases – for now," she said (*Deutsche Welle World*, Aug. 20, 2010).

A. Facebook made it possible for MALI to organise a demonstration, but it also enabled the police to stop it from taking place.

B. A group of young Moroccans called MALI fought in a battle against an army in Mohammedia near Casablanca.

C. In Morocco and many other Islamic countries, there are laws banning all eating in public places.

D. The Moroccan police consider MALI a terrorist organization and have detained many of their members indefinitely.

90. German director Christoph Schlingensief, who was also a renowned actor and artist, has died at the age of 49 after suffering from lung cancer for more than two years, according to a spokesman of the Ruhrtriennale festival. Mr Schlingensief directed numerous films, plays and operas, including an internationally recognised production of Parsifal for the Wagner summer festival in the southern German city of Bayreuth in 2004. Recently, he had been working on a project in the West African country of Burkina Faso, setting up a "village of opera" which was to combine video, live actors and music. His last major production was the Via Intolleranza II opera project in Brussels last year. He was engaged to curate Germany's pavilion at the Biennale in Venice next year (*Deutsche Welle World*, Aug. 21, 2010).

A. In 2004 Mr Schlingensief developed a "village of opera" project in Burkina Faso in West Africa.

B. German director and opera singer Christoph Schlingensief died of lung cancer at the age of 49.

C. Mr Schlingensief directed a critically acclaimed production at the Wagner festival in Bayreuth.

D. His opera production in Brussels in 2009 was very well received and won him several awards.

91. It had hardly been announced that autocratic leader Lukashenko would remain in power (it was his fourth election victory in a row, and this time his official tally was 79.7% of the votes), when more than 10,000 citizens took to the streets in the capital Minsk. An attempt to storm the government headquarters building failed. The secret police, which appeared to have been well prepared, clubbed down the demonstrators, arrested several hundred and carried off seven of the opposition presidential candidates.

Only last year, politicians in Brussels, citing the easing of political tensions in the realm of long-time dictator Lukashenko, had lifted a ban on entry into the EU imposed in 2006 on Lukashenko and about three dozen of his followers. The Europeans had argued that the Belarusian had taken some positive steps, including the release of political prisoners and the acceptance of two opposition newspapers. He was promptly invited to attend the inauguration of the EU's Eastern Partnership program in Prague. The move prompted the Minsk newspaper Komsomolskaja prawda to rejoice, calling Lukashenko "a legitimate player in European politics." (*Spiegel Online International*, English edition, 12/27/10, http://www.spiegel.de/international)

A. In Lukashenko's fourth bid for election as president, there had been at least seven opposition presidential candidates.

B. Over three dozen Belarusian government officials under Lukashenko in 2006 were banned from entry into the EU.

C. Sometime after 2006, Lukashenko had released all political prisoners and halted government censorship of the press.

D. The decision to invite Lukashenko to attend the inauguration of the EU Eastern Partnership program was unanimous.

92. Egyptian police have arrested two Italians at Cairo airport suspected of stealing a famous van Gogh painting taken from a museum earlier on Saturday, August 21. The painting, Poppy Flowers, worth an estimated 39 million euros ($50 m), was stolen from the Mahmoud Khalil museum in the Egyptian capital after it was cut from its frame. Reports say the museum's surveillance system has been out of order for some time. "The cameras had not been working for a long time, and neither had the alarm system," a museum security official told news agency AFP. This was the second time the painting had been stolen from the museum. Thieves made off with it in 1978, but it was returned a decade later. One year after that, a duplicate was sold for $43 m in London, sparking a debate in Egypt about whether the returned painting was, in fact, a fake (*Deutsche Welle World*, Aug. 22, 2010).

A. The painting was stolen in 1978 but was returned to the museum the very same year.

B. A duplicate of the painting was sold for 43 million dollars in London in 1989.

C. Worth an estimated €39 m ($50 m), van Gogh's Sunflowers has been snatched from a Cairo museum.

D. The museum's surveillance system was also out of order the first time the painting was taken.

93. Along the warm coastal lowlands of New South Wales, the yellow-bellied three-toed skink lays eggs to reproduce. But individuals of the same species living in the state's higher, colder mountains are almost all giving birth to live young. Only two other modern reptiles — another skink species and a European lizard — use both types of reproduction. Evolutionary records shows that nearly a hundred reptile lineages have independently made the transition from egg-laying to live birth in the past, and today about 20 per cent of all living snakes and lizards give birth to live young only. But modern reptiles that have live young provide only a single snapshot on a long evolutionary time line, said James Stewart, a biologist at East Tennessee State University. The dual behaviour of the yellow-bellied three-toed skink therefore offers scientists a rare opportunity to study this evolutionary change (*National Geographic*, Sept. 1, 2010).

A. The yellow-bellied three-toed skink is the only reptile that produces offspring in two ways.

B. Reptiles have become extinct on the warm coastal lowlands of New South Wales.

C. Around one-fifth of all living snakes and lizards give birth in order to live longer.

D. The yellow-bellied three-toed skink is important to science because of the stage it occupies in evolution.

94. It has been a long hard year for those living beneath the crater of Eyjafjallajokull in Iceland. When the volcano erupted in March, air passengers faced chaos as their planes were grounded amid fears that the ash, thrown high into the atmosphere, would damage aircraft. But after little more than two weeks, and a safety all-clear, life started returning to normal for airlines and their customers. The people of Iceland living near the eruption site were not so lucky. The region of south Iceland where Eyjafjallajokull is situated has a significant farming industry.

Floods, caused by lava melting glacial ice, swept down the side of the volcano and ruined farmland. Sixty hectares of the property Poula Kristin Buch farms with her husband was wiped away by the water (*BBC News*, Aug. 22, 2010).

A. An Icelandic volcano caused concerns for air passengers and devastated agricultural land.

B. Farmers in Iceland saw their fields completely destroyed by molten lava.

C. In March, an Icelandic volcano disrupted flights and caused damage to aircraft.

D. All of the land that Ms Buch works with her husband was swept away.

95. According to a report released by the UN Environmental Program (UNEP), the chemistry of the oceans is changing at a rate not seen for 65 million years. Should the rate of change continue unaltered, our oceans could be 150 percent more acidic by the end of this century, the study says.

Oceans absorb some 25 percent of global CO2 emissions, but once they do so, the carbon dioxide is transformed into carbonic acid, which accounts for the precipitous fall in pH levels found by the study. It is unclear, however, what exactly the effects of the increase in acidity might be for ocean life, but scientists are concerned that the change may harm many shell-building organisms at the bottom of the food chain. (*Spiegel Online International*, English edition, 12/03/10, http://www.spiegel.de)

A. A change to the ocean's pH balance of the magnitude described is unprecedented in the evolutionary history of our planet.

B. Scientists suspect that the ocean's level of acidity impacts the survival of shell-building organisms.

C. A twenty-five percent fall in the pH levels of the world's oceans is threatening many species of shell-building organisms.

D. An immediate 25% cut in global CO2 emissions would halt oceanic acidification and protect shell-building organisms.

96. French automakers expect this year to make little more than half the number of vehicles they did in France five years ago; German car production is around the same as it was five years ago. France expects 1.6% economic growth this year and less than 2% in 2011 and 2012, according to the European Commission; Germany is forecast to post 3.7% this year followed by 2%-plus the following two years. France's budget deficit is forecast to be about 7% of gross domestic product (GDP) in 2012; Germany's is expected to fall below 3%, according to the Organisation for Economic Cooperation and Development.

The French government is now carrying out a detailed comparison of its tax system with that of Germany, which has lower corporate and payroll taxes than France. "The point of departure for this study is convergence with Germany," France's budget minister, François Baroin, said in December. "It's to make our economy more competitive."

Germany traditionally has grown more from investment and exports, which are now booming thanks to demand from China, and it generally has run lower budget deficits than France. France, by contrast, has grown mainly through consumption over the past decade. This has been helped by public spending. The government hasn't recorded a budget surplus for more than three decades. But that model has been threatened by the last two years of economic crisis, which have pushed up France's budget deficits (*The Wall Street Journal Europe*, Jan. 3rd 2011).

A. France suffers from a far larger budget deficit in proportion to GDP than Germany does, and it lags behind its northeastern neighbour in terms of economic growth and per capita income.

B. Whereas economic growth in Germany is driven by exports and investment, France's economy – just like the United States' – has primarily been fuelled by consumption.

C. The French government is carefully examining Germany's tax regime so that it can bring

France's more in line with Germany's in order to attract more foreign business.

D. The French budget minister sees a clear link between a country's competitiveness, on the one hand, and the tax system on the other.

97. Could we "terraform" Mars — that is, transform its frozen, thin-aired surface into something friendlier and Earth-like? Should we? The first question has a clear answer: Yes, we probably could. Spacecraft, including the ones now exploring Mars, have found evidence that it was warm in its youth, with rivers draining into vast seas. And right here on Earth, we've learned how to warm a planet: just add greenhouse gases to its atmosphere. Much of the carbon dioxide that once warmed Mars is probably still there, in frozen dirt and polar ice caps, and so is the water. Perfluorocarbons, potent greenhouse gases, could be synthesized from elements in Martian dirt and air and blown into the atmosphere; by warming the planet, they would release the frozen CO2, which would amplify the warming and boost atmospheric pressure to the point where liquid water could flow (*National Geographic*, Jan. 15, 2010).

A. Scientists have found clear evidence of primitive life in the rivers and vast seas of Mars.

B. Since greenhouse gases harm Earth's environment, it is thought they should be prevented on Mars.

C. Laboratory experiments have been carried out to suggest that "terraforming" Mars is possible.

D. It is likely that both carbon dioxide and water can be found in frozen form on Mars.

98. The water separating Iceland from the rest of Europe has been choppy these past few years. After Iceland's banks collapsed in 2008, the British government used anti-terrorism laws to force Reykjavik to agree to compensation for UK and Dutch account holders. When one of Iceland's many volcanoes spewed an ash cloud westwards in April, it grounded European air traffic for a week. Now there is a new feud between the two and this time it is about the sea itself: Iceland — along with the tiny Faroe Islands nearby — has started trawling for mackerel, a stock that Norway and the EU insist is over-fished. After Iceland unilaterally raised its mackerel quota from 2,000 to 130,000 tons for the year in early August, and the Faroes raised their 25,000-ton quota to 85,000 tons, the outraged Scottish Fisheries Minister Richard Lochhead accused them of "hoovering up" stock, and warned that Iceland was jeopardizing its ambition to join the EU (*Time*, Aug. 27, 2010).

A. Iceland negotiated with several other countries in the region before it increased its mackerel quota in early August.

B. Norway and the Faroe Islands are at odds over the fishing of mackerel, with Norway arguing that the stock is shrinking.

C. In its effort to maintain sustainable numbers of different fish species, the EU has always enforced fishing quotas consistently.

D. Mr Lochhead is sympathetic to Icelandic ships needing to fish for more mackerel during difficult economic times.

99. In some ways, former British prime minister Tony Blair was Labour's most successful leader ever. No other Labour leader won three consecutive elections. After it had been 18 years in the wilderness he turned a reformed "New Labour" into a party of government. He played a significant role in bringing peace to Northern Ireland. His government devolved power to Scotland and Wales, giving them their own parliament and assembly. New Labour introduced a minimum wage and gave control of interest rates to the independent Bank of England. In an age of summitry he became one of the most recognisable leaders across the world. Mr Blair even forced changes on the

Conservative party, driving its leaders to the centre ground of politics and to supporting significant public spending. But few ex-prime ministers are the butt of so many comedians' jokes, few have been so unpopular (*CNN*, Sept. 1, 2010).

A. Despite Mr Blair's successes, he is among Britain's most unpopular former prime ministers

B. Mr Blair's Labour government kept the power to raise or lower interest rates.

C. Though he had great influence on Labour, Mr Blair affected no other parties in Britain.

D. No British prime minister other than Tony Blair has ever won three elections in a row.

100. When a group of musicians in Guca, central Serbia, launched a competition in 1961 to determine the most accomplished trumpet band in the region, it's safe to assume they had little idea what the small rural town was in for. Just four bands took part in that first contest. Almost a half century later, Guca's trumpet festival is now synonymous with the wildest street party in the Balkans and a musical event with a burgeoning international reputation. Organisers say this year's 50th edition of the competition has been the biggest ever with an estimated 800,000 visitors and some 2,000 musicians taking part. But it's beyond the festival's formal programme that Guca really swings into life, with packed streets lined with beer stands and food stalls serving sizzling grilled meats, and entire farmyards of pigs and sheep slowly cooking on spit roasts (*CNN*, Aug. 23, 2010).

A. The competition was first organised by the state, but has grown since locals started running it.

B. Trumpet playing has grown in popularity over the past 50 years in what is today Serbia.

C. The trumpet festival in Guca, central Serbia, is a celebration of music, food and drink.

D. As a rule, no pork is served during the annual trumpet festival in Guca, central Serbia.

101. Along the warm coastal lowlands of New South Wales, the yellow-bellied three-toed skink lays eggs to reproduce. But individuals of the same species living in the state's higher, colder mountains are almost all giving birth to live young. Only two other modern reptiles — another skink species and a European lizard — use both types of reproduction. Evolutionary records shows that nearly a hundred reptile lineages have independently made the transition from egg-laying to live birth in the past, and today about 20 per cent of all living snakes and lizards give birth to live young only. But modern reptiles that have live young provide only a single snapshot on a long evolutionary time line, said James Stewart, a biologist at East Tennessee State University. The dual behaviour of the yellow-bellied three-toed skink therefore offers scientists a rare opportunity to study this evolutionary change (*National Geographic*, Sept. 1, 2010).

A. The yellow-bellied three-toed skink is the only reptile that produces offspring in two ways.

B. Reptiles have become extinct on the warm coastal lowlands of New South Wales.

C. Around one-fifth of all living snakes and lizards give birth in order to live longer.

D. The yellow-bellied three-toed skink is important to science because of the stage it occupies in evolution.

102. There is something wonderfully unsettling about a plant that feasts on animals. Perhaps it is the way it shatters all expectation. Carl Linnaeus, the great 18th-century Swedish naturalist who devised our system for ordering life, rebelled at the idea. For Venus flytraps to actually eat insects, he declared, would go "against the order of nature as willed by God." The plants only catch insects by accident, he reasoned, and once a hapless bug stopped struggling, the plant would surely open its leaves and let it go free. Charles Darwin knew

better, and the topsy-turvy ways of carnivorous plants enthralled him. In 1860, soon after he encountered his first carnivorous plant — the sundew Drosera — on an English heath, the author of Origin of Species wrote, "I care more about Drosera than the origin of all the species in the world" (*National Geographic*, March 2010).

A. Linnaeus and Darwin had heated debates on the various species of animals and plants.

B. Darwin was known to have resented the Venus flytrap because of its unusual nature.

C. Both Linnaeus and Darwin were interested in carnivorous plants, but disagreed about their nature.

D. Darwin travelled the world in order to study the various species of animals and plants.

103. Faced with reports that the ocean's major commercial fish species will disappear by 2050 due to overfishing, many seafood-loving gourmets are scrapping endangered fish from their menus and cooking up tasty eco-safe species many gastronomes have never heard of. The European campaign, Mr. Goodfish, is working to highlight the numerous lesser-known or underappreciated seafood species that happen to be not only delicious but also plentiful compared to their more "noble"' cousins. Under the umbrella of the World Ocean Network, Mr. Goodfish draws together chefs, fishmongers, fishermen and scientists to promote a sustainable consumption of seafood products, and generate frequently updated recommended-species lists for professional chefs.

Recent years have also seen the emergence of fishing cooperatives like Lonxanet in Galicia, which has made sustainable fishing a value-added enterprise for its artisan fishermen. In France, the Nantes-based distributor Pêcheries Océanes, which handles some 30,000 tons of fish annually, recently partnered with Mr. Goodfish, committing to permanently carry a large selection of approved sustainable species. (*Time*, online, *http://www.time.com*)

A. The Nantes-based company Pêcheries Océanes, which handles some 30,000 tons of fish annually, is France's largest seafood distributor.

B. "Sustainable" species are defined by the World Ocean Network as those species that have populations projected to last beyond 2050.

C. The Mr. Goodfish campaign seeks to attract a broad-based coalition of scientists and those involved in seafood procurement and sales.

D. Lonxanet is Spain's only fishing cooperative, and one of only a handful in all of Europe, that is dedicated to sustainable fishing efforts.

104. Imprisoned Chinese dissident Liu Xiaobo's empty chair was a powerful symbol at the Nobel Peace Prize ceremony held in his honour. Few noticed another absence at Oslo's City Hall: Norwegian Trade Minister Trond Giske, who is in charge of talks on a groundbreaking trade pact with China. Mr Giske skipped the Dec. 10th ceremony – the highlight of the year in Norway – because he was sick, his spokeswoman, Anne Cecilie Lund, said this week. The no-show didn't raise eyebrows at the time because Norway was represented by the royal family and top members of the centre-left government, including Prime Minister Jens Stoltenberg and Foreign Minister Jonas Gahr Stoere.

Now questions are being raised about whether Mr Giske's sudden illness and equally sudden recovery – he skipped just one day of work – was an attempt to appease the infuriated Chinese government and get trade talks back on track. The minister has declined to discuss his illness, but opposition politicians are beginning to seek answers.

"If he had a cold he could just have said so. I think it is an attempt to get Norway back into trade negotiations with China," said Peter Gitmark, the opposition Conservative Party's

spokesman on human rights.

Mr Liu is serving an 11-year prison sentence for sedition after co-authoring a bold appeal for human rights and multiparty democracy known as Charter 08 (*The Wall Street Journal Europe*, Dec. 23rd 2010).

A. Mr Liu is in prison for subversion after publishing six articles on the Internet and organising the Charter 08 petition that called for political liberalisation in China.

B. Norway's opposition Conservative Party boasts a stronger track record on human rights than the centre-left party which is currently in power.

C. Critics believe that the absence of a Norwegian government minister from the ceremony was aimed at mollifying the Chinese.

D. Mr Liu's prize was placed on a symbolically empty chair on the stage at the Nobel Peace Prize ceremony.

105. Fewer than 200 rhinos were left in the north Indian state of Assam a century ago. Agriculture had taken over most of the fertile river valleys that the species depends on, and the survivors were under relentless assault by trophy hunters and poachers. Kaziranga was set aside in 1908 primarily to save the rhinos. It held maybe a dozen. Now Asia's premier rhino sanctuary and a reservoir for seeding other reserves, Kaziranga is the key to R. unicornis's future. A thundering conservation success story, the park also harbours almost 1,300 wild elephants; 1,800 Asiatic wild water buffalo, the largest remaining population anywhere; perhaps 9,000 hog deer; 800 barasinghs, or swamp deer (it's a main enclave of this vanishing species); scores of elk-like sambars; and hundreds of wild hogs (*National Geographic*, August 2010).

A. With its animals regularly killed by trophy hunters and poachers, Kaziranga is viewed as a failure.

B. Kaziranga's animals include nearly 1,300 wild elephants, 9,000 hog deer, and scores of wild goats.

C. The spread of farming was once an important factor in the ever dwindling numbers of rhinos.

D. Kaziranga is a nature preserve that was established in 1908 with only about 200 rhinos in it.

106. An Italian researcher has sparked new controversy over the world's most famous painting by claiming Leonardo da Vinci painted tiny letters into the eyes of the Mona Lisa which may finally reveal the disputed identity of his model. To arrive at a theory worthy of The Da Vinci Code, Dan Brown's 2003 bestseller, researcher Silvano Vinceti avoided the Mona Lisa's enigmatic smile and instead gazed deep into her eyes with the help of high-resolution images.

Vinceti said that the letters B or S, or possibly the initials CE, were discernible, a vital clue to identifying the model who sat for the Renaissance artist. She has often been named as Lisa Gherardini, the wife of a Florentine merchant, but Vinceti disagreed, claiming Leonardo painted the Mona Lisa in Milan. He said he would announce his conclusions next month. (*The Guardian*, online, *http://www.guardian.co.uk*)

A. There is no evidence to support the claim that the model for the Mona Lisa was Lisa Gherardini.

B. Vinceti's discovery ruled out Lisa Gherardini as Da Vinci's Mona Lisa.

C. This is the first time that anyone discovered letters inscribed into the Mona Lisa painting.

D. The location in which Da Vinci painted the Mona Lisa is one clue that may point to the model's identity.

107. A new computer program has quickly deciphered a written language last used in Biblical times — possibly opening the door to "resurrecting" ancient texts in other languages that are no longer

understood, scientists announced last week. Created by a team at the Massachusetts Institute of Technology (MIT), the program automatically translates written Ugaritic, which consists of dots and wedge-shaped stylus marks on clay tablets. The script was last used around 1200 B.C. in western Syria. Written examples of this "lost language" were discovered by archaeologists excavating the port city of Ugarit in the late 1920s. It took until 1932 for language specialists to decode the writing. Since then, the script has helped shed light on ancient Israelite culture and Biblical texts. The new program compared symbol and word frequencies and patterns in Ugaritic with those of a known language, in this case, the closely related Hebrew (*National Geographic*, July 19, 2010).

A. A computer program may one day translate texts in various long forgotten languages.

B. Ugaritic is an ancient language that is closely related to Hebrew and Aramaic.

C. Written Ugaritic has been translated for the first time using software developed at MIT.

D. The Ugaritic script was last used 1200 years ago.

108. For years, the military and law enforcement agencies have used specialized robots to disarm bombs and carry out other dangerous missions. This summer, such systems helped seal a BP well a mile below the surface of the Gulf of Mexico. Now, with rapidly falling costs, the next frontiers are the office, the hospital and the home. Mobile robots are now being used in hundreds of hospitals nationwide as the eyes, ears and voices of doctors who cannot be there in person. They are being rolled out in workplaces, allowing employees in disparate locales to communicate more easily and letting managers supervise employees from afar. And they are being tested as caregivers in assisted-living centres. Sceptics say these machines do not represent a great improvement over video teleconferencing. But advocates say the experience is substantially better, shifting control of space and time to the remote user (*New York Times*, Sept. 4, 2010).

A. Specialized robots are routinely brought in to carry out dangerous missions for the military and law enforcement.

B. Advocates of specialized robots believe they represent a minor advance over video teleconferencing.

C. Specialized robots are regularly used to do repair and maintenance work on deepwater oil and gas equipment.

D. Specialized robots are now commonly used in many hospitals, places of work and assisted-living centres.

109. The Spanish market has collapsed since 2007, with prices of new coastal homes and older houses in inland "white villages", popular with British buyers, plummeting 50% or more. Now Spain's housing ministry – which counts domestic properties as well as foreign holiday homes – reports a record-breaking 48% drop in sales between July and September 2010. This coincides with austerity measures being introduced in Spain, including the scrapping of mortgage tax relief.

In response to that, asking prices of homes on sale have plummeted as desperate sellers try to attract buyers. The property sales portal idealista.com reports that prices in 14 regions of the country fell in November, while rival website facilismo.com shows price falls across Spain for 39 months out of the last 40. (*The Guardian online, http://www.guardian.co.uk*)

A. A 48% drop in housing sales has never before been reported in Spain during any quarter.

B. Other than new coastal homes and older houses in inland "white villages," property values have been stable.

C. The number of housing units up for sale has risen proportionately in response to the drop in housing prices.

D. Idealista.com and facilismo.com are the two most widely respected sources on Spain's housing market.

110. The second extremely cold winter in a row has exposed what plumbers say is a flaw with condensing boilers, the only sort permitted to be installed since 2005 under government regulations. These are significantly more energy-efficient than traditional boilers because rather than expelling hot waste gases through a chimney they use some of this energy to heat water.

However, this process condenses moisture in the gases. The waste liquid is usually expelled into the drains via a slim plastic pipe running down an external wall – a pipe which is prone to freezing in particularly cold weather, stalling the entire system.

While thousands of plumbers have been called out in recent weeks to repair condensing boilers, if the problem is a frozen condensate pipe then it's actually relatively straightforward to sort out yourself. The trick is to gently unfreeze the pipe using either a hot water bottle, heat pads of the sort used for muscle pain, or a watering can of warm – not boiling – water. (*The Guardian, online, http://www.guardian.co.uk*)

A. Condensing boilers are not only more energy efficient but safer overall compared with traditional boilers.

B. While condensing boilers are more energy efficient compared with traditional boilers, they are also more hazardous to human life.

C. Before 2005, the government did not regulate the kind of boilers that could be installed in a home.

D. Severe environmental conditions can expose a design flaw in condensing boilers.

111. Make your password strong, with a unique jumble of letters, numbers and punctuation marks. But memorize it – never write it down. And, oh yes, change it every few months. These instructions are supposed to protect us. But they don't. Some computer security experts are advancing the heretical thought that passwords might not need to be "strong," or changed constantly. They say onerous requirements for passwords have given us a false sense of protection against potential attacks. In fact, they say, we aren't paying enough attention to more potent threats. Keylogging software, which is deposited on a PC by a virus, records all keystrokes – including the strongest passwords you can concoct – and then sends it surreptitiously to a remote location. Cormac Herley, who specializes in security-related topics, said antivirus software could detect and block many kinds of keyloggers, but "there's no guarantee that it gets everything" (*New York Times*, Sept. 4, 2010).

A. Some experts now argue that conventional wisdom on computer security is wrong since hackers have ways of detecting everything users key in.

B. Sceptics claim that the current password scare represents the latest cynical attempt to frighten computer users into spending more on their PC.

C. Mr Herley says that keylogging software may spot and stop a variety of hackers, but "there's no guarantee that it gets everything".

D. The standard view in computer security has been to create a unique password, keep it in a safe place in case you forget, and change it regularly.

112. Rebuilt after an earthquake in 1963 wiped out most of the city, Skopje, the capital of the ex-Yugoslav republic of Macedonia, was for years characterised by ugly concrete blocks and strange empty spaces. But earlier this year Nikola Gruevski's conservative government produced a video that revealed the full ambition of "Skopje 2014", its plan for a radical reinvention of the city centre. Supporters of the plans said that, after decades of stagnation, Skopje would at last get the regeneration it deserves, its heroes commemorated in marble and bronze. Sceptical critics,

used to a city where nothing much happens, sarcastically asked which triumph the proposed triumphal arch would be celebrating. Yet it is happening. New buildings are sprouting up along the banks of the Vardar river and a fresh statue is unveiled every few weeks (*The Economist*, Aug. 26, 2010).

A. Promoted by a conservative government, the "Skopje 2014" project has a nationalistic tone to it.

B. Critics of Skopje's city regeneration plans have had their predictions of inaction come true.

C. The Vardar river runs through Skopje, the capital of the former Yugoslav republic of Macedonia.

D. Skopje's concrete blocks represent the legacy of rebuilding after the destruction of World War II.

113. The Spanish government believes ETA is close to surrendering its arms but will treat any new promises of peace from the Basque terrorist group with extreme caution, said Interior Minister Alfredo Pérez Rubalcaba in an interview on Tuesday with Radio Euskadi.

ETA declared a cease-fire in September, and there is wide speculation the group will announce in coming days a commitment to lay down its arms for good. Arnaldo Otegi, the jailed leader of ETA's political wing, told The Wall Street Journal in an interview that the group is ready to give up violence and pursue a peaceful strategy to create an independent Basque state.

Mr Rubalcaba said he has heard similar comments from other political leaders close to ETA in recent weeks and that "decades of tremendous acts, of murders, can't be closed with these statements." He said it is time for the group to move from statements to acts, and he again ruled out any possibility of negotiating with ETA.

The group has announced several ceasefires in the past only to return to violence when its demands have not been met. The collapse of the latest peace process in December 2006 was a blow to the government of José Luis Rodríguez Zapatero, who had staked much of his political capital on an ETA peace deal (*The Wall Street Journal Europe*, Dec. 29th 2010).

A. ETA is an armed Basque separatist organisation that is considered a terrorist group by Spain, France, the United States and other nations.

B. Spain's Zapatero government has managed to regain some of the political capital it had lost with the failure of the last ETA peace deal.

C. Mr Rubalcaba has proven to be effective in dealing with security issues in his post as Spanish minister of the interior.

D. Political leaders associated with ETA have recently spoken of seeking a peaceful resolution to the issue of Basque independence.

114. Climate change is affecting the cultivation of Assam tea, with rising temperatures reducing yields and altering the distinctive flavour of India's most popular drink, researchers say. High hills and abundant rainfall make the north-eastern state of Assam an ideal place to grow tea, with 850 gardens over 320,000 hectares (593,000 acres) producing the majority of the country's harvest. But in the last 60 years, rainfall has fallen by more than a fifth and minimum temperature has risen by a degree to 19.5C. Mridul Hazarika, director of Tocklai Tea Research, the oldest tea research station in the world, said rainfall and minimum temperature were two of the most important factors affecting both quality and quantity of harvests. (*The Guardian*, online, *http://www.guardian.co.uk /environment*)

A. Assam tea comprises more than half of all the tea grown in India.

B. The decline in tea yields and quality in India has affected its popularity.

C. Global warming is responsible for the changing taste of Indian tea consumers.

D. Thq quality of tea grown in India is deteriorating due to short-term fluctuations in rainfall and temperature.

115. A study of 57 countries coordinated by the Global Invasive Species programme found 542 types of animals and plants were putting native wildlife at risk in places where they are not naturally found. On average, around 50 non-native species are having a negative impact on existing plants and animals in each country, ranging from nine in Equatorial Guinea to a massive 222 in New Zealand. On the list of invasive aliens are 316 plants, 101 marine species, 44 freshwater fish, 43 mammals, 23 birds and 15 types of amphibian. And the threat to native species from alien invaders is growing, the experts warned.

Invasive plants and animals are those which threaten native wildlife, by eating native species, laying eggs, damaging their habitat, spreading disease or by competing with them for the same "niche" in an ecosystem. (*The Guardian*, online, *http://www.guardian.co.uk*)

A. Worldwide, New Zealand has the greatest and Equatorial Guinea the lowest number of native species under threat from invasive species.

B. In each surveyed country the number of threatened native organisms was greater for plants than for any other type of native life-form.

C. An invasive species of plant or animal could threaten or endanger a native species without ever coming into direct contact with it.

D. All invasive alien species on Earth belong to one of the following: plants, marine species, freshwater fish, mammals, birds and amphibians.

116. Conventional geothermal power exploits naturally occurring pockets of steam or hot water, close to the Earth's surface, to generate electricity. Because such conditions are rare, the majority of today's geothermal power plants are located in rift zones or volcanically active parts of the world, such as Iceland. Engineered geothermal systems (EGS) are based on a related principle, but they work even in parts of the world that are not volcanically active, by drilling thousands of metres underground to mimic the design of natural steam or hot-water reservoirs. Wells are bored and pathways are created inside hot rocks, into which cold water is injected. The water heats up as it circulates and is then brought back to the surface, where the heat is extracted to generate electricity. Because the Earth gets hotter the deeper you drill, EGS could expand the reach of geothermal power enormously and provide access to a virtually inexhaustible energy resource (*The Economist*, Sept. 2, 2010).

A. Some conventional geothermal power plants may also be situated outside of rift zones or volcanically active regions.

B. Engineered geothermal systems (EGS) will only be successful in rift zones or volcanically active regions.

C. Though the Earth is hotter deeper down it may not be cost-effective to drill beyond a certain depth.

D. Engineered geothermal systems (EGS) work by drilling deep to find pockets of steam or hot water.

117. On Jan. 26th, Christie's South Kensington will host "The Ski Sale," with around 180 posters from European, Russian and American resorts. Vintage posters generally range from the late 1890s to the 1960s with the best prices usually achieved for the Art Deco period of the 1920s and 1930s, Ms Churcher says. Art Deco is characterized by clear, forceful lines, and, more often than not, by strong colour accents that stress a joy of life.

Posters were made to hang as advertisements for a short period; and then they were often destroyed. As a result, only a very limited number of early posters have survived, Ms Churcher explains. Designed to hit the eye with a

clear message, they oozed fun, sporting challenge and after-ski glamour in a world of mountainous, beautiful landscapes far away from cities and their daily stress.

For years, Emil Cardinaux's "Palace Hotel, St. Moritz" (1920), an image of glamorous ladies relaxing by a skating rink at this hotel mecca for the well-heeled, was a top poster at Christie's sales. It brought, at its peak in 2004, a world auction record for a ski poster at £23,900. In 2008, however, Cardinaux's work was toppled from the Christie's ski auction pinnacle when a Russian poster from 1952 by an anonymous artist fetched £36,500 against an estimate of £600-£800. It depicted a skier with racing number 21 straining for the win with red flags flying in the background (*The Wall Street Journal Europe*, Dec. 24th 2010).

A . Emil Cardinaux's "Palace Hotel, St. Moritz", an Art Deco ski poster from 1920, still holds the world record auction price for a ski poster at £23,900.

B . In 2008, despite a pre-sale low estimate, a Russian piece by an unknown illustrator beat a 2004 world record for top price paid at auction for a ski poster.

C . Vintage ski posters fetch top prices because only a small number of copies remain, as most of them were destroyed due to a change of taste over the years.

D . Ski posters from the late 1890s to the 1960s sold at auction houses like Christie's and Sotheby's usually go for tens of thousands of pounds.

118. The European Commission has long struggled to break the public's perception that it is a dry, bureaucratic ivory tower. It would rather be seen as a bold leader in vital policy debates throughout the world. To that end, as reported by Euractiv, the commission is trying to build up the brand of its president, Jose Manuel Barroso. Mr Barroso's first opportunity will come on Tuesday, 9 a.m., at the European Parliament's second home in Strasbourg, France. He will make a speech, followed by a debate. There's a hitch: "Normally, these general debates attract only a few dozen MEPs," says a parliament official. "They'd rather spend that time in their office or having meetings." To stop MEPs from checking in, then leaving – a common practice among MEPs keen to assure their €298 daily living allowance – the leaders have ordered three electronic attendance checks during the three-hour speech and debate (*Wall Street Journal*, Sept. 6, 2010).

A. Mr Barroso has arranged electronic attendance checks to ensure that MEPs remain throughout his speech.

B. According to a parliament official, the European Commission is attempting to develop its president's brand.

C. MEPs will be gathering for a speech and debate in Strasbourg, but this is not the only city in which they meet.

D. MEPs' only source of income is their living allowance of €298 per day which they do not receive if they do not turn up in parliament.

119. A former spy with the UK Secret Intelligence Service, or MI6, was sentenced on Friday to one year in prison for trying to sell top-secret information to Dutch agents. Daniel Houghton admitted violating Britain's secrecy act by trying to sell the files. The Dutch agents told their British counterparts about the approach, leading to Mr Houghton's arrest at a London hotel in March. Prosecutors said the information he was peddling included staff lists and personal details that could have endangered agents. MI6 is Britain's overseas intelligence service. Judge David Bean sentenced Mr Houghton on Friday, calling him "a strange young man" guilty of an "act of betrayal." He is expected to be released shortly because he has already served almost half of his prison time while awaiting sentencing (*Wall Street Journal*, Sept. 3, 2010).

A. Mr Houghton has waited nearly six months

for Judge Bean to pass sentence on him for violating the UK secrecy law.

B. The UK Secret Intelligence Service, or MI6, is primarily responsible for gathering intelligence domestically.

C. Mr Houghton approached Dutch agents with secret information, but they felt that it would be useless to them.

D. Though Mr Houghton broke the law, the information he was attempting to sell never placed anyone at risk.

120. Scientists have made insulin-producing cells from sperm stem cells, a technique that could one day be used to treat people with type 1 diabetes. The disease is caused by the destruction of insulin-producing cells in the pancreas, leading to low levels of the hormone that regulates sugar in the blood. It can develop at any age but usually appears before the age of 40, and particularly in childhood. Around 5-15% of all people with diabetes have type 1 diabetes, which is usually treated with, among other things, daily insulin injections.

In the latest study, G. Ian Gallicano, an associate professor at Georgetown University Medical Centre in Washington DC, transformed the early precursors for human sperm, called spermatogonial stem cells (SSCs), into beta-islet cells, which produce insulin and are normally found in the pancreas. When he transferred these cells into mice, they successfully regulated sugar levels in the rodents' blood. (*The Guardian,* online, *http://www.guardian.co.uk*)

A. The majority of type 1 diabetics are under the age of 40, and most are children.

B. Insulin-producing cells had already been made from sperm stem cells before this latest experiment.

C. Diabetics who are not type 1 are never treated with insulin injections.

D. The SSCs underwent some process through which they turned into beta-islet cells.

121. On Tuesday the Hungarian parliament, dominated by MPs from the governing centre-right Fidesz party, passed a controversial media law that will create a new media authority, called the NMHH, with powers to issue fines to media groups whose coverage is deemed to be unbalanced or an infringement upon human dignity. Editors are concerned that the new body – to comprise five appointees from the ruling right-wing Fidesz party – could also force journalists to reveal their sources in national security or public order cases.

Media freedom groups have witnessed a raft of restrictive measures across the 27-member union in recent years. A new law that came into force in Ireland on 1 January 2010 makes blasphemy a crime punishable with a fine of up to €25,000. Slovakia has also caused alarm with its 2008 Press Act, handing the minister of culture the authority to penalise editors for publishing articles that promote certain kinds of hate. (*EUobserver.com, http://euobserver.com*)

A. Conservative political forces in the 27-member union have in recent years passed laws that in various ways limit the autonomy of the press.

B. In recent years at least three laws have been enacted among the 27-member union that in various ways may limit certain kinds of speech.

C. The Hungarian law establishing the NMHH is the third of the restrictive measures passed in the 27-member union over the past several years.

D. The laws that are of greatest concern to most media freedom groups are those that establish a central governmental authority to oversee the press.

122. As Poland marks the 30th anniversary of the Solidarity movement that tore a hole in the Iron Curtain and eventually helped topple the Berlin Wall, it's worth taking a look at how much the country has changed. Many Poles still feel dissatisfied with their quality of life, and

some complain that life was better in the centrally planned economy that guaranteed employment for all, even if it didn't pay any real money. But as the daily Puls Biznesu shows today, compared to 30 years ago, Poles can afford bigger apartments, more cars and many household appliances. Over the past three decades, the average Polish consumer's buying power has increased six times. The currency is free floating and fully exchangeable, which means that in dollar terms Polish average salaries went up from a barely noticeable amount of sometimes as low as $20 during communism to more than $1,000 a month now. Average apartment space has risen by 14 square meters. (*Wall Street Journal*, Aug. 31, 2010).

A. Compared to 30 years ago, Poles enjoy an average of 14 square meters more living space.

B. The Polish currency is fixed to the US dollar and thus its value changes accordingly.

C. Poland's Solidarity movement also played an active role in Berlin under communism.

D. Since salaries have just kept pace with prices since 1980, Poles cannot afford more than before.

123. The history of Anglo-French co-operation in naval matters is not an entirely happy one. France and Britain have fought each other at sea with explosive results on plenty of occasions – most famously at the Battle of Trafalgar in 1805. Then there was the British attempt to negotiate a surrender of the French fleet in July 1940. Churchill did not want it falling into German hands and was determined to send a signal that he intended to stay in the war. The resulting brutal engagement cost more than 1,300 lives and resulted in the effective destruction of the French navy. Seventy years later a new tide of co-operation on defence is flowing back and forth between Paris and London. The UK government hopes to negotiate an arrangement by which the partners agree to co-ordinate refits of their carriers so that there is always at least one, either French or British, available from the European theatre (*Wall Street Journal*, Sept. 1, 2010).

A. As part of a new wave of defence co-operation, Britain wishes to enter into a deal with France to harmonize the timing on repair of certain of the two countries' ships.

B. The French are understandably reluctant to relinquish any of their navy's independence in the light of its sometimes turbulent history with British naval forces.

C. As part of a recent effort toward military partnership, Britain wishes to negotiate with France on co-ordinating naval exercises involving the two countries' aircraft carriers.

D. Since Churchill did not want Germany to get hold of France's naval ships, the British fought the Germans in a naval battle that led to over 1,300 deaths.

124. Croatia took a significant step towards concluding its EU accession process by closing three more negotiating chapters during a recent enlargement conference in Brussels. Finalised negotiations on the environment, justice and security, and foreign, security and defence policy mean that 28 chapters have now been closed in total.

Both the EU and Croatia aim to conclude the talks in the first half of next year and to sign the accession treaty in the autumn, although the EU has refused to set a date for Croatia to join. Enlargement commissioner Stefan Fuele said he recognized there was "a goal to conclude accession talks during the Hungarian EU presidency". But he warned there was still work to be done in Croatia to meet the remaining benchmarks, as well as in the EU where the accession treaty must be prepared for signing and ratification. (*Euobserver.com, http://waz.euobserver.com*)

A. Three out of 28 chapters have now been closed in Croatia's EU accession proceedings.

B. Although several negotiating chapters with Croatia have now been closed, defence policy is still up for discussion.

C. Delays on either side of the proceedings could possibly delay the treaty's signing beyond autumn.

D. The remaining work by Croatia involves administrative matters rather than actual reform.

125. As humans continue to evolve, scientists say our brains are actually getting smaller. The downsizing of human brains is an evolutionary fact that takes many by surprise as many assume the opposite; that our brains are growing. That was the story up to 20,000 years ago. Then, the brains of our ancestors reversed course and started getting smaller – and they've been shrinking ever since.

Cro-Magnon man, who lived in Europe 20,000 to 30,000 years ago, had the biggest brains of any human species. In comparison, today's human brain is about 10 per cent smaller. The experts aren't sure about the implications of this evolutionary trend. Some think it might be a dumbing-down process. One cognitive scientist, David Geary, argues that as human society grows increasingly complex, individuals don't need to be as intelligent in order to survive and reproduce.

But not all researchers are so pessimistic. Anthropologist Brian Hare thinks the decrease in brain size is actually an evolutionary advantage. "A smaller brain is the signature of selection against aggression," Mr Hare says. "Another way to say that is an increase in tolerance." Hare says when a population selects against aggression, they can be considered to be domesticated. And for a variety of domesticated animals like apes, dogs or turkeys, you can see certain physical characteristics emerge. Among these traits are a lighter and more slender skeleton, a flattened forehead – and decreased brain size (*NPR*, Jan. 2nd 2011).

A. While scientists appear to agree that the human brain is diminishing in size, they have differing views on what this implies.

B. Mr. Hare sees studying animals and human nature as an important aid toward designing strategies to cope with humans' darker side.

C. Domesticated animals such as apes, dogs, turkeys and horses show the development of similar physical features, including a shrinking brain.

D. Mr Geary contends that aggression plays a far less important role in survival and reproduction in an increasingly complex human society.

126. The US and EU are hoping to construct an 800-million-citizen-strong market with converging regulatory regimes whose standards will set the benchmark for product rules the world over. At a meeting of joint EU-US Transatlantic Economic Council (Tec) on Friday (17 December) described as "fantastic" by American officials, the two sides backed a plan to try to seek common recognition for each others' standards in new areas of product development, from nanotechnology to electric cars.

The two sides are to develop an 'early warning system' in which both Brussels and Washington will be made aware of new regulatory moves "upstream" in the pipeline, particularly when it comes to new technology products. While not wanting identical regulation, the two sides hope to achieve "increased regulatory co-operation". At the meeting, they agreed to a common set of principles to frame regulation development, including transparency, public participation and minimizing the burden to business. (*Euobserver.com, http://euobserver.com*)

A. By standardising their regulatory processes, the US and EU seek an alliance that will allow them to dominate the world market in emerging technologies.

B. The proposed 'early warning system' will require that Brussels and Washington modify their existing or proposed regulations so they are identical in both regions.

C. Nanotechnology and electric cars are the two emerging technologies that are of the greatest interest and hold the most promise to officials in the US and EU.

D. The US and EU reached agreement-in-principle that will guide development of processes to recognize and co-ordinate pending regulations of new technologies.

127. In the difficult summer of 2010, the German-speaking Italian province of South Tyrol is like a small beacon of prosperity surrounded by doom and gloom. Despite the economic crisis, there is almost no unemployment in the area surrounding the capital Bolzano (known in German as Bozen), and the province is debt-free. By comparison, Italy as a whole has the highest government debt, as a percentage of the country's gross domestic product (GDP), in the entire eurozone. Within the last half-century, 19 prime ministers have been sworn in in Rome. In South Tyrol, on the other hand, there has been only one change in the province's top job during the same period – from its "über-father" Silvius Magnago to its current paternalistic governor since 1989, Luis Durnwalder (*Der Spiegel*, Aug. 25, 2010).

A. With heads of government serving under three years on average over the last 50 years, Italy shows less political continuity than South Tyrol.

B. Due in part to South Tyrol's economic situation, Italy suffers under the largest government debt in proportion to GDP in the eurozone.

C. Unlike northern neighbour Austria, the German-speaking Italian province of South Tyrol actually has no government debt.

D. Long-serving South Tyrol governor Luis Durnwalder has held the Italian province's top post for well over half of the last 50 years.

128. Police in the ex-Soviet republic of Moldova have seized 1.8 kg of radioactive uranium in a garage in the capital and have arrested several people, government officials said on Tuesday. The substance was sent for tests in the United States which showed it to be uranium-238, Igor Volnitchii, a top state adviser to the government, told Reuters. "A group of criminals involved in uranium smuggling planned to sell it abroad," Mr Volnitchii said. The seized uranium was valued at 9 million euros. He said three people had been arrested and several others were being sought. Two members of the group were former police officers. He said Moldovan authorities were now waiting for tests conducted in Germany to determine the country of origin of the uranium. EU officials say Moldova's territory, which covers the rebel area of Transdniestr bordering Ukraine, is vulnerable to all types of smuggling, including narcotics and human trafficking (*France24*, Aug. 24, 2010).

A. A gang in Moldova caught attempting to smuggle 1.8 kg of radioactive uranium is probably also mixed up in narcotics trafficking.

B. Tests carried out in Germany have determined that a radioactive substance found in a Moldovan garage was uranium-238.

C. Once part of the former Soviet Union, today Moldova must contend with such problems as rebellion and drug smuggling.

D. Worth 9 million euros, the radioactive uranium uncovered in the Moldovan capital was found to have originated in neighbouring Ukraine.

129. China's remarkable growth is as apparent in beer consumption as it is in more formal economic indicators. In the space of a couple of decades the country has gone from barely touching a drop to becoming the world's biggest beer market, a considerable distance ahead of America. And beer drinking in China is growing fast, by nearly 10% a year according to Credit Suisse's World Map of Beer. This might seem like good news for the four big firms that dominate global brewing. Between them ABI, SABMiller, Carlsberg and Heineken have nearly half the world

market. But unlike America and other hugely profitable mature markets where beer drinking has levelled off or is in decline, China's drinkers provide slender profits. Still it remains a market with huge potential, though foreign brewers must now be rather tired of hearing that (*The Economist*, Aug. 17, 2010).

A. The Chinese beer market is expanding quickly, yet beer makers' profits are relatively low.

B. America's beer market is lucrative and growing, but it is not expanding as quickly as China's.

C. China has long been a beer-drinking nation, but new wealth has led to a demand for imported beer.

D. ABI is the largest of the four brewing companies that dominate the world's beer market.

130. The nota roja, a section reporting the previous day's murders and car crashes in all their bloodstained detail, is an established feature of Mexican newspapers. It is also an expanding one, as fighting over the drug trail to the United States inspires ever-greater feats of violence. Last month in the northern state of Durango, a group of prisoners was apparently released from jail for the night to murder 18 partygoers in a next-door state. A few days later, 14 inmates were murdered in a prison in Tamaulipas. In all, since Felipe Calderón sent the army against the drug gangs when he took office as president almost four years ago, some 28,000 people have been killed, the government says. There is no sign of a let-up, on either side (*The Economist*, Aug. 12, 2010).

A. Though the death toll has been high, the army appears to be winning the battle with the drug gangs.

B. 28,000 people have been killed in Mexico in clashes between the Mexican Army and drug gangs.

C. The nota roja is a section in Mexican newspapers containing readers' opinions about the violent drug wars.

D. An increasing number of people are dying in Mexico in incidents related to drug-smuggling to the United States.

131. Normally, Germany and France are close partners at the heart of Europe – but US diplomatic cables suggest a battle royal between the two allies over satellite technology, with the German space and intelligence agencies accusing the French of bad faith and looking to the United States as a future partner to develop next-generation satellites. At the heart of the rivalry is HiRos – a High Resolution Optical System – that would potentially be a leap forward in satellite surveillance. A flurry of cables obtained by WikiLeaks and published by the Norwegian newspaper Aftenposten shows German officials lobbying for a "strategic US-German partnership" in 2009 to develop the system, amid French attempts to kill it.

Some thirty pages of cables show the political maneuvering and enticing technological potential of HiRos, as well as the determination of the German space agency (DLR) to get it deployed by 2013. The cables also show the DLR's desperation to end Germany's dependence on "foreign sources of imagery."

HiRos remains in the project phase, despite the intense lobbying by German space agency and intelligence officials – and optimistic noises in 2009 that they were ready to move beyond the design phase and start "bending metal" (*CNN*, Jan. 3rd 2010).

A. While leaks of US diplomatic cables have revealed a fascinating conflict between France and Germany, they are unlikely to have caused any significant damage.

B. The leaked cables have disclosed the German space agency's resolve to push the HiRos system forward and thus put a halt to Germany's dependence on the US.

C. The Franco-German rivalry over the development of next-generation satellites represents an exception to the usual co-operation between the two countries.

D. The French have been lobbying against HiRos because they clearly wish to protect their stake in the lucrative market for satellite imagery.

132. This February, inventor Nathan Myhrvold of the investment firm Intellectual Ventures unveiled a Star Wars-inspired mosquito killer: a laser death ray. Mr Myhrvold mounts LED lamps on a fence post and uses a sensor called a charge-coupled device to monitor the field of light they create. When a disturbance in the field indicates the presence of an insect, a non-lethal laser beam is fired to determine how quickly the insect's wings beat – a trait that reliably distinguishes one species from another. Only female, malaria-bearing mosquitoes get zapped with the powerful kill laser (their wings beat at a low frequency); other insects are allowed to escape unharmed. "This is the first example of a smart insecticide," Mr Myhrvold says. "If you sprayed, you'd kill all kinds of bugs" (*Scientific American*, Aug. 19, 2010).

A. Mr Myhrvold's device can be adjusted to kill mosquitoes with other potentially harmful diseases.

B. Mr Myhrvold has invented a device that selectively destroys a potentially deadly insect.

C. A non-lethal laser beam on Mr Myhrvold's device is able to determine the size of a passing insect.

D. Mr Myhrvold has invented a device that can selectively destroy certain potentially deadly insects.

133. A farm chemical with an infamous history – causing the worst known outbreak of pesticide poisoning in North America – is being phased out under an agreement announced on Tuesday by the US Environmental Protection Agency (EPA). Manufacturer Bayer CropScience agreed to stop producing aldicarb, a highly toxic insecticide used to kill pests on cotton and several food crops, by 2015 in all world markets. Use on citrus and potatoes will be prohibited after next year. Tuesday's announcement comes 25 years after a highly publicized outbreak of aldicarb poisoning sickened more than 2,000 people who had eaten California watermelons. New EPA documents show that babies and children under five can ingest levels of the insecticide through food and water that exceed levels the agency considers safe. "Aldicarb no longer meets our rigorous food safety standards and may pose unacceptable dietary risks, especially to infants and young children," the EPA said in announcing the agreement (*Scientific American*, Aug. 18, 2010).

A. Aldicarb once may have satisfied the EPA's food safety standards, but that is no longer the case.

B. The producer of Aldicarb has consented to stop manufacturing the insecticide immediately.

C. Aldicarb has been used only on citrus fruits such as oranges, lemons and grapefruit.

D. The potential dangers of Aldicarb to human beings have only come to light recently.

134. Tundra are among Earth's coldest, harshest biomes. Tundra ecosystems are treeless regions found in the Arctic and on the tops of mountains, where the climate is cold and windy and rainfall is scant. Tundra lands are snow-covered for much of the year, until summer brings a burst of wildflowers. Mountain goats, sheep, marmots, and birds live in mountain, or alpine, tundra and feed on the low-lying plants and insects. Hardy flora like cushion plants survive on these mountain plains by growing in rock depressions where it is warmer and they are sheltered from the wind. The Arctic tundra, where the average temperature is -12 to -6 degrees Celsius, supports a variety of animal species, including Arctic foxes, polar bears, gray

wolves, caribou, snow geese and musk-oxen. The summer growing season is just 50 to 60 days, when the sun shines 24 hours a day. (*National Geographic*)

A. Rainfall is abundant in Tundra ecosystems

B. Tundra lands are snow-covered for around 300 days a year

C. Mountain goats as well as snow geese and musk-oxen live in alpine tundra areas

D. The average temperature in the Arctic tundra is -12 to -6 degrees Celsius, so it does not support any animal life

135. Poliomyelitis – a viral disease that wreaks havoc on motor neurons, often paralysing sufferers for life – was supposed to be banished from the planet a long time ago. When Jonas Salk unveiled his famed vaccine to the world in 1955, and Albert Sabin introduced an oral version shortly thereafter, inoculations began in earnest in many parts of the world, drastically lowering incidence numbers. Polio was completely eradicated in North and South America by 1994; in Australia and China by 2000; and in Europe by 2002. Even so, cultural animosities in isolated pockets of the world have conspired to keep global health authorities from stamping out the disease altogether. In 2003, for instance, the World Health Organisation's Global Polio Eradication Initiative mounted a Herculean effort to vaccinate 15 million Nigerian children. But prominent leaders from the country's Islamic community tarred and feathered the campaign, warning citizens that the vaccine was part of an imperialist US plan to keep Nigeria's population down (*Scientific American*, Aug. 18, 2010).

A. Jonas Salk discovered a vaccine against polio that did not have any significant side-effects.

B. Leaders from Nigeria's Islamic community fought a vaccination campaign in that country based on religious doctrines.

C. Soon after Jonas Salk discovered a polio vaccine, inoculation campaigns dramatically cut the number of polio cases.

D. Over 50 years since a polio vaccine was developed, the disease has been completely eliminated.

136. Deep beneath the border of France and Switzerland, the world's most massive physics machine is sending subatomic particles smashing into each other at speeds nearing the speed of light. Physicists working with the 17-mile-long Large Hadron Collider (LHC) hope it will help solve some of the universe's mysteries. But first, researchers must overcome two very mundane hurdles: how to handle all of the data the LHC generates and how to get non-scientists to care.

One physicist has a novel way to solve both problems: sound. Lily Asquith is a physicist who until recently worked with the LHC. Ms Asquith, like many physicists, spends a lot of time thinking about particles like the elusive Higgs boson – the subatomic particle that scientists say endows everything in the universe with mass. Proving the existence of the Higgs boson is one of the main goals of the collider.

In the process of the search for the Higgs, the collider generates a massive amount of information – more than 40 million pieces of data every second. So Ms Asquith was trying to figure out a new way to understand and sort through all of this data. The LHC currently produces colourful images as an output from the data – sprays of particles in different directions. "It's quite easy to step from there, really, to consider that there could be some kind of sound associated with these things," she says. Right now, Ms Asquith says, the sounds don't tell scientists very much. But she hopes that in the future, it could help them understand the data in new ways (*NPR*, Jan. 2nd 2011).

A. Built to assist in solving some of the universe's mysteries, the recently completed

Large Hadron Collider forms a 17-mile-long ring through a tunnel below the surface of France and Switzerland.

B. One scientist believes there may be a better way to organise the enormous quantity of information – over 40 million pieces of data per second – produced by the Large Hadron Collider.

C. The Large Hadron Collider, the world's largest physics machine, provides work for thousands of scientists from all over the world who conduct experiments on sub-atomic particles.

D. The Large Hadron Collider aims to shed light on unknowns of physics such as the Higgs boson and Dark Matter.

137. Scientific misconduct is defined as "fabrication, falsification or plagiarism in proposing, performing or reviewing research or in reporting research results," according to the US Office of Research Integrity (ORI). A 2009 meta-analysis of misconduct studies found that about 14 per cent of responding scientists reported having witnessed falsification by others – and 2 per cent confessed (anonymously) to having been involved in fabrication, falsification or modification of data themselves.

An inquiry into scientific misconduct often leads to research disruption, evidence confiscation and lengthy meetings, all of which can add up quickly in terms of expenses such as faculty and staff labour. A typical case might run in the neighbourhood of half a million dollars, concluded the authors of the new case study, led by Arthur Michalek of the Roswell Park Cancer Institute in Buffalo, NY. Taking as an example a real case from their own institution, they estimated the direct costs of that instance of misconduct to be about $525,000 (*Scientific American,* Aug. 17, 2010).

A. According to the US Office of Research Integrity (ORI), plagiarism in research is a form of scientific misconduct.

B. When suspected scientific misconduct is under investigation, as a rule, all evidence is seized.

C. A 2009 study found that 14 per cent of scientists had been involved in some form of scientific misconduct.

D. Research headed by Arthur Michalek received approximately half a million dollars in funding.

138. Fisheries agreements with countries outside the EU and negotiations within regional and international fisheries organisations ensure that not only the waters of the EU, but those of the whole world, are not over-fished. At the same time, they give EU fishermen access to fish in distant waters. With developing countries, the EU pays for access rights. The money raised in this way is largely invested in the fisheries industries of these countries and in building up their fish stocks. (*Europa policy*)

A. International fisheries agreements aim to keep fish populations steady off the shores of Europe and throughout the world.

B. The EU tends not to enter into talks within regional fisheries organisations, preferring instead the clout of international ones.

C. Through international fishing agreements, the EU and other wealthy nations pay developing countries to use their waters for fishing.

D. Most of the EU fisheries' money that developing countries receive is used to diversify the economy in fishing communities.

139. Each EU country is free to decide on the health policies best suited to national circumstances and traditions, but they all share common values. These include the right of everyone to the same high standards of public health and equity in access to quality health care. So it makes sense to work together on common challenges, ranging from ageing populations to obesity. The EU is also committed to taking the implications for health into account in all its policies. Moreover, diseases know no borders,

particularly in a globalised world where many of us travel widely. Joint action adds value when facing potential threats such as influenza epidemics or bioterrorism. It is also equally logical that the EU has common standards on safe food and nutrition labelling, the safety of medical equipment, blood products and organs, and the quality of air and water. (*Europa policy*)

A. Due to varying degrees of budgetary strength and of commitment among policy makers in different countries, the standard of health care is uneven in the EU.

B. While health policies may vary within the Union, all EU citizens should enjoy the right to gain access to quality health care.

C. The EU has long had common standards in such areas as safe food and nutrition labelling and the quality of air and water.

D. While the EU takes such potential dangers as bioterrorism seriously, it has not yet made health concerns a part of other areas of policy making.

140. With nearly all votes counted on Monday, a loose coalition of pro-Western parties appears to have come out ahead of the communists in Moldova's elections, but the bloc failed to secure enough votes to break a parliamentary impasse that has left the country without a president for the past year and a half.

With 95 per cent of Sunday's ballots tallied, the three top parties in the current ruling Alliance for European Integration bloc appear to have locked in 57 representatives in the 101-seat parliament, according to the state news agency Moldpres. That leaves the communists with 44 seats – enough to block any move by the Alliance to name a president. The constitution calls for the president to be chosen by at least 60 per cent of the representatives in the 101-seat parliament.

The still-uncounted votes come from Moldovans voting outside the country in the former Soviet state's third parliamentary election in two years. The election pitted the ruling Alliance bloc against a Communist Party that held a firm grip on power for most of the past decade.

The former Soviet republic earned independence from Russia in 1991, but it has remained deeply divided, with the Alliance pushing for European Union membership and the Communists hoping to build stronger ties to Moscow.

The Central Election Commission reported that more than 1.6 million registered voters had cast their ballots, with turnout standing at 59.15 per cent nationwide. That figure easily surpassed a key threshold requiring at least a third of eligible voters to submit ballots for the election to be considered valid (CNN, Nov. 29th 2010).

A. Still-uncounted ballots cast by young Moldovans living and working abroad are likely to bolster the showing of pro-Western parties.

B. Though Moldova has been independent from Russia for about two decades, its Communist politicians still wish to steer the country toward Moscow.

C. The political divide between supporters of the Alliance and the Communists in Moldova is also coloured by ethnic and linguistic differences.

D. Praised by foreign observers as fair and free, the elections in Moldova appear to have won the pro-Western Alliance 57 seats in parliament.

141. To meet the common challenges, the EU is spending more than €50m annually on activities to improve our health security, to promote good health – including reducing inequalities, and to provide more information and knowledge on health. The money goes to a wide range of issues, including planning for health emergencies, patient safety and reducing injuries and accidents. There is also funding to promote better nutrition and safe consumption of alcohol, healthy lifestyles and healthy ageing, to combat consumption of tobacco and drugs, to

prevent major diseases including HIV/AIDS and tuberculosis, and to exchange knowledge in areas such as gender issues, children's health and rare diseases. Activities to combat drug use can draw on the expertise of the European Monitoring Centre for Drugs and Drug Addiction in Lisbon. This provides the EU and its Member States with objective, reliable and comparable information on drugs and drug addiction. (*Europa policy*)

A. Tuberculosis prevention receives funding from the European Union.

B. The EU finances an effort to encourage the safe consumption of alcohol and tobacco.

C. The annual health care budget in the EU stands at approximately €50 million.

D. Though certainly considered important, no funding is yet set aside for specific women's health issues.

142. Large differences in prosperity levels exist both between and within EU countries. The most prosperous regions in terms of GDP per capita (the standard measure of well-being) are all urban – London, Brussels and Hamburg. The wealthiest country, Luxembourg, is more than seven times richer than Romania and Bulgaria, the poorest and newest EU members. The dynamic effects of EU membership, coupled with a vigorous and targeted regional policy, can bring results. The case of Ireland is particularly heartening. Its GDP, which was 64% of the EU average when it joined in 1973, is now one of the highest in the Union. One priority of regional policy is to bring living standards in the countries which have joined the EU since 2004 up to the EU average as quickly as possible. (*Europa policy*)

A. In terms of levels of prosperity among EU Member States, Luxembourg is even richer than Ireland.

B. Annual total GDP is the standard measure of well-being in comparing the relative wealth of countries and regions within the Union.

C. EU membership and a strong regional policy have already had a positive effect on living standards in Romania and Bulgaria.

D. One aim of regional policy is to help emulate the strategies of Ireland in the countries that have joined the EU since 2004.

143. Regional inequalities have various causes. They may result from longstanding handicaps imposed by geographic remoteness or by more recent social and economic change, or a combination of both. The impact of these disadvantages is frequently evident in social deprivation, poor quality schools, higher joblessness and inadequate infrastructures. In the case of some EU states, part of the handicap is a legacy of their former centrally-planned economic systems. The EU has used the entry of these countries to reorganise and restructure its regional spending. In the period from 2007 to 2013, regional spending will account for 36% of the EU budget. In cash terms, this represents spending over the seven years of nearly €350 billion. The effort focuses on three objectives: convergence, competitiveness and co-operation, which are grouped together in what is now termed Cohesion Policy. (*Europa policy*)

A. A centrally-planned economic system has represented no serious handicap in the rise of the relatively new Member State Slovenia.

B. Cohesion Policy addresses a number of key aspects of regional inequalities, including higher unemployment and inadequate education.

C. The EU budget for the 2007-2013 period amounts to almost €350 billion, 36% of which will go to resolving regional inequalities.

D. There is no connection between the accession of the poorest new members and the EU's reorganised and restructured regional spending.

144. The 12 countries which have joined the EU since 2004 will receive 51% of total regional spending between 2007 and 2013, although they represent less than one quarter of the total EU population.

The money comes from three difference sources, according to the nature of the assistance and the type of beneficiary. The European Regional Development Fund (ERDF) covers programmes involving general infrastructure, innovation, and investments. Money from the ERDF is available to the poorest regions across the EU. The European Social Fund (ESF) pays for vocational training projects and other kinds of employment assistance, and job-creation programmes. As with the ERDF, all EU countries are eligible for ESF assistance. The Cohesion Fund covers environmental and transport infrastructure projects as well as the development of renewable energy. Funding from this source is reserved for countries whose living standards are less than 90% of the EU average. This means the 12 recent newcomers plus Portugal and Greece. (*Europa policy*)

A. The Cohesion Fund pays for efforts to develop sources of renewable energy.

B. EU money available for projects in the poorest Member States comes exclusively from the Cohesion Fund.

C. The poorest regions in the EU are not necessarily part of the poorest countries.

D. The European Regional Development Fund (ERDF) finances schemes that create jobs.

145. Google agreed on Friday to delete data it inadvertently collected from unsecured Wi-Fi networks when compiling its Street View mapping service in Britain, authorities said. The British government and privacy advocates have long been concerned about the personal data Google may have collected when its Street View cars drove around the country taking pictures for the service, which shows panoramic photographic views from street level. Google admitted its vehicles inadvertently captured so-called payload data but said it contained only fragments of content, according to the Information Commissioner's Office (ICO), which examined the data in August.

The ICO agreed it was "unlikely" that the data contained significant amounts of personal information but said it was wrong for Google to have collected and stored the information. It also said the collecting of the details violated the Data Protection Act. On Friday, Google agreed to delete that data as soon as possible, the company and the ICO said: "I am very pleased to have a firm commitment from Google to work with my office to improve its handling of personal information," Information Commissioner Christopher Graham said. "We don't want another breach like the collection of payload data by Google Street View vehicles to occur again." In addition to agreeing to delete the data, Google signed a commitment to improve data handling, the ICO said (*CNN*, Nov. 19th 2010).

A . Google has not only made an agreement to destroy any personal information it has collected, but also to improve its data handling.

B. Google admitted to violating Britain's Data Protection Act when camera-equipped cars gathered huge amounts of data for its Street View service.

C. Google agreed to get rid of data it had intentionally gathered from unsecured Wi-Fi networks.

D. Britain is the most recent of several countries to address privacy issues with regard to data collected by Google's Street View service.

146. The bulk of regional spending is reserved for regions with a per capita GDP below 75% of the Union average to help improve their infrastructures and develop their economic and human potential. This concerns 17 of the 27 EU countries. On the other hand, all 27 are eligible for funding to support innovation and research, sustainable development, and job training in their less advanced regions. A small amount goes to cross-border and inter-regional co-operation projects. The idea is for regional policy to dovetail with the EU's

so-called Lisbon agenda to promote growth and jobs by making countries and regions more attractive for investments by improving accessibility, providing quality services and preserving environmental potential; encouraging innovation, entrepreneurship and the knowledge economy through the development of information and communications technologies; and creating more and better jobs by attracting more people into employment, improving workers' adaptability and increasing investment in human capital. (*Europa policy*)

A. A total of 17 of the 27 Member States have a GDP less than 75% of the Union average.

B. All 27 Member States have regions with a GDP lower than 75% of the EU average.

C. 17 of the EU's 27 Member States have at least one region with a per capita GDP below 75% of the EU average.

D. EU spending on less advanced regions has no connection to the Lisbon agenda.

147. To remain competitive, the EU needs to spend more on research and development (R&D), matching investment R&D by major competitors. In particular, EU industry needs to close the spending gap between itself and counterparts in the US and Japan to remain competitive at the cutting edge of technology and innovation. The EU is likely to fall short of its goal to close this gap by investing 3% of GDP in research by 2010. The EU must also improve its record of translating scientific knowledge into patented processes and products for use in high-tech industries. The new European Institute for Innovation and Technology will support this process by promoting partnerships which link the three sides of the 'knowledge triangle': education, innovation and research. (*Europa policy*)

A. Closing the R&D spending gap between the EU and its competitors (the US and Japan) depends on the private sector as well as on the EU itself.

B. The EU has improved on its already strong trend of applying scientific findings in high-tech industries.

C. The complicated and expensive process of obtaining a patent in the EU holds back progress in R&D.

D. The European Institute for Innovation and Technology has long promoted R&D in the Union.

148. Space has its own research budget for the first time in the Seventh Framework Programme 2007-2013 (FP7), marking the increasing importance the EU attaches to playing an independent role in space. The Global Monitoring for Environment and Security project will make it easier to use observations from space to anticipate or deal with environmental and security crises. The EU is also leading the Galileo project for the next generation of satellite global positioning systems (GPS), another area where the EU wants to develop its own technology rather than rely on other countries. The systems of the future will have a much broader range of applications than the common GPS used to reach a destination on car journeys, such as more efficient traffic management and a feature to support search-and-rescue operations. (*Europa policy*)

A. The EU currently relies almost entirely on American satellites to serve GPS devices in Europe.

B. The EU wishes to establish a more independent role in space generally and in GPS technology in particular.

C. The Global Monitoring for Environment and Security Project aims primarily to develop defensive weapons in space.

D. While the current positioning systems are widely used for search and rescue purposes, the Galileo system is purely aimed at navigation and traffic management purposes.

149. It is our governments which set tax rates on company profits and personal incomes, savings and capital gains. The EU as a whole merely keeps an eye on

these decisions to see they are fair to the EU as a whole. It pays particular attention to company taxation because of a risk that taxes could create obstacles to the smooth movement of goods, services and capital around the EU's single market. Member countries are bound by a code of conduct to prevent them from providing tax breaks which unfairly distort investment decisions, for example. (*Europa policy*)

A. The EU does not set tax rates, but it does monitor member countries' taxation policies for the good of the single market.

B. Countries in the Union are entirely free to tax individuals and business organisations at their discretion.

C. The EU encourages Member States to keep taxes on individuals low to boost consumer spending and thus stimulate the economy.

D. The EU encourages especially less advanced members to use lower or no taxes as an incentive to attract foreign-owned companies.

150. Approximately 1,000 years before Pythagoras was calculating the length of a hypotenuse, sophisticated scribes in Mesopotamia were working with the same theory to calculate the area of their farmland. Working on clay tablets, students would "write" out their math problems in cuneiform script, a method that involved making wedge-shaped impressions in the clay with a blunt reed. These tablets bear evidence of practical as well as more advanced theoretical math and show just how sophisticated the ancient Babylonians were with numbers – around one millennium before Pythagoras and Euclid were doing the same in ancient Greece. "They are the most sophisticated mathematics from anywhere in the world at that time," said historian Alexander Jones. "This is around 4,000 years ago and there's no other ancient culture at that time that we know of that is doing anything like that level of work. It seems to be going beyond anything that daily life needs," he said. Many scribes were trained in the ancient city of Nippur in what is now southern Iraq, where a large number of tablets were discovered between the mid-19th century and the 1920s. Typical problems they worked on involved calculating the area of a given field or the width of a trench (*CNN*, Dec. 17th 2010).

A. The mathematical proficiency of ancient Babylonians was rooted in the needs of their daily lives.

B. In ancient Greece about 3,000 years ago, Pythagoras was engaged in advanced mathematics.

C. With the mounting evidence that ancient Babylonians were engaged in sophisticated mathematics, historians are convinced that Pythagoras borrowed his ideas from them.

D. Many of those who created the clay tablets found in Mesopotamia received their training in Nippur, an ancient city in present-day Iraq that lies on the Euphrates River.

ANSWERS

1. C

A. Incorrect. The new test is to reduce pressure on the police and prisons. Also, the text does not state that this will result in fewer requests.

B. Insufficient information. Whilst this is raised as a concern in the text it makes no mention of how many or what proportion of requests come from such states.

C. Correct. The crime's gravity along with other factors can be taken into account.

D. Insufficient information. There is no indication in the text that this is, or is not, the case.

2. D

A. Incorrect. It is not that hot plasma is ineffective; rather, they have not been used in this area for these reasons.

B. Insufficient information. We are not told how the cold plasma achieves the results it does.

C. Insufficient information. There is no indication that Pseudomonas aeruginosa and Staphylococcus aureus survive cold plasma any longer than any other bacteria.

D. Correct. Ten times as many bacteria survive twice as long in rat wounds than on a Petri dish.

3. A

A. Correct. As time passes, more stars die and produce heavier elements which produce more colours in a star's spectrum.

B. Insufficient information. Although this may be true it does not say this.

C. Incorrect. Their blue colour merely shows that not many stars had yet died and dispersed their heavier elements.

D. Incorrect. It only states that the galaxies seen through these telescopes at this time are small and blue.

4. A

A. Correct. The aim is to achieve 3% of GDP

B. Insufficient information. There was a Council meeting on that date but we don't know that it was responsible for environmental issues.

C. Incorrect. It means higher investment in education and research, not financial markets.

D. Insufficient information. Although this was the aim of the Lisbon Agenda, the text merely states a link between competitiveness and the Lisbon Agenda – there is no mention of being the most competitive one in the world.

5. C

A. Insufficient information. Ethical guidance is cited as a crucial measure but whether it is likely to do any good or not is left unanswered.

B. Incorrect. There is a need for an international consensus against allowing this to happen.

C. Correct. It is because of the unprecedented advances that have been made.

D. Insufficient information. It is impossible to infer or refute this from the text.

6. D

A. Incorrect. Prior to the increase in coast guard patrols, more people entered Europe via Italy, France and Spain.

B. Incorrect. The text states that 31,400 entered through Greece via the 8-mile stretch near Orestiada.

C. Insufficient information. The text only states that fewer than 31,400 entered via the Canary Islands during 2006. There is no mention of whether this was the largest influx.

D. Correct. The Canary Islands had a peak in 2006 and so there must have been fewer in 2010.

7. D

A. Incorrect. This is only one of the two ways suggested in the text.

B. Insufficient information. It is unclear whether the butterfly migrates to or from North America each winter.

C. Incorrect. The text suggests that this species in fact may migrate to escape from parasites.

D. Correct. It is the difficulties caused by the

seasons, whatever they are, that is now seen as the reason for migration.

8. A

A. Correct. '…a message of confidence…' is required.

B. Insufficient information. Stabilised oil prices are listed as one area of improvement but there is no information to suggest that they were fluctuating strongly.

C. Incorrect. It states that positive signs are emerging.

D. Incorrect. These are in fact the key factors behind the pick-up.

9. B

A. Incorrect. It is '…reasonable for ozone and other pollutants…'

B. Correct. The article states that most people inhale more pollutants than indicated by standard risk assessments based on outdoor measurements.

C. Insufficient information. There is no information given for levels of inhalation 10 years ago.

D. Insufficient information. There is no indication that this is the sole domain of environmental agencies.

10. C

A. Insufficient information. The construction of the Eixample, along with the Universal Exposition, induced a sense of civic pride but there is no mention of this lasting into the 20th century.

B. Incorrect. He was a professor of architecture and also a scholar of heraldry.

C. Correct. Barcelona was the right place and right time for architects due to the wealth from industrialization.

D. Insufficient information. The text merely states that the new style was one way through which the middle class could connect with medieval history.

11. A

A. Correct. 'That extreme a temperature should have destroyed any hint of organic material inside…'

B. Incorrect. It says that amino acids have been found in a variety of carbon-rich meteorites.

C. Insufficient information. There is no mention of what the scientists were looking for at the time of their discovery.

D. Insufficient information. There is no mention of how the amino acids might have survived the intense heat.

12. C

A. Incorrect. The text is about the intention to integrate migration issues with other EU policies toward third countries.

B. Insufficient information. There is no mention of how many countries in how many continents have relations with the EU.

C. Correct. It wants '…an evaluation mechanism to monitor relations with third countries which do not cooperate…'

D. Incorrect. It reaffirms that this is already the case.

13. A

A. Correct. This is one of the areas stated as needing legislation.

B. Insufficient information. There is no comment on whether e-money is becoming more widespread.

C. Insufficient information. There is no indication that international cooperation in criminal matters is being expressed as a concern.

D. Insufficient information. It calls for consultation where appropriate but doesn't say whether copyright and related rights are such an area.

14. B

A. Insufficient information. There is no mention of whether Mastrolorenzo et al. were the first or not.

B. Correct. It states '…a recent study says most died instantly of extreme heat…'

C. Incorrect. Until now this has been the received wisdom.

D. Incorrect. The fourth surge was the first to actually reach Pompeii.

15. B

A. Incorrect. There are sixteen areas.

B. Correct. It requires harmonisation of standards which has subsequently been complemented by a policy on certification and tests.

C. Insufficient information. The product certification complements the new approach to technical harmonisation but there is no indication that it is a pre-requisite for it.

D. Incorrect. The new approach adopted in 1985 was only the start of the process.

16. D

A. Insufficient information. The process discussed certainly does but there is no mention of how much CO2 would be produced by other methods.

B. Insufficient information. The process discussed does both but alternative heating methods might not.

C. Incorrect. The heating process is only one part of it. The chemical process which sets the cement also produces CO2 which would be unaffected by the heating process.

D. Correct. The heating and setting together produce 5% of the world's CO2.

17. D

A. Insufficient information. It is not stated when the SEA was signed or when it entered into force.

B. Incorrect. It was the SEA that did this. Also, it is not clear whether the secretariat has anything to do with the European Political Cooperation.

C. Incorrect. The Dooge committee drew up a report for the Intergovernmental conference.

D. Correct. It states '…the SEA established an institutional basis for…the group of European correspondents…'

18. A

A. Correct. It states 'Without these two pieces of the puzzle in place, we will not have a deal in Copenhagen'.

B. Incorrect. 'We need to see more of that' can never be construed as 'not ambitious enough'.

C. Insufficient information. Little progress was made on the two key issues but there is no indication of whether progress was made in other areas.

D. Incorrect. An increase of 40% is much better than 26%, but it isn't double.

19. D

A. Incorrect. It aims at deferring their pay.

B. Incorrect. Britain was alone in this aim.

C. Incorrect. It states '…Sweden gave some concessions in the three most controversial areas…'

D. Correct. The aim is to defer up to 60% of their pay for up to 3 years.

20. D

A. Incorrect. This finding refutes this long-held notion.

B. Incorrect. The limbic system is critical to many functions including processing spatial relationships.

C. Insufficient information. He might well do but it can't be inferred from the text. What we do know is that he dreams of becoming a London taxi driver.

D. Correct. It recruited neighbouring regions to the cause.

21. C

A. Incorrect. The growth would only be due partly to "natural gas liquids".

B. Incorrect. They predict a rise during this period.

C. Correct. Rising oil prices, reduction in investment and moves to greener technologies are all cited as reasons.

D. Insufficient information. These reservoirs are merely one of the sources of "petroleum fuels" and no mention is made of its rank.

22. C

A. Incorrect. It is the amount dumped on the developing world that is set to triple.

B. Incorrect. These are just some of the valuable parts.

C. Correct. It is the toxic elements within the waste plus the caustic acids used to salvage it.

D. Insufficient information. China and India are two countries cited as processing this waste but there is no mention of whether or not they are the most advanced.

23. B

A. Wrong. Both Brussels and Liege are famous for their waffles. It is Belgium as a whole that is famous for its chocolate and pralines.

B. Correct. The country referred to is Belgium as a whole, while craquelin and pistolet, which are like a small cake or loaf, are listed among its specialties.

C. Wrong. There is no evidence to support this statement at all.

D. Wrong. It is mastel that is described as rusk bread with aniseed.

24. B

A. Wrong. It is the Rome Convention which protects broadcasting organisations.

B. Correct.

C. Wrong. There is no indication where these organisations have their headquarters.

D. Wrong. There is no indication that the Paris Convention affords any protection to performers but it is explicitly stated for the Rome Convention.

25. C

A. Wrong. The transport industry's contribution to GNP and employment are both 7%.

B. Wrong. The transport industry's contribution to Member States' investment is 40% which is not more than a half.

C. Correct. Passenger transport has grown 3.1% per year whereas goods have increased 2.3% per year.

D. Wrong. The average is 7% but each Member State's spending could vary wildly.

26. D

A. Incorrect. Although the number of PhDs has doubled, the US's share has dwindled.

B. Insufficient information. While the US did enroll 12 per cent of the world's students, we have no way of knowing what portion of the world's student other OECD countries enrolled as compared to the US data.

C. Insufficient information. Although this may very well be the case, this subjective opinion is not supported by the information in the text passage.

D. Correct. The text states both the US data and the OECD averages, and the US percentage increase was indeed lower than the average OECD increase.

27. C

A. Insufficient information. There is no mention of how people are increasingly comparing themselves.

B. Insufficient information. There was no strong link found but if there were exceptions they are not mentioned here.

C. Correct. He concludes that '...a correlation between countries is strong.'

D. Incorrect. He examined both aspects and reached different conclusions.

28. C

A. Wrong. Some people ("lucky oddballs") function on 4 hours sleep or even less.

B. Wrong. The text states that the flies remain motionless for many hours a day, not 8.

C. Correct. A mutation in an insect's gene which is shared by humans has been identified.

D. Wrong. The reference in the text is to scientists studying sleep for decades, not the specific issue of insect sleep.

29. A

A. Correct. Anarchists sent nearly 30 devices intended to explode on May Day, 1919.

B. Insufficient information. Luxdorph describes the event but there is no evidence to suggest that he sent it.

C. Incorrect. The first event described was in 1714 which is the 18th century.

D. Insufficient information. We are not told whether there was careful investigation or not. It may have been discovered by chance.

30. C

A. Wrong. Scientists have long suspected this. They now know it to be a fact.

B. Wrong. The probe crashed into a crater of this size. It wasn't the cause of the crater.

C. Correct. There could, of course, be more but only 90 litres has been confirmed.

D. Wrong. It has accumulated over billions of years but in ice form

31. C

A. Incorrect. He seemed to believe your language, or lack of, changed your entire perception of a concept.

B. Insufficient information. He may have been but the use of one example does not constitute 'firm belief'.

C. Correct. This is the view of the '...dominant school of post-war linguistics...'

D. Incorrect. They claim it is their language's precision that is most suitable for the rigours of legislation.

32. B

A. Wrong. The text states that agricultural production increased by 24% per capita, but the population increased by 89% in the period.

B. Correct. It states that the world population increased by 89% between these years which is fairly close to double.

C. Wrong. It cites China as a country that reached the limits of increasing arable land use "many years ago".

D. Wrong. The text states that in the past agricultural production was improved by increasing land use AND employing the best technologies available.

33. B

A. Insufficient information. We are not told that Mrs Desai is Indian nor is there any indication that there was racism in the workplace.

B. Correct. It was her 'magical turn of phrase' that galvanized her fellow workers.

C. Insufficient information. There is no mention of whether there was any union support or not.

D. Insufficient information. We have no information on whether this particular strike was successful or not.

34. B

A. Wrong. The Chrysler Building held the record of tallest building for less than a year.

B. Correct. 102 storeys were built in 410 days which is about 4 days per story. [NB: Story is the US spelling of storey.]

C. Wrong. 40 Wall Street, like the Chrysler Building, was still under construction when work began on the Empire State Building.

D. Wrong. They were "mostly" from Europe.

35. B

A. Insufficient information. We are not really given any information about the length of time he may have lived in Budapest, if at all.

B. Correct. He developed his style by combining elements of Czerny and Paganini whilst Wagner is described as a musical son.

C. Insufficient information. Despite 'Tristan' being his last word we cannot conclude that this was because he was thinking of Wagner's opera.

D. Insufficient information. We are not told whether he was a 'Romantic' style composer.

36. C

A. Wrong. It is theorized that Europa could support this quantity of life, not that it does.

B. Wrong. There is no evidence in the text that any form of life has ever existed on Europa.

C. Correct. Greenberg said that there was nothing saying there is life there now.

D. Wrong. Jupiter has many moons but it doesn't say it here.

37. A

A. Correct. The culture is believed to have started in 4000 B.C. and this site was buried 500 years later in 3500 B.C.

B. Insufficient information. There is no indication whether this is the first or 1000th discovery of this kind in Norway.

C. Incorrect. The arid climate was known about before the discovery of the site.

D. Insufficient information. There is no indication of how the artifacts compare with other sites.

38. D

A. Wrong. There is nothing in the text about the images being carved into the wood.

B. Wrong. Phnom Penh was the seat of government when the French arrived in 1863.

C. Wrong. Oudong was the seat of government from 1618 until the mid 19th century.

D. Correct. Phnom Penh is 40km south of Oudong.

39. B

A. Insufficient information. We are not told that the Central European Roma and the Gitanos have the same value system.

B. Correct. There are between 500,000 and 800,000 Gitanos living in harmony with their non-Gitano neighbours.

C. Insufficient information. Although the importance of family elders is mentioned in the text, we have no information about reverence for recently deceased.

D. Incorrect. We are told it is easier in Andalusia than in the larger cities to the north but not impossible.

40. A

A. Correct. It says that the cultural diversity has produced a culinary melting pot.

B. Wrong. A melting pot is a mixing of multiple cultures and not a cooking vessel.

C. Wrong. There is no mention of the opportunity chance to play games at the restaurant.

D. Wrong. The old town may be quiet; other parts of town are rowdier.

41. D

A. Incorrect. It is more likely that it is a protest against the ban on religious clothing.

B. Incorrect. It is civil liberty rather than national sentiment that is a concern, according to the text.

C. Insufficient information. There is no indication of when secularism was set down in law.

D. Correct. She strikes at night anonymously.

42. C

A. Insufficient information. Although it mentions that Shell was expelled by the community, there is no mention of Shell attempting to return to clear up the pollution.

B. Wrong. It states: "These days the 400 sq mile delta ... is still badly polluted".

C. Correct. It states that Shell and the government have earned $100bn (a substantial amount by any yardstick) and that it is still badly polluted.

D. Wrong. On the contrary, it states that it "barely needs refining".

43. B

A. Incorrect. The text suggests that this was tried and in made no appreciable difference.

B. Correct. In Germany, men can now choose to stay at home for up to 12 months while being paid.

C. Insufficient information. There is no mention of how many women choose to return to work compared with those who stay at home.

D. Insufficient information. The reason why a birth rate of 2.1 is required is not expounded in the article.

44. A

A. Correct. China sees this gesture as "brandishing a fist at a potential [enemy]".

B. Wrong. It was diplomatic relations between

America and Vietnam that were established 15 years ago.

C. Wrong. Danang was ONCE home to one of America's largest army bases in Vietnam.

D. Wrong. The large aircraft carrier was intended as a "striking token of reconciliation".

45. A

A. Correct. The butanol can be added to gasoline (petrol) or diesel and used in existing engines without modification.

B. Insufficient information. There is no mention of the environmental impact of the use or production of the butanol.

C. Insufficient information. There is no mention of yields from either of the two raw materials.

D. Insufficient information. There is no mention of whether byproducts from iron stills (if they exist) can be used.

46. B

A. Insufficient Information. It is not disclosed which marine invertebrates rely on sound.

B. Correct. Sound travels further than light in water and absorption of sound is decreasing as the sea gets more acidic.

C. Incorrect. The court protected the rights of the navy to test their sonar.

D. Incorrect. It is the increasing volume of shipping rather than increasingly powerful engines that appears to be the problem.

47. C

A. Insufficient information. This is probably true but it doesn't say it in the article. It says China is second but doesn't say who is first.

B. Insufficient information. There is no mention of any tension between the two neighbours, just quibbles about how the data are measured.

C. Correct. It says that China's economy was one of the biggest for nearly 2000 years and has fallen back only briefly.

D. Wrong. It is Japan's economy that has been the third largest for some time.

48. C

A. Incorrect. The text suggests that the lineage of modern humans is much more intertwined than previously thought.

B. Insufficient information. Although both these locations are cited it is not stated that they were the only places.

C. Correct. As recently as a year ago the belief was that we all came from one African exodus.

D. Incorrect. It is the presence of the ancient group's genes in modern humans that gives rise to this conclusion.

49. C

A. Wrong. Climate change is cited as a possible cause but not the only one.

B. Wrong. Deforestation is cited as a possible cause but not the only one.

C. Correct. It states that they are "spreading lethal epidemics around the world".

D. Wrong. It is a 10-year drought which has caused the worst air pollution in 70 years.

50. D

A. Incorrect. He was the first person to write a detailed account of the mounds.

B. Incorrect. They used to think this but now the mounds are 'collectively ignored'.

C. Insufficient information. The peak of the civilisation came some 300 years after it rose but we are given no information about the rapidity of its demise.

D. Correct. It was letters to Jefferson and other friends in high places that helped to spread the word.

51. A

A. Correct. There were 977 babies born from donated sperm and 82 from donated embryos.

B. Insufficient information. This is not specified. We are only told that there were 15,237 births due to IVF and DI combined.

C. Wrong. It says that 396 donors are far fewer that what is needed.

D. Wrong. It says that fewer men donate mainly because of the loss of anonymity.

52. C

A. Incorrect. The painting was done when he was 16; he was described as a master when he was 17.

B. Insufficient information. It is undoubtedly an early work of Raphael's but it doesn't state whether it was his earliest work or not.

C. Correct. He was described as such when he was 17 which would be about 1500 given that he was born in 1483.

D. Insufficient information. Both these facts are given to us but there is no defined connection between them.

53. A

A. Correct. It says that sensory information from many systems is likely stored correctly.

B. Wrong. It is the recollection and reassembly of memories that is so unreliable.

C. Insufficient information. This may or may not be true; there is no mention of it in the text.

D. Wrong. It states that you can have vivid memories of things that never happened.

54. A

A. Correct. The report says, 'The least healthy habits turn out to be eating ones…'

B. Insufficient information. Ms Arrue's heritage is not divulged in the text, only the location of the University.

C. Incorrect. The text says that they displayed more risk behaviour than expected.

D. Insufficient information. There may have been follow-up interviews but it doesn't say it.

55. B

A. Wrong. He has stated a desire to be self-sufficient by 2014, a date which is non-binding.

B. Correct. It is being "seized upon" by politicians whose electorates are increasingly against keeping troops in Afghanistan.

C. Wrong. It says that "German police trainers will continue to teach local recruits" after 2014.

D. Insufficient information. It doesn't mention the views of voters about the Taliban, only about the corruption seen in the government.

56. D

A. Incorrect. Digital ratio theory only suggests that finger length *may* be an indicator of gender.

B. Insufficient information. There is no mention of whether or not there are other paintings suspected of being drawn by children.

C. Incorrect. Digital ratio theory was proposed prior to this study.

D. Correct. It states that women's fingers are about the same length but the index finger may also be longer.

57. A

A. Correct. "The EU came under fire for its lack of cohesion..."

B. Insufficient information. There is no mention of establishing an office in Brussels or anywhere else.

C. Wrong. It states that the EU has yet to create an emergency force.

D. Wrong. Mr Sarkozy has called upon Mr Barroso to set up an EU disasters rapid reaction force.

58. C

A. Insufficient information. There is no mention of the current system being inconsistently enforced.

B. Incorrect. The text does mention that the CIA did not give the protest a colour, but this does not necessarily imply that it has taken no position on the events.

C. Correct. It is described as 'The non-partisan tax code protest campaign…'

D. Insufficient information. There is no indication given as to how long the prime minister has been in office.

59. A

A. Correct. This was the view of Dr Sam Perlo-Freeman.

B. Wrong. The survey shows that many countries are spending more on military expenditure, not actually killing more people.

C. Wrong. The report is issued every year.

D. Insufficient information. The report merely says that spending was up 5.9% on the previous year. It makes no mention of how this is distributed.

60. A

A. Correct. Cambyses sent his troops to legitimise his claim on Egypt, and this was around 525 B.C.

B. Incorrect. Herodotus wasn't born until 484 B.C., 41 years after the event.

C. Incorrect. El-Kharga is where they are thought to have visited, not known to have visited.

D. Insufficient information. The bones are stated to be human but how they met their demise is not revealed.

61. A

A. Correct. Journalists are often silenced by intimidation, brutality and murder.

B. Insufficient information. It is currently 146th out of 175 nations but there is no mention of whether this is improving or not.

C. Wrong. Reporters Without Borders is Paris-based.

D. Insufficient information. There is no mention of a fire fight or of Congolese rebels being involved.

62. C

A. Incorrect. He admitted to organising but not funding the theft.

B. Insufficient information. The sign was broken into three parts but we are not told if it was its three constituent words.

C. Correct. He was sentenced to 32 months and his accomplices got 30 months.

D. Insufficient information. We are not told whether he kept out of the limelight or not.

63. D

A. Wrong. Her problems with the Portuguese authorities were due to her age.

B. Wrong. Having won her court case in the Netherlands she has set out from Portugal or Gibraltar.

C. Wrong. The Dutch welfare authorities lost their court case and so, could not stop her.

D. Correct.

64. D

A. Insufficient information. It is the only one mentioned but it does not say it is the most advanced.

B. Incorrect. The Norwegian Broadcasting Corporation seem to be using it.

C. Insufficient information. Although the new system intends to have none of these 'features' there is no mention of whether existing ones have all of them.

D. Correct. It uses 'The same kind of peer-to-peer file sharing that made Napster famous…'

65. D

A. Wrong. Mr Williamson said that there was "little evidence" to suggest this.

B. Wrong. It showed a dip for the third time in four months.

C. Wrong. Weaker economies have introduced austerity measures. It is not the austerity measures that have weakened those economies.

D. Correct. He said that although economic recovery was slowing down, it still retained "significant forward momentum."

66. B

A. Incorrect. "...ministers are worried that schools try to boost their score..."

B. Correct. The measurements will be made on the basis of five core subjects "from the beginning of 2011".

C. Insufficient information. There is no mention of why it is called a baccalaureate.

D. Insufficient information. Although Michael Gove is the Conservative education secretary, his political affiliation is not mentioned in the article.

67. B

A. Wrong. The satellite is mapping gravity and its malfunction has nothing to do with that.

B. Correct. They remain "confident the situation can be recovered..."

C. Insufficient information. It was the main computer which experienced a processor error. The fault on the back-up computer is unspecified.

D. Insufficient information. It was struck by a glitch which may, or may not, be space debris.

68. C

A. Incorrect. This seems to be true only in the first round of IVF.

B. Incorrect. Although transferring one embryo may be the safest, we have no information on how most parents decide.

C. Correct. The main finding of the study is exactly that.

D. Insufficient information. There is no mention of the odds before the study.

69. C

A. Wrong. The court has only agreed to his extradition to the US.

B. Insufficient information. There is no indication how Russia intends to treat the man if he is returned.

C. Correct. It was a joint Thai-US sting operation which caught Mr Bout.

D. Wrong. It says that Russia will "work to secure his return".

70. D

A. Incorrect. The bailout could be €50 billion or as much as €100 billion.

B. Insufficient information. We are told that many young depart but not where to.

C. Insufficient information. We are told that '...public spending is being slashed back in a way not seen for a generation...' but not how it is being done.

D. Correct. Markets are threatening to force up the price of borrowing leaving the EU/IMF as their only option.

71. A

A. Correct. It is its fastest rate since unification in 1990.

B. Wrong. It is for its world-class machines and manufacturing products.

C. Insufficient information. The rest of the eurozone experienced a growth of 1% but there is no detail as to how this is distributed.

D. Wrong. It is two-thirds not one third.

72. B

A. Insufficient information. Women undergo a physical change in their brain but there is nothing in the text to suggest that this affects intelligence one way or the other.

B. Correct. The changes affect '...the areas that motivate a mother to take care of her baby...'

C. Insufficient information. There is no mention of whether men are affected by this or not.

D. Incorrect. Evidence shows that there is an actual change in the brain.

73. C

A. Wrong. It states that today Switzerland is "grubby" and in need of repair.

B. Wrong. The text refers to those fleeing Nazism after 1933, not 1917.

C. Correct. They met there to begin ending the Cold War.

D. Wrong. They employed "deregulated low-tax economics", not high taxes.

74. C

A. Insufficient information. It is unclear whether it was Italian or Greek police involved in the shootout.

B. Incorrect. They express solidarity with the

other groups but don't necessarily act in co-operation.

C. Correct. The bomb is described as crude and it is uncertain that their capabilities attain the level normally associated with terrorism.

D. Insufficient information. There is no indication that they are concerned with an upswing in anarchist violence.

75. B

A. Wrong. There is no mention or hint of any other regions being affected.

B. Correct. He has allocated 1 billion roubles for aid.

C. Wrong. They are still trying to put out the fires at the time of writing.

D. Insufficient information. There is no mention of the forest's susceptibility to fires.

76. C

A. Incorrect. There had been rumors about the plague long before it arrived in Italy.

B. Insufficient information. There is no mention of whether they had treatments for the symptoms or not.

C. Correct. It states that it was '...terrifyingly, indiscriminately contagious...'

D. Incorrect. It says that there were '...some larger, some smaller.'

77. A

A. Correct.

B. Insufficient information. We are not told from where the ship originally sailed.

C. Wrong. The champagne and beer were found on the same ship.

D. Wrong. It is claimed that the beer is still drinkable.

78. A

A. Correct. The agreement with Iran was snubbed by the US and its allies.

B. Insufficient information. There is no mention of any past political coups.

C. Insufficient information. There is no information given on the current state of Turkish-Israeli relations.

D. Insufficient information. We are not told that he founded the party nor when.

79. B

A. Insufficient information. We are not told anything about the importance of Catalonia to the bullfighting fraternity.

B. Correct. It had 180,000 signatures from the public.

C. Wrong. It was initiated by calls from thousands of Catalonians to include bulls in the animal protection legislation.

D. Wrong. 68 to 55 does not constitute a two-thirds majority.

80. A

A. Correct. The text suggests that this new finding is 'Contrary to some popular conceptions...'

B. Insufficient information. There is nothing in the text that states they displaced the local inhabitants.

C. Incorrect. There are several other regions listed as well.

D. Insufficient information. They were not Christian but they may well have had diverse religious beliefs.

81. A

A. Correct. It is known to cause death and paralysis.

B. Insufficient information. There is no reason given for any variation in mosquito populations.

C. Wrong. It is usually transmitted by mosquito or blood transfusion.

D. Wrong. It is only one-fifth of people who show any symptoms.

82. D

A. Insufficient information. The text does not contain information as to the exact reasons for the fall of the Western Empire.

B. Insufficient information. Constantinople was

certainly harder to attack but the text gives no indication of how often it was attacked.

C. Insufficient information. There is no indication given as to whether the fall of the Western Empire had any effect on the fall of the eastern empire.

D. Correct. The text lists multiple reasons for the higher resilience of the Eastern Empire.

83. C

A. Wrong. The guide indicates only the "must-does" on the cultural trail but it doesn't mention anything that would imply it is an "all-in exhaustive tour".

B. Insufficient information. We are only told that there are 242 churches, statues, fountains and buildings but not how many of them are churches.

C. Correct.

D. Wrong. It states that Paris has a cultural life "past and present".

84. B

A. Insufficient information. AQIM operate in their areas but there is no mention of them wanting to create their own state.

B. Correct. This is the crux of the text.

C. Wrong. AQIM only pretend to fight for people like the Tuareg.

D. Wrong. It says: "He was not the first hostage to be executed by AQIM..."

85. B

A. Incorrect. Both Louis XVI and his predecessor spent extravagantly.

B. Correct. Previously they had been exempt and there is no mention of how long this was for.

C Insufficient information. It could be surmised that they did have some influence otherwise why would the King have summoned them but no mention is made of how much.

D. Incorrect. There is only mention of unrest among the peasants and urban poor.

86. C

A. Wrong. It is defence contractors who are suspected of corruption, not the government.

B. Wrong. Germany is selling two submarines worth over a billion euros.

C. Correct. Defence contractors are suspected of paying bribes worth more than a million euros.

D. Wrong. It says that at the same time as the government approved aid for Greece, prosecutors began investigating.

87. D

A. Wrong. It states that "nearly all nuclear power reactors ... are fuelled with uranium".

B. Wrong. The IFR does not create new fuel but uses its existing fuel more completely.

C. Insufficient information. There may well be research in this area but it isn't detailed here.

D. Correct. They do this to make the fission more effective.

88. C

A. Insufficient information. The text states that many wanted reform but not necessarily a majority.

B. Incorrect. This didn't happen until Oct 3rd the following year.

C. Correct. It states that it was East Germany's first, and only, free election.

D. Insufficient information. Many wondered what they had got out of it or how it might have been done differently but there is no indication that they thought it a failure.

89. A

A. Correct. The social networking site allowed the demonstrators to organise their picnic but it also allowed the authorities to monitor it as well.

B. Wrong. MALI fought against the police who were described as being like an army waiting for terrorists.

C. Wrong. Eating in public places is only banned during daylight hours during Ramadan.

D. Wrong. The police have now closed all their cases – "for now".

90. C

A. Wrong. The Wagner festival was in 2004 and the "village of opera" project is described as something he had been working on "recently". It can be inferred that this was not in 2004.

B. Wrong. Christoph Schlingensief is described as a director, actor and artist but not an opera singer.

C. Correct. He directed Parsifal at the Bayreuth festival.

D. Insufficient information. There is no mention of any awards being won for this production.

91. A

A. Correct. Seven candidates were carried off.

B. Insufficient information. The text states that 'about' 3 dozen officials were banned not 'at least'.

C. Insufficient information. He released some political prisoners and allowed two opposition papers which may well have been subject to censorship.

D. Insufficient information. We are merely told he was invited and not informed about the majority of the vote or the unanimity of this decision.

92. B

A. Wrong. The painting was returned a decade later.

B. Correct. One year after its return in 1988 a duplicate was sold for $43m.

C. Wrong. It was Van Gogh's Poppy Flowers that was stolen.

D. Insufficient information. We are only told that the security systems have not been working "for a long time". There is no indication that this is for 32 years.

93. D

A. Wrong. It states there are two other modern reptiles that do this.

B. Wrong. The skink in question is currently alive there.

C. Insufficient information. While it is true that one-fifth of snakes bear live young, we are not told the benefit of this evolutionary change.

D. Correct. It gives scientists a rare glimpse of this evolutionary stage.

94. A

A. Correct. There were fears that the ash might damage the aircraft.

B. Wrong. It was floods caused by lava melting glacial ice which ruined farmland.

C. Insufficient information. There were fears it might damage aircraft but there is no report that it did.

D. Insufficient information. It says that 60 hectares of her land was wiped away but it doesn't indicate if this was all of her land.

95. B

A. Incorrect. It happened 65 million years ago.

B. Correct. '…scientists are concerned that the change may harm many shell-building organisms…'

C. Insufficient information. We are not told what the percentage drop in pH levels would be.

D. Insufficient information. It may well do but we aren't told that in the text.

96. D

A. Insufficient information. It states that Germany has run lower budget deficits than France but there is no information about per capita income.

B. Insufficient information. There is no information on the US economy and whether it is fuelled by consumption.

C. Incorrect. Although a comparison between tax regimes is being done, we are not told what the purpose of this exercise is.

D. Correct. He says, "It's to make our economy more competitive."

97. D

A. Insufficient information. They have found evidence of former rivers and seas but it doesn't indicate whether signs of life have been detected.

B. Wrong. Although greenhouse gasses harm the

Earth by raising its temperature, this is seen as a benefit for Mars as it is so cold.

C. Insufficient information. There is no mention of any laboratory experiments having been performed.

D. Correct. Hopefully, this would be released by raising the temperature sufficiently to melt it.

98. B

A. Wrong. It states that Iceland "unilaterally raised its mackerel quota".

B. Correct. The Faroe Islands have increased their quota and Norway, along with the EU, insists that it is already over-fished.

C. Insufficient information. There is no mention of how, or how long, the EU has implemented or enforced its fishing quotas.

D. Wrong. Mr Lochhead was "enraged".

99. A

A. Correct. It says that "few have been so unpopular".

B. Wrong. It says that they "gave control of interest rates to the independent Bank of England."

C. Wrong. It states that "Mr Blair even forced changes on the Conservative party..."

D. Insufficient information. It only states that he is the only Labour leader to win three consecutive elections.

100. C

A. Wrong. It was originally organised by a group of musicians.

B. Insufficient information. The festival has grown in popularity but we have no information on the popularity of trumpet playing in general.

C. Correct. And lots of each.

D. Wrong. There are "entire farmyards of pigs" roasting on spits.

101. D

A. Wrong. It states there are two other modern reptiles that do this.

B. Wrong. The skink in question is currently alive there.

C. Insufficient information. While it is true that one-fifth of snakes bear live young, we are not told the benefit of this evolutionary change.

D. Correct. It gives scientists a rare glimpse of this evolutionary stage.

102. C

A. Insufficient information. They certainly had contrary views but there is no indication that they ever debated this together, heatedly or otherwise.

B. Wrong. It was Linnaeus who had a problem with the Venus Flytrap.

C. Correct. They both saw them as special but had differing ideas on their adaptation.

D. Insufficient information. Those familiar with his life know that he did, but it doesn't say anything about it here.

103. C

A. Insufficient information. We are not told whether this is France's largest distributor or not.

B. Insufficient information. We are not told how the World Ocean Network defines 'sustainable'.

C. Correct. '…chefs, fishmongers, fishermen…' cover those involved in procurement and sales.

D. Insufficient information. We are not told if Lonxanet is the only one in Spain or not.

104. C

A. Insufficient information. There is no mention in the text of him publishing 6 articles on the Internet though he may well have done.

B. Insufficient information. There is no mention of relative performance between the two parties.

C. Correct. This is precisely what Peter Gitmark was saying.

D. Insufficient information. The empty chair was highly symbolic but there is nothing to suggest that the prize was placed there although, if it had been, it would have made even more impact.

105. C

A. Wrong. Kaziranga is seen as a "thundering conservation success story".

B. Insufficient information. It may or may not have scores of wild goats, we cannot tell from the text.

C. Correct. "Agriculture had taken over most of the fertile river valleys that the species depends on".

D. Wrong. When set up in 1908 there were about a dozen rhinos in it.

106. D

A. Insufficient information. The text doesn't discuss what evidence does, or does not, exist.

B. Incorrect. There is no mention of anything being ruled out.

C. Insufficient information. The text doesn't reveal whether or not Vinceti is the first to discover this.

D. Correct. The location would be a clue but unlikely to be definitive.

107. A

A. Correct. It raises the possibility of "resurrecting" ancient texts in other languages.

B. Insufficient information. It is certainly closely related to Hebrew but we have no information on its similarity to Aramaic.

C. Wrong. Specialists first decoded the language in 1932.

D. Wrong. It was last used around 1200 B.C. which is around 3200 years ago.

108 A

A. Correct.

B. Wrong. It is the sceptics who say this; the advocates believe it is a great improvement.

C. Insufficient information. It seems likely but there is no information to support this.

D. Wrong. They are, at present, being tested in these environments.

109. A

A. Correct. The 48% drop in Q3 2010 was a record-breaker.

B. Incorrect. The housing ministry, which reported the fall, counts domestic as well as foreign holiday homes both on the coast and inland.

C. Insufficient information. We are not told anything about the number of houses being put up for sale.

D. Insufficient information. We are given no information about the respectability of these organizations.

110. D

A. Insufficient information. There is no information given as to the relative safety of such boilers.

B. Incorrect. There is no suggestion that they are in any way unsafe.

C. Insufficient information. The legislation concerning condensing boilers was implemented in 2005 but we are not told whether or not it replaced existing legislation.

D. Correct. This is, indeed, the crux of the text.

111 A

A. Correct. A strong password can be useless against keylogging software.

B. Insufficient information. This is exactly what some sceptics would believe but it doesn't mention it here.

C. Wrong. Mr Herley said this of antivirus software not keylogging software.

D. Wrong. Received wisdom is not to store your password anywhere.

112. C

A. Insufficient information. There is no mention of a theme or tone for the project.

B. Wrong. It says "...it is happening. New buildings are sprouting up..."

C. Correct. We are told that Skopje is the capital of FYR Macedonia and that buildings are sprouting up along the banks of the Vardar.

D. Wrong. It is the earthquake of 1963 that is responsible for the destruction.

113. D

A. Insufficient information. Whilst this may well be true there is no evidence in the text that ETA is considered to be a terrorist group by anyone other than Spain.

B. Insufficient information. It states that the government lost political capital in 2006 when the previous ceasefire collapsed but there is no mention of any recovery of that capital.

C. Insufficient information. The article does not allude to the effectiveness of Mr Rubalcaba in his current post.

D. Correct. This is what was told to and reported by the Wall Street Journal.

114. A

A. Correct. Assam produces the majority of the country's harvest.

B. Insufficient information. There is no mention of how this has affected the quality or the popularity of the tea.

C. Incorrect. The article is not about the taste of the consumers.

D. Incorrect. Although the text does cite rainfall and temperature as two factors affecting tea quality, it does not state that this is necessarily a deterioration and the timescale cannot be called 'short term' either.

115. C

A. Incorrect. This was a study of only 57 countries not the whole world.

B. Insufficient information. In total, across all 57 countries surveyed, there were more plants than anything else. This is not necessarily the case for each individual country.

C. Correct. Competing with another species for food can endanger them without any direct contact.

D. Incorrect. This is merely the list of what they found on their study. Further searching may well find insects, molluscs, reptiles etc.

116. A

A. Correct. It states that the majority are in volcanically active regions, which implies that a few are not.

B. Wrong. It states "they work even in parts of the world that are not volcanically active..."

C. Insufficient information. There is no information about depth limits or cost-effectiveness.

D. Wrong. Wells are bored into hot rocks and water is injected.

117. B

A. Incorrect. Not since 2008.

B. Correct. At £36,500 it became the new record holder.

C. Incorrect. They were destroyed because they were only useful as advertisements for a short period – we are not given information about changing tastes.

D. Insufficient information. We are not told what usual or average prices are although given that the record was less that £23,900 until 2004 it seems unlikely.

118. C

A. Wrong. The attendance checks are to encourage MEPs to remain throughout the debate while there is nothing written in the text to suggest that Mr Barroso has arranged them.

B. Wrong. This is according to Euractiv.

C. Correct. It states that Strasbourg is the Parliament's second home.

D. Insufficient information. It does not state whether or not this is the sole source of income for the MEPs.

119. A

A. Correct. He was sentenced to one year in prison but he has already served nearly half of that.

B. Wrong. "MI6 is Britain's overseas intelligence service."

C. Insufficient information. There is nothing said about the usefulness of the information to the Dutch agents.

D. Wrong. It states: "...personal details that could have endangered agents."

120. D

A. Incorrect. Onset of the disease is usually before 40 but there is no information about proportions above or below that age.

B. Insufficient information. There is nothing in the text to support or refute this assertion but it seems unlikely.

C. Insufficient information. We are only told that type 1 sufferers are treated with insulin and not that other sufferers are not.

D. Correct. This is precisely what the text says.

121. B

A. Insufficient information. There is no indication of whether the laws were brought in by Conservative political forces or others.

B. Correct. There are three listed here amongst a 'raft' of others.

C. Incorrect. It is the latest law to be passed amongst a 'raft' of others.

D. Insufficient information. There is no indication that media freedom groups view any particular type of restriction with more concern than others.

122. A

A. Correct. Along with increased buying power.

B. Wrong. The currency is free floating and fully exchangeable.

C. Wrong. Solidarity helped topple the Berlin Wall.

D. Wrong. The average consumer's buying power has increased six times.

123. A

A. Correct. The co-ordination will ensure that at least one British or French carrier is available at all times.

B. Insufficient information. There is no indication of the French attitude towards this proposal.

C. Insufficient information. There is no mention of co-ordinating exercises or aircraft, only the refits of the ships.

D. Wrong. The British sank the French ships to stop them falling into German hands.

124. C

A. Incorrect. The latest three bring the total to 28.

B. Incorrect. Defence is listed as one of those recently closed.

C. Correct. The schedule is for autumn but there is still work to do.

D. Insufficient information. We are not told anything specific about what remains to be done.

125. A

A. Correct. There seem to be several ideas to explain the observed data.

B. Insufficient information. There is no mention of how he intends to apply this finding.

C. Insufficient information. Horses are not mentioned in the text.

D. Incorrect. Mr Geary contends that intelligence, not aggression, plays a lesser role.

126. D

A. Incorrect. They seek standardization across the world.

B. Incorrect. The early warning system will only be an opportunity, not a requirement, and identical regulations are not sought by the two regions.

C. Incorrect. Nanotechnology and electric cars are cited as two examples defining the range of products not the most important ones.

D. Correct. They seek "increased regulatory co-operation".

127. A

A. Correct. 19 prime ministers in 50 years is less than 3 years each on average.

B. Insufficient information. We are not told whether South Tyrol's situation has affected the Italian situation as a whole.

C. Insufficient information. There is no mention of whether or not Austria has any government debt.

D. Wrong. He has held the post since 1989 which is 21 years, less than half of the last 50.

128. C

A. Insufficient information. There is no information on whether they were also involved in narcotics trafficking.

B. Wrong. The tests were done in the United States.

C. Correct. It states that it is an ex-Soviet republic, it is a rebel area and prone to narcotics smuggling.

D. Insufficient information. They are awaiting results of tests in Germany to determine its origin.

129. A

A. Correct. It states "... China is growing fast, by nearly 10% a year..." but also that "...China's drinkers provide slender profits."

B. Wrong. It states that America's market has levelled off or is in decline.

C. Wrong. We are told that the market has grown from virtually nothing in just 2 decades.

D. Insufficient information. ABI is one of the 4 largest brewers but we are not told which is biggest.

130. D

A. Wrong. There is no sign of a let-up on either side.

B. Insufficient information. There is no indication how or why the 28,000 people have been killed.

C. Wrong. It is a section of the paper that details murders and violent accidents.

D. Correct. The nota roja is expanding "as fighting over the drug trail to the United States inspires ever-greater feats of violence."

131. C

A. Insufficient information. There is no indication of how damaging or long-lasting the conflict will prove to be.

B. Incorrect. Their resolve is to reduce dependency on foreign sources which are unlikely to be US based as they are teaming up with them for this project.

C. Correct. 'Normally, Germany and France are close partners…' starts the article.

D. Insufficient information. Although quite likely this is not stated in the article.

132. B

A. Insufficient information. It doesn't say whether the device can be adjusted in this way or not.

B. Correct. It selectively kills the female mosquitoes which are malarial.

C. Wrong. It determines the frequency of the insect's wing beat.

D. Wrong. It only kills those with a low frequency wing beat which identifies them as female and carrying malaria.

133. A

A. Correct. It states that it "...no longer meets our rigorous food safety standards..."

B. Wrong. It will stop producing it by 2015.

C. Wrong. Potatoes and watermelons are also mentioned.

D. Wrong. It was 25 years ago that more than 2000 people were poisoned by it.

134. B

A. Wrong. The text states that rainfall is scant.

B. Correct. It says it is snow-covered for much of the year until summer and summer lasts 50 to 60 days.

C. Wrong. Musk-oxen are listed as living in arctic tundra areas.

D. Wrong. The stated temperature is correct but it supports a variety of animal species.

135. C

A. Insufficient information. There is no information given about side-effects.

B. Wrong. They fought the campaign because of anti-US sentiment.

C. Correct. The incidence of the disease was "drastically reduced".

D. Wrong. It states that the disease was supposed to have been eradicated long ago and the latest effort was sabotaged e.g. in Nigeria.

136. B

A. Insufficient information. Although the LHC is a ring and was recently completed, neither of these facts can be inferred from the text.

B. Correct. This is, indeed, the belief of Ms Asquith.

C. Insufficient information. We are not informed of the number of scientists working on the LHC nor their nationalities.

D. Insufficient information. We are certainly told of the Higgs boson but there is no mention of Dark Matter.

137. A

A. Correct. The definition of scientific misconduct includes plagiarism in research.

B. Wrong. It states that it often leads to evidence confiscation.

C. Wrong. It states that 14% reported having witnessed falsification by other people.

D. Insufficient information. There is no mention of how much funding Mr. Michelek's research has received.

138. A

A. Correct. The agreements aim to ensure that waters are not over-fished.

B. Wrong. It states that the EU makes agreements within regional and international organisations.

C. Insufficient information. This is true of the EU but there is no information about other wealthy nations.

D. Wrong. It is largely invested in the fishing industries.

139. B

A. Wrong. The reasons given for the current inequity are "national circumstances and traditions".

B. Correct. This is the basic premise of the text.

C. Wrong. The text implies that these are goals to be achieved rather than a long standing situation.

D. Insufficient information. It states that health needs to be taken into account with other polices but there is no evidence to suggest that it isn't yet so in some areas.

140. B

A. Insufficient information. There is no indication given in the text of how the uncounted votes might be cast.

B. Correct. They wish '...to build stronger ties to Moscow.'

C. Insufficient information. There is no mention of ethnic or linguistic differences.

D. Insufficient information. There is no indication of whether the elections are perceived as fair and free or not.

141. A

A. Correct. Tuberculosis is listed as a major disease and one of their priorities.

B. Wrong. They finance an effort to combat consumption of tobacco.

C. Wrong. This is merely the budget on promoting healthy living etc.

D. Wrong. It states that there is already funding for gender issues.

142. A

A. Correct. Ireland is now one of the wealthiest countries but Luxembourg is the wealthiest.

B. Wrong. It is GDP per capita that is the standard measure.

C. Insufficient information. There is no mention of how much benefit Romania and Bulgaria have received since joining.

D. Insufficient information. It is a goal to improve the wealth of the newer members but it doesn't state whether it should be done by emulating Ireland.

143. B

A. Insufficient information. There is no specific mention of Slovenia's circumstances.

B. Correct. The Cohesion Policy focuses on convergence which means eliminating disadvantages such as "poor quality schools" and "higher joblessness".

C. Wrong. The €350 billion is 36% of their total budget.

D. Wrong. It states: "The EU has used the entry of these countries to reorganise and restructure its regional spending."

144. A

A. Correct. The Cohesion Fund is for, amongst other things, "the development of renewable energy".

B. Wrong. The money comes from three different sources, the ERDF, the ESF and the Cohesion fund.

C. Insufficient information. There is no specific information about the distribution of the poorer regions.

D. Insufficient information. The ERDF cover various types of projects which may create jobs but it doesn't explicitly say so.

145. A

A. Correct. 'In addition to agreeing to delete the data, Google signed a commitment to improve data handling…'

B. Insufficient information. We are not told about the volume of data gathered by the camera-equipped cars.

C. Incorrect. The data was unintentionally gathered.

D. Insufficient information. There is no indication that there have been any other countries addressing this issue.

146. C

A. Insufficient information. We are told the 17 countries have at least one region with a GDP below 75% of the EU average be we cannot tell whether any or all of them are below 75% overall.

B. Wrong. Only 17 do. The remaining 10 can only claim "...for funding to support innovation and research, sustainable development, and job training..."

C. Correct. The fund reserved for regions with a GDP below 75% of the EU average concerns 17 of the 27 countries.

D. Wrong. The policy is to dovetail with the Lisbon agenda.

147. A

A. Correct. The EU matches private investment so closing the gap is a joint effort.

B. Wrong. It states that the EU must improve its record in this area.

C. Insufficient information. There is no mention of how difficult the patent process is.

D. Wrong. It talks of the "new European Institute" so it cannot have long promoted anything.

148. B

A. Insufficient information. It states that the EU currently relies on other countries but there is no indication which countries they may be.

B. Correct. The EU does want to be less reliant on other countries and GPS is a key reason.

C. Insufficient information. It does state that the Global Monitoring for Environment and Security wants to "deal with … security crises" which could mean "develop defensive weapons in space" but there is no indication that this is one of the primary aims.

D. Wrong. The current system has no support for search-and-rescue. This is a proposed addition for the new system.

149. A

A. Correct. It states that they keep an eye on the decisions of governments to see that they are fair.

B. Wrong. It says that governments set the taxes but that the EU monitors them for fairness as these countries are bound by a code of conduct.

C. Insufficient information. There is no information given of how the EU might encourage taxes on individuals.

D. Wrong. A code of conduct prevents this kind of behaviour.

150. B

A. Incorrect. The text says that it was '…beyond anything that daily life needs…'

B. Correct. It says that the Babylonians were using this 4000 years ago, 1000 years before Pythagoras.

C. Insufficient information. Although the text states that Babylonians used many of the same methods, there is no indication that historians believe Pythagoras actually borrowed these ideas from them.

D. Insufficient information. There is no indication whether or not Nippur lies upon the Euphrates river.

4. Succeeding in Numerical Reasoning Tests

Introduction

It is often said that the difficulty in taking numerical reasoning tests lies not in finding the actual answer to the question but doing it within the limited time available. This observation is correct inasmuch as these tests do not require complex mathematical calculations but rather the ability to:

- *identify data relevant to answering the question from a larger set of information*
- *identify the quickest way to extract the answer from the relevant data*
- *discover one or several possible shortcuts that will allow us to arrive at the answer quickly*
- *determine the level of accuracy required to select the correct answer, and*
- *make quick mental calculations*

In order to be prepared for the above, there are certain aspects of numerical reasoning tests that we must be aware of.

First of all, the "alternative reality" of a numerical reasoning test is different from what we are used to in everyday life – relevant data is not provided in a clean format but is rather hidden among other pieces of information that we may call "noise". Our first task is to always identify what we will need to work with from the information provided and avoid getting bogged down in wondering why other data might also be present.

Secondly, such tests have a surprising tendency to reach back to basic mathematical skills that may in fact come naturally to a secondary school student but are often lost during later academic stages and at the workplace. It is essential to refresh our basic calculus (see for instance www.calculus.org or www.sosmath.com and other sites).

Also, many candidates dread the numerical reasoning test simply because it is based on mathematics and they have always considered this discipline their weakness. What we must realize here is that the "mathematical" aspect of numerical reasoning tests is rather basic – addition, subtraction, multiplication, division, fractions and percentages will always be sufficient to perform the necessary calculations. As we will see, in a large number of cases even such calculations are unnecessary and arriving at the correct answer is rather based on an intuitive insight or the realization of a relationship between figures that is in fact right in front of our eyes – we just need to learn to see it.

It is also useful to note here that, just like in the case of verbal reasoning, the broad term "numerical reasoning" may be used to designate various test types related to the handling of numbers, calculations and data, such as:

- **Computation tests** are basic tests that measure the speed at which the test-taker is able to make basic mental calculations such as addition, subtraction, multiplication and division (e.g. "how much is 45+19+52-38?").

- **Estimation tests** resemble computation tests in that the calculations to be made are very similar, but the numbers with which you have to work may be greater. The point of the test is not to measure ability to perform the actual calculation but rather the speed and accuracy at which candidates can approximate the result of the calculation. The aim is to select an answer option that will be close to what the result would be if the actual calculation was performed (e.g. 226 divided by 1000 is approximately 1/4).
- **Numerical reasoning tests** represent a higher level where the focus is not on the actual ability to make calculations but rather the insight required to find out which calculations need to be performed to arrive at the answer. In other words, applied reasoning is tested. These tests are usually text-based in which a certain scenario involving numbers is described – it is this situation that the test-taker is expected to interpret in mathematical terms. To take an example of such a scenario: "There are 300 people in a group. Each person in the group likes either coffee or tea. Five times as many people like coffee as tea. How many people in the group like tea?"
- **Data interpretation tests** are similar to the above but instead of using a text, a "scenario" or story as the input, the basis of the exercise is a data set presented in the form of a table, a chart, or any combination of these (e.g. "Based on the table's figures, how many more Spanish speaking people immigrated to Spain in 1990 than in 2000?")

EPSO's numerical reasoning tests are most closely modeled on the latter two test types. Yet it is easy to see how each subsequent test type in this "hierarchy" builds on skills and routine that is measured in a lower-level test type. Quick estimations can only be made if we can make quick calculations as well. When you are faced with text-based numerical reasoning tests and you need to find a way to arrive at the answer, once you have done that, you must actually perform the required calculations or estimations to end up with the correct figure. When it comes to data interpretation based on tables and charts, the task is very similar to those in a text-based numerical reasoning test, with the added twist of having the data presented in a tabular or graphical format.

Let's now turn our attention to a real numerical reasoning test item and see how the above skills come into play.

Mobile Phone Subscriptions in EU Member States (thousands)

	2005	**2006**	**2007**
Bulgaria	1594	1957	2451
Denmark	3799	4228	4982
Greece	5511	6824	9191
Poland	1759	1819	1928

What percentage of the mobile phone subscriptions shown did Denmark account for in 2005?

A. 10%; B. 20%; C. 30%; D. 40%; E. 50%.

Using the above sample test item, we can demonstrate how the above-described skills (data interpretation, numerical reasoning, estimation and computation) can be used to quickly and efficiently solve EPSO's numerical reasoning tests.

The first step is to interpret the data that we need to work with.

In the present case, the first step is to determine which figures from the table we actually need. The question concerns the number of mobile phone subscriptions in 2005, so we can concentrate on the 2005 column in the table knowing that all the other figures are irrelevant to the task.

Next, we need to figure out what calculations we actually need to perform – in other words, we apply our numerical reasoning skills to the task at hand. Since the question is about Denmark's share of the total number of mobile phone subscriptions in the four countries shown in the table, we need to calculate the total (by adding up the individual figures for the four countries), and then calculate Denmark's share in it (by dividing Denmark's share by the total). Finally, we need to convert the result of this division into a percentage figure (multiplying it by 100).

The next question we have to decide is whether we actually need to perform the exact above calculations at all. We can decide this by considering if there is any possibility of estimating certain results. Let's look at the four numbers we need to add up from this perspective:

1594

3799

5511

1759

Whenever making a decision about the use of estimation, we must take into account the answer options first. In our case, these are percentages which are quite far apart from one another: 10%, 20%, 30%, 40% and 50% - this will tell us that the level of accuracy required to answer the question is not too high and you can feel free to "guesstimate".

Looking at the numbers, we can see that they lend themselves quite nicely to rounding up and down. By doing this, we can arrive at some more "convenient" numbers:

1600 (rounded up)

3800 (rounded up)

5500 (rounded down)

1800 (rounded up)

Now that the numbers are easy to work with, we can perform some actual computation. Since all numbers end in 00, we can disregard those two digits and work with two-digit numbers as their relative proportions (percentages) will remain the same. Add up these four numbers to get to the total number of subscriptions:

16+38+55+18 = 127

Remember that we are looking for a percentage. This means that we do not need to add back the two zeroes – that would only be needed if we had to arrive at an actual value. Instead, we can just compare our total (127) with Denmark's number: 38.

38 / 127 = 0.296

To convert this to a percentage, simply multiply the number by 100:

0.296 x 100 = 29.6%

Remember at this point that we rounded all the numbers up and down a bit – this explains why our result is not exactly the same as any of the answer options provided. It is, however, overwhelmingly clear that it is closest to Answer C (30%), which will be the correct answer.

Let's take stock of what we did in solving this test problem:

1. We interpreted the data in the table.

2. We applied our reasoning to determine what calculations we needed to perform.
3. We made estimations to simplify our calculations.
4. Finally, we performed the actual calculations.

Hopefully, this example demonstrates how the various skills required for succeeding in numerical reasoning depend on one another. If you keep these simple principles in mind and follow the steps laid out above, you will gain a systematic approach to solving all numerical reasoning tests successfully. There are, of course, things to look out for in test items, traps to avoid and tactics to use and become accustomed to.

Based on the required skills and the aspects introduced above, we will provide an overview of the following:

- Mental calculus
- Order of magnitude
- Percentages and percentage points
- Estimation
- Equations
- Tables and charts

After reviewing these various methods and aspects, we will discuss how to approach numerical reasoning tests, what to focus on in each exercise and how to practice for the exam.

Mental Calculus

If you read through the information made available to candidates before the exam it will, based on recent data, be stated that an on-screen calculator may be used during the numerical reasoning test. EPSO may also make a physical calculator available for you to use at the exam centre. In light of this, you might be doubtful as to why it is so important to be able to perform quick mental calculations. There are several important reasons for this:

- The calculator provided may be quite slow to use and its layout may be unfamiliar to you, which might make its use counter-productive
- The calculator provided may be quite slow to use and its layout may be unfamiliar to you, which might make its use counter-productive
- There are certain calculations that are always faster to perform in your head
- Overreliance on a calculator may make you less intuitive and prevent you from realizing whether certain calculations are really required to answer the question

It is therefore strongly advised to first practice as if no calculators were provided and start to use such devices only later when you have learned all the necessary ways of carrying out calculations.

Fractions

As mentioned above, certain types of calculations can quite simply be performed more efficiently without any "technical assistance". One such example is the handling of fractions (as in the illustration below).

Consider the following scenario. We are looking for the proportion of households with broadband access among all households in Estonia. Based on the data provided, you will

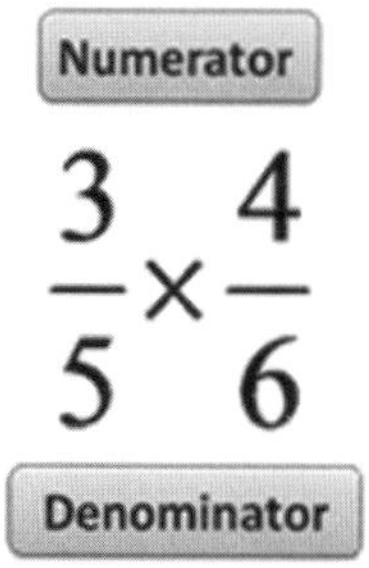

Numerator

$$\frac{3}{5} \times \frac{4}{6}$$

Denominator

realize that approximately three in five households in Estonia have an internet connection and among those, four in six have broadband access. One way of approaching this calculation would be to use the calculator to do the following:

3 ÷ 5 = 0.6 (proportion of households with internet access)

4 ÷ 6 = 0.666 (proportion of internet-connected households with broadband access, rounded to three decimal points)

0.6 * 0.666 = 0.3996 (proportion of households with broadband access among all households)

If we also have the total number of households, say 2,000,000, we then perform one additional calculation:

0.3996 * 2,000,000 = 799200

Let's see how this calculation would go without the use of a calculator, by using fractions:

3/5 x 4/6 = 12 / 30 (fractions are multiplied by multiplying the first numerator by the second numerator and the first denominator by the second denominator)

12 / 30 = 4 / 10 (we can then simplify the fraction by finding a number that both the numerator and the denominator can be divided by)

It is easy to see that the above two calculations can be performed very quickly bymental arithmetic. Also, the final figure we arrive at is extremely convenient – now we know that four in ten households have broadband internet access.

If we consider that there are 2,000,000 households, the remaining calculation will also be very simple:

2,000,000 / 10 = 200,000 (by removing one decimal, we will get the number equal to one in ten households)

200,000 x 4 = 800,000 (by multiplying that by 4, we get four-tenths of all households)

There are two observations to make here:

- We arrived at the required figure by making extremely simple calculations with easy, round numbers
- Using fractions is actually more accurate than the "calculator", because during the first method, we "truncated" one of the figures given its decimals

Calculations with Fractions

Multiplication:

$$\frac{3}{5} \times \frac{4}{6} = \frac{12}{30}$$

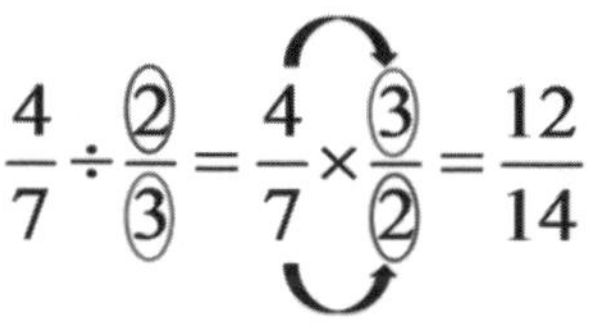

Division:

$$\frac{4}{7} \div \frac{2}{3} = \frac{4}{7} \times \frac{3}{2} = \frac{12}{14}$$

Addition and subtraction:

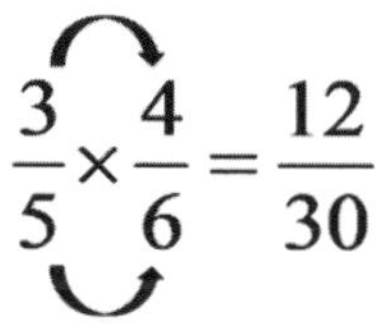

Lowest Common Multiple

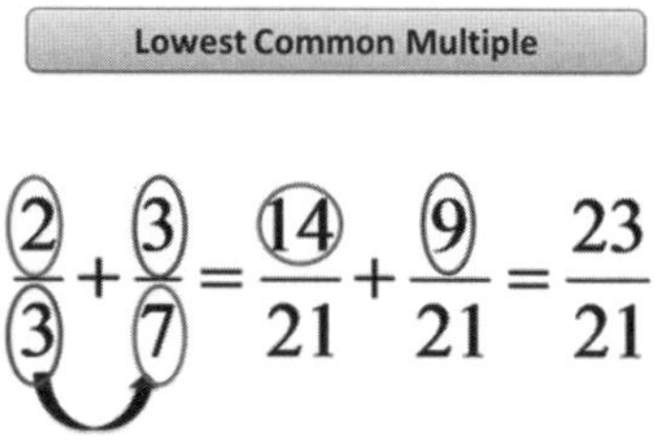

$$\frac{2}{3} + \frac{3}{7} = \frac{14}{21} + \frac{9}{21} = \frac{23}{21}$$

Multiplication

Method

If we need to multiply two fractions, we first multiply the two numerators (the numbers at the top) and then the two denominators (the numbers at the bottom).

Example of Application

Imagine that you are given a table showing Spain's population in millions. You are also given the following two pieces of information in the question text itself:

- one in five Spaniards considers sport to be their favourite hobby
- of those who consider sport as their favourite hobby, two out of three name football as their preferred choice

Your task is to calculate how many Spaniards consider football their favourite hobby. A quick answer to this question can be found using fractions.

"One in five can be described as $^1/_5$ and "two out of three" can be described as $^2/_3$. Based on this, the calculation would go as follows:

Number of Spaniards with Football as Favourite Hobby

= Population x $^1/_5$ *x* $^2/_3$ = $^2/_{15}$ *x Population*

Now we can perform a simple calculation with the data above. We divide Spain's population by 15 and multiply the result by 2, and our task is complete.

Division

Method

If we need to divide a fraction by another fraction, our first task is to turn the operation into multiplication. We do this by 'inverting' the numerator and the denominator in one of the fractions. This way, $^2/_3$ would become $^3/_2$, and so on.

Next, we multiply the two numerators and then the two denominators in the same way as we do when multiplying fractions.

Example of Application

Imagine that you are given the following information:

40% of Thailand's annual rice production is equal to half of China's annual rice consumption. If all of China's rice consumption would be covered by imports from Thailand, what percentage of Thailand's production would need to be imported?

We can transcribe the above information with fractions as follows.

$^4/_{10}$ *x Thailand's production* = $^1/_2$ *x China's consumption*

We are looking for China's total consumption in terms of Thailand's total production. This means that we want only China's total consumption on one side of the equation, so we need to divide both sides of the equation by $^1/_2$.

China's consumption = $^4/_{10} \div ^1/_2$ x Thailand's production

We can now invert the numerator and the denominator (say, in the second fraction) and then perform the multiplication as described above.

China's consumption = $\frac{4}{10} \times \frac{2}{1} = \frac{8}{10}$ *x Thailand's production*

The answer to the question is, then, that China's rice consumption is equal to 80% of Thailand's rice production.

Addition and Subtraction

Method

When adding or subtracting fractions, we need to make sure first that the denominators are the same in both fractions. We can achieve this by finding the smallest number that can be divided by both denominators. If our two denominators are 3 and 7, as in the illustration at the start of this section, that number will be 21. Once we have done that, we need to multiply the numerators by the same number as the one with which we had to multiply the denominator in the same fraction. In the illustration, the numerator in the left fraction needs to be multiplied by 7 and the numerator in the right fraction needs to be multiplied by 3.

The last step is to simply add up the two numerators.

Example of Application

Imagine that you have the following two pieces of information:

- three in ten Germans believe that the budget deficit needs to be reduced
- three in five Germans believe that the budget deficit needs to be kept at the current level

Based on the wording of the above, we can be sure that there is no overlap between the two groups – one group believes in reduction, the other in maintaining the current level.

We are looking for the following data:

What percentage of Germans believes that the budget deficit needs to be kept at the current level or reduced?

To answer the above question with fractions, we need to express "three in ten" and "three in five" in the form of fractions and then add up the two.

"three in ten" = $\frac{3}{10}$

"three in five" = $\frac{3}{5}$

The proportion we are looking for, then, is as follows:

$\frac{3}{10} + \frac{3}{5}$

We will notice that in this particular case, only the second fraction will need to be "converted". If we multiply both the numerator and the denominator of that fraction by 2, the two denominators will be identical and we can perform the addition.

$\frac{3}{10} + \frac{3}{5} = \frac{3}{10} + \frac{6}{10} = \frac{9}{10} = 90\%$

By using fractions, we can answer the question by saying that 90% of Germans believe the budget deficit needs to be reduced or at least kept at current levels.

When solving numerical reasoning tests, it is always worth considering for a second whether we can take advantage of fractions – they are an extremely powerful tool in reducing seemingly complex relationships into the simplest of calculations.

Order of Magnitude

Nuclear Electricity Generation in the EU

		Electricity Generated (millions MWh)		
	Population in 2005 (thousands)	***2005***	***2006***	***2007***
France	61013	452	446	440
Hungary	10078	163	158	150
Poland	38198	44	51	67
Ukraine	46936	87	90	93

How many MWh did France generate on average for each person in the country in 2005?

A. 0.74

B. 7.4

C. 74

D. 740

E. 7400

An order of magnitude is a scale of amounts where each amount is in a fixed ratio to the amount preceding it. The most common ratio is 1:10, which means that the next amount in a scale can be calculated by multiplying the previous figure by 10.

For example: 1, 10, 100, 1000, 10000 …and so on…

If we look at the above answer options, we can see that that is exactly the situation we have here:

0.74, 7.4, 74, 740, 7400

When we are faced with a set of numbers like the ones above, it gives us an important hint that the actual calculation of the figure may not really be necessary – all we need to figure out is the order of magnitude of the correct answer.

Let us consider the above sample test from the perspective of whether we can take advantage of this observation.

We have the following information:

- The amount of nuclear energy France generated in 2005 – in million MWh – **452**
- The population of France in thousands – **61013**

Since the answer options only differ in their order of magnitude, we can be quite flexible in rounding our number up or down to simplify our calculations.

Let us round 452 down to 450 and 61013 down to 60000. You can disregard the exact number of digits for a second. What is the relationship between the numbers 45 and 60? If you think for a second about time (45 minutes out of 60), you will realize that 45/60 is equal to three quarters. Expressed in decimal terms, this is 0.75. Our answer options include the digits 7 and 4 – this difference is caused by having rounded down the numbers.

Remember – we do not need to be particularly accurate in this case, all that we are looking for is the number of digits in the correct answer. Now turn your attention to those zeroes we disregarded so far.

Energy Production: 452 million MWh – we will need to add six zeroes here: **452,000,000 MWh**

Population: 61013 thousand – we will need to add three zeroes here: **61,013, 000**

If we turn back to our simplified figures, our calculation would look like this:

450 million divided by 60 million

We could use a calculator to obtain the result here, but let us recall what we said about time above – 45 minutes out of 60 minutes is three quarters, that is, 0.75. So, if the electricity generation was 45 million instead of 450 million, our two numbers would be:

45 million divided by 60 million – this would correspond to three quarters, that is, 0.75 – the closest answer option to this would be Answer A. We, however, removed one zero from the end of our electricity generation figure just now, which we need to add back. Adding a 'zero' to a figure is the equivalent of multiplying it by 10:

0.75 x 10 = 7.5

The above is closest to Answer B and that is the correct answer.

Percentages and Percentage points

The information in this section may seem trivial, yet mixing up two concepts (*percentage change* and *percentage point change*) can prove fatal when taking a numerical reasoning test.

Let us consider the following example (some lines are blocked out):

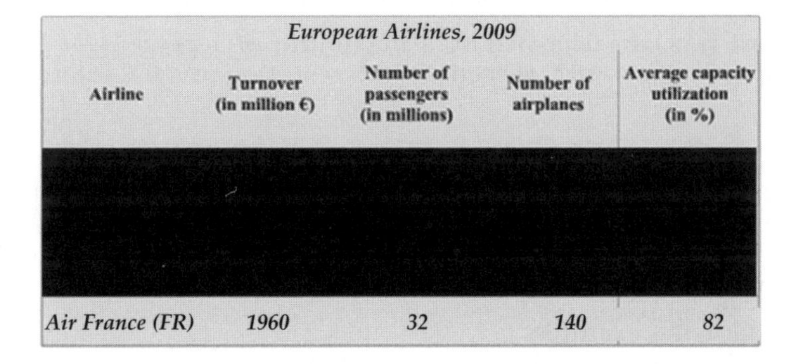

European Airlines, 2009

Airline	Turnover (in million €)	Number of passengers (in millions)	Number of airplanes	Average capacity utilization (in %)
Air France (FR)	*1960*	*32*	*140*	*82*

In many numerical reasoning tests, you will be faced with data where calculation of the correct answer will require working with percentages. A straightforward case is where one figure (for example the number of television sets in Italy) is an amount, and the other factor (for example the proportion of high-definition capable devices) is a percentage. In such cases, the calculation is obvious:

Number of television sets * Percentage of high-definition devices

Let us, however, consider another example. There are cases when both figures are proportions or percentages. What happens when the first piece of data (the capacity utilisation of Air France airplanes) and the second piece of data (the % change in capacity utilisation, for example) are both percentages?

Suppose that the question based on the above table is the following:

"How much was the capacity utilisation of Air France in 2008 if its capacity utilisation was 10% worse than in 2009?"

In the above example, where 82% capacity utilisation decreases by 10%, our natural instinct would be to perform the following calculation:

82% -10% = 72%, therefore the capacity utilisation in 2008 was 72%.

Not surprisingly, this would *not* be the correct answer. For comparison, keep in mind how we would calculate a 10% decrease of a regular amount, for example 550:

550 * (1 – 10%) = 550 * 90% = 550 * 0.9 = 495

Now apply the above logic to capacity utilisation:

82% * (1-10%) = 82% * 90% = 82% * 0.9 = 73.8%

We can see that the correct calculation yields a significantly different result from what our initial instinct suggested.

When it comes to percentage changes in values that are themselves percentages, what many people consider a 10 per cent change (for example 82% to 72%) is in fact a 10 *percentage point* change.

Through an intuitive example, we will be able to appreciate the fundamental difference between the two concepts.

Suppose that an imaginary central bank in the EU has an interest rate of 10%. Now let's take a look at possible changes to this interest rate:

- If the interest rate drops by 9 *percentage points*, the new interest rate will be 1%
- If the interest rate drops by 9 *percent*, the new interest rate will be 9.1%
- A 1% interest rate can decrease by a maximum of 1 percentage point, but it can decrease by as much as 100 per cent – both resulting in a 0% interest rate

Estimation

In a previous section, when calculating the per-capita electricity generation of France, we applied a sort of estimation to get to the correct answer. In that case, the estimation took the form of concentrating only on the number of digits in the correct answer. There are cases, however, where we need to be a little more precise than that.

Consider the following example:

European Airlines, 2009				
Airline	**Turnover (in million €)**	**Number of passengers (in millions)**	**Number of airplanes**	**Average capacity utilization (in %)**
Air France (FR)	*1960*	*32*	*140*	*82*

"Based on the above table, how many passengers would Air France have transported in 2009 if its capacity utilisation had been 10% worse?"

a) 28.8 million

b) 23.6 million

c) 35.2 million

d) 35.9 million

Again, let us first consider the less innovative (and therefore more time-consuming) way of calculating the correct answer first.
The data we will work with are:

- Number of passengers in millions
- Capacity utilisation %
- The fact that capacity utilisation decreased by 10% as compared to the actual figure in the table

The first thing we would do is calculate the new capacity utilisation. An important point to mention here is the difference between percentage change and percentage point change, as discussed above.

New capacity utilisation = 82% * (1 – 10%) = 82% * 90% = 82% * 0.9 = 73.8%

One mistake we could make here is equating the figure for new number of passengers transported with the following:

32 million * 73.8% = 32 million * 0.738 = 23.616 million

Why is the above calculation incorrect? We must bear in mind that the number 32 million is actually equal to 82% of the total capacity of Air France, since its capacity utilisation according to the table was 82%.

We also know the new capacity utilisation figure (73.8%), but we must also calculate total capacity (X). We know the following:

X * 0.82 = 32 million (82% of the total capacity is 32 million passengers)

Let's solve the equation for X:

X = 32 million / 0.82 = 39.02 million

We can now calculate the number of passengers transported at 73.8% capacity utilisation:

39.02 * 0.738 = 28.8 million

Answer A is in fact the correct answer.

While the above series of calculations were all correct, we must always be suspicious when so many raw calculations are required to get to the correct answer. Do not forget that numerical reasoning is not a mathematical exercise in the first place so this might be a hint that an easier solution may exist.
We need to make two observations here:

- Some of the data is irrelevant
- The "distance" among the values in the answer options allows for estimation

Let's look at the first problem. As the question referred to average capacity utilisation, we immediately started to work with that number. However, we should reconsider the meaning of this term. If average capacity utilisation decreases by 10%, is this not the same as saying that Air France transported 10% fewer passengers?

This immediately simplifies our calculation:

32 million passengers - 10% = 32 million passengers * 90% = 32 million passengers * 0.9

`Now let us look at the answer options again:

a) 28.8 million

b) 23.6 million

c) 35.2 million

d) 35.9 million

`Answers C and D can be immediately ruled out because those numbers are larger than the 32 million in the table, which is impossible when the capacity utilisation decreases.

Answer B has a smaller number, but if we estimate 10% of 32 million (circa 0.3 million, or exactly 0.32 million) we will immediately see that Answer B's 2.36 million is too small an amount, which leaves only Answer A as a feasible option.

The correctness of Answer A can also be verified very quickly, with a simple subtraction:

3.2 million – 0.32 million = 3.2 million – (0.2 million + 0.12 million) = 3 million – 0.12 million = 2.88 million.

The above calculation also shows an example of how to make subtractions easier. In this example, we reformulated 0.32 million as 0.2 million + 0.12 million so it became much easier to first subtract 0.2 million from 3.2 million (leaving the round number of 3 million), and then deal with the rest.

Equations

Equations might sound too mathematical, yet they are a brilliantly inventive ways of dealing with problems where multiple calculations must be made. Consider this:

"There are 12,450 applicants for an exam. Out of them, 60% pass the first round, of these 40% pass the second round, of whom the last 500 performers are excluded. Eventually how many people get a job if only the best 25% of the remaining are selected?"

a) 747

b) 518

c) 622

d) 875

One way of approaching the problem would be to perform a series of calculations. First, we would calculate 60% of 12,450, then 40% of the resulting number, then we would subtract 500 from that number, and finally, we would calculate 25% of this last intermediate amount.

By denoting the number of people who get a job (which is the answer we are looking for) by X, we can create an equation which will make our lives much easier and the calculation significantly faster:

X = (12450 * 0.6 * 0.4 – 500) * 0.25 (where 0.6 equals 60%, 0.4 equal 40%, and 0.25 equals 25%)

We can further simplify the equation:

X = (12450 * 0.24 – 500) * 0.25

Since the answer options are quite far apart, we could also use some estimations and rounding up or down:

X ≈ (12000 / 4 – 500) / 4 (where 12450 is rounded down to 12000, 0.24 is rounded up to 1/4, and 0.25 is converted to 1/4 as well)

X ≈ (3000 – 500) / 4 = 2500 / 4 = 625

625 is closest to Answer C, so that will be the correct answer.

Tables and Charts

European Airlines, 2009				
Airline	**Turnover (in million €)**	**Number of passengers (in millions)**	**Number of airplanes**	**Average capacity utilization (in %)**
Swiss (CH)	*1 570*	*19.7*	*93*	*72*
British Airways (GBR)	*2 600*	*36.8*	*13.7*	*84*
Lufthansa (GER)	*2 237*	*46.1*	*137*	*82*
Air France (FR)	*1960*	*32*	*140*	*82*

"Based on the above table, how many passengers would Air France have transported in 2009 if its capacity utilisation had been 10% worse?"

a) 28.8 million

b) 23.6 million

c) 35.2 million

d) 35.9 million

The above table may seem familiar. This is because we previously used a version of this table with some rows "blacked out" for demonstrating certain methods. In real numerical tests, however, the table always contains lots of superfluous data that you will not need for your calculations – this is what I called "noise" in the introduction. When starting to solve a numerical reasoning question, it is always important to first decide which data is necessary for the calculation because the superfluous information will just confuse you and can take valuable time if you become distracted.

European Airlines, 2009				
Airline	**Turnover (in million €)**	**Number of passengers (in millions)**	**Number of airplanes**	**Average capacity utilization (in %)**
Air France (FR)	*1960*	*32*	*140*	*82*

For this reason, it is often suggested to mentally "black out" that data from the table which you will not need. In this instance, the first thing we will realize is that we can make no use of the data about the other three airlines (SWISS, Lufthansa, British Airways).

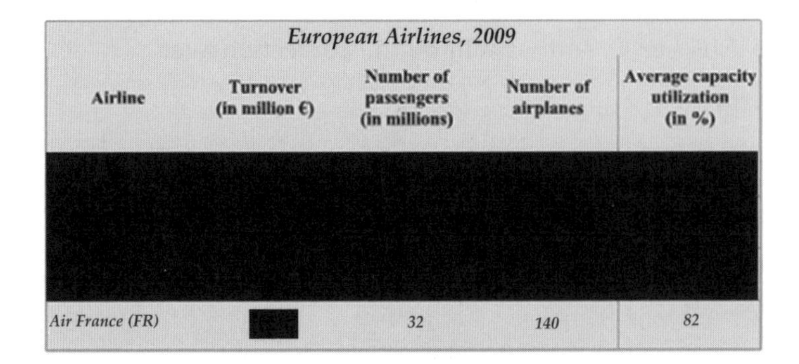

European Airlines, 2009

Airline	Turnover (in million €)	Number of passengers (in millions)	Number of airplanes	Average capacity utilization (in %)
Air France (FR)		32	140	82

Since the question refers to the number of passengers transported, we will certainly not need turnover data to answer the question:

Based on our reasoning in the section on Estimation, we will also realize that the *number of airplanes* is a superfluous figure, as is *average capacity utilisation*:

If we systematically exclude all superfluous data, the task will seem significantly less

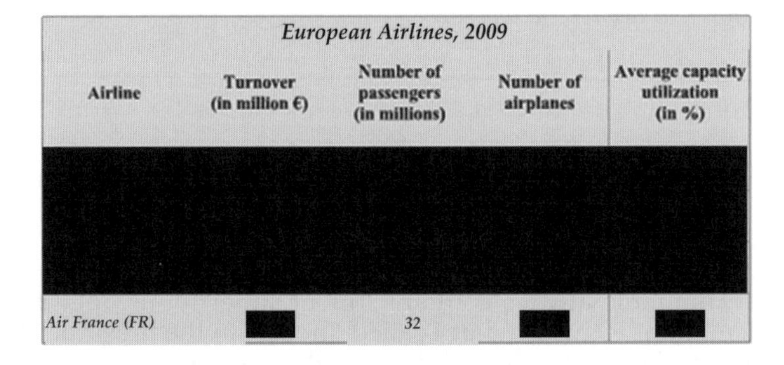

European Airlines, 2009

Airline	Turnover (in million €)	Number of passengers (in millions)	Number of airplanes	Average capacity utilization (in %)
Air France (FR)		32		

complicated. As it turns out, in our example, the table's only purpose is to tell us that Air France transported 32 million passengers in 2009. The other piece of information we will use (the 10% decrease in average capacity utilisation, and therefore 10% decrease in passengers transported) is supplied in the question, not the table.

How to Approach Numerical Reasoning Tests

The above sections demonstrated the number of factors we must consider to be able to efficiently solve the problems posed in numerical reasoning tests. Consider aspects such as the required level of accuracy, the relevance of data or the possibility of estimation, then decide the approach to take – whether to perform raw calculations, apply estimates, draw up an equation, or simply read a relationship or a trend off a chart.

As is true in the case of verbal and abstract reasoning tests, a systematic approach will make your test-taking experience much more efficient. Below, you will find a a summary of the recommended approach:

1. Read the question and the answer options first as carefully as possible.
2. The question will help you identify which data sets will be relevant and necessary for answering the question and know what to ignore.
3. Looking at the answer options will help you decide the level of accuracy required. If, for example, the values in the answer options are very far apart, you may consider estimation.
4. Based on the question, determine the relevant information and mentally "black out" the unnecessary data.
5. Having looked at the answer options and the data in the table, you can now make a final decision about whether to go for an exact figure or make an estimate, whether to use an equation, and so on.
6. Make sure you exclude all unrealistic answer options (for example numbers representing an increase when the question refers to a decrease).
7. Once you have performed your calculations, you can match the result against the remaining answer options. If you estimated, look for the answer option closest to your estimated result. If the result is significantly closer to one answer option than to all others, you were probably on the right track.

Practice Methods

Finally, a few suggestions for how to practice for the numerical reasoning test:

- Start your practice by identifying your weaknesses. Percentages? Subtraction? Estimation? Equations? Calculus in general?
- Once you have identified your weaknesses, you can pointedly practice these operations either by creating problems of your own or selecting practice tests where these calculations come into play
- Once you have gained the necessary routine using all of these methods (and maybe further ones online), you can start practicing with tests that are similar to the real exam – for example the ones in this book
- Check the available time at the real exam and the number of questions to be answered
- Start without timing yourself at first but solve the same number of test questions as at the exam (usually around 20-30). Measure the average time you require.
- Start decreasing the time needed to answer the questions so it gets closer to the time available at the exam
- Ideally, by the time of the exam, you should be able to answer more questions in the time available than required at the exam, because you cannot account for stress and other outside factors are impossible to recreate at home
- The EPSO test will be administered on a computer, which will make it much more challenging (and stranger) to take than a paper-based test where you can scribble on the paper and make quick calculations, write down equations, underline key concepts and so on – if you have access to such services, try to practice online
- Try to practice with materials that offer detailed explanations of why a certain answer option is correct and how to efficiently perform the required calculations – various textbooks and online resources offer such services.

5. Numerical Reasoning Test

150 QUESTIONS – ANSWERS follow questions

Passport Applications (Questions 1-3)				
	Population in 2005 (thousands)	*New Applications (thousands)*	*Renewal Applications (thousands)*	*Replacement Applications*
Austria	8387	72	474	9610
Belgium	10698	126	589	21080
Denmark	5481	49	378	1100
Netherlands	16653	181	1090	42900
Portugal	10732	81	432	1900

1. If the table were ordered by total number of applications per capita, which country would be in the middle?

A. Austria

B. Belgium

C. Denmark

D. Netherlands

E. Portugal

2. The population of Denmark rose by 0.2% per year between 2005 and 2010 and the per capita rate of new applications rose by 3.2% over the 5 years. How many applications for new passports were there in Denmark in 2010?

A. 49090

B. 50280

C. 50870

D. 51076

E. 51382

3. How many more passport renewal applications would Austria have needed, to have had the same per capita rate as the Netherlands?

A. 55000

B. 60000

C. 65000

D. 70000

E. 75000

Accidental Death Rates (Questions 4-6)					
	Population in 2005 (thousands)	*Number of Deaths per 100,000*			
		2004	*2005*	*2006*	*2007*
France	61013	28.1	28.2	27.9	27.1
Belgium	10415	26.9	26.4	26.2	25.5
UK	60261	23.8	23.9	23.7	22.9
Ireland	4187	34.0	34.1	33.6	31.6
Italy	58645	33.1	32.9	32.2	31.6

4. If the population of France increases by 16,000 each year, how many fewer accidental deaths were there in France in 2007 than in 2004?

A. 597

B. 610

C. 649

D. 688

E. 721

5. If the population of Ireland is increasing by 0.2% per year, what is the percentage fall in number of deaths per year from 2004 to 2007?

A. 5.5%

B. 6.0%

C. 6.5%

D. 7.0%

E. 7.5%

6. What percentage of the total deaths shown in 2005 were in Italy?

A. 20%

B. 25%

C. 30%

D. 35%

E. 40%

TABLE FOR QUESTION 7

Juices sold in 2004 (m. boxes)	*Grapefruits*	*Orange*	*Pear*
Company A	12	20	14
Company B	4	37	19
Company C	27	23	8

Income from all juices sold (millions in €)	*2003*	*2004*	*2005*
Company A	180	200	220
Company B	225	240	210
Company C	280	225	300

7. If grapefruits are the same price as oranges and a third of the price of pears how many million euros income did Company C have in 2004 from oranges?

A. 45

B. Cannot tell

C. 109

D. 69

Increase in Hungary's exports by country group, 2008 (Q. 8-10)

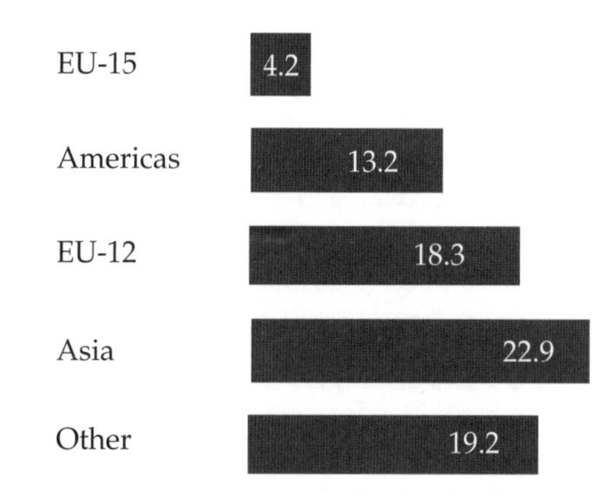

(EU-15: member states of the EU before May 1, 2004)
(EU-12: the 12 newest member states of the EU)

Distribution of Hungary's exports by country group, 2008 (Q. 8-10)

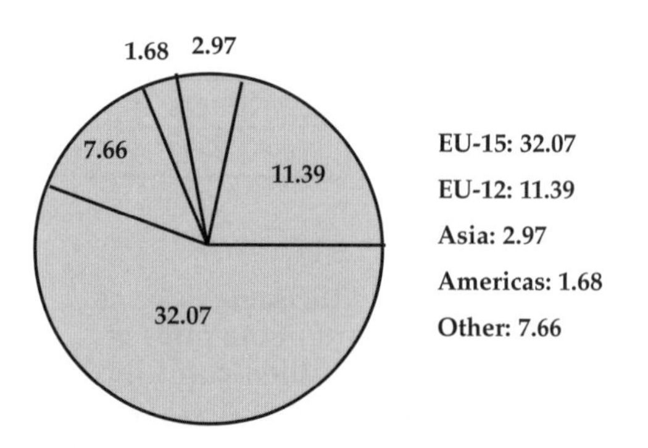

(January-September 2008, billion EUR)

(EU-15: member states of the EU before May 1, 2004)
(EU-12: the 12 newest member states of the EU)

8. Based on the diagrams, by approximately what percentage did the value of Hungarian exports to the European Union increase from the period January-September 2007 to the same period in 2008?

A. 8%
B. 11%
C. 14%
D. 23%

9. Based on the diagrams, what percentage of the value of Hungarian exports to Asia in the period January-September 2007 did the same figure for the Americas account for?

A 33%
B 52%
C 61%
D 73%

10. Based on the diagrams, how did Asia's share of Hungary's exports change from the period January-September 2007 to the same period in 2008?

A. Decreased by 9%
B. Increased by 12%
C. Decreased by 19%
D. Decreased by 23%

Child Mortality (Q. 11-13)

	No. of Under-5s in 2005 (thousands)	*No. of Under-5s in 2010 (thousands)*
Belgium	1042	1070
Czech Republic	1019	1041
Finland	524	535
Macedonia	204	205
Portugal	1055	1073

Number of under 5 deaths (Q. 11-13)

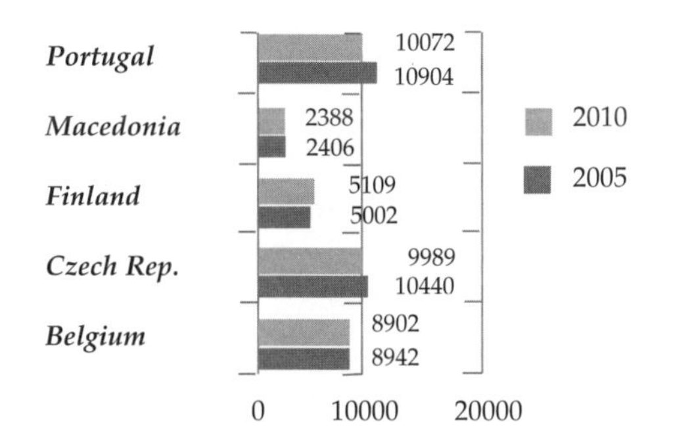

11 . If the table were ordered by deaths per 1000 children under-5 in 2005, which country would be in the middle?

A. Belgium

B. Czech Republic

C. Finland

D. Macedonia

E. Portugal

12 . What was the percentage decrease in deaths per 1000 children in Belgium from 2005 to 2010?

A. 3.1%

B. 2.7%

C. 4.2%

D. 2.1%

E. 3.8%

13. What percentage of the total under-5 deaths shown in 2010 occurred in Portugal?

A. 21.8%

B. 33.2%

C. 28.2%

D. 36.7%

E. 25.6%

Indebtedness in the Visegrad countries, 2007, Q. 14

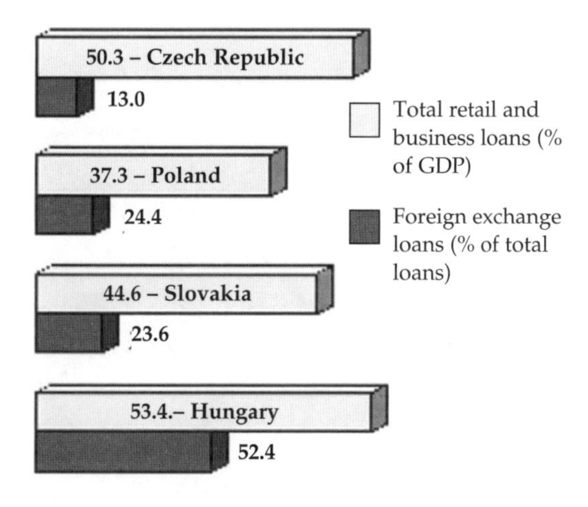

(Source: RZB Group)

14. Based on the diagram and the fact that Hungary's GDP was double that of Slovakia in 2007, how many percent less was the amount of foreign exchange loans in Slovakia than in Hungary?

A. 58%

B. 62%

C. 77%

D. 81%

TABLE FOR QUESTION 15

GDP (US$ bn) and social expenditure (% of GDP) of various countries

	1990		2005	
	GDP	*Soc.exp.*	*GDP*	*soc.exp.*
Denmark	95.1	25.1%	179.9	26.9%
France	1007.4	25.1%	1869.4	29.2%
Germany	1462.8	22.3%	2586.5	26.7%
Ireland	45.7	14.9%	160.4	16.7%
Netherlands	264.1	25.6%	572.8	20.7%
Norway	76.0	22.3%	218.7	21.6%

Source: OECD

15. Assuming that in the Netherlands, both the GDP and the absolute amount of social expenditure increased linearly (by the same amount every year) between 1990 and 2005, what percentage of the GDP did social expenditure account for in 1996?

A. 17.4% B. 22.0%

C. 22.7% D. 23.7%

E. 24.5% F. 33.5%

TABLE FOR QUESTION 16

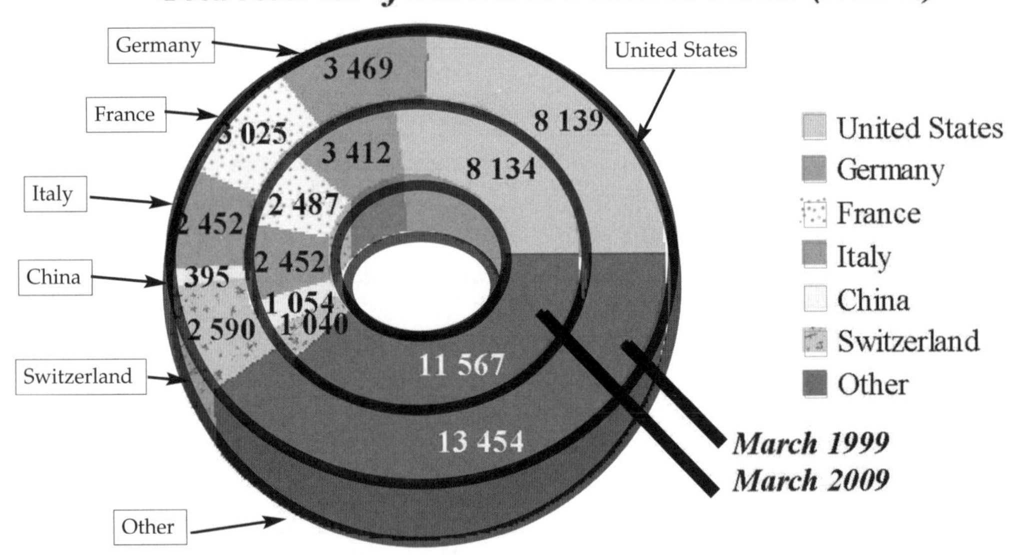

16. How did the market value of the gold reserves of Switzerland's central bank change between March 1999 and March 2009 given that in this period, the world price of gold increased from 286 USD per ounce to 886 USD per ounce? (1 ounce = 31.1 grams)

A. Increased by 0.58 billion USD

B. Increased by 5.81 billion USD

C. Increased by 58.1 billion USD

D. Decreased by 0.64 billion USD

E. Decreased by 6.42 billion USD

F. Decreased by 64.2 billion USD

TABLES FOR QUESTION 17

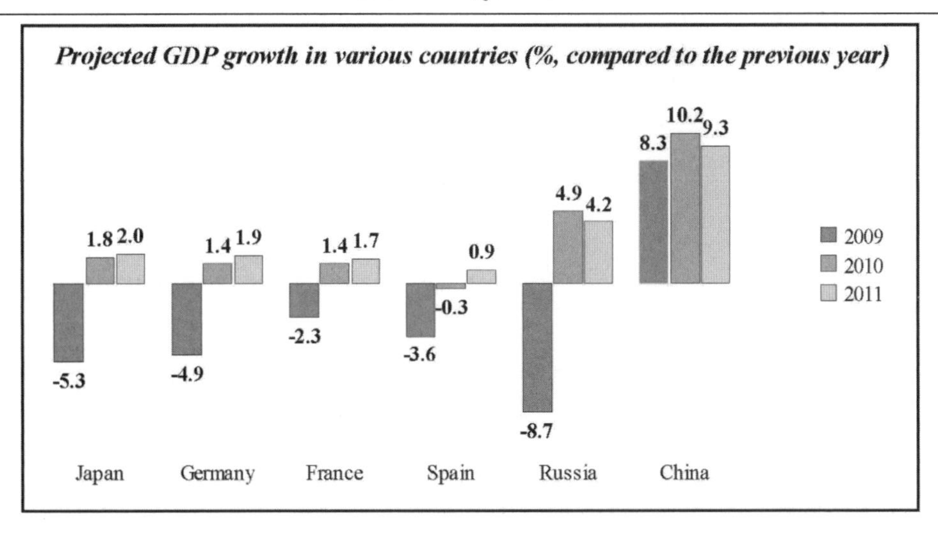

GDP of various countries, 2008 (billion USD)

China	7,992	Japan	4,340	Germany	2,925
Russia	2,271	France	2,133	Spain	1,402

17. What, expressed as a percentage of Spain's GDP, is Russia's GDP projected to be in 2011?

A. 59.6%
B. 61.7%
C. 65.2%
D. 162.0%
E. 166.7%
F. 169.4%

Paper Recycling in Europe (Q18-20)					
	Population in 2005 (thousands)	Paper Recycled (thousand tonnes)			
		2004	2005	2006	2007
Albania	3111	37	40	51	59
Channel Islands	149	4.1	4.8	4.9	5.1
Estonia	1347	26	28	31	38
Luxembourg	464	51	54	60	62
Slovenia	2001	17	18	20.2	24.1

18. If the table shown was ordered by percentage growth in recycling paper from 2004 to 2007, which country would be in the middle?

A. Albania
B. Channel Islands
C. Estonia
D. Luxembourg
E. Slovenia

19. If the population of Albania increases by 0.3% each year, what is the per capita increase in paper recycling in Albania from 2005 to 2007?

A. 28.2%
B. 46.6%
C. 31.9%
D. 51.3%
E. 39.8%

20. Assuming the populations remained constant, how many more tonnes of paper would Estonia have needed to recycle in 2007 to equal the Channel Islands' per capita recycle rate?

A. 46100 tonnes B. 38300 tonnes

C. 23900 tonnes D. 15200 tonnes

E. 8100 tonnes

TABLE FOR QUESTION 21

	Total area (sq. km)	*Population (1000s)*	*GDP/ inhabitants*	*Inflation %*
A	30 500	5 300	27 530	2.8
B	93 000	10 200	11 840	9.1
C	90 000	10 200	16 920	4.9
D	450 000	8 999	23 130	2.0
E	200 001	59 000	23 160	1.9

21. What is the average inflation rate in the five countries?

A. 2.5%

B. 4.1%

C. 5.1%

D. 6.3%

TABLE FOR QUESTION 22

PRODUCTION AND TRADE DATA IN NOVEMBER 2005 (WIRE & WIRE LTD.)

All lengths in metres (100s)	*Bare copper wire*	*Tinned copper wire*	*PTFE silver plated copper cable*	*Gold plated copper wire*
Production (100s)	100	150	30	20
Production costs per m in €	1	2	4	10
income per m in €	2	3	10	20
export (100s)	80	90	10	20

22. What is the ratio between the total production of all types of wire and the quantity sold for export?

A. 3 : 2 B. 2 : 3

C. 4 : 3 D. 3 : 4

TABLE FOR QUESTION 23

INCOME FROM CERTAIN INDUSTRIAL PRODUCTS (in billion euros)

Products	*2001*	*2002*	*2003*	*2004*	*2005*
Cars	50	52	53	55	58
Buses	33	35	32	32	32
Trucks	40	44	45	46	49
Boats	8	12	11	15	14
Airplanes	40	40	30	40	50
Helicopters	20	22	20	22	20

23. How many industries made a gain of 20% or more between 2002 and 2004?

A. 0 B. 1

C. 2 D. 3

TABLE FOR QUESTION 24

Juices sold in 2004 (m. boxes)	*Grapefruits*	*Orange*	*Pear*
Company A	12	20	14
Company B	4	37	19
Company C	27	23	8

Income from all juices sold (millions in €)	*2003*	*2004*	*2005*
Company A	180	200	220
Company B	225	240	210
Company C	280	225	300

24. How much money in million euros did Company B get in 2004 from pear juice if all juices are sold at the same price?

A. 80 B. 76

C. 120 D. 48

TABLE FOR QUESTION 25

GDP (US$ bn) and social expenditure (% of GDP) of various countries

	1990		2005	
	GDP	Soc.exp.	GDP	soc.exp.
Denmark	95.1	25.1%	179.9	26.9%
France	1007.4	25.1%	1869.4	29.2%
Germany	1462.8	22.3%	2586.5	26.7%
Ireland	45.7	14.9%	160.4	16.7%
Netherlands	264.1	25.6%	572.8	20.7%
Norway	76.0	22.3%	218.7	21.6%

Source: OECD

25. In how many of the six countries did the GDP increase by more than 200% between 1990 and 2005?

A. one B. two

C. three D. four

E. five F. six

TABLES FOR QUESTION 26

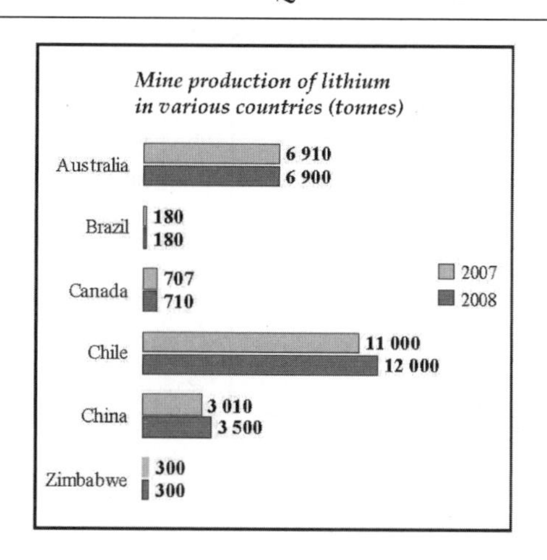

Proven lithium reserves in various countries, end of 2008 (thousand tonnes)

Australia	220	Brazil	910
Canada	360	Chile	3 000
China	1 100	Zimbabwe	27

Source: US Geological Survey

26. If the amount of lithium produced in the six countries together increases by the same percentage from 2008 to 2009 as from 2007 to 2008, how many thousand tonnes of lithium will be produced in the six countries together in 2009?

A. 20.9 B. 22.1

C. 23.6 D. 25.2

E. 26.4 F. 27.4

TABLE FOR QUESTION 27

Total population and population projections (end of year, million inhabitants)

	2007	2020	2040	2060
EU 27	495.1	513.8	520.1	505.7
Belgium	10.6	11.3	12.0	12.3
Czech Republic	10.3	10.5	10.2	9.5
Poland	38.1	38.0	35.2	31.1
Romania	21.6	20.8	19.2	16.9
Sweden	9.1	9.9	10.5	10.9
United Kingdom	60.9	65.7	72.0	76.7

27. Assuming that the population of Sweden increases by the same amount every year between 2020 and 2040, in which year is it projected to exceed 10 million for the first time?

A. 2024 B. 2027

C. 2029 D. 2031

E. 2033 F. 2036

EUROPEAN POPULATION STATISTICS (QUESTIONS 28-29)

		Population (%)		
	Population (thousands)	*Urban*	*Over 60*	*Under 15*
Country A	3140	47	13	24
Country B	7590	71	24	13
Country C	5120	81	27	16

28. How many people in country B are aged between 15 and 60?

A. 5.4 million
B. 1.82 million
C. 0.99 million
D. 4.78 million
E. 2.81 million

29. In country C 256,000 people are over the age of 75. What percentage of the population is this?

A. 5%
B. 10%
C. 15%
D. 20%
E. 25%

BRITISH BIRDS OF PREY POPULATIONS (QUESTION 30)

	2007	2008	2009
Buzzards	2200	2299	2296
Hawks	6140	6020	6090
Kestrels	450	470	517
Kites	790	792	707
Owls	1800	1850	1870
Totals	11380	11431	11480

30. In 2009 what percentage of the birds of prey listed were buzzards?

A. 4%
B. 8%
C. 12%
D. 16%
E. 20%

SOLAR POWER GENERATION IN VARIOUS COUNTRIES (MILLONS OF KWH) (QUESTIONS 31-32)

	2006	2007	2008
France	12	16	24
Germany	36	38	42
Greece	33	36	44
Spain	23	27	34
UK	8	11	16

31. What is France's share of the total solar power generation in 2008?

A. 10%
B. 15%
C. 20%
D. 25%
E. 30%

32. By how many million KWh did the overall generation of solar power increase between 2006 and 2007 across these five countries?

A. 4
B. 32
C. 12
D. 10
E. 16

SPENDING ON EDUCATION IN EUROPE (QUESTIONS 33-35)

	Population in 2005 (thousands)	No. Students in 2005 (thousands)
Bosnia	3781	635
Cyprus	836	146
Iceland	295.7	56
Slovakia	5386	969

Spending per Student in Euros (Q 33-35)

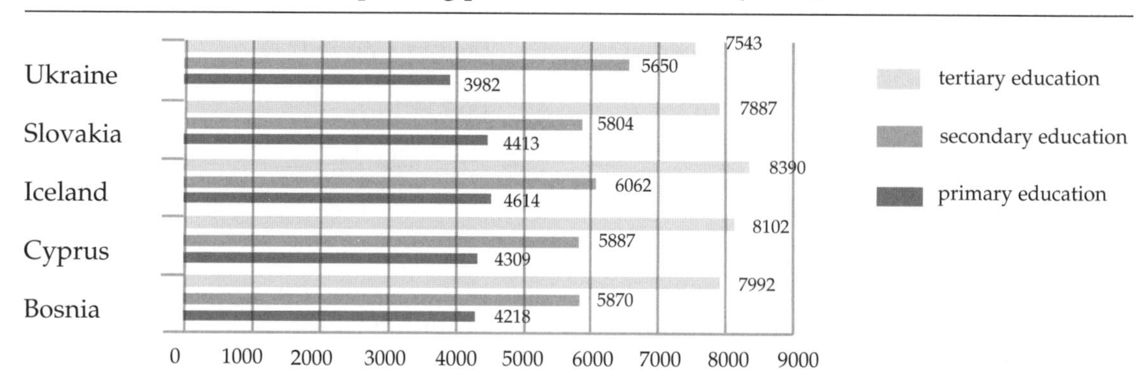

33. If 40% of students in Cyprus are at primary school and 36% at secondary school, what is the total per capita spending on education in Cyprus in 2005?

A. 1220 Euro B. 1178 Euro

C. 1010 Euro D. 986 Euro

E. 912 Euro

34. If 42% of Bosnian students and 38% of Slovakian students are at primary school, how much more does Slovakia spend on primary education than Bosnia?

A. 500 million Euro B. 450 mil Euro

C. 400 million Euro D. 350 mil Euro

E. 300 million Euro

35. If Iceland and Ukraine each have 35.2% of their student population attending secondary schools, how much more does Iceland spend on secondary education per capita than Ukraine?

A. 240 euro B. 137 euro

C. 97 euro D. 142 euro

E. 190 euro

European Marriage Rates (Q36-38)

	Population in 2005 (thousands)	*Percentage Unmarried*
Denmark	5417	28.2
Georgia	4465	24.1
Hungary	10078	26.9
Netherlands	16316	31.4

Number of marriages (Q 36-38)

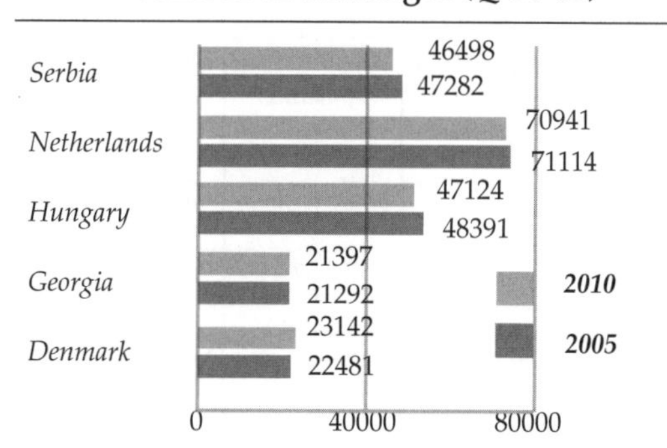

36. If 21.4% of the Danish population is under the minimum age to marry, what percentage of the eligible population got married in 2005? (You must be over the minimum age and unmarried to be eligible to get married.)

A. 3.2% B. 9.8%

C. 12.7% D. 6.1%

E. 8.4%

37. If the population of Hungary decreased by 100,000 between 2005 and 2010, what was the change in marriages per capita over the same period?

A. Up 3.2% B. Up 1.6%

C. Stayed the same D. Down 1.6%

E. Down 3.2%

38. If the percentage of the population that is unmarried in the Netherlands dropped to 30.9% in 2010 but the percentage of those getting married remained the same as in 2005, what was the change in the population over that time?

A. Up 223 000 B. Up 112 000

C. Stayed the same D. Down 112 000

E. Down 223 000

European Births and Infant Mortality (Q39-41)

	Population in 2005 (thousands)	*Births (thousands)*		*Died under age of 1 week*	
		2004	*2005*	*2004*	*2005*
Ireland	4187	72.4	73.1	78	73
France	61013	914	918	1202	1173
Greece	11064	159	160	207	191
Spain	43060	537	542	499	507
Germany	82409	1204	1194	1019	1002

39. If the table shown was ordered by number of births per 100,000 population in 2005, which country would be in the middle?

A. Ireland B. France

C. Greece D. Spain

E. Germany

40. If the population of Spain decreased by 0.2% from 2004 to 2005, what was the change in per capita birth rate over the same period?

A. Up 1.13% B. Up 0.56%

C. Stayed the same D. Down 0.56%

E. Down 1.13%

41. By how much did the number of deaths under the age of 1 week per 1000 births drop in Germany from 2004 to 2005?

A. 2.6% B. 1.2%

C. 2.1% D. 0.84%

E. 0.12%

Police Officers in Europe (Questions 42-44)

	Population in 2005 (thousands)	*Number of Policemen (thousands)*		
		2000	*2005*	*2010*
Greece	11064	42.6	44.1	39.9
France	61013	416	410	409
Italy	58645	401	422	424
Germany	82409	490	487	494
Ireland	4187	27.7	28.1	28.7

42. Which country has the fewest policemen per 1,000 population in 2005?

A. Greece B. France

C. Italy D. Germany

E. Ireland

43. If the population of Ireland rises 1.8% each year from 2005 to 2010, what is the percentage change in policemen per capita over that period?

A. Up 6.6% B. Up 1.6%

C. Stays the same D. Down 1.6%
E. Down 6.6%

44. If the number of policemen per capita in Italy remains constant between 2005 and 2010, what happened to the population of Italy over the same period?

A. Up 320,000 B. Up 285,000
C. Up 210,000 D. Up 157,000
E. Up 96,000

Child Vaccination Uptake (%) 2008 (Q. 45-47)

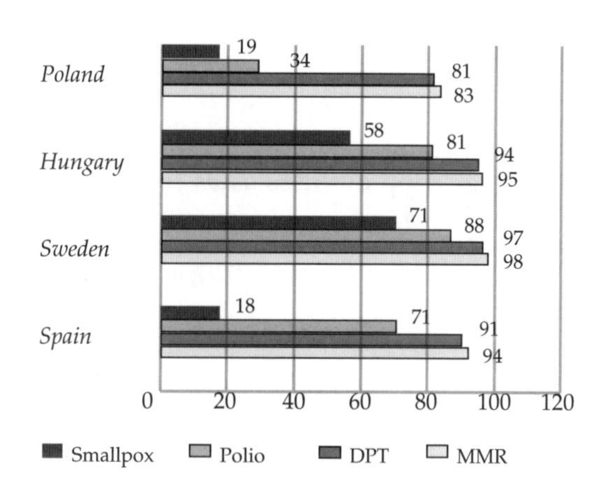

No. of children (thousands (Q. 45-47)

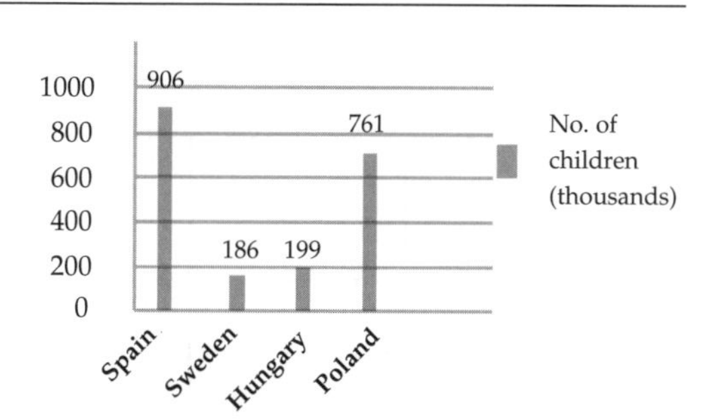

45. How many more children in Hungary had the DPT vaccine than in Sweden?

A. 9123 B. 7259
C. 6640 D. 5827
E. 4720

46. The number of children who received the polio vaccine in Poland in 2008 dropped by 10% from the number in 2005 despite the total number of children rising by 6% over the same period. What was the percentage uptake of the polio vaccine in Poland in 2005?

A. 37% B. 38%
C. 39% D. 40%
E. 41%

47. What is the minimum number of children in Spain who could have had both the MMR and DPT vaccines but not the polio vaccine in 2008?

A. 127,000 B. 241,000
C. 26,000 D. 91,000
E. 172,000

48. What is the per capita increase in domestic solar power generation in the UK from 2005 to 2010?

A. 9 956% B. 10 281%
C. 11 018% D. 11 946%
E. 12 556%

49. What is the per capita growth in installations in Ireland from 2005 to 2010?

A. 523% B. 496%
C. 465% D. 402%
E. 387%

Domestic Solar power Installations (Questions 48-50)						
	2005 (thousands)			*2010 (thousands)*		
	Population	*Installations*	*Kw Generated*	*Population*	*Installations*	*Kw Generated*
Germany	82409	1549	1859	82057	1794	2523
Ireland	4187	0.6	0.7	4589	4.1	7.4
Luxembourg	464	2.2	2.6	492	2.9	5.2
Spain	43060	1.8	2.1	45317	3.1	6.3
UK	60261	1.4	1.7	61899	112.1	221

50. What was the growth in average generation per installation in Germany from 2005 to 2010?

A. 2.6% B. 12.9%

C. 17% D. 22%

E. 28%

51. If the cost of a video in France rose from €14 in 2000 to €16 in 2005 and the population rose by 1.2m over the same period, what was the decrease in per capita spending on videos during that time?

A. €12.36 B. €17.02

C. €21.00 D. €23.28

E. €25.19

52. If the cost of videos in Austria and Spain was €15 in 2005, how many more videos would need to have been sold in Spain for them to have the same spending per capita as Austria?

A. 0.2 million B. 0.63 million

C. 1.91 million D. 1.38 million

E. 0.91 million

53. Which country had the greatest percentage drop in video sales from 1990 to 2010

A. Austria B. Belgium

C. France D. Spain

E. UK

European Video Sales (Questions 51-53)						
	Population in 2005 (thousands)	*Number of Videos Sold (millions)*				
		1990	*1995*	*2000*	*2005*	*2010*
Austria	8232	14.7	18.9	19.0	7.4	0.3
Belgium	10415	20.2	27.1	26.8	7.7	0.4
France	61013	112	141	137	42.2	1.2
Spain	43060	74.1	79.8	81.2	37.8	1.4
UK	60261	132	157	142	48.6	0.9

INTERNET USAGE IN EUROPE (QUESTIONS 54-55)

	Population in 2005 (thousands)	Number of Internet Users (in thousands) 2004	2005	2006
Belgium	10415	7995	8020	8542
Bulgaria	7739	4392	4512	4902
Romania	21635	13450	13842	14660
Switzerland	7441	4942	5334	5892

54. By how much did the number of internet users in Romania grow between 2004 and 2006?

A. 9% B. 18%

C. 12% D. 10%

E. 4%

55. What percentage of the population of Belgium had access to the internet in 2005?

A. 25% B. 43%

C. 57% D. 68%

E. 77%

EU ALCOHOL PRODUCTION IN 2005 (QUESTIONS 56-57)

	Population in 2005 (thousands)	Production (thousand hectolitres) Wine	Spirits	Beer
France	61013	53440	1741	17200
Germany	82409	9450	4056	95000
Spain	43060	32430	1766	30200
Switzerland	7441	1000	57	3600

56. If the Swiss drink half of the wine produced in their country what is the average amount consumed per person?

A. 0.067 litres B. 0.67 litres

C. 6.7 litres D. 67 litres

E. 670 litres

57. What percentage of the total beer produced by the countries in this table is produced by Germany?

A. 65% B. 29%

C. 73% D. 38%

E. 95%

MOBILE PHONE SUBSCRIPTIONS IN THE EU COUNTRIES (THOUSANDS)(QUESTIONS 58-59)

	2005	2006	2007
Bulgaria	1594	1957	2451
Denmark	3799	4228	4982
Greece	5511	6824	9191
Poland	1759	1819	1928

58. What percentage of the mobile phone subscriptions shown did Denmark account for in 2005?

A. 10% B. 20%

C. 30% D. 40%

E. 50%

59. If the population of Bulgaria in 2007 was 3.77 million, how many mobile phone subscriptions were there per hundred people?

A. 23 B. 31

C. 42 D. 55

E. 65

National Healthcare Funding – € millions (Questions 60-62)

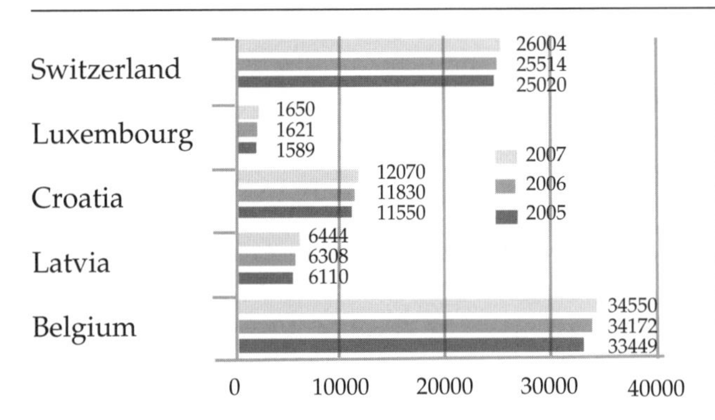

National Populations 2005 (thousands)	
Belgium	10415
Latvia	2292
Croatia	4443
Luxembourg	464
Switzerland	7441

60. What is the difference in per capita healthcare funding between Belgium and Switzerland in 2005?

A. €27 B. €84
C. €129 D. €151
E. €173

61. If the table were ordered by per capita funding in 2005, which country would be in the middle?

A. Belgium B. Latvia
C. Croatia D. Luxembourg
E. Switzerland

62. If the population of Latvia decreases by 0.5% each year, what is the increase in per capita funding from 2005 to 2007?

A. 1.2% B. 6.5%
C. 3.1% D. 4.8%
E. 2.6%

---

63. If the population of Croatia increased by 8000 from 2004 to 2005, what was the change in accidental deaths per capita in Croatia over the same period?

A. Up more than 1% B. Up less than 1%
C. Exactly the same D. Down less than 1%
E. Down more than 1%

64. What was the change in non-road related deaths in Romania between 2004 and 2005?

A. Up 20% B. Up 10%

European Accidental Deaths (Questions 63-65)

	Population in 2005 (thousands)	*Total Accidental Deaths*		*Accidental Road Deaths*	
		2004	*2005*	*2004*	*2005*
Bulgaria	7739	2391	2429	2107	2044
Croatia	4443	1418	1421	864	851
Finland	5244	1391	1320	1007	994
Romania	21635	6821	6211	5891	5467
Switzerland	7441	2122	2298	1749	1822

C. Stayed the same D. Down 10%

E. Down 20%

65. How many fewer accidental deaths would Bulgaria have needed to record in 2005 to have had the same per capita rate as Switzerland?

A. 70 B. 45

C. 39 D. 14

E. 8

66. What is the change in the combined number of doctors and nurses per 100,000 population in Italy from 2005 to 2010?

A. Down 12.5 B. Down 1.25

C. Moved less than 1 D. Up 1.25

E. Up 12.5

67. How many more nurses would France have needed in 2010 to have the same per capita ratio as the UK?

A. 200 B. 250

C. 300 D. 350

E. 400

68. What is the percentage increase in the number of nurses per capita in Belgium from 2005 to 2010?

A. 1% B. 2%

C. 3% D. 4%

E. 5%

EU VACCINE TRADE IN 2008 (QUESTIONS 69-70)

	Trade US$ (millions)		Weight (tonnes)	
	Imports	Exports	Imports	Exports
France	506	1811	1019	3976
Italy	267	276	387	482
Spain	417	126	704	245
UK	1387	1132	14634	647

69. What percentage of the shown exports by weight does Italy account for?

A. 2.3% B. 15%

C. 4.8% D. 9%

E. 8%

70. What is the average price per gramme of vaccine exported from the UK?

A. $1.75 B. $2.21

C. $0.23 D. $14.91

E. $6.23

Hospital Staff (Questions 66-68)

	2005 (thousands)			*2010 (thousands)*		
	Population	*Doctors*	*Nurses*	*Population*	*Doctors*	*Nurses*
Belgium	10415	16.1	42	10697	16.4	44
France	61013	92.3	281	62637	94.1	284
Germany	82409	118	310	82057	118	307
Italy	58645	79	261	60098	83.1	273
UK	60261	74.5	279	61899	74.2	281

Nuclear Electricity Generation in the EU (Questions 71-72)				
	Population in 2005 (millions)	*Electricity Generated (millions MWh)*		
		2005	*2006*	*2007*
France	61013	452	446	440
Hungary	10078	163	158	150
Poland	38198	44	51	67
Ukraine	46936	87	90	93

71. How many MWh did France generate on average for each person in France in 2005?

A. 0.74 B. 7.4

C. 74 D. 740

E. 7400

72. What percentage of the total nuclear power generation did Hungary account for in 2007?

A. 10% B. 15%

C. 20% D. 25%

E. 30%

Municipal Waste Collection (thousand tonnes) (Q 73-74)			
	2005	*2006*	*2007*
Austria	2713	2981	3002
Ireland	595	627	719
Norway	716	931	1014
Slovenia	1386	1326	1354

73. What percentage of waste collection did Ireland account for across these countries in 2005?

A. 11% B. 5.95%

C. 18% D. 7%

E. 14%

74. If Slovenia had grown its waste collection by 5% between 2006 and 2007, how many more tonnes of waste would it have collected in 2007?

A. 18100 tonnes B. 27200 tonnes

C. 1392 tonnes D. 38300 tonnes

E. 2289 tonnes

Students in Tertiary Education (Q 75-76)				
		Female proportion of student population (%)		
	Student Population in 2007 (thousands)	*2005*	*2006*	*2007*
Austria	1090	55.2	55.3	55.3
Germany	2445	53.5	54.9	54.2
Luxembourg	171	50.9	51.7	52.4
Serbia	723	55.6	54.2	53.9

75. Assuming the population was constant, how many females were in tertiary education in Luxembourg in 2005?

A. 8700 B. 33600

C. 89600 D. 87000

E. 63200

76. What was the percentage growth in female student numbers in Germany between 2005 and 2006?

A. 1.4% B. 0.2%

C. 10.6% D. 5.2%

E. 2.6%

ACCIDENTAL DEATH RATES IN EUROPE (QUESTIONS 77-78)

		Deaths Per 100,000 Population		
	2006 Population (thousands)	2005	2006	2007
Belgium	10400	21	18	16
Italy	58645	49	37	39
Spain	43060	15	21	19
Slovakia	8187	21	23	26

77. How many more people died accidentally in Slovakia in 2006 than in Belgium in the same year?

A. 5 B. 11

C. 29 D. 35

E. 49

78. If the population remained unchanged, how many fewer people died accidentally in Italy in 2007 than in 2005?

A. 5 B. 59

C. 586 D. 5865

E. 58645

VIOLENT CRIME IN EUROPE (QUESTIONS 79-80)

	2005 Population (thousands)	*Number of crimes committed* 2005	2006	2007
France	61013	58122	58595	59073
Ireland	4187	3105	3270	3532
Malta	403	305	316	357
Portugal	10529	11017	11256	11046

79. Which country had the highest violent crime rate (i.e. per head of population) in 2005?

A. France B. Ireland

C. Malta D. Portugal

E. Impossible to tell from the data

80. What was the average violent crime rate (the number of violent crimes per 100,000 of population) across these four countries in 2005?

A. 0.02 B. 0.14

C. 3.7 D. 21

E. 95

SALES OF CHEESE IN EUROPE (QUESTIONS 81-82)

	Cheese sold (thousand tonnes) 2005	2006	2007
Aldi	523	591	671
Carrefour	110	115	121
Lidl	618	581	570
Sainsbury's	294	327	348

81. If 6 million people shopped at Carrefour during 2007, how much cheese did each person buy on average?

A. 20 grammes B. 200 grammes

C. 2 Kg D. 20 Kg

E. 200 Kg

82. What percentage of the total cheese sold in these supermarkets in 2005 was sold by Lidl?

A. 40% B. 38%

C. 36% D. 34%

E. 32%

PATENT APPLICATIONS IN EUROPE (QUESTIONS 83-84)

	2005	2006	2007
France	12471	12486	12508
Germany	32837	33936	33187
Italy	12601	12280	12984
Spain	8175	8155	8293
Total	66084	66857	66972

83. What percentage of all the patents filed over the three years were filed by Germany?

A. 40% B. 45%

C. 50% D. 55%

E. 60%

84. Which country had the greatest growth per capita in patent applications between 2005 and 2006?

A. France B. Germany

C. Italy D. Spain

E. Impossible to tell from the data

SPENDING ON OLD AGE BENEFITS (QUESTIONS 85-86)

	Population in 2005 (thousands)	*Euros per inhabitant* 2005	2006	2007
Estonia	5346	1033	1055	1089
Georgia	4219	911	1059	1022
Latvia	2240	1008	1250	1297
Ukraine	45433	1096	1125	1296

85. Which country spent the most on old age benefits in 2005?

A. Estonia B. Georgia

C. Latvia D. Ukraine

E. Impossible to tell from the data

86. What is the percentage increase in spending per capita in Georgia between 2005 and 2007?

A. 12% B. 15%

C. 9% D. 7%

E. 19%

Internet Users in the UK (thousands) (Questions 87-89)

	2000	*2005*	*2010*
Dial-up	2800	2650	1072
ADSL Broadband	1742	12389	31839
Cable Broadband	860	1349	2987
3G	0	0	1047

87. If half of the dial-up users in 2000 upgraded to ADSL broadband and a further 340,000 upgraded to cable broadband, what percentage of the 2005 dial-up users are new?

A. 45% B. 50%

C. 55% D. 60%

E. 65%

88. What percentage of internet users use cable broadband in 2010?

A. 6.9% B. 8.1%

C. 7.3% D. 9.1%

E. 8.8%

89. If cable broadband experiences the same growth between 2010 and 2015 as it did between 2005 and 2010, how many cable broadband users will there be in 2015?

A. 8.5 million B. 12.2 million

C. 9.1 million D. 7.6 million

E. 10.4 million

90. If nobody owns more than 3 cars in Belarus, how many cars are there in total in Belarus?

A. 2.93 million B. 3.76 million

Cars per Household (Questions 90-92)					
	Total Households (thousands)	*Number of Households with... (thousands)*			
		0 Cars	*1 car*	*2 cars*	*3+ cars*
Belarus	4123	627	3241	250	5
Czech Rep	4704	86	3214	1396	8
Greece	4887	202	3501	1179	5
Hungary	4615	91	3214	1303	7
Sweden	4039	33	2027	1892	87

C. 4.02 million D. 4.73 million

E. 5.12 million

91. Across the five countries shown, what proportion of households have no car at all?

A. 1.9% B. 3.1%

C. 4.6% D. 5.1%

E. 5.8%

92. If there are 6.08 million cars in Sweden and no household owns more than 4 cars, how many households have precisely 4 cars?

A. 2000 B. 4000

C. 6000 D. 8000

E. 10000

93. How many more people abstain or drink very little (less than 5 units) in Croatia than in Georgia?

A. 9500 B. 12200

C. 3400 D. 18100

E. 7900

94. If you selected a person entirely at random in Albania, what are the odds that they drink less than 10 units of alcohol per week?

A. Evens B. 2 to 1

C. 3 to 1 D. 4 to 1

E. 5 to 1

95. If the table were ordered by the number of people who drink between 20 and 40

Weekly Alcohol Consumption (Questions 93-95)						
	Population (thousands)	*Population consuming units* of alcohol (%)*				
		0-5	*5-10*	*10-20*	*20-40*	*40+*
Albania	3111	18.1	6.3	30.2	31.6	13.8
Croatia	4443	17.9	9.1	41.9	23.8	7.3
Georgia	4465	17.6	4.7	28.6	31.4	17.7
Norway	4635	18.2	2.9	14.8	41.6	22.5
Slovakia	5386	19.4	12.1	47.2	19.3	2.0

* 1 unit of alcohol is 10ml of ethanol which is the equivalent of a 25ml shot of a 40% proof spirit.

units per week, which country would be in the middle?

A. Albania B. Croatia

C. Georgia D. Norway

E. Slovakia

---

96. If the chart were ordered by percentage growth of prison population from 2004 to 2006, which country would be in the middle?

A. Austria B. Croatia

C. Georgia D. Lithuania

E. Switzerland

97. If the population of Switzerland is increasing by 30,000 each year, what is the percentage decrease in prisoners per capita from 2004 to 2006?

A. 1.2% B. 3.9%

C. 5.9% D. 0.8%

E. 2.2%

98. How many more prisoners would Austria have needed in 2004 to have had precisely 30% of the total in all five countries?

A. 132 B. 917

C. 24 D. 270

E. 503

GLOBAL DISASTER AID IN 2009 (QUESTIONS 99-100)

		Aid Donated (tonnes)		
	Population (thousands)	*Local[1]*	*Indirect[2]*	*Direct[3]*
Austria	9588	12504	1012	648
Czech Republic	10411	2321	6781	2901
Hungary	9973	6292	1019	871
Portugal	10732	9821	19223	561

1. Purchased in the country in need.
2. Purchased elsewhere and shipped.
3. Shipped directly from donating country.

99. What percentage of Portugal's aid contribution was purchased locally in the country in need?

A. A half B. A third

C. A quarter D. Two fifths

E. Three fifths

100. What percentage of the total direct aid was funded by Austria?

A. 25% B. 22%

Prison Populations (Q 96-98)

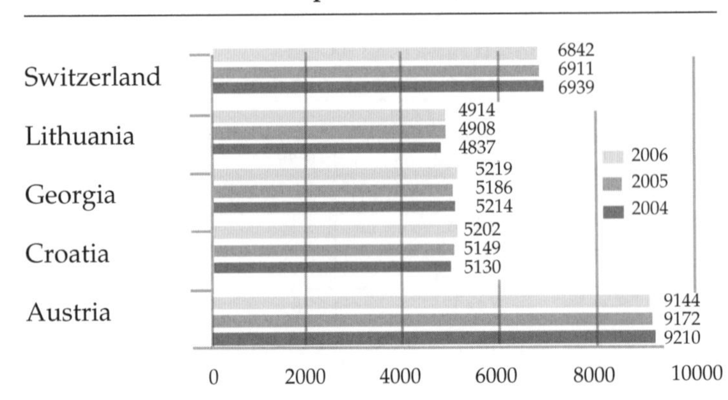

Populations in 2005 (thousands)	
Austria	8232
Croatia	4443
Georgia	4465
Lithuania	3416
Switzerland	7441

C. 19% D. 16%

E. 13%

BIRTH RATES AROUND EUROPE (QUESTIONS 101-102)

	Population in 2005 (thousands)	Births per thousand population 2000	2005	2010
Croatia	4443	15.4	14.1	12.1
Finland	5244	14.1	12.2	11.3
Ireland	4187	15.5	14.4	12.8
Slovakia	5386	13.1	11.9	11.1

101. Which country had the most births in 2005?

A. Croatia B. Finland

C. Ireland D. Slovakia

E. Impossible to tell from the data

102. How many more children were born in Croatia in 2010 than in Ireland in the same year (assuming that both populations remained constant)?

A. 166 B. 201

C. 23 D. 190

E. 82

CHURCH ATTENDANCE AROUND EUROPE (QUESTIONS 103-104)

	Population in 2005 (thousands)	Churchgoers (%) 2000	2005	2010
France	61013	18.4	16.2	15.6
Greece	11064	22.1	22.1	21.9
Italy	58645	16.8	16.7	15.9
Spain	43060	18.2	18.1	17.9

103. Which country had the most churchgoers in 2005?

A. France B. Greece

C. Italy D. Spain

E. Impossible to tell from the data

104. What was the percentage drop in church attendance in Italy between 2005 and 2010?

A. 2.3% B. 7.1%

C. 4.8% D. 6.2%

E. 8.1%

Satellite Dishes in Europe (thousands) (Questions 105-107)

	Population in 2005 (thousands)	2005	2006	2007
Bosnia	3781	32.1	34.7	35.7
Denmark	5417	102	109	112
Greece	11064	327	381	390
Netherlands	16316	1294	1422	1504
Portugal	10547	836	907	1002

105. If the table were ordered by percentage growth in the number of dishes, which country would be in the middle?

A. Bosnia B. Denmark

C. Greece D. Netherlands

E. Portugal

106. How many more satellite dish installations would Greece have needed in 2007 to have had the same growth as Portugal from 2005 to 2007?

A. 1930 B. 2579

C. 3120 D. 502

E. 1123

107. If the population of Bosnia decreases by 4000 each year, what is the increase in per capita installations of dishes from 2005 to 2007?

A. 12.6% B. 11.5%

C. 10.1% D. 9.7%

E. 9.2%

SALES OF WINE IN THE UK (QUESTIONS 108-109)

	Wine sold (million litres)		
	2007	2008	2009
Asda	470	478	490
Morrisons	210	215	221
Sainsbury's	525	516	529
Tesco	895	927	918

108. Which supermarket had the largest percentage growth in sales of wine between 2007 and 2009?

A. Asda B. Morrisons

C. Sainsbury's D. Tesco

E. Impossible to tell from the data

109. How much more wine would Asda have had to have sold in 2009 to have achieved a 10% rise in sales from 2007?

A. 2700 litres B. 27 thousand litres

C. 270 thousand litres D. 2.7 million litres

E. 27 million litres

SHOE SALES AROUND EUROPE (QUESTION 110)

		Sales (million euro)		
	Population in 2005 (thousands)	*2004*	*2005*	*2006*
Belgium	7739	208	212	232
Greece	11064	222	231	233
Italy	58645	2280	2340	2771
Netherlands	16316	589	600	606

110. How much extra did the average Greek spend on shoes in 2006 than in 2004 assuming the population remained constant? (Figures in the table should be rounded for ease of calculation)

A. 1 euro B. 2 euro

C. 3 euro D. 4 euro

E. 5 euro

INSTALLED TELEPHONE LINES IN EUROPE (QUESTIONS 111-112)

		Number of lines (thousands)		
	Population in 2005 (thousands)	2005	2006	2007
Andorra	80	35.4	36.5	37.2
Luxembourg	464	245	247	249
Malta	398	200	210	230
San Marino	30	20.8	21	21.1

111. Which country had the lowest number of telephone lines per head of population in 2005?

A. Andorra B. Luxembourg

C. Malta D. San Marino

E. Impossible to tell from the data

112. What percentage of telephone lines shown in the table were in Luxembourg in 2006?

A. 53%   B. 48%
C. 30%   D. 65%
E. 44%

NATURAL DEATH RATES ACROSS EUROPE (QUESTIONS 113-114)

	Population in 2005 (thousands)	*Number of Deaths (per hundred thousand)* 1985	1995	2005
Latvia	2292	23.4	24.1	21.7
Liechtenstein	35	18.7	18.8	17.2
Lithuania	3416	27.1	26.9	24.1
Luxembourg	464	17.2	17.1	16.9

113. If the population of Latvia was the same in 2005 as in 1995, how many fewer deaths were there in Latvia in 2005 than in 1995?

A. 6   B. 12
C. 102   D. 41
E. 55

114. How many people died of natural causes in Liechtenstein in 2005?

A. 6   B. 12
C. 102   D. 41
E. 55

Mobile Phone Ownership (%) (Questions 115-117)

	Population in 2005 (thousands)	*Number of phones owned* 0	1	2	3+
France	61013	16.4	71.6	8.4	3.6
Germany	82409	18.9	81.2	8.1	1.8
Italy	58645	11.2	68.3	19.2	1.3
Spain	43060	19.1	80.2	0.6	0.1
UK	60261	17.2	79.6	3.0	0.2

115. How many people do not own a mobile phone in total across the five countries?

A. 10 million   B. 20 million
C. 30 million   D. 40 million
E. 50 million

116. If there are 52 million mobile phones in the UK and nobody owns more than 4 phones, how many people own exactly 4 phones?

A. 32000   B. 55000
C. 51000   D. 41000
E. 22000

117. How many more people don't own multiple phones in Italy than in Spain?

A. 1.21 million   B. 980 thousand
C. 2.94 million   D. 672 thousand
E. 3.84 million

EUROSTAR JOURNEY TIMES (HH:MM) (QUESTION 118)

From \ To->	Brussels	Geneva	London	Luxembourg	Paris
Brussels	-	X	01:56	X	01:22
Geneva	X	-	07:54	X	03:28
London	02:22	06:48	-	05:45	02:25
Luxembourg	X	X	05:45	-	02:16
Paris	01:20	03:33	02:15	02:39	-

118. How much shorter is the Paris to London journey than the Paris to Luxembourg trip?

A. 5%   B. 10%
C. 15%   D. 20%
E. 25%

OCTOGENERIANS IN EUROPE (%) (QUESTIONS 119-120)

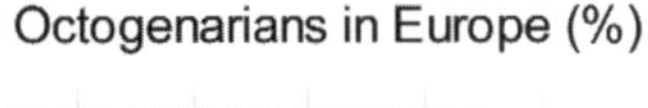

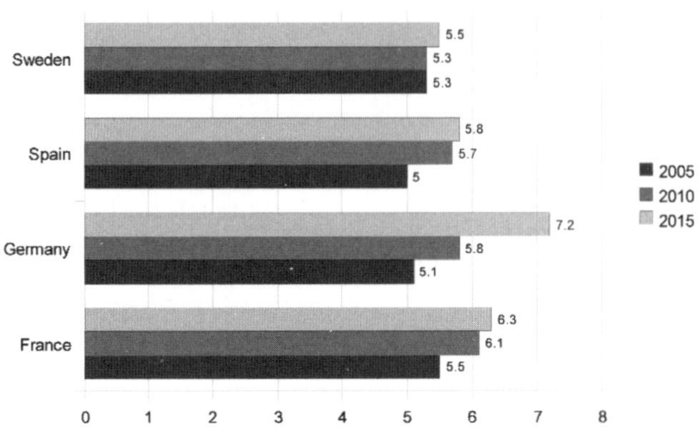

119. What is the growth rate of octogenarians in Spain between 2005 and 2015?

A. 5%
B. 5.8%
C. 0.8%
D. 16%
E. 13.8%

120. If the population of Sweden is 9.3 million and it remains constant, how many more octogenarians will there be in Sweden in 2015 than in 2005?

A. 18600
B. 12200
C. 1800
D. 21400
E. 9600

Divorce rate per 100,000 (Q 121-123)

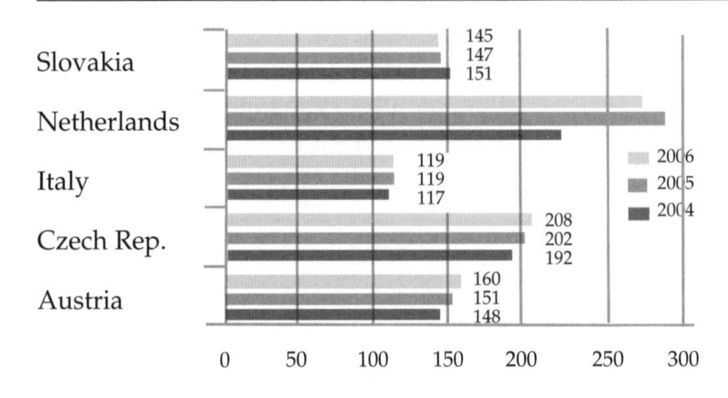

Populations in 2005 (thousands)	
Austria	8232
Czech Rep	10195
Italy	58645
Netherlands	16316
Slovakia	5386

121. How many more people got divorced in the Czech Republic than in Austria in 2005?

A. 17231 B. 8164
C. 10239 D. 3012
E. 5218

122. If the population of Slovakia is increasing by 5000 each year, what is the percentage decrease in the number of divorces from 2004 to 2006?

A. 0.2% B. 0.9%
C. 1.7% D. 2.9%
E. 3.8%

123. What is the percentage increase in divorces per capita in the Netherlands from 2004 to 2006?

A. 13.4% B. 12.9%
C. 11.7% D. 10.3%
E. 9.7%

Wine Consumption (Questions 124-126)

	Population in 2005 (thousands)	*Litres Consumed (millions)*			
		1995	*2000*	*2005*	*2010*
Belgium	10415	84	107	126	131
France	61013	1204	1381	1487	1527
Germany	82409	502	578	614	707
Portugal	10547	168	174	192	215
UK	60261	484	715	910	1146

124. Which country in the table had a growth rate in consumption of twice that of another country in the table from 1995 to 2010?

A. Belgium B. France
C. Germany D. Portugal
E. UK

125. If the population of France has steadily increased by 200,000 every year from 1995, what is the increase in consumption per capita from 1995 to 2000?

A. 20.7% B. 15.8%
C. 12.8% D. 10.6%
E. 9.9%

126. What is the overall growth rate of wine consumption from 1995 to 2010 across all five countries?

A. 23.2% B. 52.6%
C. 19.8% D. 31.9%
E. 28.1%

Heart Attack Survival Rates (%) (Q. 127-129)

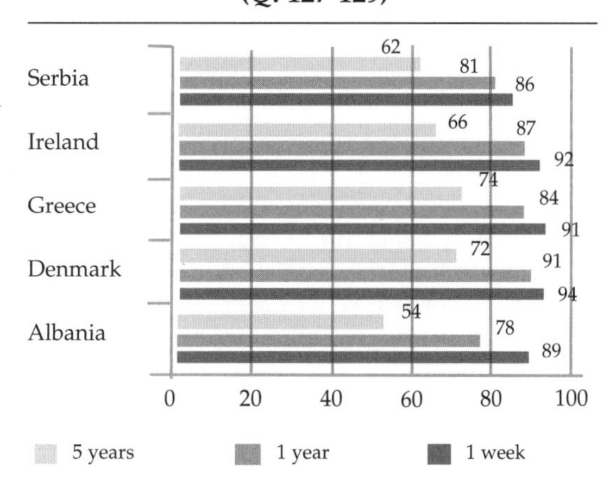

Heart Attacks in 2005

	Population in 2005 (thousands	*Number of Heart Attacks*
Albania	3111	4748
Denmark	5417	5014
Greece	11064	8128
Ireland	4187	6042
Serbia	9856	12314

127. How many more people died within 1 year of their heart attack in Albania than in Ireland?

A. 121 B. 482
C. 90 D. 259
E. 106

128. How many fewer heart attacks would Serbia have needed to record to have exactly one third of all recorded heart attacks on the table?

A. 258 B. 391
C. 27 D. 402
E. 198

129. What is the difference in the number of heart attacks per 100,000 people in Denmark and Greece?

A. 1 B. 12
C. 19 D. 23
E. 34

130. In 2003 Legoland, in Denmark, had 1.2 million visitors, half of which were from abroad. What proportion of Denmark's foreign visitors went to Legoland?

A. A half B. A third
C. A quarter D. A fifth
E. A sixth

131. If the Norway population was 4.7m in 2005, how many visitors per head of population did Norway receive that year?

A. 0.33 B. 1.8
C. 1.3 D. 0.56
E. 2.37

POPULATIONS IN EUROPE (QUESTIONS 132-133)

	Area in km2 (thousands)	*Population (thousands)* 2002	2005	2008
Belgium	30	10310	10440	10667
France	540	61426	62773	63983
Portugal	91	10329	10529	10618
Spain	499	40970	43038	45067

132. What was the average population density, in people per square kilometre, in Belgium in 2005?

A. 0.348 B. 3.48
C. 34.8 D. 348
E. 3480

VISITORS TO SCANDINAVIA (THOUSANDS) (QUESTIONS 130-131)

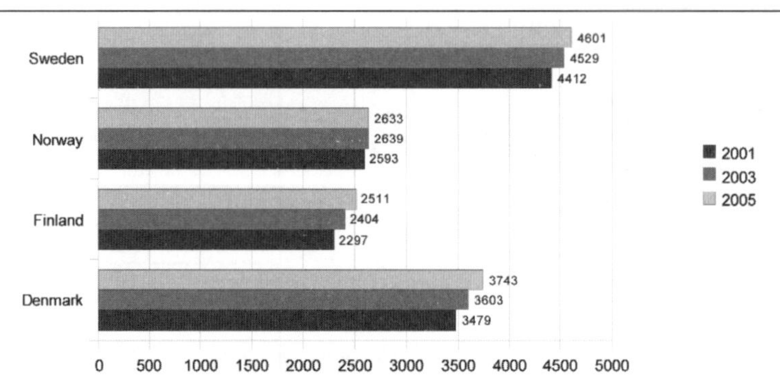

133. How many more people lived in these countries in 2008 than in 2002?

A. 1.2m B. 3.9m

C. 5.7m D. 6.8m

E. 7.3m

MARRIAGES IN EUROPE (QUESTIONS 134-135)

	Population in 2005 (thousands)	*Number of Marriages 2004*	*2005*	*2006*
Ireland	4187	20233	20209	19887
Italy	58645	234600	235200	233900
Slovakia	5386	15809	15628	15680
Switzerland	7441	18211	18202	17919

134. What is the largest percentage increase in marriages in any country on the table between any two years?

A. 0.11% B. 0.22%

C. 0.33% D. 0.44%

E. 0.55%

135. What is the percentage drop in the number of marriages in Switzerland between 2004 and 2006?

A. 1.6% B. 2.1%

C. 2.8% D. 3.1%

E. 3.4%

136. What is the difference in marriages per 1000 people in Ireland and Italy in 2005?

A. 0.1 B. 0.8

C. 1.4 D. 3.6

E. 5.2

137. How many more men wear size 9 shoes than size 8 in the UK?

A. 1.55m B. 1.15m

C. 975000 D. 823000

E. 735000

FREQUENCY OF MEN'S SHOE SIZE IN THE UK (Q. 137)

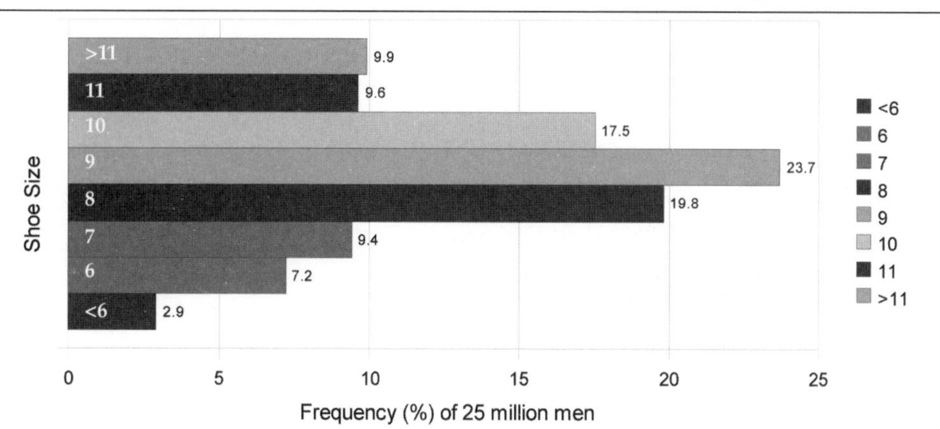

UNEMPLOYMENT IN EUROPE IN 2008 (Q 138-139)

		Unemployed (thousands)		*Proportion of workforce (%)*	
	Population (thousands)	*Men*	*Women*	*Men*	*Women*
France	61813	1163	1266	8	10
Italy	59545	902	987	6	10
Spain	44560	863	1050	7	12
UK	61260	817	580	5	4

138. What was the total size of the workforce in Italy in 2008?

A. 59.5m B. 24.9m

C. 1.9m D. 23.8m

E. 37.2m

139. How many more women than men were unemployed across these four countries in 2008?

A. 22000 B. 39000

C. 64000 D. 97000

E. 138000

140. If the population of Iceland changes equally each year between 2004 and 2007 and the total amount of chocolate consumed in 2007 is the same as in 2004, what was the population of Iceland in 2007?

A. 302 000 B. 304 000

C. 306 000 D. 308 000

E. 310 000

141. How much more chocolate was consumed in Cyprus than in Malta in 2005?

A. 621.2 Kg B. 6212 Kg

C. 62.12 tonnes D. 621.2 tonnes

E. 6212 tonnes

142. If the population of Monaco rises by 200 per year, what is the growth in total chocolate consumed from 2004 to 2007?

WIND POWER GENERATION (KWH MILLIONS) (Q 143)

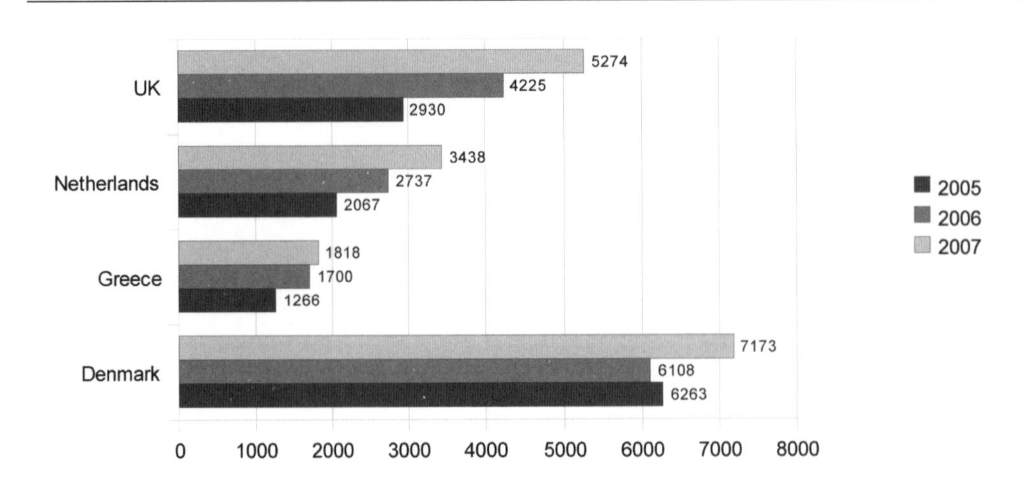

Chocolate Consumption (Q 140-142)					
	Population in 2005 (thousands	*Annual Consumption (Kg/person)*			
		2004	*2005*	*2006*	*2007*
Andorra	79.8	3.7	3.9	3.7	3.6
Cyprus	836	1.8	1.9	2.1	2.3
Iceland	296	4.4	4.2	4.2	4.1
Malta	403	2.1	2.4	2.3	2.4
Monaco	32.5	5.7	5.8	5.8	5.9

A. 2.2% B. 5.4%

C. 3.9% D. 2.0%

E. 4.3%

143. How much more wind power than Greece did the Netherlands produce, as a percentage, in 2006?

A. 19% B. 72%

C. 57% D. 43%

E. 61%

SPENDING ON EDUCATION IN EUROPE (QUESTIONS 144-145)

Amount spent in Euros (millions)

	Population in 2005 (thousands)	2004	2005	2006
Belgium	10415	12384	12394	12723
Estonia	1347	827	911	996
Norway	4635	4848	5012	5221
Slovakia	5386	6222	6318	6581

144. Which country had the highest growth (in %) in spending on education between 2004 and 2006?

A. Belgium B. Estonia

C. Norway D. Slovakia

E. Impossible to tell from the data

145. What is the overall growth in spending on education between 2005 and 2006?

A. 1.1% B. 5.2%

C. 4.1% D. 3.6%

E. 2.9%

SPENDING ON HEALTHCARE IN EUROPE (Q 146)

Amount spent in Euros (millions)

	Population in 2005 (thousands)	*2004*	*2005*	*2006*
France	61013	175800	179200	181300
Ireland	4187	11398	11893	12302
Poland	38198	12671	15188	16872
Switzerland	7441	24281	24612	25010

146. What is the growth in spending on healthcare in Switzerland between 2004 and 2006?

A. 3.5% B. 3.0%

C. 2.5% D. 2.0%

E. 1.5%

147. Which country had the lowest growth in rail passenger numbers between 2006 and 2007?

A. France B. Germany

C. Italy D. UK

E. Impossible to tell from the data

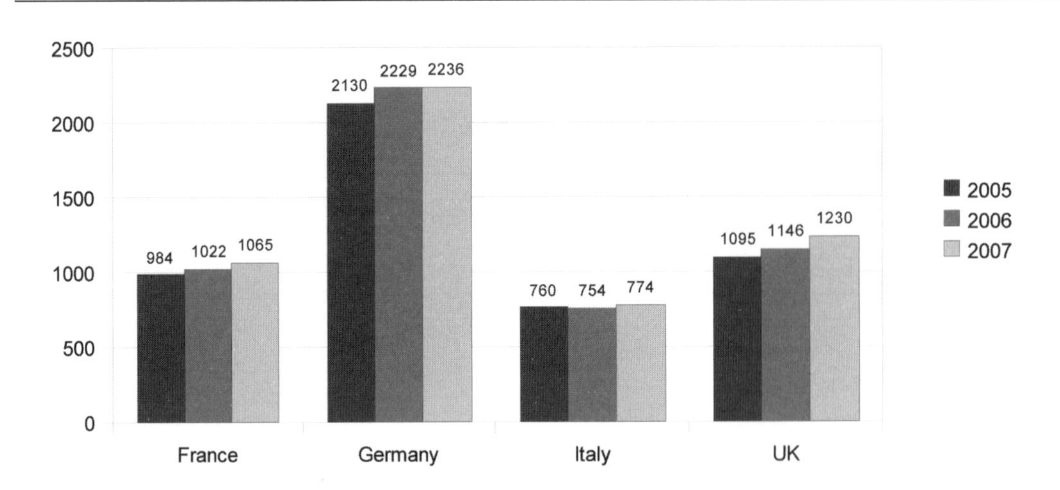

Single Parent Families (Questions 148-150)

	Families in 2005 (thousand)*	*Number of single parent families (per 1000)*			
		2003	***2005***	***2007***	***2009***
Bulgaria	1018	27.1	27.4	27.6	27.9
Estonia	226	13.4	14.1	13.9	14.4
France	9281	38.1	39.7	40.2	43.6
Poland	5724	19.8	18.9	19.1	19.4
Spain	6804	8.7	8.8	9.1	9.3

**Families with at least one child under the age of 18.*

148. If the table were ordered by percentage increase in single parent families per 1000 families from 2003 to 2009, which country would be in the middle?

A. Bulgaria B. Estonia
C. France D. Poland
E. Spain

149. If the population of Poland decreases by 15000 each year, what is the change in the number of single parent families in Poland from 2003 to 2009?

A. 4048 B. 12304
C. 7192 D. 6023
E. 8122

150. What percentage of single parent families shown in the table in 2005 are French?

A. 49.5% B. 54.7%
C. 59.2% D. 64.9%
E. 68.2%

ANSWERS

1. B

To calculate total per capita rate, add the numbers of applications together for each country (note the final column is not in thousands) and divide by the population. This gives values of 0.066, 0.069, 0.078, 0.079 and 0.048 respectively.

2. D

The per capita rate of new applications in 2005 is 49/5481 which increased by 3.2% which gives a per capita rate of (49*1.032)/5481 in 2010. Multiply this by the 2010 population which is 5481*1.0025. This gives a total of 51076.

3. E

If the number required by Austria is X then (X/8387)=(1090/16653). Therefore, X=549 (thousand) which is 75000 more than they actually had.

4. A

The number of deaths is the rate multiplied by the population. The difference is (28.1*(610.13-0.16)-(27.1*(610.13+2*0.16))=597.

5. C

The number of deaths per year is the rate multiplied by the population. This gives (34*(41.87/1.002))=1421 for 2004 and (31.6*(41.87*1.0022)) =1328 for 2007. The percentage fall is the difference (1421-1328) divided by the starting value (1421) and multiplied by 100 which gives 6.5%.

6. D

The number of deaths in each country is the rate multiplied by the population. The percentage in Italy is the Italian total divided by the overall total and multiplied by 100. So, (32.9*586.45)/((28.2*610.13)+(26.4*104.15)+(23.9*602.61)+(34.1*41.87)+(32.9+586.45)) gives 35%.

7. D

You need to find the proportion that the income from oranges represents in the total income of 225 million euros. As the price of each pear is three times the price of a grapefruit (or orange), replace the pears' values with grapefruits' values when adding the quantities sold, as in: 27 + 23 + (3 * 8) = 74 (to get a total of price units, rather than product units).

The oranges' income therefore makes up a 23 : 74 share of the three fruits total income, thus: (225 / 74) * 23 = approximately 3 * 23 = 69.

8. A

In the period January-September 2008, the value of Hungarian exports to the EU was equal to 11.39 billion EUR (the value of export to the EU-12) + 32.07 billion EUR (the value of export to the EU-15) = 43.46 billion EUR. The same figure for the previous year was (11.39 / 1.183) + (32.07 / 1.042) = 9.63 + 30.78 = 40.41 (billion EUR), which means that an increase by 43.46 / 40.41 - 1 = 8% took place.

9. C

In the period January-September 2007, the value of Hungarian exports to Asia was equal to 2.97 / 1.229 = 2.42 (billion EUR), while the same figure for the Americas equalled 1.68 / 1.132 = 1.48 (billion EUR). The latter figure amounts to 1.48 / 2.42 = 61% of the former one.

10. B

Comparing the increases in the value of Hungarian exports to the different country groups with the help of the bar graph, it can be seen that it was exports to Asia which increased by the greatest percentage. This already shows that Asia's share in the total exports of Hungary grew, and since only one of the four answers refers to an increase, this must be the correct one as well.

11. B

The deaths per 1000 is simply the number of deaths divided by the population in thousands. This gives values of 8.6, 10.2, 9.5 11.8 and 10.3 respectively.

12. A

The deaths per 1000 children for each year is the number of deaths divided by the population. The percentage decrease is the difference between these divided by the 2005 figure and multiplied by 100. Thus, 100*((8942/1042)-(8902/1070))/(8942/1042)= 3.1%.

13. D

The percentage of deaths in Portugal is the number in Portugal divided by the total of all five countries and multiplied by 100. Thus, 100*10072/ (8902+9989+5109+2388+10072)=36.7%.

14. D

Denoting Slovakia's GDP by x, the total amount of loans in 2007 was 0.446x in Slovakia and 0.534 * 2x = 1.068x in Hungary. Thus, foreign exchange loans amounted to 0.236 * 0.446x = 0.1053x in Slovakia and 0.524 * 1.068x = 0.5596x in Hungary; the former figure is 1 - 0.1053x / 0.5596x = 1 - 0.1053 / 0.5596 = 81% less than the latter one.

15. C

Between 1990 and 2005, the GDP of the Netherlands increased from 264.1 billion USD to 572.8 billion USD - an increase of 308.7 billion USD – 20.58 billion for each year 1990-2005. Similarly, social expenditure grew from 25.6% of 264.1 billion = 67.61 billion to 20.7% of 572.8 billion = 118.57 billion, which corresponds to a total increase of 118.57 – 67.61 = 50.96 (billion USD) and an annual increase of 50.96 / 15 = 3.40 (billion USD). In 1996, the GDP of the Netherlands was equal to 264.1 + 6 * 20.58 = 387.58 billion, while the social expenditure equalled 67.61 + 6 * 3.40 = 88.01 billion. Social expenditure divided by GDP and multiplied by 100 gives the percentage that social expenditure represents of GDP, as in 88.01 / 387.58 = 0.227 = (0.227 * 100) % = 22.7%.

16. B

1 tonne = 1,000 kg and 1 kg = 1,000 grams, therefore 1 tonne = 1,000,000 grams. 1 ounce = 31.1 grams, so 1 gram is 1 / 31.1 ounces. Therefore 1 tonne = 1,000,000 grams * 1 / 31.1 = 32,154 ounces. The amount of Switzerland's gold reserves changed from 2,590 tonnes or 83.28 million ounces (as in 2,590 * 32,154 = 83,278,860) in March 1999 to 1,054 tonnes or 33.44 million ounces (as in 1,040 * 32,154 = 33,440,160) in March 2009. The value of the reserves changed from 23.82 billion USD or 23,818 million USD (as in 83.28 million ounces * 286 USD per ounce) in 1999 to 29.63 billion USD or 29,628 million USD (as in 33.44 million ounces * 886 USD per ounce) in 2009. This is an increase of 5.81 billion USD.

17. E

Russia's GDP is projected to decrease in 2009 by 8.7% from 2,271 billion USD in 2008 and will thus equal 2,271 * (100% – 8.7%) = 2,271 * 91.3% = 2,271 * (91.3 / 100) = (2,271 * 0.913) (billion USD). The 2010 GDP will equal 104.9 % of (2,271 * 0.913) or (2,271 * 0.913) * 104.9% = (2,271 * 0.913) * (104.9 / 100) = (2,271 * 0.913 * 1.049) (billion USD). The 2011 GDP will be 104.2% of the 2010 projected GDP and equal (2,271 * 0.913 * 1.049) * (104.2 / 100) = 2,271 * 0.913 * 1.049 * 1.042 = 2,266.4 (billion USD). Similarly, Spain's 2011 GDP is projected to be 1,402 * 0.964 * 0.997 * 1.009 = 1,359.6 (billion USD). Thus, Russia's 2011 GDP will represent 22,66.4 / 1,359.6 = 1.667 = (1.667 * 100) % = 166.7% of Spain's.

18. E

The percentage growth is the difference between the 2007 and 2004 figure divided by the 2004 figure and multiplied by 100. This gives values of 59%, 24%, 46%, 22% and 42% respectively.

19. B

The per capita rate is the volume of paper recycled

divided by the population. The rate of increase is the difference between the rates divided by the starting rate and multiplied by 100. This gives 100*(59/3111*1.0032)-(40/3111))/(40/3111)=46.6%.

20. E

The Channel Islands' per capita rate is 5.1/149 tonnes per person. Therefore Estonia would have to recycle 1347*(5.1/149)=46100 tonnes which is 8100 tonnes more than they actually did.

21. B

Add the inflation rates and divide by the number of countries:
(2.8 + 9.1 + 4.9 + 2 + 1.9) / 5 = 4.14

22. A

As we are looking for proportions, we can use the figures given in 00s:
Total wire produced = 100 + 150 + 30 + 20 = **300**
Total wire exported = 80 + 90 + 10 + 20 = **200**
Production : export = 300 : 200 = 3 : 2

23. B

Cars: gain of 3bn or 6% (3 / 52 = 0.06)
Buses: no gain in income
Trucks: gain of 2bn or 5% (2 / 44 = 0.05)
Boats: gain of 3bn or 25% (3 / 12 = 0.25)
Airplanes: no gain in income
Helicopters: no gain in income

24. B

Company B received 240 million euros for all juices sold in 2004. Pear juice represented a proportion of that, as in: 19 / (19 + 4 + 37) = 19 / 60
240 * (19 / 60) = (240 / 60) * 19 = 76 million euros

25. A

If a figure increases by 200%, it is tripled (x + 200% = x + (200/100) * x = x + 2x = 3x); thus, we need to look for countries whose GDP more than tripled between 1990 and 2005. Taking a quick look at the data, we can see that Ireland is the only country which satisfies this condition (160.4 > 3 * 45.7, since 3 * 45.7 is less than 3 * 50 = 150; or more precisely, 160.4 / 45.7 = 3.51 > 3).

26. D

The amount of lithium produced in the six countries together was equal to 6 910 + 180 + 707 + 11 000 + 3 010 + 300 = 22 107 (tonnes) in 2007 and 6 900 + 180 + 710 + 12 000 + 3500 + 300 = 23 590 (tonnes) in 2008. Since 23 590 / 22 107 = 1.067, an increase by (1.067 * 100) % – 100% = 106.7% – 100% = 6.7% took place in the production between 2007 and 2008. The amount of lithium produced in 2009 will thus equal 23 590 tonnes + 6.7% = 25 171 tonnes = 25.2 thousand tonnes.

27. A

Between 2020 and 2040, the population of Sweden is projected to increase from 9.9 million to 10.5 million, = 0.6 million, giving an annual increase of 0.6 million / (2040 – 2020) = 0.6 million / 20 = 0.03 million. In order to exceed 10 million, the population has to increase by at least 10 million – 9.9 million = 0.1 million compared to 2020, i.e. 0.1 million / 0.03 million = 0.1 / 0.03 = 10 / 3 = 3 1/3 years. Thus, the population will exceed 10 million in the course of the fourth year - i.e. 2024.

28. D

This is the total population (100%) minus those over 60 (24%) minus those under 15 (13%) which is 63%. We then need to multiply this by the population (7590 thousand and divide by 100 to convert the value from the percentage. 7590*63/100 = 4781.7 thousand = 4.78 million.

29. A

256 (thousand) in a population of 5120 (thousand) is 256/5120 = 0.05. This is multiplied by 100 to make it a percentage which is 5%.

30. E

The number of buzzards in 2009 was 2296 out of a total population of 11480 birds. This is 2296/11480 = 0.2. Multiply by 100 to convert to a percentage which equals 20%.

31. B

France generated 24MKWh out of a total of (24+42+44+34+16) = 160MKWh. This is a proportion of 24/160 = 0.15. To express this as a percentage, multiply by 100 which is 15%.

32. E

The total generated in 2007 was (16+38+36+27+11) = 128 and the total generated in 2006 was (12+35+35+23+7) = 112. This is an increase of (128-112) = 16MKWh.

33. C

The total spending will be the number of students in each stage of education multiplied by the spending per student. The number of students in each stage is the total number of students multiplied by the proportion. This gives Total=(146*(8102*0.24) +(5887*0.36)+(4309*0.4))=845K. Divide this by the population to get the per capita amount => 845K/836 = 1010 Euro/person.

34. A

The total spending for each country is the total number of student multiplied by the percentage of students in that stage multiplied by the spending per student. For Slovakia this is (969000*0.38*4413)=1.6 billion Euro. For Bosnia it is (635000*0.42*4218)=1.1bn euro, a difference of 500 million euro.

35. B

The per capita spending is the number of students multiplied by the cost per student and divided by the population. As the proportion of students in secondary education in both countries is the same, it can be ignored. For Iceland this is (6062*56) /295.7=1148. For Ukraine it is (5650*8401)/46936 =1011, a difference of 137 euro.

36. D

In Denmark there are (28.2-21.4)% of 5417000 people who are eligible which is 368 356. Divide this into the number who married and multiply by 100 to get 6.1%.

37. D

The per capita marriage rate is the number of marriages divided by the population. The percentage change is the difference in rates divided by the 2005 rate and multiplied by 100. Thus, 100*((47124/9978)(48391/10078))/(48391/10078)=-1.6%.

38. A

Let X be the population in 2010. The number of unmarried people is the unmarried percentage multiplied by the population and the percentage of those getting married is the number of marriages divided by the number of unmarried people. So, 71.114/(16316*0.314) =70.941/(X*0.309). Re-arrange and solve, X=16539(thousand) which is up 223 000.

39. E

The births per 100,000 is the number of births divided by the population and multiplied by 100,000. This gives values of 1746, 1505, 1446, 1259 and 1449 respectively.

40. A

The per capita birth rate is the number of births divided by the population. The percentage change is the difference between the two rates divided by the 2004 rate and multiplied by 100. This gives 100*((542/43060)(537/(43060/0.998)))/(537/(43060 /0.998))=+1.13%

41. D

The deaths per thousand births is simply the number of deaths divided by the number of births (as stated in thousands). The drop in rate is the difference between the two years divided by the 2004 rate and multiplied by 100. Thus, ((1002/1194)-(1019/1203))/(1019/1204)=0.84%.

42. A

The number of policemen per 1,000 is the number of policemen divided by the population and multiplied by 1000. However, it can easily be seen that France and Italy have about 10 times as many policemen and only 6 times the population of Greece. Likewise Germany has 12 times the policemen and 8 times the population. Ireland has over half the number of policemen but less than half the population.

43. E

The per capita rate of policemen is the number of policemen divided by the population. The change is the difference in rates divided by the 2005 rate and multiplied by 100 to make it a percentage. Thus, 100*((28.7/(4187*1.0185))-(28.1/4187))/(28.1/4187)=-6.6%.

44. B

Let X be the population of Italy in 2010. The per capita rate is the number of policemen divided by the population. So, (424/X)=(422/60098). X=60383 which is 285 (thousand) more than in 2005.

45. C

The number of children receiving a vaccine is the percentage uptake multiplied by the population. So, (199*0.94)-(186*0.97)=187.06-180.42=6.64 which is in thousands.

46. D

The number of children receiving the vaccine in 2008 was (761000*0.34)=258740 which was 10% lower than in 2005 which was (258740/0.9)=287489. The number of children in total increased by 6% so there were (761000/1.06)=717925 in 2005. The percentage uptake in 2005 was therefore, 100*(287489/717925)=40%.

47. A

The minimum number is when there is no overlap between the groups. This is the total number of children minus (those who didn't have MMR plus those who didn't have DPT plus those that did have Polio). This is 906-(906*(0.06+0.09+0.71)) =906*0.14. This gives 127 (thousand).

48. E

The per capita generation is the amount generated divide by the population. The percentage increase is the difference between the two years divided by the 2005 value and multiplied by 100. This gives 100*((221/61899)-(1.7/60261))/(1.7/60261)=12556%.

49. A

The per capita installations is the number of installations divided by the population. The growth is the difference between the two years divided by the 2005 value and multiplied by 100. This is 100*((4.1/4589)-(0.6/4187))/(0.6/4187)=523%.

50. C

The generation per installation is the amount produced divided by the number of installations. The growth is the difference between the two years divided by the 2005 value and multiplied by 100. This gives 100*((2523/1794)-(1859/1549))/(1859/1549)=17%.

51. C

The per capita spending is the total amount spent on videos (number of videos multiplied by cost per video) divided by the population. For 2000 it was (137*14)/(61.013-1.2)=32.07 and for 2005 it was (42.2*16)/(61.013)=11.07, a difference of 21 euro.

52. E

As the cost of videos in both countries is the same it can be ignored. Let X be total number of videos needed to be sold in Spain. Then, X/43060 =7.4/8232 => X=38.71 million which is 0.91 million more than was actually sold.

53. E

The percentage drop is the number of difference between the number of videos sold in 1990 and 2010 divided by the number sold in 1990 and then multiplied by 100 to make it a percentage. This gives values of 98%, 98%, 98.9% 98.1% and 99.3% respectively.

54. A

In Romania the users grew from 13,450,000 to 14,660,000. This is an increase of 1,210,000. To express this as a percentage we divide the increase by the starting value and multiply by 100. So, 100*(1210000/13450000) = 9%.

55. E

The proportion of the population using the internet is 8020/10415 = 0.77 (both numbers are in thousands so we can round to thousands). To make a percentage we multiply by 100 to get 77%.

56. C

As the units for wine production and population are all in thousands then they can safely be ignored. The wine produced in Switzerland is 1000 hectolitres, half of which (50000 litres) is drunk by 7441 people. This is an average of 50000/7441 = 6.7 litres per person.

57. A

The percentage produced by Germany is 95000 divided by the total amount produced which is (17200+95000+30200+3600) = 146000 and then multiplied by 100. This is 100*(95000/146000) = 65%.

58. C

The proportion of subscriptions accounted for by Denmark is 3799 divided by the total of all subscriptions for that year, (1594+3799+5511+1759) = 12663 which is 3799/12663 = 0.3. To make this a percentage then multiply by 100 which is 30%.

59. E

In 2007 there were 2451 (thousand) subscriptions in Bulgaria between 3770 (thousand) people. The (thousands) can be ignored. So there are 2451/3770 = 0.65 subscriptions per person or 65 per hundred people.

60. D

The per capita funding is the total amount spent divided by the population. This gives a difference of (33449/10415)-(25020/7441)=0.151. This needs to be multiplied by 1000 to make it into Euros/person.

61. A

The per capita funding is the total amount spent divided by the population. This gives values of 3212, 2666, 2600, 3425 and 3362 respectively.

62. B

The per capita funding is the total amount spent divided by the population. The increase is the difference between the two years divided by the 2005 value and multiplied by 100. This gives 100*((6444/(2292*0.9952))-(6110/2292))/(6110/2292) =6.5%.

63. B

The per capita death rate is the total number of deaths divided by the population. The change is the difference between the two years divided by the 2004 value multiplied by 100. This gives 100*((1421/4443)-(1418/(4443-8)))/(1418/(4443-8))=+0.03%.

64. E

The non-road related deaths is the total deaths minus the road related deaths. The change is the difference between the two years divided by the 2004 value and multiplied by 100. Thus, 100*((6211-5467)-(6821-5891))/(6821-5891)=-20%.

65. C

The per capita death rate is the total number of deaths divided by the population. Let X be the number of deaths required in Bulgaria in 2005. (X/7739)=(2298/7441). Re-arrange and solve and X=2390 which is 39 fewer than actually recorded.

66. E

The medical staff per 100,000 is the total doctors and nurses divided by the population and multiplied by 100,000.. For 2005 it is 100000* ((79+261)/58645)=580. For 2010 it is 100000*((83.1+273)/60098)=592.5. The change is an increase of 12.5 staff per 100,000 people.

67. D

The per capita ratio is the number of nurses divided by the population. Let X be the number of nurses required in France in 2010. Then, (X/62637) =(281/60098) +> X=284350 which is 350 more than the actual figure.

68. B

The per capita ratio is the number of nurses divided by the population. The change is the difference between the two years divided by the 2005 value and multiplied by 100. So, 100*((44/10697)-(42/10415))/(42/10415)=2%.

69. D

The proportion of exports by weight accounted for by Italy is 482 divided by the total exports, (3976+482+245+647) = 5350. 482/5350 = 0.09 which is multiplied by 100 to make it a percentage, 9%.

70. A

The UK exported 647 tonnes of vaccines for $1132m. One tonne is one million grammes and so the cost per gramme is simply 1132/647 = $1.75 per gramme.

71. B

France generated 452 million MWh of electricity for 61.013 million people. This is an average of 452/61.013 = 7.4 MWh per person.

72. C

Hungary generated 150 million MWh out of a total of (440+150+67+93) = 750 million MWh. This is 150/750 = 0.2 which is multiplied by 100 to make it a percentage, 20%.

73. A

Ireland collected 595 (thousand) tonnes out of a total of (2812+595+716+1287) = 5410 (thousand) tonnes. This is a proportion of 595/5410 = 0.11 which is multiplied by 100 to make it a percentage of 11%.

74. D

In 2006 Slovenia collected 1326 (thousand) tonnes of waste. If they collect 5% more in 2007 then they would have collected 1326*1.05 = 1392.3 (thousand) tonnes. They actually collected 1354 (thousand) tonnes which is a difference of 38.3 (thousand) tonnes.

75. D

The student population in 2005 was 171000 of which 50.9% were female. So, we multiply these together and divide by 100 to convert from a percentage to get 87000.

76. E

The female student proportion grew from 53.5% to 54.9% which is an increase of 1.4 percentage points. To calculate the percentage rise, divide the increase by the starting level and multiply by 100. So, 100*(1.4/53.5) = 2.6%.

77. B

In Slovakia there were 23 deaths per 100,000 people so the total number of deaths is (8187 (thousand) * 23 / 100(thousand)) = 1883. In Belgium it was (10400*18/100) = 1872 which is a difference of 11.

78. D

The death rate dropped from 49 to 39 per 100,000 population, a drop of 10 per 100,000 or 1 per 10000. So, the actual drop in deaths is 58645 (thousand) divided by 10000 or 58645/10 which is 5865.

79. D

The crime rate is the number of crimes divided by the population. From this it can clearly be seen that only Portugal will produce a number that is greater than 1 per thousand and must, therefore, be the highest.

80. E

The average rate is the total number of crimes (58122+3105+305+11017) = 72549 divided by the total population (61013+4187+403+10529) = 76132 which is 0.95 per thousand which is 95 per hundred thousand.

81. D

The average amount per customer is the total amount bought divided by the number of customers. This gives 121000 tonnes divided by 6 million which is 121Kg divided by 6 or 20 Kg per person.

82. A

Lidl sold 618 (thousand) tonnes out of a total of (523+110+618+294) = 1545 (thousand) tonnes. The percentage is then 100*618/1545 = 40%.

83. C

The number of patents filed by Germany was (32837+33936+33187) = 99960. The total number filed was (66084+66857+66972)= 199913. The percentage is, therefore, 100*99960/199913 = 50%.

84. E

To calculate the per capita patent filing we need to know the populations of the countries so there is no way of calculating this.

85. D

The amount spent is the spending per inhabitant multiplied by the population. The population of Ukraine dwarfs the other three countries combined and, therefore, so does its spending.

86. A

The percentage increase is the amount of increase divided by the starting point and then multiplied by 100. This gives 100*(1022-911)/911 = 12%.

87. D

Of the 2.8m dial-up users in 2000 1.4m are left for ADSL and 340,000 are left for cable leaving 1.06m. In 2005 there are 2.65m users of which 1.06m are existing users and 1.59m are new. As a percentage this is 100*(1.59/2.65)=60%.

88. B

The percentage of cable users is the number of cable users divided by the total number of users and multiplied by 100. Thus, 100*2987/(1072+31839+2987+1047) => 298700/36945=8.1%.

89. A

The growth is the difference in the number of users between two years divided by the initial number of users. Let X be the number of users in 2015 then, (X-

2987)/2987=(2987-1049)/1049. => X=2987+2987*(2987-1049)/1049 => X=8505 (thousand).

90. B

As no one owns more than 3 cars then the total number of cars is simply the number of people multiplied by the number of cars summed across all columns. This is 3241+(250*2)+(5*3)=3756 (thousand) cars.

91. C

This is simply the total number of people with no cars divided by the total number of households in the five countries. Thus, (627+86+202+91+33)/(4123+4704+4887+4615+4039) => 1039/22368 = 0.046 which is 4.6%.

92. D

The total number of cars is the number of households multiplied by the number of cars per household summed across the line. If the number in the '3+ cars' column is assumed to be just 3 cars then the difference between the total and 6.08m is the number of households with 4 cars. Thus, 6080-2027-(1892*2)-(87*3)=8 (thousand).

93. A

The number of small drinkers is the percentage multiplied by the population. This gives (4443*0.179)-(4465*0.176)=795.3-785.8=9.5 (thousand).

94. C

The percentage of drinkers who drink 0-5 or 5-10 units is (18.1+6.3)=24.4 which is just about 1 quarter which means there are 3 times as many people who drink more than 10 units.

95. C

The number of people drinking 20-40 units is the percentage in that column multiplied by the population. This gives values of 983, 1057, 1402, 1928 and 1039 respectively.

96. C

The percentage growth is the 2006 difference between the 2004 and the 2006 population divided by the 2004 population and multiplied by 100. However, by simple inspection it can be seen that Austria and Switzerland both had a drop in prison population and Croatia and Lithuania had relatively large increases compared to Georgia. Therefore Georgia will be in the middle.

97. E

The per capita population of prisoners is the number of prisoners divided by the population. The percentage growth is the difference in the two values divided by the 2004 value and multiplied by 100. So, 100*((6842/(7441+30))/(6939/(7441-30))/(6939/(7441-30))=-2.2%.

98. D

Let X be the number of prisoners required. Then, X=0.3*(X+5130+5214+4837+6939). Re-arrange to get X=0.3*22120/0.7 => X=9480 which is 270 more than the actual figure.

99. B

The local contribution is 9821 tonnes and their total contribution is (9821+19223+561) = 29605 and so the proportion of local aid is 9821/29605 = 0.33, which is a third.

100. E

The total direct aid is (648+2901+871+561) = 4981 tonnes, of which, Austria's contribution was 648 tonnes. This gives a proportion of 648/4981 = 0.13. To make this a percentage we multiply by 100 to get 13%.

101. D

The number of births is the rate multiplied by the population. This gives values of 62646, 63977, 60293 and 64093 respectively and so Slovakia had the most births.

102. A

The number of births is the rate multiplied by the population. So, for Croatia this gives (4443*12.1) = 53760 and for Ireland it is (4187*12.8) = 53594. This is a difference of 166.

103. A

The number of churchgoers is the percentage multiplied by the population. Greece has such a small population compared to the others it need not be calculated. The other three give values of 9.88m, 9.79m and 7.79m, hence France has the most churchgoers.

104. C

The percentage drop in attendance is the difference in attendance divided by the starting value and multiplied by 100 to make it a percentage. Thus: 100*(16.7-15.9)/16.7 = 4.8%.

105. D

The percentage growth is the difference between the two percentages divided by the 2005 value and multiplied by 100. This gives values of 11.2, 9.8, 19.3, 16.2 and 19.9 respectively.

106. A

Let X be the number of dishes that Greece needs. The growth can be expressed as (X-327)/327 which needs to equal the Portuguese growth which is (1002-836)/836. So, X=327+(166*327)/836 => X=391.93 which is 1.93 (thousand) more than the actual figure.

107. B

The per capita installations is the number of installations divided by the population. The growth is the difference in these numbers divided by the 2005 value and multiplied by 100. This gives 100*((35.7/3773)-(32.1/3781))/(32.1/3781)=11.5%.

108. B

The percentage growth is the increase in sales divided by the starting level and then multiplied by 100. As this is a comparison rather than an absolute value that is sought, the *100 can be omitted. This gives expressions of 20/470, 11/210, 4/525 and 24/895 respectively and from among these options the result for 11/210, Morrisons' growth, is clearly the largest.

109. E

A growth of 10% would have increased Asda's sales from 470 to 470*1.1 = 517. They actually sold 490, a difference of 27 in million litres.

110. A

The increase in spending is (233-222) = 11 million euro and there are 11 million inhabitants and so the increase is 1 euro per person.

111. A

The number of phone lines per head of population is the number of lines divided by the population of the country. However, from simple inspection it can be seen that only Andorra will produce a result below one half (0.5) and must, therefore, be the lowest.

112. B

The percentage of lines in Luxembourg is the number of lines there (247) divided by the total number of lines (36.5+247+210+21) = 514.5 and then multiplied by 100 to make it a percentage. So, 100*247/514.5 = 48%.

113. E

The death rate fell from 24.1 to 21.7 per 100,000 over the period, a difference of 2.4.

The number of deaths is the death rate (2.4) multiplied by the population (2,292,000) and divided by (100000) as the rate is per 100,000. This gives 2292*2.4/100 = 55.

114. A

The number of deaths is the death rate (17.2) multiplied by the population (35000) and divided by (100000) as the rate is per 100,000. This gives 35*17.2/100 = 6.

115. E

This is the percentage of people who own 0 phones multiplied by the population summed across all five countries. So, (61013*0.164)+(82409*0.189)+(58645*0.112)+(43060*0.191)+ (60261*0.172)=50739 (thousand) or 50 million.

116. B

The total number of phones is the number of people multiplied by the number of phones per person summed across the line. If the number in the '3+' column is assumed to be just 3 phones then the difference between the total and 52m is the number of people with precisely 4 phones. Thus, 52000-(60261*0.796)-(60261*0.03*2)-(60261*0.002*3)=55 (thousand).

117. E

The number of people who don't own multiple phones is the percentage of people who own either 0 or 1 phone multiplied by the population. Thus, 58545*(0.112+0.683)-43060*(0.191+0.802)=3864 (thousand).

118. C

The two journey times are 135 minutes and 159 minutes. To calculate how much shorter the first one is, divide the difference by the longer time and multiply by 100 to make it a percentage. Thus, 100*(159-135)/159 = 15%.

119. D

The growth is the difference between the two values (5.8-5.0) divided by the starting value (5.0) and multiplied by 100 to make it a percentage. This gives 16%.

120. A

The increase in the number of octogenarians is the increase in the rate (5.5%-5.3%) which is 0.2% multiplied by the population (9.3m). This gives 18600.

121. B

The number of people getting divorced is the rate (per hundred thousand) multiplied by the population (thousands) and divided by 100. The difference is (202*10195)/100-(151*8232)/100 = 8164.

122. E

The number of divorces is the rate multiplied by the population divided by 100. The percentage decrease is the difference between the two years divided by the 2004 value and multiplied by 100. This is 100*((145*(5386+5)/100)-((151*5386-5)/100))/(151*(5386-5)/100) which gives -3.8%.

123. A

The per capita rate is the rate in the chart divided by 100,000. The percentage increase is the difference in per capita rates divided by the 2004 rate and multiplied by 100. As we are dividing the per capita rate by a per capita rate then the 100,000s cancel out and are not required. So, 100*(254-224)/224 = 13.4%.

124. A

The growth rate in consumption is the difference between the 2010 and 1995 value divided by the 1995 value. This gives values of 56, 26.8, 40.8, 28 and 137. This shows Belgium with a growth rate twice that of Portugal.

125. C

The consumption per capita is the amount consumed divided by the population. The increase is the difference in per capita rates divided by the 1995 rate and multiplied by 100. This gives 100*((1381/(61013-1000))-(1204/(61013-2000)))/(1204/(61013-2000))=12.8%.

126. B

The growth is the total consumption in 2010 minus the total in 1995 divided by the total in 1995 and then multiplied by 100. The 1995 total is (84+1204+502+168+484) =2442, the 2010 total is (131+1527+707+215+1146)=3726. The growth is 100*(3726-2442)/2442=52.6%.

127. D

The number of people who died is the percentage of people who didn't survive one week multiplied by the number of people who had a heart attack. This gives a difference of (4748*0.22)-(6042*0.13) =259.

128. A

Let the number required be X, then X/(X+4748+5014+8128+6042) =1/3. Re-arrange and X=(4748+5014+8128+6042)/2 => X=11966 which is 348 less than actually recorded.

129. C

The number of heart attacks per 100,000 is the number of heart attacks divided by the population and multiplied by 100. This gives 100*((5014/5417)-(8128/11064))=19.

130. E

Half of 1.2m is 0.6m or 600 thousand. There were 3603 thousand visitors to Denmark and so the proportion of foreign visitors is 600/3603 which is one sixth.

131. D

The per head visitor ratio is the number of visitors divided by the population. This gives (2633/4700) when both are in thousands. This is 0.56 visitors per head of population.

132. D

The average density is the total population divided by the total area. Thus, 10440 (thousand) is divided by 30 (thousand) which gives 348 people per square kilometre.

133. E

The increase in population is the total population for 2008 (10667+63983+10618+ 45067) = 130335 (thousand) minus the total population for 2002 (10310+61426+10329+40970) = 123035 (thousand). 130335-123035 = 7300 (thousand) or 7.3 million.

134. C

The percentage increase between any two years is the difference divided by the starting value and multiplied by 100. By inspection one can see that there are only two occasions in the table where an increase occurs: Italy 04-05 and Slovakia 05-06. The former gives a growth of 100*600/234600 = 0.26% and the latter gives 100*52/15628 = 0.33%.

135. A

The percentage drop in marriages is the difference in numbers between the two years divided by the starting value and multiplied by 100. Thus: 100*(18211-17919)/18211 = 1.6%.

136. B

The number of marriages per thousand people is simply the number of marriages divided by the population (in thousands). So, for Ireland it is

20209/4187 = 4.83 and for Italy it is 235200/58645 = 4.01; the difference is about 0.8.

137. C

The difference in the number of men wearing size 8 and size 9 shoes is the difference in percentages divided by 100 and multiplied by the number of men. This gives 25m*(23.7-19.8)/100 = 975000.

138. B

The workforce is the number of unemployed divided by the percentage of the workforce that is unemployed and multiplied by 100. This has to be done for both men and women and then added together. So, (902/0.06) + (987/0.1) = 24900 (thousand) or 24.9m.

139. E

The total number of women unemployed is (1266+987+1050+580) = 3883 and the total number of men unemployed is (1163+902+863+817) = 3745. This is a difference of 138 (thousand).

140. E

Let the yearly increase in population be X. The total volume of chocolate consumed is the per capita consumption multiplied by the population. The population in 2004 is (296-X) and in 2007 is (296+2*X). So, (4.4*(296-X))=(4.1*(296+2*X)). Rearrange and X=(296*(4.4-4.1))/12.6) which is 7. So the population increase by 7 thousand per year and so is 310 000 in 2007.

141. D

The amount consumed is the amount per person multiplied by the population. This gives (836*1.9)-(403*2.4)= 1588.4-967.2 = 621.2. The consumption is in Kg/person but the population is in 1000s so this is 621.2 thousand Kg or 621.2 tonnes.

142. B

The amount consumed is the per capita rate multiplied by the population. The growth is the difference between the two years divided by the 2004 rate and multiplied by 100. Thus, 100*(5.9*(32.5+0.4))-(5.7*(32.5-0.2)))/(5.7*(32.5-0.2))=5.4%.

143. E

Greece produced 1700kWh and the Netherlands 2737kWh. The difference is 1037kWh which is (1037/1700) = 0.61 times more. Multiply by 100 to convert to a percentage of 61%.

144. B

The growth is the difference between the values for the two years divided by the starting level and multiplied by 100. However, we can see from inspection that Belgium has a growth of about 350/12000 which is very small, Norway is nearly 400/4800 which is less than 10% and Slovakia is about 350/6000 which is about 5%. In contrast, Estonia is about 170/800 which is about 20%, far more than the others.

145. D

The overall growth between 2005 and 2006 is the total spent in 2006 (12723+996+5221+6581) = 25521 minus the total spent in 2005 (12394+911+5012+6318) = 24635 divided by the 2005 spending and multiplied by 100 to convert to a percentage. This gives 100*(25521-24635)/24635 = 3.6%.

146. B

The growth is the difference in values divided by the starting value and multiplied by 100 to convert to a percentage. This gives 100*(25010-24281)/24281 = 3%.

147. B

The growth is the difference in numbers for the two

years divided by the starting value. However, simple inspection shows that Germany's growth is so small that it appears flat on the graph and so is, therefore, the smallest increase. Along with their highest starting value this must make theirs the lowest growth.

148. E

The increase is the difference between the 2009 value and the 2003 value divided by the 2003 value and multiplied by 100. This gives values of 3, 7.5, 14.4, -2 and 6.9 respectively for the five countries.

149. A

The number of single parents is the rate per 1000 multiplied by the number of families. This gives (19.8*(572+30))-(19.4*(5724-60))=4048.

150. D

The percentage of French single parents is the number of French single parents divided by the total number of single parents and multiplied by 100. This is (100*(39.7*9281))/((27.4*1018)+(14.1*226)+(39.7*9281)*(18.9*5724)+(8.8*6804))= 368456*100/567594 = 64.9%.

6. Succeeding in Abstract Reasoning Tests

When first faced with an abstract reasoning test such as the one on this page, it can be a daunting experience. In each EPSO abstract reasoning test, you will see a text-based question (something similar to "Which of the following figures comes next in the series?"). Your eyes will scan the shapes in a haphazard fashion. You look at the first image, then the second. You quickly glance at the "answer figures" and get an idea. You then check all the shapes against that idea to find out whether it works. Then you realize that the figure you carefully selected would only fit the prospective pattern if just one figure in the question was a little bit different. Now it's time to start all over again.

Just as in the case of verbal reasoning tests, a systematic approach can produce results much more reliably and quickly. As part of such a systematic approach, we must mention that there are various abstract reasoning test types, depending on:

- the use or avoidance of colours
- the logical relationship between the various figures, whether they are part of a series, a grid, or if there is one figure which is the odd-one-out
- the number of dimensions in the test (two- or three-dimensional tests both exist)

Fortunately, it is now known that EPSO have chosen a type of abstract reasoning test that is very well defined:

- only black-and-white images are used (possibly with various shades of grey)
- only two-dimensional tests are given
- only series-type questions are used
- five items of the series are shown, and the candidate must select the next item in the series
- there are usually five answer options (though EPSO may vary this).

A typical abstract reasoning question: *Which figure is next in the series?*

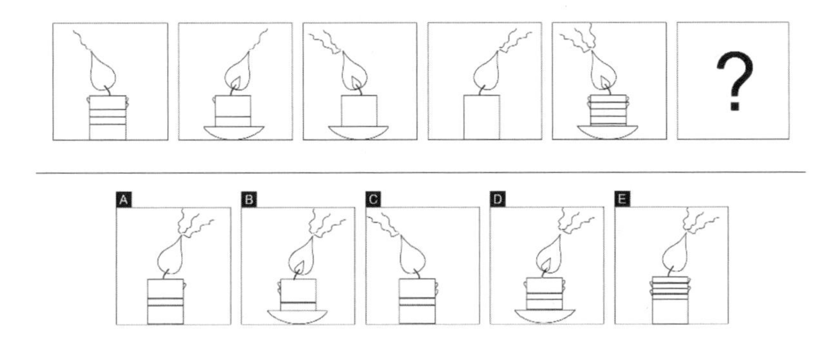

In abstract reasoning tests, it is extremely useful to identify the components. Let us look at these one-by one:

- Building blocks: the building blocks of abstract reasoning tests are twofold:
  - Shapes and patterns are the actual visual objects that are used to construct the figures in the test: triangles, squares, circles, everyday objects (flowers, flasks, houses, and so on), as well as the physical properties of these objects (stripes, dotted or solid fill patterns, and so on)
  - Operations are various visual changes that these objects can undergo, such as colour inversion, multiplication, rotation, change of position, and countless others
- Rules: the rules of an abstract reasoning test are its essential component – they are the text-based description of what the relationship between the various shapes and patterns is, and between the various figures of an exercise

  In this chapter, we will:

- Introduce how abstract reasoning tests are designed: insight into the thought process that is behind the creation of abstract reasoning tests will be very valuable when you are on the other side, that is, when taking such tests
- Introduce the various building blocks, typical shapes, patterns and operations that you will encounter in abstract reasoning tests
- Discuss how to approach abstract reasoning tests
- Provide tips on how to prepare for them

By quickly identifying the building blocks of the test and systematically looking for the above patterns and operations in each test question, you will be able to identify the rules that the question author invented to create the figures and the answer options. Consequently, you will be able to "generate" or "anticipate" the correct figure in your mind without even looking at the options. This method is highly reliable since you will not select one of the figures as the correct answer just because that particular shape seems the best or most suitable option: you will also have independent confirmation, that is, the rule and the figure you came up with yourself.

How Are Abstract Reasoning Tests Designed?

In this section, we will provide a look into the "workshop" of abstract reasoning test designers and, through a real test example, introduce how abstract reasoning exercises are designed.

As mentioned earlier, EPSO uses the series test type exclusively in its competitions. In this type of abstract reasoning test, the question is looking for the one figure that correctly completes a series of figures. A series is an abstract mathematical concept which describes a rule that will correctly predict any item in an ordered set of items. If we identify the rule, we will not just be able to tell which figure will be the sixth one (as in the example above), but also the ninth or the sixteenth one.

When designing an abstract reasoning test, there are specific steps to take:

1. The author decides what shapes and patterns will be used in the tests. Based on the sample test above, let's say we will use an everyday object (a candle) in our abstract reasoning test. This will give us a good variety of objects to work with: the candle itself, candlewick, flame, smoke, possibly a dish to hold the candle in, wax drops coming down the sides of the candle, and so on.
2. Next, the author has to keep in mind the difficulty of the test to be designed. It is

expected that in EPSO competitions for Administrators, the difficulty of the abstract reasoning test will fall into the "medium" and "hard" difficulty categories. The importance of difficulty during design lies in the fact that the number of different rules the author will come up with will determine the difficulty of the test.

3. Once the rules and the shapes/operations are identified and drawn, the author needs to come up with the one correct and several incorrect answer options. The incorrect options must not all be "completely wrong" – in a good (that is, tricky) abstract reasoning test, some of the incorrect answers are *almost* correct.

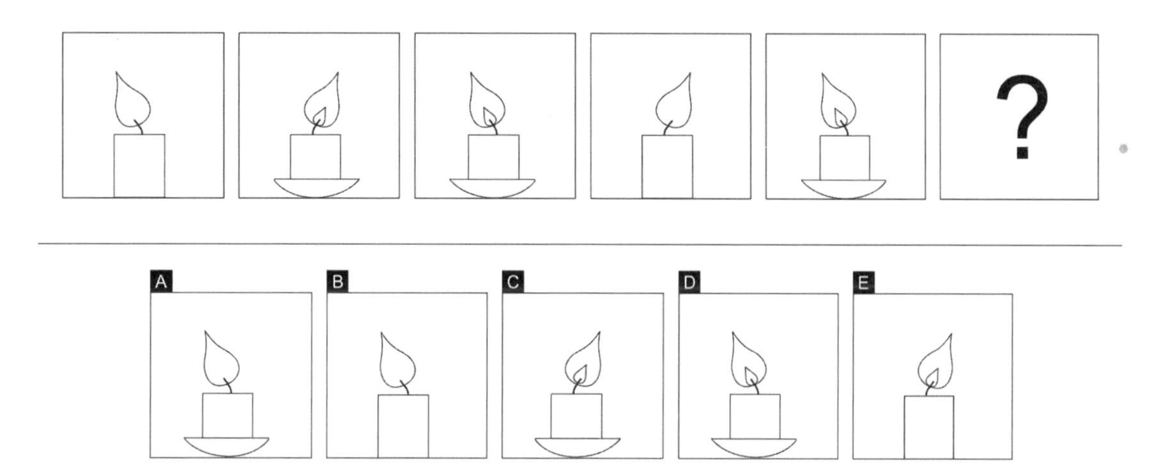

Consider the sample item above. We can identify the following building blocks:

- Candle with or without a dish
- Flame leaning left or right
- Candlewick with or without a "cone" around it

The first regularity you may notice is the direction of the flame. We might describe this as follows:

Rule #1: The candle flame alternates leaning left and right.

While this observation is certainly correct, it does not explain the presence or absence of the cone around the candlewick or the presence or absence of the dish under the candle. The appearance of these objects does not seem to follow any logical pattern.

We can, however, notice a rule in the relationship between these two objects which we might word as follows:

If the candle is on a dish, a cone is visible over the candlewick.

Our new rule, then, should be:

Rule #1: The candle flame alternates leaning left and right and if the candle is on a dish, a cone is visible over the candlewick.

We might at this point ask what will determine the appearance of the dish, but if we turn our attention to the answer options, we will realize that this will not be necessary.

- we are looking for a candle with a right-leaning flame: this immediately excludes A, B, and D

- we are looking for a figure where both the cone and the dish are either present or absent: this excludes E because it only features a cone but no dish

This will leave us with Answer C as the only possible correct answer. There are two very important observations to make here:

- Certain building blocks or patterns may not be relevant for the rule of the test – in our case, there is no logic governing which figures will feature the cone and the dish. Such irrelevant patterns are added to the test as *distractors* designed to make it more difficult to identify those components that are indeed relevant
- Some of the incorrect answer options are *less incorrect* than others: in our case, Answer E correctly included a right-leaning candle flame and was incorrect only because the dish and the cone did not appear together

The above sample item was a relatively easy one. It is, however, possible and usual to create more difficult versions of a test using the same essential components.

Let's see how we could make this test item a bit harder.

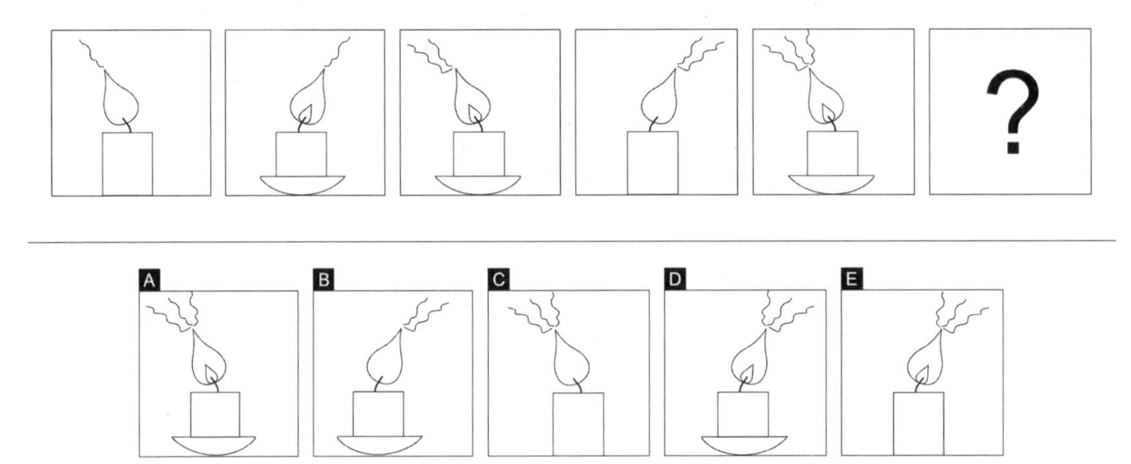

If you look at the above sample item, you will immediately realize that a new building block was included: smoke.

Before we identify the rule governing the smoke, notice that the rule we came up with above still holds:

Rule #1: The candle flame alternates leaning left and right and if the candle is on a dish, a cone is visible over the candlewick.

This rule, however, does not explain the number of wisps of smoke in the figures – consequently, any number of different images could be correct.

We need to identify the second rule:

Rule #2: The number of wisps of smoke increases by 1 every other turn.

Based on these two rules, we can correctly predict that the correct answer will have:

- Right-leaning flame
- Three wisps of smoke
- A dish and a cone or no dish and no cone

The only answer option that matches this description is Answer D.

We can make the test item even harder by introducing a few additional components:

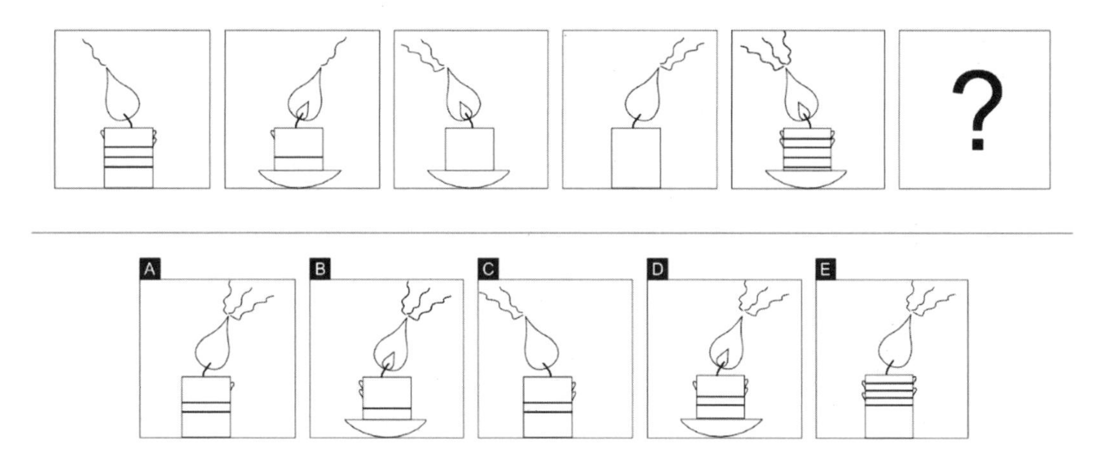

Notice that, again, a new rule must have been introduced because Rules #1 and #2 would be satisfied by Answer A, Answer B, Answer D and Answer E as well. In other words, we can only exclude Answer C based on the first two rules.

If we analyse the figures, we will notice that the number of stripes on the candles is always equal to the number of wax drips on the sides of the candle and, again, there seems to be no logic in how many wax drops appear in each image. We can describe this regularity as follows:

Rule #3: The number of stripes on the candle corresponds to the number of wax drips down the sides.

This rule will exclude Answer A (1 wax drip, two stripes), Answer B (2 wax drips, one stripe) and Answer D (3 wax drips, two stripes) as well, leaving Answer E as the only possible correct option.

As a summary, let us overview what techniques we can use to glimpse the thought process of the creator of the test item:

- Determining the building blocks (candle, dish, etc.) and the number of rules
- Watching out for distractors (e.g. the dish sometimes appears and sometimes does not)
- Eliminating answer options based on each rule we can identify

Patterns and Operations

Now that we have covered the basic components of abstract reasoning tests and the way they are designed, it is time to turn to the various patterns and operations that you must be aware of and able to recognize in order to quickly and efficiently take and successfully pass abstract reasoning tests. It is of course impossible to take stock of all possible shapes and patterns, but we try to give a comprehensive overlook in the next section.

Rotation

The example top right on the next page shows a simple rotation by 90° clockwise. You can gain the necessary routine in identifying rotations by taking the time to sit down

with a piece of paper and a pencil, draw various shapes and then redraw them after rotating them various degrees in either direction, clockwise or counter-clockwise.

The example below left shows a different kind of rotation. In strict geometrical terms, the relationship between the two figures is not rotation at all, yet for convenience's sake, we will discuss it in this section.

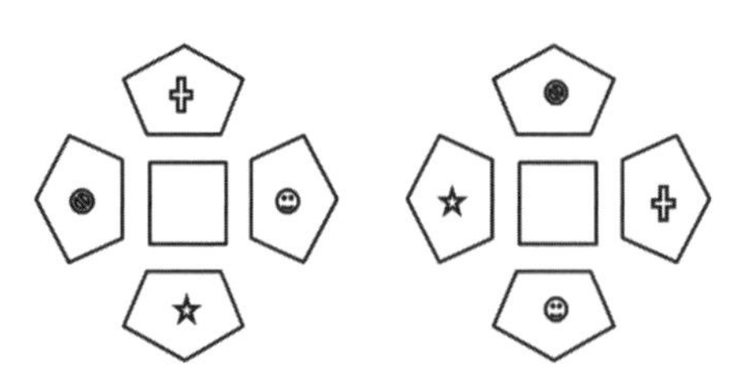

In the two figures, the small icons in the four pentagons around the rectangle in the middle swap places by each icon taking the place originally occupied by its neighbour in a clockwise direction. In some sense, we can say that the icons "rotate" along an imaginary circle running through the centres of the pentagons.

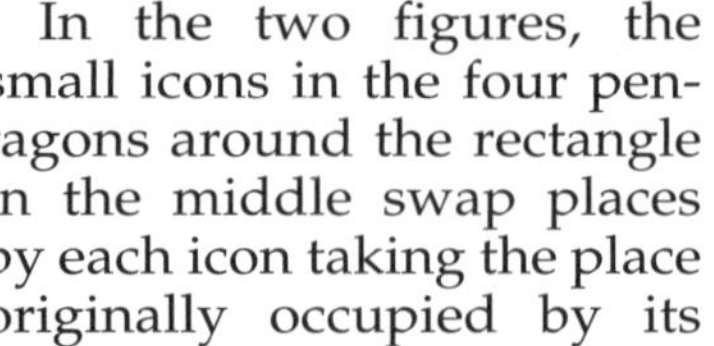

Axial Reflection

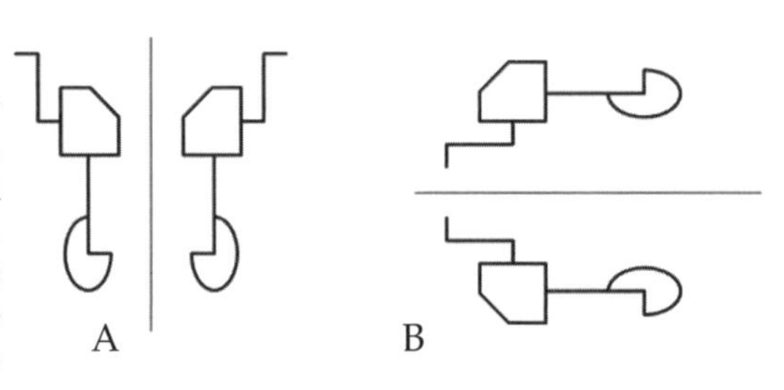

The two examples on the right show the geometrical operation called "axial reflection". The thin lines between the two figures in each of the two sets represent an imaginary mirror. In the first set A, the figure on the right is the reflection of the figure on the left in the "mirror" in the middle and vice versa. This is an example of a horizontal reflection.

Set B represents a so-called vertical reflection. While for demonstration's sake the examples show the horizontal reflection side by side and the vertical reflection with one figure below the other, in real tests this may not always be the case.

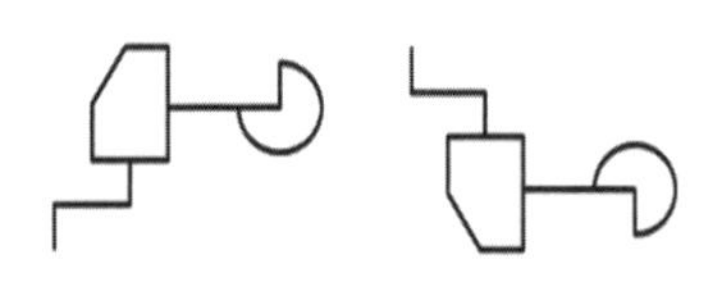

In the example on the left, the figure on the right is still the vertical "reflection" of the figure on the left, but the placement of the second figure does not correspond with where it would actually be in a strictly geometrical sense, that is, below the first image – this makes it harder to consider the relationship between the two figures as a reflection.

You can practice the recognition of this operation in the same cost-effective way as described above for rotations – all you need is paper, a pencil and loads of patience.

Patterns and Inversion

"Which of the following figures completes the series?"

In the example on the right, a new component is introduced – patterns. The example features three shapes:

- Stars
- Ellipses
- Rhombuses

We also notice three distinct patterns or *"fills"*:

- No fill (or solid white fill)
- Solid black fill
- Dots

Looking at the sample test, we notice that two "operations" take place:

- The shapes in each figure change places according to some rule
- The patterns (or fill) of the rhombuses and the ellipses also change according to some rule
- The pattern (or fill) of the star never changes

After further observation, we can establish the following rule regarding the patterns:

"If a rhombus has a dotted pattern, change it to solid black in the next step. If it has a solid black fill, change it to a dotted pattern in the next step. If an ellipse has a dotted pattern, change it to solid white in the next step. If it has a solid white fill, change it to a dotted pattern in the next step. Always leave the star's pattern unchanged."

There are of course many other combinations possible, involving more types of patterns and different relationships between them. Another typical case is the so-called inversion. In such tests, the solid colour fill (usually black or white) of each shape and object turns into its exact opposite, just like looking at pictures in a photo negative. Every shape with black fill becomes white, and vice versa.

The other component of our rule for the above example has to do with the positions of the shapes in relation to each other. We will discuss this in the next section.

Translation

In geometry, translation is an operation where each and every point of a shape is moved to a specified distance in a specified direction.

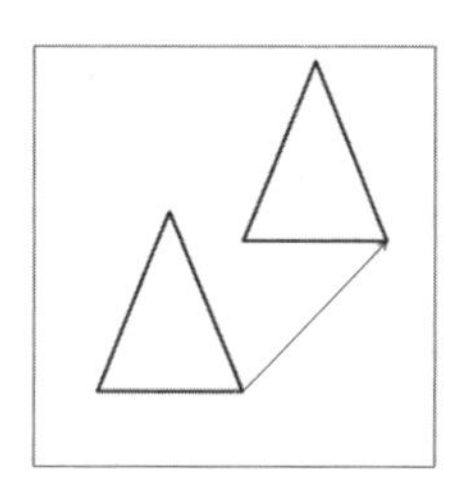

In the example on the right, each point of the triangle at the bottom is moved (or "translated") to the same distance and in the same direction, as indicated by the arrow or "vector" connecting the two shapes. The vector is only shown here for demonstration purposes and would not be visible in a real exercise. We must also keep in mind that the movement sometimes occurs along an actual shape that is part of the figure:

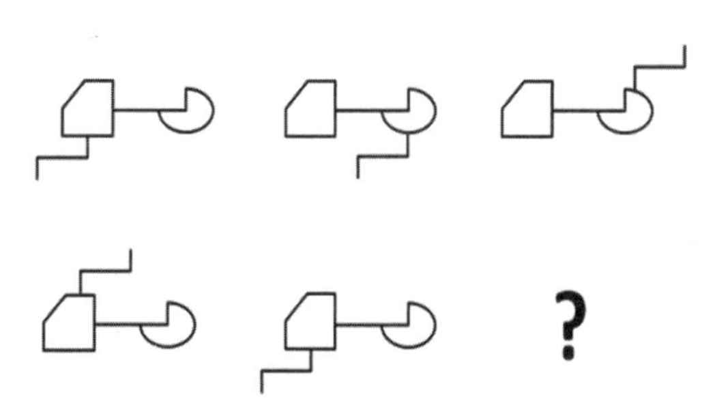

In the example on the left, the zigzagging line "migrates" around the other shapes in a counter-clockwise order. The movement is not a rotation or a reflection – the points of the zigzagging line are simply moved at a certain distance in a certain direction in each step of the series. Therefore the correct answer is a shape that is the same as the middle one in the top row.

Similarly to rotation, there is also a geometrically less accurate meaning of the term "translation". Looking at the sample question with the star, the ellipse and the rhombus, we may notice the following rule governing the placement of the three shapes in the figures of the series:

"Move each of the three shapes one position up. If the shape is already in the top position, it will now occupy the bottom position in the figure."

In the example, the six answer options were intentionally deleted. Based on the method described earlier in this chapter, we can mentally generate the correct figure based on the two rules we established for the series (copied below for convenience).

Rule #1:

"If a rhombus has a dotted pattern, change it to solid black. If it has a solid black fill, change it to a dotted pattern. If an ellipse has a dotted pattern, change it to solid white. If it has a solid white fill, change it to a dotted pattern. Always leave the star's pattern unchanged."

In the fifth item in the series (the figure that will take the place of the question mark), then, the ellipse will become dotted and the rhombus will become solid black. The star will remain white.

Rule #2:

"Move each of the three shapes one position up. If the shape is already in the top position, it will now occupy the bottom position in the figure."

In the figure we are looking for, the now black rhombus will take the bottom position, the now dotted ellipse will go to the middle, and the still white star will move to the top position.

Angles

In geometry, an angle is defined as a figure formed by two lines extending from the same point. In simple geometry, angles are usually given as being any number that is larger than zero and smaller than 360°.

When it comes to abstract reasoning tests, we need to be aware of angles for various reasons. In the case of identifying rotations, the rotation is usually done at a certain angle: 45°, 90° (also called a "right angle"), 180°, or 270°. Of course, rotation at any angle is possible, but due to the difficulty in identifying "custom" angles (say, 67°), such rotations are not likely to appear in EPSO's abstract reasoning tests.

When establishing the "rule" for a test question, we must always think about angles as well.

Consider the example below:

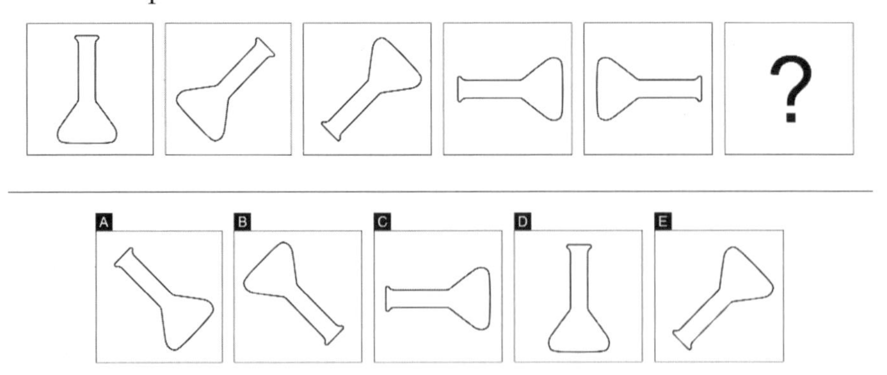

If we look at the images in the sample test above, we see a flask in various positions. After some further observation, we will notice that the flasks in the second, third and further figures are rotated at certain angles when compared to the flask in the first figure. We might describe this regularity based on angles as follows:

Rule #1: The flask is rotated around a fixed point 45 then 180 degrees, and then the cycle repeats.

Visual Arithmetic

The last typical abstract reasoning component we discuss here is sometimes referred to as visual arithmetic.

If we look at the figure extracted from a real abstract reasoning test, we see a large outer rectangle with seven smaller rectangles along its sides. The top left rectangle is shaded, and there are various shapes in the other rectangles (the fact that not all rectangles contain shapes is not relevant for our purposes now).

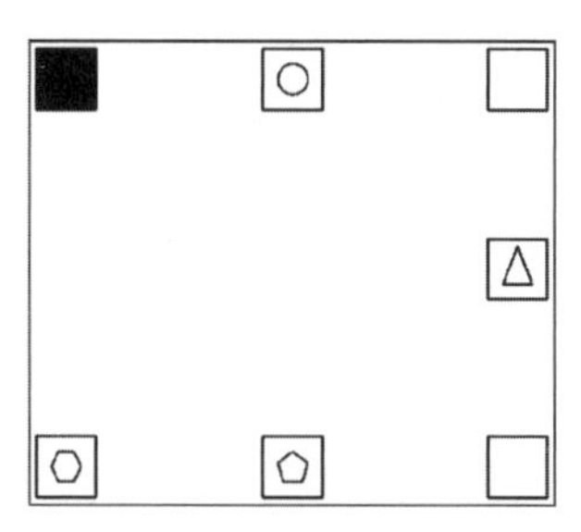

What is the rule that could govern which kind of shape appears in each of the small rectangles? One tactic we can follow in items similar to the above is to first count the number of sides the shapes have. Obviously, the triangle has three sides, the pentagon has five and the hexagon has six. How many sides should we "allocate" to the circle? Let's worry about that a bit later.

The other question is what determines why a certain shape is placed in a certain position in the figure. Counting can again help us out. If we count the distance (defined as the number of rectangles) between the shapes and the shaded rectangle in a clockwise direction, we will notice that the position with the triangle, for example, is three steps away, the position with the rectangle is five shapes away, and so on.

We can now identify a rule:

The distance of a rectangle defined as the number of steps to be taken clockwise from the shaded rectangle is indicated by the number of sides the shape has inside that rectangle.

It is important to bear in mind that EPSO's abstract reasoning tests, similarly to all such well-designed tests, attempt to measure the candidate's intuition and intelligence both visually (identification of shapes, patterns, and so on) and logically (e.g. identifying relationships and numerical regularities).

Summary, Combinations and Approaches

In this chapter, we have overviewed various aspects of abstract reasoning tests:

- Test design, difficulty, rules and distractors
- Building blocks: operations, rules and patterns (rotation, reflection, angles, visual arithmetic, and so on)

Based on the difficulty of the test and the building blocks used, it is easy to see how many different combinations of tests can be created:

- A test with three rules based on rotation, pentagons, triangles and three different patterns (shaded, striped and dotted)
- A test with a single rule based on the number of circles inside a square
- A test with two rules involving windows on a house and the color of the chimney

The above list could of course be continued almost infinitely. The examples above were just meant to demonstrate the sheer number of building block and rule combinations that you as an EPSO test-taker can face. This is exactly why it is crucial to practice and familiarize yourself with an efficient method for identifying both the building blocks and the combination of rules that govern the given exercise – and of course to spot and then disregard distractor elements that do not play a role in establishing the rules of the test item.

Hints for Practicing

- If you feel that a geometrical operation (reflection, rotation, angles, etc.) is one of your weak points, do not shy away from sitting down with some paper and a pencil and draw various shapes and perform the operations on them until they become routine and you are able to recognize a 90°degree clockwise rotation of a complex shape in a couple of seconds
- Once you are familiar with all of the typical rules and operations as detailed above, start practicing on actual test questions, for example the ones in this book.
- Since abstract reasoning tests are all about shapes, it is especially important to try to model the infrastructure of the exam while practicing – the EPSO test will be administered on a computer, which will make it harder (and stranger) to take than a paper-based test where you can scribble on the paper (even though you will be given scrap paper in the exam centre). If you have access to such services, try also to practice online.

  It is also important to develop a systematic approach that you can take when solving each and every abstract reasoning test. One recommended approach is summarized below.

1. Quickly glance through the set of figures. Do not yet spend much time looking at the answer options at this stage.
2. Run through all the rules, operations and patterns you familiarised yourself with during practice and try to apply them to the set of figures. Start with the one that, based on glancing at the figures, intuitively seems the most promising "lead".
3. If you believe you have found the rule or rules governing the exercise, try to "generate" the correct answer figure in your mind or draw a sketch on a scrap paper.
4. Look at the answer options provided and match them against the one you came up with yourself. If a test item is based on multiple rules, you may still be able to exclude one or two of the answer options based on only the first rule. If you are able to do that, you can continue looking for the second rule with a smaller set of answer options to work with – thereby speeding up the process one rule at a time.
5. If you have found a match (and only one), you can mark that as the correct answer. If there are no matches, or multiple matches to your rule(s), they probably have a flaw. Apply your rule to all the figures in the test – this will most likely reveal the flaw, which you can then correct and "generate" a new, hopefully correct, answer figure in your mind.
6. While practicing, you may consider writing every idea and step down for each exercise to make sure you are aware of the logic and rules at play.

In the following chapter, you will find 100 abstract reasoning questions that you can use to start practicing right away.

7. Abstract Reasoning Test

100 Questions – Answers follow on from Question 100

In each question you must choose which of the figures in the bottom line - A, B, C, D or E - completes the series in the top line.

The following questions vary greatly in their level of difficulty. Please note that those that have one rule as a solution are considered as "easy" level, those with two rules are "medium" level, three rules are considered to be "hard" questions and those with four rules are "extremely hard".

The most important thing is to come to understand the type of logic the questions use. Do not despair if you cannot find the solution immediately, especially for the "very hard" questions!

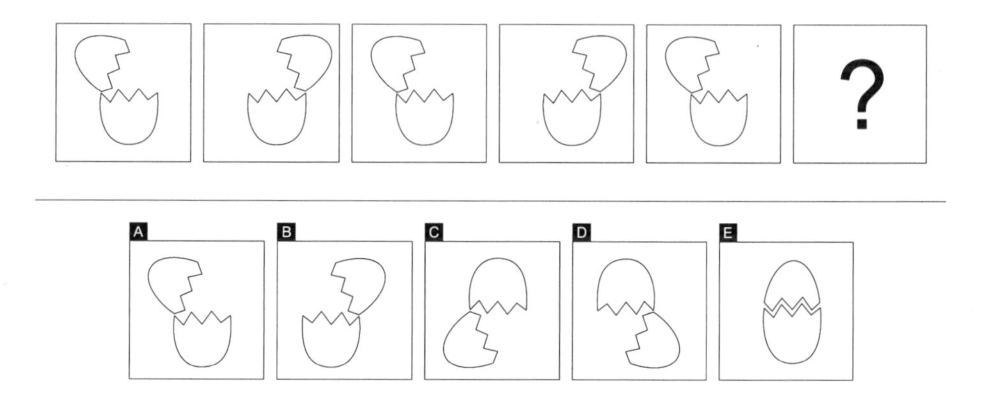

1 Which figure completes the series above?

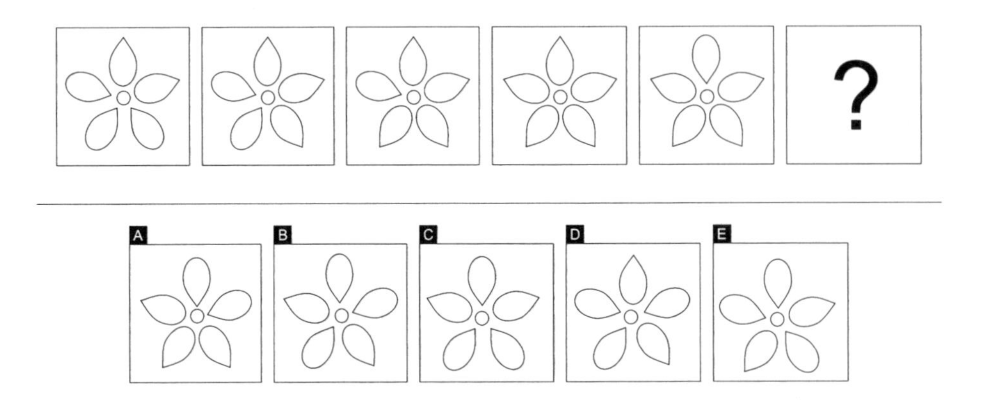

2 Which figure completes the series above?

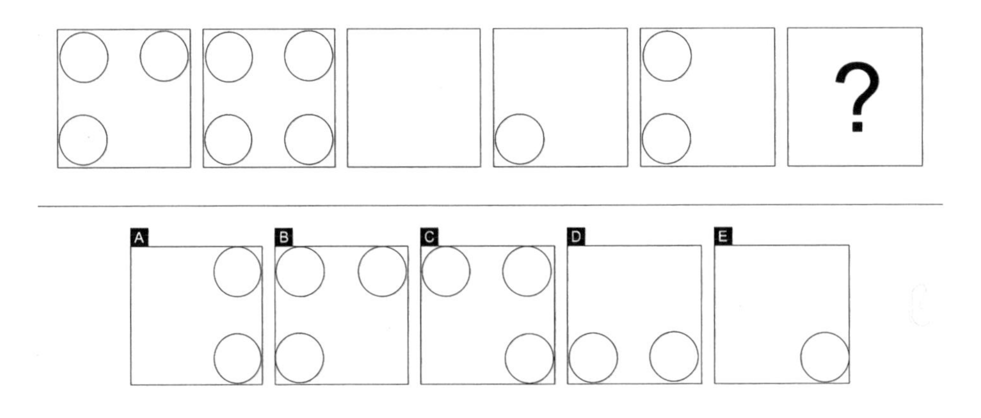

3 Which figure completes the series above?

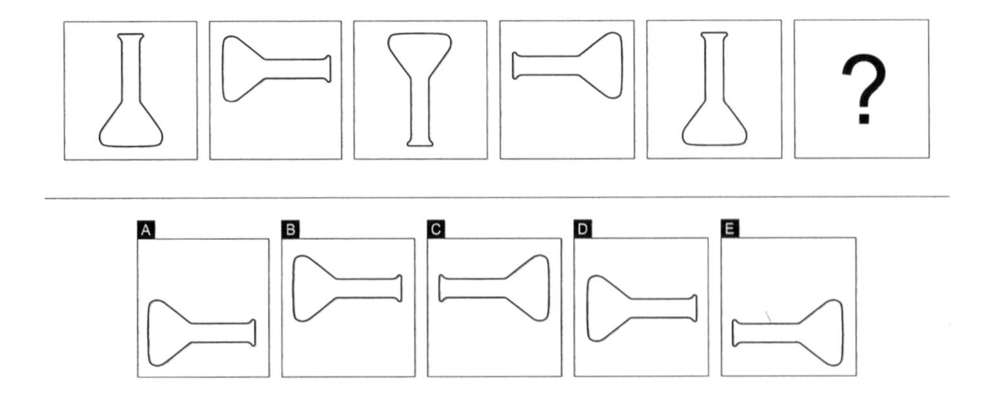

4 Which figure completes the series above?

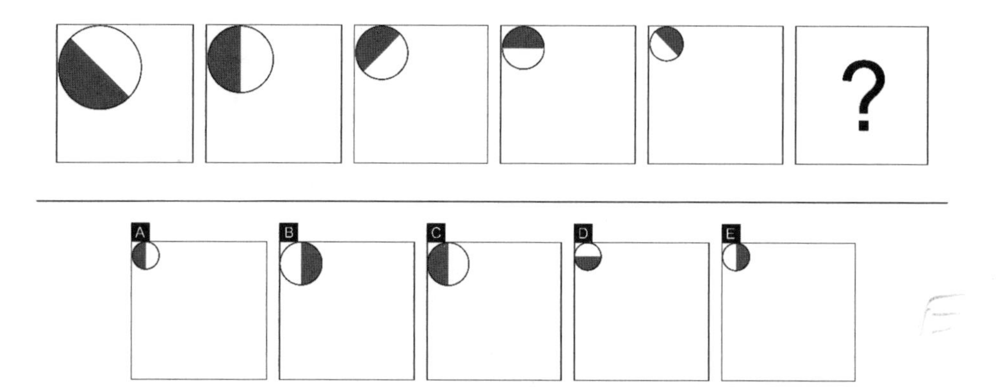

5 Which figure completes the series above?

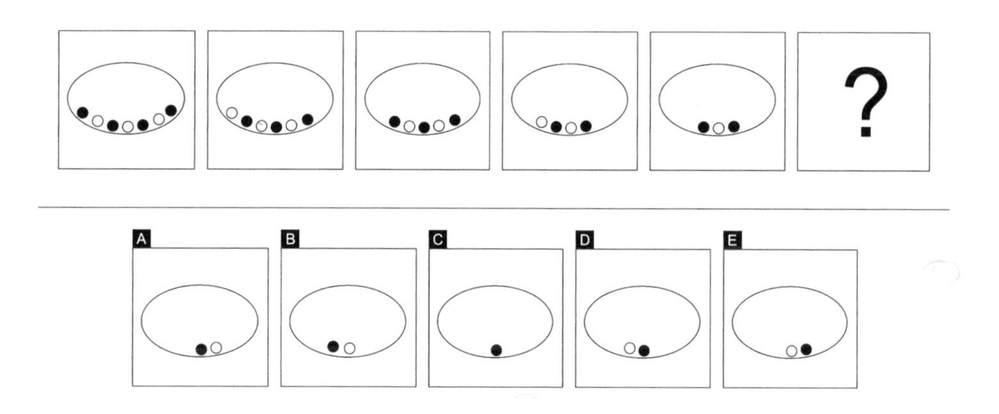

6 Which figure completes the series above?

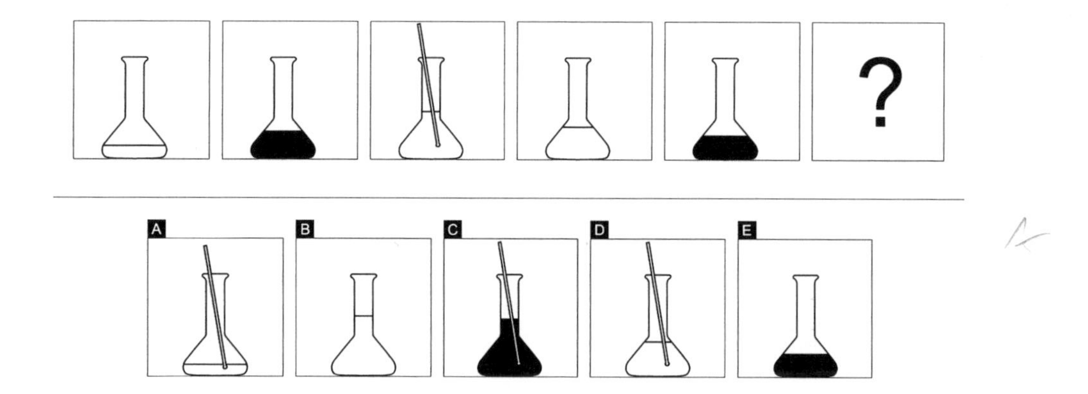

7 Which figure completes the series above?

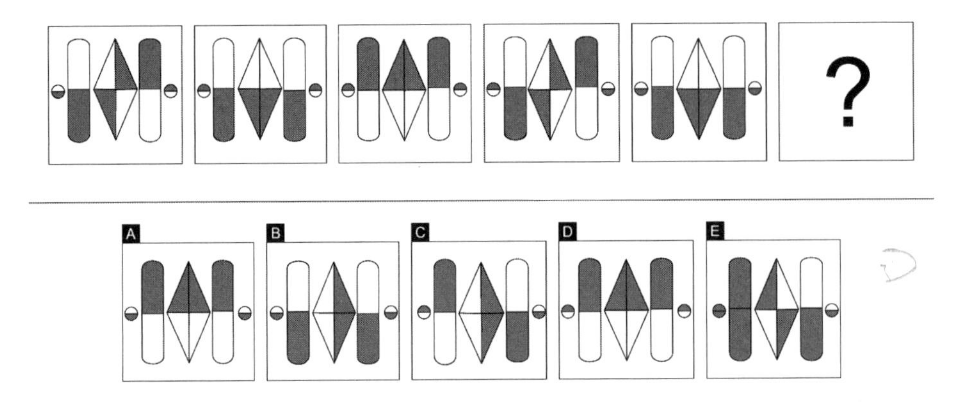

8 Which figure completes the series above?

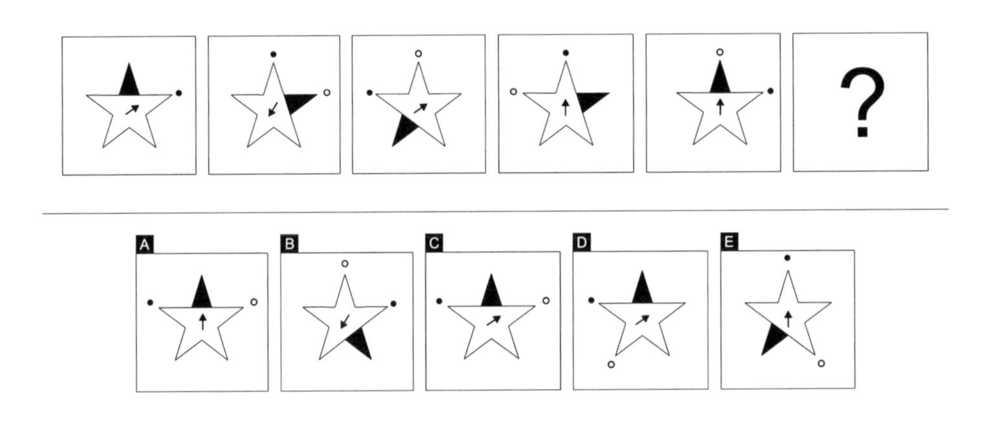

9 Which figure completes the series above?

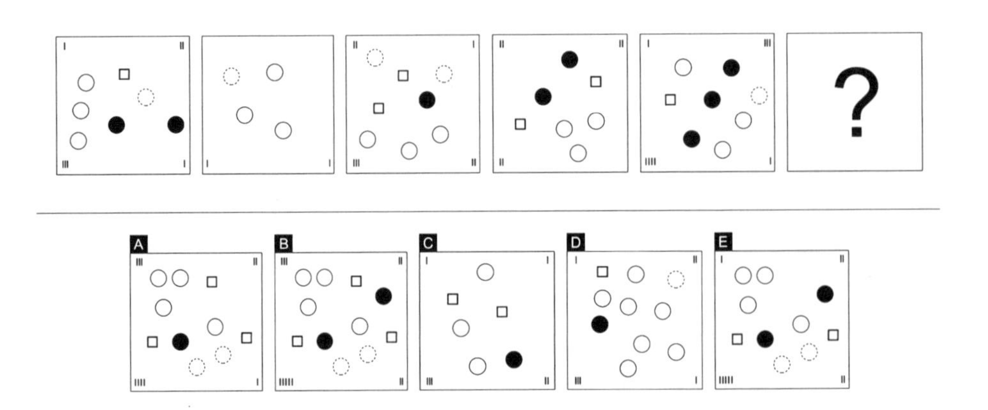

10 Which figure completes the series above?

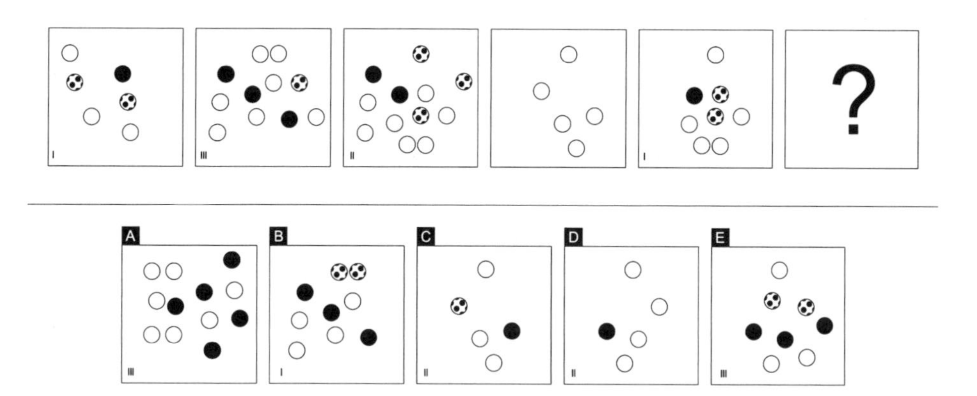

11 Which figure completes the series above?

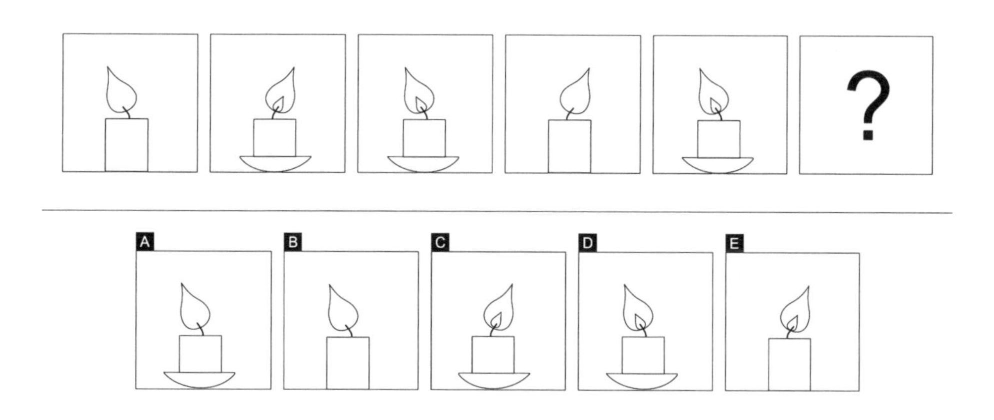

12 Which figure completes the series above?

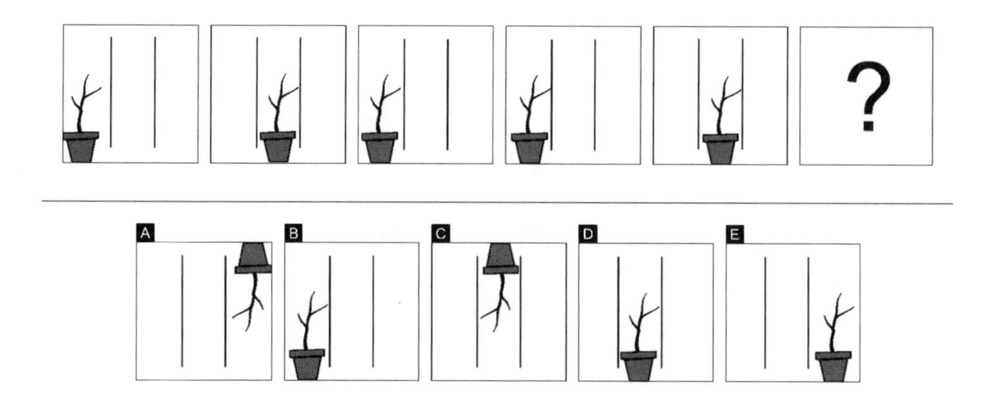

13 Which figure completes the series above?

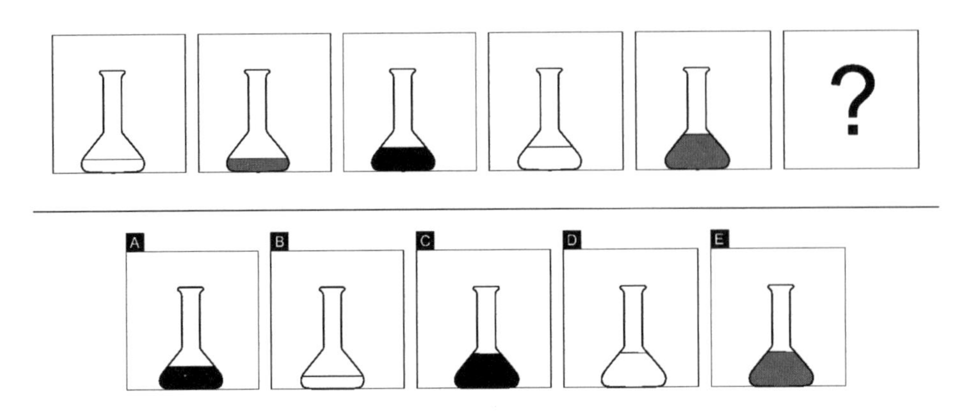

14 Which figure completes the series above?

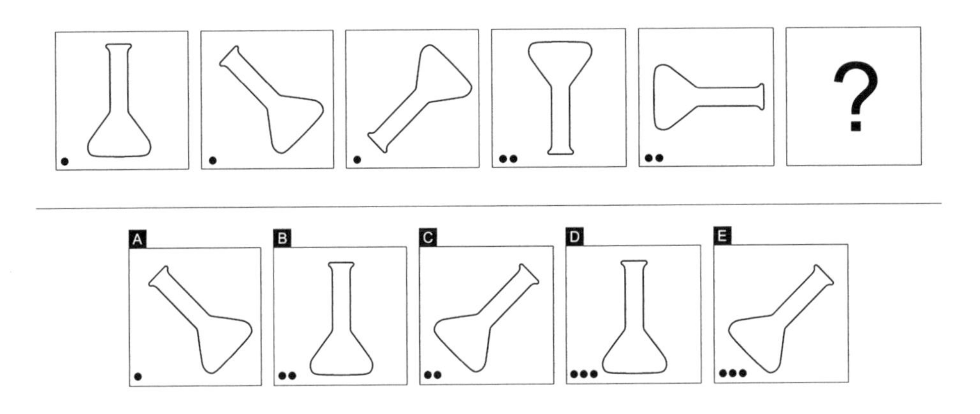

15 Which figure completes the series above?

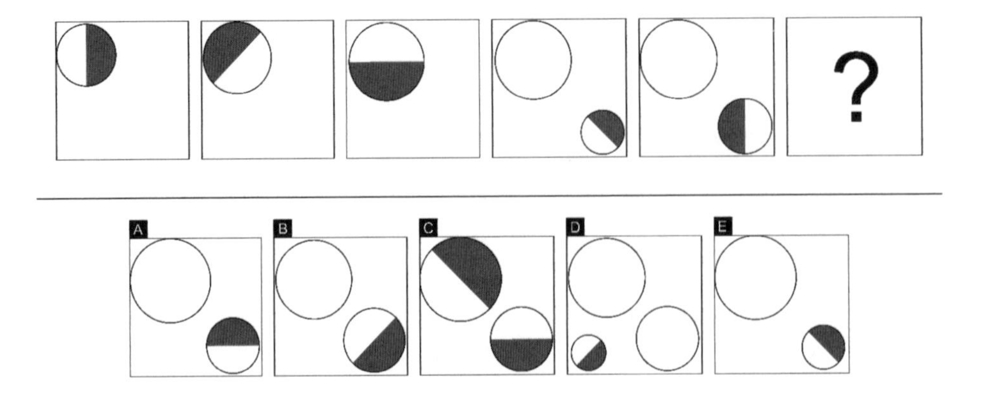

16 Which figure completes the series above?

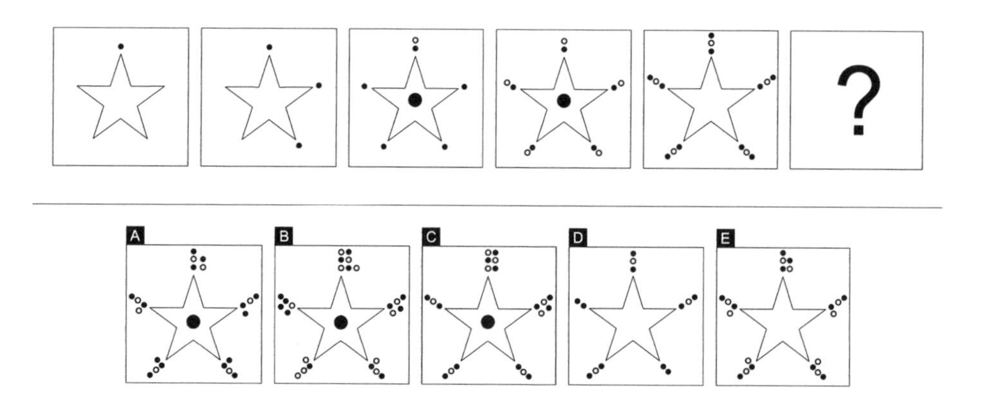

17 Which figure completes the series above?

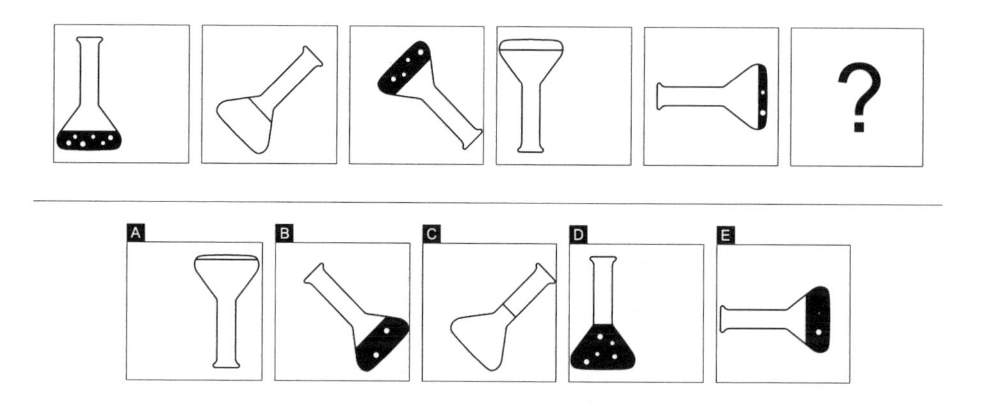

18 Which figure completes the series above?

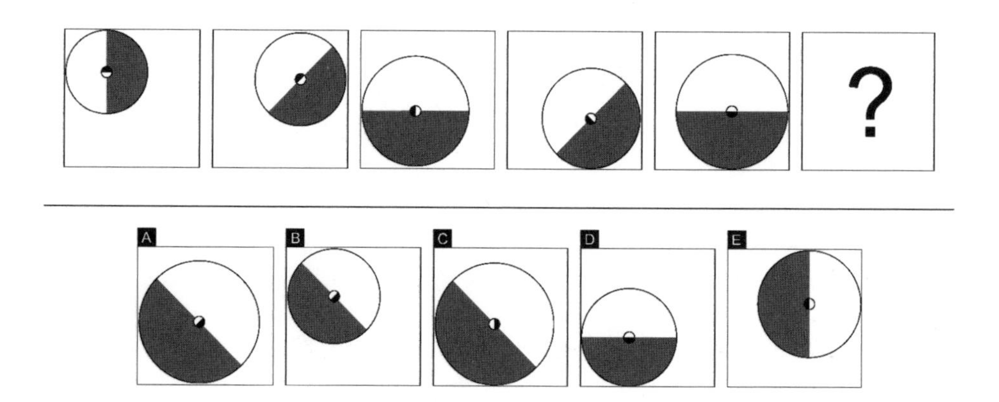

19 Which figure completes the series above?

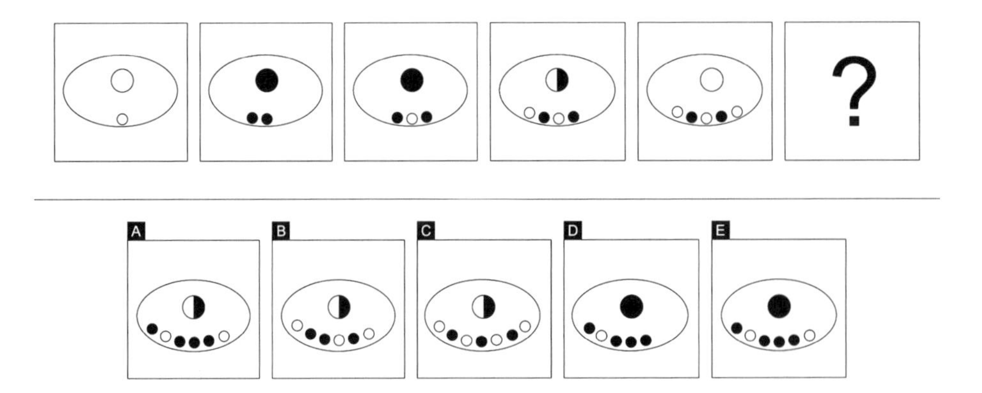

20 Which figure completes the series above?

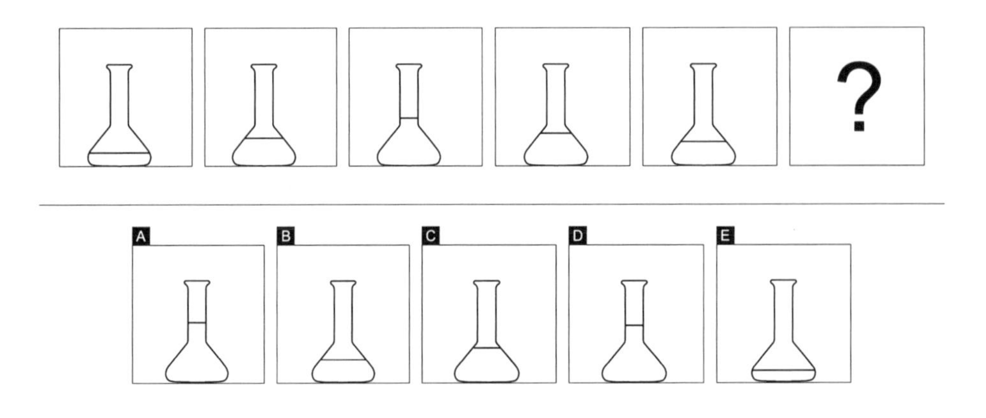

21 Which figure completes the series above?

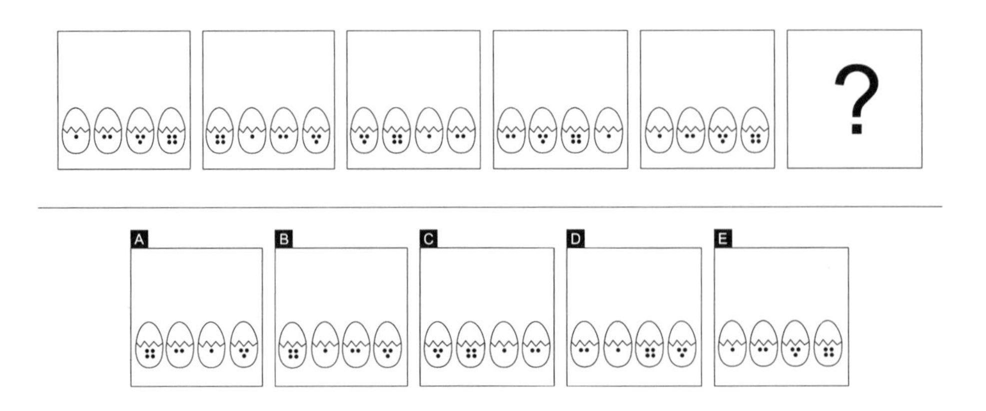

22 Which figure completes the series above?

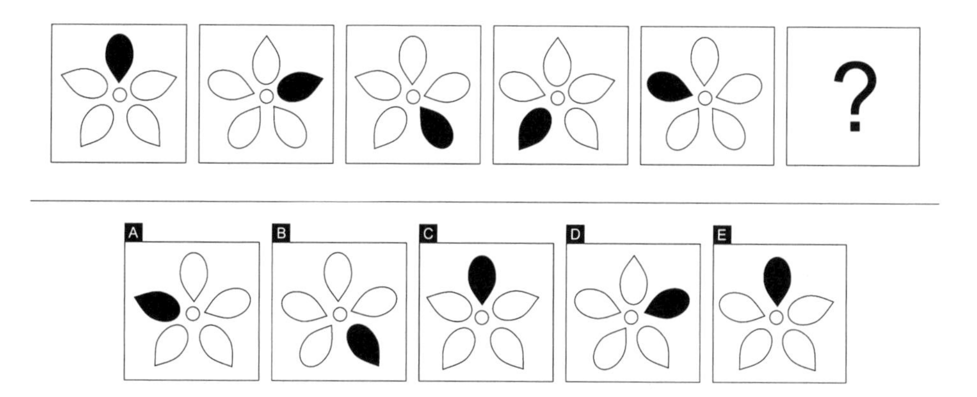

23 Which figure completes the series above?

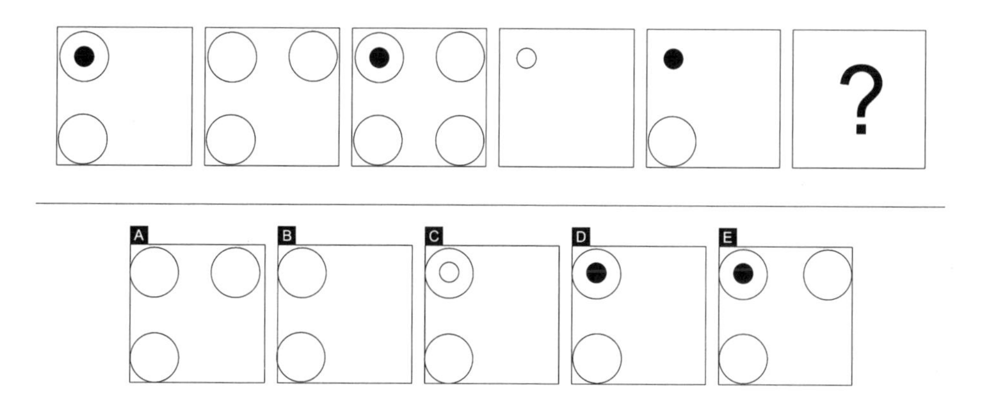

24 Which figure completes the series above?

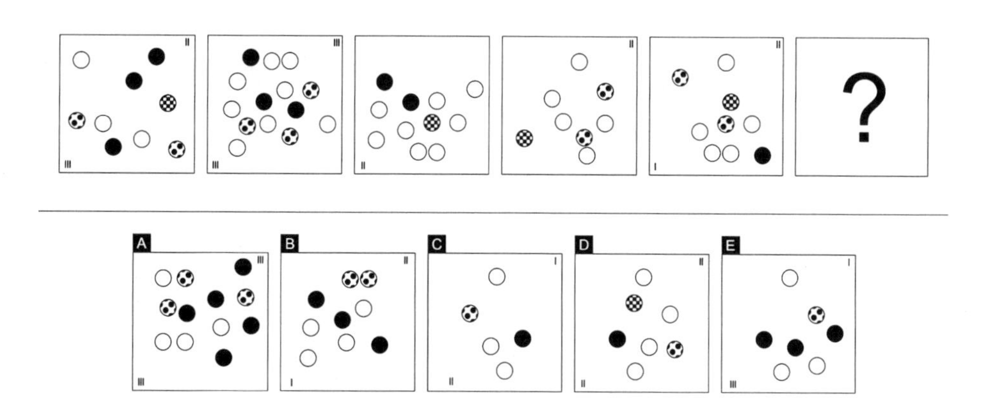

25 Which figure completes the series above?

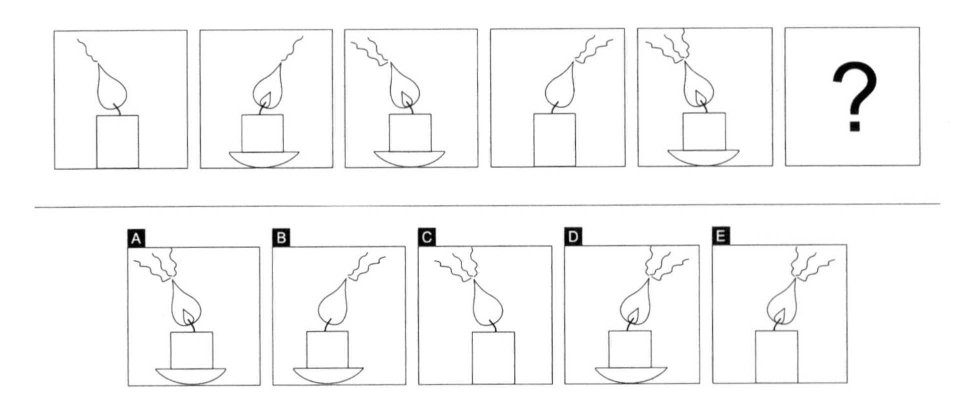

26 Which figure completes the series above?

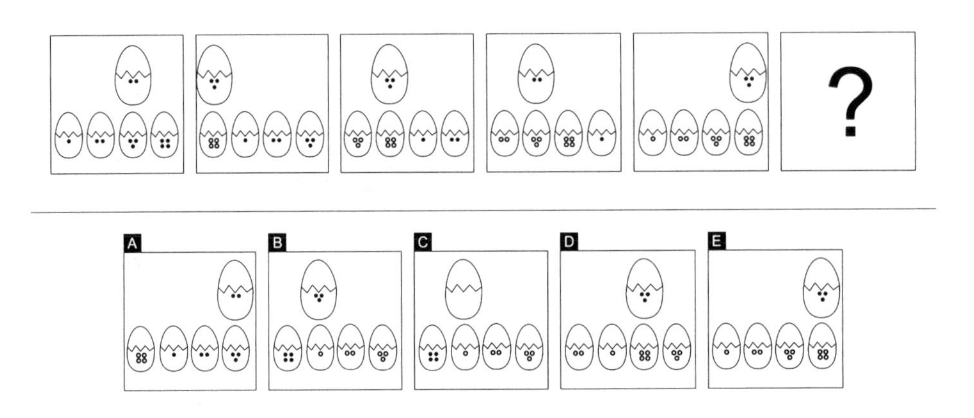

27 Which figure completes the series above?

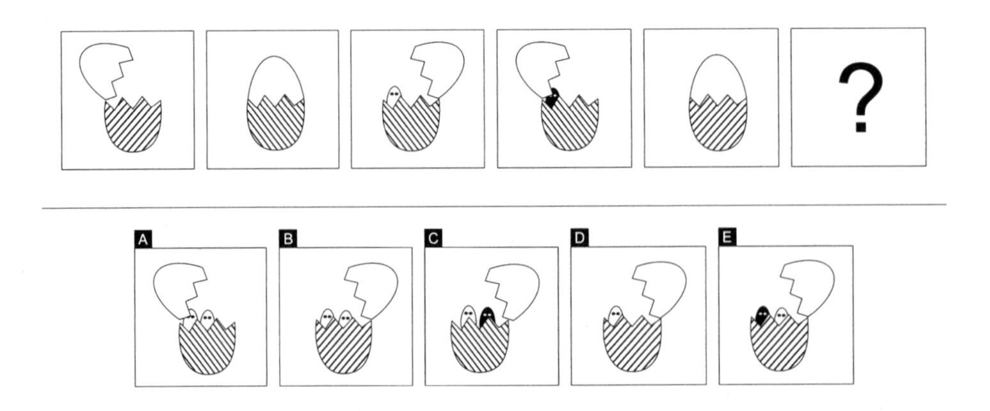

28 Which figure completes the series above?

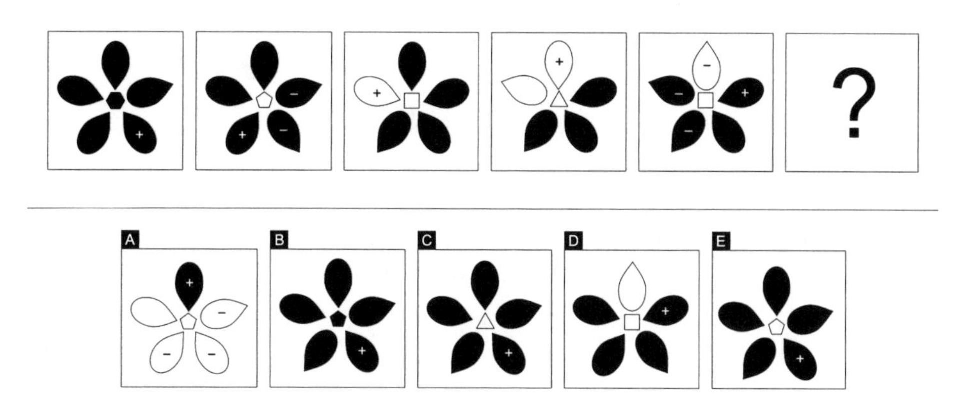

29 Which figure completes the series above?

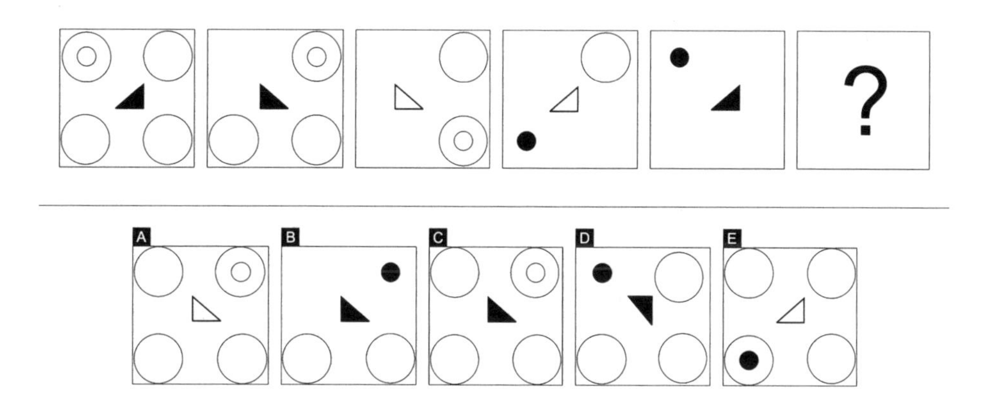

30 Which figure completes the series above?

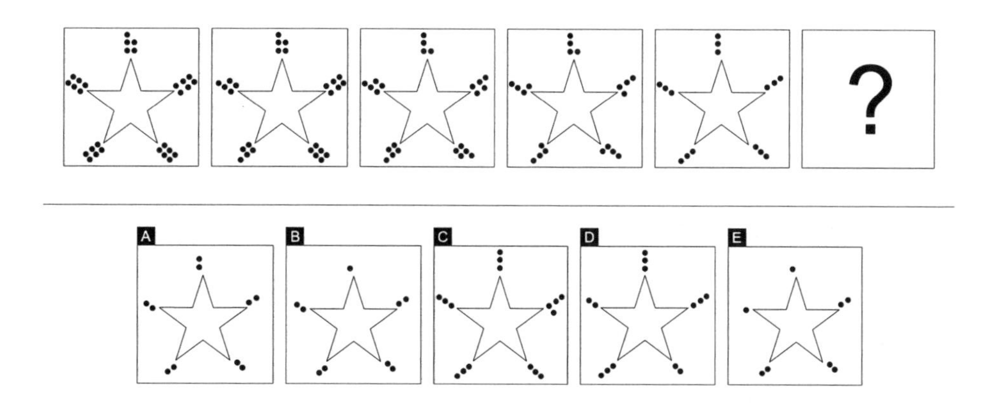

31 Which figure completes the series above?

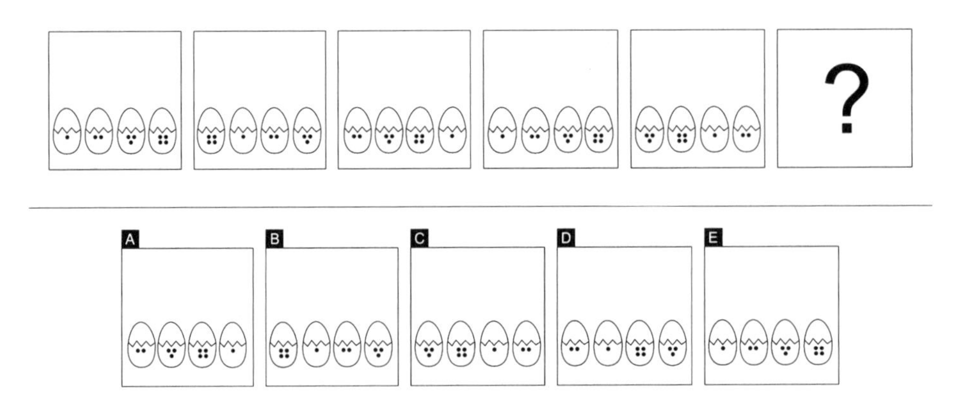

32 Which figure completes the series above?

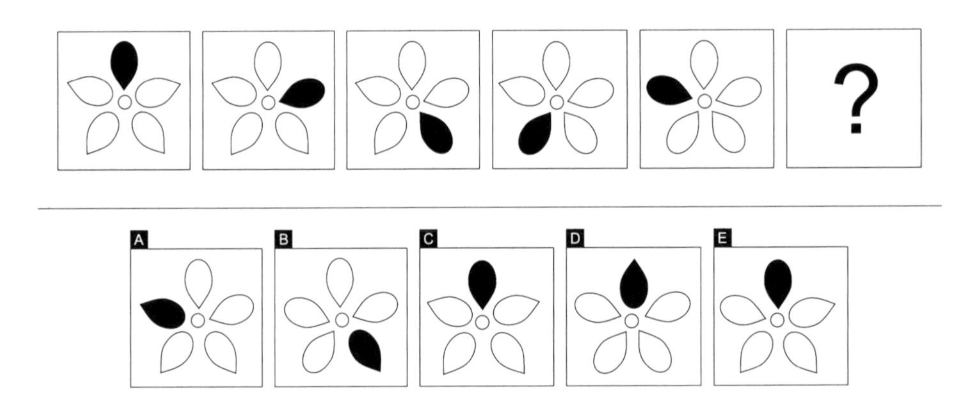

33 Which figure completes the series above?

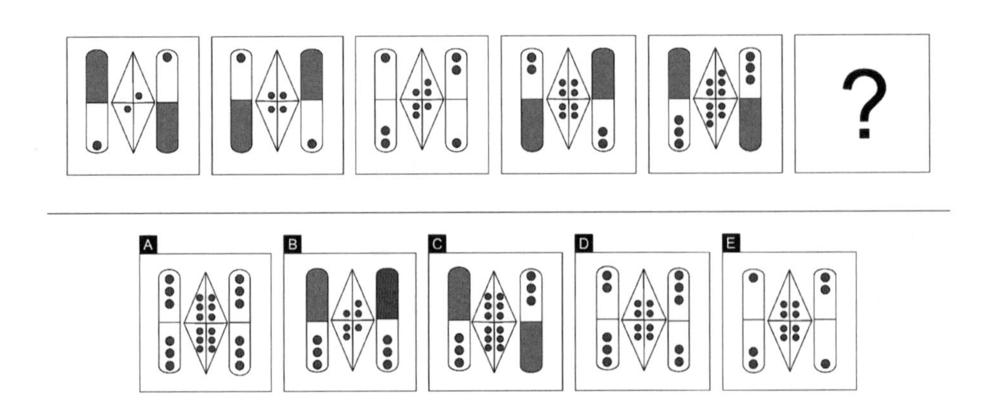

34 Which figure completes the series above?

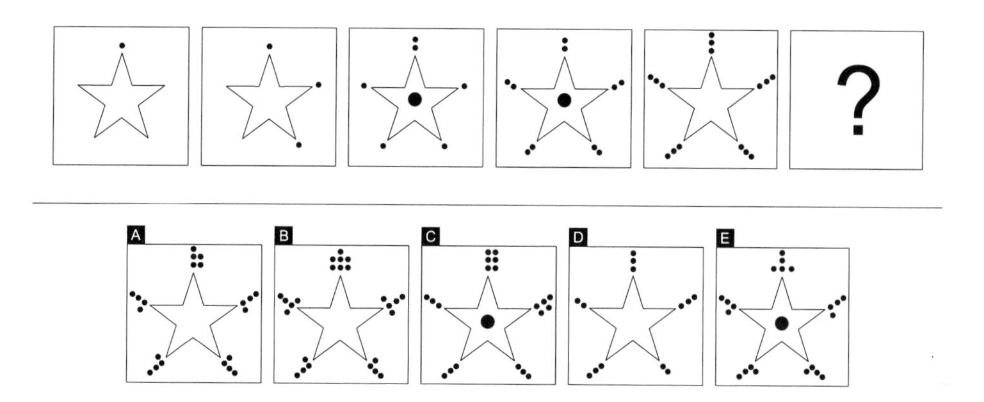

35 Which figure completes the series above?

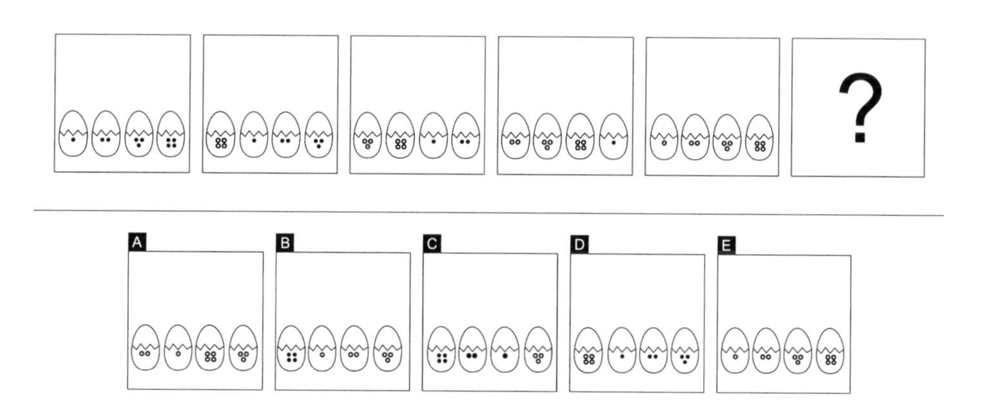

36 Which figure completes the series above?

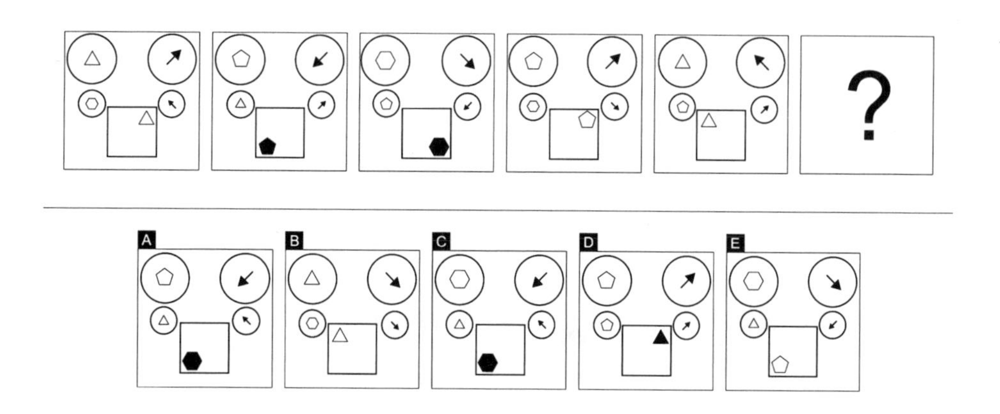

37 Which figure completes the series above?

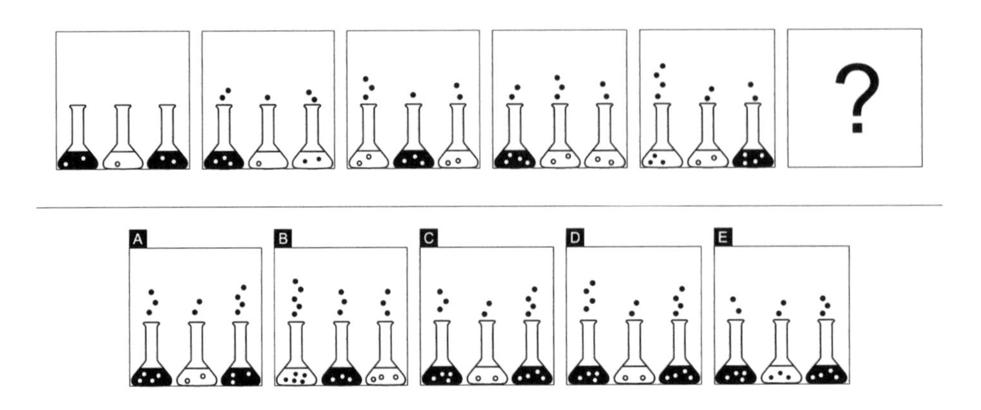

38 Which figure completes the series above?

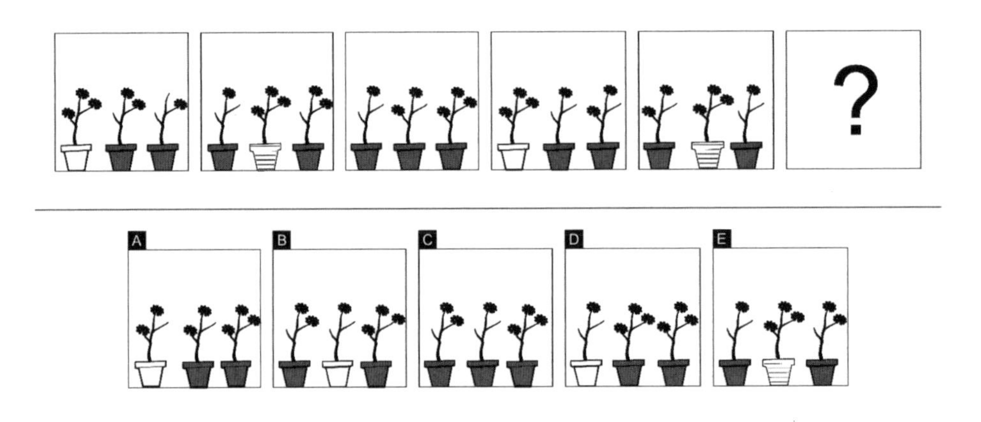

39 Which figure completes the series above?

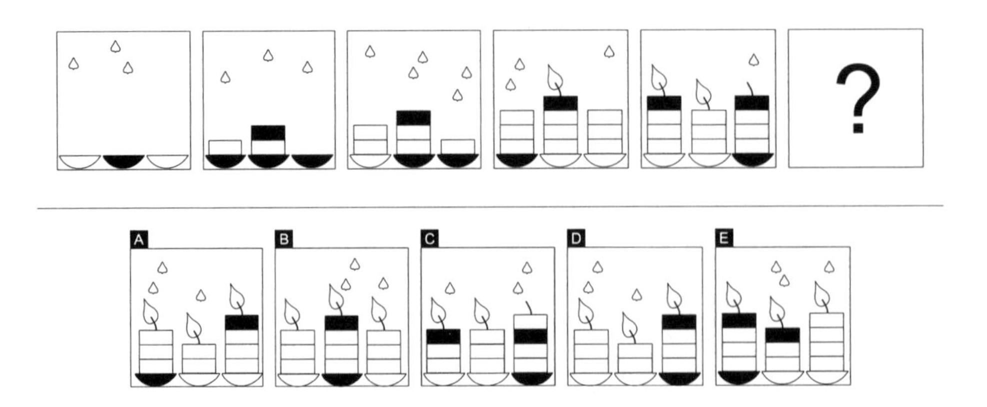

40 Which figure completes the series above?

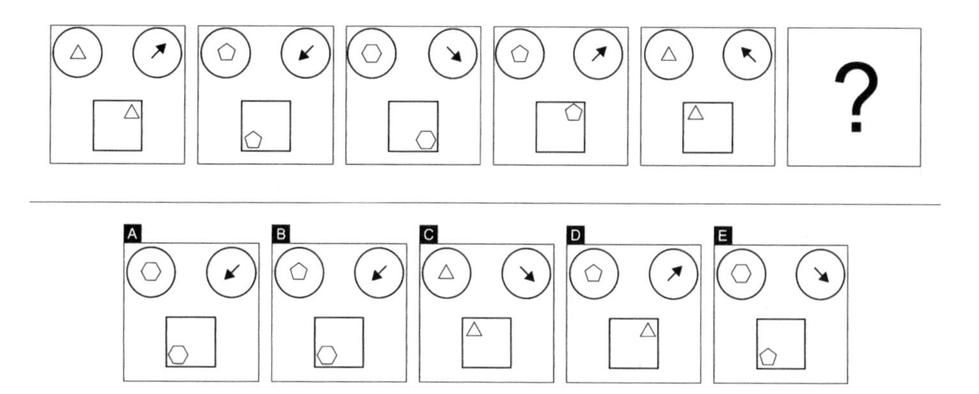

41 Which figure completes the series above?

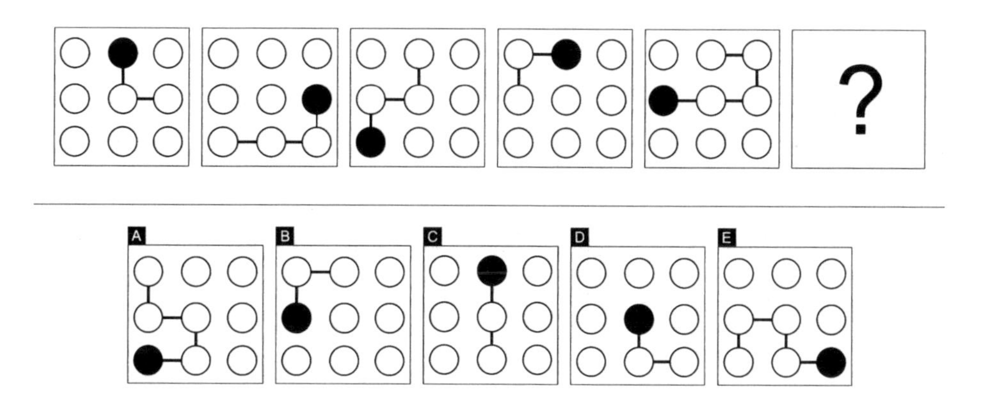

42 Which figure completes the series above?

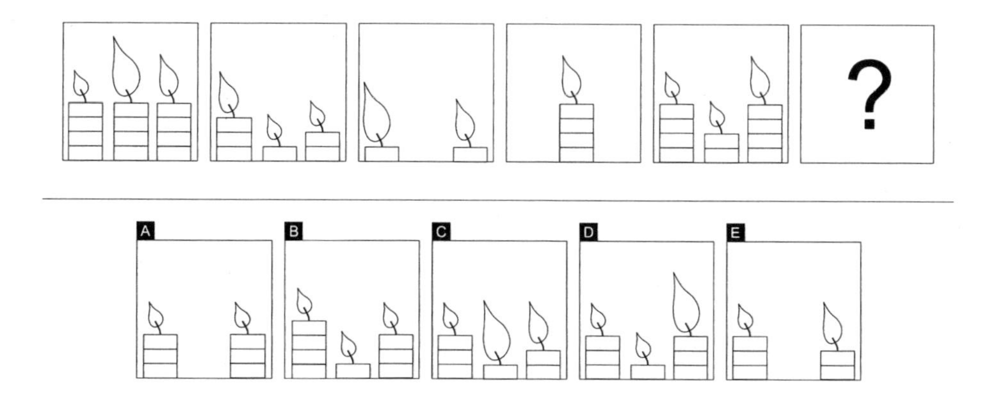

43 Which figure completes the series above?

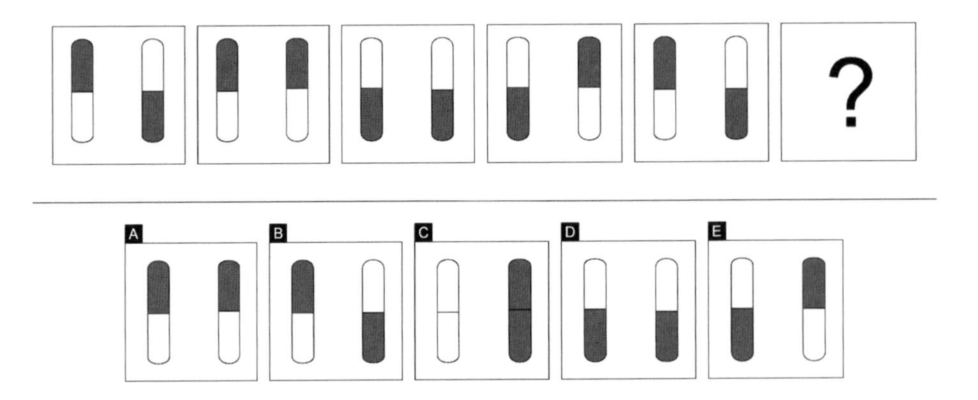

44 Which figure completes the series above?

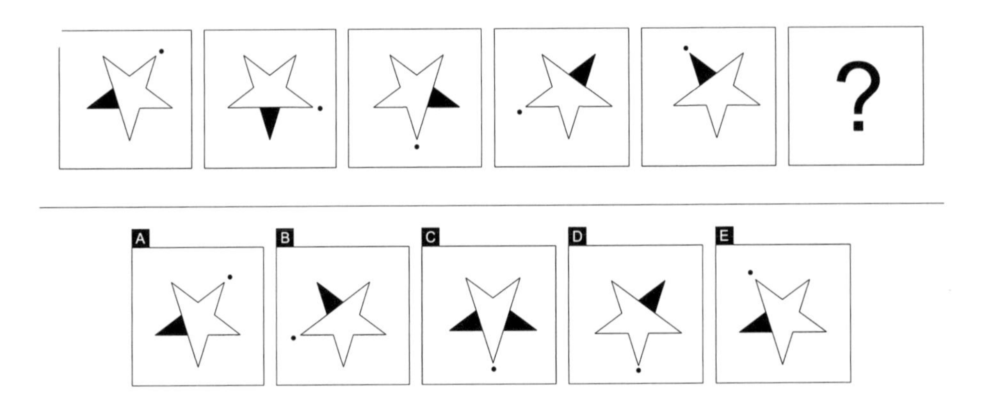

45 Which figure completes the series above?

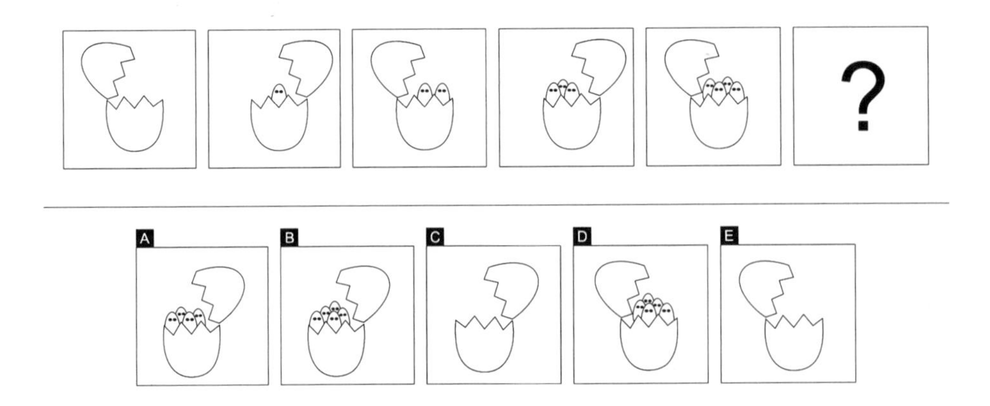

46 Which figure completes the series above?

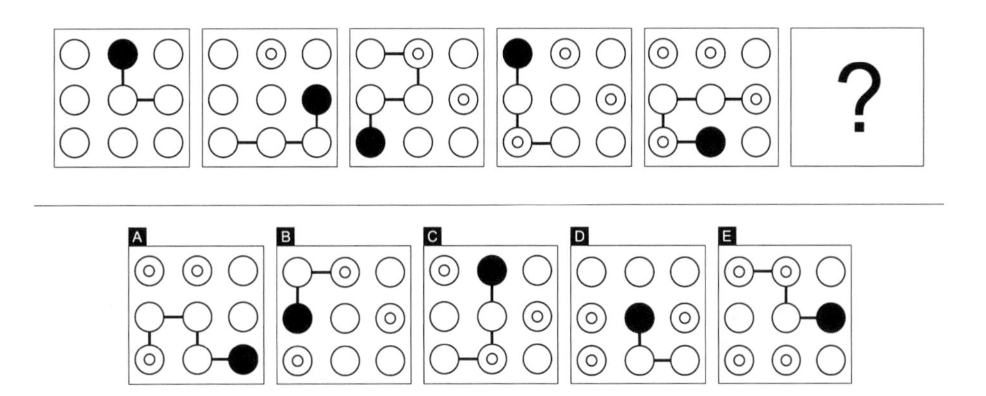

47 Which figure completes the series above?

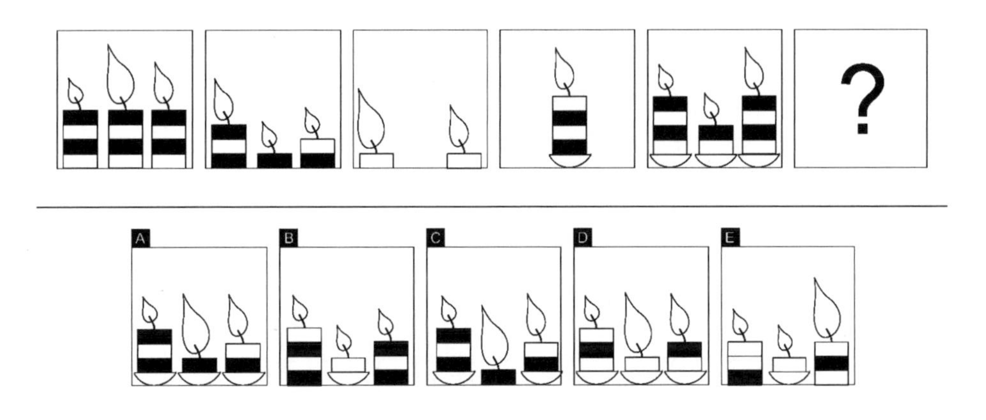

48 Which figure completes the series above?

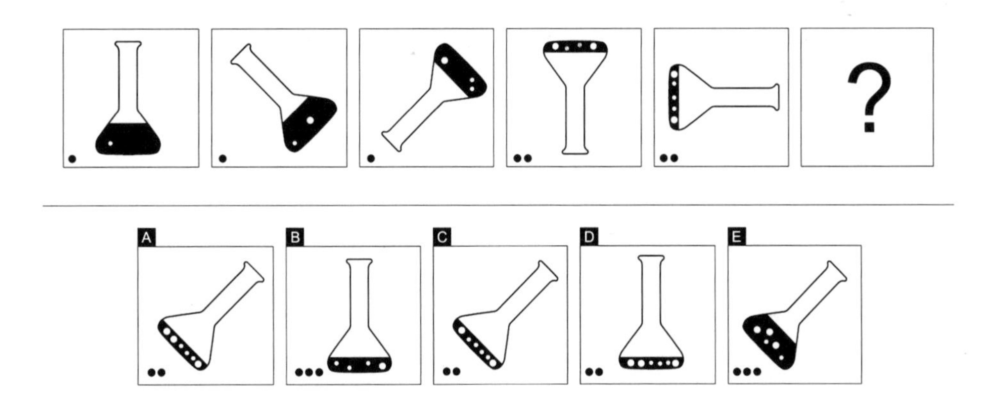

49 Which figure completes the series above?

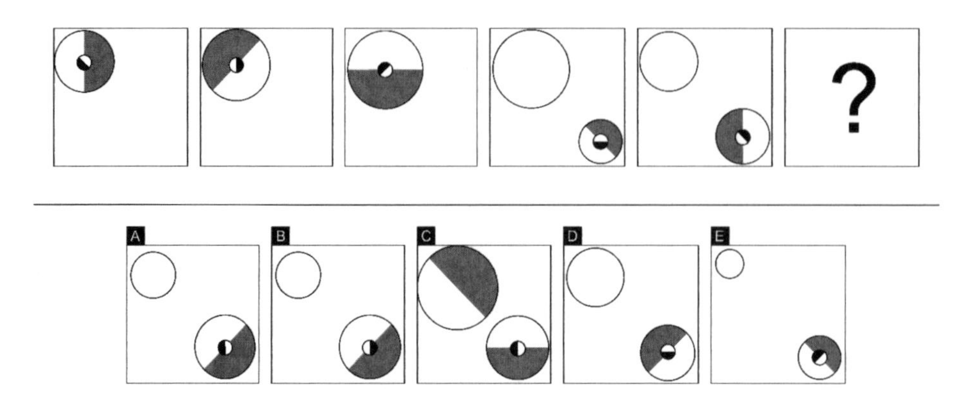

50 Which figure completes the series above?

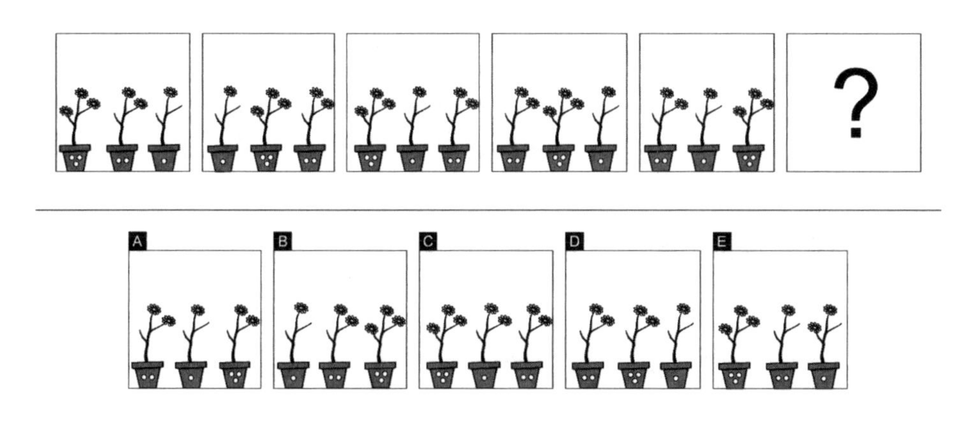

51 Which figure completes the series above?

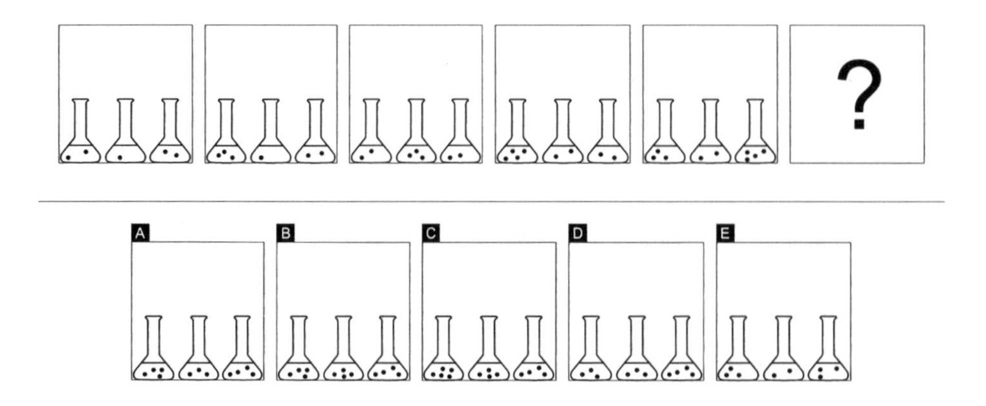

52 Which figure completes the series above?

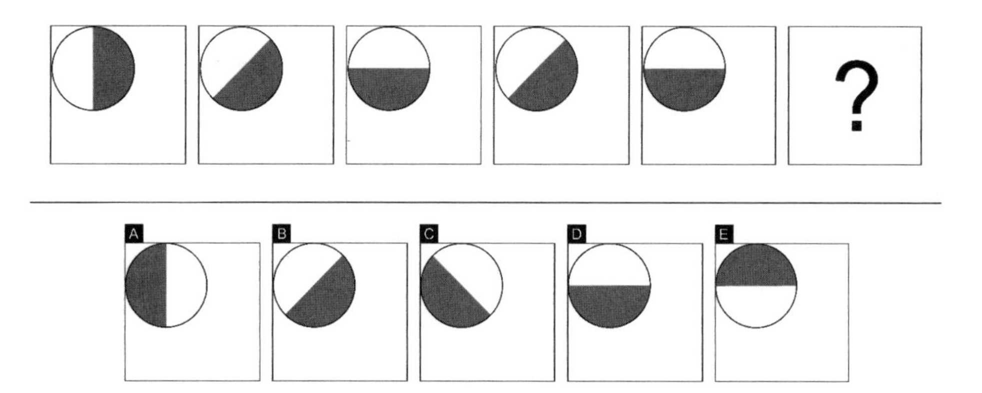

53 Which figure completes the series above?

54 Which figure completes the series above?

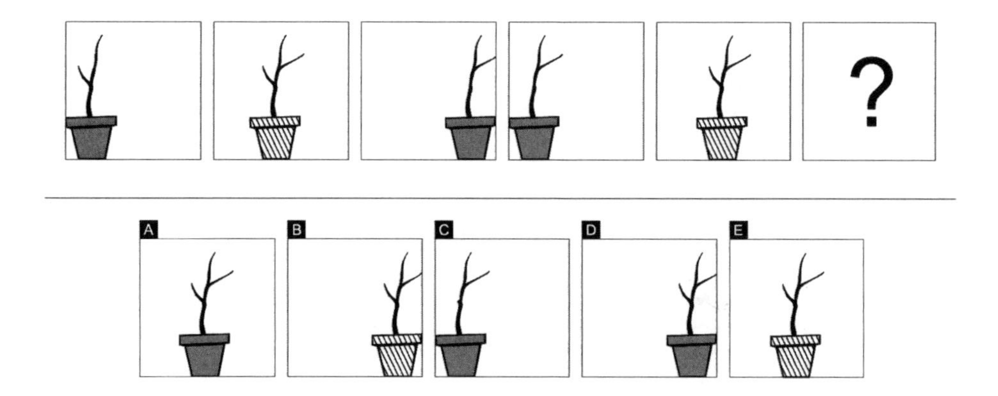

55 Which figure completes the series above?

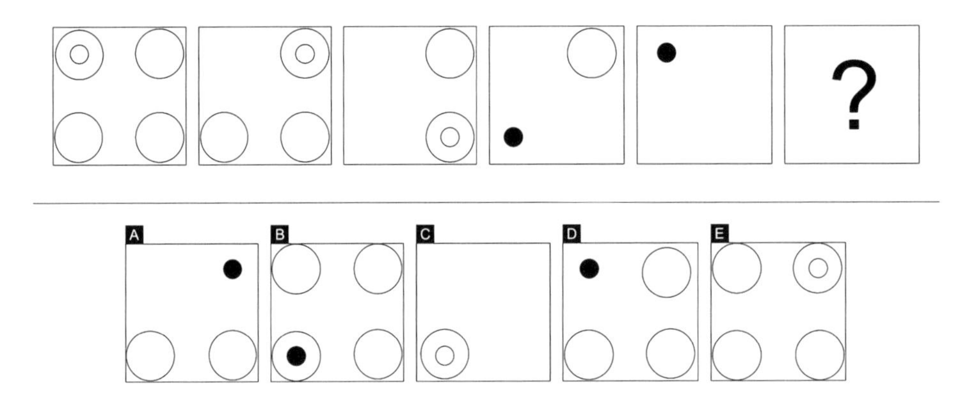

56 Which figure completes the series above?

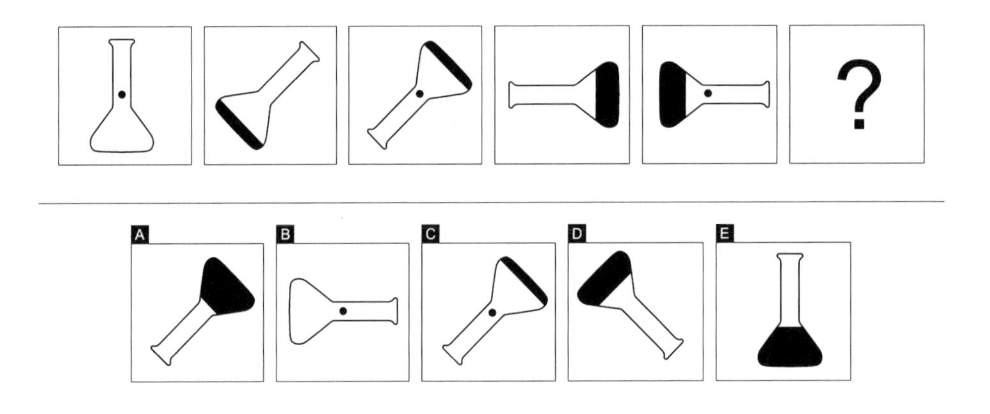

57 Which figure completes the series above?

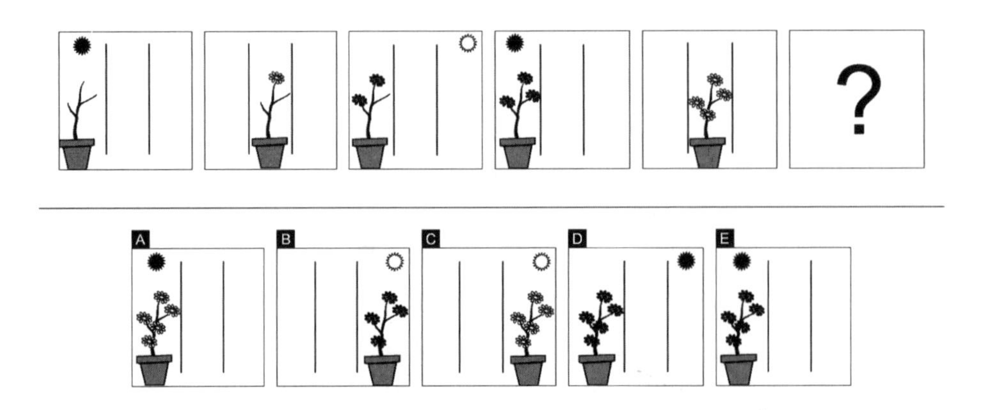

58 Which figure completes the series above?

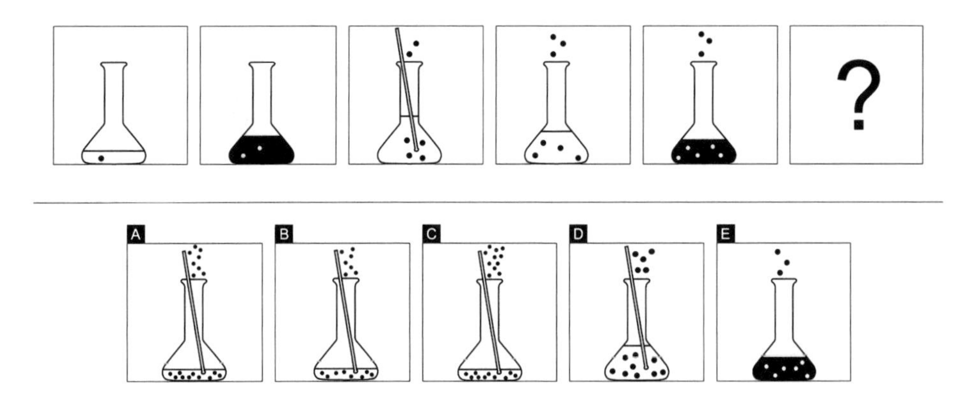

59 Which figure completes the series above?

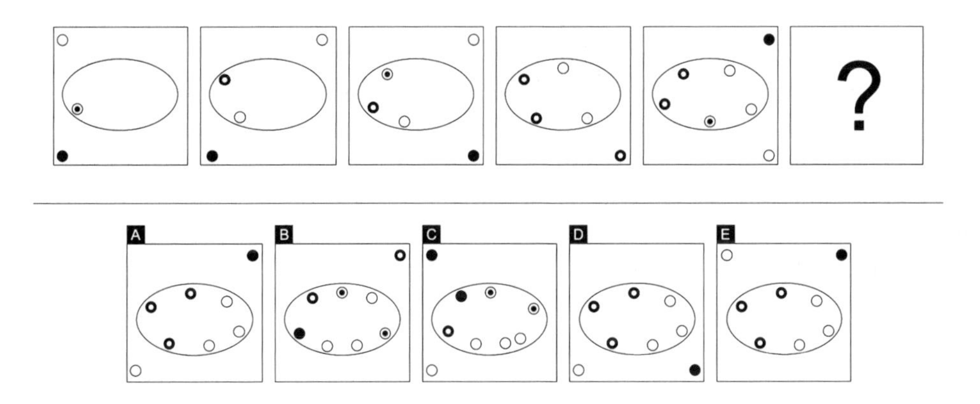

60 Which figure completes the series above?

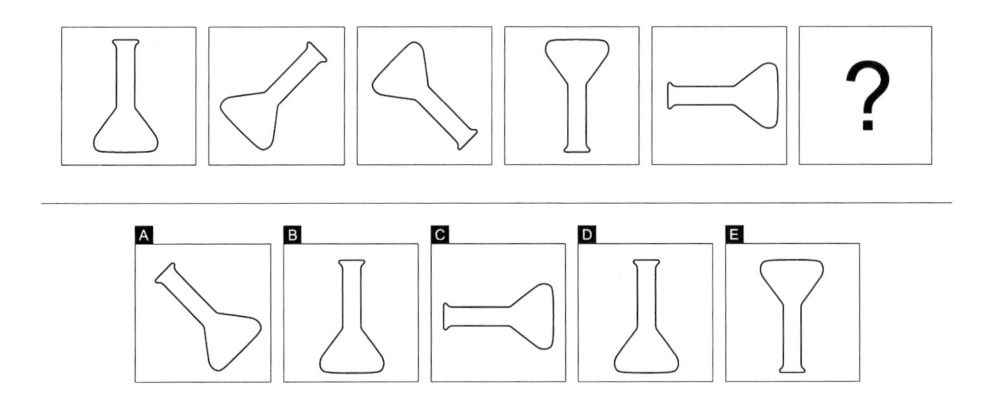

61 Which figure completes the series above?

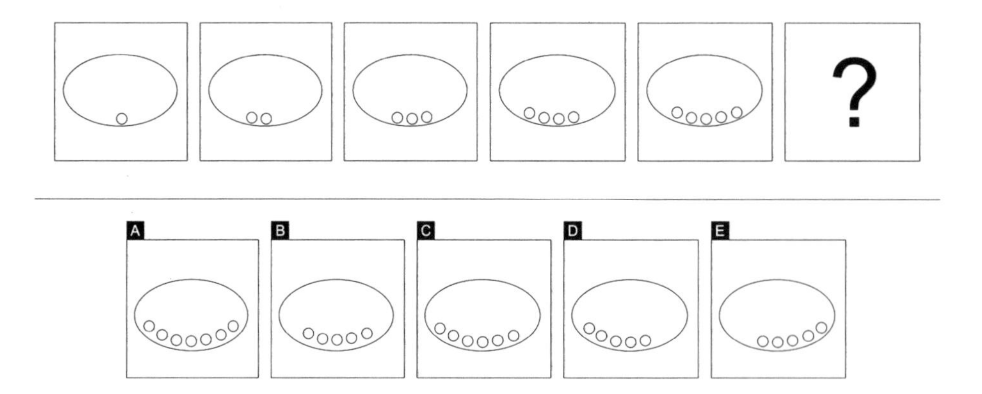

62 Which figure completes the series above?

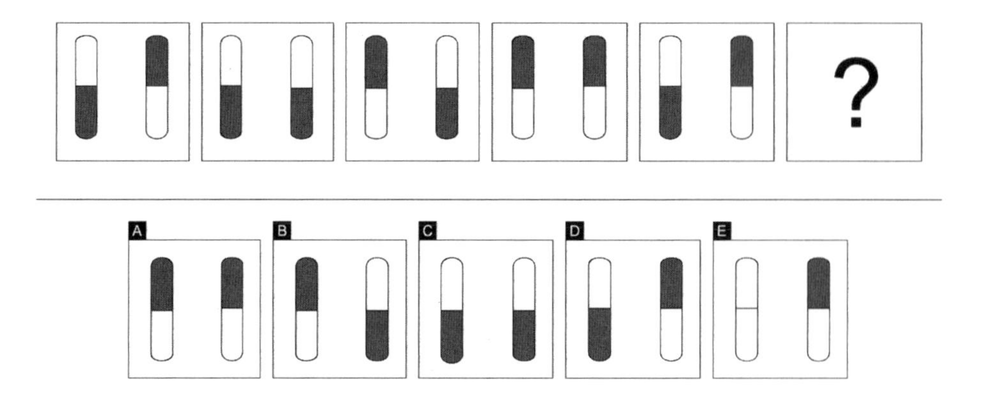

63 Which figure completes the series above?

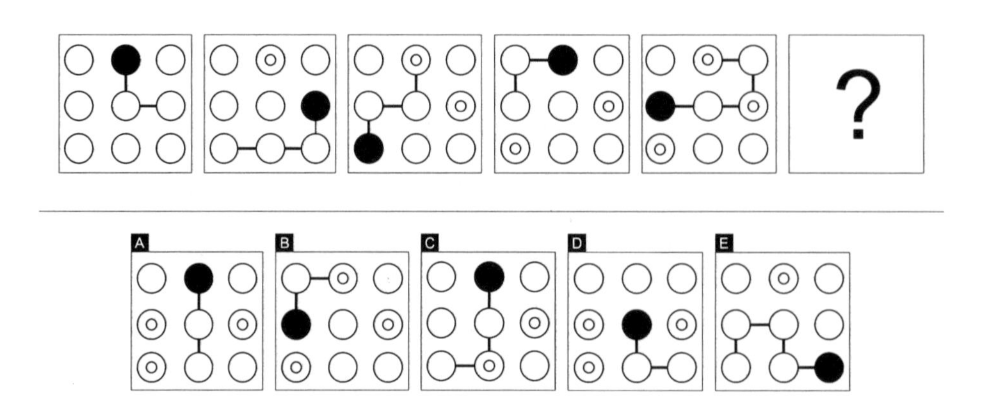

64 Which figure completes the series above?

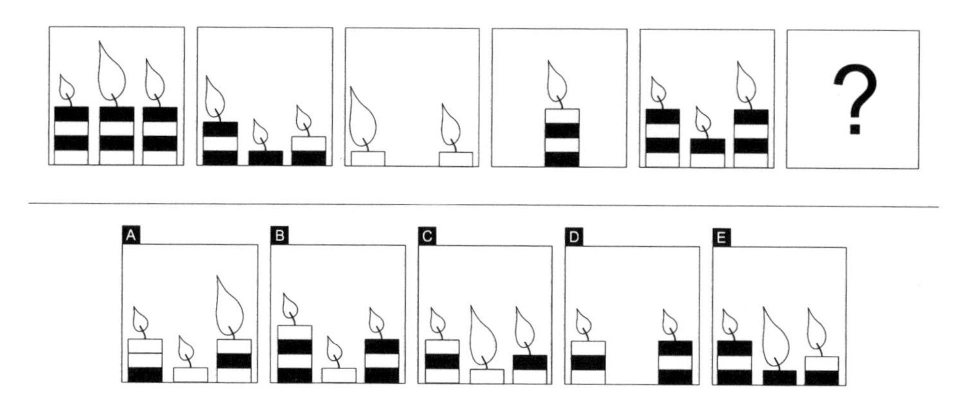

65 Which figure completes the series above?

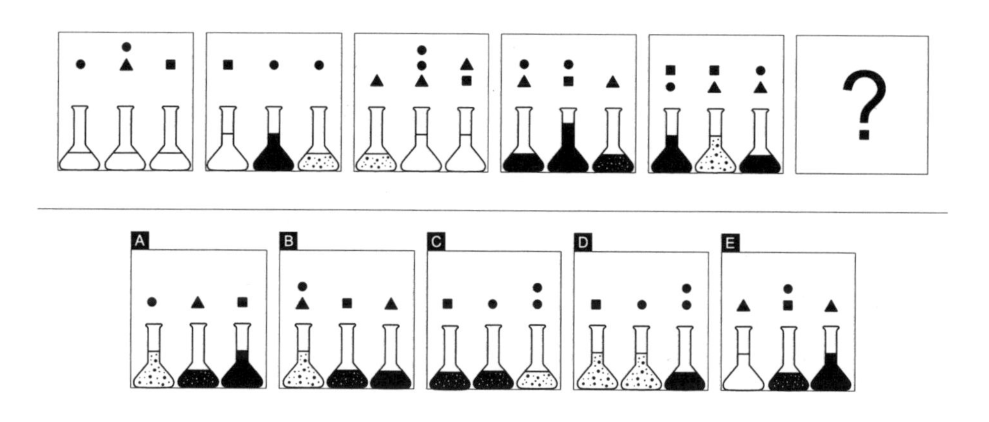

66 Which figure completes the series above?

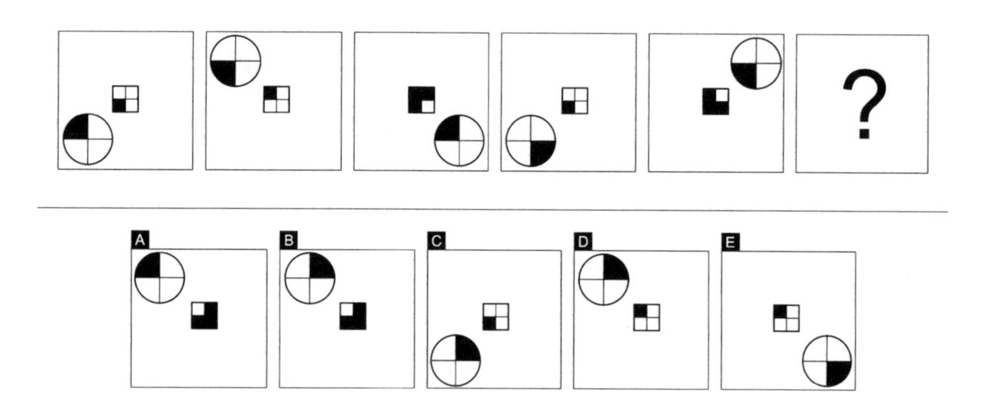

67 Which figure completes the series above?

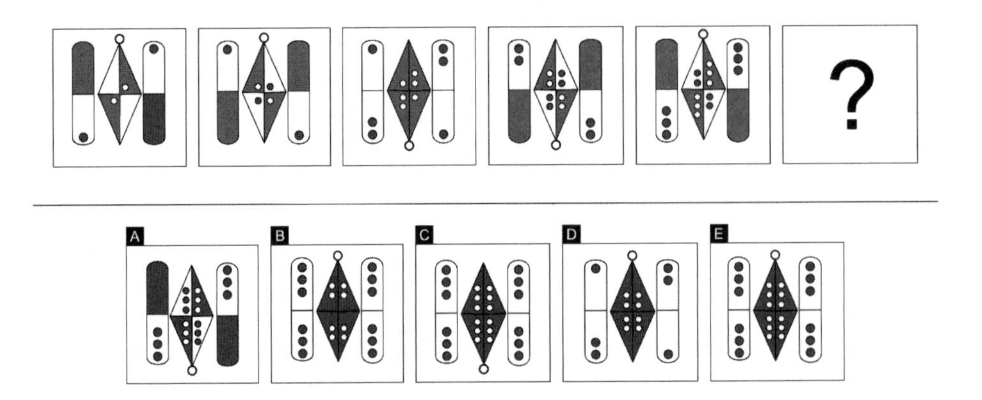

68 Which figure completes the series above?

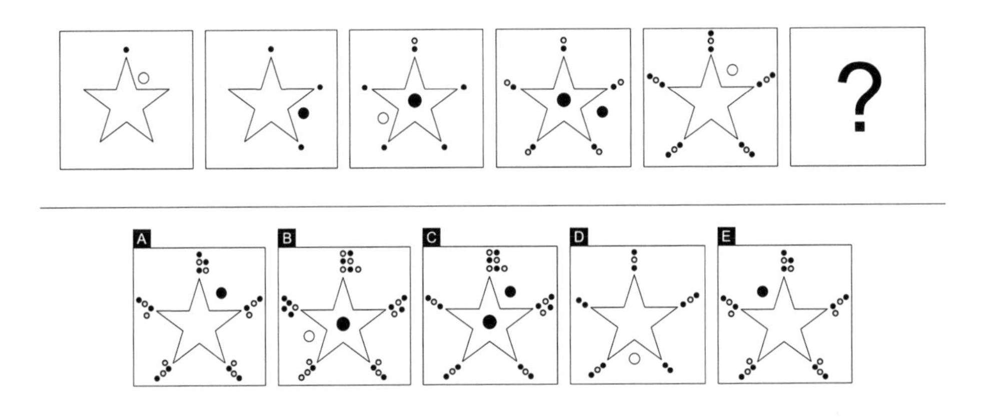

69 Which figure completes the series above?

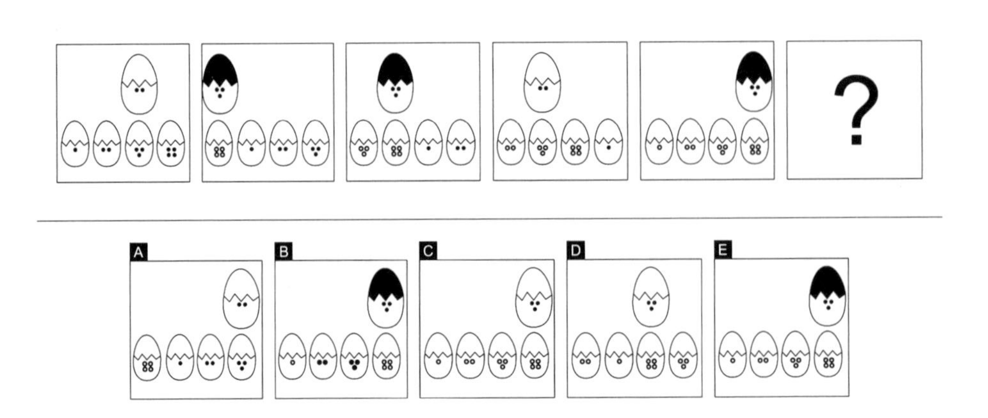

70 Which figure completes the series above?

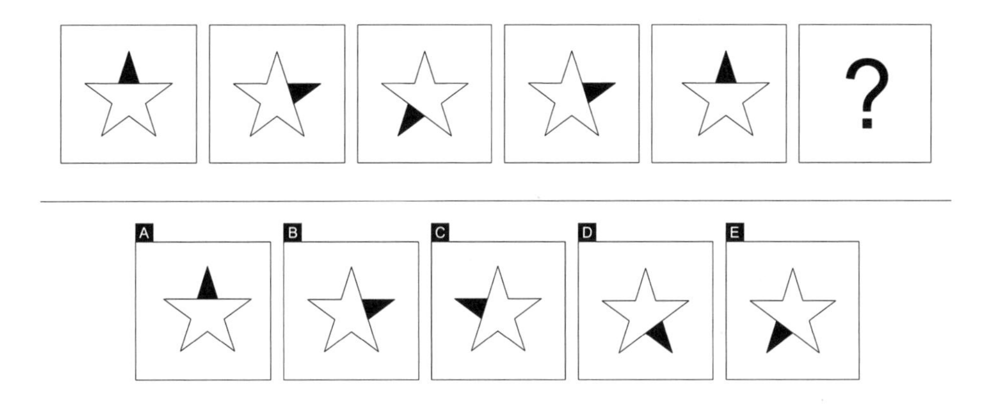

71 Which figure completes the series above?

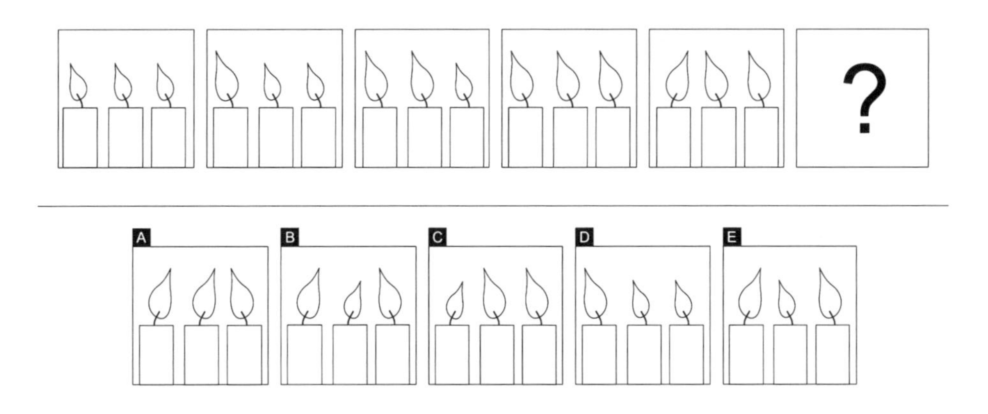

72 Which figure completes the series above?

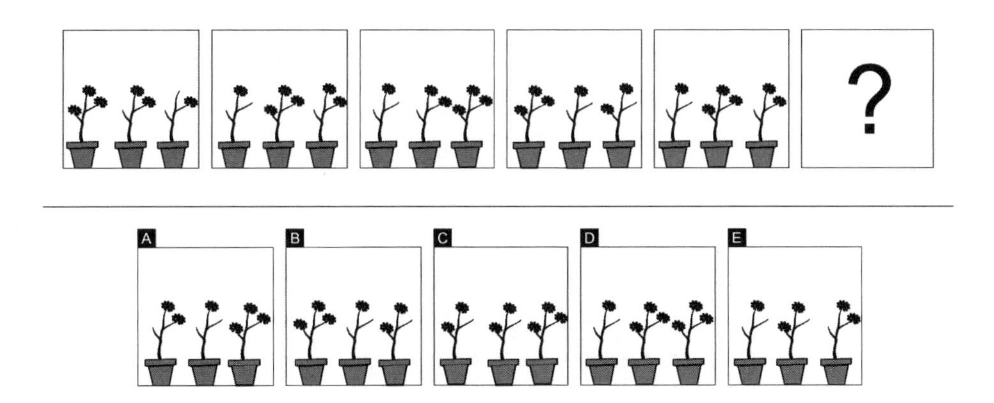

73 Which figure completes the series above?

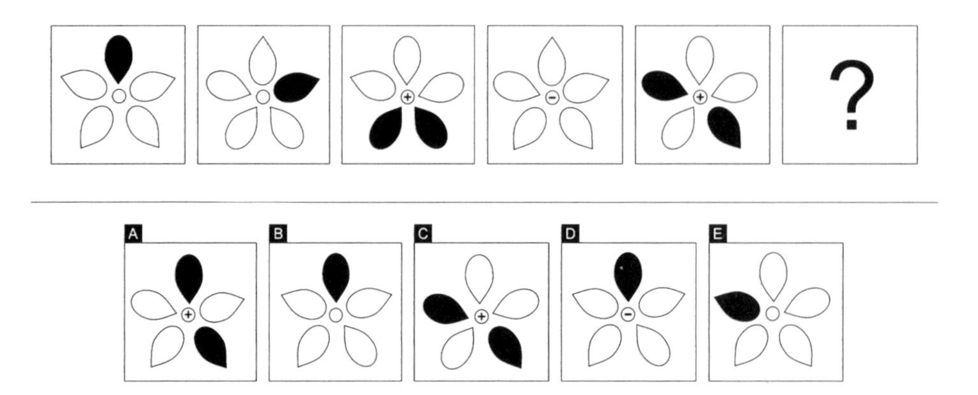

74 Which figure completes the series above?

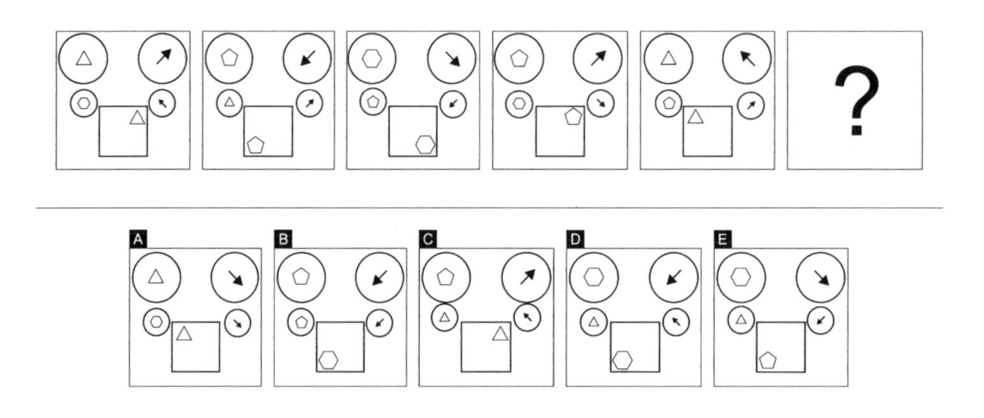

75 Which figure completes the series above?

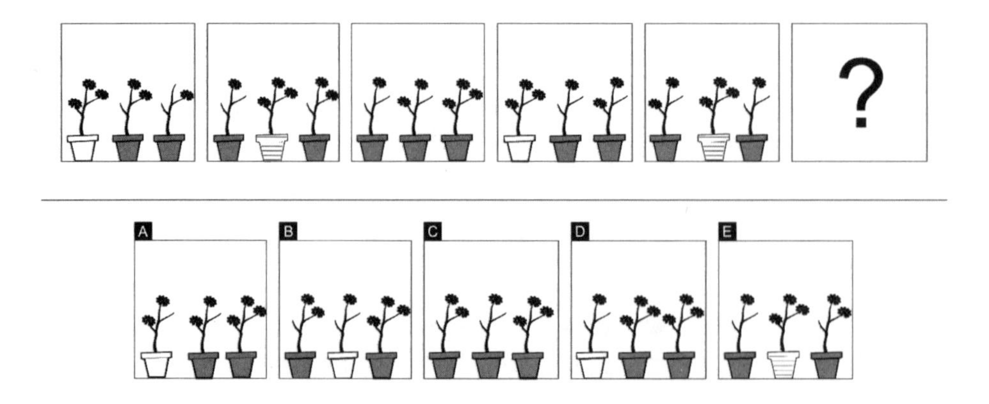

76 Which figure completes the series above?

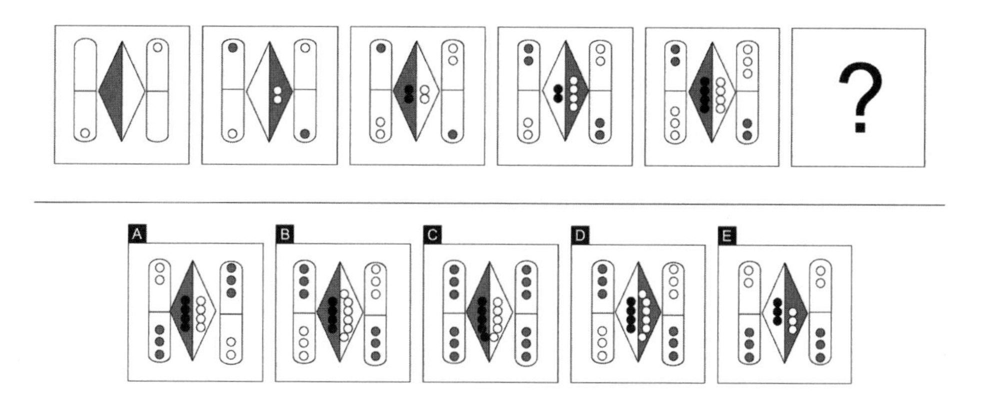

77 Which figure completes the series above?

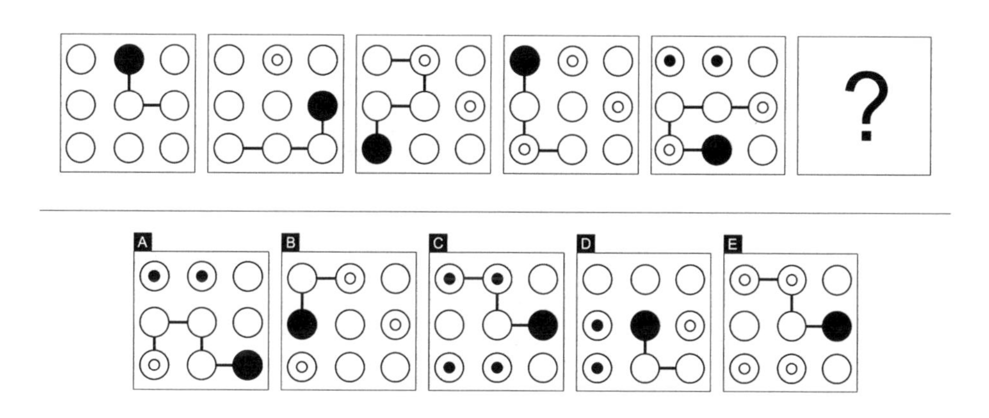

78 Which figure completes the series above?

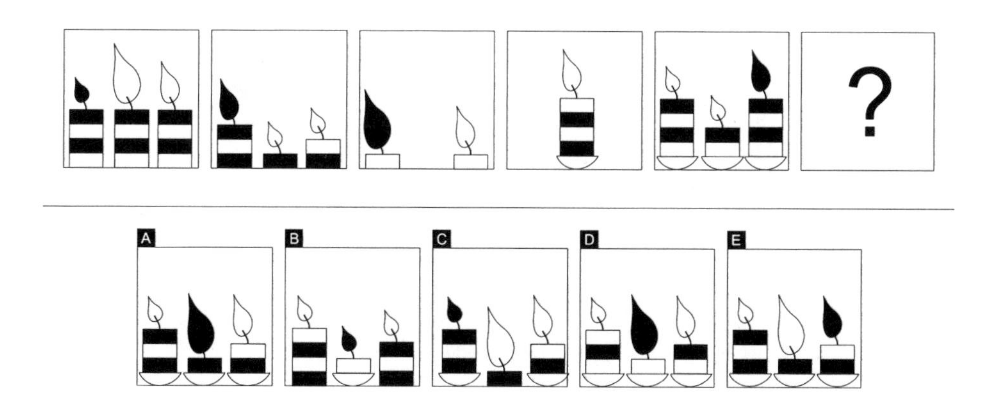

79 Which figure completes the series above?

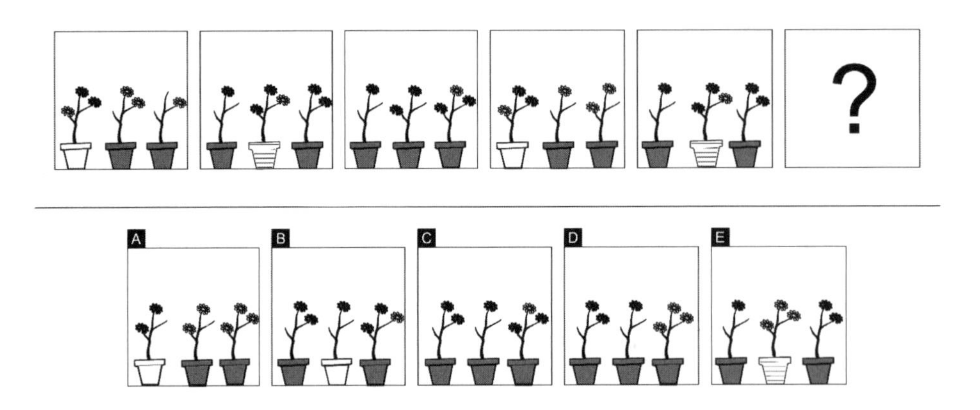

80 Which figure completes the series above?

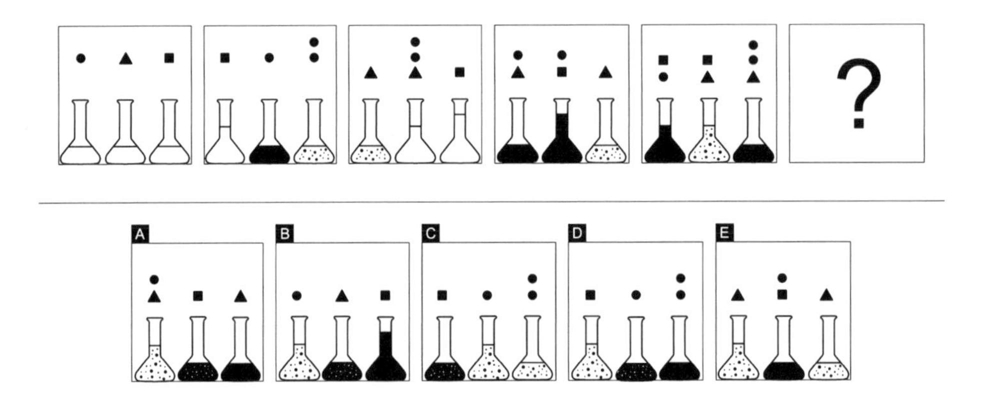

81 Which figure completes the series above?

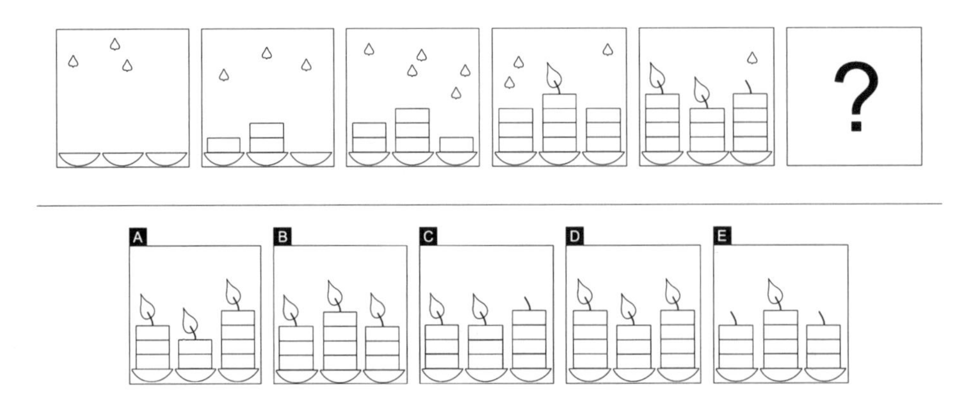

82 Which figure completes the series above?

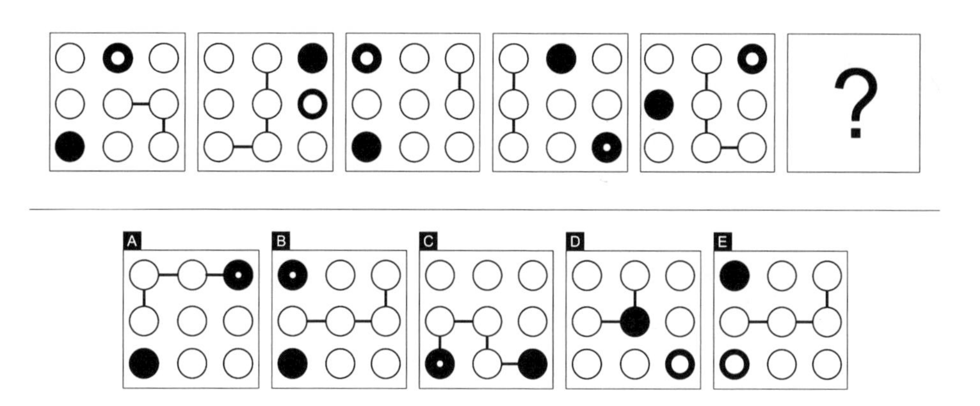

83 Which figure completes the series above?

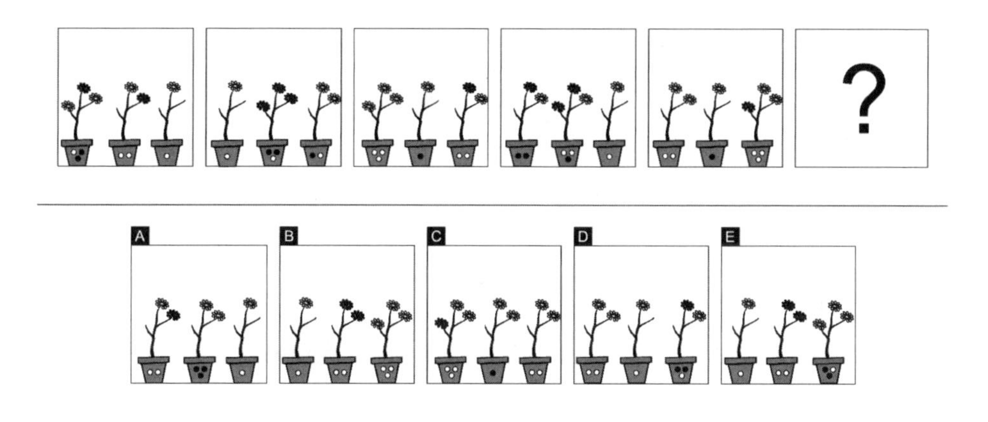

84 Which figure completes the series above?

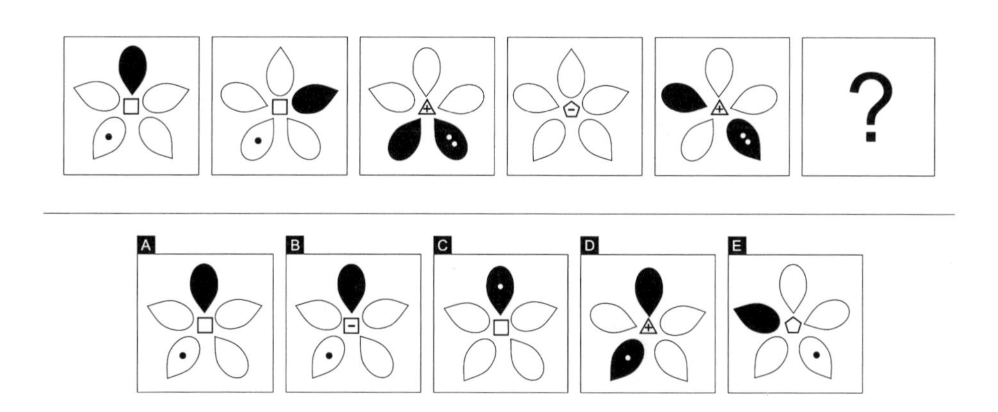

85 Which figure completes the series above?

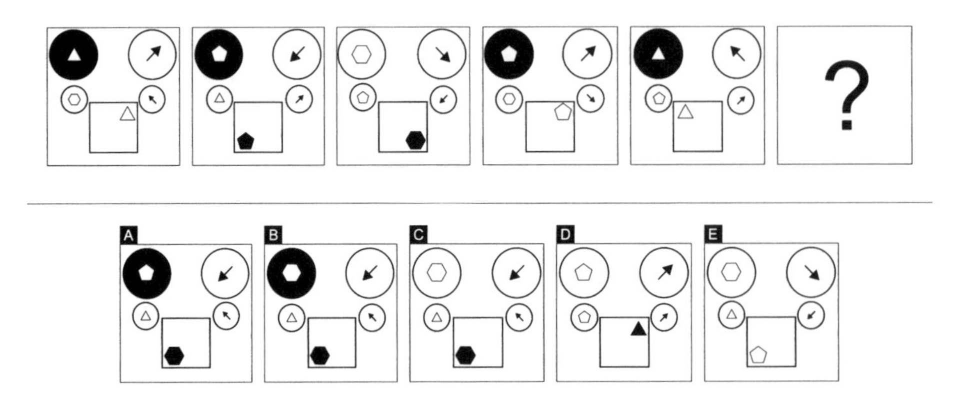

86 Which figure completes the series above?

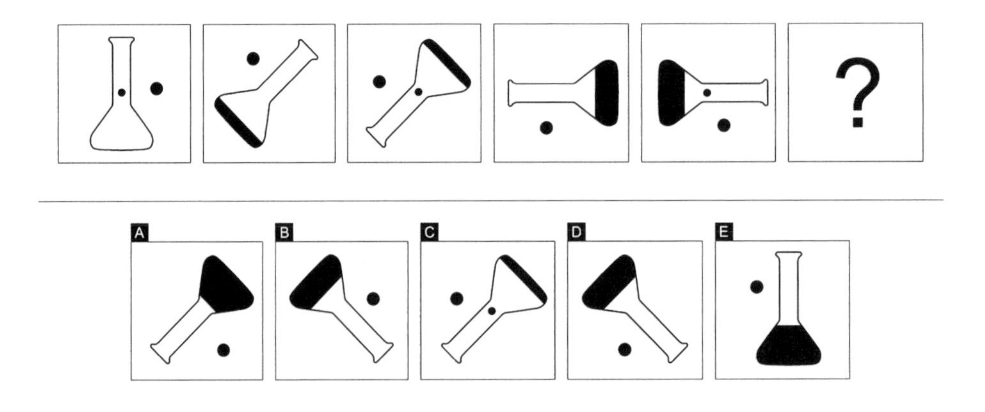

87 Which figure completes the series above?

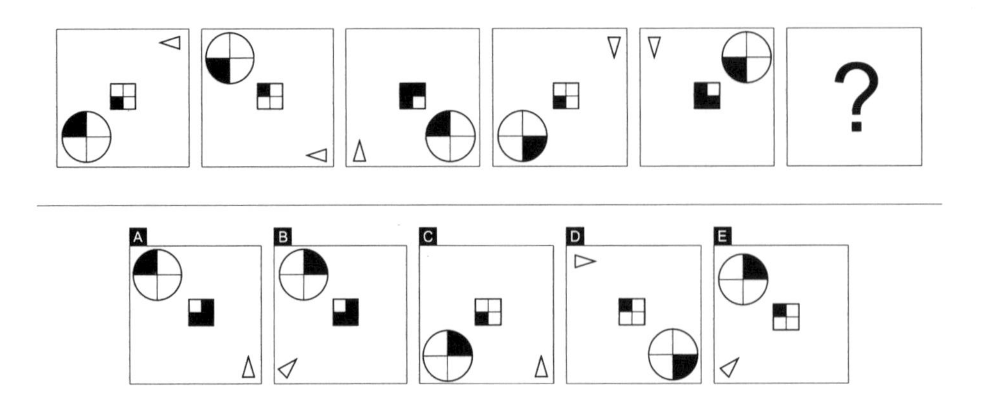

88 Which figure completes the series above?

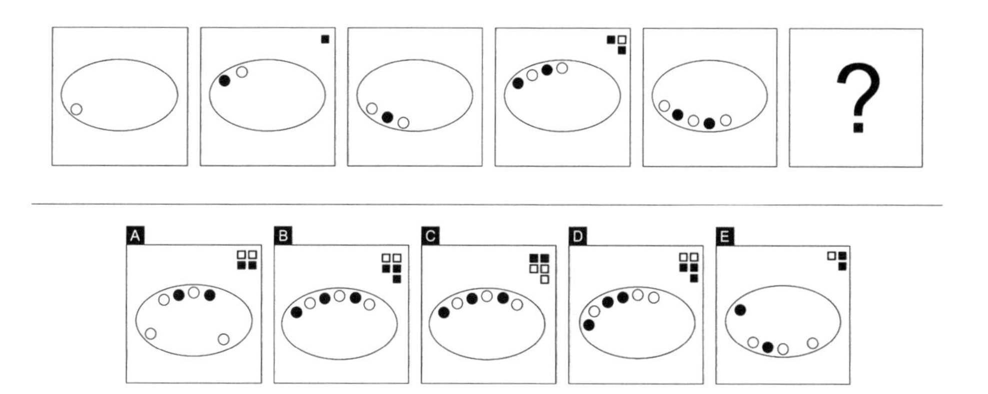

89 Which figure completes the series above?

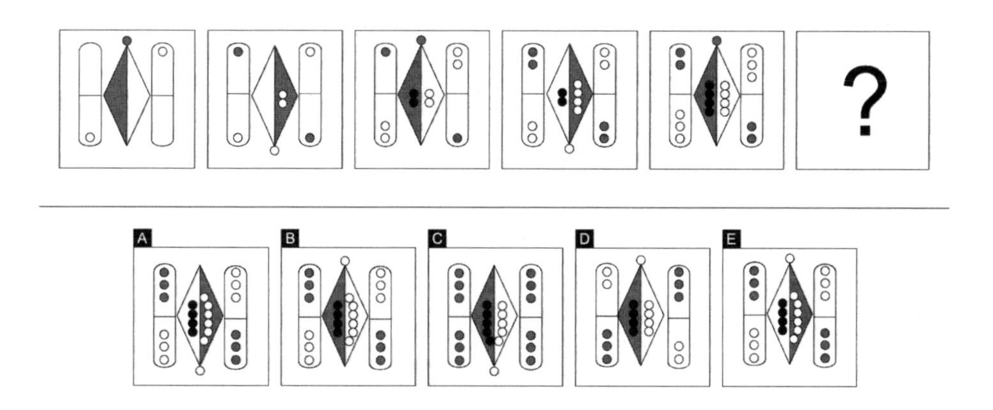

90 Which figure completes the series above?

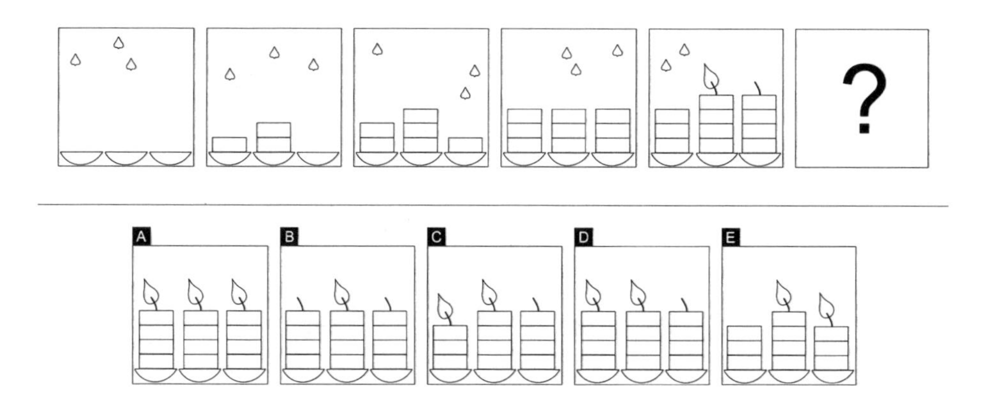

91 Which figure completes the series above?

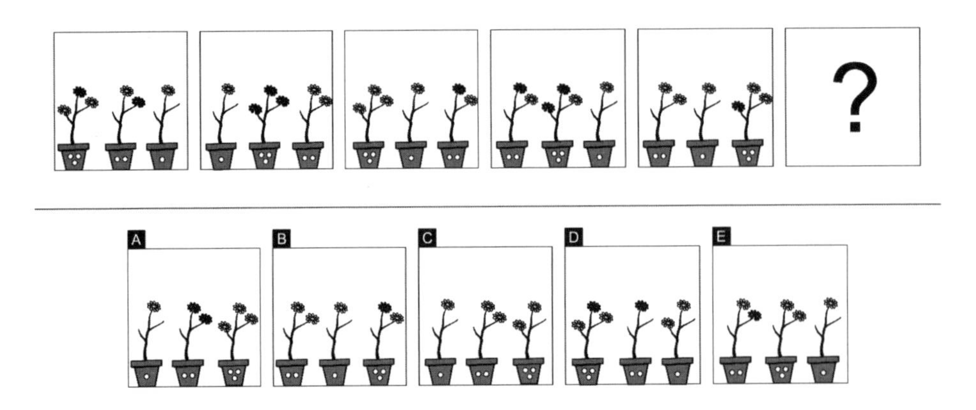

92 Which figure completes the series above?

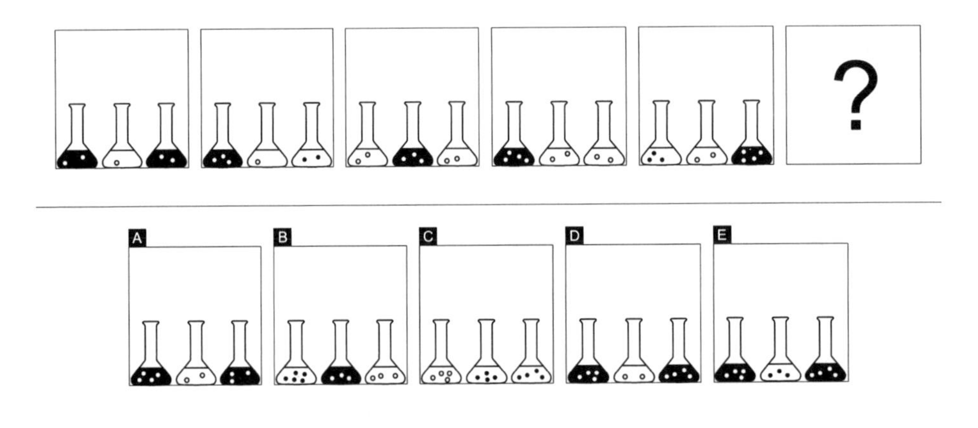

93 Which figure completes the series above?

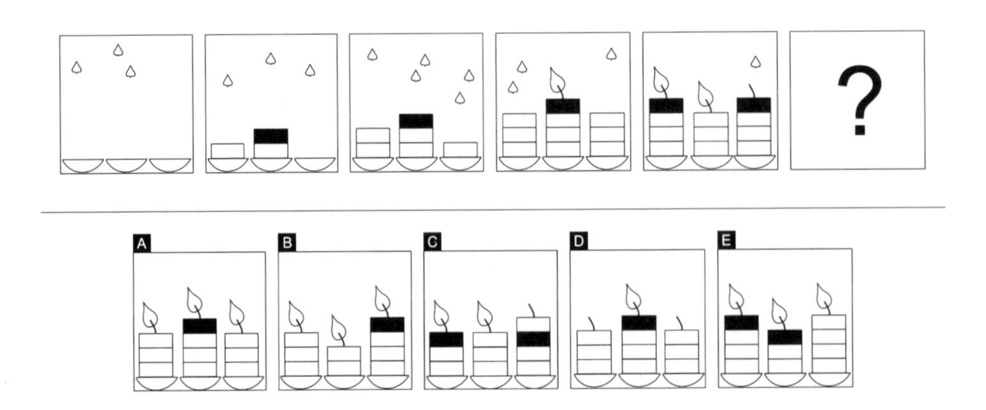

94 Which figure completes the series above?

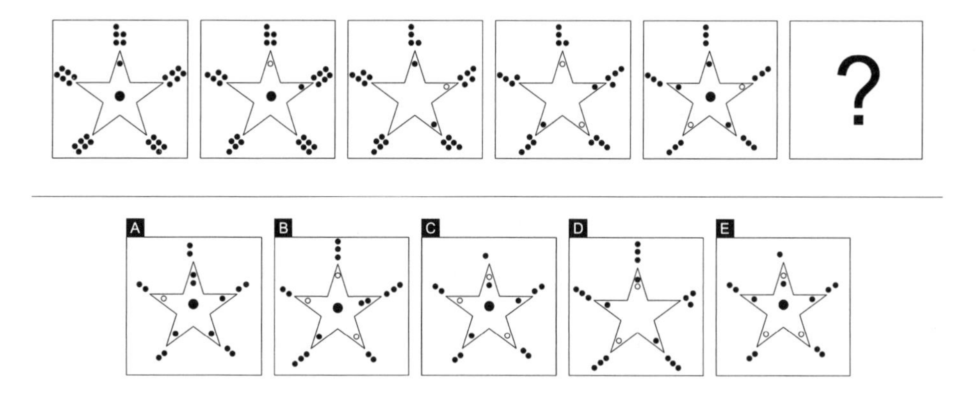

95 Which figure completes the series above?

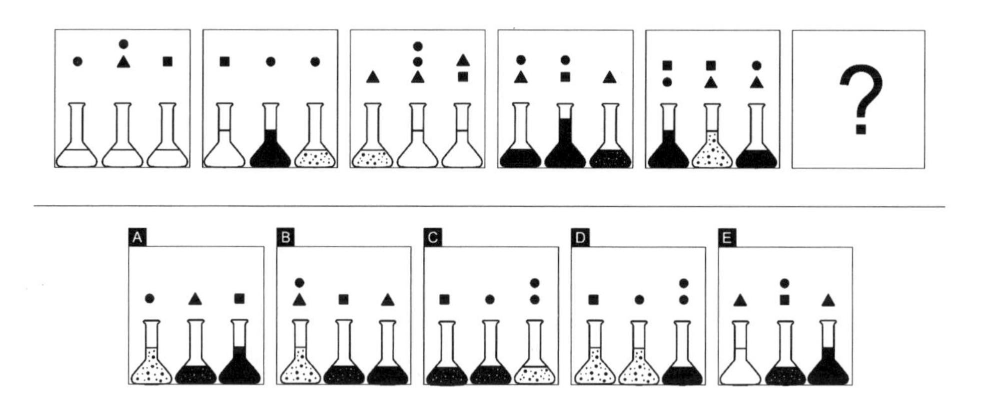

96 Which figure completes the series above?

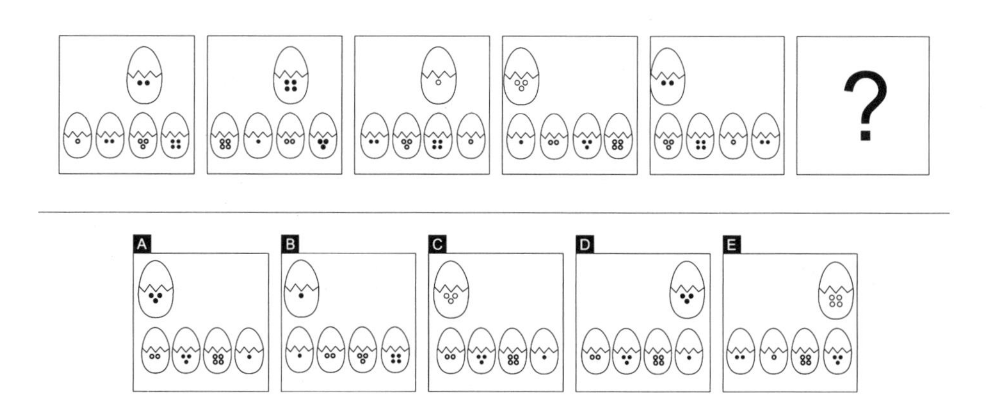

97 Which figure completes the series above?

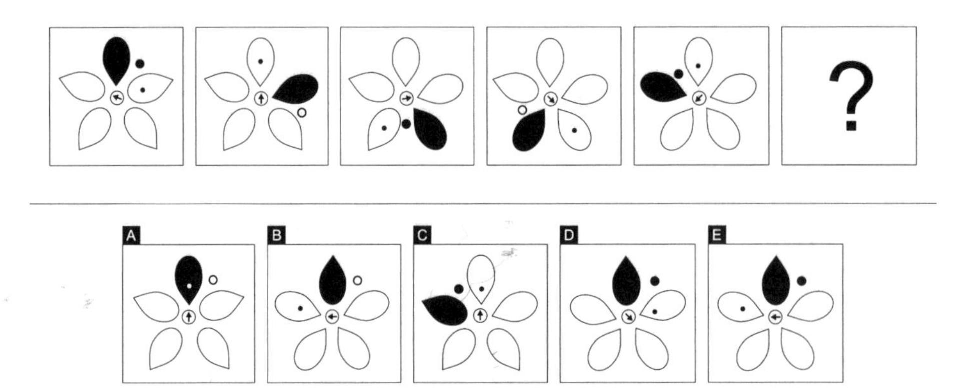

98 Which figure completes the series above?

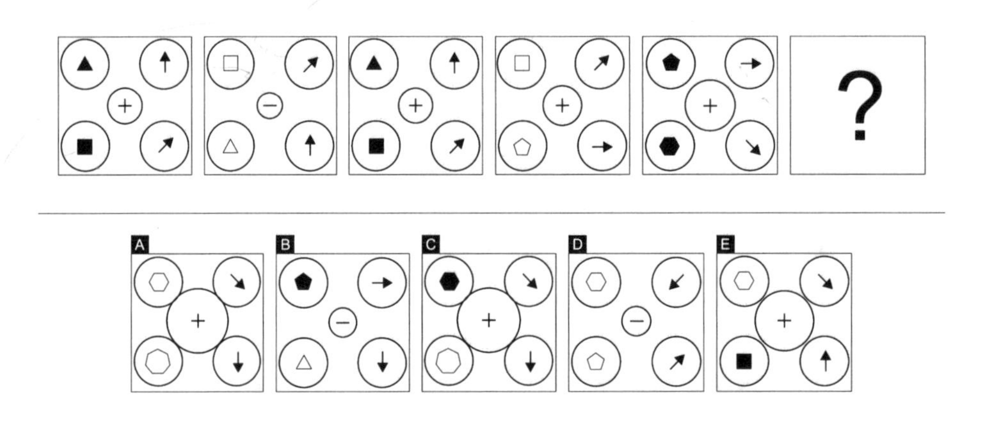

99 Which figure completes the series above?

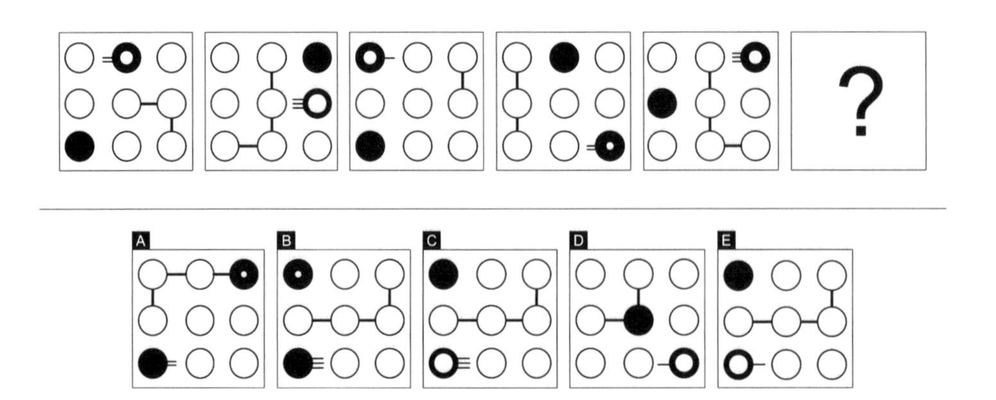

100 Which figure completes the series above?

ANSWERS

1 B

Rule 1: The top half of the egg alternates from left to right.

2 A

Rule 1: The petals invert in turn clockwise.

3 B

Rule 1: A circle is added to each corner in turn, clockwise. When all 4 corners are full, the next turn is blank before starting again.

4 B

Rule 1: The flask is rotating 90° clockwise every time.

Rule 2: Looking at the picture with the flask the correct way up, it moves between three positions (left, centre and right). It moves as far as it can in one direction before changing direction. The sequence shown is from the centre to the left to the centre to the right to the centre. The next move would therefore be to the left.

5 E

Rule 1: The shaded area of the circle is rotating 45° clockwise every time.

Rule 2: The circle is getting smaller every time.

6 D

Rule 1: One circle is removed each time. This alternates between the circle furthest to the right and the one furthest to the left.

Rule 2: The circles alternate between being shaded and unshaded. The circle furthest to the right is always shaded.

7 A

Rule 1: the flask levels go up for three turns and then down for another three turns.

Rule 2: during the second stage of the rising fluid level and the second stage of falling fluid level, the fluid is shaded.

Rule 3: at the highest and lowest levels (the last level of rising and the last level of falling) there is a stirring stick in the pots (alternatively, we could say that the stirring stick appears after the fluid was shaded).

8 A

Rule 1: First, the left pill is inverted, and then the right one. After this stage, both pills are flipped within the same turn and the cycle repeats.

Rule 2: the four quadrants of the central shape reflect the shading of the two shapes on its sides.

Rule 3: the shading of the circles next to the shapes on the sides alternates between reflecting the actual shading of the shapes and the inverted version.

9 C

Rule 1: the shaded section moves an increasing number of points in a clockwise direction every turn.

Rule 2: the shaded circle outside the star alternates between being 1 step after or before (going clockwise) the shaded section of the star.

Rule 3: an unshaded circle appears in every turn showing where the shaded circle was in the previous turn.

Rule 4: an arrow inside the star points to the arm which is going to become shaded in the next turn.

10 B

Rule 1: the tallies in the lower left corners show how many extra circles are present in each figure in addition to the standard three white circles.

Rule 2: the tallies in the upper right corners show how many of the extra circles are shaded.

Rule 3: the tallies in the lower right corners show how many circles with a dotted outline are added.

Rule 4: tallies in the upper left corners show the number of added unshaded squares to the image.

11 E

Rule 1: The number of circles filled in black is shown in tallies in the bottom L corner.

12 C

Rule 1: The candle flame alternates leaning left and right and if the candle is on a dish, a cone is visible over the candlewick

13 E

Rule 1: the potted plant takes an increasing number of steps to the right. When it reaches the right edge of the image, the movement continues from the left again.

14 C

Rule 1: The flask levels go up; two turns at low, two turns at medium, two at high.

Rule 2: The shading of liquid in the flask alternates from white to pale to dark to white, etc.

15 C

Rule 1: the flask alternates between rotating 45 and 90 degrees counter-clockwise each turn around a fixed center.

Rule 2: every time the top of the flask passes the 12 o'clock and 6 o'clock position, a black circle is added to the bottom of the picture.

16 B

Rule 1: in every turn, the shading rotates 45 degrees in a clockwise direction, and after the rotation took place the shaded and unshaded sections switch places.

Rule 2: the circle grows in size for three turns, after which it creates a smaller circle and its shading is transferred to the new circle. In the following turn, the shading rotation continues in the new (small) circle, while the old one remains empty.

17 E

Rule 1 In every turn, an increasing number of circles are added one by one to the points of the star going in a clockwise direction. If there is already a circle at a given point of the star, the new one is added above or next to it.

Rule 2: a black circle appears inside the star if the total number of circles outside the star is even.

Rule 3: every even numbered circle added to a given point of the star is unshaded.

18 A

Rule 1: First, the flask rotates 45 degrees clockwise, and in the next turn it rotates 90 degrees clockwise.

Rule 2: the flask starts on the left side of the figure and takes one step to the right in each turn. When it reaches the right edge of the figure, the movement starts again from the left.

Rule 3: the level of the liquid gets higher in all stages where the flask is the right way up (that is, bottom of the flask at the bottom, top at the top), and gets lower in all stages when it is upside down. The level remains the same when the flask is completely horizontal.

Rule 4: starting with the first turn, the liquid inside the flask is dark in every other turn. In addition, the liquid starts with 6 bubbles (which can only be seen when the liquid is shaded) and loses two bubbles in every shaded turn.

19 A

Rule 1: the shading rotates 45 degrees clockwise for two turns, then 45 degrees counter-clockwise for one turn.

Rule 2: while the shading rotates clockwise, the circle is getting bigger, and while the shading rotates counter-clockwise, the circle is getting smaller. The changes in the size of the circle are not uniform.

Rule 3: the circle goes around the corners of the square in a clockwise direction, increasing the steps it takes by 1 every turn.

Rule 4: the shading inside the small circle rotates 45 degrees anticlockwise every turn.

20 E

Rule 1: a single circle is added to the bottom of the oval in each turn – from the second image, the new circle is first added to the left of the original one, then to its right.

Rule 2: the newly added circles alternate between being shaded and un-shaded. The alternations for the circles added to the left and to the right side are counted separately. The first circle added to the left will be shaded, then the next circle added to the right will be shaded, but the second circle added to the left will be unshaded, and so on. The central circle remains unshaded throughout the series. Simply put: the newly added circles must carry a pattern that maintains every second circle as shaded.

Rule 3: the large circle in the center is shaded if there are more shaded circles in the given figure than unshaded ones. If there are an equal number of shaded and unshaded circles, the large circle is half shaded and if there are fewer shaded circles, it is unshaded.

21 E

Rule 1: the flask levels go up for three turns and then down for another three turns.

22 B

Rule 1: there are four eggs, each marked with 1, 2, 3 and 4 circles respectively. In every turn the egg on the far left side moves one step to the right, pushing the other eggs to the right.

23 C

Rule 1: in every turn going clockwise the shading of the next petal changes and every petal with the exception of the shaded ones is inverted.

24 B

Rule 1: A circle is added to each corner in turn, clockwise. When all 4 corners are full, the next turn is blank before starting again.

Rule 2: A smaller circle top L alternates black and white. When it is white, it is not visible against the larger circle (if applicable)

25 E

Rule 1: The number of circles filled in black is shown in tallies in the bottom L corner.

Rule 2: The number of spotty circles is shown in tallies in the top R corner. The numbers of chequered and plain circles are irrelevant.

26 D

Rule 1: The candle flame alternates leaning left and right and if the candle is on a dish, a cone is visible over the candlewick

Rule 2: The number of wisps of smoke increases by 1 every other turn

27 C

Rule 1: there are four eggs, each marked with 1, 2, 3 and 4 circles respectively. Every turn the egg on the far left side moves one step to the right pushing the other eggs to the right.

Rule 2: In each egg that disappeared on the right side and reappeared on the left again, the circles change shading.

Rule 3: a large egg randomly appears above one of the small eggs and it has as many circles as the small egg under it has, minus one (i.e. if the small egg under it has 1 circle, the large egg will have no circles).

28 B

Rule 1: the top half of the egg alternates between being on the left, in the middle closing the egg and on the right.

Rule 2: In every turn after the egg was closed, a new chick appears inside the egg.

Rule 3: the stripes on the bottom half of the egg change direction in every turn when the egg is closed.

Rule 4: the chicks change their shading every turn they appear.

29 E

Rule 1: In every turn, going clockwise, a petal is inverted which then stays that way, and every third turn, every previously inverted petal with the exception of the currently flipped one is flipped back.

Rule 2: in each turn, the petal that will be flipped in the next turn is marked with a + sign and the petals that will be flipped back (in the third and sixth turns) are marked by – signs in the preceding turn.

Rule 3: the central shape loses a side until it becomes a triangle and then gains a side every turn until it becomes a hexagon.

Rule 4: the number of sides the central shape has also equals the number of petals shaded in a given turn. If the shape has six sides (which is more than the number of petals) the shape itself is shaded.

30 C

Rule 1: in every turn, a large circle is removed from one of the corners going in an anticlockwise direction. Once every circle has been removed, there is a blank turn, where no circles appear, before the series starts again.

Rule 2: a smaller circle inside the large ones is going around in a clockwise direction, and if it lands on a space where the large circle is missing, it becomes shaded.

Rule 3: the right angle of the triangle in the middle is pointing diagonally away from the circle with the smaller circle inside.

Rule 4: the triangle is shaded if the small circle is in one of the upper corners.

31 B

Rule 1: each point of the star has six circles above it, and each turn an increasing number of these circles are taken away going in an anticlockwise direction. Each turn only a single circle can be removed from a given point.

32 A

Rule 1: there are four eggs, each marked with 1, 2, 3 and 4 circles respectively. Each turn the egg on the far left side takes one then two steps to the right pushing the rest of the eggs to the right.

33 D

Rule 1: in every turn, the shading goes around in a clockwise direction by one step at a time, and the petal which is shaded in a given turn is inverted. The following turn the shading moves onward but the petal stays inverted.

34 A

Rule 1: the shadings invert every turn on both pill shapes and every third turn the shading is removed from them. Each turn a single circle is added to each non shaded section. These circles remain there even though they cannot be seen when the shading is over them.

Rule 2: the central shape's quadrants gain circles based on how many circles the two shapes on the sides have.

35 A

Rule 1: every turn an increasing number of circles are added to the points of the star going in a clockwise direction. Each turn only one circle can be added to a given point and if there is already a circle there the new one is added above or next to it.

Rule 2: a circle appears inside the star if there is an even number of circles outside the star.

36 B

Rule 1: there are four eggs, each marked with 1, 2, 3 and 4 circles respectively. In every turn the egg on the far left side moves one step to the right, pushing the other eggs to the right.

Rule 2: In each egg that disappeared on the right side and reappeared on the left again, the circles change shading.

37 C

Rule 1: there are two circles in the upper half of the image and a square at the bottom. The left circle shows a shape and the right one a directional arrow. The square will have the shape which appeared in the upper left circle in one of its corners based on where the directional arrow pointed.

Rule 2: two small circles below the large ones show the shape and the directional arrow from the previous turn.

Rule 3: the shape in the square is shaded if it has more sides than the previous one had.

38 C

Rule 1: there are three flasks in each figure and in each turn, the number of bubbles they have grows by one. At the beginning there are five bubbles altogether and their distribution is random.

Rule 2: All flasks with the highest number of bubbles in a given figure become shaded.

Rule 3: in the flask with the lowest number of bubbles, the bubbles are unshaded. If there is more than one flask with the same low number of bubbles, all of their bubbles are unshaded.

Rule 4: in each turn, the bubbles above the flasks represent the number of bubbles that were inside the flasks in the previous turn.

39 C

Rule 1: there are three pots of plants, and they can have either one, two or three flowers on them. The one with three flowers starts on the left side and every turn it moves one step to the right. The positions of the other two flowers are random and irrelevant.

Rule 2: if the plant with the three flowers appears on the far left side, its pot is unshaded, if it appears in the middle, the pot is striped, and if it appears on the far right side, the pot is shaded. All other pots are always shaded.

40 A

Rule 1: there are three dishes on the image and a random number of wax drops are dripping on them. Every drip turns into a candle segment in the following turn. Once a candle reaches four segments a flame appears above it. Further wax drops above this candle will melt before reaching the candle, therefore will have no effect on it.

Rule 2: in every turn, after a candle has started burning, it will lose one segment per turn.

Rule 3: in every turn, top segments of those candles are shaded which are the highest in a given figure. If there is more than one candle with the same maximum height, the top segments of all those candles are shaded.

Rule 4: The number of wax drops above each candle determines the shading of the dishes under the candles. Locate the candles in each figure over which the highest number of wax drops is falling (for example two or three) – that is the candles whose dish will be shaded. If there is more than one candle with the same number of wax drops, their dishes will be shaded too.

41 A

Rule 1: there are two circles in the upper half of the image and a square at the bottom. The left circle shows a shape and the right one a directional arrow. The square will have the shape which appeared in the upper left circle in one of its corners based on where the directional arrow pointed.

42 C

Rule 1: there are 3x3 circles in the image and one of the circles is shaded. Links between the circles show the route the shaded circle will take the following turn. In the next turn, a new route is planned.

43 C

Rule 1: there are three candles, each divided into four segments. The flame above them has three levels; small, medium and high. If a candle burns with a small flame it loses one segment the following turn, two segments with medium flame and three with high. If a candle completely burned down, it reappears the next turn with all four segments.

44 A

Rule 1: The pill shape on the left is inverted every other time.

Rule 2: The pill shape on the right is inverted every time.

45 A

Rule 1: The shaded section of the star moves one point anti-clockwise each time.

Rule 2: At the same time, a spot rotates 1 point clockwise.

46 B

Rule 1: The top half of the egg alternates from left to right

Rule 2: The number of chicks in the egg increases by 1 each time

47 E

Rule 1: there are 3x3 circles in the image and one of the circles is shaded. Links between the circles show the route the shaded circle will take the following turn. In the next turn, a new route is planned.

Rule 2: a dot appears in every previous station of the shaded circle.

Rule 3: in every odd turn, the shaded circle takes an even number of steps and every even turn it takes an odd number of steps.

48 A

Rule 1: there are three candles, each divided into four segments. The flame above them has three levels; small, medium and high. If a candle burns with a small flame it loses one segment the following turn, two segments with medium flame and three with high. If a candle completely burned down, it reappears the next turn with all four segments.

Rule 2: every odd turn the even segments of the candles are shaded, while every even turn the odd segments are (counting from the bottom).

Rule 3: Every second time a candle appears in a given position (left, centre or right), a dish will appear under the candle in that position.

49 A

Rule 1: the flask alternates between rotating 45 and 90 degrees counter-clockwise each turn around a fixed center.

Rule 2: every time the top of the flask passes the 12 o'clock and 6 o'clock positions, a black circle is added at the bottom of the picture.

Rule 3: every time the flask is upside down (that is, its top side is lower than its bottom side), the level of the liquid inside it decreases – in all other positions, the level of the liquid remains unchanged.

Rule 4: in every odd turn, a small bubble appears inside the flask and in every even turn, a larger one appears.

50 A

Rule 1: The shading of the circle that appears first rotates 45 degrees in a clockwise direction, and after the rotation took place, the shaded and unshaded sections switch places.

Rule 2: The circle grows in size for three turns, after which it spawns a smaller circle and its shading is transferred to the new circle. In the following turn, the shading rotation continues in the new (small) circle, while the original circle remains empty.

Rule 3: the empty circle becomes smaller in every turn after it has transferred its shading.

Rule 4: the shading of the small circles in the center of the larger one always mimics the shading of the larger circle in the previous turn.

51 B

Rule 1: there are three potted flowers, each pot marked with one, two and three dots. In every turn, the pots randomly change places and the plants inside them have as many flowers as the number of dots on their pots.

52 D

Rule 1: there are three flasks in each figure and in each turn, the number of bubbles inside them in total grows by one. At the beginning, there are five bubbles altogether and their distribution is random.

53 C

Rule 1: the shading rotates 45 degrees clockwise for two turns, then 45 degrees anticlockwise for one turn.

54 C

Rule 1: The petals invert in turn clockwise

Rule 2: The cross denotes the petal will disappear in the next frame for one complete cycle. The placing of the cross is random

55 B

Rule 1: The plant pot alternates position, L, middle, R each turn.

Rule 2: If the pot is shaded, the plant has 1 twig. If the pot is striped the plant has 2 twigs.

56 E

Rule 1: in every turn, a circle is removed going in an anticlockwise direction. Once every circle has been removed, there is a blank turn, where no circles appear, before the series starts again.

Rule 2: a smaller circle inside the large ones is going around in a clockwise direction, and if it lands on a space where the large circle is missing it becomes shaded.

57 D

Rule 1: the flask alternates between rotating 45 and 180 degrees clockwise every turn around a fixed center.

Rule 2: if the top of the flask passes either the 12'o clock or 6 o'clock positions in a given turn, the center around which the flask rotates is shown in that turn.

Rule 3: the flask starts as empty and every time the flask is not angled down the level of the liquid inside it increases.

58 E

Rule 1: the potted plant has three stations where it can stand (left, middle and right). Starting on the left it takes an increasing number of steps to the right (when it reaches the right edge of the figure, the movement continues from the left again).

Rule 2: the plant has as many flowers as the number of steps it took in a given turn.

Rule 3: whenever the sun appears, the flowers are shaded.

Rule 4: the sun is shaded if it appears on the left side of the image.

59 A

Rule 1: the flask levels go up for three turns and then down for another three turns.

Rule 2: during the second stage of the rising fluid level and the second stage of falling fluid level, the fluid is shaded.

Rule 3: at the highest and lowest levels (the last level of rising and the last level of falling) there is a stirring stick in the pots (alternatively, we could say that the stirring stick appears after the fluid was shaded).

Rule 4: there is an increasing number of bubbles inside (and above) the flasks. The number of bubbles increases by one in each turn, and if there is a stirring stick in a given figure, it also doubles the number of bubbles (after the regular + 1 bubbles has been added).

60 A

Rule 1: every turn a new circle gets added to the oval shape. The already existing circles change their position every turn, first moving to the top of the oval shape, then back to the bottom, and so on.

Rule 2: Once a circle has appeared, it first gains a small black dot inside, then its silhouette becomes thicker in the next turn. Once a circle has reached this stage, it remains that way for the rest of the series.

Rule 3: Outside the oval, the unshaded circle starting in the top left corner takes a step in a clockwise direction in every even turn, while the shaded circle starting in the bottom left corner takes a step in an anticlockwise direction in every odd turn. If they happen to meet in a corner, the two circles unite and form a circle with a thick black silhouette.

61 A

Rule 1: first the flask rotates 45 then 90 degrees clockwise.

62 C

Rule 1: a single circle is added each turn, first to the left of the original one, then to the right.

63 C

Rule 1: first, the left shape is inverted (this results in the first image), then the right one, and this alternation repeats throughout the series.

64 A

Rule 1: there are 3x3 circles in the image and one of the circles is shaded. Links between the circles show the route the shaded circle will take the following turn. In the next turn, a new route is planned.

Rule 2: a dot appears in every previous station of the shaded circle.

65 E

Rule 1: there are three candles, each divided into four segments. The flame above them has three levels; small, medium and high. If a candle burns with a small flame it loses one segment the following turn, two segments with medium flame and three with high. If a candle completely burned down, it reappears the next turn with all four segments.

Rule 2: every odd turn the even segments of the candles are shaded, while every even turn the odd segments are (counting from the bottom).

66 A

Rule 1: there are three flasks in each figure, and in every turn, different components are dropped into them, which have different effects on the flasks, as visible in the following turn. If a triangle is dropped inside the flask, the liquid becomes shaded; a square makes the flask bubbly, while the circle raises the level of the liquid inside the flask. In every turn, the dropped components are selected randomly, the liquid is reset to its default state between turns, and more than one component can be dropped in any given flask.

Rule 2: in every even turn, an odd number of components are dropped into the flasks altogether, while every odd turn an even number of components are dropped.

67 D

Rule 1: a circle divided into four segments wanders around the four corners of the square randomly and the corner in which the circle appeared the previous turn marks the section which gets shaded inside the circle.

Rule 2: a square (also divided into four segments) appears in the middle of the image, and one of its segments becomes shaded – this is based on which corner of the main square the circle stands at in the given turn.

Rule 3: the shading of the square becomes inverted (the shaded section becomes unshaded and the unshaded section becomes shaded) if the shading in the square and the shading in the circle are in diagonally opposite segments.

68 E

Rule 1: the shading of the pills inverts in every turn; in every third turn the shading is removed from them completely.

Rule 2: the number of circles in the pills is equivalent to the circles in the central shape's closest quadrants, but when the given segment of the pill is shaded, the circles are invisible.

Rule 3: the central shape's shading is the opposite of the two pills on the sides. The circles inside it can be seen even through the shading (as opposed to the ones in the pills).

Rule 4: the outer circle stays above the central shape for two turns, then below it for another two.

69 A

Rule 1: in every turn, an increasing number of circles is added to the points of the star going in a clockwise direction. If there is already a circle at a given point, the new one is added above or next to it.

Rule 2: a circle appears inside the star if there is an even number of circles outside the star.

Rule 3: every second circle added to a given point of the star is shaded.

Rule 4: a circle outside the star goes around in a clockwise direction increasing the steps it takes between the arms of the star by one in every turn. In addition, it changes its shading as well in every turn.

70 E

Rule 1: there are four small eggs, each marked with 1, 2, 3 and 4 circles respectively. In every turn, the egg on the far left side moves one step to the right pushing the other eggs to the right (the rightmost egg always reappears on the left).

Rule 2: In each egg that disappeared on the right side and reappeared on the left again, the circles change their shading.

Rule 3: a large egg randomly appears above one of the small eggs and it has one less circle inside it than does the smaller egg under it (i.e. if the small egg under it has 1 circle, the large egg will have no circles).

Rule 4: the upper half of the large egg is shaded if it has an odd number of circles in the lower half.

71 A

Rule 1: the shaded section moves an increasing number of points in a clockwise direction every turn.

72 A

Rule 1: the three candles each start with a low flame, and in every turn, starting from the left, the flame of one of the candles increases. When all flames already increased, they start changing the direction in which they face one by one starting from the left.

73 A

Rule 1: there are three pots of plants, and they can have either one, two or three flowers on them. The one with three flowers starts on the left side and in every turn it moves one step to the right. The positions of the other two flowers are random and irrelevant.

74 B

Rule 1: the petal turns clockwise; in every turn, the shading of one or more petals may change depending on the sign in the middle of the flower. The petal turns even when it is not shaded (i.e. when "invisible").

Rule 2: if there is a plus (+) sign in the middle of the image, two petals will be shaded instead of the standard one, and if there is a minus (–) sign in the middle, no shading will take place in that turn. In the absence of a sign in the middle, 1 petal will become shaded. The special signs do not necessarily appear in every turn, and the same sign cannot appear on the next turn if it showed up on the previous one.

75 D

Rule 1: there are two circles in the upper half of the image and a square at the bottom. The left circle shows a shape and the right one a directional arrow. The square will have the shape which appeared in the upper left circle in one of its corners based on where the directional arrow pointed.

Rule 2: two small circles below the large ones show the shape and the directional arrow from the previous turn.

76 C

Rule 1: there are three pots of plants, and they can have either one, two or three flowers on them. The one with three flowers starts on the left side and every turn it moves one step to the right. The positions of the other two flowers are random and irrelevant.

Rule 2: if the plant with the three flowers appears on the far left side, its pot is unshaded, if it appears in the middle, the pot is stripped, and if it appears on the far right side, the pot is shaded. All other pots are always shaded.

77 D

Rule 1: in every turn, an unshaded circle is added to the top section of the right shape, and a shaded circle to the bottom section of the same shape in the following turn. The two sections of the left shape contain identical numbers of shaded and unshaded circles, but their places are flipped; the shaded circles appear in the upper section, while the unshaded ones appear in the lower section.

Rule 2: the central shape is divided into two segments (left and right), and theses segments show

how many circles the shapes on the sides had (the left side 'collects' the shaded circles and the right side 'collects' the unshaded circles) in the previous turn.

Rule 3: in every turn, a different side of the central shape is shaded.

78 C

Rule 1: there are 3x3 circles in each figure and one of the circles is shaded. Links between the circles show the route the shading will take the following turn. In the next turn, a new route is planned.

Rule 2: a circle appears in every previous station of the shaded circle.

Rule 3: in every odd turn, the indicate route of the shaded circle contains an even number of steps and in every even turn, it contains an odd number of steps.

Rule 4: dots representing previously shaded circles become shaded if there are more than one in a row.

79 A

Rule 1: there are three candles, each divided into four segments. The flame above them has three levels; low, medium and high. If a candle burns with a low flame it loses one segment the following turn, two segments with medium flame and three with high. If a candle completely burned down, it reappears the next turn with all four segments.

Rule 2: in every odd turn, the even segments of the candles are shaded, while in every even turn, the odd segments are unshaded (counting from the bottom).

Rule 3: Every second time a candle appears in a given position (left, center or right), a dish will appear under the candle in that position.

Rule 4: In each figure, a type of flame may be shaded. First, the low-level flame is shaded, then the medium, then the high one, and then the cycle repeats. If the necessary type of flame is not present in a figure, the shading is not visible either. That is why there is no shading in figure #4 (there is no low-level flame), and that is why the medium-level flame is shaded in figure #5.

80 C

Rule 1: there are three pots of plants, and they can have either one, two or three flowers on them. The one with three flowers starts on the left side and every turn it moves one step to the right. The positions of the other two flowers are random and irrelevant.

Rule 2: if the plant with the three flowers appears on the far left side, its pot is unshaded, if it appears in the middle, the pot is striped, and if it appears on the far right side, the pot is shaded. All other pots are always shaded.

Rule 3: whenever the pot of the plant with the three flowers is unshaded (that is, it is on the far left side) the flowers of the other two pots become unshaded too.

Rule 4: starting from the bottom and moving upwards, each turn a new flower is unshaded on the plant with three flowers.

81 B

Rule 1: there are three flasks in each figure, and in every turn, different components are dropped into them, which have different effects on the flasks, as visible in the following turn. If a triangle is dropped inside the flask, the liquid becomes shaded; a square makes the flask bubbly, while the circle raises the level of the liquid inside the flask. In every turn, the dropped components are selected randomly, the liquid is reset to its default state between turns, and more than one component can be dropped in any given flask.

82 A

Rule 1: there are three dishes in each figure and a random number of wax drops are dripping on them. Every drip turns into a candle segment the following turn. Once a candle reaches four segments a flame appears above it.

Rule 2: in every turn, after a candle has started burning, it will lose one segment per turn.

83 E

Rule 1: in every turn, two circles are randomly shaded on the 3x3 table and links are drawn between the two shaded circles of the previous turn.

Rule 2: small white dots appear inside the shaded circles in every turn. In odd turns, they appear in the upper shaded circle, while in even turns, they appear inside lower shaded circle.

Rule 3: the small circles inside the big ones change their size from turn to turn; they grow for two turns then shrink for the next two.

84 E

Rule 1: there are three potted flowers, each pot marked with one, two and three dots. In every turn, the pots randomly change places and the plants inside them have as many flowers as the number of dots on their pots.

Rule 2: in every turn, flowers are randomly shaded based on the number of dots the middle pot has.

Rule 3: the dots on the pots are randomly shaded based on how many dots the pot in the middle has in a given turn.

85 A

Rule 1: in every turn, one or more random petals are shaded. With the exception of these petals, all other petals have been flipped from their previous positions.

Rule 2: if there is a plus (+) sign in the middle of the image, two petals will be shaded instead of the standard 1, and if there is a minus (-) sign in the middle, no shading will take place in that turn. In the absence of a sign in the middle, 1 petal will become shaded. The special signs do not necessarily appear in every turn.

Rule 3: the shape in the center has as many sides as the number of unshaded petals in the figure.

Rule 4: a number of circles appearing in each figure is based on how many shaded petals there are in the given figure. The position of the circles corresponds to the number of unshaded petals, counting clockwise from the top petal (if, for example, there are 3 unshaded petals, the circles will appear in the third petal counting clockwise from the top one).

86 C

Rule 1: there are two circles in the upper half of the image and a square at the bottom. The left circle shows a shape and the right one a directional arrow. The square will include a shape which appears in the upper left circle in one of its corners based on where the directional arrow points in the same figure.

Rule 2: two small circles below the large ones show the shape and the directional arrow from the previous turn.

Rule 3: the shape in the square is shaded if it has more sides than the previous one had.

Rule 4: the upper left circle is shaded if the shape inside it has an odd number of sides.

87 B

Rule 1: the flask alternates between rotating 45 and 180 degrees clockwise every turn around a fixed center.

Rule 2: if the top of the flask passes either the 12'o clock or 6 o'clock positions in a given turn, the center around which the flask rotates is shown in that turn.

Rule 3: the flask starts as empty, and every time the flask is not upside down (that is, its top is higher than its bottom), the level of the liquid inside it increases.

Rule 4: a small black circle alternates between appearing to the left then to the right of the flask as viewed from position of the flask.

88 E

Rule 1: a circle divided into four segments wanders around the four corners of the outer square randomly and the corner in which the circle appeared the previous turn marks the section which gets shaded inside the circle.

Rule 2: a square (also divided into four segments) appears in the middle of the image with one or more of its segments shaded – this is based on which corner of the outer square the circle stands at in the given turn.

Rule 3: the shading of the square is reversed (the shaded section becomes unshaded and the unshaded section becomes shaded) if the shading in the square and the shading in the circle are in diagonally opposite segments.

Rule 4: a triangle pointing to the circle's previous position appears in every turn in a random corner.

89 B

Rule 1: In every turn, a new circle is added to the oval – first to the bottom, then in the next turn to the top. The already existing circles change their positions in every turn, either going to the top or the bottom of the oval shape according to their previous positions.

Rule 2: when a circle changes its position, it becomes shaded. At the next position change, it again becomes unshaded, and so on. Circles that freshly appear in the image always appear unshaded.

Rule 3: in every even turn, small squares appear outside the oval shape, in the top right corner. The number of squares is equal to the number of circles that were present inside the oval shape in the previous turn.

Rule 4: the number of shaded and unshaded squares is the inverse of the number of shaded and unshaded circles inside the oval in the previous turn.

90 A

Rule 1: in every turn, an unshaded circle is added to the top section of the right shape, and a shaded circle to the bottom section of the same shape in the following turn. The two sections of the left shape contain identical numbers of shaded and unshaded circles, but their places are flipped; the shaded circles appear in the upper section, while the unshaded ones appear in the lower section.

Rule 2: the central shape is divided into two segments (left and right), and these segments show how many circles the shapes on the sides had (the left side 'collects' the shaded circles and the right side collects the unshaded circles) in the previous turn.

Rule 3: in every turn, a different side of the central shape is shaded.

Rule 4: A circle appears attached to either the top or the bottom of the central shape in every turn. The shading of this circle and its position (top or bottom) is the opposite of the shading and position of the circle that appears in the left pill in the given figure.

91 D

Rule 1: there are three dishes in the image and a random number of wax drops are dripping on them. Every drip turns into a candle segment the following turn. Once a candle reaches four segments a flame appears above it. Further wax drops above this candle will melt before reaching the candle, therefore will have no effect on it.

92 A

Rule 1: there are three potted flowers, each pot marked with one, two and three dots. In every turn, the pots randomly change places and the plants inside them have as many flowers as the number of dots on their pots.

Rule 2: in every turn, flowers are randomly shaded based on the number of dots the middle pot has.

93 D

Rule 1: there are three flasks on the picture and each turn the number of bubbles they have grow by one. At the beginning there are five bubbles altogether and their distribution is random.

Rule 2: every turn the flask with the highest number of bubbles becomes shaded (the bubbles become white). If there is more than one flask with the highest number of bubbles, all of them become shaded.

Rule 3: in the flask with the lowest number of bubbles, the bubbles are unshaded. If there is more than one flask with the same low number of bubbles, all of their bubbles are unshaded.

94 B

Rule 1: there are three dishes in the image and a random number of wax drops are dripping on them. Every drip turns into a candle segment the following turn. Once a candle reaches four segments a flame appears above it. Further wax drops above this candle will melt before reaching the candle, therefore will have no effect on it.

Rule 2: in every turn, after a candle has started burning, it will lose one segment per turn.

Rule 3: in every turn, the highest candle segment is shaded. If there are more segments of equal maximum height, all of them are shaded.

95 C

Rule 1: Each point of the star originally had six circles attached to it. In each figure, an increasing number of circles are removed from the image going in a counter-clockwise direction. In the first figure, one circle is already removed from the 12'o clock position. In the second figure, a total of two circles are removed (one each from the next two points of the star going clockwise), then three, and so on.

Rule 2: a large black circle appears inside the star every time the total number of circles outside the star is an odd number.

Rule 3: in every turn, a circle is added to an inner point of the star going in a clockwise direction.

Rule 4: the circles added inside the star change their shading in every turn.

96 B

Rule 1: there are three flasks in each figure, and in every turn, different components are dropped into them, which have different effects on the flasks, as visible in the following turn. If a triangle is dropped inside the flask, the liquid becomes shaded; a square makes the flask bubbly, while the circle raises the level of the liquid inside the flask. In every turn, the dropped components are selected randomly, the liquid is reset to its default state between turns, and more than one component can be dropped in any given flask.

Rule 2: in every even turn, an odd number of components are dropped into the flasks altogether, while every odd turn an even number of components are dropped.

97 A

Rule 1: there are four eggs, each marked with 1, 2, 3 and 4 circles respectively. In each turn, the egg on the far left side takes one and then two steps to the right, pushing the rest of the eggs to the right as well, and then the cycle repeats.

Rule 2: First, the circles in those eggs are shaded where the number of circles is even. Then, in the next turn, the circles in those eggs are shaded where the number of circles is odd, and then the cycle repeats.

Rule 3: a large central egg has a random number of circles inside it (between one and four), and the number of circles shows above which small egg it will appear the following turn (above the one with the same number of circles).

Rule 4: the shading of the circles in the large egg is the opposite of that of the circles appearing in the small egg underneath.

98 B

Rule 1: in every turn, the shading on the petals goes around in a clockwise direction by one step at a time, and the petal which is shaded in a given turn is inverted. In the following turn, the shading moves onward but the petal stays inverted.

Rule 2: an arrow in the middle shows which petal was shaded in the previous turn.

Rule 3: in every odd turn, a black dot appears on the petal that will be shaded in the next turn. In every even turn, the black dot appears on the petal that was shaded in the previous turn.

Rule 4: a single circle is going around between the petals of the flowers in a clockwise direction, and each time the black dot is in a neighbouring petal, it becomes shaded as well.

99 A

Rule 1: there are five circles in each figure. The upper left circle has a shape, the upper right a directional arrow, while the circle in the middle has either a plus (+) or a minus (-) sign in it. The sign shows what happens with the shape (loses a side or gains a side) shown in the upper left circle and the result is shown in the lower left circle. The directional arrow in the upper right circle changes its facing depending on whether there was a + sign in the central circle (the directional arrow rotates 45 degrees in a clockwise direction) or a - sign (the directional arrow rotates 45 degrees in an anticlockwise direction), and again, the result is shown in the lower right circle. The bottom two results will then form the upper shapes of the next image.

Rule 2: the central circle grows in size if there's a + sign in it, and shrinks if it is a - sign.

Rule 3: the lower left shape is shaded if it has an even number of sides.

Rule 4: the shape in the upper left circle is shaded if it has an odd number of sides.

100 C

Rule 1: in every turn, two circles are randomly shaded on the 3x3 table and links are drawn between the two shaded circles of the previous turn.

Rule 2: small white dots appear inside the shaded circles in every turn. In odd turns, they appear in the upper shaded circle, while in even turns, they appear inside lower shaded circle.

Rule 3: the small circles inside the big ones change their size from turn to turn; they grow for two turns then shrink for the next two.

Rule 4: in each turn, a number of lines appears on the surface of the shaded circle with the dot in it. The number of these lines equals the number of the lines representing the route between the connected circles in the given turn.

8. Succeeding in Situational Judgement Tests

Situational judgement tests (or SJTs for short) present candidates with a series of hypothetical but realistic work-based scenarios in which they are required to make a decision. It is important to understand that even though called "tests", they are very different in nature from the verbal, numerical and abstract reasoning tests you will face during the recruitment process as they measure how you evaluate certain situations instead of testing your harder analytical skills and behaviours.

Situational judgement tests are employed because they can be used to consistently and fairly assess at an early stage behavioural attributes such as decision-making ability and interpersonal skills that are difficult to measure by other techniques.

SJTs are a fast-growing area in the selection and development field. The basic idea of presenting a relevant hypothetical situation has been in use in recruitment since the early 1900s, but SJTs in a format comparable to today's SJTs have been more prevalent since the 1940s, used in particular for predicting supervisory and managerial potential.

More recent research has found that SJTs are strong predictors of real-life job performance. This means that in the development or review of SJTs, those people doing well in the tests were also the people who performed well in role. Not only that, but SJTs seems to measure an additional aspect of performance that is not measured by other assessment tools such as ability tests or personality questionnaires. This suggests that the SJTs are tapping into a different skill, and one that is highly relevant to job performance.

According to EPSO, situational judgement tests will be used prior to the assessment phase, as part of the computer-based pre-selection process for Assistant and Administrator profiles. However, it is important to note SJTs will not be eliminatory at the pre-selection stage. They are only taken into account if the candidate is accepted for the assessment phase; otherwise the conclusions that can be drawn from them are not communicated to the applicant. One reason why SJTs are administered in the pre-selection phase is technical, as it is more convenient to have candidates respond to multiple choice questions in an exam centre than later in the assessment phase.

Theory behind Situational Judgement Tests

At the heart of social psychology is the idea that what makes us human is our ability to make sense of social situations. When we evaluate an important or new situation most of us try to understand the intentions of others in the situation, and possible causal explanations, to guide our response (e.g. "How would you react if you discovered that your colleague had leaked some confidential information to the press?").

Social psychology theory also holds that there is a similarity in how people evaluate situations, and that most people will have a shared expectation of what is an *appropriate* response. This theory forms the basis of why situational judgement tests can be used to provide an indicator of our likely behaviour in an EU job-context or elsewhere. By presenting the candidate with relevant hypothetical scenarios and a set of responses which have been previously scored for their level of effectiveness, it is possible to assess how appropriate the candidate's response selection is, and to use this information to predict their likely behavioural response if faced with similar situations in the role.

What They Measure

The name "situational judgement test" suggests that what is being measured is indeed "situational judgement" even though little research has been done to explore exactly what type of personal quality is being measured by SJTs. However, some evidence exists that what SJTs are actually tapping into is an aspect of "practical intelligence" or "general intelligence". It is likely that SJTs are indeed multi-dimensional; they measure a number of different constructs including social or behavioural judgement, practical or general intelligence and aspects of personality such as conscientiousness. In the EPSO assessment process the SJT has been specifically developed for the purpose of measuring the candidate's situational judgement in relation to selected EPSO competencies.

How They Are Developed

Robust situational judgement tests are developed in the same way as other psychometric tests. The particular job profiles EPSO is seeking to recruit for are analysed by experts to understand what type of workplace situations occur that are critical to achieving good performance outcomes. This is done by interviewing current EU officials, heads of unit, directors and subject matter experts to gain a number of perspectives on what is important and what would be effective behaviour.

At the same time, examples of how less effective behaviour could lead to less desirable outcomes are gathered. Once these situations are identified, they are written up as possible test scenarios: a paragraph or two that summarises the situation and a range of four or more response options (from *most desirable* to *least desirable*). The scenario and response options are crafted so that there is no "obvious" answer and even the "undesirable" options sound plausible. This is necessary to avoid "obvious" answers or the risk that candidates would be able to easily identify the "desired" answer.

Careful consideration is given to the design of the test introduction and instructions and the scenario wording, format and content. It is well known that in the case of public opinion surveys, how the question is formulated will significantly influence the answer. As this is certainly true for SJTs as well, even subtle details of presentation must be thought through carefully.

It is important that the SJT design fits within the organisational setting and the assessment process, and that it reflects realistic elements of the job role in question. However, EPSO has said that its situational judgement tests are designed so that they require no specialist knowledge to complete: they will be purely behaviourally-based assessments.

How They Work

The theory of planned behaviour states that an individual's behaviour in the past is a good predictor of their likely behaviour in the future. As with a standard competency based interview, this is the basis on which a situational judgement test is used to predict a candidate's job performance or suitability for the given job profile.

For each given situational judgement test, a *scoring key* is developed so that the candidate's response can be compared against this key. Initially, this can be developed by making rational judgements as to which are the most and least preferred responses to each scenario, based on the job analysis data collected in the design process and from additional evaluations made by subject matter experts.

The SJT can then be *validated* by demonstrating a clear relationship between good performance in the test and real-life good performance in the role. In order to validate the test design, and to select which scenarios will be in the final test, groups of existing job holders such as – for example – Administrators in the European Commission or Assistants in the Committee of the Regions will be tested on the sample scenarios and their responses will be compared to their real-life competency-based job performance (as judged by their superior's appraisal ratings).

Those scenarios for which the high performers have consistently selected the most preferred response as their *own* most preferred response will be selected as good ones for the final test. If there are scenarios for which high performers consistently select different responses, these will be brought into question as to their appropriateness and dropped from the test. When used in the organisation's assessment process, the candidate's score in the SJT will be based on their performance across all scenarios within the test and a score will be given to each competency in question.

What They Look Like

When sitting the test, you will be presented with a number of seemingly equally-viable alternative courses of action and be asked to choose the most and least appropriate in your opinion; the questions will have limited or no direct relevance to the European Union but they will most likely relate to realistic workplace situations and working within hierarchies and with colleagues.

I would anticipate that each of the "situations" would measure one of the key competencies for the job (although you would not be informed which is being measured when answering each question) and also cross-check the consistency of your answers. Consequently, each competency will need to be measured more than once in order to reliably estimate your ability and therefore more than one scenario will relate to each competency. The test will have been designed especially for EPSO by expert occupational psychologists and I expect that it will contain from twenty-five to fifty questions.

Here is a sample SJT test scenario, designed to measure a generic "planning"-type competency (which is not itself a specific EPSO competency, but see below for a comprehensive sample test and explanations based on the EPSO competency framework). I have also included what I would judge to be the most and least effective courses of action (although this could vary according to exact competency definitions):

You have been approached by your superior and asked to deliver a project within a very tight deadline. You are pleased that your head of unit has approached you to work on the project but are concerned about delivering it within the timeframe given. What do you do?

A. Review and reprioritise the projects you are currently involved in so you can start work on the new project straight away.

B. Schedule a meeting with your head of unit to discuss options for delivering the project, suggesting colleagues that you would like to involve to ensure the project is delivered within the timeframe given. (**Most Effective**)

C. Develop a plan outlining how you intend approaching the project and use this to emphasise to your head of unit your concern about the deadline and ask if it can be extended.

D. Delegate the task to another person, stressing to them the importance of meeting the deadline. Retain an overview so that you can track progress and keep the ultimate credit for the work. (**Least Effective**)

The Candidate Experience

SJTs contribute to the assessment by being a two-way process for EPSO and the candidate.

EPSO can evaluate the candidate's responses to the scenarios against the structured scoring key and evaluate the extent to which the candidate's behaviour is likely to fit in with the competencies and way of working at the EU institutions.

The candidate is also able to take a view of what it would be like to work with the EU by reflecting after the test on the types of scenarios and response options presented. These may provide a general insight into what situations or behaviours might be expected in the role. Reviewing this chapter and trying out some of the practice questions later on is likely to prove beneficial for you: those candidates who are familiar with SJTs have been found to view the experience of completing SJTs as part of an assessment process more positively than those without that familiarity.

How to Prepare

It is difficult to prepare in advance of taking an SJT: a response to a situation that may be appropriate in one role may be inappropriate in another (e.g. the way you would react to a critique from your supervisor is very different from your reaction to an issue raised by an EU citizen affected by a policy you are covering). Therefore, your answers should draw from your intuitive, *honest* responses about how you would address such situations.

However, reviewing some practice questions (see sample test later in the chapter) can help to alleviate stress and allow you to focus on the *content* of the questions once you start the real test, rather than spending time becoming familiar with the *format*. Also, ensure that you are familiar with the EPSO competencies, as I anticipate that each scenario will be based around one of these. By doing this, you will be more aware of what is likely to be looked for across all the questions. Once again, however, it should be reiterated that you must be honest in your responses and not spend time trying to second-guess what is being looked for.

If you wished to, you could look up some reference material on current best practice thinking on areas related to the competencies being assessed. For example, as there is an EPSO competency entitled "leadership" for Administrator grades (defined as "Manages, develops and motivates people to achieve results"), you may benefit from doing some background reading on how to motivate a team, issue clear directions or give developmental feedback as there is likely to be a question scenario based around this competency. Ideas for research topics on the other competencies are as follows (see also recommended resources below):

- **Analysis and Problem Solving** – *Identifies the critical facts in complex issues and develops creative and practical solutions.* Research areas such as troubleshooting techniques, how to approach dealing with large amounts of information, techniques to stimulate creative problem solving, how to gather appropriate information.
- **Communicating** – *Communicates clearly and precisely both orally and in writing.* Research areas such as public speaking techniques, best practice in internal communications within organisations, how to engage an audience.
- **Delivering Quality and Results** – *Takes personal responsibility and initiative for delivering work to a high standard of quality within set procedures.* Research areas such as how to effectively balance quality and deadlines, how to judge when rules or procedures might be bent or broken.
- **Learning and Development** – *Develops and improves personal skills and knowledge of the*

organisation and its environment. Research areas such as general self-improvement techniques, self-motivation, how to learn from mistakes, how to seek feedback from colleagues, how an organisation can use its learning capital.

- **Prioritising and Organising** – *Prioritises the most important tasks, works flexibly and organises own workload efficiently.* Research areas such as project management tools and techniques, how to prioritise effectively, how to distinguish the important from the urgent, how to respond to shifting deadlines and goalposts, when and how to delegate.
- **Resilience** – *Remains effective under a heavy workload, handles organisational frustrations positively and adapts to a changing work environment.* Research areas such as how to stay calm under pressure, how to keep an optimistic outlook, how to respond to criticism, how to balance work and home life, how to cope with ambiguity.
- **Working with Others** – *Works co-operatively with others in teams and across organisational boundaries and respects differences between people.* Research areas such as effective team working, working across organisational boundaries, how to support others.

However, it should be noted that this will be a lot of background work and it would be unrealistic to expect to become an expert in all of these areas prior to the assessment if you are not already. A better tactic might be to decide which one or two competency areas are your prime areas for development and focus upon these.

Tips for the Assessment itself

Several tips mentioned in the verbal reasoning chapter can be successfully applied for SJTs as well. Review and adapt those hints to match the specialties of SJTs.

- **Read Everything**: Read the scenario and each of the possible answers fully before responding. You may find that the answer that originally seemed to be the best does not turn out to be upon closer inspection. Remember that the options will be carefully worded and watch out for subtle differences in wording that could differentiate a truly exceptional response from an adequate one. If possible, try to judge which EPSO competency is being assessed so you have a good idea about what qualities they will be looking for you to emphasise.
- **Relative Answers**: Bear in mind that you are being asked to make *relative* judgements: you are not asked to say which courses of action are right or wrong. In other words, you may find that *all* of the possible responses are appropriate to some degree. In this case, just rank them in order of appropriateness to help you make the "most effective" and "least effective" decision.
- **Limited Context**: As with verbal reasoning exams, try not to bring in outside knowledge – base your responses solely on the information contained within the scenario itself. This is because your outside experience may colour your response in a way that means it is not relevant to the question being posed. To take a light-hearted example, you may know that in your team at work, they are all huge fans of pizza and therefore this would be a good way of motivating them. However, in the SJT test item, there may be no reference to this and the best way to motivate a team may well be to give a motivational talk. Therefore, your outside experience might negatively impact on your ability to perform well in the test.
- **Outcome Focus**: Take the time to consider what the possible *outcomes* would be, both positive and negative, of each of the courses of action you are considering. This will help you to narrow down the choices.
- **Communication is Key**: When a situation is described where you need to choose

between handing responsibility for discussing an issue to your superior or discussing an issue with another party face-to-face, it is likely that the latter option will be preferred.

- **Internal Issues**: In a situation involving a conflict, try to look for options that favour keeping a certain issue in-house and involve only those affected by it; your loyalty to your unit or institution is highly valued.
- **Stay Positive**: When faced with a problem that may be resolved by making someone take the blame, avoid the temptation and try to act as fair as possible even if that means a disadvantage for you in the short term.

Though the primary focus of situational judgement tests is not your factual knowledge of EU procedures or administrative practice, it is advisable to read through the Code of Good Administrative Behaviour of EU officials. This includes fundamental principles such as lawfulness, proportionality, non-discrimination, consistency, objectivity and others which can *indirectly* help in your judgement of the questions. Another valuable source is EPSO's very own statement of the values based on which it aims to conduct its mission : integrity, ambition, professionalism, quality service, diversity and respect. If you bear these in mind when making your "situational judgement", it will surely yield the best result.

In the following pages, you can find a sample situational judgement Test with detailed explanations, based on EPSO's competency framework.

SAMPLE SITUATIONAL JUDGEMENT TEST

In this sample situational judgement test, you will be presented with **eight different situations**, along with a set of **four possible courses of action for each**. Instead of providing a comprehensive test that could evaluate your competency strengths and weaknesses (which is anyway close to impossible without a professional assessor's personal feedback or a dynamic evaluation tool), the goal is to give you a feel for what these tests are like so when facing the real exam, you can focus more on the content and not be surprised by the form.

Apart from the hints and techniques suggested above, we would also recommend that you *try to identify which EPSO competency is being assessed* before choosing one option that you think would be the most desirable and one option that would be the least desirable course of action in each situation. The above list of competencies should help you properly understand the detailed characteristics of each competency and thus assist in making your choice. The reason I recommend this approach is that this will help you to focus your response on the correct area instead of assuming a different context that might lead to misinterpretation. As a final note, I have written these scenarios so that they are likely to measure some of the qualities looked for under each of the EPSO competencies. However, these are not necessarily the exact format you will face as the number of answer options or other details might change. This nevertheless does not affect the core idea and methodology of SJTs, so the sample tests below should prove helpful whatever the final EPSO format is.

Situation One

You are scheduled to join a new unit next week, having requested a transfer from your current role as you had begun to feel as if your work was becoming rather predictable and dull. You are looking forward to your new role, but are aware that there are some areas of knowledge that you need to work on in order to perform effectively. There is no formal induction process into the new role. Which of the following are you most likely to do?

A. Wait until you begin in the new role as you have always learnt best "on the job" in the past.

B. Speak to other people who actually do the new job to find out what they think is important to know. Then plan your learning accordingly.

C. Meet with your new superior to discuss where your strengths and weaknesses may lie and then plan your learning accordingly.

D. As you already have some idea of where you need to improve, begin research on these areas straight away to avoid taking up other people's time.

Situation Two

You are in a meeting, trying to get your point of view heard, when another person interrupts you saying that you are "talking nonsense" and then puts forward his views instead. The group all agree with the other person's idea even though you did not finish describing yours and you feel it still has merit. Moreover, the other person's plan has some obvious flaws. The group is about to move onto another topic of conversation; what are you most likely to do?

A. State that you, likewise, feel that the other person's idea is "nonsense" as well and that if he hadn't interrupted so rudely, he might have had a chance to hear your idea as well. Then proceed to give your views.

B. As the group is about to move on, don't hold up the meeting by disagreeing now, but send round an email that outlines your alternative idea afterwards, asking for feedback and whether you could call a subsequent meeting to discuss.

C. Let them proceed with the other person's idea, as it is the group consensus decision. However, do some preparation in advance to manage the fall-out when things go wrong.

D. Despite holding up the meeting, you state clearly and firmly that whilst you appreciate the other person's idea has merit, there are some drawbacks and you would like to suggest an alternative. Then proceed to give your views.

Situation Three

You are working as part of a team to discuss how to resolve a problem that has occurred with a technical system. The conversation seems to be going nowhere, with lots of people suggesting their own solutions but no-one listening. About halfway through you notice that the technical expert who was responsible for the problem has been quiet for most of the meeting, only contributing the occasional fact when asked by others. You know he is shy as you have worked with him for a while, but you definitely feel he could be contributing more. What do you do?

A. Explain that you feel the meeting is not achieving its objectives and you are running out of time. Summarise what has been discussed and then say that you want to make sure that everyone's views are heard. Then ask for the technical expert's views directly in front of the rest of the group.

B. Make a note of the fact that the technical expert not only caused the problem, but was also unhelpful in resolving the issue. Feed this back to him and his superior following the meeting.

C. Ask him for his views immediately and assertively. The meeting is already halfway through and you do not wish to waste any more time on discussions that might be irrelevant.

D. Suggest that the group pause for a moment and refocus on the purpose of the meeting. Then ask if anyone would like to comment on what we have covered so far whilst looking at the technical expert in the hope that they will take the opportunity to speak.

Situation Four

You are new to the role and one of your team members comes to you for an urgent decision. Apparently, they are in a heated debate with someone from another team about the best way to implement a new piece of software. Your team member has presented you with a large amount of information that they say backs up their case and asks you to give them your support at a project meeting tomorrow. What do you do next?

A. Demonstrate your faith in your team member's judgement and promise to give your full support at the meeting.

B. Ask if the meeting can be postponed so that you have a chance to look through the information and analyse it in more detail before arriving at a decision about what to do.

C. Go and see the individual from the other team to get their side of the story before making up your mind about what to do.

D. Start from scratch in analysing the situation for yourself and see if you can suggest something that meets both party's needs.

Situation Five

You are leading a team that is feeling quite overworked due to stretching deadlines and sheer quantity of work. You have managed them for quite a while and have developed a friendly, informal relationship with its members. Recently, a new head of unit joined who you report to. They have just told you that you need to give your team additional tasks to complete by the end of the month and also that some of their benefits, such as free lunches on a Friday, will need to be stopped. How would you approach the situation?

A. Convey all the messages from your new head of unit verbatim. Refuse to enter into debate with the team and restate your position calmly but firmly.

B. Convey the messages from your new superior but apologetically, to your team. Recommend to them that they accept the changes with little fuss for the sake of their career, as well as your own.

C. Talk to the team informally about the state of the organisation in general before moving on to discuss the changes that need to be made. Listen to their views and offer support where possible.

D. Hold back from giving the messages until the workload has lessened a little. Instead, take on the extra work yourself and fund the Friday lunch from your own pocket in order to avoid demotivating the team.

Situation Six

You have just been given responsibility for overseeing a special project team that has been put together to work on a large piece of translation work over the next 6 months. You have worked with everyone before and you feel you know their strengths and weaknesses. They are all hard workers and you are confident they have the motivation to do an excellent job. However, you do know that the commissioning client is likely to change the specification of the project as time progresses, so you want to keep things flexible. How would you approach the management of the team?

A. Gather the team together at the start and reiterate the faith you have in their ability to deliver. Avoid patronising them by telling them exactly what is expected of them. Ask for regular updates from them and hold ad hoc meetings to check on progress.

B. Identify the key milestones, risks and contingencies facing the project in partnership with the team and pull together a formal project plan that you can all refer to as the project progresses.

C. Instruct the team to begin by working towards the first deadline target, without looking too far into the future so that you can respond flexibly to the client's changing requests.

D. Start with a broad plan, but then arrange one-to-one meetings with every team member on a daily basis in order to check on progress and assign new tasks and responsibilities as they arrive from the client.

Situation Seven

You have been asked by your superior to give a presentation to some senior stakeholders about a piece of work you were responsible for delivering. What would be the most important part of your preparation?

A. Try to understand more about what the senior stakeholders are interested in so that you can adapt your presentation to suit.

B. Rehearse your presentation with a colleague a number of times until you feet completely confident in its delivery.

C. Try to identify the key messages you wish to deliver and then plan how to convey these clearly and concisely.

D. Do some research into the kind of props you could use to make the presentation more interactive in order to really capture the audience's attention.

Situation Eight

You are responsible for compiling the results of an important opinion survey that is running behind schedule and you are due to present the findings in two days' time. The work required is fairly basic data entry with some simple calculations required to get average scores. You already have a full diary and are feeling exhausted, your superior is away on holiday and you have no additional budget to spend. How do you approach the situation?

A. Decide to request an extra temporary member of staff anyway and worry about the budget later: delivering the project on time is the most important issue.

B. Scale back the scope of the project and report on what you have been able to complete in the available time and then give a follow-up presentation at a later date that covers subsequent work.

C. Work additional hours yourself in order to get the data entered, even if you already have a very busy schedule.

D. See if some extra resource is available from another team to help with the data entry.

Answers with Explanations

Situation One

EPSO Competency: Learning and Development

Which did you think were the most and least desirable courses of action?

The most appropriate answer in this case is **Option C**. By understanding where your strengths and weaknesses lie and getting an expert opinion on this too, you will have the ideal base upon which to plan your development. You new superior is the ideal source, although you may also get some input from your current superior to help the discussion.

Option B might be useful, but the advice is likely to be quite general, rather than applied to you specifically. Also, the people in the job may not be performing all the tasks in the way in which the head of unit wishes them to be performed.

Option A may be a possibility, especially if you have a preference for active learning. However, this should follow from Option C, not replace it. It also reflects a rather ad hoc approach to personal development, rather than a planned, well considered one.

By choosing **Option D**, you will have missed out on the valuable chance to have your own opinion on what to develop validated or challenged by another, therefore this is likely to be the least effective course of action. Ruling out this course of action because it may take up people's time before you have even checked with them is a missed opportunity.

Situation Two

EPSO Competency: Resilience

Which did you think were the most and least desirable courses of action?

The most appropriate answer in this case is **Option D**. It demonstrates great resilience to not only come back against a challenger that everyone else has agreed with, but also to do so in a calm and measured manner. It will be far more efficient to raise the point now, even if it means extending the meeting, as it ensures all subsequent discussions are relevant.

Option A is likely to simply cause antagonism by being equally rude in return. Although your views will be heard by the group, they will also note your emotional reaction and may hesitate about engaging with you or challenging you in the future. Additionally, the person you were originally in conflict with may then feel obliged to argue back just because of the approach you adopted, in order to maintain his pride.

Option B may be acceptable, depending upon the timescales available, but it would show greater resilience to address the issue there and then, face to face. It also runs the risk of the rest of the meeting being unproductive because it will be based on the premise that the alternative idea will be adopted.

However, **Option C** is probably the least desirable as because you failed to speak out, now an entire project's success is at risk: Option C almost feels like you are getting your own back on the other person through spite. It also shows a tendency to shy away from confrontation, which shows a lack of personal confidence.

Situation Three

EPSO Competency: Working With Others

Which did you think were the most and least desirable courses of action?

The most appropriate answer in this case is **Option A**. By pausing the meeting and summarising, this gives the chance to ensure everyone has the same understanding so far and also allows a pause for the technical expert to speak. Choosing Option A not only demonstrates empathy on your part, it also shows a certain drive to help the team achieve its goals.

Option B shows no real attempt to aid the team-working process and is therefore the least desirable option. It also abdicates responsibility for resolving the issue there and then yourself which would have aided the team-working process.

Option C shows a certain lack of appreciation for the technical expert's current mindset: this action may embarrass him and/or lead to him being unable to contribute by feeling too exposed. Introducing a pause in proceedings and then asking the technical expert to contribute in a non-threatening way shows far greater emotional intelligence.

Option D is unlikely to be successful as it seems from the scenario information that the technical expert is so shy or embarrassed they may not pick up on your cue to speak. More direct action is needed to encourage their contribution.

Situation Four

EPSO Competency: Analysis and Problem Solving

Which did you think were the most and least desirable courses of action?

The most effective action in this case is **Option B**. It is likely to be unrealistic for you to make a sound judgement before you have reviewed the evidence and it sounds like there is not only complex data to analyse, but also some internal politics to consider before reaching a conclusion. There does not seem to be an urgent deadline for a decision, besides the scheduled meeting, and therefore a delay would probably be acceptable.

The least effective is **Option A**: this shows perhaps a tendency to shy away from detailed analysis and does not take into account the possible biases of your team members in presenting their views to you. Although it may demonstrate unwavering loyalty to your team, it may result in a less than optimum outcome – especially considering you are new to the role and you presumably know little about your team members' trustworthiness to date.

Option C would be a potentially good course of action at some point, as it will help not only give you a balanced view but also build bridges with the other team and help reduce conflict. However, to go and see them before having first reviewed your team member's documentation and doing some preparation may result in you not having all the facts to hand. Therefore it would be better to do Option B first.

Option D is a possibility if you had a lot of time, but it seems an uneconomical way of problem solving if a lot of the research has already been conducted. It would be better to capitalise on the existing information, even if it is biased, and then once you have reviewed all the evidence you can then decide if a full analysis from scratch is required or not.

Situation Five

EPSO Competency: Leadership

Which did you think were the most and least desirable courses of action?

The most appropriate answer in this case is **Option C**, which shows you are prepared to deliver tough messages when necessary but are also open to listening and offering support where possible. You also give credit to the team by talking about the wider issues the organisation is facing so that they understand the rationale for the decision.

Although it represents a very informal, friendly approach, **Option B** does not present a united management front to the team and is unlikely to motivate them. It may make the team worried due to your reference to their careers being in jeopardy. Also, it may get back to your new manager and cause problems in your relationship.

Option A shows that you are prepared to deliver tough messages and direction but it is such a shift from your usual style, it is likely to cause the team to question your behaviour and feel unsettled as a result. The fact that you are unwilling to debate means that the team are unable to even vent their frustrations and feelings to you and are therefore more likely to do so to each other. If you do not know how your team are feeling you are not well-placed to deal with it.

Option D is interesting as it will avoid further demotivation in the short term: however, the team is already feeling over-worked so this is unlikely to turn this around into a motivated team. It also shows an unwillingness to deliver tough messages from the top and could cause you difficulties if your new head of unit found out. You are likely to become more tired and stressed due to the extra work, which will reduce your effectiveness as a leader. For these reasons, Option D is probably the least desirable.

Situation Six

EPSO Competency: Prioritising and Organising

Which did you think were the most and least desirable courses of action?

The most appropriate answer in this case is **Option B**. Despite the fact that project scope is likely to change, in order to stand the best chance of successful delivery, an initial project plan with milestones, risks and contingencies is required. By involving the project team, not only will you formulate a better plan but you will gain their buy-in to it and show how you value their expertise. You can always build contingencies into the plan from an early stage to try and pre-empt any difficulties.

Option A reflects too much of a relaxed approach and this lack of planning is likely to lead to difficulties later on due to a lack of clarity over deliverables. Whilst you may expect this to lead to your team feeling empowered, it is actually likely to make them feel a little directionless and therefore possibly demotivated and certainly less productive.

Option C reflects a very "short-termist" approach. It may mean that some time is saved in planning, but it would be more effective to consider all the steps required in the lead up to the ultimate objective rather than dealing with each in isolation. Without a view of the bigger picture, it is impossible to plan effectively for each stage in isolation. Option C is therefore probably the least effective course of action.

Option D reflects a micro-management approach that is likely to make the team members feel a lack of empowerment, as well as taking up a lot of your time. If you are meeting that regularly with your team and issuing frequent changes of direction or new tasks, this may cause frustration: better to meet less frequently and have time to consolidate all the feedback from the commissioning client into coherent, larger pieces of information that could be fed back to all – e.g. at a team meeting.

Situation Seven

EPSO Competency: Communicating

Which did you think were the most and least desirable courses of action?

The most appropriate answer in this case is **Option A**. Finding out what your audience wants to get from your presentation will inform all of your subsequent preparation, so it is important to be clear on this first. For example, they may be interested in a highly detailed breakdown of financials, or just a quick high-level overview. They may wish to have time to ask you lots of questions, or they may just wish you to present to them and then they will go away and discuss.

Option B will be useful: by practising the presentation you will be more confident and fluent on the day. However, the question asks for the most important part of your preparation and in this case, practice is not the key element.

Option C will also be a critical stage in preparing to give the presentation: understanding your key messages will dictate the entire structure of your presentation. However, like Option B, remember the question asks for the most important part of your preparation. Option C is something you would do after Option A, which would help to shape how you present your key messages.

Option D may or may not be useful, depending upon what Option A reveals. Some audiences will welcome such aids to maintaining interest, for other audiences it will be perceived as possibly patronising or time-wasting. Until you know more about what your audience want to get out of the discussion, you will not know whether such props will be useful so Option D is probably the least appropriate in this instance.

Remember: all options can be desirable; there won't always be an obviously 'wrong' response!

Situation Eight

EPSO Competency: Delivering Quality and Results

Which did you think were the most and least desirable courses of action?

The most appropriate answer in this case is **Option D**. If extra resource is available from another team, this should help to ensure the deadline is met and with no additional cost implications. If the extra resource is not available, you are still free to pursue one of the other options, meaning that this gives you the most possible flexibility.

Despite demonstrating drive and determination, **Option C** runs the risks of errors being made due to fatigue. There is the additional risk that the other work you have on the go will also suffer as a result. Therefore, this answer falls down on the quality focus aspects.

Choosing **Option B** means that you fail to deliver the project objective. There is no indication that this course of action will be acceptable in the scenario and it is likely to be unsatisfactory to the stakeholders. Therefore it is probably the least appropriate answer.

Option A shows initiative, and should get the project delivered on time and with less chance of mistakes than working extra hours yourself (although a temp will still need to be fully briefed). However the extra budget goes beyond the remit of the project and this is therefore not an ideal solution as you will not have worked within the project objectives.

PART III

THE ASSESSMENT CENTRE

1. About Assessment Centres and Exercises

What is an Assessment Centre?

An "Assessment Centre" (or AC for short) is a way of assessing potential performance in a role; applied to a group of participants by trained assessors using various diagnostic tools. Assessment Centres were first used in the 1950s and are now regularly used by organisations to assess staff, whether for recruitment, personal development or internal promotion. In essence, an Assessment Centre consists of asking candidates to complete a varied set of exercises which are designed to simulate different aspects of a role and work environment.

Candidates are observed by a team of assessors who make judgements on the candidates' performance by completing a set of standardised competency rating forms which describe what "good" and "poor" performance looks like. As an EU exam candidate you will be observed by a number of assessors throughout the event, to minimise the likelihood of any bias on the part of assessors. According to the Chartered Institute of Personnel and Development's "Recruitment, Retention and Turnover Survey", 34% of employers now use Assessment Centres when recruiting managers, professionals or graduates. This figure will inevitably grow as organisations seek to make more accurate selection and promotion decisions.

Assessment Centres are one of the most fair, objective and effective ways of identifying high-potential candidates who will fit in with a role and an organisation's culture. Research shows them to be far more predictive of future job performance than individual tasks, such as an interview. This is because a number of different assessors get to see you perform over a relatively long period of time and have the chance to see what you can *actually* do in a variety of situations (rather than what you might *say* you do in an interview).

An additional advantage that I have found when running ACs is that they offer potential employees a realistic preview of the types of tasks they will be required to perform in the role. On a number of occasions when feeding-back to candidates they have told me that, regardless of how they actually performed at the Assessment Centre, they have decided that the role is not for them as they did not enjoy the tasks they were required to perform. This is obviously only going to benefit you in the long-run: it is far better for you to decide now that you are less well suited to a particular EU role than once you have accepted an offer and are in the post.

For those of you that are interested in the research angle, I have included a table below that summarises research conducted at the University of Manchester by Dr. Mike Smith and Prof. Ivan Robertson. It compares the predictive power of a range of assessment methods. To help you interpret it, a score of zero suggests that the prediction is no better than random chance. A score of one would mean that the selection technique offered a perfect prediction of future performance. You can see from this table that no technique is perfect but that Assessment Centres offer the best chance to predict future performance effectively.

From reviewing the information EPSO has published on its website and the EPSO Development Plan "Roadmap for Implementation", it appears that the EPSO Centres will typically last between half a day and one day, depending upon the role. In my experience, a single Assessment Centre usually contains up to twelve people, although EPSO may

Predictive Power of Various Assessment Methods

(Mike Smith/Ivan Robertson, University of Manchester)

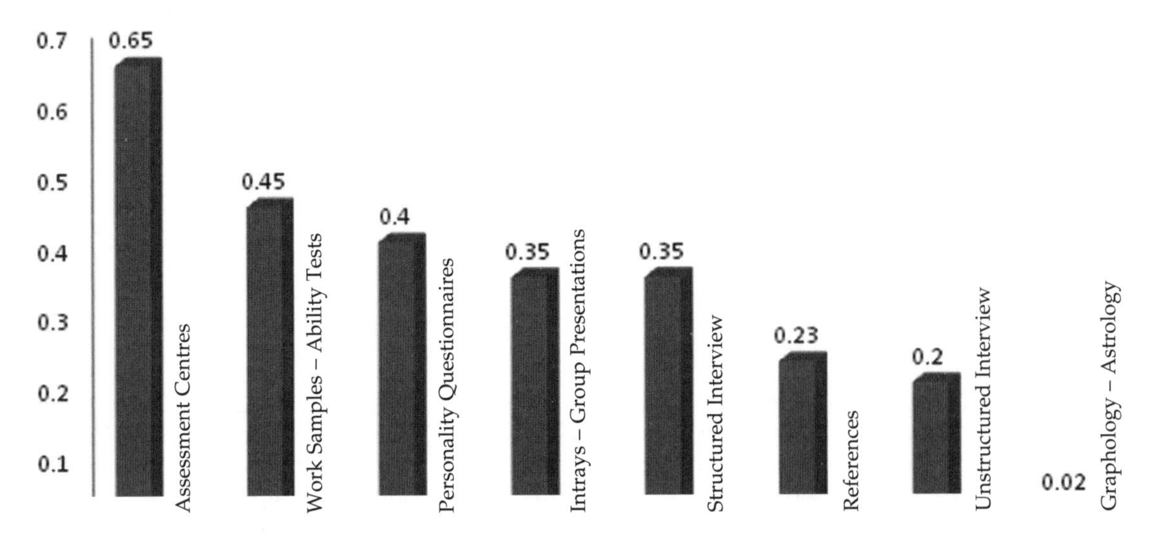

decide to run multiple streams on the same day given the large number of candidates. The Centres will be conducted by EPSO personnel who have been trained by an external body in best Assessment Centre practice, and they might be assisted by accredited external consultants. Assessment Centres are time consuming and expensive affairs: for this reason, they are the last stage in the EPSO selection process so that there are smaller numbers of preselected candidates to deal with.

I hope that these opening comments have given you some confidence in the validity of the process. In the chapters that follow, I will be revealing a large number of hints and tips to help you perform well at an Assessment Centre. Some of these are based upon knowledge of actual EPSO processes gained from publicly available sources; other hints are drawn from my experience of designing and running Assessment Centres and what types of behaviours have earned candidates a positive result in similar past situations.

You should bear in mind two important points when reading these chapters. Firstly, it is hard to "fake" a good performance at an Assessment Centre. Trying to act in a manner completely contrary to your natural style over an eight hour period and across multiple assessments can be mentally taxing and may actually cause your performance to suffer. If the behaviours you are trying to convey do not come at all naturally, you will be found out. Secondly, it is contrary to both your and EPSO's interests to find yourself in a role for which you are neither behaviourally nor motivationally suited. As well as underperforming, you are likely to experience greater levels of stress and job dissatisfaction if you are placed in a role that you are not well suited to.

That said, it is possible to prepare yourself for what is coming in the Centre by reading the advice in the following chapters and thinking about your approach in advance. I tend to actually encourage this for all prospective Assessment Centre candidates, as it places everyone on a "level playing field" and minimises the likelihood that the Assessment Centre process causes a poor performance, rather than it being a true reflection of someone's ability. By going into the event with your eyes open and having planned how you can show off your strengths to their maximum advantage, you will give yourself the best possible chance for success, not to mention that the assessment tasks will not take you by surprise if you are fully aware of what to expect.

The Role of Competencies

EPSO states that from now on EU staff selection procedures are to be competency driven, and no longer purely based on knowledge. This is certainly because research has found that the ability to learn and retain knowledge is only one small aspect of the personal qualities that go towards making a successful employee. The way I tend to define competencies is "groupings of related behaviours, traits and motivations that each predict successful performance in a particular aspect of a role". From the EPSO website, it appears that the EPSO process is built around a set of competencies that are relevant to all roles within the organisation to some extent. In my experience, it is often decided that some competencies are more or less important for certain roles and will therefore carry more or less weight in the final decision making process.

The EPSO competencies and definitions are as follows (with titles and definitions taken from the EPSO website). I have also provided an example of where each competency might be well measured:

Analysis and Problem Solving – *Identifies the critical facts in complex issues and develops creative and practical solutions.* This competency would be well measured in a **case study exercise**. For example, positive behaviours would include making correct calculations using numerical data presented in charts (such as Eurostat tables, financial data from an EU policy's impact assessment report or other) and poorer behaviour would include taking only a surface look at issues and missing subtleties such as politically contentious aspects, long-term ramifications of short-term decisions or missing the inherent relations between different groups of data. (For example: a table on the transposition ratio of an EU directive by Member States may be telling about a certain country's compliance with EU rules but it must be examined in relation to other data such as the number of infringement procedures against it; if both tables are provided, you will be expected to cross-check your assumptions before drawing any conclusion). *See the feedback and scoring guide in the Case Study chapter below.*

Communicating – *Communicates clearly and precisely both orally and in writing.* The most natural places for this competency to be measured would be the **presentation (oral communication) and case study (written communication)**. I would expect better responses to not only be grammatically correct, but also to convey something of the passion and conviction of the views of the candidate, especially if you are requested to represent a certain role that in fact means taking a certain position on an issue. For example, a sentence like "We was recommending more money be spent" is grammatically poor and emotionally sparse. A better way of expressing the same concept would be "I believe it is essential that we allocate more funds to the international trade development project to guarantee its success". The fundamental principles of communication apply: your message must be clear, sufficiently concrete, and underpinned by strong relevant arguments and data; it must be well structured both visually and logically, and its presentation should be done in a compelling manner. *See further tips on effective oral and written communication in the Group Exercise, Case Study and other chapters below.*

Delivering Quality and Results – *Takes personal responsibility and initiative for delivering work to a high standard of quality within set procedures.* This competency could be measured in the **group exercise**: for example, positive actions could include spurring the group on to meet the time limit for the task by introducing time- and project-management methods into the exercise (adding milestones, allocating time for the exercise and other ideas, even in a relatively short one hour exercise setting). Poorer actions could be trying to bring the meeting to a premature close before the possible options had all been discussed and evaluated fully, or arbitrarily interpreting the rules set by the assessors – for example if your task is to "identify the three best courses of action", you should not identify two or rather four by saying "that number was only a suggestion".

Learning and Development – *Develops and improves personal skills and knowledge of the organisation and its environment.* In my opinion, this is best assessed by self-report in the **interview**, as it is hard to simulate these behaviours in a day-long Assessment Centre. Better candidate responses would include examples of when they have proactively decided to undergo additional learning or training to enhance their employability or skills, such as enrolling in a seminar on the EU financial regulation or in a team management course; this may be shown by presenting the self-development books you have recently read or mentioning the wine tasting course you signed up for. A poorer candidate response would show little evidence of attempting to proactively improve their knowledge or skills, outside what has been mandated by their studies or employment, or talking negatively of the "burdens" posed by the trainings your current or previous employer "imposed" on you. *A large number of tips and hints can be found in the chapter on Structured Interviews.*

Prioritising and Organising – *Prioritises the most important tasks, works flexibly and organises own workload efficiently.* I would typically expect this type of competency to be measured well by a **case study exercise**. From the large amount of data you are presented with in such an exercise, it will be important to identify key priorities – in other words, those requiring immediate action (e.g. short deadline items). A less strong performance on this competency would likely be indicated by a haphazard approach to tasks (or in the case of the case study, an unstructured way of digesting the large amount of data you will be presented with), or tackling them in the order they are presented to you in the background briefing documentation rather than by their importance. *More ideas and hints will be offered in the chapters on the Case Study and Group Exercise below.*

Resilience – *Remains effective under a heavy workload, handles organisational frustrations positively and adapts to a changing work environment.* As it would be unethical to place candidates under excessive stress during an assessment, I frequently try to measure this through an **interview**, where I can ask candidates about previous stressful experiences they have encountered. Therefore it is crucial that you try to recall such experiences when preparing for the Assessment Centre so that you will not be left without any ideas when the question is put to you. A better response might be if a candidate were to describe a time when they remained calm and focused when faced with a tight deadline and multiple competing demands (e.g. your boss assigned you two projects where the deadlines seemed unrealistic). A poorer response would be if a candidate described an emotional outburst they had made towards a colleague when under pressure without also providing a more positive approach or a creative idea of how the situation was resolved. In addition to the interview, I sometimes try to simulate a relatively low-level of stress by asking candidates a series of challenging questions after their presentation: I will even express contrary opinions on purpose to see how they respond. *More tips will be offered in the chapter on the Structured Interview below.*

Working with Others – *Works co-operatively with others in teams and across organisational boundaries and respects differences between people.* This competency would be well measured by a **group exercise**. Effective behaviours could then include both the immediate interactions I see between group members, as well as whether candidates make the more abstract consideration of which stakeholders to consult as part of their plans. (In an EU context, this means you will not only be expected to show a co-operative approach with your fellow candidates, but also to understand the decision-making procedures and stakeholder consultation mechanisms of the European Commission and other institutions; this should then be integrated into your approach.) Poorer responses would include interrupting or belittling other candidates' responses in a non-professional way (e.g. by saying "this idea doesn't make any sense") or failing to draw quieter members into the conversation. *You will find further ideas about how to make the most of this competency in the chapter about the Case Study and Group Exercise.*

The final competency applies only to Administrator grades (and not to Assistant levels):

Leadership – *Manages, develops and motivates people to achieve results.* I could envisage this competency being measured in **a number of exercises**. As an example, if we take a presentation where the candidate needs to instruct a team on how to respond to a crisis (e.g. a flood destroys several villages in rural Spain and they ask for the release of emergency funds from the European Commission), I would expect a good performance to include passionate language, a clear set of directions for others to follow and perhaps some provision being made for developing people's skill sets in the process. A poorer response would include only one motivation tactic, applied to everyone (e.g. the threat of delayed promotion) and very vague or top-level instructions (e.g. "check the EU crisis management operating manual and act accordingly") that said nothing of how they could be implemented "on the ground".

In terms of how the competencies are actually used, as part of the Assessment Centre design, they are "mapped" to each of the Assessment Centre exercises, depending upon where they would be best observed. EPSO specifies that each of the above competencies will be observed twice over the course of the event. This is a good idea, as it prevents someone's rating being overly affected by a particularly bad or good performance in just one exercise.

Below, I have created a simple artificial example assessment matrix, to show how this might look. A "tick" denotes that a competency will be measured by a particular exercise at the Assessment Centre. Please note that this is just for illustration purposes and does not necessarily eflect the actual EPSO assessment matrix.

Exercise	**Situational Judgement Test**	**Case Study**	**Presentation**	**Group Exercise**	**Interview**
Competency					
Planning	✓	✓	✓		
Teamwork	✓			✓	✓
Analysis	✓	✓			✓
Influencing	✓		✓	✓	

As a general rule, in order to help assessors score the candidate's performance on each exercise, each competency will then be further defined by a range of positive and negative indicators on a bipolar scale. For example, here are three possible indicators for a generic "Planning"-type competency (non EPSO-specific):

Sample Competency Name: Planning			
Sample Competency Description: Adopts a methodical and structured approach to work.			
	Negative Indicators		**Positive Indicators**
–	Only sets an end goal, no checkpoints along the way	–	Sets clear checkpoints to track progress
–	Plans contain no contingency time	–	Builds contingency into plans
–	Treats all tasks as equally important – fails to prioritise	–	Assigns appropriate priorities to issues
	... etc		... etc

In my experience, I tend to include up to 10 paired positive or negative indicators for each competency. The exact EPSO indicators have been kept confidential to maintain the integrity of the testing process.

Then, once the Assessment Centre is underway, assessors will make copious notes on everything you say and do during each exercise. Afterwards, they will rate you on each competency that has been linked to each particular exercise on the matrix, using a prescribed performance scale. In my experience they usually follow a 1-5 rating, for example:

1	2	3	4	5
Poor. Meets all of the negative indicators.	**Development Need.** Meets more than half of the negative indicators.	**Acceptable.** Meets about half of the positive indicators.	**Good.** Meets more than half of the positive indicators.	**Excellent.** Meets all of the positive indicators.

Following an Assessment Centre we would all meet as a group of assessors to discuss the results for each candidate and reach a group consensus about each candidate's ratings for each competency.

How to Maximise Your Chance of Success

In order to give your best possible performance, I recommend the first step to be researching the details of the Assessment Centre EPSO has prepared for your role or profile – length, activities, etc. This will be either provided in your invitation letter or on the EPSO website. As with any selection process, thorough preparation is the key to maximising the outcome of your assessment. As a next step, read and consider the general guidance about how to approach Assessment Centres given below, before proceeding to the exercise-specific guidance I provide later.

How to Prepare

- **Invitation Letter**: Read the invitation letter/e-mail carefully as this will tell you what exactly to expect at the centre though in a less detailed form.
- **Research**: Make sure you carry out some research on the EU and EPSO websites, and on the internet in general (e.g. relevant news articles, job discussion boards; see further information in other chapters of this book and recommended websites below).
- **EU Knowledge**: Apart from techniques, I strongly suggest that you try to learn and remember key details about the EU's history, institutions, decision-making system, structure and policies. This will help you speak the right "language" of an international public administration and you can also relate to the case study much better if you are familiar with the big picture.
- **Questions**: It is also worth thinking of a few questions you can ask if given an opportunity. You might, for example, find yourself seated at lunch beside an assessor: if you have prepared a selection of questions and topics for discussion relating to the role or the EU, you will make a strong impression (even though this will not form part of the formal assessment). If you have a contact in the EU, phone them up and talk to them about the role and what it is like to work there, or you can also find blogs and Facebook pages with such content.
- **EPSO Competencies**: Think about what skills and attributes EPSO is looking for. Review the competency framework, job description or other material sent to you, with

the objective of identifying the main skills and attributes required to be successful in the post. Write out a bullet-point checklist of these core capabilities to help fix them clearly in your mind, because the exercises in the Assessment Centre will be designed to measure your abilities in these areas.

- **Local Preparation Resources**: Check with a Brussels-based or your local careers service or training firms, as some run workshops and presentations on how to successfully prepare for Assessment Centres. See if you can practice similar exercises and gain feedback before attending. There are also various online training services that you can access from anywhere in the world (just google EPSO training).
- **CV**: Look over your application and CV to refresh your memory about their contents – a surprising number of candidates fail to refresh their CV or leave unprofessional typos and inconsistencies within. As this is something you can certainly avoid, better do so.
- **Practicalities**: Think about the practical things such as travel arrangements, timings and what you are going to wear. Deciding upon these in advance will reduce stress closer to the time. (As the Assessment Centres are located in Brussels, you should always find out whether public transport companies are planning a strike or some protest event in the EU/Schuman area for the day of your assessment or whether certain sections of the metro or bus lines are expected to be temporarily unavailable; by no means should you risk arriving late in the early morning traffic jam.)
- **Introduction**: At the beginning of an Assessment Centre, all delegates are normally asked to introduce themselves and then they may be asked to briefly tell the others about themselves. So it is good practice to prepare a 30-60 second introductory pitch about yourself and your background beforehand. Say something memorable, preferably about an achievement related to the job profile you are aiming at. But do bear in mind that you will only have about 60 seconds maximum, so practise beforehand and keep it short and sharp.
- **Special Needs**: Make it clear well before the session if you have any special needs so that there is a chance to make appropriate amendments to the process. For example, large text versions of the materials should be available for anyone who is visually impaired or extra time may be available for people with dyslexia. Access considerations will be important for wheelchair users. EPSO will be used to making such adaptations and it will only benefit your performance on the day, so do let them know. If you require reading glasses or a hearing aid, please be sure to take these with you.
- **Relax**: Make sure you have a good night's sleep before the Assessment Centre; being tired will impact on your performance. This also means that you should try not to take an early morning flight or train but arrive in town the day before.
- **Know Yourself**: Take some time for self-awareness raising and reflection. Being aware of your own development areas is the first step to being able to address them. How much of an awareness and understanding do you actually have about your behaviour in certain situations? Are you already aware of any development needs? For example, if you're part of a group charged with completing a task, how do you behave? Do you have a tendency to be nervous and lost for words? Nervous and talk too much? Bossy? Passive? Find it hard to get your point heard? Is your picture of yourself accurate? It may be worth consulting with other people who know you well, to help identify any development points you could work on. Consider what you need to work on in advance of the Assessment Centre and find opportunities to practise and gain feedback on your progress.
- **Positive Thinking**: Maintain a positive frame of mind. Whilst you need to visualise yourself being successful in completing an Assessment Centre to guard against lack of

confidence, over confidence can have a detrimental effect on candidates where they fail to pay sufficient attention to the tasks. Perhaps try some thought experiments in advance where you work through various scenarios that could arise at the Assessment Centre and picture how you would deal with those successfully. For example, how would you respond if the person you are making a presentation to says that they disagree with your viewpoint? This will not only help reduce tension but also assist in dealing with these situations should they arise in reality.

- **Simulation**: Another good method could be simulating certain exercises with a friend or other exam candidates; the help of someone knowledgeable in recruitment could certainly help but even without such person you can test or "challenge" each other in a simulated environment.
- **Communication Skills**: Good communication skills are always helpful, no matter what the exercise. Many applicants attending Assessment Centres can find it quite daunting when first confronted with a new group of individuals, especially when they feel that they are in direct competition, so they tend to keep a low profile at first. But this is an opportunity to get noticed, and it will be looked upon very favourably if you are seen to be mingling with the group when the opportunity arises. Have a think about this when preparing for the day. Prepare some questions that you feel comfortable to ask the other individuals in the group. Aim to talk to as many of the other candidates as you can – including a range of nationalities, ages and genders – before the end of the day because this will be noted, not to mention the valuable pieces of information you can gather as well, including your impressions of the others' skills, background and experience vis-à-vis your own. (An excellent collection of articles and books on the "fine art of small talk" can be found under http://www.debrafine.com/articles.html)
- **Open Questions**: Also, showing that you are confident, friendly and proactive will come across well with the other candidates which may bode well for any group activities. Remember that any questions you ask should be open and straightforward to encourage a dialogue. Open questions that start with "what", "why", "how", "where" and "when" should be a good start.
- **Honesty**: Make sure you remember how to use any technology applications and speak all languages that you have mentioned in your CV (if you listed basic knowledge of Croatian to make a better impression, don't risk being caught by an assessor who just started his beginner's course and may wish to test his knowledge with you!).

Tips for the Assessment Itself

- **Dress Code**: Unless otherwise instructed, wear business dress.
- **Contingency Plan**: Build plenty of time into your journey for unexpected delays. Make sure you set off with the full address of your destination and a contact telephone number. If you are delayed and are going to be late, ring to advise the Assessment Centre as soon as you can – though this is definitely not going to compensate for setting out late or unprepared.
- **Checklist**: Ensure you take with you anything that you have been asked to bring, such as photographic ID.
- **Instructions**: At the beginning of the assessment, you should receive an initial briefing about the timetable of exercises, location of rooms etc. Prior to each exercise, you will be given instructions describing the task, your role, timeframes, equipment etc. Take time to think and absorb this information. Follow any instructions carefully and ask questions if there is something you do not understand or wish to understand further.

- **Remember Names**: It may be useful to make a note of the names of the EPSO representatives you meet, and when in conversation with assessors or candidates drop those names into conversation.
- **Socialise**: Talk to the other candidates. Remember that you are not necessarily in competition with the other candidates so treat them as allies rather than rivals. *If you all perform well, you might all be successful.* Your performances will all be judged against the competency indicators, not against each other; therefore this is a crucial issue to bear in mind.
- **Approach Each Exercise Afresh**: Do not be dismayed if you struggle in some of the exercises. The Assessment Centre is designed to thoroughly explore all of the attributes for the job, so you might find that you do not perform as well as you hope to in every single exercise. If you feel that you have let yourself down on some of the exercises, do not dwell on your mistakes and agonise over them, because that will create a negative attitude that might bring down your overall performance. Just accept it, and concentrate fully on the next task, seeing this as a new opportunity to demonstrate your potential. Remember that many candidates will have a slow start, and very few, if any, will perform well on all of the tasks. You can still score highly over the whole event, even if you have performed badly in one exercise.
- **Be Yourself**: It's much easier and fairer to be yourself, rather than putting on an act. It's very easy to fall into the trap of making assumptions about what the assessor is looking for in a new recruit and trying to second-guess what they want to hear or see. The best approach is to be yourself at all times. It has been proven that when you behave normally, rather than trying to create a false image of yourself, you will come across as being a lot more relaxed and confident, and will therefore present a better picture of yourself. If "the real you" is not what EPSO is looking for in that particular competition, the profile is obviously not meant for you, so perhaps you should reconsider which other EPSO profile or position your skills, style, background and aspirations make you best suited to.
- **Stay Calm**: Remember it is normal to feel nervous before the day. A shaky voice or clammy hands are not unusual symptoms and therefore it is recommended that you arrive ten to fifteen minutes early to give yourself time to relax. Be polite to everyone you meet. Stay calm, focused and positive throughout the Assessment Centre.
- **Lunch Break**: You are not being formally observed during breaks and lunch, but you should remain professional at all times. Do not over-indulge, become flippant or overconfident. Take the opportunity to ask questions, talk to other candidates or assessors and show a strong interest in the position.
- **Mobile Phone**: Turn off your mobile phone (and make silent any other electronic device that beeps) before the start of the assessment session.
- **Time Limit**: The exercises will have strict time limits. Make sure to bring a watch with you and check the clock carefully during timed exercises – over-running may be penalised (or not allowed). Try to work through the tasks quickly but accurately. Use all of the time allocated to you and make sure to plan your time prudently before starting an exercise (e.g. if you have 40 minutes available, split it into 10-25-5 minute segments to allow enough time for an outline, drafting and revision). Even if you have finished the task, take the final few minutes to review your response (or preparation work in the case of preparing to give a presentation).
- **Decision Timescale**: EPSO should let you know when they expect to have made a decision and how you will be notified of the end result but do not be scared to ask if this has not been made clear.

- **Positive Ending**: Remember to thank the assessors for their time before you leave.

After the Assessment

- **Enquiries**: If you do not hear from EPSO by the deadline stated (or two to three weeks later at the latest), write or telephone to enquire whether a decision has been made.
- **Reserve List**: If you are placed on the reserve list, your name will appear on the EPSO website and be published in the Official Journal of the EU. Once this happens, you are eligible to be recruited by any EU institution (see more details in the relevant chapter on the recruitment procedure and flagging system).
- **Job Offer**: Once you receive an offer, make sure it is the right role and job profile for you before accepting. Take into consideration the following; they may all impact on what makes the offer you accept the right decision for you.
  - **Job Content** (while this is largely determined by the exam you are sitting, it may nevertheless differ greatly depending on what the actual job is, so it's worth asking for more details and trying to search online for this profile; it is also worth checking the Directorate General's or institution's organigram online to see the type of positions that exist there).
  - **Location** (are you willing to relocate to Luxembourg? Or to a Commission delegation in e.g. Sri Lanka, Japan or elsewhere?)
  - **Working Hours** (while the Staff Regulations of EU officials have strict rules on working hours, the intensity can vary according to the job profile; if you deal with for example CO_2 emissions or external trade, it may require more intensive day-to-day work than some other administrative job profiles)
  - **Salary Level** (this is almost exclusively determined by the competition's grade that you were sitting for, though smaller adjustments called "steps" within a given grade are possible, based on your work experience)
  - **Mobility Requirement** (if the work is in the European Parliament or in another institution but dealing with Parliamentary affairs, it probably means you will have to spend four days a month in Strasbourg; or if you work for e.g. the Commission's Directorate General for Trade, you will most likely be required to travel extensively)
  - Impression of the **organisational culture** of the institution or directorate
- **Keep Rejection in Perspective**: If you are unsuccessful – do not take it personally! You are simply not the most suitable applicant for that specific position at the current time; you can of course apply again for an EU exam any time in the future.
- **Feedback**: Gaining feedback is an essential part of the Assessment Centre process. Even if you do not get the job, remember that attending the Assessment Centre is a significant learning experience for you, and feedback can provide invaluable insights for the future. EPSO does offer feedback to all candidates, so be sure to ask for formal feedback at a later stage. There is also no harm in using the day as a networking opportunity, with both the panel and the other delegates. Your career is a long path and you never know when or where these people may turn up in the future.
- **Self-development**: Learn from your mistakes. Once the dust has settled after the Assessment Centre, take stock of the situation. Summon up the courage to be brutally honest with yourself: make a list of areas with room for improvement, and then take appropriate action. Knowing yourself is one of the keys to success, because if you can identify the gaps in your knowledge (e.g. you realise that you need to know more

about the Court of Justice case-law or European public finances), pinpoint the skills you need to gain or develop (e.g. improve your time management skills or work better in a team under pressure), and then rectify these deficiencies by attending training or enrolling in various courses, you will greatly improve your attractiveness and value to the EU and other organisations in your chosen field. Once you have addressed these areas, you will enter the next Assessment Centre with much greater confidence, and greater chance of success.

Lastly, as assessors we do understand that Assessment Centres can be daunting and will do all that we can to put you at ease. It may help to bear in mind that it is only those people who have passed through the preliminary selection stages and those that EPSO thinks are more likely to successfully carry out the job that are asked to attend – so be confident and positive. Indeed, the Assessment Centre as a whole should be viewed as a two-way process. Use it as an opportunity to find out what you want to know about the role and the organisation. Judge the extent to which you enjoy the tasks you are required to perform and the extent to which you gel with the EPSO or EU representatives you meet.

2. EPSO Assessment Exercise: The Group Exercise

Description and Purpose

Group exercises typically involve you working with other candidates (usually between four and eight) as part of a team to resolve a presented issue. These are the most effective simulations for measuring interpersonal skills and behaviours such as group leadership, teamwork, negotiation, and group problem-solving skills.

There are two primary types of group exercise: unassigned role and assigned role. In unassigned role group exercises, candidates are all given exactly the same background information and are all placed within the same role at the simulated organisation. There are no pre-determined conflicting agendas and this type of group exercise is most appropriate when assessors are interested in general team-working abilities.

When assessors wish to assess behaviour in more challenging group situations, for example where it is necessary to persuade and negotiate or when political sensitivities and directly conflicting viewpoints are present, then an assigned role group exercise scenario is chosen. In this type of group exercise, each candidate receives the same "core" background information, but then also receives some information that is unique to their brief that the others do not know about. This will be designed so that it contradicts the aims or purposes of at least one other group member. In this instance, the assessors will be particularly interested in how participants are able to convey and promote their own positions and defend them against others' objections, whilst also remaining focused on the overall objectives of the group and striving to achieve a consensus.

In terms of the expected outcome from such a discussion, this can vary. Sometimes there is nothing tangible to be produced by the end: the group just needs to reach a verbally-agreed consensus. In other exercises, an assessor will come in at the end to hear a short verbal presentation of the group's decision and probe your responses. In my experience, most commonly the group needs to produce a short, bullet-pointed summary of their decisions, supposedly to be sent to a key stakeholder following the meeting. Superbly written prose is not expected and this summary is not assessed: it is merely used as a tool to help focus participants' minds and also to test your time management skills still further.

How to Prepare

It can be difficult to prepare for group exercises, especially as you have no prior idea about the composition of the group (the other candidates) and the types of behaviours required from each of you may be quite different. For example, you will need to show different personal qualities if there is one especially frequent contributor to the group who threatens to take over the whole discussion compared to a group where there are people all expressing a lot of conflicting views and priorities.

It can be useful to ask for feedback beforehand from those who know you well on what role you tend to play in a group situation. "Group situation" can refer to either your work or social life. It is worth considering issues such as the following: Are you the one who always suggests where to go next when out with friends? Or do you tend to follow the group decision? Do you tend to clash with others in a group if you have a strong opinion or do you tend to avoid conflict at all costs? Do you like having a close ally with whom you can share feelings about the group as a whole? Or do you prefer being everyone's friend? Do you always try to make sure everyone in the group is included in a conversation or does it make no difference for you if some are quiet or inactive?

All of these traits will have positive and negative implications: how might your typical behaviours impact upon your performance at the Assessment Centre? Generally, I find the key is being interpersonally flexible. For example, you may need to become more directive and assertive when faced with a group that is failing to reach decisions quickly enough ("I suggest we focus on the task at hand as we are running short of time" or "I guess we should split the tasks among us as follows…"). Equally, you may also need to be more facilitative and questioning ("what do you think about developing a public consultation on the research policy?" or "why not do a checklist of issues that must be considered when launching a tender procedure?") in a group that is making quicker, less reasoned decisions. Make a conscious effort to behave in a manner opposite to your "natural" style when in group settings and gain feedback on how effective you were from someone else.

Tips for the Assessment Itself

- **Preparation Time**: You will generally get time up-front to read the background documentation. Use this wisely and make rough notes on key messages you wish to discuss with the group. However, be aware that the time for this preparation is set deliberately short: you will not be given enough time to read and digest it all in extreme detail. It would not reflect well on you to spend the first five minutes of the discussion with your head down in your notes, catching up on reading the background information!
- **Understand What is Being Asked**: Do not rush into a group exercise without first pausing to analyse and discuss the scenario. Planning and preparation are always the keys to success, so make sure that you review the situation described in the brief with the group before you rush into solving the problem. Start by analysing and qualifying the question, so that everyone is clear on *exactly* what is required from the exercise (e.g. if the exercise requires you to outline ideas for a negotiation strategy with the Council of Ministers, make sure you do not misinterpret the task by adding the European Parliament as well; or, if the exercise requires you to describe the state of play on a certain piece of legislation on biofuels, make sure you keep your focus on the policy at hand instead of the underlying legislative procedures or going off at a tangent about wind energy). Then show clearly the thought processes and procedures you followed to arrive at your proposed solution.
- **The Real Problem**: An excellent way of keeping focus is by asking a simple yet powerful question: "what is the real problem we need to solve?" As an example, suppose you need to send a letter that has to arrive at its destination within a day. This means you would need to rush to the post office by bus to reach it before it closes. If you miss the bus, you could start thinking what other means of transport you could take, whether it is worth paying for a taxi etc. However, the real issue is to get the mail to its addressee in time, so if you focus your attention on solving this instead of sticking to your original line of action, you can come up with creative solutions such as finding a person who is going to the addressee anyway and asking him to take the letter. The same is true in a group exercise: make sure you are crystal clear about what the *real* problem is that you are requested to resolve.
- **The Beginning**: Many group discussions begin with each person outlining their view of the presented material and a proposed solution. This is a good way to start but be

sure that a) this does not take up too much of the allotted time and b) each person has the chance to contribute equally.

- **Team Skills**: The best way to impress the assessors is to show yourself to be a good team player – flexible, full of ideas but willing to listen to and help expand the ideas of others. This requires constant self-reflection and a good sense of proportion.
- **Be Active**: You need to contribute, otherwise assessors will not be able to judge your performance; but you must not dominate. Be assertive, but not aggressive. If you are aware that you are usually a shy person who does not speak up, do your best to participate. If you know that you can sometimes be overbearing in groups, hold that tendency in check. Recognise other people's contributions both verbally and non-verbally (e.g. by saying "I think this is a very good point and we should take it on board", or conveying positive body language towards other team members by turning towards them, showing positive gestures, taking notes when they are speaking etc).
- **Be Clear**: Speak clearly and confidently; if you have a tendency to speak fast, practice beforehand to consciously slow down. You may wish to record your voice while talking freely about a certain subject and then evaluate yourself (do not read any text but try to express your thoughts as they arise; this creates a certain pressure similar to the one you will be facing at the Assessment Centre).
- **Listen**: Listen and do not interrupt. Be aware of what others in the group are contributing and acknowledge their views ("This idea about launching an information campaign to underline our communication efforts is very appealing"). You could try to draw out quieter members and seek their views ("You seem to have some reservations about this approach, is that correct?"). Be sure to appear interested and attentive whatever topic is being discussed.
- **Note-taking**: Be wary of offering to be the note-taker or the one who marks the group's ideas on the flipchart – this can frequently mean a tendency to contribute less. If you do offer to take the post, ensure that you still contribute effectively and make it to your benefit by coordinating and/or leading the group's efforts. If handled effectively, it can result in you being adopted as the de facto leader of the group.
- **Be Diplomatic**: If one person is behaving in a dominant way, do not shout at them, but try to make sure that everybody gets a chance to share their thoughts ("Many thanks for your input; I was wondering if others could share their views as well"). Be prepared to compromise. Make your points and if criticised, be prepared to stand up for yourself and diplomatically argue why your opinions are valid ("I understand you are a bit sceptical about this idea, and in fact I used to have reservations myself as well; but evidence has shown that all facts reinforce this approach and I am positive this is the right way to proceed"). Ensure that any criticism you give is constructive.
- **Time Management**: Keep an eye on the time and stay focused on the overall objective ("We have covered points 1 and 2 so far and came to the following conclusions [...] As we have twenty minutes left, I suggest we focus on the remaining items in the following way..."). From time to time, try to summarise the group's progress; this can also improve your stature as an effective member of the group by taking stock of where you are. If you need to produce something by the end of the discussion (e.g. a written summary), ensure that you leave enough time for this in your planning.
- **Sharing Tasks**: If you're working in a small group you could divide up the tasks between you. You could suggest or "nominate" someone to assess any new information passed to the group during the course of the exercise. You could also ask for a volunteer note-keeper though try to avoid making others feel you are too bossy.

- **Self-Assess**: about halfway through the group exercise, check the impact you are having on the discussion – is it visible, sufficient, too little? Make adjustments accordingly.
- **Eye Contact**: Assessors are trained not to hold eye contact with group members, or to respond to comments made during the course of the group discussion (even humorous ones!) even if partially addressed to them. Do not be disheartened if your contributions do not seem to be having an effect on the assessors: they are merely trying to ensure that they do not unduly influence your behaviour and that they remain as objective outside observers.
- **Missing Candidates**: On occasion, a candidate may drop out from the Assessment Centre. In this case, all participants in a group exercise may be given their brief and asked to consider it as part of their overall decision. Do just as you would in real-life if someone could not be present: ensure that their views are represented fairly in their absence.
- **Leadership Scenarios**: Occasionally, when the organisation is particularly interested in testing your leadership skills (e.g. if you participate in the Assessment Centre when applying for a Head of Unit or Director post), you may be asked to chair a meeting or act as leader of your group. Once again there will be a set task but this time you will be expected to be in charge and to lead the others to success. This is what the assessors will be looking for:
  - A good leader *delegates*. The task cannot be done by you alone. You must divide up the work between the others and ensure proper follow-up and quality control of the delivery.
  - You may wish to read about the so-called *"Situational Leadership"* approach: it provides that each subordinate or employee must be treated according to two main factors, namely their level of knowledge of the issue at hand and their level of willingness to act. The four combinations (willing/unwilling, knows/does not know) demand the adoption of very different management approaches.
  - A good leader uses the *strengths of others*. You must identify the strengths of the individuals in your group (which may be a challenging task given that you have no prior knowledge of your group's members) and use them in appropriate ways.
  - A good leader takes an *overview*. Do not get too involved in actioning things. It's better to monitor what's going on and then suggest changes at a later stage if required.

SAMPLE GROUP EXERCISE

In the following section, we have provided an example of the type of brief you may be faced with if a group exercise forms part of your assessment process. We have chosen a very broad topic that assumes no specialist knowledge on the part of the candidate – which can also be expected for your group exercise though the actual one will of course be somewhat different or it may even be unrelated to EU affairs. After the candidate brief, we have included some examples of positive and negative behaviours that assessors would be looking for against a couple of competencies likely to be assessed by this exercise.

Group Exercise – Introduction

In the introduction to the group exercise, you will be briefed with a set of instructions that will also be provided for you on a printed page. Do not turn over the page until you are asked to do so. Feel free to ask questions if anything is unclear after the introduction: but be mindful that a lot of the information you will need is in the subsequent reading material. Once the exercise starts, however, the administrator may refuse to answer questions so do make sure to find out everything that you wish to know about how the exercise will run.

Following is an example of the type of candidate brief you may receive at your Assessment Centre. All the names of individuals and other data in the documents have been invented for the purpose of the exercise.

Group Exercise – Candidate Brief

This booklet contains all the practical information that you will need to complete this exercise.

- *You are a member of an EU Task Force that is part of a wider initiative aimed at raising awareness in schoolchildren of the importance of environmental concerns across the EU. This is a very high profile initiative that has been signed up to by all Member States in the European Council.*
- *Your role as a group is to evaluate a range of proposals for the EU and recommend two of them: one to be implemented straight away, another to be phased in after 6 months.*
- *Each member of the group will be given the same information – some background information and then six proposals that have been developed for your consideration by various inter-institutional working groups.*

You have 15 minutes to prepare and 45 minutes to discuss the proposals.

By the end of the meeting you must:

- *Agree on the two proposals to recommend to the two European Commissioners responsible for Climate Action and for Education, Training and Youth.*
- *Establish key benefits/advantages and risk/disadvantages for each of the recommended proposals.*
- *Argue, with reasons, for the proposal to go ahead with immediately and which to implement in six months' time.*
- *Consider the implementation of your proposals and highlight:*
  - *Who (if anyone) you wish to consult prior to implementation.*
  - *What strategies need to be developed to ensure the success of the proposals in terms of implementation, stakeholder buy-in etc.*
- *You do not need to produce a written record, but need to be prepared to talk the Commissioners clearly through your ideas if requested.*
- *You are asked not to appoint a formal chairperson for the discussion.*

PLEASE DO NOT TURN OVER UNTIL YOU ARE ASKED TO DO SO

[Disclaimer: Names and other information below are fictitious and only serve demonstration purposes for the group exercise. Material should not be considered as representing the official position of any institution or body mentioned below.]

Group Exercise – Candidate Background File

From: Andrea WERNER [Head of Unit, DG Climate Action]
To: [Your Name]
Date: 4th November 201X
Subject: Task Force Meeting
Importance: High

Hello [Your Name],

Welcome to the Task Force. I am confident that the team members we have pulled together represent some of the brightest talent we currently possess and I look forward to hearing about how you present and argue for your views at the upcoming Task Force Meeting today.

As you may have heard, I am scheduled to speak to the press on the 6th November in order to outline our proposals regarding raising awareness of environmental issues in schools across the EU over the next twelve months starting 1st January. Despite our best efforts in this area, recent survey results suggest that the important messages regarding recycling, carbon emissions and conservation are not as effective as we would like them to be. Some drastic action is obviously called for.

I know you have a variety of working groups who will be submitting proposals for the Task Force to consider at the meeting. I would be keen to hear your recommendations on which two proposals to implement – one that will be a "quick win" and show immediate results, the other that we can implement in six months' time or so, to build upon the success of the first. I also need to know why you discounted the other options.

I would like to remind you that the stated aim of the Task Force is that every child in the EU will not only be aware of the impact of environmental damage, but will be involved in active steps to reduce it, both in and outside school. We wish to ensure the EU is a beacon for best practice for this and to be a model for nations around the world.

I would also like to stress that you are free to choose whichever recommendation you feel is best and what is more, you are free to modify proposals if this is felt to provide the optimum intervention. However, the Task Force cannot simply combine interventions as they stand, as this would prove too costly. The exact implementation cost of each proposal has not been calculated exactly, but estimates suggest they will be broadly similar in cost.

From: Florin MARKOSZ [Assistant Policy Officer, DG Climate Action]
To: [Your Name]
Date: 4th November 200X
Subject: Information for the meeting

Dear [Your Name],

In advance of your Task Force meeting, I have pulled together a short dossier of materials that summarise some relevant facts, opinions and information that will be useful for your discussion. This includes some emails I drew from your inbox that were relevant. I hope this is of some use in planning for your meeting with Ms. Werner.

continued...

1) Market Research

The results of a Eurobarometer poll conducted on over 5,000 under-13's across Europe in July 200X are summarised below.

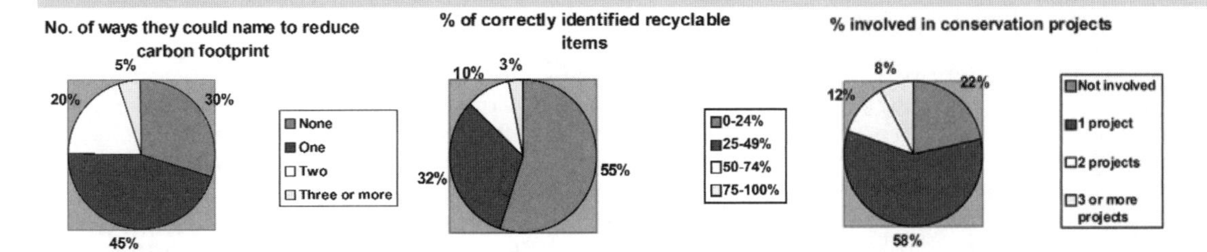

From: Angelika PETKOVA [Policy Officer, DG Communication]
To: [Your Name]
Date: 3rd November 200X
Subject: Information for Meeting

Dear [Your Name],

I just thought I would send you a quick message to let you know that somehow, some of the inter-institutional working group's draft ideas for discussion by the Task Force have been leaked to the Press and have been received in a generally negative light. The main problem seems to be the perception that the EU is "interfering" in the affairs of Member States and there is fear that these measures will be imposed in a blanket, "one-size-fits-all" manner across the EU, with little regard for local initiatives, customs or situations.

One euro-sceptic pressure group in particular, "Keep Our Children Innocent", believes that we should not be talking about these issues at all to children under the age of 13, as it only serves to frighten them about something that is largely out of their hands. Whilst research suggests that talking about such issues to children at a young age is actually critical in helping them to develop an awareness and concern about such issues in the future; "Keep Our Children Innocent" is actually currently enjoying a fair degree of support from the public and press in several countries: although how much this is a reaction against EU intervention in general is unclear.

On the positive side, recent claims of malpractice by scientists in the manipulation of climate change data does not seem to have had an overt effect on public opinion, with the majority (64%) agreeing that we are damaging the environment and feeling that Governments need to act in order to reverse this effect. Of those in favour, 88% would be willing to pay (increased taxes, cost of goods etc) in order to see this implemented.

I hope you find this information helpful.

Kind Regards,

Angelika

----

continued...

From: Luciano DECOCCO [Joint Research Centre]
To: [Your Name]
Date: 2nd November 200X
Subject: Research from Italy

Dear [Your Name],

I thought you might be interested in the results of some research we have conducted into the effects of introducing classroom-based learning sessions specifically upon environmental awareness into schools in Italy. This long term study looked at environmental knowledge and tendency to get involved in conservation-type activity amongst children of school age who had attended such classes. Previous research in other European countries had shown that there was no clear link between the two; however, this latest research found that those children who had attended such classes were 60% more knowledgeable about environmental issues than their peers.

Additionally, they were 13% more likely to get involved in environmental projects outside school at post-13 age and 8% more likely to encourage this type of behaviour in others. There was also a link shown between those children involved in conservation-type activities being 35% less likely to be involved in anti-social behaviour: which is obviously a political hot topic at the moment. The changes are thought to be due to the focus in Italy on a far more practical, hands-on approach to learning about the issues, rather than the more theoretical manner that has tended to be taught in the past.

Considering the picture geographically, pro-environment activity is higher in the rural areas of the country, compared to urban areas. One recommendation to emerge is that opportunities must be created for those in urban areas to get involved in conservation work to a greater degree – especially if it helps to reduce anti-social behaviour.

Finally, a number of other contributory factors were shown to link with environmental-type activities in under-13's, including parental role modelling of environmentally-friendly behaviours and availability of local facilities to help with activities such as recycling, conservation etc.

Kind regards,

Luciano

The Six Proposals

Option One

In a number of selected schools across the EU, all school children are to be given "Green Vouchers" that they can take home and give to their parents to exchange for products marked with an "Environmentally friendly" sticker from the given country's largest supermarket chain. These tokens will be redeemable only at the aforementioned supermarket and only for the specified items. The idea behind this is that if parents can be encouraged to eat and shop in a more environmentally-conscious way, then this will act as a positive role model for their children.

continued...

By giving the token to the children, rather than directly to adults, they can get involved in the process themselves and will be given a list of the included items so that they can express their own preferences. It is hoped that the increased profits for environmentally-friendly manufacturers will also encourage more firms to adopt these practices in future. The only note of concern here is that DG Competition or the Legal Service may challenge the use of just one supermarket, so we may need to approach others for their involvement.

Option Two

This involves taxing school suppliers more heavily who supply goods that are shown to use excess packaging, travel over long distances or are in other ways harmful to the environment. This will not be visible to children, unless it is also accompanied by an awareness-raising campaign in which they are informed of the EU's plans and are taken through a series of planned activities designed to highlight exactly what types of activities are being taxed more heavily and why this is. On the other hand taxation is a sensitive matter these days and it is subject to unanimous decision in the Council.

This serves a dual purpose, as it not only encourages suppliers to become more environmentally-conscious, it provides children with an insight into how business and taxation work in relation to an issue they are likely to feel passionately about. There is the possibility that industry bodies may well challenge what they perceive to be an unfair targeting practice of those suppliers who are not able to change to more environmentally-friendly practices in a short timescale and the EU's limited competence in this field may also pose challenges.

Option Three

This involves the creation of local "Environment Centres" in major cities that schools, as well as private individuals, are able to visit. These will be interactive, multimedia exhibition centres that are all centred on the general theme of environmental care, as well as including details of local initiatives and how local residents can get involved. These will be conveniently sited so that people are able to drop in easily.

The Centres will be updated frequently to keep them fresh and to encourage repeat visits. They will be staffed by local experts who are able to provide information and guided tours on request. There will be ten such centres set up initially in major European cities. Once their benefits have been proven, they will be rolled out to smaller cities and towns across the EU. The note of caution here is that when such Centres have been set up in the past by national governmental bodies for other purposes (e.g. local history), they have not always been successful and embarrassing closures have been necessary.

Option Four

This proposal involves installing a range of electronic monitors at schools and pupils' homes that provide a real-time output of the amount of energy being used in the buildings. Coupled with structured instruction sessions in schools, this will provide a very real view of the impact of changing behaviours on energy consumption. These have been trialled very successfully in homes and have demonstrated a drop in energy consumption of up to 40%. This is an intervention that not only educates but has a tangible and immediate effect on the environment as well. The main concern here is that the technology is still in its early stages and may well become obsolete over the next couple of years as more advanced energy-efficiency measuring techniques are developed, along with the challenges of public tendering and logistics.

Option Five

Creating funding for an additional one thousand research scholarships across the EU, aimed at investigating environmental issues. Links would be made between the research institutions and local schools whereby the researchers are required to come into the schools periodically and present their findings in a fun, interactive manner. Children could also visit the research institutions and observe the research being conducted first-hand.

continued...

This would serve multiple additional purposes: the results of the research could actually be used to help resolve environmental issues; researchers get to draw upon the children to help in data collection and other activities while children would gain exposure to further establishments which should encourage them to continue in their education. The key drawback here is that the people at research institutions are not likely to have had experience dealing with young children and making learning fun for them. Therefore, time consuming and expensive up-skilling is likely to be required.

Option Six

This proposal involves increased funding to schools to provide in-house expertise in order to raise children's environmental awareness. This is the route that has been traditionally followed, but it is recommended that EU-level funding is doubled over the next twelve months in order to ensure that resource is sufficient to guarantee greater success. Experts predict that this additional funding could be enough to improve children's environmental awareness and behaviour and may therefore be reflected in improved subsequent survey results.

Some of the ways the money will be spent include: sending all teachers on environmental awareness training courses, recommending to national governments the introduction of new compulsory sessions on the subject as part of the school curriculum and making the subject of "Environmental Conservation" a formally assessed subject that pupils can take under 13. It will also cover school trips and on-site environmental projects. The main concern here is that this has already been tried in a few Member States and some people are concerned this is simply "throwing good money after bad"; wasting money on initiatives that have already been shown to be ineffective.

Scoring Guide

The following section outlines some examples of what good and poor behaviour might look like for a couple of the competencies (working in a team; leading and inspiring others) likely to be assessed in an exercise like this.

Competency Area: Working in a Team

This competency area is concerned with how effectively a candidate works with other people – be they colleagues, external contractors or other stakeholders. It measures co-operative tendencies as well as general interpersonal sensitivity. It also covers how effectively a candidate may utilise the diverse skills and backgrounds of others.

Scoring Criteria:

For this competency, the following would be indicators of a **positive response**:

- Includes relevant others in decision making (e.g. mentions relevant possible internal and external stakeholders as well as other group members; consults with other members of the group on how they view the issue; proposes public consultations with stakeholders such as NGOs or policy makers regarding school education and awareness raising on the above topics)
- Praises the contributions of others (e.g. when someone outlines their views or comes up with a feasible proposal, the candidate responds with "good point" or "I did not think of this from such a perspective, thanks for bringing this up" and shows no sign of jealousy or irritation)
- Works co-operatively across organisational areas (e.g. suggests working collabora-

tively with DG Communication or the Joint Research Centre to ensure the success of the initiatives; happy to spread the responsibility and potential credit to bodies outside his or her own Task Force)

- Actively listens to others (e.g. does not interrupt whilst others in the group are talking; nods, makes eye contact, takes notes of others' ideas and recalls these when underlining certain points; summarises what they have just said, e.g. "So if I understand you correctly, you suggest a public consultation in the European Parliament, is that right?")
- Effectively utilises the diverse range of backgrounds, skills and motivations of the team (e.g. makes reference to others' knowledge or views, for example "I know you are keen on getting the private sector involved Michel, so I am wondering how else could we do this?" or "You mentioned you had worked as a journalist before, maybe you would have a suggestion on how to improve our programme's public image?")
- Shows a concern for the emotional state of others (e.g. notices other group members' body language and asks them about it, for example "Sue, you don't appear quite convinced by this argument, can I ask why?")

The following would be indicators of a **poor response**:

- Makes decisions in isolation without consulting others (e.g. breaks off into a pair to discuss the issues and ignores other group members' input)
- Ignores or belittles the contributions of others (e.g. says "That's ridiculous, that will never work" to another group member or "I'm sorry but what you are suggesting is complete nonsense")
- Adopts a silo mentality, does not co-operate with other organisational areas (e.g. fails to consider other parts of the Commission or other EU institutions, national governments or external bodies)
- Ignores others (e.g. does not seek to build upon others' contributions and repeats his or her own ideas without considering others' viewpoints)
- Fails to consider individual differences in background, skills or motivations (e.g. does not attempt to find common ground when there are disagreements or fails to consider others' individual sensitivities or personal convictions)
- Shows no concern for or ignores the emotional state of others (e.g. does not attempt to draw quieter members of the group into the conversation or ignores others' body language)

Competency Area: Leading and Inspiring Others

This competency area is concerned with how effectively a candidate can issue directions as well as motivate colleagues. It is about delivering clear feedback messages as well as taking responsibility for the personal development of others.

Scoring Criteria:

For this competency, the following would be indicators of a **positive response**:

- Role models positive organisational behaviours for others (e.g. talks positively about the importance of raising environmental awareness, for example says "This issue is extremely important and I am positive we can do a lot about it")
- Effective at motivating others (e.g. draws other people in; speaks in an enthused

manner, for example "I find this a terrific project: I am glad to work with such a dedicated team")

- Issues clear directions for others to follow without being overly dominant (e.g. allocates timekeeping or note keeping responsibilities to one person; splits tasks among the team for higher efficiency or talks about how other stakeholders would be briefed)
- Prepared to deliver tough messages when necessary (e.g. prepared to voice disagreements with other group members in a sensitive manner, for example "This seems to be a good point but if we look at Option 3, I am afraid it is impossible to execute in the way you propose. I hope you also agree that it should be reconsidered in its current form.")

The following would be indicators of a **poor response**:

- Fails to role model positive behaviours, or actively role models undesirable behaviours (e.g. belittles the importance of the Task Force's aims or questions the rationale behind the exercise)
- Demotivates others or fails to try and motivate them (e.g. makes no attempt to drive the group discussion forward to meet objectives or refuses to cooperate actively with group members)
- Issues unclear or no instructions (e.g. makes no suggestions on how to delegate tasks, does not aim to come up with positive suggestions when asked)
- Shies away from delivering tough messages (e.g. voices no disagreements, agrees with various contradicting opinions, afraid of outlining ambitious goals)

3. EPSO Assessment Exercise: The Case Study

Description and Purpose

On its website, EPSO describes the case study exercise as: *"a comprehensive case study related to the field for which the candidates applied in order to test professional skills and knowledge"*.

A case study exercise will involve being given tons of information to be read through within a seemingly impossible time limit, about a work-related scenario. It will be presented in a dossier form and you will be invited to consider the evidence before presenting your hypotheses and solutions. You may also be given additional information to assess and respond to throughout the allocated time.

With a case study (a) the output is usually a report, rather than a prioritisation and list of decisions and (b) it is designed primarily to test relevant technical or specialist knowledge in relation to the role, rather than broad behavioural competencies such as organisation skills and others (although the latter are often measured as well).

How to Prepare

- Part of the aim of the exercise is to see how you cope with the unfamiliar, but research will still boost your confidence and help you tackle issues in a more informed way. Check the list of recommended websites in this book and EPSO's own site for sample case studies and recent press releases as they may relate to the topic of case study; for more details, look at the sample case study exercise later in this chapter and the general tips and resources for covering EU affairs in earlier chapters of this book.

  At the same time, I strongly recommend familiarizing yourself with the terminology, expressions, main concepts and ideas of your field (e.g. if you are sitting the Law exam, make sure to revise the fundamentals of EU law, major case law, EU legal principles, fundamentals of institutional and competition law, the competencies of the General Court, the European Court of Justice and the Civil Service Tribunal, etc.). The key issue here is to have the right vocabulary and knowledge of the basic developments in your domain, so that you can include references in your written assignment that will show to the assessors your proficiency in and in-depth understanding of your field. The same is true for all other domains: just because the case study does not require any specific preparation, it should not mean you completely avoid revising textbooks or browsing through specific online resources, especially the European Commission's and European Parliament's website.

Tips for the Assessment Itself

- **Background Knowledge**: The case study is the only exercise where your background knowledge of the field (Public Administration, Finance, Statistics, Economics, Law or other) can and should be used to demonstrate your ability to work in this domain. Make sure to be aware of all relevant topics of your chosen domain; see recommended resources in this book and online.

- **Unlimited Context**: Though it may seem in contradiction to the above tip, you will be asked to respond to the questions in the dossier using primarily (but not exclusively) the background notes provided. The aim of these background materials is to help with your assessment of the situation and provide you with additional information in case you are unfamiliar with some of the facts. However, unlike e.g. verbal reasoning exercises, you must apply and demonstrate some of your existing knowledge of the subject as well since the dossier is "only" a useful asset but not an isolated or limited paradigm in which you are requested to work.
- **Relevant Information**: As the case study dossiers tend to include longer extracts from Court judgements (Lawyer field), Eurostat tables (Economist or Finance field), Commission White Papers or Communications (Public Administration or other fields), several parts of these documents *will not be relevant* for your exercise and purposefully so. Do not be afraid to disregard superfluous information and only underline or mark the relevant data or facts. Similarly to numerical reasoning tables where you may only need to look at two cells in a complex table, you may only need to consider a few sections of the dossier to answer the questions correctly.
- **Notes**: Make rough notes either on the documents themselves or on scrap paper as you read the background information in order to help structure your thoughts and for quick reference later.
- **Administration**: These exercises are generally administered in a less standardised manner than other Assessment Centre exercises, so do ask questions if any terms used are unclear or if you are unsure what you need to do.
- **Focus on the Question**: Make sure you answer the question posed, not what you would have *liked* the question to have been (e.g. if the dossier concerns the Services Directive's effect on the EU's internal market policy, do not cover issues related to the Lisbon Treaty's new horizontal provisions). Read the question extremely thoroughly and avoid any arbitrary interpretation thereof (e.g. if the question mentions "steps foreseen for the next five years", make sure you do not cover issues beyond this timescale).
- **Every Word Matters**: each word and expression has an important meaning in the question, therefore make sure you answer everything that you were instructed to cover (e.g. if the question has multiple segments such as "who, on which legal bases and against which institution may launch an action for damages", make sure your answer includes a section on each of the three main items).
- **Your Opinion**: if the question refers to "your opinion", make sure you state a position on the issue and not just recall facts or information. Be cautious, however, about taking a radical view or hurting anyone's sensitivities if you decide to challenge an EU action.
- **Facts vs. Assumptions**: Bear in mind that you may not have all the information at hand that you would need; you are usually safe to make reasonable assumptions, but make it clear when you are doing so and where further information would be desirable ("It can reasonably be assumed from the file that..." as opposed to "It is known that...").
- **Use Arguments**: When underlining a certain point to answer the questions in the dossier, always try to gather facts and specific information from the file (e.g. "Based on the provisions of Article 8 of Directive X, it was not possible for company Y to

apply for this grant." or "As seen from the vacancies shown in the organigram of this Directorate, Mr. X could be appointed deputy Head of Unit in December.")

- **Stay Within Context**: Stay focused on the case study, and do not get sidetracked into talking about the wider outside-world situation unless asked to do so (e.g. if the case study concerns the new mobile phone transmission standards, keep the mention of global telecommunication trends to the minimum).
- **Time Keeping**: Keep track of how much time you have got left. Just like in other exercises, always be aware of the time remaining and do not get held up by a single task or exercise. Furthermore, be very careful in how you allocate your time – as you most likely will be given 1 hour and 30 minutes to complete a task, try to create a time plan as follows: from the 90 minutes you have, spend 10 on understanding the question and browsing through the dossier; spend another 25 on marking the relevant parts and drafting an outline of the answers, and then 50 minutes actually writing down your thoughts in an organised and final format. This leaves you with 5 minutes to proof-read and double-check your work which is extremely little but still gives you a timetable to work to.
- **Use Bullet Points**: You will not need to write full sentences while "digesting" the dossier; even in the written submission you can use itemised, well-structured lists that evaluators will appreciate for their clarity. Moreover, assessors love to have clear structures when they read through dozens of papers: it not only assists their task but also transmits the message that you have a clear, structured way of thinking and were able to grasp the essence of the issues in question.
- **Abbreviations**: If you use abbreviations of events, names or institutions referenced in the dossier, make sure you know exactly what they refer to and include a short legend or key to avoid misunderstandings.
- **Spell Check**: If your assessors read your notes or paper, make sure to use words that you are confident of spelling correctly. Choose simpler versions of synonyms and, for example, use "various" rather than "miscellaneous" if in doubt about its spelling.
- **Write Legibly**: Though this is certainly not an issue you will be scored on, it will make the assessors' life much easier if you do your best to write legibly even towards the end of the exercise when time pressure and fatigue may start to take their toll on you.
- **Length**: there is no pre-determined page length that is expected of you (not least because candidates' handwriting differs greatly) but generally 2-4 pages in A4 format is expected. As long as you provide the answers to all questions, the overall length is less of a concern.

Sample Case Study Exercise

In the case study, you will encounter a comprehensive dossier with various sources of information that may include legal documents, scientific reports, statistical charts or any other document that EPSO considers relevant to your exam's profile.

We have created a sample case study dossier below and included background information relating to **six different role profiles**. For the sake of this exercise and to offer a comprehensive overview of the major exam profiles, we think these will prove to be helpful in this context.

The case study exercise is the main task that tests your expert knowledge of your chosen field. Unlike the group exercise, the case study will require your personal *individual* input without using anyone's help. Consequently, you are not only allowed to use your background knowledge but *absolutely encouraged to do so*; the aim is to demonstrate how prepared you are professionally to work as an EU official such as Auditor or Scientific Administrator.

Apart from the evaluators' enhanced focus on the content of your written answers, they will evaluate other aspects as well, such as the quality of your arguments, the sophistication and spelling of your writing, your ability to analyse complex information in a relatively short time and present facts and personal judgements in a clear and concise manner.

At the end of this section, you will find a sample case study answer with comments and an evaluation sheet so that you can draw conclusions from it and avoid any pitfalls.

Case Study - Candidate Brief

You will find the following elements in the dossier:

1. EU Press Release: Environment Council Conclusions [extract] (Dec 2009)
2. EU Press Release: Copenhagen Climate Conference – Key EU Objectives (Dec 2009)
3. EU Press Release: European Commission sets out strategy to reinvigorate global action after Copenhagen (March 2010)
4. European Council Presidency Conclusions [extract] (Oct 2009)
5. EU Press Release: European Union Welcomes Cancun Agreeement (December 2010)
6. Eurostat Data Charts (2009)

Based on this information and your background knowledge, answer in writing the following sample questions listed in the table for your profile. Based on which EPSO competition you had applied for, we suggest answering all three questions belonging to that group. You may nevertheless wish to have a look at questions put for other profiles as you may be encouraged to conduct further research into the dossier and approach the same issues from multiple angles.

There is no strict format to follow for your response, but you should ensure that whatever structure you choose is clear and addresses the points raised in the questions. Your target audience is your head of unit in your new role: so, a certain level of knowledge can be inferred, but you should explain all jargon used. You should spend up to one and a half hours in total for reading the background information and producing your responses.

Base your answers on the attached dossier but you are also encouraged to use your professional knowledge of the subject.

Public Administration / Human Resources profile

Question 1 Briefly describe the EU's position in the run-up to the Copenhagen and Cancún Summits of December 2009 and 2010 and its post-summit evaluation.

Question 2 If you were in charge of the strategic human resource management of the EU institutions, what kind of changes (reorganisation, staffing, HR initiatives) would you propose until 2020 in regard to tackling the effects of climate change on the administrative side?

Question 3 In your view, what are the major geopolitical challenges of Europe's energy dependence and low level of renewable sources? Do you think the steps foreseen for the next five years are suitable to remedy the problem?

Law Profile

Question 1 Summarise the legal nature of the commitments EU leaders have pledged to fight climate change from a legal perspective.

Question 2 Should the above legal and political commitments not be respected, who, on which legal bases and against which institution, may launch an action for damages? Include references to case-law in your answer.

Question 3 In your view, which rules and principles of the EU competition policy and internal market rules could be used to ensure that Member States respect the pledges made shortly before and at the Copenhagen and Cancún Summits?

Economics profile

Question 1 Briefly summarise the state of play and main challenges of the EU's climate change financing with special regard to Member States' public finances and the negotiations on the EU's 2013-2020 framework budget.

Question 2 In your view and based on the historical data provided, how would an increase in energy tax rates affect the use of renewable energy sources?

Question 3 Creating an EU carbon market has spill-over effects on European competitiveness, FDI and external trade. In your view, which are the main challenges and how can they be best tackled, with particular reference to the EU2020 strategy?

Audit or Finance Profile

Question 1 Outline from a performance audit perspective the risks inherent to innovative financing of the EU's climate change policy.

Question 2 Regarding the EU's carbon market and the ETS, which principles apply to ensure the sound management of EU public finances? Also provide examples.

Question 3 Which financial control mechanisms are applied for EU funds allocated to 3rd countries in order to assist them to tackle or mitigate the effects of climate change? In your opinion how could these be improved?

Statistics Profile

Question 1 How do demographic trends in the European Union affect, directly or indirectly, climate change financing?

Question 2 You are requested to present correlations between energy tax rates, greenhouse gas emissions and air pollution to your superior who is giving a presentation to a non-expert international audience. Which information would you highlight and how?

Question 3 The press in some EU Member States has been skeptical about the scientific validity of certain data included in your dossier. Provide arguments why Eurostat's methodology is perfectly reliable.

continued...

Scientific Researcher Profile

Question 1 Summarise the major threats caused by the effects of climate change and the increasing use of bio-fuel on the European food chain.

Question 2 If you were required to draft an impact assessment on the effects of having the current levels of non-renewable energy sources unregulated in the EU, what scientific arguments would you base your assessment upon?

IQuestion 3 In your opinion, what are the major public health challenges created by rising temperatures in comparison with the situation 20-30 years ago? How should these be addressed on a policy level?

Background Dossier

File #1

IP/09/1997
Brussels, 22 December 2009

Environment: Council Conclusions

European Environment Commissioner Stavros Dimas joined the Presidency in concluding that the Copenhagen Accord is a first step towards a legally binding global climate agreement. Commissioner Dimas welcomed conclusions on international biological diversity beyond 2010 and on combination effects of chemicals, adopted by today's Environment Council.

Commissioner Dimas said: "A lot of work still needs to be done. We must now ensure that the Copenhagen Accord becomes operational and as such constitutes the core of a new climate treaty. Regardless of what happens internationally, the EU will continue to implement its climate policy. As well as contributing to Europe's environmental sustainability, this will help the EU gain a first mover advantage on the road to building a low-carbon economy."

Copenhagen climate conference

Commissioner Dimas joined the Presidency in concluding that the Copenhagen Accord is a first step towards a legally binding global climate agreement. He said that although the Accord fell well short of the level of ambition that was needed to prevent dangerous climate change, it contained many of the elements the European Union had fought for. This includes recognition of the 2 degree Celsius objective, economy-wide emission reduction targets for developed countries and mitigation action by developing countries by 31 January 2010, and a substantial finance package of USD 30 billion for the coming three years and USD 100 billion by 2020. It also provides for a mechanism to accelerate technology cooperation. He said a crucial first step would be to ensure that all key parties confirm their endorsement of the Accord and notify their targets or actions by 31 January 2010.

continued...

International biological diversity beyond 2010

Commissioner Dimas welcomed Council conclusions on a post-2010 global vision and target for biodiversity. The conclusions agree on key strategic principles which should inform the debate. These call for measurable, achievable, realistic and time-bound targets based on the best available science. The loss of biodiversity is as great a threat as climate change to the environment, our quality of life and economic prosperity. Besides its intrinsic value, biodiversity also has an important role to play in mitigating and adapting to climate change through the capacity of ecosystems to store carbon dioxide and protect societies against the impacts of climate change. 2010, the International Year of Biodiversity, will be a crucial year for biodiversity policy. Commissioner Dimas said the conclusions would help the Commission in its work at international level and in the run up to the 10th Conference of the Parties to the Convention on Biological Diversity (CBD) in October 2010 in Nagoya, Japan, where the new global target will be adopted. The Commission is currently preparing a Communication setting out options for a post-2010 EU vision and target which it aims to present in January.

File #2

MEMO/09/534
Brussels, 2 December 2009

The Copenhagen climate conference: key EU objectives

International negotiations were launched at the end of 2007 to draw up a United Nations agreement on tackling climate change for the period after 2012, when the first commitment period of the Kyoto Protocol expires. The EU wants these negotiations to result in a comprehensive, ambitious, fair, science-based and legally binding global treaty.

The new treaty should aim to ensure global warming is kept below 2°C above the pre-industrial temperature. It should cover all elements of the 2007 Bali Action Plan, which set the agenda and scope of the international negotiations.

Given the slow progress made in the negotiations to date, and a lack of consensus about the shape of the eventual agreement, it is now unlikely that the treaty can be finalised at the UN climate change conference in Copenhagen on 7-18 December as originally planned.

The EU's goal is therefore to make as much progress as possible in Copenhagen towards a full treaty and to reach an ambitious and comprehensive political agreement covering all its key elements.

This agreement would shape the full contours of the final outcome of the negotiating process, provide the guidance needed to elaborate it into a legal text, and specify both a process for doing so and, if possible, the shape of the legal agreement to be reached.

From the EU's viewpoint, the Copenhagen agreement will need to cover four elements:

1. Pledges on emissions and finance

The two central pledges that developed and developing countries alike will be expected to make in Copenhagen are their contributions in terms of mitigating their greenhouse gas emissions and of providing financial assistance, particularly to the poorest and most vulnerable developing countries.

On mitigation, developed countries should make ambitious, binding and quantified emission limitation or reduction commitments. To keep the 2°C target within reach, these commitments need to amount to a cut in collective emissions from developed countries in the order of 30% below 1990 levels by 2020.

Action is also needed by developing countries. In particular the more economically advanced developing countries should pledge ambitious, quantified mitigation actions. Overall developing country pledges should amount to a substantial deviation - in the order of 15-30% - below the currently predicted growth rate in their collective emissions by 2020.

continued...

The EU has committed unconditionally to cut its emissions to at least 20% below 1990 levels by 2020 and is implementing this goal through the climate and energy package (IP/09/628). It has also committed to scale up its emission cut to 30% provided other industrialised countries agree to make comparable reductions and developing countries contribute adequately to the global effort according to their responsibilities and respective capabilities.

Regarding finance, a deal is needed on both "fast start" financing to help developing countries strengthen their capacities to tackle climate change in the short term (2010-2012) and a significant scaling up of public and private financial flows to developing countries from 2013. The EU is ready to contribute its fair share of both.

Total international public finance required by developing countries to combat climate change is estimated by the European Commission in the range of €22-50 billion per year by 2020 under a global agreement that is in line with the EU's level of ambition. The EU wants contributions to be shared fairly on the basis of a comprehensive global key reflecting contributing countries' emission levels and ability to pay (GDP). All countries except the least developed should contribute, but developing countries would be net beneficiaries.

It is vital that both mitigation and financial commitments are captured in the Copenhagen agreement in the strongest possible manner. The best way to do this is to include them in a Decision by the Confererence of Parties (COP) of the UN Framework Convention on Climate Change (UNFCCC).

2. Key architectural components of the future treaty

The key architectural components of the future treaty need to be agreed because they can significantly affect how ambitious the mitigation pledges are in practice. They are also needed to ensure the pledges are implemented.

These key architectural components include the following:

- A procedure for codifying emission mitigation contributions by developed and developing countries and for reviewing and updating them;
- Targets for reducing global emissions from the international aviation and maritime transport sectors, an international arrangement to address emissions of hydrofluorocarbon gases (HFCs) and a work programme for the agriculture sector;
- A framework for action on adaptation to climate change;
- A framework for reducing emissions from deforestation and forest degradation (REDD) and promoting conservation, sustainable management of forests and enhancement of forest carbon stocks (REDD+) in developing countries;
- Accounting rules for emission changes due to land use, land-use change and forestry (LULUCF) in developed countries;
- The role of low carbon growth plans and nationally appropriate mitigation actions (NAMAs);
- The role and use of carbon markets, including reform of the Clean Development Mechanism and Joint Implementation mechanism and the establishment of sectoral carbon market mechanisms;
- Institutional arrangements for the management and matching up of international financial resources with developing countries' financing needs;
- A framework for stepping up international cooperation on technology;
- The length of the treaty's commitment period; starting levels for measuring emission reductions; treatment of the surplus of national emission rights (assigned amount units) from the Kyoto Protocol's first commitment period; and a framework of rules on compliance;

continued...

- Strengthened rules on monitoring, reporting and verification (MRV) of action on mitigation and adaptation and of related support.

The conference should anchor political agreements on each of these elements in the text of an overarching COP Decision.

3. A "fast start" deal

The implementation of key elements of the Copenhagen agreement should start immediately after the conference, facilitated by the provision of targeted "fast start" financial support to developing countries.

Possible elements of the "fast start" deal are:

- Preparation of low carbon growth plans and NAMAs, including financing to support these activities;
- Readiness for REDD, including financing for capacity building and elaboration of national forest inventories;
- Implementation of the adaptation action framework, including the set-up of any institutions and provision of financing to developing countries for further adaptation plans and their implementation;
- Preparations for implementing sectoral carbon market mechanisms, including capacity building for the monitoring and reporting of emissions from key sectors in advanced developing countries;
- Preparations for the implementation of a strengthened system of monitoring, reporting and review (MRV).

Each of these elements could be elaborated through separate Decisions taken by the COP.

4. The follow-up process

The international negotiations have been organised on two parallel "tracks" under the UNFCCC and the Kyoto Protocol respectively. The Copenhagen agreement needs to decide on a single track for the follow-up process.

The EU has made clear it wants to see a single, new, legally binding treaty as the outcome of the current two-track process. The treaty should contain all the essential elements of the Kyoto Protocol plus further emission commitments by all developed countries, including the US, and emission actions by developing countries. It should be capable of universal ratification.

The EU has several reasons for this preference:

- Universal participation: a single instrument favours universal participation because only one ratification process would be required. By contrast, an agreement involving two or more instruments would run the risk of them not achieving an identical number of ratifications and of not entering into force at the same time.
- Consistency: A single instrument enables consistency because it avoids separate parallel international regimes.
- Institutions: a single instrument would offer better opportunities to streamline the international institutional framework for addressing climate change, avoiding duplication and waste of resources.
- Carbon market: a single instrument would promote greater certainty for the international carbon market, given the risk of a fragmented international climate regime if two or more instruments require ratification.
- Differentiation: a single instrument does not preclude the differentiation of obligations between different countries.

File #3

IP/10/255

Brussels, 9 March 2010

Climate change: European Commission sets out strategy to reinvigorate global action after Copenhagen

The European Commission today set out a strategy to help maintain the momentum of global efforts to tackle climate change. The Communication proposes that the EU swiftly begin implementing last December's Copenhagen Accord, in particular 'fast start' financial assistance to developing countries. In parallel the EU should continue to press for a robust and legally binding global agreement that involves all countries in real climate action. This will require integrating the Copenhagen Accord into the UN negotiations and addressing the weaknesses in the Kyoto Protocol. Active outreach by the EU will be key to promoting support for the UN negotiations and the Commission will undertake this effort in close contact with the Council and with the support of the European Parliament.

Commission President José Manuel Barroso said: "The Commission is determined to keep up the momentum for global action on climate change; Today's communication sets out a clear strategy on the next steps needed to reinvigorate the international negotiations and engage our partners in this path. I will call on the next European Council to support this strategy building also on further consultations that I have asked Commissioner Hedegaard to undertake with key international partners."

Connie Hedegaard, Commissioner for Climate Action, said: "Climate change can be controlled only if all major emitters take action. Obviously nobody would stronger than myself hope that we could get everything done in Mexico, but the signals coming out of various capitals of big emitters unfortunately do not make that likely. In Copenhagen the world had a unique chance and did not use this to its full. We now have to secure the momentum and to do our utmost to get specific and substantial results out of Cancun and to secure no later than in South Africa an agreement on the legal form. Copenhagen was a step forward. Even if the Copenhagen Accord fell short of Europe's ambitions, the increasing support for it around the world gives the EU the opportunity to build on this and channel it into action. The most convincing leadership Europe can show is to take tangible and determined action to become the most climate friendly region in the world, which will also strengthen our energy security, stimulate greener economic growth and create new jobs.

Negotiations roadmap

The Communication proposes a roadmap for the UN negotiating process which will restart in April. The political guidance in the Copenhagen Accord – which was not formally adopted as a UN decision – needs to be integrated into the UN negotiating texts that contain the basis of the future global climate agreement. The EU would be ready to reach a legally binding global deal at the UN climate conference in Cancun, Mexico, at the end of this year, but the Commission recognises that differences between countries may delay an agreement until 2011. EU is ready but the world might not be, and therefore our approach has to be step-wise.

Copenhagen Accord

The Copenhagen Accord is a step towards the EU's goal of a legally binding global climate agreement, which should take effect in 2013 at the end of the Kyoto Protocol's first commitment period. The Accord endorses the EU's core objective of keeping global warming below 2°C above the pre-industrial temperature in order to prevent the worst impacts of climate change.

continued...

File #3 - continuation

To date industrialised and developing countries representing more than 80% of global greenhouse gases emissions have inscribed their emission targets or actions in the Accord. This shows the determination of a majority of nations to step up their action against climate change.

Environmental integrity

The international negotiations must ensure the future global agreement will have a high level of environmental integrity and will actually keep warming below 2°C. The Kyoto Protocol remains the central building block of the UN process but the limited number of countries it covers, and its serious weaknesses, must be addressed. If allowed to continue these weaknesses, which concern accounting rules for forestry emissions and the handling of surplus national emission rights from the 2008-2012 period, would risk reducing industrialised countries' current emission reduction pledges to almost zero.

EU leadership

The Commission believes the EU must show leadership by taking tangible action to become the most climate friendly region of the world as part of the Europe 2020 strategy proposed on 3 March (see IP/10/225). The EU has committed to a 20% emissions cut below 1990 levels by 2020, and to scaling up this reduction to 30% if other major economies agree to do their fair share of the global effort. Ahead of the June European Council, the Commission will prepare an analysis of what practical policies would be required to implement the 30% emission reduction. The Commission will later outline a pathway for the EU's transition to becoming a low-carbon economy by 2050. Consistent with the EU 2020 strategy, the goal is to come with intelligent solutions that benefit not only climate change, but also energy security and job creation.

Delivering 'fast-start' funding

The Commission suggests that the EU starts implementing the Copenhagen Accord. Swift implementation of the EU's commitment to provide €2.4 billion in 'fast start' financial assistance to developing countries annually in 2010-2012 is essential both to the EU's credibility and to enhancing recipient countries' capacities to address climate change. The Commission is ready to help ensure the EU's assistance is well coordinated .

Advancing carbon markets

The Communication underlines that the EU should continue to work to advance the development of the international carbon market, which is essential for driving low-carbon investments and reducing global emissions cost-effectively. The carbon market can also generate major financial flows to developing countries.

Stepping up outreach

The EU will need to bolster its outreach in order to build confidence that a global deal can be reached and to explore specific action-oriented decisions that can be taken in Cancun. The Commission will undertake this outreach in close contact with the Council and its Presidency, and would encourage and assist the European Parliament to engage fully with parliamentarians from key partner countries.

For further information:

http://ec.europa.eu/environment/climat/future_action_com.htm

File #4

Brussels European Council
29/30 October 2009
Presidency Conclusions

[extract]

II. Climate change

4. The climate is changing faster than expected and the risks this poses can already be seen. We are experiencing widespread melting of ice, rising global sea levels and increased frequency, intensity and duration of floods, droughts and heat waves.
5. Just weeks away from the Copenhagen Conference, the European Union is more than ever fully determined to play a leading role and contribute to reaching a global, ambitious and comprehensive agreement. All parties to the negotiation need to inject new momentum into the process and the pace of the negotiations must be stepped up.
6. The Copenhagen agreement needs to include provisions on the 2°C objective, ambitious emission reduction commitments by developed countries, appropriate mitigation action by developing countries, adaptation, technology and a deal on financing, as outlined below. The European Council emphasises the need for a legally binding agreement for the period starting 1 January 2013 that builds on the Kyoto Protocol and incorporates all its essentials. The European Council also recognises that all countries, including those not presently bound by the Kyoto Protocol, should take immediate action.
7. The European Council calls upon all Parties to embrace the 2°C objective and to agree to global emission reductions of at least 50%, and aggregate developed country emission reductions of at least 80-95%, as part of such global emission reductions, by 2050 compared to 1990 levels; such objectives should provide both the aspiration and the yardstick to establish mid-term goals, subject to regular scientific review. It supports an EU objective, in the context of necessary reductions according to the IPCC by developed countries as a group, to reduce emissions by 80-95% by 2050 compared to 1990 levels.
8. The European Union is at the forefront of efforts to fight climate change. It is committed to take a decision to move to a 30% reduction by 2020 compared to 1990 levels, as its conditional offer with a view to a global and comprehensive agreement for the period beyond 2012, provided that other developed countries commit themselves to comparable emission reductions and that developing countries contribute adequately according to their responsibilities and respective capabilities.
9. Action by the European Union alone will not be enough. A comprehensive and ambitious agreement can only be reached if all parties contribute to the process. Other developed countries should also demonstrate their leadership and commit to ambitious emission reductions and step up their current pledges. Developing countries, especially the more advanced, should commit to appropriate mitigation action, reflecting their common but differentiated responsibilities and respective capabilities. The European Council underlines the need for measuring, reporting and verification (MRV) of mitigation actions in all countries.
10. Adaptation is a necessary element that must be comprehensively addressed in a Copenhagen agreement. The European Council recalls the proposal to create a Framework for Action on Adaptation as part of this agreement. It underlines the need to scale up support for adaptation in developing countries, until and beyond 2012, focusing on countries and regions that are particularly vulnerable to the adverse impacts of climate change.
11. The European Council underlines the importance of creating incentives to engage the private sector in technology cooperation. R&D must be substantially scaled up, global technology objectives established and safe and sustainable technologies diffused.
12. A deal on financing will be a central part of an agreement in Copenhagen. A gradual but significant increase in additional public and private financial flows is needed to help developing countries implement ambitious mitigation and adaptation strategies.

continued...

13. The EU is ready to take its fair share of the global effort by setting an ambitious mitigation target, allowing for offsets and providing its fair share of public support. The European Council endorses the Commission estimate that the total net incremental costs of mitigation and adaptation in developing countries could amount to around EUR 100 billion annually by 2020, to be met through a combination of their own efforts, the international carbon market and international public finance.
14. The overall level of the international public support required is estimated to lie in the range of EUR 22 to 50 billion per year by 2020, subject to a fair burden sharing at the global level in line with the distribution key to be agreed by Parties, a governance arrangement and delivery towards specific mitigation actions and ambitious Low Carbon Development Strategies/Low Carbon Growth Plans. This range could be narrowed down in view of the Copenhagen summit.
15. An effective and efficient institutional framework for governance has to be developed at the forefront of financing. The European Council supports the establishment of a high-level forum/body to be set up under the guidance of the UNFCCC to inter alia provide an overview of international sources for climate financing in developing countries.
16. All countries, except the least developed, should contribute to international public financing, through a comprehensive global distribution key based on emission levels and on GDP to reflect both responsibility for global emissions and ability to pay, with a considerable weight on emission levels. The weight on emissions should increase over time to allow for adjustments of economies. The EU and its Member States are ready to take on their resulting fair share of total international public finance.
17. The European Council stresses that fast-start international public support is important in the context of a comprehensive, balanced and ambitious Copenhagen agreement. The purpose should be to prepare for effective and efficient action in the medium and longer term and avoid delay of ambitious action, with a special emphasis on least developed countries. Taking note of the Commission estimate that a global financing of EUR 5-7 billion per year for the first three years is needed following an ambitious agreement in Copenhagen, the European Council underlines that a figure will be determined in the light of the outcome of the Copenhagen conference. The EU and its Member States in this context are ready to contribute their fair share of these costs. The European Council stresses that this contribution will be conditional on other key players making comparable efforts.
18. The European Council notes that during the current commitment period under the Kyoto Protocol a significant amount of unused Assigned Amount Units is likely to accrue. This issue must be addressed, in a non-discriminatory manner treating European and non-European countries equally, and so that the handling of the AAU surplus does not affect the environmental integrity of a Copenhagen agreement.
19. Private financing will be stimulated by developing a broad and liquid carbon market based on robust cap-and-trade systems in developed countries, a reformed CDM and sectoral crediting and trading mechanisms for action in developing countries.
20. The European Council stresses the role of mitigation actions in land use, land use change and forestry and in particular through creating incentives for reduced deforestation and forest degradation and for the sustainable management of forests in developing countries. A performance based mechanism which recognises verified emission reductions should be established.
21. It recalls that the risk of carbon leakage is analysed and addressed in the new ETS Directive (Directive 2009/29/EC) so that, to preserve the environmental integrity of the EU's policies, in the light of the outcome of the international negotiations and the extent to which these lead to global greenhouse gas reductions, it is possible to consider appropriate measures to be taken in compliance with international trade rules. An ambitious international agreement remains the best way of addressing this issue.
22. The European Council notes the Commission's draft decision containing a list of sectors and subsectors deemed to be exposed to a significant risk of carbon leakage based on the criteria set out in the new ETS Directive (Directive 2009/29/EC). It notes that a sector or sub-sector may be added to the list, on the basis of new information, if it satisfies the relevant criteria. The list will be reviewed in light of the outcome of the international climate change negotiations.

continued...

23. In parallel with deliveries of climate financing all international parties should commit that such financing would not undermine or jeopardize the fight against poverty and continued progress towards the Millennium Development Goals. Innovative financing can play a role in ensuring predictable flows of financing for sustainable development, especially towards the poorest and most vulnerable countries.
24. The European Council endorses the conclusions adopted by the Council on 21 October 2009 (14790/09), which together with these European Council conclusions and the attached guidelines give the European Union a strong negotiating position. It will allow the European Union to play a constructive role during the final phase of the negotiating process, in particular on key issues such as financing, technology transfer, adaptation, mitigation and good governance.
25. The European Council invites the Presidency to take the necessary steps to maintain a strong negotiating position throughout the process and will review the situation at its meeting in December in order to take the necessary decisions in the light of the early stages of the Copenhagen conference.

File #5 (ttp://ec.europa.eu/environment/climat/pdf/future_action/com_2009_475.pdf)

IP/10/1699

Cancún, 11 December 2010

European Union welcomes Cancún Agreement as important step towards global framework for climate action

The European Union welcomes the positive results of the Cancún climate conference. The balanced and substantive package of decisions adopted today, known as the Cancún Agreement, represents an important further step on the road to building a comprehensive and legally binding framework for climate action for the period after 2012.

Connie Hedegaard, European Commissioner for Climate Action, said: "The EU came to Cancun to get a substantial package of action-oriented decisions and keep the international climate change negotiations on track. We have helped to deliver the successful outcome the world expected and needed. But the two weeks in Cancún have shown once again how slow and difficult the process is. Everyone needs to be aware that we still have a long and challenging journey ahead of us to reach the goal of a legally binding global climate framework".

Joke Schauvliege, Flemish Minister for Environment, Nature and Culture, who represents the Belgian presidency of the Council of the European Union at Cancún, said: "The EU has worked tirelessly to be a bridge-builder in Cancún while also advancing its positions. The EU has reported transparently on the progress it has made in mobilising the 7.2 billion euros of fast-start funding it has pledged over 2010-2012 and we will continue to do so on an annual basis. We congratulate the Mexican Presidency on conducting an exemplary conference."

The Cancún Agreement builds on the decisions taken a year ago in Copenhagen and also sets out processes for making further progress in the future. It represents a well balanced compromise between different interests within the United Nations system. Key elements of the package include:

- Acknowledgement for the first time in a UN document that global warming must be kept below 2°C compared to the pre-industrial temperature, and establishment of a process to define a date for global emissions to peak and a global emissions reduction goal for 2050;

- The emission pledges of developed and developing countries have been anchored in the UN process and a process set out to help clarify them. The text also recognises that overall mitigation efforts need to be scaled up in order to stay within the 2°C ceiling;

- Agreement to launch a process to strengthen the transparency of actions to reduce or limit emissions so that overall progress can be tracked more effectively;
- Confirmation of the goal that developed countries will mobilise US$ 100 billion in climate funding for developing countries annually by 2020, and establishment of a Green Climate Fund through which much of the funding will be channelled;
- Agreement on the Cancún Adaptation Framework to enhance action on adaptation to climate change;
- Launch of a "REDD+" mechanism enabling action to reduce emissions from deforestation and forest degradation in developing countries;
- Agreement to consider setting up new carbon market mechanisms going beyond a project-based approach;
- Establishment of a Technology Mechanism, including a Technology Executive Committee and a Climate Technology Center and Network, to enhance technology development and transfer;
- Establishment of a clear process for reviewing the adequacy of the goal of keeping global warming below 2°C, including consideration of strengthening the goal to 1.5°C, to be concluded in 2015;
- Extension of the work of the ad hoc working groups under the UN climate change convention and the Kyoto Protocol for a further year while leaving open the legal form of the eventual outcome of the negotiations.

Following pages File #6, Statistical Tables

1. Share of renewables in gross inland energy consumption – [tsdcc110]; *Renewable Energies*

	1996	1997	1998	1999	2000	2001	2002	2003	2004	2005	2006	2007
European Union (27 countries)	5.2	5.4	5.5	5.6	5.8	5.8 (p)	5.7 (p)	6	6.4	6.7	7.1	7.8
European Union (25 countries)	5.1	5.3	5.4	5.5	5.7	5.8 (p)	5.7 (p)	6	6.3	6.5	7	7.8
European Union (15 countries)	5.3	5.5	5.6	5.7	5.9	5.9 (p)	5.8 (p)	6.1	6.5	6.7	7.2	8
Belgium	1.2	1.2	1.3	1.3	1.3	1.5	1.5	1.9	2	2.4	2.9	3.1
Bulgaria	2	2.3	3.4	3.5	4.2	3.6	4.4	4.8	5.2	5.6	5.5	4.7
Czech Republic	1.4	1.6	1.6	1.9	1.5	1.7	2	3.3	3.9	4	4.3	4.7
Denmark	7.2	8.3	8.8	9.7	10.9	11.4	12.4	13.5	15.1	16.4	15.6	17.3
Germany (including ex-GDR from 1991)	1.9	2.2	2.4	2.5	2.8	3	3.4	3.9	4.5	5.1	6	8.3
Estonia	10	10.3	9.5	10.4	10.3	10.6	11	10.6	10.6	10.6	9.8	10
Ireland	1.5	1.5	1.8	1.6	1.6	1.6	1.7	1.6	1.8	2.4	2.7	2.9
Greece	5.4	5.2	4.9	5.3	5	4.5	4.7	5.1	5	5.2	5.7	5
Spain	7	6.3	6.1	5.2	5.7	6.5	5.4	6.9	6.3	6	6.5	7
France	7.3	7.1	7	7.2	7	6.9	6.3	6.5	6.5	6.3	6.6	7
Italy	5.2	5.3	5.4	5.8	5.2	5.5	5.3	5.8	6.8	6.5	7	6.9
Cyprus	2	2	1.9	1.9	1.8	1.8	1.8	1.8	2	1.9	1.9	2.4
Latvia	26.5	29.5	32.6	31.8	31.8	31.7	31.3	30.9	33.1	33	31	29.7
Lithuania	5.7	6.1	6.5	7.9	9.2	8.4	8.1	7.9	8	8.8	9.3	8.9
Luxembourg (Grand-Duché)	1.1	1.4	1.5	1.3	1.6	1.3	1.4	1.4	1.6	1.6	1.7	2.5
Hungary	1.9	2	1.9	1.9	2.1	1.9	3.4	3.4	3.6	4.4	4.8	5.3
Malta	:	:	:	:	:	:	:	:	:	:	:	:
Netherlands	1.8	2	2.2	2.3	2.4	2.4 (p)	2.6 (p)	2.6	2.8	3.4	3.6	3.6
Austria	20.3	20.8	20.6	22.9	22.8	22.2	22.1	19.8	20.8	21.1	22.3	23.8
Poland	3.7	3.8	4.1	4	4.2	4.5	4.6	4.5	4.7	4.8	5.1	5.1
Portugal	18.6	17.3	16.1	13.5	15.3	16.1	13.9	16.9	14.7	13.2	17.1	17.6
Romania	8	10.7	11.2	11.9	10.9	9.3	9.7	9.9	11.5	12.6	11.7	11.9
Slovenia	9.8	8.1	8.6	8.6	12.3	11.5	10.5	10.3	11.5	10.6	10.5	10
Slovakia	2.5	2.5	2.5	2.7	2.8	4	3.7	3.3	3.9	4.3	4.6	5.5
Finland	19.8	20.5	21.7	22.1	23.8	22.4	21.8	20.9	23	23.1	22.7	22.6
Sweden	23.4	27.4	28	27	31.4	28.3	26.3	25.3	25.7	29.6	29.4	30.9
United Kingdom	0.8	0.9	1	1.1	1.1	1.1	1.2	1.3	1.5	1.7	1.9	2.1
Croatia	13.9	10.9	10.5	11.3	11.2	10.7	9.2	9	11	10.1	9.9	7.4
Turkey	16.6	15.8	15.8	15	13.1	13.2	13.4	12.6	13.2	11.9	11.1	9.5
Iceland	65.4	66.7	67.4	71.2	71.3	73.1	72.7	72.7	72.2	72.9	74.9 (p)	:
Norway	43.2	43.6	43.9	44.7	50.9	44	51.7	38.2	37.6	40.3	46.5	46.7
Switzerland	15.2	16.2	15.5	16.9	16.4	17.6	17.2	15.8	15.8	13.9	18.3	18.2

:=Not available p=Provisional value ; Source: Eurostat

2. Implicit tax rate on energy – [tsdcc360]; *Euros per tonne of oil equivalent*

	1996	1997	1998	1999	2000	2001	2002	2003	2004	2005	2006	2007
European Union (27 countries)	:	:	:	172.5	171.8	166.6	171.6	169.4	168.2	165.4	164.4	164.7
European Union (25 countries)	154.9	160.0	164.7	175.6	175.2	170.4	175.8	173.6	172.4	169.4	168.4	168.4
Belgium	99.8	96.8	97.0	98.0	92.4	90.4	95.0	94.7	103.8	107.0	102.8	111.6
Bulgaria	:	:	:	31.9	36.4	44.5	35.5	46.9	57.7	52.9	53.2	65.8
Czech Republic	49.9	47.2	48.7	53.6	55.2	64.3	74.6	72.1	78.9	93.5	99.5	108.5
Denmark	233.3	233.8	264.3	301.4	313.7	319.0	326.0	323.8	319.1	306.7	296.4	286.2
Germany (including ex-GDR from 1991)	154.9	151.3	152.1	179.7	192.7	198.3	208.3	221.0	213.3	206.5	202.0	203.7
Estonia	17.1	21.3	33.3	32.3	32.2	42.0	42.8	46.4	56.0	65.5	68.9	70.8
Ireland	141.5	159.1	154.3	153.5	140.5	117.4	136.7	142.0	155.9	151.7	147.9	147.9
Greece	197.1	181.2	152.5	141.6	117.3	114.5	104.7	101.9	102.9	100.2	96.0	101.6
Spain	150.3	140.5	148.7	151.3	137.8	130.6	133.5	129.8	125.0	119.3	119.8	118.1
France	172.1	172.2	172.9	179.8	172.9	158.1	172.7	165.9	168.7	162.8	161.9	157.9
Italy	287.4	291.9	274.8	274.2	248.7	234.2	225.6	226.4	213.8	208.2	210.3	199.2
Cyprus	30.4	28.8	31.3	33.2	43.1	59.6	62.2	116.8	131.9	128.2	125.5	122.6
Latvia	21.3	29.1	47.3	43.6	48.3	42.6	45.8	47.0	51.3	55.1	52.9	49.4
Lithuania	18.0	25.3	38.9	55.3	58.0	65.4	77.5	83.1	80.0	78.2	74.4	77.4
Luxembourg (Grand-Duché)	158.1	160.4	169.0	170.6	164.3	167.3	172.2	177.6	181.0	177.7	167.8	167.4
Hungary	83.0	83.2	91.5	88.0	79.7	77.9	85.8	86.1	84.7	87.3	86.1	102.8
Malta	69.5	81.7	140.6	152.6	142.2	179.8	156.4	119.3	118.4	127.1	138.3	197.5
Netherlands	120.0	133.0	138.5	153.4	154.4	155.4	157.6	160.6	169.1	181.5	193.6	178.4
Austria	120.5	140.6	133.1	137.7	141.8	146.2	148.1	147.0	156.1	149.6	141.4	150.5
Poland	37.7	34.9	42.8	51.5	58.9	64.7	72.9	66.6	66.6	84.1	87.5	101.4
Portugal	184.9	166.6	170.2	158.3	111.8	129.9	150.0	156.7	141.7	148.8	148.1	149.1
Romania	:	:	77.4	79.8	58.2	27.9	22.3	22.1	24.4	24.7	26.2	32.5
Slovenia	161.6	165.6	201.4	167.8	118.3	126.1	126.7	118.9	118.4	114.5	113.7	123.8
Slovakia	37.2	38.1	37.3	36.9	42.4	35.2	40.8	52.9	60.2	65.0	67.8	77.3
Finland	101.9	111.7	108.2	113.8	108.7	111.0	111.8	110.8	110.5	111.6	105.0	104.2
Sweden	177.4	173.8	178.3	182.3	182.0	176.7	187.1	195.2	198.8	196.9	199.6	196.5
United Kingdom	154.0	192.3	217.8	229.4	249.5	235.0	239.0	214.1	220.8	212.2	211.3	218.0
Norway	:	:	:	:	:	:	187.7	178.0	155.0	162.4	160.7	155.2

:=Not available ; Source: Eurostat

3. Indicators for Air Pollution and Climate Change (source: EEA)

Total Greenhouse Gas Emissions (in CO_2 equivalent) indexed on actual base year = 100

	1996	1997	1998	1999	2000	2001	2002	2003	2004	2005	2006	2007
European Union (27 countries)	95.6	93.7	92.7	90.8	90.8	91.8	91.0	92.6	92.6	91.9	91.8	90.7
European Union (25 countries)	:	:	:	:	:	:	:	:	:	:	:	:
European Union (15 countries)	98.7	97.2	97.6	96.1	96.3	97.4	96.8	98.0	98.0	97.1	96.5	95.0
Euro area (EA11-2...	:	:	:	:	:	:	:	:	:	:	:	:
Euro area (15 cou...	:	:	:	:	:	:	:	:	:	:	:	:
Euro area (12 cou...	:	:	:	:	:	:	:	:	:	:	:	:
Belgium	105.5	99.6	103.5	99.1	99.6	99.4	98.1	100.0	99.9	97.4	93.7	90.1
Bulgaria	65.4	63.2	56.4	52.4	52.2	52.4	50.2	54.1	53.6	53.6	54.2	57.2
Czech Republic	82.3	78.8	74.6	72.4	75.8	76.9	74.7	75.1	75.7	75.3	76.8	77.6
Denmark	129.1	115.1	109.1	104.7	97.8	100.1	99.0	106.3	97.7	91.6	102.5	96.1
Germany (includin...	89.6	86.6	84.6	81.9	81.8	83.2	81.7	81.7	80.9	78.6	79.5	77.6
Estonia	51.1	50.0	46.1	42.9	43.1	43.6	42.4	46.6	47.7	46.1	45.0	51.7
Ireland	110.1	113.0	118.2	121.0	124.0	127.1	123.7	123.3	123.4	126.3	125.3	124.5
Greece	106.0	110.4	115.4	115.0	118.8	119.8	119.4	122.7	122.8	123.2	119.7	123.2
Spain	107.7	114.8	118.5	128.2	133.1	133.2	139.1	141.6	147.0	152.2	149.5	152.6
France	101.3	100.1	102.5	99.6	98.7	99.0	97.4	97.9	97.9	98.2	96.1	94.2
Italy	101.1	102.3	104.4	105.5	106.3	107.4	107.5	110.4	111.0	111.0	108.9	106.9
Cyprus	133.3	136.4	148.6	163.4	170.9	170.2	170.6	171.2	174.7	180.3	182.4	185.3
Latvia	48.7	46.5	44.5	41.4	39.0	41.5	41.5	42.1	42.2	43.3	45.0	46.6
Lithuania	46.8	45.7	47.5	42.0	38.8	40.9	41.7	42.2	43.7	45.7	46.3	50.1

continues overleaf

Indicators for Air Pollution and Climate Change (source: EEA) -cont.

	1996	1997	1998	1999	2000	2001	2002	2003	2004	2005	2006	2007
Luxembourg (Grand...	79.4	74.7	68.5	71.5	75.7	78.1	86.1	89.4	100.9	101.7	101.0	98.1
Hungary	71.0	69.3	69.1	69.3	67.6	69.1	67.6	70.4	69.2	69.7	68.3	65.8
Malta	126.7	127.2	128.1	132.6	126.9	132.6	134.9	142.5	141.1	144.2	145.3	149.0
Netherlands	109.2	106.0	106.7	101.0	100.7	101.3	101.1	101.7	102.4	99.6	97.9	97.4
Austria	105.7	105.2	104.4	102.4	102.6	107.6	110.1	117.8	116.1	117.4	115.8	111.3
Poland	80.7	79.7	73.4	71.1	69.0	68.3	65.9	68.1	68.2	68.6	70.9	70.8
Portugal	112.9	118.8	127.0	139.2	135.8	139.6	147.6	139.3	143.4	148.3	140.8	136.1
Romania	67.2	59.9	53.5	47.3	48.7	50.5	52.7	55.2	55.9	53.7	55.3	54.7
Slovenia	94.8	96.4	95.1	91.7	92.9	97.2	98.5	97.0	98.5	100.1	101.1	101.8
Slovakia	70.9	69.3	70.0	68.7	67.2	69.5	68.0	69.7	69.4	68.5	67.9	65.2
Finland	108.7	106.6	101.6	100.7	97.9	105.3	108.2	119.0	113.4	96.8	112.6	110.3
Sweden	107.0	100.6	101.1	96.5	94.5	95.3	96.4	97.3	96.6	93.1	92.7	90.7
United Kingdom	94.4	91.2	90.7	86.5	86.8	87.2	84.5	85.1	84.8	84.1	83.5	82.0
Croatia	74.8	79.2	79.6	83.2	82.7	86.6	89.7	95.4	95.1	97.0	98.1	103.2
Turkey	142.4	150.3	150.9	151.0	164.6	154.1	159.1	168.3	174.4	183.7	195.6	219.1
Iceland	96.7	101.4	104.9	111.7	110.8	109.9	110.6	109.6	111.1	109.7	125.8	134.9
Liechtenstein	103.7	109.1	114.1	113.9	111.0	110.8	113.0	117.5	117.8	118.0	119.0	106.1
Norway	106.2	106.1	106.3	108.4	107.5	110.0	107.4	108.8	110.3	108.2	107.8	110.9
Switzerland	98.0	96.5	98.9	99.3	97.8	99.4	97.5	99.4	100.4	101.7	100.7	97.1
United States	:	:	:	:	:	:	:	:	:	:	:	:
Japan	:	:	:	:	:	:	:	:	:	:	:	:

Special values:

- *not applicable or real zero or zero by default*
0 *less than half of the unit used*
: *not available*

4. Electricity generated from renewable sources - [tsien050]; *% of gross electricity consumption*

	1997	1998	1999	2000	2001	2002	2003	2004	2005	2006	2007	2010
European Union (27 countries)	13.1	13.4	13.4	13.8	14.4	12.9	12.9	13.9	14.0	14.6	15.6	21.0
European Union (25 countries)	12.8	13.1	13.1	13.7	14.2	12.7	12.7	13.7	13.6	14.3	15.5	21.0
European Union (15 countries)	13.8	14.0	14.0	14.6	15.2	13.5	13.7	14.7	14.5	15.3	16.6	22.0
Belgium	1.0	1.1	1.4	1.5	1.6	1.8	1.8	2.1	2.8	3.9	4.2	6.0
Bulgaria	7.0	8.1	7.7	7.4	4.7	6.0	7.8	8.9	11.8	11.2	7.5	11.0
Czech Republic	3.5	3.2	3.8	3.6	4.0	4.6	2.8	4.0	4.5	4.9	4.7	8.0
Denmark	8.9	11.7	13.3	16.7	17.3	19.9	23.2	27.1	28.3	26.0	29.0	29.0
Germany (including ex-GDR from 1991)	4.3	4.8	5.5	6.5	6.5	8.1	8.2	9.5	10.5	12.0	15.1	12.5
Estonia	0.1	0.2	0.2	0.3	0.2	0.5	0.6	0.7	1.1	1.4	1.5	5.1
Ireland	3.8	5.5	5.0	4.9	4.2	5.4	4.3	5.1	6.8	8.5	9.3	13.2
Greece	8.6	7.9	9.5	7.7	5.2	6.2	9.7	9.5	10.0	12.1	6.8	20.1
Spain	19.7	18.6	12.8	15.7	20.7	13.8	21.7	18.5	15.0	17.7	20.0	29.4
France	15.2	14.4	16.5	15.1	16.5	13.7	13.0	12.9	11.3	12.5	13.3	21.0
Italy	16.0	15.6	16.9	16.0	16.8	14.3	13.7	15.9	14.1	14.5	13.7	22.55
Cyprus	0.0	0.0	0.0	0.0	0.0	0.0	0.0	0.0	0.0	0.0	0.0	6.0
Latvia	46.7	68.2	45.5	47.7	46.1	39.3	35.4	47.1	48.4	37.7	36.4	49.3
Lithuania	2.6	3.6	3.8	3.4	3.0	3.2	2.8	3.5	3.9	3.6	4.6	7.0
Luxembourg (Grand-Duché)	2.0	2.5	2.5	2.9	1.6	2.8	2.3	3.2	3.2	3.4	3.7	5.7
Hungary	0.8	0.7	1.1	0.7	0.8	0.7	0.9	2.3	4.6	3.7	4.6	3.6
Malta	0.0	0.0	0.0	0.0	0.0	0.0	0.0	0.0	0.0	0.0	0.0	5.0
Netherlands	3.5	3.8	3.4	3.9	4.0	3.6	4.7	5.7	7.5	7.9	7.6	9.0
Austria	67.5	67.9	71.3	72.4	67.2	66.1	53.1	58.7	57.4	56.6	59.8	78.1
Poland	1.8	2.1	1.9	1.7	2.0	2.0	1.6	2.1	2.9	2.9	3.5	7.5
Portugal	38.3	36.0	20.5	29.4	34.2	20.8	36.4	24.4	16.0	29.4	30.1	39.0
Romania	30.5	35.0	36.7	28.8	28.4	30.8	24.3	29.9	35.8	31.4	26.9	33.0
Slovenia	26.9	29.2	31.6	31.7	30.5	25.4	22.0	29.1	24.2	24.4	22.1	33.6
Slovakia	14.5	15.5	16.3	16.9	17.9	19.2	12.4	14.4	16.7	16.6	16.6	31.0
Finland	25.3	27.4	26.3	28.5	25.7	23.7	21.8	28.3	26.9	24.0	26.0	31.5
Sweden	49.1	52.4	50.6	55.4	54.1	46.9	39.9	46.1	54.3	48.2	52.1	60.0
United Kingdom	1.9	2.4	2.7	2.7	2.5	2.9	2.8	3.7	4.3	4.6	5.1	10.0
Croatia	38.8	38.3	45.1	40.0	42.7	33.9	29.4	41.0	36.2	33.4	23.0	:
Turkey	38.1	37.3	29.5	24.3	19.1	25.6	25.2	30.9	24.7	25.5	19.2	:
Iceland	99.9	99.9	99.9	99.9	100.0	99.9	99.9	100.0	99.9	100.0	:	:
Norway	95.3	96.2	100.7	112.2	96.2	107.3	92.1	89.7	108.4	98.4	106.1	:
United States	:	:	:	:	:	:	:	:	:	:	:	:
Japan	:	:	:	:	:	:	:	:	:	:	:	:
Former Yugoslav Republic of Macedonia, the	:	:	:	:	:	:	:	:	:	:	:	:
Switzerland	:	:	:	:	:	:	:	:	:	:	:	:

:=Not available ; Source: Eurostat

For the sake of practice, only read this part after completing the exercise above

Scoring Guide

Please find below a sample top-level scoring guide we created for this case study exercise; it is similar to the one EPSO is likely to use.

Professional Knowledge Aspects

By way of example, we indicate for each criterion a 1-5 scale where 1 is the worst, 5 is the best; in reality, the weight of each criterion is different given the variations in their relative importance. An overall score from 1-5 would then be awarded based upon the spread of scores across all criteria.

- *Presentation of the main issues at stake (1-5)*
  - Did the candidate answer all aspects of the questions?
  - Did the candidate provide a comprehensive presentation of the political, legal, economic, financial, technical or scientific issues?
- *Overall knowledge of the specialist field (1-5)*
  - Did the candidate provide specific legal or technical references? (Research data, case-law, legislative instruments, historic facts, etc.)
  - Did the candidate demonstrate an in-depth understanding of the chosen field by providing examples, facts, names, data or other?
- *Considering the EU perspective and understanding the international context (1-5)*
  - Did the candidate consider the wider EU context of the issues? (Considering an overall EU approach instead of national or regional one; implications for various Member States and neighbouring countries, long-term effects of a policy or initiative etc.)
  - Did the candidate mention international examples, current events, place the information in a global context? (Linking current affairs to the facts of the file; mentioning international organisations' perspectives; diplomatic efforts, political events etc.)
- *Knowledge of and references to arguments not included in the dossiers (1-5)*
  - Did the candidate demonstrate a solid understanding of the specialist field? (Confident use of terminology, concepts, ideas; reference to renowned achievers in the field etc.)
  - Did the candidate refer to important facts, legislation, research or other information demonstrating their familiarity with the topic? (Mention of publications, public events, industry best practices and policies etc.)
- *Correct references to, conclusions from and interpretation of data (1-5)*
  - Did the candidate use their knowledge to interpret the charts, statistics, financial and economic data correctly?
  - Did the candidate demonstrate a thorough understanding of the cross-references and draw the right conclusions from them?

Competency Aspects

In this section, we have provided a range of indicators that assessors would be looking for against a couple of the behavioural competencies likely to be assessed by this exercise.

Competency Title: Communicating With Clarity

For this competency, the following would be indicators of a **positive response**:

- Writes clearly, precisely and fluently. Arguments remained consistent throughout. Response is well structured (e.g. sets out response under headings, includes summary at end)
- Uses the correct balance of detail and conciseness (e.g. paraphrases information in the brief rather than simply repeating it)
- Avoids jargon (or explains it if used)
- Communicates in a manner that captures the attention and interest of the audience (e.g. poses rhetorical questions, writes in a lively style)
- Can identify and convey the key points of an argument. Uses professional, relevant and high quality ideas to back up arguments (e.g. the key points are stressed in an introduction and then again in the conclusion)
- Tailors writing style so that it is appropriate to target audience (e.g. explains jargon, but not in a patronising manner; understands the priorities and perspective of the target audience and adapts the message accordingly)

The following would be indicators of a **poor response**:

- Writes unclearly, imprecisely or in a disjointed manner. Arguments were inconsistent at times. Response is poorly structured (e.g. response reads as a stream of consciousness, hard to follow. Recommendations contradict themselves at times)
- Is either overly detailed or overly brief in their communications (e.g. repeats large chunks of the background brief, or alternatively writes very little making it hard to follow what is being said)
- Uses jargon without explanation
- Communicates in a manner that is dull, flat or uninteresting to read (e.g. simply lists facts in bullet point form throughout)
- Fails to identify or convey the key points of an argument (e.g. writes as if all aspects equally important)
- Adopts a writing style that is inappropriate to the target audience (e.g. too informal or too brief)

Competency Title – Planning and Organising

For this competency, the following would be indicators of a **positive response**:

- Describes how they would conduct preparation in advance of implementing actions (e.g. who they would speak to, which stakeholders to consult, how they would identify the financial and human resources required)
- Prioritises tasks appropriately (e.g. distinguishes the important from the urgent)

- Sets realistic deadlines and milestones (e.g. not too far in the future, but not unrealistically short)
- Describes how progress would be monitored (e.g. through meetings, emails, project plans, milestones)
- Considers how they would respond to last minute changes (e.g. if resources become unavailable or cash-flow problems occur)
- Manages own workload effectively – i.e. completes a reasonable amount of work in the time available for the exercise (e.g. at least 5 written sides)

The following would be indicators of a **poor response**:

- Advocates proceeding to action immediately before any further research is conducted (e.g. fails to identify possible risks or issues that need to be resolved before starting work, does not read relevant parts of the background materials)
- Makes incorrect prioritisation judgements (e.g. focuses on relatively unimportant issues to a disproportionate degree in their response while ignoring important issues)
- Sets overly ambitious or overly lengthy deadlines and milestones
- Allows projects to proceed without outlining how they would be monitored (e.g. covers this at a very broad level, "we will keep an eye on things as they progress" or not at all).
- Has not allowed contingencies for changing circumstances
- Works inefficiently or becomes overwhelmed with workload (e.g. finishes early and produces a small amount of work; or runs out of time and produces an unfinished response)

Sample answers for the Public Administration Profile follow on pages 324-331.

Analysing and Problem Solving **EPSO definition - Identifies the critical facts in complex issues and develops creative and practical solutions.**			
Positive indicators	*Example*	*Negative indicators*	*Example*
Copes well with complexity. For example, shows evidence of fully understanding and dealing with all the issues in the brief. Noticed subtle messages in the information by looking across various sources.	"The EU's climate action programme includes a fine set of measures to tackle the 2°C global warming threshold, a 20% emission cut below 1990 levels, a fast-start financial assistance of 2.4 billion € to developing countries and to advance carbon markets. This has repercussions on the EU's framework budget (smart allocation of funds), its administrative capacities (recruiting climate experts, creating new units, focusing on research and communication), all the while having energy security and sourcing independence from Russia as the second goal in mind, apart from environmental considerations."	**Becomes confused by complexity**. For example does not deal with all the issues in the brief. Misunderstands some aspects. Misses some subtle messages in the information, makes generalised or superficial conclusions and uses clichés.	"The EU's climate action programme aims at preventing developing countries from reaching European levels of CO2 emissions. This affects many countries and European leaders must be aware of the repercussions of their actions. Biofuels are very important in creating a varied source of energy."
Makes correct calculations from data presented in charts (e.g. financial data, Eurostat data)	"If we look at the trend regarding the use of renewable sources for generating electricity, we see a growing trend (of almost 5 percentage points) in the EU's 27 Member States over the last few years, while the share of renewables in the energy consumption has also increased. This shows a positive trend in the European uptake of such sources."	**Makes incorrect calculations.**	"According to the European Environmental Agency, Spain, Cyprus and Malta were the most polluted countries in 2007 by having the highest amount of greenhouse gas emissions."
Challenges data put before them. For example, notices that a survey was only conducted in one nationality, or was done 5 years ago and recommends re-doing it. Notices where political biases may lie and uses this to question people's claims.	"It is to be noted that the 2009 European Council Presidency conclusions naturally had a different approach given its timing, that is, weeks before the Copenhagen conference which proved to be a partial success and was only concluded a year later in Cancún. Therefore the timing of the 5-7 billion EUR earmarked global financing had to be restructured in light of the protracted negotiations."	**Accepts all data at face value.** For example, opinions are treated as fact; data that is obviously old or biased in some way is simply accepted	"The European Commission has already managed to reduce the greenhouse gas emissions via a perfectly viable carbon trading scheme in the EU by 12% and will surely reach its goal of 20% reduction in the coming years."
Identifies the root cause of issues. For example, whilst the data presented may seem to be suggesting a quick and simple solution to a problem, further consideration reveals that more favourable alternatives are available.	"The fundamental motive of the EU's climate change policy, as also reinforced by the European Commission's press release, is to find a balanced solution between mitigating the effects of climate change while acknowledging the needs of the least developed countries in sharing the burden and creating a financially viable system of incentives and taxes in Europe."	**Operates at a surface level** – does not seek to identify root causes. For example, seems to have skim-read the data, only deals with most obvious presenting issues and does so in a simplistic manner, without considering alternatives, implications or risks	"The climate change priorities are focusing on reducing heatwaves, taxing polluters and making life easier for every side of the globe."

Analysing and Problem Solving

EPSO definition - Identifies the critical facts in complex issues and develops creative and practical solutions.

Positive indicators	*Example*	*Negative indicators*	*Example*
Considers multiple options for resolving issues. For example, one way that is simple and less risky; one that has never been tried before and is complex but perhaps has a bigger payoff. Considers pros and cons of each including both short term and long term.	"The EU's approach can be multifold by leveraging the EU budget in financing innovative carbon capture solutions, innovation in the field of renewable energy research, coordinating policy solutions on a global scale under the UNFCC, creating financial instruments such as public-private funding, carbon market and international financing to decrease emissions and divert energy use to renewable."	**Considers only one way to resolve issues.** For example, just one option presented, no evidence of considering pros and cons of alternatives. Considers only short or only long term impact.	"I believe the only possible solution for tackling climate change is taxing carbon emissions. I see no drawbacks to this. "
Suggests creative ideas. For example, something that is not even hinted at in the brief.	"I think that the approach regarding the least developed nations could be coupled with a micro-finance scheme where farmers and production workers, whose job would be most threatened by the closing of high-emission facilities, could be redirected to new fields of activity and encouraged to start their own ventures."	**Suggests standard, conventional ideas.** For example, suggests staying with the current way things are from the brief, or only uses ideas already hinted at in the brief.	"The new structures on behalf of the Commission could be created in-house, by allocating sufficient internal resources to managing climate change efforts. No new staff would need to be recruited."
Makes practical, workable suggestions. For example, in terms of time, cost, people, expertise, location, degree of change required, stakeholder reaction.	"Providing economic incentives by tax rebates to EU energy consumers can, within 10 years, lead to a 2 percentage point increase in renewable source uptake and achieve the EU's 30% ultimate reduction goal, along with an average 4% lower pollution compared to 2007 data."	**Suggestions are impractical** or unworkable. For example, an idea that would work 'in a perfect world' but fails to take into account the realities of the present-day situation.	"Reaching the 30% reduction goal can be easily achieved if every second person in the EU started using public transportation instead of cars."
Gathers relevant information to inform decision making. For example, not only considers all evidence in the brief that is relevant, but suggests what other data would be desirable and how this would be acquired.	"Based on the information regarding the implicit tax rate on energy and the total greenhouse gas emissions in the period 2005-2007, we can draw the conclusions that the Commission's approach is realistic. However, if we knew the amount of import in renewable sources from neighbouring non-EU countries, we could better assess the spill-over effects of the energy policy on our neighbourhood and trade policies."	**Fails to gather relevant information to inform decision making**. For example, either considers all information from the brief indiscriminately or specifically uses information that is irrelevant from the brief. Makes no attempt to describe what further information would be desirable.	"To decide whether the climate change policy is a unique one or if it should be considered as part of a larger context, it is enough to look at the UN's confirmation that developed countries will mobilise US$ 100 billion in climate funding for developing countries annually by 2020."

Communication **EPSO definition - Communicates clearly and precisely both orally and in writing**			
Positive indicators	*Example*	*Negative indicators*	*Example*
Writes clearly and fluently. For example, avoids or explains jargon to an appropriate level. Clear structure to the response. Produces a reasonable length of response for the time available. Gives sufficient supporting rationale for assertions.	"Europe's climate policy is well aware of the efforts made by the UNFCC (United Nations Framework Convention on Climate Change, the basic agreement, amended by the Kyoto protocol, on fighting climate change on a global level). The EU has equally considered the Least Developed Nations' (or LDPs') needs by planning to allocate significant funds to compensate for their efforts."	**Writes unclearly or inefficiently.** For example, uses jargon and technical terms with no explanations (n.b. some of this may be acceptable due to the technical knowledge element of the task). Repeats self. Unclear in the points they are trying to make. Structure is very loose or nonexistent. Response is either very verbose or very brief.	"I don't think that any EFTA country would agree to the concessions that the EU has made at the COP. Nobody likes being instructed. This doesn't work. Both the UN and the LDPs must see where their efforts are going and what the OECD members are thinking."
Uses the correct balance of detail and conciseness. For example, summarises the information in the background brief well, and when appropriate in order to support their arguments.	"The REDD+ mechanism is a new element in the system. It refers to a system that aims to fight deforestation and its effect on emissions. It operates under the UN's auspices and has a number of detailed initiatives that could be subject to another discussion paper."	**Is either overly detailed or overly brief in their communications.** For example, simply repeats information from the brief verbatim (or omits any reference to background information at all)	"As the European Commission's press release, issued after the Cancún agreement, says, the agreement builds on the decisions taken a year earlier in Copenhagen and also sets out processes for making further progress in the future. It represents a well balanced compromise between different interests within the United Nations system."
Communicates in a manner that captures the attention and interest of the audience. For example, uses anecdotes, metaphors, differing sentence lengths, bullet points, passionate language.	"The Cancún Agreement in advancing the EU's climate change efforts are similar to the Treaty of Nice that opened the way for the EU's most significant enlargement towards central and eastern Europe: it did not make it happen but it sure laid the legal foundations for it to happen."	**Communicates in a manner that fails to capture the attention and interest of the audience.** For example, uses a very dry style with little passion on display. Long passages of unbroken text.	"The carbon market has been a tool in leveraging the will of private sector entities in reducing their emissions without having negative repercussions on their business productivity; it also created a method that could be used elsewhere in the world, though the financial crisis lessened their economic attractiveness."

Communication **EPSO definition - Communicates clearly and precisely both orally and in writing**			
Positive indicators	*Example*	*Negative indicators*	*Example*
Can identify and convey the key points of an argument. For example, perhaps uses headings or bullets to convey this. Presents a convincing case.	"The following key concepts need to be considered when discussing the EU's climate change efforts: • IPCC • CDM • AAU • EU ETS These abbreviated terms (definitions to follow) are regularly referred to in all documents relating to the issue."	**Fails to identify or convey the key points of an argument.** For example, simply gives a recommendation with no attempt to persuade. Alternatively, attempts to persuade are based upon a poor premise.	"The EU 2020 strategy should have a stronger focus on energy independence and on establishing public administration governance structures that are capable of achieving this goal."
Uses English (or other chosen language) **to a suitable level of proficiency.**	"Some European governments seemed to be having second thoughts after signing the Cancún Agreement; they were nevertheless bound by their obligation to meet the jointly agreed and in fact ambitious goals."	**Uses English** (or other chosen language) **poorly,** many elementary mistakes in grammar, punctuation, spelling and word usage.	"The Cancún Agreement was a good thing. Members state was hesitants to execute them, so they wanted more change to be done later. This was no successful."

Delivering Quality and Results **EPSO definition - Takes personal responsibility and initiative for delivering work to a high standard of quality within set procedures**			
Positive indicators	*Example*	*Negative indicators*	*Example*
Takes responsibility for meeting objectives. For example, makes a lot of 'I' statements – 'I will speak to X' or 'I would ensure that Y was considered'. This requires the scenario to be set up correctly. Also, answers the question posed.	"If it was my task to create an organisational strategy for the EU institutions to tackle climate change policies efficiently, I would start by screening existing structures and their relevance to delivering results. I would request input within three months from the European Environmental Agency as they are well placed for expert input."	**Allows objectives to be missed due to failing to take responsibility.** For example, assumes no responsibility for tasks, simply makes recommendations for others. Also, answers a question different to that which was posed.	"The various European Commission directorates need to provide ideas on creating an efficient carbon market for the post-2020 period. They should all come up with good hints that would be then merged into a concept document."
Maintains quality standards to at least an acceptable level. For example, in the drive to, say, save costs – finds ways to maintain the quality of what is being delivered	"Administrative structures should be cost-efficient and future-proof. This means in practice that existing staff should be re-allocated to new units so their institutional memory is kept. While costs must be kept in a budget-neutral manner, staff training is a key element in ensuring the project's success."	**Allows quality standards to slip** to an unacceptable level. For example, in a drive to broaden a committee's remit, schedules too much into their responsibilities to allow them to perform all tasks to a good level.	"I would suggest creating an inter-institutional committee on EU level that would be the ultimate decision-maker in all issues related to climate financing. This committee would not be allowed to delegate any of its powers so that it can always stay on top things. Budget cannot be an issue here."
Follows established guidelines and procedures where appropriate. For example, quotes relevant legislation or conventions quoted in the background brief and from their own knowledge.	"The re-structuring of the HR systems must duly follow the procedures established by the Staff Regulations and include staff consultations, trade union meetings, endorsement by the staff committee and the European Parliament's budgetary scrutiny. Stakeholder buy-in and the legality of the new structure cannot be ensured by any other manner."	**Breaks with established guidelines and procedures in an inappropriate manner**. For example, suggests breaking with established procedure without considering the wider consequences. Recommendations are illegal or do not follow EU recommendations.	"A novel and speedy way of creating the strategic HR system is circumventing the existing procedures and setting up an entirely new entity. Though this may be less welcome by the European Parliament, climate change requires urgent action that cannot be hamstrung by the slowness of internal procedures."
Acts without waiting to be told: takes the initiative. For example, makes decisions on important issues (appropriately) that will ensure a problem does not escalate due to inaction or bureaucracy.	"The measures to be taken need the approval of my hierarchy. However, should this be an unexpectedly long process, I would take the liberty to proceed with certain measures that are not controversial and do not require a formal signature."	**Fails to act before receiving instructions**: misses opportunities to take the initiative. For example, fails to take a firm decision, defers to the assessor or their manager, or some other body.	"Strategic human resources cannot be decided by anyone else but the given institution's top officials. They need to know how to proceed, and they should delegate certain tasks to their subordinates if that seems to be the right action. I cannot do more on my level."

Delivering Quality and Results (continued) **EPSO definition - Takes personal responsibility and initiative for delivering work to a high standard of quality within set procedures**			
Positive indicators	*Example*	*Negative indicators*	*Example*
Thrives in challenging situations. For example, speaks with enthusiasm about how the present issue can be resolved. Completes all work in the time available.	"Finding alternative energy sources should be seen as a quest for gold: we know it is out there, and we will find it soon. It must not be viewed through one angle: new types of energy sources from new countries should be sought, and the discovery of novel processing methods is also the way forward. The current situation can and should be challenged."	**Avoids, or becomes demotivated by challenging situations.** For example, sounds defeatist: 'we've tried this before and it did not work', pessimistic about the chances of success. Fails to complete the task.	"If Central Asian countries are unwilling to enter into negotiations with the EU about providing natural resources for export, we cannot do much more to convince them. This seems to be an uphill struggle that has little hope of success."
Seeks to continually exceed expectations. For example, describes what they would do above and beyond the objective set for the in the case study brief, or what would be expected of them from stakeholders.	"Apart from the ideas listed above, I would suggest further measures to provide a stronger European performance in tackling climate change. As shown by various Eurobarometer polls, wider communications campaign can lead to citizen support, while education initiatives for elementary school students can enhance long-term awareness among the next generation of energy users."	**Does the bare minimum of work to be considered acceptable.** For example, gives a very brief, simplistic answer to the problem posed in the case study. No evidence of seeking to impress / delight stakeholders.	"One measure seems enough to reach the emission reduction goals. Cutting carbon quotas for companies must be an efficient tool and I am positive it will bring the desired results."

Prioritising and Organising **EPSO definition - Prioritises the most important tasks, works flexibly and organises own workload efficiently**			
Positive indicators	*Example*	*Negative indicators*	*Example*
Prioritises tasks appropriately. For example, there will be more and less important items in the case study file: candidate spends more time and effort dealing with the more important tasks than the less important ones.	"It seems that before creating any strategic organigrams for the new administrative structures, the final form of climate change efforts needs to be consolidated so the human resources will reflect the needs and not vice versa. My analysis therefore begins with a brief introduction to the final form of climate change efforts."	**Makes incorrect prioritisation judgements**. For example, spends too long discussing issues that are peripheral to the main point at hand. Appears to deal with items in the order they are presented in the brief rather than prioritising them.	"I have decided to answer each question in the presented order. As the issue of energy diversification seemed very important, I have spelled it out in greater detail."
Sets realistic deadlines and milestones. For example, considers all possible impacts on a project when setting deadlines such as unforeseen crises, availability of stakeholders, technology issues, illness etc	"When thinking about the HR strategy for the next decade regarding climate change priorities, I would adopt a step-by-step approach. This needs to consider the EU institutional system, as well as the summer recess and elections of the European Parliament, the European Commission's internal decision-making deadlines and other administrative arrangements with the local government of Brussels."	**Fails to set realistic deadlines and milestones**. For example, naively sets very short turnaround times for task completion which show a lack of consideration of possible delays	"I am confident that any strategic HR issue can be dealt with in a six-month period, even if there are delays or difficulties."
Monitors progress. For example, describes how and when the success of the implementation of their ideas would be reviewed. Expect this to be on a periodic basis during the implementation, not just at the end.	"When it comes to European actions to implement the Cancún Agreement, we need to build in certain evaluations of the state of play, possibly every three years. Apart from these mid-term reviews, a six-monthly stocktaking exercise should also be foreseen."	**Allows projects to continue without monitoring**. For example, makes no reference to project review meetings or any other method for reviewing how well their recommendations are being delivered.	"Once the implementation of the Cancún Agreement starts, it will be the responsibility of the EU institutions and Member States alike to execute what they signed up for. Hopefully no major disappointment will happen in 2020 before the final deadline is reached."
Adapts to changes in plans effectively. For example, describes what they have in mind as a contingency if certain events arise.	"Should any of the above actions become unfeasible or impossible to be put in action, an ad hoc emergency meeting is foreseen that can be conveyed within a week."	**Becomes flustered and ineffective** when plans need to change. For example, makes no reference to contingency planning.	"Should this not be possible, unfortunately there is little that can be done to remedy the situation."
Conducts preparation in advance. For example, schedules in plan, do, review time.	If the recruitment of new staff is needed, this requires an in-depth analysis of the tasks and profiles we are seeking to fill in. Climate change experts can come from a broad range of fields, therefore proper planning and execution is crucial. Should we fail to identify a sufficient number of candidates within 6 months, existing staff should be trained to fit new roles.	**Fails to prepare in advance.** For example, simply makes statements like 'I will do X and then the next day I will go to Y' with no time built in (or reference made) to planning.	I would announce the recruitment of global warming experts, along with diplomats who have experience in international negotiations. Once the human resources are in place, we can start allocating them to their new roles.

Applying Knowledge in the Field			
Positive indicators	***Example***	***Negative indicators***	***Example***
Evidences a **sound understanding** of the basic principles of their chosen specialism area. Refers to the **latest developments** in their field of specialism; shows **breadth and depth of knowledge**	"It is essential to see the underlying events that have led to the Cancún Agreement as follows (...)"	Response reveals **fundamental gaps** in knowledge of specialist area, or an actual misunderstanding of some basic principles. References are all **out of date** or just do not reflect the latest thinking; shows a **narrow** range of knowledge; shows a **superficial**, surface level of knowledge.	"Global warming has nothing to do with biofuels as the first one belongs to the environmental domain while the latter is clearly an energy issue. Moreover, using 1990 as a benchmark of reduction is not suitable for biofuels as they were not used back then."
References their knowledge sources in some way.	"As Eurostat's 2002 figures show, (...)"; "The UN has also confirmed in its press statements issued after the 2009 Copenhagen and 2010 Cancún Agreements that the potential benefits can reach 4.5% higher gains than (...)"	**Makes no references** to add credence to their recommendations.	"The UN said it supports these measures (...)"; "It is known that CO2 emissions have decreased over the years (...)"
Demonstrates awareness of relevant legislation	"The EU has been operating on the basis of the 2009/29/EC directive, also known as the ETS (or Emission Trading System) directive."	Response shows **lack of awareness of relevant legislation**	"The EU has no formal legal measure in place to regulate the emission trading, though various declarations have been made on this issue."

4. EPSO Assessment Exercise: The Oral Presentation

Presentation exercises are designed to measure your ability to organise and structure information, to communicate clearly and concisely and to remain resilient under questioning. At the EPSO Assessment Centre, you will be asked to present on a topic in front of your fellow candidates and the assessors. It is therefore similar to a public speaking exercise that you may be required to do once recruited, to showcase to your colleagues a certain file you have been working on.

How to Prepare

As you will not know the topic of the case study (and therefore, the presentation) in advance, it is difficult to prepare from a content perspective, except by following the same preparation as advised for the case study and the general tips for preparation. You can, however, consider your personal presenting style in advance by asking others for feedback on the strengths and weaknesses of your communication style and how you tend to present information.

Practising giving presentations can be unappealing for some people, but it is definitely worth considering it. Try to find opportunities to do so in advance of the Assessment Centre in order to reduce any tension or fear: even if you just present on a familiar topic to supportive friends or family members, it can still be extremely useful. You may also wish to have yourself recorded on video and then analyse your body language, voice strength and pace of speech, content vocabulary and other factors that assessors will be looking at. You ideally wish to get to the stage that:

- You are comfortable speaking from memory with only the need for brief prompts or bullet points on index cards.
- You can ensure a presentation you give runs to a set time.
- You feel comfortable projecting your voice and speaking at a measured pace.
- Through feedback, you are aware of any distracting habits you may have, such as fiddling with your hair or repeating a particular phrase or expression (e.g. "yeah", "uhm" or "you know": these are much more common than most people imagine, it's just that speakers hardly ever notice these themselves). You should aim at least to get to the stage where you become consciously aware when they are happening and can take steps to stop them.

If you are able to, try to anticipate the type of questions you might get from your audience and think about how you will respond to these. For example, if there are any particular hot topics for your area of expertise at the moment that might arise, what are your personal views on them and how would you back these views up with facts?

Tips for the Assessment Itself

- **Stay Calm**: If you feel nervous on the day before giving your presentation, practise deep breathing and rehearse your opening sentences. If you are very nervous, standing behind a lectern or table may help you to feel less vulnerable, as well as giving you something to lean on and somewhere to place your notes. If a lectern or table is not available, then take in some of the background papers to hold in order to keep your hands still. Alternatively, you may wish to hold a pen in your hand that can take help you control your hand movements or form a "barrier" in front of your body if held by both hands; though this is not particularly advisable from a body language point of view, it can help you subconsciously feel less exposed.
- **No Need to Rush**: Do not start until you are ready. If you're nervous, your body will scream at you to begin and get it over with. What then tends to happen is that you start when neither you nor the audience is ready. Take your time. Before you say anything, pause, take a couple of calm, deep breaths and look around the audience. When they are settled and ready, you can begin.
- **Structure**: There is an old expression that goes: "say what you are going to say, say it, then say what you just said". In other words, give your presentation a beginning, middle and an end in a consciously structured manner. A good structure will make you feel secure and is helpful to the audience too: they will know where they are and what's to come. This also refers to the outline you prepare for yourself: some key concepts, bullet points and reminders are sufficient to help you keep the flow.
- **Opening Styles**: You can choose various opening styles for the start of your presentation as follows:
  - You might start with a surprising fact: "Did you know that 3 out of 10 EU citizens do not believe in climate change?"
  - You might start with a personal element: "When I was a teenager, I always dreamed about becoming a lawyer. Now that I have become one, I am very excited to analyse the latest case law in this field."
  - You might refer to an event: "When President Barroso announced the Commission proposals to tackle the financial crisis, he suggested that..."
  - You might recall a story: "Two months ago one early morning, three people gathered in a meeting room of the European Parliament to discuss something crucial for the EU's future. These three were..."
  - You can be factual: "In 2005 when the Constitutional Treaty was rejected in two EU Member States, nobody thought it could be revived again."
  - You might develop your opening based on a mixture of the above.
- **Plan Your Time**: Assuming you have ten minutes in total, you would spend the first minute outlining what you will be discussing. The main content section will take a further eight minutes: enough for six to eight main points. The end should be a summary conclusion of what you have covered. Invite questions from the audience and when that's finished, thank them for their attention.
- **Cut, Cut, Cut**: Be ruthless with the content. Inevitably, preparing a presentation will involve you assembling too much information from your background research. Remember what it feels like to listen to a speaker. Too much information and you begin to switch off. Prune your talk to the essentials. You might want to break it into

no more than three memorable points you want your audience to take away with them. If you have too much information it's also much harder to keep to time.

- **Be Specific**: It is crucial to add concrete examples to support each of your points. When talking about e.g. the EU's performance audit efforts, make sure to provide specific projects you are familiar with or ones that you learned from the dossier; or when discussing the EU's plans to cut CO_2 emissions from cars, you can mention specific emission figures, thresholds, or a simple but powerful example of "if you have an X car, its emissions will be regulated as follows, therefore when doing your shopping next weekend, think of the added value this policy has triggered". This will help your audience visualise your words and remember them much better.
- **Flash Cards**: If you feel you have the time, try writing your notes on numbered pieces of paper torn into card-shapes. You can then move each card to the bottom of the pile when you have used it, and will always keep your place.
- **Body Language**: Even if you do not feel confident, try to look as if you are by keeping your shoulders down, by not speaking too quickly, by looking up as much as you can (even if you are reading from notes) at every member of the panel and by smiling occasionally. Less experienced presenters have a tendency to speed up as they talk especially as the end of their allotted time approaches: try to speak clearly and at a measured pace. If you feel yourself start to rush, pause and get yourself back on track.
- **When in the Spotlight**: Think about whether you will move during your presentation and if so, how you will do it. Keep hand gestures smooth, and do not block any visual aids (if used): a common mistake is to stand in between your presentation (if projected) and the video device.
- **Guiding Purpose**: If you are asked to make a recommendation or give a view, make this the starting point of your presentation, and then present your reasoning and analysis. For example, if you are asked to give your views on whether or not setting up a new EU Patent Court is a good idea, you can start by a strong (but always diplomatic) argument for or against and build your entire presentation on supporting this position. However, always make sure not to be personal or give views that may be hurtful to anyone's personal or professional feelings (by the latter I mean saying things like "unit X or institution Y is useless as they only slow down the policy making").
- **Your Tone**: Try to vary the tone of your voice so that you do not speak in a monotonous way. This can be done by carefully inserted "pauses" in your speech that will certainly attract attention if done right; you may also vary the pitch or tone of your voice to further enhance the audience's attention.
- **Outline**: Give an introductory outline of your presentation, and make sure you keep to this. Avoid introducing a completely new subject without warning halfway through, or changing the tone of your presentation for no clear reason.
- **Verbal Connections**: Use links to lead logically from one section to the next: e.g. "while we are on the subject of…"; "in view of…"; "as for…"; "before moving on to…"; "in spite of…"
- **Adapt Style**: Make sure the presentation is delivered in an appropriate style for the target audience: depending on whether the assessors are experts in your field, you must adapt your vocabulary, examples, expressions and facts accordingly. (It may have a detrimental effect on your evaluation if for example you are asked to present a communication strategy for the introduction of the euro in a Member State and you use expressions such as "convergence criteria" to a non-expert audience.) Keep things sharp, succinct and to the point. Do not over elaborate, or waffle for the sake of using

up time or showing off knowledge for its own sake. Also, it is important to be articulate, and not to use slang (such as "the new regulation was viewed as a really cool one by the industry"). Throughout your presentation you must be professional.

- **Concreteness**: Provide specific examples from the background brief or from your outside knowledge. These give the audience something to think about and an interesting source for the later question-and-answer session.
- **Easy Style**: You may wish to include some light humour, but always ensure that it is appropriate to the presentation subject and to the audience. Needless to say, it is completely inappropriate to make cynical comments or voice stereotypes about an EU Member State, race, religion or other sensitive matters.
- **Delivery**: Aim for a conversational delivery, using brief notes or bullet points, rather than memorising and reciting, or reading from a prepared sheet. Try to establish eye contact with everyone around you and aim to read their body language to gain reinforcement or feedback.
- **What You Think**: Do not be afraid to express your opinions. When you are expressing opinion rather than stating facts, remember to make this clear by using expressions such as "I believe that"; "in my opinion"; "to my mind". You can show how strong your beliefs are by slightly amending some of these expressions, "I firmly believe that"; "I strongly believe that"; "We are absolutely certain that"; "We are pretty sure that".
- **Stay on Track**: Make sure that you only cover topics in your presentation that you know and understand at least fairly well. Do not choose to introduce a subject you are less familiar with because you think it will be more impressive: you may well run into difficulties when questioned in more detail following the presentation. It is better to present confidently on topics about which you feel comfortable.
- **Pauses**: Pause slightly between points to show the audience when you are about to move on to a different subject. Allow pauses for audience reaction or possibly, questions. Pauses are also an extremely useful tool to gain the audience's attention: if used wisely, a pause of a few seconds will allow everyone to catch up and focus their attention on you again.
- **Corrections**: Do not be put off if you make a mistake during the presentation (e.g. you realise you mixed up the date a Treaty was signed). Apologise quickly and move on.
- **Interactivity**: Consider some aspect of audience participation. Some degree of interaction tends to make a presentation more interesting, although be aware that some assessors will prefer to leave questions or comments until the end of your presentation and they may be reluctant to act as a "normal" audience that could be drawn into the presentation.
- **Repeat**: At the end of your presentation, rephrase the original question (or title of your presentation) and answer it with your conclusion. Thank your audience, smile and offer a chance for questions to be asked.
- **Stay on Time**: Keeping track of time is important during your presentation. Giving a short presentation looks like a candidate is under-prepared. Giving a long presentation runs the risk of boring or agitating your assessors (or being cut short).
- **Visual Aids**: Use the visual aids effectively. You may be allowed to use a flipchart to support your presentation. There are certain things to bear in mind when using visual aids:
- – **Illustrate**: They must be visual; do not put too much written information on a flipchart. A clear heading and a couple of bullet points is plenty. Try to use

simple diagrams, charts or graphs to illustrate your points. Keep the style straightforward and professional.

- – **Support**: They must be a support and not a crutch; only use visual aids to clarify what you are saying. You want the audience to concentrate on you and not on the visuals.
- – **Talk Ahead**: Do not talk to visual aids; when you feel nervous, it is very easy to do this with the result that you turn your back to the audience. Always talk to the audience and not to the flipchart.
- – **Less is More**: Keep the number of flipchart sheets to a minimum with no more than a few concise bullet points to each one.
- – **Easy to See**: Ensure that you use bold colours that will easily be seen even from far and write clearly in a large font (e.g. not yellow, light blue etc) This small piece of advice can have an important effect on the success of your presentation.
- **Stay Professional**: Remain calm under questioning and do not become defensive or nervous even if your views are challenged. The assessors are testing to see how you react under pressure so try to remain calm and relaxed in your responses.
- **Ask Back**: Do not be afraid to ask the assessor to clarify questions if you do not understand them. If you genuinely cannot respond to a difficult question, thank the assessor for raising the point, acknowledge its relevance, and concede this is not something you can offer an opinion on at the present time, but suggest that this is something you would be prepared to follow up later.

Sample Presentation Exercise

In the following section, we discuss how the presentation exercise would run at an EPSO Assessment Centre. No, or little, extra background information will be provided. The key objective is to present a particular issue covered in your background brief in a concise, clear and engaging manner and then to answer a series of questions (some deliberately quite challenging) from an observer.

Here, we have briefly outlined how the presentation brief may be presented, before going on to outline how the questions may be phrased. Following this, we provide sample scoring criteria for a couple of the competencies likely to be measured by this exercise.

Candidate Brief

We would now like you to spend 20 minutes preparing to present your views relating to one of the questions posed. You can choose which of the three questions to focus your presentation around.

You will have up to 15 minutes to make the presentation itself, followed by up to a further 15 minutes of questioning. Flipchart paper can be used but not PowerPoint.

Please note that you will be presenting to your direct supervisor, who is interested to hear your views and will provide robust questioning to ensure the issues are fully understood.

Presentation – Likely Questions

The types of questions you will face by the assessor following your presentation are likely to be split into two types. Firstly, there will be more general ones seeking more information about your approach and challenging you to see how you perform under pressure. The second type will be more specialised in nature and will focus upon testing your knowledge of the subject area in more depth. Independent of your selected profile, it is advisable to carefully consider the answers to these probing questions and do some research on the issues, institutions and procedures raised therein.

Some of the general questions and challenges you can expect to face are as follows (some of these will depend upon whether or not you have included them already in your presentation):

General and Probing Questions

- Have you considered the impact of [a topic not covered in your presentation – e.g. broader economic picture, staffing issues, lack of resources, potential repercussions on other EU policies]?
- What alternative options did you consider? Why did you discard them?
- I am not convinced that [specific recommendation you made] is the right way to proceed. Have you considered [alternative option] instead?
- Why do we need to act at all? What is the problem with allowing things to continue as they are?
- Talk me through the [financial, people, resource] implications of your proposal in more detail.
- I am not sure how popular this will be with other stakeholders [e.g. staff, the public, NGOs]. What arguments can you propose that would help me to persuade them that this is a good idea?
- What are the longer-term implications of your proposals?
- What concerns do you have over the long-term viability of your proposals?
- How might your proposal affect EU activities in other areas?
- What other information would you have liked to help reach your decision? Why?
- What was the most important factor in making your decision, as far as you are concerned?
- How would you communicate your proposals both internally and externally?
- What do you see as your role in this project going forward?
- What external knowledge or expertise would we need to bring in?
- What do you see as the biggest risk in your plan? How do you propose that we manage it?
- What contingencies do you think are needed?

EU and Specialist Questions

- Would your proposal respect the subsidiarity principle?
- Are you sure it is the EU that needs to act and not the Member States themselves?

- How does your proposal affect our goals of economic and environmental sustainability?
- Do you think an impact assessment would be necessary for this proposal? Why?
- Do you know what the G20 or UN position is on this issue?
- How would the European Parliament approach this matter? Would that be different from the Commission's perspective?
- The budgetary implications may raise concerns at the European Court of Auditors. How would you address these?
- How can these initiatives get approved faster in the EU decision-making procedures?
- Would these issues be regulated under the comitology procedures? Why?
- What is the European Council President's and the rotating Presidency's role in this field?
- If your proposal is challenged on legal or procedural grounds, to whom can you turn for legal opinion and in case of need, legal remedy?
- If the proposed budget proves to be insufficient, how can the EU budget be amended?
- Should a Member State fail to enact this policy, what measures can be taken to enforce compliance?
- This approach may not be in line with the Financial Regulations. What do you think?
- What role does the Economic and Social Committee have in this issue?
- Where does this policy fit in the European Commission's legislative and work programme?

Scoring Guide

The following section outlines some examples of what good and poor behaviour might look like for a couple of the competencies likely to be assessed in an exercise like this.

Competency Area: Coping Under Pressure

This competency area is concerned with how a candidate responds to pressure at work. It includes the extent to which they display their feelings and their general levels of optimism. It also measures how well they respond to changing circumstances.

For this competency, the following would be indicators of a **positive response**:

- Remains calm under pressure. Keeps negative emotions under control even when challenging questions are put (e.g. remains composed throughout, speaks evenly and body language is under control)
- Maintains an optimistic, positive outlook (e.g. talks with enthusiasm about the challenges ahead; tone of voice and body language are in line with the positive mood of what is being said)
- Reacts positively to change (e.g. sees the opportunities in a change situation; proposes change on own initiative; understands the value in a new proposal)
- Responds confidently and non-defensively to criticism (e.g. thanks the assessor for their question and responds in a positive, energised way; turns challenging questions into an opportunity to dispel doubt)

- Tolerates ambiguity in work content or organisational situation (e.g. prepared to make decisions on the basis of limited information)

The following would be indicators of a **poor response**:

- Becomes stressed under pressure. Displays negative emotions inappropriately (e.g. goes red, fiddles with pen or papers while presenting, has difficulty finding the right words)
- Maintains a negative, pessimistic outlook (e.g. is cynical about the likely success of their proposed solution; words and tone express doubt or lack of true commitment)
- Reacts negatively to change (e.g. proposes keeping things the way they are currently and expresses doubt about the consequences of change)
- Responds defensively to criticism (e.g. becomes defensive when challenged in the questioning phase, raises voice in frustration, questions assessor's credentials).
- Intolerant of ambiguity in work content or organisational situation (e.g. requests much more information before willing to make a firm decision)

Competency Area: Communicating With Clarity

This competency area is concerned with how effectively a candidate communicates facts and opinions to others. It includes both oral and written communication. Effective communication is measured not just by clarity and accuracy, but also by successfully gaining the interest and attention of the audience and by adapting to suit their needs.

For this competency, the following would be indicators of a **positive response**:

- Speaks clearly and fluently (e.g. pronounces words clearly and speaks in a fluent manner)
- Uses the correct balance of detail and conciseness (e.g. does not go into the same amount of detail as the written response; yet still uses the full time available for the presentation)
- Avoids jargon (or explains it if uses)
- Communicates in a manner that captures the attention and interest of the audience (e.g. uses personal anecdotes and facts; raising and lowering of pitch and pace; uses moderate humour)
- Can identify and convey the key points of an argument (e.g. structures presentation around these or makes them clear in some way; uses repetition)
- Picks up from audience cues and changes style to suit (e.g. notices if the assessor is taking notes and slows down or becomes more serious in response to serious questions)

The following would be indicators of a **poor response**:

- Speaks unclearly and hesitantly (e.g. pauses frequently during presentation to check notes, becomes tongue-tied over certain words and phrases)
- Is either overly detailed or overly brief in their communications (e.g. includes lots of small details that mean the presentation overruns or time is not used effectively. Alternatively, finishes the presentation very early and misses the opportunity to give more information as a result)
- Uses jargon without explanation

- Communicates in a manner that fails to capture the attention and interest of the audience (e.g. speaks in a monotone; uses only basic facts with no attempt to embellish)
- Fails to identify or convey the key points of an argument (e.g. assessor is unclear on the rationale behind a proposed course of action by the end of the presentation)
- Fails to pick up on audience cues or change style to suit (e.g. makes jokes at inappropriate points such as when the assessor is expressing scepticism; speaks very fast throughout when assessor is looking confused or flustered trying to keep up)

5. EPSO Assessment Exercise: The Structured Interview

Description and Purpose

The interview must surely be the most widely-used selection tool. Its use is based on the idea that past behaviour is a good indicator of future performance. Most organisations now include at least one interview at the Assessment Centre, even when there has been a previous interview stage.

Interviews come in a variety of formats and can be one-to-one or panel, formal or informal, general or technical, competence-based or biographically-based, structured or more open and flexible. The interview is generally classed by assessors as a "secondary" source of evidence. This means that it carries less weight in the overall decision as performance is based upon the candidate's own self-report (rather than directly observed behaviours). This also means that it is the easiest exercise to perform well in, so this really is your best opportunity to shine.

The interview format used by EPSO is described as a "competency-based structured interview". It contains questions related to three to four of the competencies that are relevant to the role being recruited for. EPSO states that a structured interview is used as part of the recruitment process for all EU institution roles including Administrators, Specialists and Linguists alike, and most likely for Head of Unit tests as well.

It is also indicated that they are planning to link the interview to the outcome of the earlier situational judgement test (SJT) (where one has been included in the pre-selection stage; see more information on these tests in Part II). What I infer from this is that in these cases the interviewer will focus especially upon those competencies that a candidate performed less well on during the SJT, by asking more questions or probing the candidate's responses to a greater depth. This will help the assessor to ascertain whether this is a real development need for the candidate, or whether there is sufficient evidence from the interview to allay any concerns.

The fact that the interview is "structured" means that it will follow a consistent format across all candidates. This is in contrast to a more fluid, unstructured exploration of a candidate's CV that other organisations use. Research suggests that taking a structured approach offers the best chance to predict future behaviour. In practice, this means that everyone will receive the same instructions; the interviews will be the same length and will usually focus on the same competency areas (and thus cover the same questions).

The interviewer will ask you to talk about example situations where you have demonstrated the relevant competencies. For example, a question for a generic "Teamwork" competency may be as follows:

- *"Tell me about a time when you had to deal with conflict within a team you were part of"*

The interviewer is then likely to ask follow-up probing questions in order to explore your responses more fully. The exact probes asked will vary depending upon your answer to the starter question. For example:

- *"Tell me about a time when you had to deal with conflict within a team you were part of"*

– *"What caused the conflict?"*
– *"What did you do?"*
– *"What was the outcome?"*
– *"With hindsight, what would you do differently?"*

How to Prepare

Consider the types of questions you may be asked based upon the previously outlined EPSO competencies and have a think about relevant situations you can draw upon from education, work and leisure activities. A helpful way to do this may be to ensure that you have a good, detailed example to fill each of the four quadrants below. This is a completed example, but you are strongly advised to create your own.

EXPERIENCE TYPE		EXPERIENCE FOCUS	
		PEOPLE	**TASK**
	POSITIVE	*E.g.* • *Working successfully with team on final year project* • *(EPSO competencies – Working With Others, Analysis and Problem Solving, Prioritising and Organising)*	*E.g.* • *Project managing end of year university ball* • *(EPSO competencies – Prioritising and Organising, Delivering Quality and Results, Resilience)*
	NEGATIVE	*E.g.* • *Relationship troubles with other charity workers.* • *(EPSO competencies – Communicating, Working With Others)*	*E.g.* • *Data analysis for end of year project – not knowing the correct statistical techniques.* • *(EPSO competencies – Learning and Development, Resilience)*

Consider Your Experiences: First, consider and write down your key achievements and general life experiences in a structured manner. Which of those were task focused and which were people focused? By task focused, I mean those experiences that were primarily related to resolving a problem or issue or delivering a result (such as launching a marketing campaign or compiling a risk analysis) that involved minimal contact with others. By people focused, I mean those experiences that had a large component of interactions with others such as a joint drafting exercise, a team meeting that you coordinated etc.

Find Positive and Negative Examples: Then, try to consider experiences of both a positive and a less positive nature or outcome (and how you learned and grew from the negative experience). This is valuable in case you are asked to describe a time when things did not go so well (e.g. "please tell me about a mistake you made at your current workplace and describe how you reacted to it"), and avoids you becoming flustered or put off by the question. For these types of questions, you need to ensure that you can talk about how you either overcame the negative experience on that occasion, or have done so in subsequent similar situations.

Link with Competencies: Next, make a note against each example, indicating which of the EPSO competencies they are relevant to. Using this method, you should have a comprehensive list of examples for the interview. If you have had previous interviews for other posts at other employers, consider how you could have improved your approach and how you could have answered certain questions more effectively.

Prepare for Follow-up Questions: Be aware that sometimes an interviewer will simply ask you for a second example once you have already described one situation. This is designed to find out if a candidate only has one "star answer" for a competency. Make sure that you are not caught out by this and have multiple examples in mind. Prepare answers to classic "difficult" questions such as "what are your biggest weaknesses"?

Further sample questions can include:

- *What is your main motivation for working in the EU?*
- *What makes you suitable for an EU post?*
- *What role or position do you see yourself in, in 5-10 years?*
- *Can you describe situations where you acted in a pro-active manner?*
- *What would you do if you discovered that your colleagues were breaking some administrative rules?*
- *Describe a stressful situation in your current job. How did you react to it?*
- *What does success mean to you?*

Your Questions: Apart from being asked, consider what questions you may wish to ask the interviewer about the EU institution and the role if you are given the opportunity at the end of the interview (or at any point during the Assessment Centre). Be mindful of the impression your questions give. Making your first question one that enquires about holidays or the next pay rise may give the interviewer the impression that you are not intrinsically interested in either the EU institution or the role.

Likewise, try not to ask questions to which answers could easily be obtained by a bit of basic research (e.g. what a certain institution deals with). Asking about the organisation's future strategies (such as a unit's future tasks after the changes of the Lisbon Treaty) in a particular area may be a more suitable question. It is a good idea to have some questions prepared (even if you already have the answers): it will show you are keen to learn about the organisation from the interviewer and will allow them to feel good about themselves when providing you with the information you seek.

Such questions could refer to the interviewer's experience about how the EU's continuous enlargement has changed the institutions' organisational culture; you may ask about the changes in policy focus triggered by the global financial crisis; or you may choose to ask about life in Brussels (Luxembourg or elsewhere) for young families etc.

You could also try a few more testing questions such as how they differentiate the opportunities they offer from those available at other organisations or what they think the most challenging part of the job profile of an administrator (or assistant or linguist) is. However, only use questions where you have a genuine interest in the answer – avoid questions that are merely designed to impress, as you may not be able to follow up with further thoughtful questions or responses if the interviewer gives a fuller response than you expected them to.

Tips for the Assessment itself

- **Introduction**: The interviewer is likely to inform you which competencies are to be covered during the interview (it is acceptable to ask if they do not give this information – although they will not necessarily reveal this). If you have become familiar with the EPSO competencies in advance, then you can ensure that your responses are tailored around the competency under discussion and that you provide relevant answers that help both your assessment and the assessor's job as well. For example, if you are asked a question under the Prioritising and Organising competency, do not spend a long time describing your teamwork with your other group members: focus your answers on the planning, prioritising, monitoring and organising-type behaviours that you displayed at the time.
- **Active Listening**: You should listen carefully to what you are being asked; it is perfectly acceptable for you to take a moment to think before responding (you can always say to the interviewer: "If I understand your question correctly, you are asking if [...]. Let me think about that for a moment..." which wins you time to think the issue over).
- **Clarification**: If you are unsure what information a question is aimed at getting from you, ask for clarification: "could you please clarify what you'd like to learn about me here?"
- **Respond to the Question**: Keep your answers focused (e.g. when asked about your most recent work experience regarding workplace conflicts, do not start by introducing your CV and professional background or how you got your most recent job; keep your focus on the question with only a few words on the overall context). Begin with a broad outline of the situation, and then proceed to give details about what behaviours and personal qualities you displayed rather than spending a lot of time describing technical details (for example "I arranged... I instructed... I persuaded..." are all good, but avoid going into details such as "I used my knowledge of EU employment policies, specifically regarding the working time directive that deals with the following list of issues...[long explanation follows]").
- **Personal Achievements**: The interviewer is interested in what you did personally, so make sure this is clear and avoid using collective terms such as "we (made a project plan)" or "the group (came up with the solution)" or "company X launched (an initiative)". Instead, make statements such as "I (suggested we begin with a project plan)". This can be hard if the situation you are describing was genuinely a group process, but you should always be clear about the role you played in helping a group arrive at its decision. At the same time, avoid giving the impression of being an overly confident or egocentric candidate.
- **Respond Concisely**: In order to allow the interviewer time to probe your response if required, focus your answers. For example, if you were responsible for a particular piece of legal translation work, outline the situation in around five sentences ("I was given the task of ensuring the timely and precise translation of a tender procedure"), what you did in another five ("I created a project plan and milestones, identified the team members, outlined the work methodology...") and the outcome in another five ("we managed to deliver the translation within deadline"). The interviewer is then free to probe you around the specific details they are interested in. If you are not sure whether you have given enough information, you can always ask. If your answers are too verbose, you may damage your chances because if what you are saying is irrele-

vant to the competency (e.g. you explained in detail the IT applications used for the translation while the question essentially focused on project management skills), the interviewer will have less time to ask questions about the areas they really need to understand. In short, keep your focus strictly on the management and interpersonal side of the events.

- **Confidentiality**: Do not disclose the name of the company or organisation you mention in your responses; it is enough to say "when I worked for a firm" or "when I was a project manager" unless the interviewer wishes to know more. Similarly, never disclose the full name of a person with whom you had a conflict or use him or her as an example to describe a situation.
- **Stick to the Point**: Resist the temptation to describe a situation in unnecessary detail (e.g. "I had a Spanish colleague who had just moved to Latvia where he was travelling in neighbouring countries almost every weekend") unless certain facts are relevant because they affected or explained a certain behaviour you wish to emphasize.
- **Methodology and Motivation**: When asked "how did you respond to this situation", aim to provide an answer that concentrates on the methodology or motivation side ("I understood there is a tension between us so I tried to discuss the situation face to face") instead of describing unrelated facts ("I proposed we have lunch in the company canteen as it had just opened on the sixth floor"); when asked "how did you facilitate the teamwork" avoid fact-driven but less relevant answers such as "I heard from the IT department that Microsoft had come out with a great program that runs on Windows XP, so given that we had this operating system, it sounded like a good idea". Instead, focus on your behaviours, solutions, methods, motivation, feelings and ideas.
- **Taking Notes**: It is important to allow the interviewer to write down as much information as possible in order to assess your answers afterwards. Watch the interviewer's note taking. If they seem to be having trouble keeping up with your answers, you should slow down, pause and allow them to catch up. Conversely, if they have stopped taking notes, or put their pen down, this indicates they are likely to have all the information they need on for this competency *or* you are currently giving them detail that is irrelevant. Pause, and perhaps ask if what you are telling them is useful and relevant.
- **Be Honest**: Interviewers are trained to probe your responses; if you are embellishing the truth then they may well find out as you begin to falter under increasingly detailed questioning.
- **Trick Questions**: You will seldom, if ever, be asked "trick" questions in a professionally run interview.
- **EU Jargon**: Explain any jargon or acronyms you use. Avoid using slang expressions. For example, if you are sitting a competition for general administrators and you use the term "absorption capacity", make sure you show that you understand it by explaining its meaning in plain terms; similarly, if you are sitting a specialist competition for e.g. data protection officials, your interviewer may not be an expert in that field even if he or she is an EU official, therefore try to read the interviewer's non-verbal cues regarding their knowledge of the field and adjust your vocabulary accordingly. Similarly, if you talk about previous work and use industry jargon such as "the PHP programmer had a conflict with the Java scripter", make sure you do not overload the interviewer with expressions they may not be familiar with.
- **Stay Calm**: Aggressive interviewers are probably just acting and looking for your response; staying calm and professional is the best way to respond to this.

- **Loyalty**: Never belittle or give away secrets of any past or present employers – the interviewer will see this as unprofessional and be concerned about you doing the same if you were to leave the role you are applying for. For example, avoid saying something like "I left my last company because it was run by people who were incompetent".
- **If Stuck:** If you find you are completely stuck for an answer and do not have an example to offer, then it is worthwhile trying to make one of your other experiences "fit" the question if at all possible. You may begin by saying "I have never experienced precisely that situation, but let me tell you about a similar situation when..." Even if your response does not help you on this particular competency, it should count as further evidence towards other competencies covered by the interview, not to mention your resourcefulness.
- **Body Language**: Consider your body language during the interview: this is one of the key aspects interviewers will observe and weigh in almost as much as your words. Keep your arms unfolded and adopt a generally "open" posture. Lean slightly forward in the chair and maintain good eye contact with the interviewer (even if they themselves break eye contact to make notes). Smile, nod and repeat back their questions to show you are listening. Be careful of your body language "leaking signals" that you are uncomfortable with a question or subject area: for example, avoid pained expressions when asked a difficult question – look interested, motivated and positive instead. A good exercise can be a simulation with a friend who, while asking you questions, takes notes on your body language and you analyse it together afterwards. You may also wish to have yourself recorded and then try to improve your overall performance; a professional coach can also be of great help.
- **Flash Cards**: Some interviewers may allow you to refer to "prompt cards" (or "flash cards") during the interview. It is worthwhile preparing some of these in advance: you can always check with the interviewer if these are acceptable at the beginning of the session. Keep them short and focused: one or two words bullet-pointed against each of the competencies to help remind you of relevant examples. Do not fall into the trap of writing out examples verbatim and then simply reading your notes out loud during the interview: this will not impress the interviewer and will make you less agile and able to respond to follow-up probing questions.

Sample Structured Interview

In the following section, we have provided a sample structured interview of the type that you will be facing as part of the EPSO recruitment process. We have begun with an outline of the typical topics to be covered in the introduction to the interview. We have then gone on to provide examples of the type of questions you may be faced with, followed by all competency areas we identified that are reflective of the types of areas looked for as part of the EPSO recruitment process. It should be stressed that these are of course not the exact questions you will be facing as part of your structured interview; however, they should be very useful in understanding the likely question format. They will also help you consider how you may be able to best phrase your skills and experience to fit with the way these types of interview are structured. After the questions, we have provided example candidate answers to two of the questions so that you can actually have a go at assessing a response against typical assessor guidelines and see how your rating compares to that of an actual assessor.

Interview Introduction

When the interview starts, you will be given a short introduction by the interviewer. This is designed to give you information about how the interview will run, put you at ease and allow you to ask any questions you have about the interview process. It is unlikely that there will be time to discuss the role in depth at the structured interview stage: check with the interviewer whether such questions are appropriate if you wish, but they may best be saved for another time.

The interviewer will cover the following topics in the introduction:

- **Time Available**: It can be up to one hour 30 minutes, though given the large number of EPSO candidates, it will likely be shorter, around 45 minutes. The interviewer may tell you that they will move you on if they feel they have enough information on a particular competency. Some interviewers are better at this than others, so make it easy for them by keeping your answers concise and then asking them if they would like any more information.
- **Definition of a structured interview**: This will introduce the format of the session and explain what a competency is. They may describe the EPSO competencies at this point.
- **Notes**: The interviewer is likely to inform you that they will be taking notes throughout and to ask you to excuse them if they break eye contact.
- **"Warm up" Questions**: Before the formal competency-based questions begin, you may be asked some more general questions designed to "warm you up" before the interview proper begins. These may or may not be assessed. Questions like "Tell me about your studies" or "What was the subject of your dissertation" are less likely to be assessed than a question like "Tell me what motivated you to apply for this role".

Questioning

This sample interview is split into eight competency areas. Each competency has two "starter questions": these would be asked of all candidates. They are then followed by a selection of probing follow-up questions. These are designed to not only gain more detail about an example, but also to really test those candidates who have fabricated their answers: it is likely they will falter under this level of detailed questioning.

Competency Area One: Harnessing the Power of Development

This competency area is concerned with how well a candidate utilises the power of learning. This includes learning and developing personally, as well as managing the learning of the organisation.

Question One: Tell me about a time that you proactively decided to expand your knowledge of a certain subject.
[Possible situations to think of: you were assigned a task by your boss and you did extra in-depth research online, interviewed industry experts and wrote studies on the topic out of your own personal curiosity; you signed up to a course outside work as you were so motivated to learn about a subject; you volunteered to give lectures on a topic and prepared a presentation about it.]

Follow-up Probes:

- Why was it important to do so?
- What approach did you take? Why?
- What difficulties did you encounter?
- How successful were you?
- What would you have done differently, with hindsight?
- How have you applied this since?

Question Two: Tell me about a time you received valid negative feedback about the work you completed.
[Possible situations to think of: you were not precise enough in your written report and your superior called your attention to the problem; you failed to fully respect or negligently overlooked a certain rule which caused some loss to your company; you did not act or talk properly in a professional meeting and your superior discussed ways of improvement with you; you did not organise your work efficiently and you missed a deadline or forgot about a task which caused delays or tensions in the team.]

Follow-up Probes:

- How did you find out how the other person felt about your work?
- How did you feel when you received the feedback?
- How did you respond?
- With the benefit of hindsight, how might you have handled the situation differently?
- What further feedback have you received on this area since that time?

Competency Area Two: Planning and Organising

This competency area is concerned with how well a candidate manages time and resources in order to achieve their objectives. It includes both initiating projects and keeping them running to schedule once they are underway.

Question One: Tell me about a time when an unexpected problem arose during a project that you were responsible for resolving.

[Possible issues to think of: a certain note or background briefing you were asked to prepare and a critical input was not provided to you in time; you were requested to organise an event and unforeseen extra expenses arose; a computer or server collapsed in a critical period of executing a certain task; a person whose contribution was crucial to the project refused to participate or declined to take part; personal conflicts within a team prevented the project from timely and accurate delivery.]

Follow-up Probes:

- How did you become aware of the problem?
- What was its potential impact on the project?
- How did you respond?
- What was the outcome?
- What feedback did you receive on the project?
- With the benefit of hindsight, how could you have improved your handling of the situation?
- How have you applied this learning since?

Question Two: Tell me about a particular project or task you were involved with in which taking a planned approach was essential.
[Possible issues to think of: you were asked to organise a consultation or conference and this required practical planning efforts; you were asked to create a strategic financial or marketing forecast for your organisation; the completion of a compliance or a special qualification course while working full time required in-depth time management and planning; a certain project such as redecorating a house or a work-related issue in which the sequence of steps and creation of milestones was of crucial importance and it required proper step-by-step planning.]

Follow-up Probes:

- What factors did you need to take into account in your planning?
- How did you do this?
- How did you track progress?
- What was the outcome?
- What feedback did you receive?
- With the benefit of hindsight, what would you have done differently?
- How have you applied this learning since?

Competency Area Three: Coping Under Pressure

This competency area is concerned with how a candidate responds to pressure at work. It includes the extent to which they display their feelings and their general levels of optimism. It also measures how well they respond to changing circumstances.

Question One: Tell me about a time you were working under intense time pressure to complete a project or task.

[Possible issues to think of: an event that had to be ready by a certain non-negotiable deadline (anniversary, Christmas party, national holiday, exam); a business project or legal obligation where any delay would have caused significant loss of revenue or reputation or downgrading in rating (tax report deadline, application for a tender, legal obligations)]

Follow-up Probes:

- How had this situation arisen?
- How did it make you feel?
- How did this situation affect your behaviour?
- What was the outcome?
- With the benefit of hindsight, how could you have approached the situation differently?
- How have you applied this learning in subsequent similar situations?

Question Two: Tell me about a time that you felt particularly disappointed or let down in a work situation.
[Possible issues to think of: a promise regarding your possible promotion was not kept; a work input you really counted on did not arrive at all or came too late; you expected a certain project to be completed in time but it was not; you had an assumption (that you would get a better office room or you would be asked to take part in a new project team or you would be sent on your company's annual bonus trip) and expected it to happen in a certain way but it did not, thus you felt exposed (and possibly a little naïve).]

Follow-up Probes:

- How did your emotions manifest themselves?
- How did this affect your behaviour?
- How did others react to your behaviour?
- How did you "move on" from this situation?
- With the benefit of hindsight, how might you have handled this situation differently?
- How have you applied this learning in subsequent similar situations?

Competency Area Four: Working in a Team

This competency area is concerned with how effectively a candidate works with other people – be they colleagues, officials from other EU institutions or other stakeholders. It measures co-operative tendencies as well as general interpersonal sensitivity. It also covers how effectively a candidate may utilise the diverse skills and backgrounds of others.

Question One: Tell me about a time when you experienced a difficulty in a working relationship with someone
[Possible issues to think of: you had a conflict with someone above or below you in the hierarchy (manager or secretary) due to a misconception of your position or role in the organisation; a colleague seemed jealous of your job profile or your benefits or the way you were treated by your superiors and thus harboured negative feelings about you; due to miscommunication, conflicts arose in a project team working under tense circumstances and heavy time pressure.]

Follow-up Probes:

- Had the relationship always been difficult? If not, what prompted the change?
- What made it difficult?
- How did you respond to the situation?
- How did the other party respond?
- What was the ultimate outcome?
- What feedback did you receive from others on how you handled the situation?
- With the benefit of hindsight, how would you have approached the situation differently?
- How have you applied this learning in subsequent similar situations?

Question Two: Tell me about a time when you needed to work as part of a team to accomplish an objective.
[Possible issues to think of: the organisation of an event or delivery of a development project was assigned to you and two other colleagues to work in a team; you were part of the team or you were asked to lead it; conflicts and management techniques required handling team members who were more senior than you and did not accept your authority; you had different concepts or ideas than the coordinator or leader of the team; some team members failed to deliver their share in the proper quality or in time and the way you handled this; rivalry between the team members.]

Follow-up Probes:

- What role did you play in the team?
- To what extent did you tailor your approach towards different group members?
- How did you decide on decisions facing the group?
- What differences of opinion arose? How did you deal with these?
- What did you do to facilitate the teamwork process?
- What was the outcome?
- With the benefit of hindsight, what would you have done differently?
- How have you applied this learning to subsequent similar situations?

Competency Area Five: Communicating with Clarity

This competency area is concerned with how effectively a candidate communicates facts and opinions to others. It includes both oral and written communication. Effective communication is measured not just by clarity and accuracy, but also by successfully gaining the interest and attention of the audience and by adapting to suit their needs.

Question One: Tell me about a time that it was important that your communication captured the attention and interest of another party.
[Possible issues to think of: you had to make an important presentation to secure buy-in or funding from others; you needed to convey important health and safety information; your communication was going to resolve an important training needs gap; you were facing a particularly cynical or stubborn audience who had proven to be resistant to the idea you were presenting in the past.]

Follow-up Probes:

- How did you know what would appeal to the other party?

- What tactics did you employ?
- What reaction did you get? How do you know?
- What was the outcome?
- With the benefit of hindsight, what would you have done differently?
- How have you applied this learning to subsequent similar situations?

Question Two: Tell me about a time when you had to communicate a complex concept in layman's terms.
[Possible issues to think of: you were explaining technical aspects of your role to a non-expert audience during a job interview, during a networking event or at a conference; your manager wished to know the impact of a technical issue without hearing the detail behind it; a new starter in your department required training in a new system or process; you were seeking buy-in from stakeholders to the value of what you were proposing, but they would not respond well to lots of technical details.]

Follow-up Probes:

- How did you know the other party would find the content complex?
- How did you approach the task?
- Why did you decide on the approach you took?
- To what extent do you feel you were successful? How do you know?
- With the benefit of hindsight, what would you have done differently?
- How have you applied this learning to subsequent similar situations?

Competency Area Six: Analysing and Creating Solutions

This competency area is concerned with how a candidate approaches the resolution of complex issues. A systematic approach to gathering relevant informaion and then formulating solutions that are both innovative and pragmatic is important. It also includes the creation of multiple alternative courses of action where possible.

Question One: Tell me about a time that you had a large amount of information to analyse.
[Possible issues to think of: you were new to a role and needed to assimilate lots of information relating to your daily tasks, organisational structure, systems and stakeholders quickly; you were preparing a report for your superior or a stakeholder about a particular issue where it was important to consult a wide range of sources and media; you were responsible for financially reporting on the performance of a venture; you personally conducted a research project that entailed large amounts of data (e.g. survey results, observations).]

Follow-up Probes:

- What type of information was it?
- How did you approach the task?
- How did you distinguish essential from non-essential information?
- To what extent did you trust the information you were presented with? How did this affect your approach?
- How did you feel while conducting the task?

- What was the outcome?
- With the benefit of hindsight, what would you have done differently?
- How have you applied this learning to subsequent similar situations?

Question Two: Tell me about a time when you successfully resolved a key problem or issue that you were facing at work.
[Possible issues to think of: a persistent problem with an inefficient process was overcome by an innovative solution you suggested; a project encountered an obstacle that could have threatened to stop the project in its tracks but you found a way round it no-one else had thought of; you were tasked with finding ways of making a task more commercially efficient; a team you managed were facing persistent absence issues which you successfully investigated and then resolved.]

Follow-up Probes:

- What made this problem an important one to resolve?
- What did you suggest? How did you arrive at this suggestion?
- How innovative would you rate your idea as being?
- How well did it work in practice?
- What feedback did you receive?
- With the benefit of hindsight, what would you have done differently?
- How have you applied this learning to subsequent similar situations?

Competency Area Seven: Focusing on Delivery

This competency area is concerned with how effectively a candidate meets their work objectives to a high standard of quality. It covers the extent to which they are proactive and thrive in challenging situations. It also includes the extent to which candidates follow relevant rules and regulations where appropriate.

Question One: Describe to me your most challenging work project to date.
[Possible issues to think of: a challenging situation in which you took the initiative and acted proactively to achieve a good project outcome; a project you managed where you made sure procedures were followed and/or quality standards were met in the face of pressure to do otherwise; a recent example of when you took responsibility for meeting stretching project milestones and objectives.]

Follow-up Probes:

- What made it challenging?
- How did this make you feel and act?
- How did your behaviour and attitude compare to others in the same situation?
- What were the delivery expectations? To what extent were these met?
- What feedback did you receive?
- With the benefit of hindsight, what would you have done differently?
- How have you applied this learning to subsequent similar situations?

Question Two: Tell me about a time when you had to make a judgement call between meeting a deadline and quality of the end product.

[Possible issues to think of: a time when you took on responsibility for an existing project that was running behind schedule, and had to evaluate what was essential and what could be done to a lesser degree in order to meet the deadline; a time when the client's requirements changed but the deadline remained, and you had to balance quality of the additional output requirements with meeting the strict deadline.]

Follow-up Probes:

- Why was such a judgement call necessary?
- What did you decide?
- What was the impact of your decision?
- What steps did you take to mitigate the impact of this?
- What feedback did you receive?
- With the benefit of hindsight, what would you have done differently?
- How have you applied this learning to subsequent similar situations?

Competency Area Eight: Leading and Inspiring Others

This competency area is concerned with the extent to which the candidate acts as a motivational leader of others and includes such activities as issuing instructions, spotting and developing talent and giving tough feedback messages when necessary.

Question One: Describe a time that you led a team who were demotivated.
[Possible issues to think of: new to a company, you took responsibility for a team that were disengaged and you were able to reengage them over time; you led a team through time of organisational restructure; you led an underperforming team and managed to raise levels of motivation and performance simultaneously.]

Follow-up Probes:

- What was the context?
- How did you respond to the situation?
- To what extent was this effective?
- What was the mixture between "push" and "pull" tactics?
- What problems did you encounter? How did you respond?
- What feedback did you receive?
- With the benefit of hindsight, what would you have done differently?
- How have you applied this learning to subsequent similar situations?

Question Two: Talk me through a time that you significantly contributed to another person's personal development.
[Possible issues to think of: you managed a previously high performer who had become disengaged in their role; a time when you were responsible for a graduate or person new to their role; a time when you managed an underperformer, providing constructive feedback and establishing a realistic personal development plan.]

Follow-up Probes:

- How were their development needs identified in the first instance?

- What strategies did you adopt?
- What was the impact?
- What was the person's feedback to you?
- How long-lasting were your interventions?
- With the benefit of hindsight, what would you have done differently?
- How have you applied this learning to subsequent similar situations?

Summaries, Ending the Interview

After each competency is completed, the interviewer is likely to summarise your examples back to you, to check that they have understood correctly. This is your chance to correct any misunderstanding or add in additional important information that has been left out – so listen carefully. They may also ask if you have anything else to add around this competency. Only give them extra information if you have a really good example that you simply could not give through the questions they asked – otherwise, this could cut into the time you have available on other competencies.

Once all the questions have been asked, the interviewer may again offer you the chance to contribute final examples (although this is less common): again, only do so if you have a relevant, fantastic example that you were not able to give in answer to the questions posed. Keep it short and simple – the interviewer will ask for more information if they need it. Assuming there are no opportunities for questioning the interviewer about the role at this stage, you should thank them for their time and move onto the next exercise in your schedule.

Sample Candidate Responses

In this section, we have included sample summary transcripts for a candidate's answers around three of the competencies. Read their responses and then using the scoring criteria we provide afterwards, try to decide how well you think the candidate has performed. Then, read the Assessment of Performance section to see how your views compare to those of a professional assessor.

In each of the examples that follow we have focused on the candidate's response to the question and follow up probes and, for ease of reading, have omitted the probes themselves from the text.

Competency Area Four: Working in a Team

Question: Tell me about a time when you experienced a difficulty in a working relationship with someone

Sample Candidate Response: Let me have a think.... Yes, when I was working as a project manager for company X, there was a colleague in particular who I struggled to build a really good relationship with. He was the same level in the hierarchy as me but I was relatively new to the firm. Despite my behaving in what I felt was a professional and competent manner, this person used to frequently make little sarcastic comments to me and did not seek to include me when interesting new pieces of work came up. I got on well with other members of staff, so I don't know why there was a problem with him in particular.

I did make attempts to try and help the relationship, for example I would include him on emails when I suggested a social evening out to a nice Japanese restaurant. However, it all came to be an open conflict when a project report we had been assigned to work on together was not delivered by the deadline. This person had not informed me of some critical information, which meant I had much shorter timescales than I realised; I was really frustrated especially because I was supposed to go on holiday after handing in the report. When this happened, I made sure that my manager was aware of the background to the situation and I told my colleague I was disappointed he had not kept me informed as communication is key to the type of work we are involved in.

Things did change a little after this incident. Even though I was really upset, I decided to change tactic and stopped inviting him to social events, but instead set up review meetings and milestones in our diaries whenever we were working on a project together to make sure no important points got missed. Overall, I think it was just one of those things – you can't expect to get on with everyone, can you? We were very different people and I think we now have a professional relationship: but we will never be best of friends or anything.

Scoring Criteria

For this competency, the following would be indicators of a **positive response**:

- Includes relevant others in decision making
- Praises the contributions of others
- Works co-operatively across organisational areas
- Actively listens to others
- Effectively utilises the diverse range of backgrounds, skills and motivations of their team
- Shows a concern for the emotional state of others

The following would be indicators of a **poor response**:

- Makes decisions in isolation without consulting others
- Ignores or belittles the contributions of others
- Adopts a silo mentality, does not co-operate with other organisational areas
- Ignores others
- Works with others without regard to individual differences in background, skills or motivations
- Shows no concern for the emotional state of others

Assessment of performance: So, how well did you feel the example candidate did? Overall, assessors would be likely to grade this as a poorer response against the scoring criteria. On the positive side, the candidate did make an attempt (however small) to build the relationship through the social event invitations and the candidate also put measures in place to improve future communication. However, there was far more scope for the candidate to have openly explored the other party's feelings and motives for behaving in the way that he did. The candidate allowed the interpersonal relationship issue to get in the way of collaborative decision making, which ultimately had a detrimental effect on delivery.

Competency Area Two: Planning and Organising

Question: Tell me about a particular project or task you were involved with, in which taking a planned approach was essential

Sample Candidate Response: In my last role, I was given responsibility for organising the translation of a range of promotional literature for a forthcoming international conference on global migration. I needed to consider a lot of factors such as when I was going to speak to the original copywriters, completing the actual translations, how to identify and approach peer-reviewers, setting up the back-translation process and allowing time for amendments. I decided that the best thing to do would be to set up a project plan in Microsoft Project. I identified each of the required tasks and I highlighted where the potential pitfalls were. I set deadlines and checkpoints but also built in additional time to allow for unforeseen events that could arise. I made sure to assign responsibilities and stakeholders to each of the tasks.

I did find that certain events arose that threw the plan off a little. For example, the back-translation took longer than expected which reduced the time I had available for amendments. I have to admit, this got me rather worried as I feel the final stage is the most critical for identifying those final errors that can detract from the quality of a professional finished product. As a result, I asked the back-translators to send me through their work in sections immediately as it was completed, rather than waiting until it was all ready; so that I could also begin the review and amendment process immediately. In hindsight, this was not such a good idea, because as the back translation progressed I found that they would frequently revisit their earlier work in the light of the more recent translations and terminology and send me over multiple updated versions which became difficult to track. If I were faced with a similar situation in the future, I would simply work extended hours once the back translation was complete, or perhaps see if I could bring on extra human or IT resource.

In the end, the promotional leaflets were ready by the deadline and met with great feedback from my manager and conference delegates.

Scoring Criteria

For this competency, the following would be indicators of a **positive response**:

- Prioritises tasks appropriately
- Sets realistic deadlines and milestones
- Monitors progress
- Adapts to changes in plans effectively
- Manages own workload effectively
- Conducts preparation in advance

The following would be indicators of a **poor response**:

- Makes incorrect prioritisation judgements
- Fails to set realistic deadlines and milestones

- Allows projects to continue without monitoring
- Becomes flustered and ineffective when plans need to change
- Works inefficiently or becomes overwhelmed with workload
- Fails to prepare in advance

Assessment of performance: Overall, assessors would be likely to grade this as a good response against the scoring criteria. On the positive side, the candidate adopted a highly planned approach to the task by identifying the key stages, setting up monitoring procedures and allowing contingency time. The project was also delivered by the deadline and met with positive feedback. There was, however, some indication that the candidate panicked when faced with changing circumstances and worked in a less efficient manner, even though they did recognise this and said they would follow a different approach in the future.

Competency Area Three: Leading and Inspiring Others

Question: Talk me through a time that you significantly contributed to another person's personal development.

Sample Candidate Response: I had been recently promoted to team leader of a team of four researchers. Three of these were high performing and one was thought by my predecessor to need performance managing. For this individual, although in the past they had been a strong performer in high demand, performance had been trailing off and my predecessor had just received strong feedback from a client that they were unreliable, never returned calls quickly and gave scant information in their reports, which were often riddled with errors. This feedback had not yet been passed on to the researcher.

Our organisational values promoted leading by example, listening to and collaborating with others. With this in mind I held a team meeting and shared my own vision for the team and department, including what I perceived my own strengths to be and what would be my focus for personal development. I asked the team what they saw as the future for the department and how we might work together to achieve this. I then met one to one with each of the researchers, asking how they found the role; what they found engaging and less engaging about the role; what motivated them; what their strengths were currently and where they felt they would benefit from development.

For the poor performing team member, I ensured I listened to their responses to understand how they considered they were doing in role, and what might engage them further. I decided not to share the client feedback with them as this might have ruined the rapport we were building and upset the researcher unnecessarily. The researcher did ask for a role description as they felt that the role requirements were not clear, but I explained I did not think these were available and I thought that they should have a good idea of what the role entails by now. We agreed an individual development plan focusing on utilising their strengths further, and also building on their weaker area of time management and attention to detail. The researcher attended a time management workshop and met with me for monthly coaching sessions, and six months later received positive feedback from the same client that had previously been negative. In hindsight, perhaps I should have spoken with HR to see if there were role descriptions, but there was a lot on my agenda at the time and the moment passed.

Scoring Criteria

For this competency, the following would be indicators of a **positive response**:

- Role models positive organisational behaviours for others
- Effective at motivating others
- Creates targeted development opportunities for others
- Issues clear directions for others to follow
- Spots and nurtures potential future talent
- Prepared to deliver tough messages when necessary

The following would be indicators of a **poor response**:

- Fails to role model positive behaviours, or actively role models undesirable behaviours
- Demotivates others (or fails to try and motivate them)
- Fails to create targeted development opportunities for others
- Issues unclear (or no) instructions
- Fails to spot or nurture potential future talent
- Shies away from delivering tough messages

Assessment of performance: Overall, assessors would be likely to grade this as an average response against the scoring criteria. On the positive side, the candidate invested time and energy as team leader in understanding the individual team member in order to provide targeted development for them, recognising their potential and nurturing this talent. The candidate gave consideration to the organisational values and ensured these were modelled in their own behaviour. There was however a clear opportunity for the candidate to deliver the tougher message of the client feedback, which they shied away from. The researcher sought clearer direction around what was expected of them in their role, which the candidate also failed to provide.

6. Sample Assessment Centre Reports

In the following chapter, I have included a couple of sample reports against the EPSO competency headings that summarise some fictional candidates' performance at an Assessment Centre to be administered by EPSO. Such reports would be used internally to compare candidates' performances to help make the decision and also would be used to give feedback directly to the candidates themselves.

You will be offered the chance of a written feedback report following the Centre, and since they can be very useful, do request one. If you are unsuccessful at the Centre, a feedback report can help to illuminate your strengths and weaknesses and you can use this to improve your performance at Assessment Centres in the future and also use the findings for personal development in the highlighted fields. If you are successful, then it will often form the basis of your first personal development discussion with your new superior.

As stated, the two candidates are fictional, and the exercises quoted are not necessarily the exact ones that will be used to measure each competency. However, they seem reasonable mappings and this will give you an indication of what an EPSO summary report could look like.

I have included two reports – one representing a good performance overall, the other representing a poorer performance (although of course there is variation within each). **The ratings for each competency are rated on a 1-5 scale: 5 being a perfect performance, 1 being a very poor performance.**

Example Report # 1 – Mr X

Summary

Overall, Mr X performed well at the Assessment Centre and he is recommended as a potential candidate to be placed on the reserve list of EPSO competition XX/YY.

His key **strengths** emerged as follows:

- Strong quality focus and drive
- Strong at keeping his professional knowledge up to date
- Remains calm and focused on delivery when under pressure
- Strong analytical skills and formulates creative solutions
- Good teamworking and networking ability
- Communicates clearly and in an entertaining way
- Comfortable directing the work of others and motivating them
- Good understanding of EU institutions, his specialist field and the global context

His key **development needs** emerged as follows:

- Needs to focus more on personal development of soft skills
- Creative ideas need to be more practical to implement

– Needs to try and predict and manage project risks before they occur
– Remember to always include contingencies in project planning
– Would benefit from developing greater confidence when his ideas are challenged in a group situation
– More attention to be given to the right terminology, EU jargon and names of institutions

More detailed ratings by competency follow below.

Delivering Quality and Results

In the **Group Exercise**, Mr X's time checks ensured that the group remained focused and driven in achieving the meeting's objectives to choose the right course of action. When discussing the project implementation, Mr X refused the other group members' demands to compromise on quality, instead insisting that a creative way around the problems must be found. However, in the end a solution was not found by the group and he agreed with the consensus decision to make some compromises. A couple of times he pointed out where the group's suggestions might be at odds with EU directives or regulations but seemed to find good legal reasoning to remedy the issues, which underlined his subject matter expertise.

In the **Case Study**, Mr X outlined how he would implement his proposal and included quality control procedures at various points such as review meetings and peer review of documentation, inter-service consultations with various DGs etc. He mentioned various cross-cutting EU policies and procedures that he would adhere to in the implementation. He sought to add additional value by mentioning a number of additional spin-off projects that could be considered as a result of the research conducted in the main project.

Overall Rating: 5

Learning and Development

In the **Structured Interview**, Mr X described a number of ways he kept his professional knowledge up to date, including reviewing relevant Brussels-based and international press and television such as Euronews, attending policy conferences organised by various think-tanks and networking with peers at special events. Mr X is frequently consulted by his peers regarding latest policy developments and therefore likes to stay at the forefront of research developments.

Mr X was less strong on developing his softer skills. He tends to receive feedback on an ad hoc basis and never sought to collect this proactively in a structured way. He has sought to develop some of his interpersonal skills, such as influencing, but this tended to consist of just attending a relevant training course with little evidence of putting what he has learnt into practice subsequently. He showed little interest in pursuing such courses if he were to become an EU official.

Overall Rating: 3

Resilience

In the **Oral Presentation**, Mr X remained confident and composed under questioning. When the assessor stated they disagreed with Mr X's recommendation, Mr X remained calm and asked for more information. He listened, nodding and then proceeded to state: "I understand your perspective and your concerns are valid". He then went on to explain how the assessor's concerns could be overcome in a measured and relaxed way.

In the **Structured Interview**, Mr X described an occasion where he needed to work for a prolonged period of extended hours due to a last minute change to a brief on a report he was producing. Despite feeling it was going to be difficult to complete, he rearranged his calendar and worked evenings and weekends to ensure the report was finished on time and to specification. This did make Mr X feel quite tired for a while afterwards, but he feels the extra effort was rewarded with a report that was very well received. He showed a generally strong commitment to working intensively if a job must be done within a tight deadline.

Overall Rating: 5

Analysis and Problem Solving

In the **Case Study** exercise, Mr X conducted an in-depth analysis of the background information presented and uncovered a number of important themes and trends from the dossier. His solutions showed real creativity as well as the ability to think of the longer-term implications of current courses of action. He presented a number of possible alternatives, evaluated their pros and cons and then came to a reasoned judgement about which to recommend. Some of his ideas sounded good, but were unlikely to be practical to implement as his approach was overly high-level and less sensitive to the realities of EU decision-making; he sometimes failed to take account of the Treaty of Lisbon changes. At the same time however, Mr X managed to identify pitfalls relating to institutional changes in the balance of power between the European Council President and the rotating Presidency of the Council; he proposed various lines of action which underlined his good sense of solution-oriented thinking. His budgetary calculations were also 100% accurate.

In the **Structured Interview**, Mr X described many examples of complex analytical work that he has conducted as part of his role as scientific researcher. He is adept at both quantitative and qualitative analysis and is comfortable switching between longer-term analysis work and short term data crunching. He gave concrete examples from his previous work experience of where he had made recommendations on the basis of his analysis that were subsequently taken up and implemented successfully, but he failed to show a real conviction that the success was attributable to his novel approach rather than other external factors.

Overall Rating: 4

Working With Others

In the **Group Exercise**, Mr X showed consideration and empathy with his fellow group members. He did not interrupt while they were speaking and built upon their ideas, showing that he was listening. There was one member of the group who was very quiet and Mr X sought to bring her into the conversation on a number of occasions by asking her for her views. When Mr X disagreed with someone, he always expressed an appreciation for their perspective before putting forward his alternative.

In the **Structured Interview**, Mr X described how it was important for him in his last role to build relationships quickly when he arrived, as there were a number of projects nearing completion that he needed to oversee. He did this effectively and proactively through a series of e-mails and meetings. He described some potentially contentious situations, such as dealing with trade union representatives, which he handled with maturity and tact and resulted in a positive outcome for both sides.

He sees networking as a crucial part of getting his agenda heard, as well as being useful from a personal development perspective. He has managed a small team for the past year and has found it interesting to get to know each person's unique motivations. He has used this knowledge to help successfully influence their behaviour. He also showed a great interest in working in an international environment and in public administration.

Overall Rating: 5

Communicating

In the **Group Exercise**, Mr X contributed frequently and clearly. His contributions were concise and to the point and they succeeded in capturing the attention of the other group members. He asked other group members for their views and praised the contributions of others.

He did not attempt to summarise the group's progress, which could have been helpful. Mr X allowed others the space to contribute and showed active listening by nodding his head and making eye contact, along with positive body language gestures.

In the **Oral Presentation**, Mr X structured his points in an easy to follow manner. He began the presentation with an overview of what he wanted to cover, with section headings, and then proceeded to go through his sections clearly. He ended with a short conclusion and summary which tied up the presentation clearly. He spoke at an appropriate volume and speed and varied his tone which kept the audience engaged. He did not use any visual aids such as flipcharts, which would have been beneficial, but his varied tone of voice made up for this to a certain extent. However, his clear signals when moving from one section to the next made the presentation easy to follow.

Overall Rating: 4

Prioritising and Organising

In the **Structured Interview**, Mr X described how he was responsible for the implementation of a 4-month project and described a number of concrete project management tools and techniques he employed in order to ensure delivery. A number of crises arose during the project and Mr X showed flexibility in changing and updating the plan to accommodate these changes while keeping the deadline and budget to requirement. Many of these crises could have been foreseen and planned for, which Mr X recognises with hindsight while drawing a few conclusions for next time.

In the **Case Study**, Mr X set clear priorities for which issues he would address first and which could wait until later. He set some tentative dates and milestones for implementation, although he did not build any contingency time into his plans. However, the time allocated for tasks seemed realistic. Mr X assigned responsibilities for tasks to individuals and set clear standards for delivery. The overall style, content and quality of the case study was of a high standard, though he did not mention two crucial EU policy initiatives in the field which could have improved the paper's level.

Overall Rating: 4

Leadership

In the **Group Exercise**, Mr X spoke first and suggested that all the group members speak in turn to give their views before the discussion started. The other group members agreed with his proposal. He also volunteered to be the timekeeper and moved the group on in their discussions on three occasions. However, at times other group members talked over Mr X and he did nothing to try and counteract this and would be quiet for a little while afterwards. However, he did encourage the group along the way by saying things like "I think we are doing very well" and "we only have to discuss one more issue and then I think we have this situation resolved". He also pointed out the strong and weak points of certain proposals by group members, based on his in-depth EU knowledge.

In the **Oral Presentation**, Mr X outlined a number of plans to keep staff motivated during the change period. These included 1:1 meetings, team building events and access to further personal development opportunities. He outlined his vision for the unit in 3 years' time, which was inspiring and a rare initiative among other candidates. He also detailed how he would cascade this vision down to others in the organisation through literature, online tools and talks.

Overall Rating: 4

EU and Professional Knowledge

In the **Case Study**, Mr X demonstrated a solid knowledge of the chosen EU policy by outlining the international context of his analysis, adding further arguments to those found in the background dossier and pointing to European trends in the field. While focusing on the subject matter, he discussed at length the role of the European Commission in policy formation and understood well the shared competencies with Member States. Referencing the correct Treaty articles added a lot of value to the written report.

In the **Oral Presentation**, however, Mr X seemed less confident regarding the use of the right terminology (often confusing expert "committees" with "commissions") and failed to answer a question on comitology procedures. His remarks on the European Central Bank's role in economic governance were imprecise and rather superficial, and he could not identify the Commissioner responsible for research policy either.

Overall Rating: 4

Example Report # 2 – Mr Y

Summary

Overall, Mr Y performed fairly poorly at the Assessment Centre and he is *not recommended* as a potential candidate to be placed on the reserve list of EPSO competition XX-YY.

His key **strengths** emerged as follows:

- Strong ability to identify possible sources of risk
- Generally high level of analytical skills, but needs to watch out for rushing his decision-making
- Proposes practical, workable solutions
- Can probably continue to operate effectively when under pressure, except where people interaction is involved
- Reacts flexibly to project issues as they arise
- Knowledge of EU structures and policy making tools

His key **development needs** emerged as follows:

- Develop greater positivity about reaching objectives
- Needs to ensure that he delivers on expectations
- Would benefit from a more focused approach to developing knowledge and skills
- Needs to work on controlling his defensiveness when challenged
- He generally prefers to work in isolation: when in a team environment he may show his frustrations openly
- Would benefit from developing his presentation skills in order to engage audiences more fully
- Would benefit from taking a more structured approach to managing projects
- Needs to develop a greater range of motivational strategies in addition to penalising poor performance
- Learn about EU policies, legislation, decision-making rules in depth
- Make sure he clearly understands the different competencies of various EU institutions

More detailed ratings by competency follow below.

Delivering Quality and Results

In the **Group Exercise**, Mr Y advocated taking a number of shortcuts in order to finish the discussion on time (for example, by saying "let's talk about the budget at a later meeting" and "it's more important to finish on time even if we cannot cover all issues"). He also suggested that it was not that important to deliver the project 100% to the original specification, as long as something was delivered by the deadline.

He was quite negative about the group's chances of reaching a workable decision by the end of the meeting and at points he seemed to have given up: throwing his hands in the air in exasperation, sitting back and crossing his arms.

In the **Case Study**, although Mr Y did not seem to contravene any EU policies or guidelines in his recommendations, he did not explicitly refer to the need to follow them in his response either. He mentioned a number of possible risks to the policy change being delivered, but he gave a vague response on how to mitigate these risks ("review things as they develop"). He produced a reasonable length of response in the time available but he used overly general common-sense language ("this policy change is very important to meet our long-term goals") without quoting sufficient evidence from the dossier.

Overall Rating: 2

Learning and Development

In the **Structured Interview**, Mr Y seemed to adopt a rather casual approach to self development. All of his information sources (such as internal bulletins, e-newsletters) seemed to be delivered to him: he showed little evidence of proactively seeking out sources of information to keep abreast of developments.

He sometimes attends events where he can network, where he stated that he sometimes picks up some useful information. In terms of his personal development, Mr Y adopts a similar approach. He got rather defensive in the interview when asked about his development areas, stating "I don't have any" and showed discontent over the need to attend compulsory training courses ("they are quite a waste of time"). When pushed, he admitted to having feedback from his supervisor that he can be a little intimidating towards others, so he has tried to be more welcoming since. He has not sought any feedback on how he has progressed on this since.

Overall Rating: 1

Resilience

In the **Oral Presentation**, Mr Y became flustered and went red when his views were challenged. When the assessor put forward an alternative course of action, Mr Y simply responded "Well, that's your view and you're entitled to it… even if it is wrong" without any further explanation or quoting any evidence. He showed a cynical approach about the limited room for manoeuvre of a single EU official in a situation where his hierarchy opposes a proposed course of action.

In the **Structured Interview**, Mr Y stated that he never becomes stressed under pressure and gave a number of examples of when he was working to very tight deadlines and he kept calm and succeeded in getting a resolution. His tactic in these situations tends to be to work harder and not to think about even trying for a work-life balance, which stops him from feeling frustrated.

Overall Rating: 2

Analysis and Problem Solving

In the **Case Study** exercise, Mr Y uncovered all the main points from the background information, although he seemed to miss some of the subtler information in the dataset. His solutions all sounded practical and workable, although they were not particularly innovative and did not add any background knowledge that could have demonstrated his in-depth understanding of the topic and its complexities. Mr Y's suggestions were all presented at a fairly superficial, top-line level: there was more scope for him to give detail on how they would be implemented in practice. He tended to shy away from detailed calculations of financials however, and also mixed up a number of terms and institutions ("European Council" with the "Council of Ministers"; "decree" with "regulation"; "European Institute of Technology" with the "Research Executive Agency" etc.).

In the **Structured Interview**, Mr Y described a situation where he was faced with a large body of information from a service provider which was intended to justify a project overspend. Mr X knew that he could not absorb this information quickly, so he decided to make a quick decision based upon gut-feel and awarded the extra funds. However, later on, it became clear that he had made an error and it ended up costing his department unnecessary extra money. From this experience, Mr X learned about the importance of double checking figures and asking for extra time if you need it to conduct appropriate analysis.

Overall Rating: 3

Working With Others

In the **Group Exercise**, Mr Y has more potential to significantly improve his team-working skills. He forgot other group members' names, causing him to point at people when referring to their ideas. Once the group seemed to be reaching a consensus on how to spend the budget, which was contrary to his views, Mr Y seemed to withdraw from the discussion about subsequent points and demonstrated closed body language. When he became particularly passionate about a point, Mr Y raised his voice almost into a shout and banged the table with emphasis a couple of times. This intimidated other group members and created an adversarial team atmosphere.

In the **Structured Interview**, Mr Y described how he generally enjoys working as part of a team. However, his examples frequently included instances of him choosing to take a piece of work for himself and completing this in isolation before returning to present it to the other group members, rather than true teamwork. He stated that he generally dislikes networking as he sees it as "fake" although he does have a sizeable network of contacts in the scientific community through previous work conducted together. He says that he generally feels the best approach when there is conflict is to move on and not dwell on it: which shows a certain reluctance to deal with these issues openly.

Overall Rating: 1

Communicating

In the **Group Exercise**, Mr Y made a number of contributions, although these were mainly criticisms of others' ideas or pointing out why they would not work, and were also of poor quality in terms of content and relevance to EU issues. He spent much of the meeting with his head down, reviewing his notes, which made some of his communications unclear and people asked him to repeat his point on a number of occasions. When challenged, he defended his views forcefully, although this did make him appear defensive and other members of the group seemed a little hesitant to include him in the discussion afterwards.

In the **Oral Presentation**, Mr Y did not follow a clear structure, instead just launching straight into his recommendations and the detailed analysis behind them. His visuals (flipcharts) were hard to read and at times he simply just read out what was written on them, without adding any further detail. His style showed an appropriate level of formality and he explained the jargon he used though the definitions or examples were not always precise. For example, he tried to define the "ordinary legislative procedure" but he confused it with the "consent procedure". He did not include a summary at the end, instead just ending abruptly and saying "and that's it". He spoke in a monotone throughout and this lack of variation in pitch and pace led to the audience feeling quite uninterested.

Overall Rating: 2

Prioritising and Organising

In the **Case Study**, Mr Y was clear about the need for a planned implementation, but did not go into details about what such as plan would look like. He did not refer sufficiently to the data contained in the background dossier but rather used its textual parts as inspiration.

He mentioned some key stakeholders and what actions he would assign to them, but he failed to take EU transparency rules into account. He gave a very thorough, considered view of the risks facing the plan's implementation as he made some suggestions for how to overcome these. He mentioned the importance of contingency time but when outlining the timeline, he failed to take this into account.

In the **Structured Interview**, Mr Y described how he prefers to take a flexible approach to managing projects as he feels that project plans only end up getting changed at some point anyway. He tends to set high-level objectives but not go into the detail and relies upon others to use their initiative. He recognises that this does not suit everyone's style but mentioned a rather bullying approach by saying "this doesn't depend on whether others like it or not, it depends on me pushing them". He described a number of times when he has been able to react to events as they occurred and did not then subsequently have to go back and amend the plan. However, he also describes some confusion from others he is working with regarding project progress, which he just says is a matter of them "just needing to speak to me more".

Overall Rating: 2

Leadership

In the **Group Exercise**, Mr Y tended to let others take a leadership position and he made no effort to guide the group's discussion or to suggest a process to follow. He did not encourage the group – in actual fact on a couple of occasions he simply said "we don't have enough time to discuss this properly" which caused an awkward pause in the discussion. He did volunteer to write some ideas up on the flipchart towards the end, but this meant that he stopped contributing completely as his whole time was spent writing up other people's ideas. He many times misspelled words and technical terms, which caused some dismay among group members. He also showed a high level of scepticism about the European Parliament's weight and role in the decision-making system, which put his commitment to EU integration into question.

In the **Oral Presentation**, Mr Y spoke at length about how he would keep staff motivated through close supervision and penalising those who did not meet their performance targets. He mentioned the importance of providing positive incentives too, but did not go into detail about how this would work in practice. Mr Y did outline his vision for the area over the next 3 years, which included some exciting technological changes.

Overall Rating: 2

EU and Professional Knowledge

In the **Oral Presentation**, Mr Y demonstrated an acceptable level of understanding how EU institutions and bodies operate. When questioned about the Office for Harmonisation in the Internal Market (OHIM), he confused it with the European Patent Office which seriously diminished the quality his performance. Later on, even though Mr Y could list a few cases handled by the European Union Civil Service Tribunal, his remarks on the Staff Regulations showed he does not really know the deeper meaning of certain terms and concepts.

In the **Case Study**, Mr Y provided some interesting insights on the human resources aspects of his proposals; however, he did not cover any of the policy-relevant issues that were required in the exam question. He correctly listed various DGs and the Committee of the Region, but he failed to include any reference to the Council of Ministers and the European Data Protection Supervisor. His remarks on the Commission's Green Paper and the long-term effect of the proposed changes were insightful, though his explanation why an impact assessment would have been needed showed he had only superficial knowledge of this topic.

Overall Rating: 3

Further Reference

A wide range of useful links to videos, interviews, sample exercises etc. that can help your preparation can be found on ***www.eu-testbook.com***